Japanese Aircraft

This Mitsubishi Army Type 87 Light Bomber was an adaptation of the very successful Navy Type 13 Carrier Attack Bombers of 1923. When combat developed in Manchuria in 1931, these bombers participated in early ground support roles.

Japanese Aircraft
1910–1941

Robert C Mikesh & Shorzoe Abe

NAVAL
INSTITUTE
PRESS

© Robert C Mikesh & Shorzoe Abe 1990

First published in Great Britain by
Putnam Aeronautical Books, an imprint of
Conway Maritime Press Ltd
24 Bride Lane, Fleet Street
London EC4Y 8DR

Published and distributed in the United States
of America and Canada by the Naval Institute Press
Annapolis, Maryland 21402

Library of Congress Catalog Card No. 90-60496

ISBN 1-55750-563-2

This edition is authorized for sale only in
the United States and its territories and possessions,
and Canada

Manufactured in Great Britain

Contents

Preface

For the vast number of Japanese aeroplanes types that were built during the period covered by this book, it is disappointing that more has not been written in English. Differences in language and translation difficulties have been the primary cause, leaving Japanese aviation pioneers and the early formation of the Japanese aviation industry virtually unknown to the rest of the world. It is hoped, therefore, that this book will bring to a wider audience a new insight into the background of early aviation history in Japan.

Included in this coverage are all the Japanese aircraft built in Japan (some unsuccessful but nevertheless meaningful in some respect) as well as the few in number that were built in Europe and the United States to a specification created in Japan but that affected further development of the design as a Japanese aircraft. Not included are gliders and lighter-than-air craft.

As the research for this book progressed, there was a strong inclination to analyse various trends in Japanese aviation development and accomplishments in perspective with similar happenings throughout the world that may have influenced these events. This would have been conjecture on the part of the authors, for, at this late date, there are a few ways of knowing to what degree foreign events were known to the Japanese individuals concerned. Communication and the flood of media news events were not as we know them today. Therefore, any correlation with these happenings must be left to the reader and not referred to here where they may be construed as fact.

Another discouraging element in the study of Japanese aircraft is the complicated methods used throughout its history such as the terminology and multiple systems used in identifying their aircraft. Not only are these strange and hard to pro-nounce designations, but they are meaningless unless there is an understanding of their usage. In the case of military aircraft in particular, more than one designation system was used simultaneously, and these often overlapped during periods of change. This adds considerable confusion and it is hoped that the following explanations will help clarify some of these problems.

Army Identification System

In the earlier years of aviation, there was little concern for an identification system. The manufacturer's preference or that which was most suited for the respective aircraft type was used. As Japan started producing its own military aircraft which were often adaptations of imported types, some sort of new identification system was needed. This was developed by the first producer of Army aircraft, a section of the Army called the Provisional Military Balloon Research Association (or Society). Their aircraft were subsequently identified by the kanji character for Kai meaning Association, followed by a consecutive number as new aircraft were developed.

Conversions of foreign aircraft in Japan such as Maurice Farmans could hardly lose their originator's identity. Therefore, to identify these aeroplanes, the first Japanese character of their name was used; in this case Mo. (Phonetic pronunciation of Maurice when put into Japanese and using only the first character to identify the type, translation back into English is Mo rather than Ma.) Consequently, Mo Shiki translated means Type (Shiki) Mo or Maurice Farman Type. The same applies to So Shiki or Sopwith Type.

Although aircraft imported into Japan are beyond the scope of this book, it is appropriate that the identifying systems be discussed here, since they have a bearing on Japanese types or modifications of foreign designs. The first apparent organized form to standardize an Army designation system for Japanese aircraft went into effect in December 1921. This consisted of a kana character selectively assigned to manufacturers of these aircraft. Japanese alphabets are not easily adaptable as a numbering system like the English alphabet, due to variations in sequence of characters. Consequently a fairly understandable Chinese alphabet of kanji characters was used as follows.

Kanji Character	Pro-nounced	English Equivalent	Manu-facturer
甲	Ko	A	Nieuport
乙	Otsu	B	Salmson
丙	Hei	C	SPAD
丁	Tei	D	Farman
戊	Bo	E	Caudron
己	Ki	F	Hanriot

With this explanation the reader can translate for himself the meaning of these prefix terms. As an example, it would be correct in the case of the Nieuport fighter to refer to it as Type A4. However, rather than to translate names and designations to where they could lose their Japanese identity, the Japanese nomenclatures such as Type Ko 4 for the same aeroplane will be retained in this coverage.

That system soon became outdated and by 1927, a type-number system was adopted which was based upon the Japanese calendar year. This was followed by an additional Kitai number system that went into effect in 1932. Both systems remained throughout the Pacific War and will be described in greater detail.

Navy Identification System

In the earlier years of Naval aircraft, three designation systems were used over a six and a half year period. This led to considerable confusion because the same designations were given different meanings. These were in the form of Japanese katakana characters of I, Ro, Ha, Ni, etc, a type of consecutive lettering or numbering used for these three systems during the periods shown below. This type of lettering system used the suffix 'go' which was equivalent to 'type'. To further identify the aircraft with respect to modifications, these designations were followed by gata (or kata) which meant sub-type or model and were preceded by a consecutive Japanese letter as changes were made, ie Ko-gata, Otsu-gata (A-model, B-model). This usage was similar to that of the Army, but in the case of the Navy it meant the order of acceptance, not manufacturer.

Beginning October 1915

I-go: Trainer powered by a 70hp class engine.

Ro-go: Larger aircraft powered by a 100hp class engine.

Ha-go: Experimental aircraft.

Beginning June 1917

I-go: Farman-type small model.

Ro-go: Farman-type large model.

Ha-go: Sopwith-type, Deperdussin-type.

Ni-go: Aircraft with folding-wing mechanism.

Ho-go: Experimental aircraft.

Beginning November 1918 to January 1922

I-go: Trainer.

Ro-go: Reconnaissance aircraft.

Ha-go: Pursuit aircraft of enemy aircraft.

Ni-go: Attack aircraft of enemy surface ships.

A better understanding of the above will be found when reviewing Navy aircraft of those periods using these designations.

As the tempo of developing new designs continued, this system became outdated. The Navy soon adopted an identifying system based upon a year identity followed by a type description. The year of Taisho, was used as a Type number up through that calendar period and as far as Showa 3 (1928), changing then to the last two digits for the year of Japan. An example would be Navy Type 13 Seaplane Trainer for 1924.

During the Showa period beginning with Showa 6 (1931), every new design proposal by the Navy was identified by the year of its proposal and tied to the kanji Shi of the word Shisaku literally meaning trial manufacture. As a consequence, with several manufacturers producing an experimental aeroplane to the same design specification and having the same Shi number, confusion was caused. Only after acceptance of the aircraft was it given a Type number with a descriptive nomenclature describing its mission. This Type numbering system for Army aircraft began in 1927 with Type 87: for Navy aircraft beginning in 1929 with Type 89. It was not intended that these were to be a common numbering system for both branches of Service. (See Appendix B for calendar/type conversions.)

Army and Navy Systems

By coincidence or not, both Services selected the national era method for dating the year-type for their aircraft starting in 1927–1929 respectively. This national era system of numbering years was conceived after the Meiji Restoration of 1868 that established retroactive numbers that began with the founding of the imperial dynasty set by tradition at 660 BC. This chronology was used sporadically as a way of dating, much like that used with the Gregorian calendar system. As such, it had its greatest play in 1940 when the government celebrated what it proclaimed to be the 2,600th anniversary of the founding of the Japanese State.

In using this calendar system, only the last two digits and, later, only one digit of the year were used. A Type 98 aircraft would have been accepted in the year 2598, equivalent to 1938. The Zero fighter, for instance, accepted as a carrier-borne fighter by the Navy in the year 2600, became the Navy Type O Carrier Based Fighter, using only the last digit subsequently at this turn of the calendar, thus bringing about the name Zero Fighter. The Army, on the other hand, used Type 100 when the year 2600 arrived, dropping back to the use of a single digit as with Type 1

for the year that followed.

This was a long and cumbersome way of identifying Navy aircraft. To solve the problem, the Navy devised what is termed the short designation system. The Navy had admired the US Navy methods and its aeroplanes in the 1930s, and adopted that system of identifying its own aircraft. This consisted of a letter to identify the mission-type, followed by a number which consecutively identified the acceptance sequence, then a letter identifying the manufacturer, and the fourth character was the numbered modification. Both the long and the short form were used simultaneously, which confuses the issue when using a mix of both.

In addition to the Army using a Type and number designation as already described, they also used a shortened version known as the Kitai or Airframe numbering system. This consisted of the first character of the word Kitai, being Ki followed by consecutive numbers that were issued to each experimental Army aircraft type regardless of manufacturer. After acceptance, and even after it was no longer an experimental type aircraft, these Ki numbers were retained as a shortened identity for each aircraft type throughout its operational existence, in conjunction with the longer designation, which was a type-number and word description.

With this complication of dual identifying systems, it is little wonder that during the Pacific War the Allied forces created their own identifying system for Japanese aircraft. This was a collection of easy to remember male and female names assigned to each type, regardless of the branch of Service. These were referred to as Allied Code Names, and with this system the problem was generally solved. After the war, the Japanese themselves often used this code name method for simplicity.

Any attempt to provide in one volume comprehensive descriptions and histories of all Japanese aircraft up to the start of the Pacific War would be impossible. Since most of the aircraft employed in that war were designed within the period covered by this volume, but are adequately described in Dr René Francillon's *Japanese Aircraft of the Pacific War*, mention of these types is made here only where appropriate. A full list of those aeroplanes which eventually served in the Pacific War appears in Appendix A together with the date when the first of their type was completed or flown.

Much is contained here about the men that influenced the design of the Japanese aircraft, and who built them, as well as about the venturesome aviators and the budding companies who advanced aviation in Japan.

Acknowledgements

To present this large quantity of Japanese aircraft, most of them never before recorded in English, would have been impossible without access to Japanese-language material and its translation. It was essential therefore that this become a team effort and to include a Japanese sharing an interest in the history of Japanese aviation. From as early as the mid-1950s, the two authors corresponded on this subject, with Shorzoe Abe then an aeronautical engineer with the Japanese Defence Agency in Tokyo and Robert Mikesh an Air Force officer and pilot. Mikesh was later assigned to Japan on two assignments totalling seven years and the two often worked closely on research into Japanese aviation. In recent years, they recognized the need for English coverage of the subject and agreed on co-authorship. Time available was a problem, Shorzoe Abe being a senior staff member in a large engineering firm in Kobe, and later assigned to Singapore, and Robert Mikesh being Senior Curator for Aeronautics, National Air and Space Museum in Washington, DC. Gathering and co-ordinating the data was no simple matter, complicated by the working distance of half a world apart.

This work has also become a collaborative effort by many individuals, and the authors gratefully acknowledge the generous help extended to them over the years, without which it would lack many of its most interesting items.

Most importantly, the greatest source for our material is from Tadashi Nozawa's eight-volume series of books entitled *Encyclopedia of Japanese Aircraft 1900–1945*, for which co-author Shorzoe Abe worked as a member of the editorial team. This work in Japanese, with the aid of many contributors, will always be recognized as a prime source of early Japanese aviation history.

Colleagues at the National Air and Space Museum were most helpful and include Dr Howard Wolko, Russell Lee, Rick Leyes, William Hardaker, Norman Moore and Herbert Brownstein. Others who have contributed include Stephane Nicholaou, John Underwood, Hideya Ando, (Mrs) Valaya Sintatiyakorn, and Colonel Akihiko Hayashi, JASDF, Embassy of Japan, Washington, DC.

Special thanks go to the person whose name seldom appears in a publication, yet whose contribution is so important, that being the editor. In this case it is John Stroud, whose outstanding ability shaped this book not only from his personal understanding of the subject but his ability to formulate this material into a meaningful form.

To our respective wives, Ramona and Tomoko, go our individual and collective debts of thanks. Both unstintingly gave up their claim on time we would otherwise have shared with them. Without their encouragement and faithful help, our book could not have been completed.

RCM and SA
Washington, DC and Kobe, Japan,
1990

The Early Years

To the English-speaking world, Japanese aviation is generally measured in time from just before the Pacific War in the 1940s. Little was known about Japanese aviation technology before that time, due for the most part to lack of interest or need; but it was also by Japanese design that the military powers controlling Japan's aviation wished to conceal the potential under development in preparation for war. The purpose of this book is to fill that gap in information by describing individual aircraft that were manufactured in Japan from the very beginning to those just before the Pacific War. To do this properly, a background of the early development of Japanese aviation is essential so as to have a better understanding of how and why many of these companies were formed.

The Beginning of Aviation In Japan

In the formative years of aviation, Japan was like any other country participating in the development of the aeroplane. Japan had its share of dreamers and experimenters, individuals that stood out from the rest. But when the technology emerged to the point that balloons and heavier-than-air craft were taking on prominence, development of aviation in Japan became predominantly that of élite civilians and group-efforts within the military establishment. Only a few achievements could be credited to civil endeavours, while in other aviation-developing countries individuals and civilian companies were the ones responsible for aviation progress. The reason was that Japan was quick to recognize the use of the aeroplane as an instrument of war; therefore the military took the lead in the development of aircraft and saw to their production.

Like other nations with long histories, Japan's first tale of flying can be found in its early myths. One recalls the story of Icarus and Daedalus in forming wings from feathers and wax with which to fly from the island of Crete. This is comparable to a mythical Sky Ship that carried the Sons of the Heavenly God to create Japan. This myth was described in *Nihon Shoki*, one of the oldest books on Japanese history, published in AD 720.*

Leonardo da Vinci is looked upon by most historians as having designed the first craft intended to ascend under its own power into the air in the 1500s. Of course the envisioned design would not work, for he knew then that it lacked sufficient power, but his concepts put down on paper showed creative thoughts of man travelling through the air. The Japanese look upon Gennai Hiraga (1726–1779) in this light, whereby he too recorded his thoughts of a ship capable of flight. Hiraga had inventive talents in many engineering subjects, but later research revealed that his concept of flight may have stemmed from a model airship that he bought from a Dutchman in Nagasaki, Kyushu.

Artificial wings became more realistic in the Japanese legend contained in *Fude-no-susabi (Random Writings with Writing Brush)*. In a story told by Suzan Kan (1748–1827), there was a man named Kokichi Ukita, a hyogu-shi† who lived in Okayama in southwestern Japan. Kokichi, a man of very modest means, fabricated a set of wings mostly from paper, and, in about 1785, allegedly took flight. Having modelled his wings like those of a captured dove, with a mechanical mechanism to flap the wings, Kokichi is said to have often flown from his roof-top over nearby fields. One evening when seeing an out-door party, he swooped down to determine whether any of his friends were among the group. In so doing, he flew too close to the ground and crashed in their midst. When seeing this winged-man from the sky before them, all those in attendance fled the party, leaving Kokichi to enjoy the feast of fine food and saké to the fullest. Later, when the incident became known to the police, Kokichi was arrested since it was decreed that his crime was in doing what ordinary men do not do – even if it were but a joke. To begin life anew, he moved to Shizuoka, changed his name to Bikosai and became a dentist. The story goes that he continued his experiments, this time with a helicopter-like machine. His efforts were again discovered by the police, and with samurai-like ruthlessness, they beheaded him.

Within this same period of the late 1700s, Shuto Asato of Okinawa experimented with an ornithopter of his own design. He used foot power so as to more efficiently flap the wings. But power for flight was still in the future. Other experimenters with the ornithopter principle, such as the families of Tarodaifu Toda-ya of Edo (Tokyo), Mikatana-ya, and Rigen Nagasawa, are among those recorded in the Japanese history of aviation experiments during the feudal days under the Tokugawa military dynasty in the 17th and 18th centuries.

During the Meiji era that followed (1868–1911), this 'time of enlightenment' makes note of the ornithopter designed by Heishiro Iwata of Nagano Prefecture, who recorded his invention with the Department of Technology. The fact that the machine was not successful caused his effort to be ignored at the time, but in retrospect this did not diminish the early

---

*Nihon Shoki literally means the written history of Japan, a book believed to be the first to be written after the development of written characters introduced from China as Kanji with Japanese adaptations that became Kana letters.

†Hyogu-shi is a craftsman that attaches paper-covers to shoji screens and fusuma doors.

concept of manned flight. Advancing still further, Taneyasu Matsumori of Yamagata Prefecture built a helicopter, an ornithopter referred to as the 'Bird Ship', and other creations; all were unsuccessful, but were stepping-stones to the future.

Ultimately, success in carrying man into the air was achieved with balloons, first in Europe and then in the United States. Japan's first balloon was made by Buheita Azabu and Shinpachi Baba of the Japanese Navy. It was a coal-gas filled airtight coated-silk balloon, fabricated on the athletic field at the Naval Academy at Tsukiji, Tokyo. With this balloon, Baba made the first captive ascent in April 1876 from nearby Sainyogahara Field. This was 93 years after the Montgolfiers had demonstrated their balloon in Paris as the first human flight, and showed that ballooning did not become the rage, worldwide, overnight.

Within a year of this first balloon ascent in Japan, a plan came into being to put this method of flight to good use. In February 1877, the rebel force under General Takamori Saigo attacked and isolated the government forces at the Kumamoto Castle in central Kyushu. A frantic effort was begun at the Naval Academy to make balloons that would drift over the castle and thus re-establish contact. Buheita Azabu and other naval engineers fabricated the first of several balloons, which when flown by Baba, reached a maximum height of 218 m (715ft) on 21 May, 1877. The second balloon also achieved success, but before either was deployed in combat, the conflict ended in favour of the government forces.

The Japanese Army became equally enthusiastic over the use of balloons as a combat weapon. For such a demonstration, 2-Lt Shinroku Ishimoto ascended to a height of 91m (298ft) at military ceremonies at the Army Academy in Ichigaya, Tokyo, on 10 June, 1878, but activity diminished until 1890 when Sotoichi Saito of Tsuruoka City submitted plans for his light balloon proposal to the Army as an item of military equipment.

By the late 1800s, ballooning attracted attention in Japan, an

interest created by the Englishman Charles Spencer when he travelled to Japan in November 1890 to make demonstration flights. His ascents over Tokyo and Yokohama were finished off with him leaving the balloon in spectacular parachute jumps during a series of public demonstrations, and his demonstration at the Imperial Palace Plaza became a nation-wide sensation.

In the next month, Thomas Baldwin, from the United States and noted for his early aviation work with balloons and airships, made similar balloon ascents and parachute jumps over Tokyo. By now, the nation was crazy about ballooning and this interest seemed to have been sparked overnight, and to heighten the excitement the Kabuki star, Kikugoro V, staged a drama about a balloonist at the Kabuki-za Theatre in Tokyo to satisfy his fans.

Recognizing the importance of the balloon, the Japanese Army placed an order with the Frenchman, Gabriel Yon, to supply one gas-filled balloon, complete with mooring car and a gas generator. The envelope had a capacity of 320 cu m (11,300cu ft). In 1897 at Wakayama City south of Osaka, Isaburo Yamada had designed and was test flying a balloon of a kite* configuration. This, too, interested the Japanese Army, and he was given assistance by Col Tokutaro Kodama and 1-Lt Kumao Tokunaga. When the balloon was perfected, Yamada recognized its potential and acquired a patent for it in May 1900.

Based upon Yamada's design, the Army, in September 1900, began manufacture of the balloon that they

This scale model of an aircraft shows the modern concept as envisioned in 1891 by Kazuhachi Ninomiya. This rubber-powered model flew 10m, but Japanese officials were not impressed with this proof of concept of flight.

termed the Purely Japanese Type Kite Balloon. Having an envelope capacity of 693cu m (24,473cu ft), the balloon carried two men to a recorded height of 400m (1,312ft), on 24 December, 1900. The Army's interest was by now captivated with the potential of such flights. In the wake of this success, Lt Kumao Tokunaga made a flight to a height of 300m (984ft) aboard an Army kite balloon at graduation ceremonies of the Army Artillery and Engineering School held on 23 December, 1901.

With the outbreak of the Russo-Japanese War on 9 February, 1904, orders were placed with Yamada in June of that year for the manufacture of two Purely Japanese Type Kite Balloons. These were used during the attacks on the fortress at Port Arthur, on the Liaotung Peninsula of China, making no less than fourteen observation flights in the course of the battles. Recognizing their worth in combat, the Army established a balloon unit at Nakano Village on the western edge of Tokyo in October 1907.

The man most acclaimed for powered heavier-than-air-flight in Japan is Kazuhachi Ninomiya (born in 1865). Ninomiya became the

*An elongated captive balloon having an empennage in the form of gas-filled lobes to keep it headed into the wind, thus usually deriving increased lift from the inclination of its longitudinal axis to the wind.

first Japanese to fly a rubber-powered model aeroplane, on 29 April, 1891. The wings of his craft were shaped like those of a crow, since as a youth in Ehime Prefecture, Ninomiya had studied the crow's flying characteristics in his efforts to solve the mysteries of flight. After this first success with his model, he made an even larger model aeroplane with a wing span of 3.2m (10ft 6in) powered with a clock spring driving a pusher propeller. Since it was inspired by the shape of an insect called Tamamushi, his craft was given that name.

Because of its success, Ninomiya offered the plans of his aeroplane to the Army, with which he was now serving during the Sino-Japanese War (1894–95). He saw the potential of such a man-carrying flying machine as an aerial spotter but his proposal fell upon deaf ears. Dejected, on leaving the Army Ninomiya joined a pharmaceutical company in the hope of saving enough to build his own man-carrying aircraft, but upon hearing of the success of the Wright brothers in 1903, he abandoned his efforts.

As time passed, Lt-Gen Gaishi Nagaoka, former Chief of Staff of the Ohshima Army Brigade during the war, and who was responsible for rejecting Ninomiya's plans, made him a public apology, and in 1925 he was officially commended by the Minister of Communications and awarded a medal of merit by the Teikoku Hiko Kyokai (Imperial Flying Association:)* as Japan's aviation pioneer. In return, Ninomiya, who was by then an executive in the pharmaceutical company, established a shrine dedicated to the development of aviation in Japan.

Lighter-than-air development had much to do with influencing

*The Teikoku Hiko Kyokai (Imperial Flying Association) was formed in January 1913 by Col Ikutaro Inoue of the Provisional Military Balloon Research Association. This had been preceded by a similar organization known as the Nihon Koku Kyokai (Aviation Society of Japan) formed on 25 November, 1912, under the leadership of retired Navy Lieut-Cdr Onokichi Isobe. To preclude having two associations devoted to the development of civil aviation, they combined on 23 April, 1913, retaining the one name, Imperial Flying Association. First chairman was Army Lt-Gen Gaishi Nagaoka.

Lighter-than-air craft brought about the first successful Japanese experiments in man-carrying flight in 1877. This Yamada Airship No.2 was completed in early 1911 as one of many Japanese airship experiments.

Japanese thinking about flight. In April 1909, the Englishman Benjamin Hamilton went to Japan to demonstrate his airship. In June of that year, at Tokyo's Ueno Park, he made the first airship flight in Japan, and this strongly influenced Isaburo Yamada to design his own airship based on what he had seen and learned from Hamilton. After a year and a half, the Yamada Airship No.1 was completed. This airship had a capacity of 1,600cu m (56,504cu ft) and was powered by a 14hp automobile engine.

During a test flight on 8 September, 1910, in Tokyo, the Yamada No.1 Airship was forced to land at the Aoyama Military Parade Grounds because of a hydrogen-gas leak. Yamada's second airship was destroyed by an explosion on 23 March, 1911, before its second flight, but his third airship made a number of successful demonstration flights around the city of Tokyo that same year. In time, this airship, having served its purpose, was sold to China where it was flown on occasions over the Hankow-Wuchang area.

Other early flights in Japan included the glider flights of Navy Lieut Shiro Aihara. With the assistance of the French Military Attaché, 2-Lt Leprieur, who had witnessed flights in France, they built a glider using bamboo for the structure, and made gliding tests with an automobile as a tug in December 1909

The first gliding flights in Japan were made by this bamboo-frame glider in December 1909 at Ueno Park, Tokyo, a year in advance of the first powered flight in Japan.

The first flight of an aeroplane in Japan took place on 19 December, 1910, piloted by Capt Yoshitoshi Tokugawa. The aeroplane was an imported Henri Farman biplane.

at Ueno Park. This was the first glider flight in Japan.*

Provisional Military Balloon Research Association

Demonstration flights by the Wrights in the United States, and in France in particular, were being publicized throughout the world. A few air-minded people in Japan were strongly influenced by these reports, among them General Seiki Terauchi, Minister of the Army. He established within the military structure the Rinji Gunyo Kikyu Kenkyu Kai (Provisional Military Balloon Research Association)† on 30 July, 1909, under the leadership of Lt-Gen Gaishi Nagaoka. Members of that Association were selected from the Army, Navy, Tokyo Imperial University, and the Central Meteorological Observatory, and there were fourteen members in all. They established their work at Tokorozawa, a city 18 miles northwest of the centre of Tokyo.

Despite the name of this Association indicating its sole interest to be in lighter-than-air flight, much of its attention was in powered heavier-than-air craft, and it was the only Japanese organization to direct its efforts towards this new means of flight. In addition, both the

Army and the Navy had their separate testing units, using the Association's joint findings to advance their own causes. They sent Capt Yoshitoshi Tokugawa to France and Capt Kumazo Hino to Germany in April 1910 for pilot training and to purchase aircraft for each to bring back to Japan. After learning to fly, Tokugawa brought from France an Henri Farman biplane with a 50hp Gnome engine, while Hino had acquired in Germany a Hans Grade monoplane, powered by a 24hp Grade engine.

In makeshift tents at the Yoyogi Parade Grounds in Tokyo, assembly of the two machines was started on 11 December, 1910. In anticipation, 100,000 spectators flocked to the parade grounds daily to be on hand for the flights. On 14 December, Capt Hino accidentally flew a distance of 100m at a height of 2m when taxi-ing, but this was not recognized as an official flight.

On the morning of 19 December, 1910, with a wet battery strapped to his back for engine ignition, Capt Tokugawa started taxi-ing his Farman biplane at 7.55. After a run of 30m, the aeroplane took to the air, reaching a height of 70m. Tokugawa made two circuits of the parade grounds and after about four minutes he landed safely amid thunderous applause. At 1.30 that afternoon, Capt Hino flew his Grade monoplane for one minute and twenty seconds, after an engine problem prevented his making a morning flight as had Tokugawa. Thus, that day marked the first powered heavier-than-air flights, bringing modern aviation to Japan,

and a commemorative monument was erected on the site that also served as the grounds for the 1964 Olympic Games in Tokyo.

These aerial demonstrations captured public interest and turned attention towards aviation as a military weapon. The Army established an aviation section and, in April 1911, an airfield was laid out at Tokorozawa where the Provisional Military Balloon Research Association was located. The Army purchased a Blériot monoplane with a 50hp Gnome engine and a German-made Wright biplane, powered by a Wright 30hp engine, and Capts Tokugawa and Hino flew these aeroplanes before a daily crowd of onlookers. As a result, the airfield at Tokorozawa became the focal point of early aviation development in Japan.

From Tokorozawa, the first cross-country flight was made by Capt Tokugawa when on 9 June, 1911, he flew with another officer in the Henri Farman biplane to Kawagoe and back in 35 minutes, covering 26 miles. On the same day, Tokugawa again left Tokorozawa with the Blériot monoplane but crashed near Kawagoe, making this the first aircraft accident in Japan.

At this point in 1911, the Provisional Military Balloon Research Association (PMBRA) began building a series of heavier-than-air craft of their own, thus marking the start of the aircraft manufacturing effort in Japan, although most were one-of-a-kind, hand-built machines.

The PMBRA did not totally abandon lighter-than-air technology. Recognizing Yamada's successful airships, they designed an airship and contracted Yamada to fabricate the envelope, and the Hiraoka Iron Works to make the gondola. This became the Type I Airship and was powered by a

*Aihara was one of three Naval officers assigned to the Provisional Military Balloon Research Association. In this capacity, he was sent to Germany on 19 February, 1910, to study aeronautics. While on a training flight on 4 January, 1911, he was thrown from the aeroplane during an emergency landing and died from injuries four days later.

†Some sources use the term Provisional Military Balloon Research Society, and other word combinations, influenced by the word Kai having a literal translation of Society as well as Association.

60hp Wolseley water-cooled engine. Its first flight was on 25 October, 1911, with Navy Sub-Lieut Chikuhei Nakajima* at the controls and with three others on board. He flew the airship over Tokorozawa at a height of 170m (557ft) for 15 minutes, covering an air distance of 5 miles. Soon after, this airship was flown for an extended period of 1hr and 41min, covering about 20 miles.

Impressed with the capacity of airships, the PMBRA imported a Parseval non-rigid airship from Germany in June 1912. During its manufacture for Japan, the PMBRA sent a team of engineers to Germany to learn about the design and fabrication techniques that were used. This airship was the thirteenth such craft designed by August von Parseval. It was test flown in Japan for the first time on 30 August, 1912, with German pilot Schubert and Capt Masuda at the controls and carrying two other men. For its day, this was a large airship, measuring 76.7m (251ft 7in) in length and 16m (52ft 6in) maximum diameter. Carrying a crew of four to twelve, and powered by two 150hp Maybach water-cooled engines, the airship's performance included a cruising speed of 35kt (40.3mph), a service ceiling of 2,000m (6,562ft) and a range of 700nm (808sm), with an airborne endurance of 20 hours; remarkable figures for 1912. The popular airship, however, was heavily damaged when it crashed on the roof top of a building on 28 March, 1913, in a landing mishap at Tokyo's Aoyama Parade Grounds, where it was to take part in a static and flying display for the Army and members of the Japanese Government.

Heavier-than-air craft remained dominant in the thinking among PMBRA members, and much experimentation was generated. In these efforts a number of aircraft were built at Tokorozawa that led to progressive development and improvement in aerodynamics.†

*Nakajima was to establish his own aircraft company in 1917.

†After 1912, the PMBRA served as the Army's point of aircraft acquisition and experimentation, most of the results of which were officially adopted by the Army; the Navy, on the other hand, adopted none of these designs.

Establishment of Japanese Naval Aviation

Although the Provisional Military Balloon Research Assoiation had been established as a joint Army-Navy organization, the Army remained dominant. Along with four civilian members within its fourteen member committee, there were only three Naval officers. Dissatisfied with this and for other reasons, the Navy members resigned in June 1912 after three years and established their own organization, the Kaigun Kokujutsu Kenkyu Kai (Naval Aeronautical Research Association). This separation was fostered by the typical ill-feeling between Army and Navy experienced in other countries; however in Japan, this resentment continued to deepen, becoming a feature that undermined Japanese air power up to and during the Pacific War.

The newly formed Naval Association took the same initial steps as did the PMBRA, in that they sent officers to other countries to become pilots and learn about aircraft design. Lieuts Sankichi Kohno, Tadaharu Yamada, and Chikuhei Nakajima were sent to the Curtiss flying school in the United States, and Lieuts Kanehiko Umekita and Masahiko Kohama went to France. After their flying instruction, Lieut Yozo Kaneko, who had preceded the others to learn to fly balloons and airships, brought back from France two Maurice Farman seaplanes, mounted on Henri Farman floats, and Lieut Sankichi Kohno brought two Curtiss seaplanes from the United States.

The aeroplanes were assembled at Oppama near Yokosuka in October 1912, thus establishing Oppama as the birthplace of naval aviation and the first Japanese Naval Air Station. To test their new wings, Lieut Kaneko made the first flight, of 15 minutes, of a Naval aircraft in Japan on 6 October and reached an altitude of 30m (100ft). The later-arriving Curtiss 1912 seaplane was hurriedly assembled and flown for the first time by Lieut Kohno on 2 November. This was all in preparation for the first grand naval review under Emperor Taisho which took place

off Yokohama on 12 November. Kaneko piloted the Farman floatplane from Oppama and made an alighting and take-off demonstration near the Imperial Ship *Chikuma* before returning to Oppama. Kohno departed from calmer waters at Yokohama in the Curtiss floatplane and made a circuit over the naval ships in review. Thus, these two lieutenants made the first powered flights in Japan by the Japanese naval air service.

Pioneers in Civil Aviation

Many accounts of the development of Japanese aviation credit the military's awareness of the aeroplane as a weapon of war and therefore the sponsor of most of its progress. This is true, but there were also many civilian pioneers involved in aviation in the early years. Civilians were not welcome in military circles unless they had direct military involvement through contracts or social status. As a result, the military services and the civil experimenters and builders went their separate ways. Most of the civilian efforts went unnoticed because their efforts came to an early end, since activities that later resulted in larger production of aircraft were usually supported by military interests.

Among those early pioneers in civil aviation was Baron Sanji Narahara, a naval engineer and a member of the PMBRA. In October 1910, before the historic flight by Capt Tokugawa, Narahara completed a biplane but it failed to fly. He was assisted by other pioneers such as Einosuke Shirato, Otojiro Itoh, who later became a dominant manufacturer of civil aircraft, Ginjiro Goto and Saken Kawebe, all of whom became leaders in civil aviation in the following few years. Narahara's second aeroplane did fly on 5 May, 1911, and this became the first successful aeroplane to be made in Japan. His four aeroplanes are described in the section of this book under his name. Another baron, Ujihiro Iga, constructed a glider which he tested on 14 February, 1911, at the Itabashi Horse

Race Track in Tokyo, pulled by an automobile; Iga's powered aeroplane failed in an attempt to fly in late 1911 at the Yoyogi Parade Grounds.

While in Paris to take piano lessons, Baron Kiyotake Shigeno also learned to fly at the de Boysson flying school and became the second Japanese to obtain an international pilot's licence, after Capt Tokugawa. While in France, he built his own aircraft and took it to Japan in August 1912. His aeroplane and success are described later. There were other pioneers such as Tetsusaburo Tsuzuku, Shinzo Morita and Sotoichi Saito, who made painstaking efforts to design and construct their own aeroplanes. Little can be credited to their efforts in advancing aviation in Japan other than their obvious interest in aviation and their own design interpretations which were so necessary in the pioneering period. All these attempts are described later under the names of each manufacturer.

Japanese women gaze with curiosity at the newly introduced Mitsubishi Army Type 92 Reconnaissance Aircraft in 1932 as Japan concentrated more on increasing its buildup of military forces (S. Nicolaou)

Civil flying activities continued during these pioneering days, and inspired the First Civil Flying Meet, sponsored by the newly formed Imperial Flying Association and The *Asahi Shimbun* (a Tokyo/Osaka newspaper) which took place on 13–14 June, 1914, at the Naruo Horse Race Track near Osaka. For the event, pilots were limited to those who had international pilot licences, thus only five pilots competed. French-educated Tsunesaburo Ogita entered with his Morane-Saulnier monoplane; US-trained pilots Takayuki Takasou, Ikunosuke Umino, and Juichi Sakamoto entered with their Curtiss pusher, Christofferson flying-boat, and Martin tractor, respectively. Lieut-Cdr Isobe, IJN (Ret), of the Imperial Flying Association participated with that organization's Kaizo Rumpler Taube. Before 270,000 spectators, the two-day competition recorded the longest flight, which was 31min 22sec, and the highest altitude, 2,003m (6,571ft). As part of the attraction, Lieut-Cdr Isobe flew the Taube monoplane without contest restrictions, registering a flying time of 1hr 34min. (*see* Isobe Rumpler Taube Aeroplane)

The First World War

By 1914, both the Army and the Navy had expanded their aviation sections, whereby the Army had sixteen aircraft and the Navy had twelve. With the outbreak of the First World War, Japan declared war against Germany according to the provisions of the Anglo-Japanese Alliance Agreement. Aboard the *Wakamiya*, Japan's first seaplane tender, a contingent of the naval air arm reached Chiao-chou Bay on 1 September, 1914, to attack the German occupied area of China. Aircraft on board were one three-seat and three two-seat Maurice Farman seaplanes. Upon arrival they launched the first naval air operation in actual war. This was also the first time that Japanese military aeroplanes made combat sorties.

On 5 September, the Farman three-seater piloted by Lieut Hideho Wada, and a Farman two-seater flown by Sub-Lieut Masaru Fujise, made reconnaissance flights over Chiao-chou Bay and confirmed that the expected German cruiser *Emden* was not in one of the inlets. They also reported the exact number of German ships that were at anchor, along with other valuable informa-

tion that could only be obtained through aerial surveillance. With aerial bombs made from ordinary gun shells, they sank a German torpedo-boat within the Bay. This type of aerial-bombing warfare had yet to be experienced on the European fronts.

The Army involvement comprised four Maurice Farman 1913 aircraft and one Nieuport NG2 monoplane. Bad weather delayed construction of the base at the port city of Lungkou in Shantung Province, China, and the first wartime sorties by the Army aircraft were not made until 21 September. Two Maurice Farman biplanes and one Nieuport monoplane dropped three makeshift bombs on an enemy camp on their first combat mission.

The first aerial combat in which Japanese military aeroplanes engaged took place on 13 October. With the news that a German Rumpler Taube was approaching, three Army Farmans took off and

In Japan prewar air travel was considered a major event and used mostly by government officials and wealthy businessmen. Minister of Communications Koizumi and his wife prepare to board the Aichi AB-1 of Tokyo Koku Yuso KK at Tokyo for Shimoda in 1936. Three 'air girls' were employed for this service as the first in Japan.

tried to encircle the enemy aeroplane. The Navy aircraft came to attack the German from the rear, but the Taube evaded by outclimbing its pursuers and went into cloud at 3,000m. The German Navy pilot, Sub-Lieut Günter Pluschow later flew the Taube to Haichow to refuel, but neutral Chinese confiscated his aeroplane. Pluschow therefore set fire to the aircraft so that it would not fall into enemy hands. When the war ended, the Japanese Army and Navy had flown 86 and 49 sorties respectively, ending Japan's brief combat period.

Postwar Expansion

With the cessation of hostilities and the ability to assess wartime experience, it was obvious to Japanese military leaders that their respective air arms were far short of world standards both in training and equipment. The Army was the first to initiate a modernization programme with the purchase of warsurplus Nieuport and SPAD fighter aircraft in April 1918. These were used only for training, the pilots spending their time in purposeless flying since they lacked the knowledge of how to use their aircraft as a military force.

To solve the problem, the Army

invited French military instructors of the l'Armée de l'Air to Japan in January 1919 to train Japanese Army pilots. As a goodwill gesture under the leadership of Col Jean Paul Faure, a team of sixty-three French instructors took with them more modern aircraft, such as a number of Breguets, Salmsons, Nieuports, Caudrons and SPAD XIIIs. Instruction was given in aerial combat, gunnery, reconnaissance and bombing. The results of this training exceeded expectations. As a result of this French mission there came not only a new system of training pilots for Army aviation, but the drawing up of a plan for modernization of its equipment, and the provision of definite standards for military aircraft. After nine months of intensive training, the French instructors left for home in September 1919.

The Japanese Navy took note of the transformation achieved in the Army by foreign instructors and the introduction to new equipment. Taking into account the Japanese opinion that French Army aviation was better geared to fighting over land masses, and that British military aviation was more adept at operations over water, the Japanese Navy requested the help of a British military group to provide Navy instruction. Arriving in April

1921, a group of twenty-nine instructors, with Col the Master of Sempill, in charge, they began their training programme at Kasumigaura, the Navy's first air base for both landplane and seaplane operations, located 35 miles northeast of Tokyo.

The British intructors trained Japanese Naval pilots in torpedo-bombing, aerial photography, air tactics and other related operations. Of great importance, they taught the necessity of land-based operations to support naval operations as well as to operate independently of fleet activities. From the beginning the Navy had been equipped only with seaplanes, but, as more was learned about European aviation, it began to appreciate the value of Naval land-based aricraft. The British group introduced a number of new types of aircraft into Japanese service including the Avro 504K trainer, Short reconnaissance seaplane, Gloster Sparrowhawk fighter, Parnall Panther reconnaissance biplane, Sopwith Cuckoo and Blackburn Swift torpedo aircraft, and Supermarine Channel and F.5 flying-boats. Some of these were later produced in Japan and remained in service for a number of years.

This influence brought to Japan by the French and British air missions was to affect Japanese military aviation and its aircraft design in many ways and for many years to come. This led to the need for aircraft to be manufactured in Japan and continuing development of new designs, and as a result brought about the formation of Japanese manufacturing companies. As these companies were formed, many military engineers left the service at an early age to join them and this military influence was very apparent. The companies which flourished were those which met the needs of the military agency that supported them. Civilian endeavour was restricted by military influence and a limited market. Numerous companies were formed to manufacture aircraft and, in alphabetical order, their histories and products are described in Section II.

Early Privately-built aircraft

All aircraft described in this early section were of limited quantity, mostly single examples. Products of these lessor known companies and individuals may be regarded by some as in the category of home-built aircraft. Nevertheless, they all contributed to the history of Japanese aviation and where possible are recorded here. Some that were built were incapable of flight; if these did not lead to successful aircraft by that builder, they are only recorded here in a few rare examples.

These early aircraft are described in alphabetical order by the name of the builder/owner; a listing that terminates around the time of the First World War. After that time, most of these pioneers no longer built aircraft.

Awazu Flight Research Studio (Awazu Hiko Kenkyusho)

Minoru Awazu, an aviation enthusiast, was the third son of one of the chief guardians of the Ohtani families of the Higashi Honganji Temple in Kyoto and this social status gave Awazu the opportunity to pursue interests which were denied to those whose primary purpose had to be that of survival. He founded the Kyoto Flight Education Society, and because of his continued enthusiasm, this expanded to the manufacture of aeroplanes and later, to a flying training business.

Using his educational background acquired at an industrial arts school, he made a makeshift workshop in a room in the temple and, around 1918, established an aeroplane company that he called the Awazu Flight Research Studio. With his first and only aeroplane, and a taxi-ing trainer, Awazu embarked upon the flying training business at the area that was known as Katsuragawa Airfield (later called Awazu Flying School) on the dry bed of the Katsura River in Kyoto, managed by aviator Ginzo Nojima.

Awazu No.2 *Seicho-go* Aeroplane

Having acquired a 70hp Mercedes Daimler engine confiscated from the Germans during the Japanese-German encounters in Tsingtao in China, Awazu and Nojima began the design of their new aeroplane. The propeller and the radiator were fashioned according to technical documents brought back from China with the engine. When their design was completed, construction was turned over to Terutaka Tamai, a younger brother of the late Seitaro Tamai, an established builder of aeroplanes under this name. (*see* Tamai).

When the aeroplane was completed in March 1919, the high-priest of the Higashi Honganji Temple, Kouen Ohtani, named it the *Seicho-go*, meaning *Bluebird*. To have a safe place for making its first flight, the aeroplane was moved by rail to Tokyo and the sandy triangular ground at Haneda where Seitaro Tamai had established a flying field for his Nippon Flying School. Satisfied with success after several flights made by Terutaka Tamai, Awazu had the aeroplane shipped again, this time to Yokkaichi on Ise Bay, south of Nagoya, home of the Tamai family and aircraft factory.

On a commemorative flight on 26 August, 1919, however, after taking off from the Chikko reclaimed ground, Tamai had to make an emergency landing due to rapidly deteriorating weather, and the aeroplane turned over upon landing. After repair, he made a flight over Kyoto from the Fukakusa Parade Grounds in October 1919 at Awazu's request, and delivered the aeroplane to Awazu.

With the aeroplane to hand, Awazu Flight Research Studio became the Awazu Flying School at the so-called Katsuragawa Airfield situated on the Katsura Riverbed. For flying training, he used this *Seicho-go* Aeroplane and the

Awazu No.2 Seicho-go *Aeroplane.*
Seicho *on the tail means* Bluebird.

35hp Franklin powered Awazu No.3 Ground Taxi-ing Trainer. As instructors, he acquired the services of Sadajiro Okamoto and Fumisaburo Kataoka, both former members of the Tamai Airfield.

This location for flight training became impractical when the river filled, causing interruption of flying lessons. After much criticism from the students, flying was moved to the Fukakusa Parade Grounds in Kyoto, but coupled with poor management influenced by Awazu's weak and vacillating character, many students left the school and eventually the airfield and flying school were closed.

Converting the *Seicho-go* to a floatplane, Awazu used the aeroplane on nearby Lake Biwa, the first seaplane operation there, and established a seaplane base.

Single-engine tractor biplane. Wooden structure with fabric covering. Two seats in open cockpits.

70hp Mercedes Daimler four-cylinder inline water-cooled engine, driving a two-bladed wooden propeller.

Span 11.54m (37ft 10¼in); length 7.22m (23ft 8¼in); height 2.88m (9ft 4¾in); wing area 27.7sq m (298.17sq ft).

Empty weight 453kg (998lb); loaded weight 726kg (1,600lb).

Maximum speed 61kt (70mph); climb to 1,000m (3,280ft) in 10min; endurance 1hr.

One built, in March 1919.

The Fujinawa Orenco Aeroplane closely resembled this American-built Orenco Tourister Type F, four-seat aeroplane.

Fujinawa (Privately-built)

Born in Takada City, Niigata Prefecture, and later becoming a manager of an electrical business in Asakusa, Tokyo, Eiichi Fujinawa enrolled in the Oguri Flying School at Susaki Airfield in Tokyo in August 1920, taking flying lessons in a Curtiss Jenny. He acquired licence No.1 as a pilot 3rd class on 23 May, 1921, under the new regulations established by the Aviation Bureau the month before. With this as a start, he established the Tokyo Aviation Training Centre and made preparations to manufacture aircraft at his factory in Mikawajima, Tokyo.

Fujinawa Orenco Aeroplane

Under the guidance of B Sc Aijiro Hara and Army assistant-engineer Seiichi Kawamoto, and with the design skill of Norio Tsukiji, the company built a biplane that closely resembled the postwar US-built Orenco Tourister, Type F aeroplane (formerly Ordnance Engineering Corporation). Both were four-seat aircraft with two tandem open cockpits for two people in each and with dual controls in the rear cockpit. A 180hp Hispano-Suiza engine purchased from Sale & Frazar Ltd, a British importing company, powered the Fujinawa aeroplane.

The Fujinawa Orenco was completed in November 1921 and flight tested at Tsudanuma, Chiba Prefecture, and then used as Fujinawa's personal aeroplane for further flight training. In his effort to be upgraded to pilot 2nd class, he made a flight in which he became enveloped in a dense fog, crashed at sea and was killed.

No technical data are known for this aeroplane.

Hino (Privately-built)

One of the members of the Provisional Military Balloon Research Association (PMBRA) established in 1909, was Army Capt (Infantry) Kumazo Hino from Hitoyoshi, Kumamoto Prefecture. As has already been described in the section on the PMBRA and in the introduction to this history, Hino was the first Japanese to make a flight in Japan (although recorded as unofficial). His interest in aviation long preceded his official preparation for his flight, and also prevailed long after, to the extent that it interfered with his official duties. His personal attempts in building aircraft ended in failure, but these failures led to the success of others' and are therefore worthy of record.

Hino No.1 Aeroplane

Aside from his official duties, Hino studied foreign reports on the design and building of aircraft, an interest in which he was deeply involved. Obtaining space at the Hayashida Wood Works at Gokencho, Ushigome-ku, Tokyo, in late 1909, he began building his single-seat aeroplane. The structural members were made of bamboo and Japanese cypress (hinoki), giving

Hino No.1 Aeroplane.

the aeroplane a wing span of 8m (26ft 3in) and length of 5m (16ft 5in). He designed and built his own engine for his project called the Hino two-cycle engine developing 8hp and installed it as a tractor on the front of the airframe. Empty weight of the aeroplane was 110kg (242lb) and when loaded it weighed 180kg (396lb). From 6 to 18 March, 1910, at Toyamagahara in Tokyo, he relentlessly attempted to make the aeroplane become airborne, but because of insufficient power, it would only taxi. Nevertheless, the PMBRA purchased the aeroplane from Hino so that it could be used for further experiments.

Hino No.2 Aeroplane.

Hino No.2 Aeroplane

It was after Capts Hino and Tokugawa were sent to Europe to study aviation and each to bring back an aeroplane, that Hino began the design on his second attempt to build a successful aeroplane of his own. A year after his part in the history-making first flight in Japan in 1910, he built an aero-engine in a laboratory of the Tokyo Army Technical School during his time off between military duties. This engine was a water-cooled, pre-compression four-cylinder 30hp type, but actually developed only 18hp.

While developing this engine, he devoted much attention to the building of his second aeroplane in which the engine was to be installed. The aeroplane was a monoplane with a canoe-like pod to accommodate the pilot and the pusher engine. It had a wing span of 9.20m (30ft 2½in) and length of 5.70m (18ft 8½in). A skid extended from the undercarriage rearward to support the empennage. This design was purely original in all aspects.

Test flights were attempted from 23 to 25 May, 1911, at the Aoyama Parade Grounds but without success. After modifications, further attempts were made at the Yoyogi Parade Grounds from 23 to 25 August, sponsored by the Kokumin Shimbunsha (Nation's Newspaper) to bring attention to aviation, but again without success. Tests were repeated at Kawasaki Stadium, but the aeroplane refused to fly. The reason for failure was insufficient engine power, for it produced approximately half of what was expected. Empty, the aeroplane weighed 170kg (374lb) and loaded it weighed 320kg (705lb).

Obsessed with these efforts to the detriment of his military duties, the situation was resolved when he was promoted to Major and was reassigned to an infantry regiment in Fukuoka in December 1911. The PMBRA also purchased this aeroplane for their experiments.

Hino No.3 and No.4 *Kamikaze-go* Aeroplane

Hino's efforts to construct a successful aeroplane continued while at Fukuoka. What became the Hino No.3 Aeroplane was actually a modification of an Iga *Maitsuru-go*. He first tested the aeroplane at Fukuoka on 20 April, 1912, with poor results, then modified it into a seaplane with 2.20m (7ft 2½in) long floats. Giving the aeroplane the designation Hino No.3 Kai or No.4 *Kamikaze-go*, he made attempts to fly on 25 September, 1912, at Nezumijima Island near Nagasaki, but again, his aeroplane would not become airborne. Disappointed with three consecutive failures and being criticized for being distracted from his military responsibilities, Hino gave up his interest in aviation. His interest was

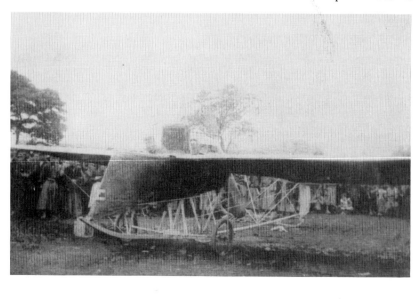

Hino No.3 Aeroplane equipped with floats and called Hino No.3 kai or No.4 Kamikaze-go.

rekindled and he created a tailess glider in 1937, the development of which was taken over by Kayaba Manufacturing Works (Kayaba Seisakusho) and then by Hidemasa Kimura of the Aeronautical Research Institute of Tokyo Imperial University. Designated HK-1 (Hino Kayaba), it was built by Itoh Aeroplane Co Ltd.

Kumazo Hino, despite the lack of success with his early designs is looked upon as a major pioneer of Japanese aviation. He died on 15 January, 1946, at his home in Azabu, Tokyo, at the age of 67.

Hoshino (Privately-built)

Yonezo Hoshino of Tamachi, Akasaka-ku, Tokyo, was a graduate from Sloane Flying School at Hempstead, Long Island, USA, in 1913 from which he earned international licence No.231. He returned to Japan in July of that year.

Hoshino Aeroplane

With financial assistance from Kanzaburo Aijima, a member of the Japanese Diet, he built his first and original design of a tractor biplane in a warehouse of the Yamashina Maritime Industry Co (Yamashina Kaiji Kogyo Kaisha) in Kobiki-machi, Kyobashi-ku, Tokyo. In appearance it resembled an early Curtiss tractor biplane, having its ailerons mounted at mid-point on the wing struts. This single-seat aeroplane had a wing span of 12m (39ft 4½in), was 7.90m (25ft 11in) long, and had an empty weight of 390kg (860lb). It had two mainwheels and a small one at the front of the skid provided to prevent nose-overs. For an engine, always the most critical factor in building an aeroplane, Hoshino borrowed a 50hp Gnome air-cooled rotary from his friend Tetsusaburo Tsuzuku, also a builder of aircraft.

Completed in August 1914, Hoshino's aeroplane was first flown very successfully at Inage across the bay from Tokyo. During a later flight on 13 September of that year, he attempted a flight to Tokyo, but while flying in fog and having to stay very close to the surface to maintain visual contact around Tsukijima, his port wingtip hit a post that was standing in the water, and he was forced to make an emergency landing nearby on a muddy area of reclaimed land. This enforced landing damaged the nose and propeller of the aeroplane and Hoshino was injured.

After the aeroplane was repaired, he redesignated it Hoshino No.2 Aeroplane, although only minor changes had been made. Beginning in October 1914, he took the aeroplane on an exhibition tour starting at Shizuoka and Gifu. Again, Hoshino sustained injuries and damaged his aeroplane when the engine failed on 31 October. With repairs made, undaunted he flew on to Hamamatsu, Maisaka and Hamanako, all on 30 November, and to Fukui on 10 to 12 December. By now, however, he was committed to return the borrowed engine to Tsuzuku who needed it to power an aeroplane ordered by the Chinese revolutionary army. Thus, without an engine, he was also without an aeroplane, so he assisted his friend Tetsusaburo Tsuzuku with the delivery of the Tsuzuku No.3 Aeroplane to Shantung in northeast China, and served as an instructor pilot.

The Hoshino No.2 Aeroplane remained at Inage, was soon given a 70hp Gnome rotary engine and converted into a two-seat aircraft. It is known to have flown from the Tokyo Aoyama Parade Grounds on 22 September, 1916, in this configuration, but no further details are known.

Hoshino Aeroplane.

Ichimori
(Privately-built)

Yoshinori Ichimori was born into a wealthy family in Higashi Tengajaya, Osaka. An early hobby was that of automobiles and related driving. Soon, his attention turned to aviation and in early February 1919 he acquired the Tamura Tractor from the estate of the late Toshikazu Tamura. After it was destroyed (*see* Shirato *Takeru-go* Aeroplane) his desire was to build an aircraft of his own and in order to do so he constructed a building on the family property.

Ichimori Monocoque Aeroplane

In early 1919, Ichimori purchased a US-built 100hp Maxim engine around which he designed a biplane with the help of a close friend and aviator, Ginzo Nojima. This had a single-seat fuselage with monocoque construction which closely resembled the Pfalz D XII fighter of the First World War. Since very little plywood was available in Japan, he made his own laminations with three-layers of Japanese cypress (hinoki) with isinglass, imported from the United States, as an

Ichimori Monocoque Aeroplane.

adhesive. The wing design used the USA 2 aerofoil and the wings and empennage were fabric covered. Dope was applied to the fabric surfaces. For a homebuilt-aeroplane the design was impressive.

Completing his aircraft in November 1919, Ichimori prepared it for flight at Okinohara Airfield in Yokkaichi, southeast of Lake Biwa. While Noburu Fujiwara was preparing to make the maiden flight and about to start the engine, the aircraft caught fire as the result of a fuel leak and was completely destroyed in less than a minute, the loss of an investment of 18,000 yen. (*see* other misfortunes of Noburu Fujiwara under Itoh Emi 6 Aeroplane.)

Single-engine homebuilt biplane. Fuselage of plywood monocoque construction, wings and empennage of wood with fabric covering. Pilot in open cockpit.

Ichimori Skylark *Sport-plane.*

100hp Maximotor six-cylinder inline water-cooled engine, driving a two-bladed wooden propeller.

Span upper 8.84m (29ft), lower 8.53m (27ft 11½in); length 6.55m (21ft 5¾in); wing area 25.55sqm (275.026sq ft).

Empty weight 499kg (1,100lb); loaded weight 683kg (1,505lb).

Maximum speed 78kt (90mph); minimum speed 39kt (45mph); endurance 2½hr. Estimated figures.

One built in 1919.

Ichimori *Skylark* Sport-plane

Putting aside thoughts of his costly loss of the Monocoque Aeroplane, Ichimori purchased a 70hp Erros eight-cylinder vee water-cooled engine from Ginzo Nojima who had bought it in Tsingtao. With this he planned a new design for a small single-seat light-plane that he named *Skylark*.

When completed, and flown by Fumisaburo Kataoka, he reported that it was a difficult aeroplane to fly because of its poor design. After modifications were made, it apparently had acceptable flying qualities, but nothing further is known about this aeroplane.

Ichimori retained his interest in aviation through the purchase of the Shirato *Takeru-go* Aeroplane from Toshikazu Tamura, a transaction negotiated by his fellow aviation enthusiast, Ginzo Nojima. After modifications, this aeroplane was redesignated the Ichimori Tractor. Its activities and fate that followed are described as the Shirato *Takeru-go* Aeroplane. Although wealthy at the beginning of his aviation ventures, Ichimori's money supply dwindled and he returned to his automobile driving interests. He became ill and died in April 1925.

Iga
(Privately-built)

One of three barons in early Japanese aviation history, Ujihiro Iga was a family member of the Tosa-Sukumo clan, born around 1886. During his enlistment in the Army, he had an idea for a flying machine that could be used as a scout. He applied for a patent for his idea on 23 April, 1910, which was granted on 4 October of that year (Pat N.18633). After his discharge from the Army in March 1911 he built a model of his concept that he called the Iga Flying Device which closely resembled a biplane.

Iga's next venture was a monoplane glider with bamboo frame and fabric covering. The glider had an 8m (26ft 3in) wing span and weighed 90kg (198½lb). This was tested by being towed behind a car at Itabashi Race Track, Tokyo, on 16 March, 1911, with perhaps little success since the undercarriage was damaged during this attempt and nothing further was recorded.

Iga *Maitsuru-go* Aeroplane

In the summer of 1911, Baron Iga began the construction of a powered monoplane. At that time, a publishing company, the Science World Co (Kagaku Sekai Sha) was promoting aviation by publishing a special issue called *Air Flying*. The editor, Orito, became a sponsor of Iga and his flying machine, and the financier of the publishing company, Kihei Yanagihara, supported part of the construction expense. For an engine, Narazo Shimazu, the manager of Tankin, the long-established ornamental silverware store in Osaka, had built an Anzani fan-type three-cylinder 25hp engine which was then used for this aeroplane.

Named *Maitsuru-go* Aeroplane, meaning *Dancing Crane*, it closely resembled a reduced-span Blériot monoplane. Iga had written to Louis Blériot who kindly sent him drawings of his aeroplane which he used as reference. With this design concept, the flexibility of the wings was gained by using bamboo for wing ribs whose fabrication was assisted by a master bow-maker, Yasaku Ishizu. When completed in December 1911, it could truthfully be said that this aeroplane was built entirely from Japanese materials, something of note in these early times of Japanese-built machines.

On 24 December, 1911, a test flight attempt was made at the Tokyo Yoyogi Military Parade Grounds, being witnessed by Dr Aikichi Tanakadate* and Capt Yoshitoshi Tokugawa, the latter having been the first man to fly in Japan the year before. Causing disappointment but not surprise, the aeroplane did not fly, because of engine problems, the norm in these early days rather than the exception.

Following this attempt, Iga ended his aviation research at his family's insistence. As a result, the

Iga Maitsuru-go *Aeroplane.*

airframe was handed over to Capt Kumazo Hino, the strong advocate of aviation and a member of the Provisional Military Balloon Research Association. (*see* Hino No.3 Aeroplane.)

Single-engine Blériot-type monoplane. Primarily bamboo construction with fabric covering. Pilot in open cockpit.

25hp Shimazu Anzani-type three-cylinder fan-type air-cooled engine, driving a two-bladed wooden propeller.

Span 8m (26ft 3in); length 7.50m (24ft 7¼in).

Empty weight 205kg (452lb).

One built in December 1911.

Inagaki
(Privately-built)

Inagaki Tractor

Yasuji Inagaki, was the second son of Buntaro Inagaki, a civil contractor in Kyoto. It was Yasuji Inagaki's intention to design and build a biplane as a home-type

*Dr A Tanakadate was a renowned professor at Tokyo Imperial University and a member of the PMBRA. He was known for his advocacy of Japan using alphabetical letters in all writing instead of kanji and kana.

Inagaki Tractor.

project. As problems with the aeroplane continued to develop so did Inagaki's frustrations, Otojiro Itoh of the Itoh aircraft company was asked to assist with the project and make the aeroplane flyable at the Yokaichi Airfield, followed by exhibition flights over Kyoto.

Itoh accepted the request but with the provision that his work be done at his company location at Inage, in Chiba Prefecture, and that no deadline be set for the date of the test flight. The fee would have been somewhere between 500 and 600 yen. Reluctantly, Inagaki sent the airframe to Inage where Itoh began his work. This included almost rebuilding the fuselage for the increased strength thought to be necessary, along with other modifications. To assure a better chance of success, Itoh installed his 80hp Hall-Scott engine. After three months, the task was completed.

The aeroplane was test flown on 7 August, 1917, by Itoh attaining a rewarding altitude of at least 30m (100ft). With this success and his continued obligation to Inagaki, Itoh planned exhibition flights at Kyoto for the middle of September of that year as agreed, but Inagaki was not meeting his promise to Itoh for payment. As a result, on 14 December, 1917, Itoh removed his engine from the aeroplane after test flying it at Osaka in conjunction with his own demonstration flights in the Itoh Emi 2 Aeroplane. Inagaki frequently asked Itoh to make further demonstrations of his aeroplane at Kyoto the next January, but Itoh refused.

Ishibashi
(Privately-built)

Following the end of the First World War, one of Japan's popular civil pilots was Katsunami Ishibashi, frequently being in the news in speed-flying events. In mid-1920, Ishibashi returned from France after military service in the French Army as a flying officer during the war. On 25 August of that year, through the French Embassy in Tokyo, he purchased three SPAD XIIIs that were on board the Russian warship *Maguryov* which had taken refuge at the end of the war in the Japanese port of Moji in the strait between Kyushu and Honshu. Ishibashi shipped the aircraft to the Nihon Hikoki Seisakusho (later Nakajima Aeroplane Co) hangars at Ojima Airfield near the Ohta factory. As so often happened in those early times, a hangar fire developed, on

18 August, 1921, and consumed everything including Ishibashi's three SPADs.

Ishibashi SPAD XIII Racing Aircraft

In an effort to make good some of the loss of the three SPAD XIIIs, Ishibashi built a Japanese version of the type by using salvaged parts and making new parts and structures from manufacturing drawings. Assisting him were his engineer Tsuruzo Takeda and apprentice Ryo Kitazato. Unable to replace the 220hp Hispano-Suiza engine, he bought a 180hp Hispano from Sale & Frazar Ltd as a substitute. A larger fuel tank was installed in the under-fuselage of this single-seat aeroplane to extend the range for his planned competitions. This gave the aeroplane a much fatter appearance than the standard SPAD XIII.

Upon completion, Ishibashi entered the Fourth Prize-winning Airmail Flying Contest which was flown between Kanazawa on the central northwest coast and Hiroshima on the southwest coast of Honshu on 3 November, 1921. On the way, he was forced to make an emergency landing at Fukuyama, Hiroshima Prefecture, because of lack of fuel caused by stronger than expected headwinds. A year later, Ishibashi entered his aeroplane in the Tokyo–Osaka Airmail Round-robin Flight Competition. It demonstrated its superior performance with its high speed capability but lost the first place because of an infringement of the rules.

Ishibashi SPAD XIII Racing Aeroplane.

Isobe
(Privately-built)

Born on 14 August, 1877, at Zaimoku-cho, Kanazawa City, Ishikawa Prefecture, Onokichi Isobe developed his interest in aviation around 1908 when he was the chief engineer of the third reserve ship *Anekawa* as a Lieut-Cdr in the Japanese Navy. While stationed aboard this ship, he designed and built a small glider equipped with floats that he would drop, with ballast, from the ship to alight on the water. Since this worked successfully, he then attempted to tow the model behind a torpedo-boat but this ended in failure.

At his request, Isobe was reassigned to the first reserve ship *Otoha* (formerly a cruiser) with home port at Yokosuka. On this assignment, his senior officer was Cdr Odagiri, an officer who shared his interest in aeronautical theory and gave Isobe encouragement and assistance.

Isobe Seaplane

Onokichi Isobe designed and built a Henri Farman type seaplane with help from seamen stationed at, and materials acquired from, the Yokosuka Naval Engineering School. A most noticeable feature of this biplane design was the use of a single-interplane strut instead of the conventional two parallel struts. This was accomplished by using bracing-wires to prevent vertical twisting of the wing on the single strut. It was a seaplane glider at first, equipped with a pair of inflatable rubber-lined canvas floats made for him by the Meiji Rubber Co in Shinagawa, Tokyo. For this combined design, he applied for a patent on 8 April, 1910, which was granted on 16 November of that year (No.18825) as the Isobe Aeroplane.

When used as a two-seat glider, it was launched on the water at Shirahama beach, at Yokosuka, on 19 April, 1910. After confirming

its stability while afloat, Isobe then had it towed by a steamboat at a speed of approximately 18 knots. The glider became airborne to a height of about 3m and flew for approximately 60m. At that point the glider went out of control and hit the water, wingtip first. Although this test ended in failure, it proved that an aeroplane could take off from and alight on the water in this fashion. It was to be another year before imported aircraft would be flown by the Navy for the first time from the Naval facility at Oppama. It is assumed that this Isobe aircraft was eventually repaired and had an engine installed.

Isobe No.2 Aeroplane

With this taste of success, Isobe began immediately to build his second man-carrying aircraft. As soon as the airframe was completed, he asked the Provisional Military Balloon Research Association to let him borrow an engine for his new aeroplane. This request from outside the PMBRA was granted reluctantly, for the members looked upon Isobe's work as that of an amateur and unauthorized. It was with the help of Dr Aikichi Tanakadate that assistance was granted. (*see* Iga *Maitsuro-go* Aeroplane for details of Tanakadate)

A number of taxi-ing tests were made at Shirahama beach, but when Admiral Sotokichi Uryu, Commander of Yokosuka Naval Station, was there, Isobe attempted to fly the aeroplane, but at the point of take off, the nose dug into the water and the aircraft turned over due to a

Although of very poor quality, this rare photograph gives some idea of the layout of the Isobe No.2 Aeroplane.

design flaw in the control system and was severely damaged. Isobe planned to build a No.3 Aeroplane to correct the flaws that were suspected, but with his personal funds already exhausted, he was forced to abandon further plans. He left the Navy on 1 December, 1911, at age 33.

Single-engine tractor biplane seaplane with fore and aft stabilizers. Wooden structure with fabric-covered wings and empennage. Pilot seated in open structure.

25hp Anzani three-cylinder fan-type air-cooled engine, driving a two-bladed wooden propeller.

Span 8m (26ft 3in); length 8.30m (27ft 2¾in); height 2.70m (8ft 10¼in).

Empty weight 410kg (903lb).

One built in April 1910.

Isobe Rumpler Taube Aeroplane

After resigning from the Navy, Onokichi Isobe was one of the principals in the establishment of the Imperial Flying Association formed on 23 April, 1913. The Association sponsored his travel to Germany to receive flying instruction, and to buy two Rumpler Taubes through Mitsui & Co.

When Japan became involved in the First World War, the Army purchased these two aeroplanes from the Association in October 1914 and sent them with an Army contingent to the Tsingtao campaign and Isobe was engaged by the Army to accompany the two aeroplanes and serve as an instructor. One Taube was damaged when flown by 2-Lt Jiro Takeda while still in Japan during flying training, and the other, to be flown by Isobe, arrived at Tsingtao too late to participate in the battle.

Now that the Association was without its aeroplanes, it purchased a 90hp Austro Daimler six-cylinder inline water-cooled engine from Britain for use in a Japanese-version of the Rumpler Taube they built in the Imperial Flying Association's hangar at Tokorozawa. Taking charge of design, Isobe made modifications to modernize the structure to some degree. Instead of having the flexible dove-like wings with negative incidence at the wingtips for control, Isobe incorporated hinged-ailerons. The empennage had hinged flying control surfaces instead of the larger flexible bamboo structure of the original Taube. The forward half of the two-seat fuselage structure was made of welded-steel tubing, the rear section having a wooden framework. The sides of the cockpit and part of the wing root where the pilot's position was located were covered with celluloid sheeting to provide a downward view.

This aeroplane, completed on 5 April, 1915, was commonly called the Kaizo (meaning modified) Rumpler Taube, and used mostly by Isobe and Toriumi in their engineering work with the Association. Later it was used as a trainer by students Yukiteru Ozaki and Takeji Senno. (*see* Ozaki Aeroplane) On 30 May, 1915, while Isobe was

Isobe Rumpler Taube Aeroplane.

flying solo at Tokorozawa, a gust of wind caused the port wing of the Taube to strike the ground, causing heavy damage to the aircraft. Only the front part of the fuselage and its engine could be salvaged. The parts were stored for a while and later used in the Ozaki *Soga-go* Aeroplane. Following the loss of its aeroplanes the Imperial Flying Association was soon re-equipped with Type Mo 1913 and Type Mo-4 aircraft through the assistance of the Army.

One month after his accident with the Kaizo Rumpler Taube, Onokichi Isobe resigned from the Imperial Flying Association and joined the French Army. He entered the Premier Regiment Étranger* before being assigned as a pilot with SPA 57. Flying Nieuport 11 Bébés with this unit, (Flight) Lieutenant Isobe was severely wounded on 6 March, 1917, while on patrol. For his service, he was awarded the Légion d'Honneur and Croix de Guerre with citations that described him in part as being '… as a foreigner fighting for the cause of France, he showed exemplary military qualities in the Squadron by demonstrating his aggressiveness in combat.' He resigned from the French Army in December 1917 and withdrew from aviation, but became involved again in Japan by establishing the Nippon Glider Club (later Nippon Glider Association) in April 1929 as an active promoter of sailplane activities. He died on 14 February, 1957, at the age of 80.

*All foreigners were inducted into the Légion Étrangère (Foreign Legion) before joining operational units.

Izaki, also Sempu Flying School (Privately-built) (Sempu Hiko Gakko)

When aviator Tsunesaburo Ogita returned to Japan from France in May 1914, he took with him an 80hp Le Rhône powered Morane-Saulnier MS 5 monoplane. He won first prize in the altitude category by reaching 2,000m at the First Civil Flying Meet, at Naruo in June 1914. Later, on 2 September, 1914, when he made an exhibition flight over Kyoto City, he was honoured by His Highness Prince Fushimi by giving his aeroplane the name *Sempu*, (meaning cut the wind with a wing).

With this aeroplane, Ogita established the Sempu Flying School in Yokaichi, near Ohtsu by Lake Biwa. After nearly eight months of flying in Japan, the aeroplane crashed soon after taking off from the Fukakusa Military Parade Grounds in Kyoto on 3 January, 1915. It struck the ground at the nearby Army ordnance arsenal, killing Ogita and his assistant Shigeharu O-hashi, and was destroyed. The parts were collected and, along with spares for the aeroplane, were stored at the nearby Kyoto Flight Sponsorship Society (Kyoto Hiko Koenkai).

No.2 *Sempu-go* Aeroplane

One month after the fatal crash, the Kyoto Flight Sponsorship Society decided in February 1915 to build an aeroplane from the remaining parts. With a working budget of 2,500 yen, Shozo Izaki and five flying students set about the task of rebuilding. The same 80hp Le Rhône rotary engine was used, but the repair of the engine by the

Shimazu Motor company in Osaka delayed completion of the aeroplane until that August. It was called the No.2 *Sempu-go* Aeroplane in honour of Ogita.

Initial test flights were made by Army 2-Lt (Reserve) Kyubei Kumaki and Shozo Izaki at the Okinohara ground in Yokaichi. The aeroplane proved very successful and caught the interest of a number of foreign aviators. The first of these was the American pilot Charles F Niles, when, on 31 January, 1916, he set Japan's altitude record of 3,050m (10,000ft) with this aeroplane. Later one of the team members of the Miss Katherine Stinson aerobatic circus, pilot engineer Frank Champion, remained in Japan after the team returned to the United States in May 1917. His plan was to make a nonstop flight between Naruo and Tokyo flying the No.2 *Sempu-go.* In preparation, he equipped the aeroplane with a fuel tank to give a duration of six hours, sufficient for the flight.

He took off from Naruo on 3 June, 1917, but while en route two emergency landings were made, one near Yokaichi and finally at Hamamatsu because of engine problems. The aeroplane had to be dismantled and returned to Yokaichi by rail for repair. When operational again and while performing in an aerobatic exhibition by Frank Champion on 30 October, 1917, over Kouchi City, Shikoku Island, the aeroplane disintegrated and Champion was killed in the crash.

Single-engine shoulder-wing monoplane. Wooden structure with fabric covering. Two in open cockpits.

80hp Le Rhône nine-cylinder air-cooled rotary engine, driving a two-bladed wooden propeller.

Span 9.30m (30ft 6in); length 6.58m (21ft 7in); wing area 14.5sq m (156.08sq ft).

Loaded weight 550kg (1,212lb).

Maximum speed 70kt (81mph); service ceiling 3,000m (9,843ft); normal endurance 1½hr.

One built in June 1915.

Maruoka
(Privately-built)

Man-powered Screw Wing Machine

The oldest heavier-than-air flying machine in Japan, for which there is a photograph, is one designed and built by Katsura Maruoka. He was a son of Kanji Maruoka, Governor of Kouchi Prefecture and was both a poet and an inventor. While living in San-ban-cho, Koujimachi, Tokyo, during 1902 and 1903 Katsura Maruoka and a friend, Daisaburo Matsushita, built a contra-rotating wing device that they called a Man-powered Screw Wing Machine. The rotor-blades were made of wood and the framework structure was of steel pipe.

Recognizing that obtaining sufficient power would be a major problem, and lacking a proper engine in Japan at that time,

Maruoka Man-powered Screw Wing Machine.

Maruoka resorted to man-power through a bicycle pedal drive system. At the handle-bar level were horizontal stabilizing wings for control. Although unsuccessful, it is worthy of note that this attempt to achieve vertical flight was made in Japan at such an early date. In appearance the craft was similar to Igor Sikorsky's 1910 engine-driven helicopter which also failed.

Morita
(Privately-built)

Shinzo Morita is credited with having made and flown, in 1911, the first aeroplane to be demonstrated in the heavily populated Kansai area of Japan which includes the cities of Osaka, Kyoto, Nara and others. This was only four months after the first flights in Japan, at Tokyo, that were made with imported aeroplanes.

Morita was born on 28 January, 1879, the son of a leather wholesale dealer in Karamono-machi, Higashi-ku, Osaka. Coming from an affluent family, he was educated by Prof Yukichi Fukuzawa, founder of Keio Gijuku University in Tokyo, and excelled in English and French.

Izaki No.2 Sempu-go *Aeroplane.*

He left Japan in 1900 at the age of 21 for eight years' additional study in the United States at a New York university. Later, while in Europe to visit the International Fair in Brussels, he bought a French Grégoire Gyp 45hp engine made in Belgium, and took it with him to Japan in the spring of 1910. With the intention of building an aeroplane for this engine, he rented space at the Osaka Joto Military Parade Grounds.

Morita Aeroplane

Obtaining the assistance of draughtsman Mitsuzo Ohnishi and Noboru Tarao and Sensuke Shimizu, they designed an aeroplane based on the Blériot and Antoinette monoplanes. The Morita had shoulder-mounted wings and a wooden frame fuselage with the rear portion left uncovered. The Grégoire engine was mounted on the nose inverted and partially faired over with an aluminium cowling. The two-wheel undercarriage had short skids to prevent nosing-over upon landing.

The aeroplane was completed in April 1911 and flown for the first time on 24 April. During one of Morita's flights that followed, one of 100m in distance and 3m in altitude, his wingtip grazed a boy who was crossing in front of him on a bicycle. Because of this accident, and having thought at first that he had killed the boy, family pressures persuaded Morita to do no further flying. As a result, he started a model aeroplane business at Matsuyamachi, Osaka, which was the first in the Kansai area. Soon after, he published a book entitled *Mokei Hikoki* (*Model Aeroplane*) with Mitsuzo Ohnishi, the first such publication in Japan.

Morita Aeroplane.

As for the rare and therefore valuable Grégoire aero-engine, it passed from owner to owner, being installed in the aeroplanes of Shigesaburo Torigai, Otojiro Itoh, and Asao Fukunaga helping them to make their names in Japanese aviation.

Single-engine tractor-type shoulder-wing monoplane. Wooden structure with fabric covering. Pilot in open cockpit.

45hp Grégoire Gyp four-cylinder water-cooled inverted inline engine, driving a two-bladed wooden propeller.

Span 9.30m (30ft 6in); length 7.40m (24ft 3¼in).

Empty weight 290kg (639.339lb).

Maximum speed 41kt (47mph) (calculated figures).

One built in April 1911.

Narahara, also Tokyo Aeroplane Manufacturing Works (Tokyo Hikoki Seisakusho)

Sanji Narahara was born on 29 December, 1876, the second son of Baron Shigeru Narahara, the Governor of Okinawa Prefecture and retainer of the Satsuma clan. Around the time that he graduated from the Faculty of Ordnance of Tokyo Imperial University, he had already published his own design for an aeroplane. In April 1908 he joined the Navy and was assigned to the Yokosuka Naval Arsenal as a Naval

Assistant Engineer. Because of his recognized talent for aviation he became a member of the Provisional Military Balloon Research Association organized in 1909.

Separate from his official work with the PMBRA, Narahara started building his aeroplane in his father's garden, then at Shio-cho, Yotsuya, Tokyo. After his first aeroplane, and unable to continue building aircraft there, Narahara established the Tokyo Hikoki Seisakusho (Tokyo Aeroplane Manufacturing Works) in Tsunohazu, Shinjuku, Tokyo. An early project at this factory was the manufacture of 3m diameter airship propellers for the PMBRA. This established Narahara and his company as a factory for the Association.

Narahara No.1 Aeroplane

Consulting foreign aeronautical publications and using his own inventive qualities, Narahara designed an aeroplane, beginning in May 1910, seven months before Captains Tokugawa and Hino made the first aeroplane flights in Japan.

The aeroplane was of unusual configuration, being a highly-staggered tractor biplane with very shallow gap. The double-surfaced wings were so arranged that the trailing edge of the upper wings was only slightly aft of the leading edge of the lower wing. The bamboo open structure of the fuselage was wire-braced and supported a forward-facing 25hp Anzani engine at the nose. In addition to horizontal and vertical tail surfaces there was an outrigged forward horizontal surface believed to have acted as the elevator. This was of wide-span and carried widely separated vertical triangular surfaces near its tips said to prevent sideslipping. There were two mainwheels of Blériot type and a large-diameter tailwheel. Originally the undercarriage comprised twin mainwheels each side of a skid. The fabric surfaces were coated with a paint made from grass paste as a primer, and shibu (an astringent juice) as a finish. Construction took approximately six months to complete.

Narahara No.2 Aeroplane.

On 24, 30 and 31 October, 1910, Narahara attempted to fly the aeroplane at Toyamagahara Military Parade Grounds in Tokyo, but the best it could achieve was a height of about 30cm (1ft). Narahara concluded that the aeroplane was underpowered because although he had placed an order for a 50hp Gnome engine through a trading company, a 25hp Anzani had been delivered. In despair, Narahara sold the aeroplane to the PMBRA for ground operational study.

Single-engine tractor biplane. Bamboo and wood construction with fabric covering. Pilot in open structure.

25hp Anzani three-cylinder air-cooled fan-type radial engine, driving a two-bladed wooden propeller.

Span, upper 11.30m (37ft 1in), lower 9.30m (30ft 6in); chord 1.50m (4ft 11in); length 7.20m (23ft 7½in).

Empty weight 310kg (683lb).

One built in 1910.

Narahara No.1 Aeroplane.

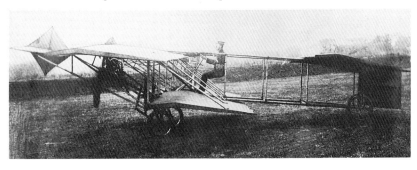

Narahara No.2 Aeroplane

In early 1911, Sanji Narahara ordered for a second time a 50hp Gnome engine and this was delivered. For this engine he designed a new aircraft that he called the No.2 Aeroplane. Influenced by new British and French designs, Narahara introduced some dihedral to the wing and fitted ailerons. Once again, he used a tractor layout and placed the pilot's seat in an open-pod behind the engine, using booms on which to mount the tail. Because of reports of pilots being injured by splintered bamboo in mishaps in other countries, Narahara substituted wooden structural members.

The aeroplane was taken to Tokorozawa Flight Test Grounds, newly established as the first airfield in Japan. On 5 May, 1911, Narahara succeeded in flying this aeroplane, five months after two imported aircraft had made the first flights in Japan. Narahara's flight covered 60m (200ft) at about 4m in height, establishing the first flight recorded by a Japanese-made aeroplane. This historic event ended

with a slight mishap when an under-carriage strut broke upon landing and damaged the propeller.

In later flights, the aeroplane recorded a maximum air distance of approximately 600m (nearly 2,000ft) at a height of approximately 60m (200ft). This was regarded as an amazing altitude since most early flying attempts were made at approximately 5m (16ft) height and on a straight-line course. It was with this aeroplane that the first civilian flying training was undertaken. Some of the students, including Einosuke Shirato, Umejiro Imamura, Ginjiro Goto, and Saito, were later to become well known in Japanese aviation.

Single-engine tractor biplane with engine/pilot pod. Wooden structure with fabric covering. Pilot in open structure.

50hp Gnome seven-cylinder air-cooled rotary engine, driving a two-bladed wooden propeller.

Span, upper 10m (32ft 9½in), lower 9.20m (30ft 2¼in); length 10m (32ft 9½in); height 2.80m (9ft 2¼in).

Empty weight 430kg (948lb); loaded weight 550kg (1,212lb).

One built in May 1911.

Narahara No.3 Aeroplane

The Narahara No.3 Aeroplane was made from reassembled parts taken from the worn and damaged No.2 Aeroplane after its many training flights. This new aeroplane was a two-seat trainer with a more orthodox fuselage instead of the pod and tail boom layout. Initially, the structure was left uncovered, but when it was covered it was of the highest quality used on any of the Narahara aeroplanes, being a layer of silk over a layer of cotton with the weaves diagonal and bonded. Wing dihedral was eliminated and the ailerons consisted of the 'pull-down only' type for both the No.2 and No.3 Aeroplanes. A more rugged undercarriage with four wheels and landing skids were incorporated. The Gnome engine was from the No.2 Aeroplane.

This aeroplane also flew successfully and became a trainer not only

Narahara No.3 Aeroplane.

for the previously mentioned Einosuke Shirato, who later established
the Shirato Aeroplane Research
Studio, but also for Otojiro Itoh,
eventually of Itoh Aeroplane Research Studio, and Saken Kawabe,
later to be Principal of the Toa
Professional Flying School, who
also assisted Narahara with his
work.

A gust of wind destroyed the
No.3 Aeroplane while it was on the
ground in September 1911. This
incident, along with reports from
other countries about aeroplane
crashes and pilot fatalities, brought
about Narahara's family's insistence he should not continue flying
and since he was more interested in
the design and building of aircraft
he agreed. Therefore, Einosuke

The Narahara No.3 after the entire
fuselage was covered.

Shirato became the instructor while
Narahara concentrated on the building of other aeroplanes. By this
time, Narahara had left the Navy
with an equivalent engineering rank
of Navy Lieutenant, Architect.

Narahara No.4 *Ohtori-go* Aeroplane

In the autumn of 1911, Narahara's
group was joined by Shuhei Iwamoto, later a professor of Tokyo
University, and Kiyoshi Shiga,
BSc. By March 1912 they had created the Narahara No.4 Aeroplane
with the help of Saken Kawabe,
Otojiro Itoh and Ginjiro Goto,
themselves to become notable in
aviation. The aeroplane was built at
the Orient Aeroplane Company
(Toyo Hikoki Shokai), having its
office in Kyobashi, Tokyo.* The
factory was then located at Fukagawa (near or at Susaki Airfield)

and final assembly was made at
Tokorozawa where it was to be
flown. It received the name of
Ohtori-go, after a champion sumo-
wrestler, *Ohtori*, at the request of
the sponsor who supported the
project.

The aeroplane performed well
and was taken on exhibition tours,
with flights at major cities throughout Japan to demonstrate what was
referred to as their 'Japanese-made
civil aeroplane'. Since there were no
airfields in Japan at this time, flights
were made from race tracks or military parade grounds of such relatively small size that landings and
take offs were very near the spectators. During the first of these exhibition flights on 13 April, 1912, at
Kawasaki Race Track, Kanagawa
Prefecture, a failing engine caused
the aeroplane to land short, allowing a wingtip to strike a school boy,
breaking his arm.

The aeroplane was again demon-
strated on 11 and 12 May for His
Highness the Crown Prince (later
Emperor Taisho) and his three sons
(one to later become Emperor Showa
[Hirohito]) along with Field Mar-
shal Aritomo Yamagata and many
other high-ranking officers at the
Aoyama Military Parade Grounds.
These demonstrations brought
Narahara an award by the Imperial
House, the first distinction given to
someone involved in Japanese civil
aviation.

The last exhibition flight by the
Ohtori No.4 was in Seoul, Korea,
on 3 and 4 April, 1913.

Single-engine tractor training biplane. Wooden structure with fabric
covering. Pupil and instructor in open
cockpit.

50hp Gnome seven-cylinder air-
cooled rotary engine, driving a two-
bladed wooden propeller.

Span, upper 11.40m (37ft 5in),
lower 9.30m (30ft 6in); length 7m
(22ft 11½in); height 2.80m (9ft 2¼in);

*Narahara disliked business management and left
such details to his manager, Sadajiro Sumiyoshi,
for the operation of the Tokyo Hikoki Seisakusho.
Mismanagement brought bankruptcy to the
company in February 1911. With financial support
by Jihei Takai, a stock speculator, and Tohma, an
industrial chemicals dealer, Narahara established
the Toyo Hikoki Shokai.

Narahara No.4 Ohtori-go *Aeroplane.*

Nishida
(Privately-built)

Matsuzo Nishida, who later changed his first name to Nakaemon, was a well-known aeroplane enthusiast in the Kansai (Osaka) area who became active shortly after the First World War. He closely followed the patterns set by aeroplane builders Minoru Awazu and Yoshinori Ichimori. He was from an affluent family, being the nephew of Madam Yone Suzuki, a wealthy merchant 'queen' in Semba, the commercial district of Osaka.

Nishida organized the Kansai Flight Research Society in 1919, constructed a workshop on his own land in Mikuni Village, a northern suburb of Osaka, and built a small single-seat sports monoplane, powered by a modified 16hp Harley motorcycle engine. The aeroplane proved to be underpowered, lacked certain design qualities, and therefore did not fly. His work was not taken seriously at first and looked upon simply as an enthusiast's hobby.

wing area 39sq m (419.8sq ft).
   Empty weight 470kg (1,036lb).
   Maximum speed 38kt (44mph).
   One built in 1912.

In May 1912, Narahara established Japan's first civil aerodrome, on the sandy beach at low tide by Inage in Chiba Prefecture, because the airfield at Tokorozara had been declared to be used only by the Provisional Military Balloon Research Association.

While the Narahara No.4 *Ohtori-go* was touring Japan with demonstration flights by Shirato, the Narahara No.5 *Ohtori Nisei-go* (meaning *Ohtori* the 2nd) was built. It was almost identical to the No.4 but was powered by a 70hp Gnome rotary engine and had a

strengthened undercarriage. This aeroplane was completed in June 1913 and made exhibition flights at Ibaragi, Toyama, Ishikawa and Niigata from June to September that year.

Sanji Narahara eventually retired completely from aviation at his family's insistence. His aviation activities were first taken over by Einosuke Shirato who then began manufacturing aeroplanes under his own name and provided flying training at Inage beach. In addition to Shirato's activities, Otojiro Itoh also became known for his aviation endeavours, and between the two, a new era of civil aviation began in 1913 stemming from Narahara's works and now centred at the Shirato/Itoh Airfields.

Nishida Sport Aeroplane

Undaunted, Nishida built a second aeroplane, this time a single-seat biplane powered by a 30hp Specky four-cylinder air-cooled inline engine. This aeroplane is reported to have been successful. It was flown at low altitude by Kinzo Negishi from reclaimed land near the mouth of the Kizu River in Osaka. Details of the flight and of the aeroplane are uncertain.

Following this apparent success, Nishida used family funding to support his aviation business and established the Nishida Aeroplane Research Studio on this same land, which was then called Kizugawa Airfield, in April 1923. From surplus Army and Navy aircraft stocks he purchased a Sopwith, Avro 504, Salmson and a Nieuport, which he used for advertising, sightseeing rides, aerial photography,

This view of the Narahara No.4 Ohtori-go *shows the drooped ailerons.*

and flying training. He hired Isegoro Miyazawa from Shirato Airfield as his chief pilot, and Tatsumi Kodera, Toshio Ishino, Yoshio Takemura, and Masayuki Fujiwara as his other pilots.

An inflight collision between two of his aeroplanes shortly after a formation take off in 1932 cost the lives of two pilots, Miyazawa and Fujiwara. This, coupled with severe damage caused by a typhoon and a high tide in the Kansai area in September 1934, brought an end to his flying business, and his remaining equipment was sold to the Tokyo Aeroplane Manufacturing Works.

Ogawa No.2 Aeroplane.

Ogawa (Privately-built)

Saburo Ogawa of Hirono-cho, Kagoshima City, was born on 18 November, 1896. Being an aeroplane enthusiast, at age 20 he began the design and manufacture of a biplane by studying his foreign aviation magazines. His efforts as a private home-builder of aircraft were not successful initially, but were typical of that time.

Ogawa No.1 Aeroplane

Ogawa's first attempt at designing and building an aeroplane was a biplane, powered by a 7hp modified motorcycle engine. It had a wing span of 7m and when empty weighed 120kg. Assisting him were his friends Misao Nakoshi and Yoshiji Masuda, who helped bring the project to completion in March 1917. Their most arduous task was the propeller which was made from laminated oak, and difficult to carve.

Causing them grave disappointment, their aeroplane did not fly, but it was recognized that insufficient power was the problem; their enjoyment came in using the aeroplane as a taxi-ing trainer.

Ogawa No.2 Aeroplane

Beginning in July 1917, Ogawa began modifications to his Aeroplane by installing a 16hp Excelsior two-cylinder air-cooled engine. Skids were attached to the undercarriage to prevent nosing over. Tomio Wakita assisted with this work, for he had additional skills due to having studied at a flying school at Haneda. When the modifications were completed in June 1918, Ogawa's No.2 Aeroplane was given the name *Taiyo-go*, meaning *Sun*.

When all was ready for the first flight, Wakita was to be the pilot because of his previous experience. The aeroplane flew for about 50m a short distance off the ground, but suddenly a wing dipped, and it crashed, causing severe damage to the aeroplane but no serious injury to Wakita.

Ogawa No.3 Taxi-ing Trainer.

Ogawa No.3 Taxi-ing Trainer

Following the failure of the No.2 Aeroplane, Ogawa made the No.3 which was entirely different, being of canard layout. Powered by the 16hp Excelsior engine taken from the No.2, it too was underpowered and would not fly, and therefore used as a taxi-ing trainer only. This aeroplane was unique in that it had large bicycle wheels in tricycle configuration, giving a smooth ride across the ground.

Still having a strong desire to fly, Ogawa became employed by Japan Aeroplane Works Co Ltd (Nakajima) as a mechanic. During his off-duty time, he took flying lessons at the Nakajima Flight Training Centre in Ohta, Gumma Prefecture, beginning in 1919 and received his training under Yozo Sato and Kintaro Iinuma. He earned his pilot 3rd Class licence on 16 August, 1921, and continued to be an employee of the Nakajima Aeroplane Co.

Ogawa No.5 Trainer

This trainer was basically a lightweight version of the Nakajima Type 5 trainer being mass produced by Nakajima as an Army and civil trainer. Ogawa modified this design in 1921 by not only reducing its weight, but giving negative stagger to the wings by moving the top wing further aft. This was necessary to compensate for the shift in centre of gravity which had been moved to the rear because of a lighter-weight engine than the 150hp Hall-Scott used in the basic design. The engine was an Army surplus 70hp Renault engine from a Type Mo-4 pusher aircraft with the cooling fan removed, but with cooling air ducts added.

Ogawa left Nakajima to become self-employed by using this aeroplane for exhibition flying. He named his aeroplane the *Nanshu-go* (*Southern Land*) and went first to his home town, Kagoshima, in December 1921 to give flying demonstrations. There, he established the Ogawa Flight Training Centre on reclaimed land along Nakashioya beach near Taniyama Village, adjacent to Kagoshima Bay in southern Kyushu. Few students enrolled because of the high cost of the training. Management problems developed and Ogawa retired from aviation. About this time, Ogawa had planned a single-seat sports aeroplane with a 50hp engine, but apparently this was not built.

On 7 November, 1961, at the age of 65, Ogawa died at his home in Musashino City, Tokyo.

Ogawa No.5 Trainer.

Oguri-Curtiss Jenny Trainer with a Japanese flag on an outer wing strut.

Oguri (Privately-built)

Tsunetaro Oguri was born in Handa-cho, Chita-gun, Aichi Prefecture, in 1886. He graduated from the Curtiss Flying School in the United States, obtaining international licence No.908, and became an instructor at the Keane Flying School while in America. Returning to Japan in 1918, he took with him an engine, a propeller and major parts and drawings for a Curtiss JN-4 Jenny with which he intended to build an aeroplane. In the meantime, he was employed as a test pilot for the Provisional Military Balloon Research Association at Tokorozawa.

Oguri-Curtiss Jenny Trainer

Oguri contracted with the Akabane Aeroplane Manufacturing Works at Kishi Airfield, to build him an aeroplane from parts of the Curtiss JN-4 Jenny, presumably a Canadian-built Canuck, he had acquired in the United States. When completed, it was flown at the Susaki reclaimed ground in Tokyo on 26 December, 1919. It performed well, demonstrating its aerobatic qualities, including loops.

With this aeroplane, Oguri established the Oguri Flying School at Susaki in June 1920. To distinguish his aeroplane from other competing fliers, he painted on it a black-cat insignia, basing it on one he had seen on aeroplanes in the United States.* In Japan, he was often referred to as 'the American-minded pilot.' He made his flying activities as visible as possible by practices such as special cross-country flights including Tokyo to Shizuoka, 100 miles to the southwest, and generally catering to female passengers. He lost his aeroplane, however, in a crash in which he was injured, while giving a flight to a geisha. While seated in the pupil's cockpit she became frightened, clung to the control column and

*Presumed to have been patterned after the 85th Canadian Training Squadron which served in both Canada and Texas in 1917–18.

caused Oguri to lose control of the aeroplane.

Single-engine biplane trainer. Wooden structure with fabric covering. Pupil and instructor in open cockpits.

90hp Curtiss OX-5 eight-cylinder water-cooled engine, driving a two-bladed wooden propeller.

Span, upper 14.55m (47ft 9in), lower 11.32m (37ft 1¾in); length 8.11m (26ft 7¼in); height 3.31m (10ft 10¼in).

Empty weight 711kg (1,567lb); loaded weight 975kg (2,149lb).

Maximum speed 65kt (75mph); landing speed 39kt (45mph); service ceiling 3,300m (10,826ft).

One built in December 1919.

Oguri No.2 Trainer

In order to participate in the Tokyo to Osaka Round-robin Flight Competition in April 1920. Tsunetaro Oguri designed and built what he called his No.2 Aeroplane which was powered by a 180hp Hispano-Suiza engine purchased from the British importing company Sale & Frazar Ltd. Construction was assisted by Yoshihei Ogawa and Kanji Tateishi, both having been trained in aeronautics in the United States. Because of delays in scheduling the competion, he was forced to withdraw for reasons not recorded.

With this change in plan, he modified the aeroplane by reducing the size of the wings and made it a standard two-seat trainer and very

Oguri No.2 Trainer, with the typical black cat insignia on the fuselage side.

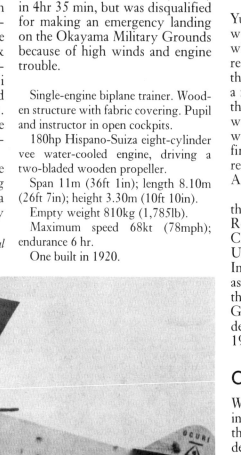

similar to the Curtiss Jenny. A larger radiator than a Jenny's gave it an almost SPAD appearance. With these modifications, Oguri entered his aeroplane in the Imperial Flying Association's Fourth Prize-winning Airmail Flying Contest between Kanazawa and Hiroshima on 3 November, 1921. He flew the course of 232nm (268sm) in 4hr 35 min, but was disqualified for making an emergency landing on the Okayama Military Grounds because of high winds and engine trouble.

Single-engine biplane trainer. Wooden structure with fabric covering. Pupil and instructor in open cockpits.

180hp Hispano-Suiza eight-cylinder vee water-cooled engine, driving a two-bladed wooden propeller.

Span 11m (36ft 1in); length 8.10m (26ft 7in); height 3.30m (10ft 10in).

Empty weight 810kg (1,785lb).

Maximum speed 68kt (78mph); endurance 6 hr.

One built in 1920.

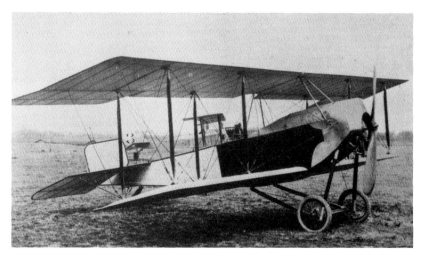

Ozaki Tractor Biplane.

Ozaki (Privately-built)

Yukiteru Ozaki was of the class of wealthy and influential Japanese who could devote his time and resources to aviation. Born the third son of Yukio 'Gakudo' Ozaki, a noted politician and a member of the Diet from Mie Prefecture, he was privileged in that he could train with and graduate from the Army's first pilot training class at the request of the Imperial Flying Association.

When Syun Wen, the leader of the revolutionary army of the Republic of China, purchased a Christofferson biplane from the United States, and requested the Imperial Flying Association to assemble it in Japan, Ozaki made the test flights at the Joto Military Grounds in Osaka. It was then delivered to the Chinese in August 1916.

Ozaki Tractor Biplane

With this aviation experience and influence, Ozaki used a hangar of the PMBRA at Tokorozawa and designed and built a light private aeroplane under guidance of Army Lt Morikichi Sakamoto. The aeroplane was powered by an 80hp Shimazu-Le Rhône engine which

Narazo Shimazu had just won as first prize at the Japanese-made aero-engine contest sponsored by the Imperial Flying Association. The building of this aeroplane was undertaken by the Association's chief engineer Toriumi almost in parallel with the Ozaki *Soga-go* Aeroplane yet to be described. Design work was begun in July 1916 and the aeroplane was completed in March 1917.

To simplify the aeroplane's transport by rail, the fuselage could be separated at mid-point. As a two-seat aircraft, it was expected to be able to fly for 40mins, but with only a pilot, and added fuel in the front cockpit, it could fly for 3hr at a maximum speed estimated to be 66kt (76mph).

In August 1917 when His Imperial Highness Prince Takehiko Yamashina visited Tokorozawa, Ozaki attempted to fly the aeroplane for the first time, but a broken axle prevented take off. Seemingly, no further attempts were made, for the aeroplane was stored for a while at his father's home. It was later purchased by supporters of the anti-communist Russian Capt Semiyonov, who attempted to invade Siberia early in 1920. Ozaki accompanied the aeroplane to Siberia, but when the attempted invasion failed, he returned home with the engine only, which he sold to the Itoh Aeroplane Research Studio.

Single-engine biplane trainer. Wooden frame structure with fabric covering. Wing with RAF 6 aerofoil. Instructor

Ozaki Soga-go *Aeroplane.*

and pupil in single open cockpits.

80hp Shimazu-Le Rhône nine cylinder air-cooled rotary engine, driving a two-bladed wooden propeller.

Span, upper 10m (32ft 9½in), lower 8m (26ft 3in); length 6.50m (21ft 4in); wing area 27sq m (290.63sq ft).

Loaded weight 570kg (1,256lb).

Maximum speed 66kt (76mph); climb to 2,000m (6,562ft) in 10min; normal endurance 40min, 3hr as single-seater with added fuel.

One built in March 1917.

Ozaki *Soga-go* Aeroplane

This all-new aeroplane was built in the hangar at Tokorozawa almost in parallel with the Ozaki Tractor Biplane. As a result of accidents with the Kaizo Rumpler Taube belonging to the Imperial Flying Association, it re-equipped with Type Mo-4 trainers as an interim type until deciding in 1916 to have a new trainer designed and built. A major finance contributor was Ichiro Soga, a rice speculator in Dojima, Osaka, and therefore the Association named the new biplane the *Soga-go*. Chief engineer for the project was Yukiteru Ozaki with guidance from Army Lt Morikichi Sakamoto.

Based on the Christofferson biplane, ailerons were installed on the upper wing only, originally extending from the trailing edge but later to be inset. A steel-tube frame was used for the forward part of the fuselage, and the undercarriage was taken from the Kaizo Rumpler Taube. When completed in April

1917 at Tokorozawa, it was not only larger than the Ozaki Tractor Biplane, but nearly twice the weight, yet with only 10hp more.

At the request of Ichiro Soga the aeroplane was taken to Osaka where it was to make its first flight from the Joto Parade Grounds, following ceremonies for the occasion to be held on 22 April, 1917. But defects were discovered in the carburettor, the location of the fuel tank was faulty, and the undercarriage structure was felt to be inadequate. As a result, flying at Osaka was limited to one flight, and the aeroplane was returned to Tokorozawa for modifications.

On 3 June, 1917, Ozaki participated in a flying exhibition in the 300th Year Fair at Nagaoka City, Niigata Prefecture, sponsored by the Association. Immediately after take off, the engine lost power and an emergency landing had to be made on a sand bank along the Shinano River, causing the aeroplane to turn over and sustain heavy damage. When repaired, a number of major modifications were made to the *Soga-go*, which included the fitting of smaller wings. It was then used by the Association exclusively under the name No.2 *Soga-go*.

Single-engine biplane trainer. Mixed wooden and steel-tube fuselage and wooden framed wings with fabric covering. Pilot in open cockpit.

90hp Austro-Daimler six-cylinder water-cooled inline engine, driving a two-bladed wooden propeller.

Span, upper 12.98m (42ft 7in), lower 10m (32ft 9½in); length 7.98m (26ft 2¼in); wing area 35sq m (376.75sq ft).

Loaded weight 760kg (1,675lb).

Maximum speed 61kt (71mph); endurance 5½hr.

One built in April 1917.

Data for the original *Soga-go*.

Having limited success with these two aircraft, Ozaki retired from aviation and followed his father's political activities as his secretary. After 22 years and still highly respected in aviation circles, he flew in the sole remaining Type Mo-6 biplane at the First Aviation Day Pageant at Haneda Airport, on 28 September, 1940, making this the

commemorative last flight of this early aircraft. In 1947, he was elected a member of the House of Counsellors, and when aviation activities resumed in Japan following the Pacific War he was appointed an advisor to Japan Air Lines, and vice-chairman to Japan Aviation Association. He died in June 1964 aged 76.

Saito
(Privately-built)

Saigai Aeroplane

Sotoichi Saito of Tsuruoka City, Yamagata Prefecture, had been involved in the development of balloon flight since 1889. In 1910 he bought a 50hp Gnome engine from France so that he could study aero-engines. He later acquired a patent for a 'Flying Machine' and manufactured an aircraft resembling a Blériot monoplane. Helping with this project was Shotaro Ueda. (*see* Ueda aircraft).

The aeroplane contained some rather innovative features. For protection against inflight fire, the fuel tank was installed on struts high above the rear fuselage at a considerable distance from the engine. Another feature was that in the event of an inflight emergency, a cable could be pulled, causing the fuselage and engine to separate from the wings leaving the pilot

Saigai Aeroplane.

Shigeno Wakadori-go *Aeroplane.*

still seated on the wing section which was to act as a parachute.

Saito named his aeroplane the *Saigai*, an acronym derived from his own name.* In June 1912 he tested the aeroplane on the dry bed of the Akagawa River in Tsuruoka City. The aeroplane, piloted by Suketaro Koya, was put on a special railway track for take off. Koya was probably selected because of his engine experience in operating the *Mogami Maru* river boat. Soon after becoming airborne, Koya felt that further flight would be risky and pulled the emergency cord, thus destroying the aeroplane. The Gnome engine was salvaged and installed in the Tamai 3 Aeroplane in 1917, in which the pilot, Seitaro Tamai, was killed. The engine then passed to Shigesaburo Torigai, and still later was installed in the Tsurubane No.2 Aeroplane of Otojiro Itoh, which made the first loop by a Japanese civil aeroplane when piloted by Toyotaro Yamagata in 1918.

Single-engine monoplane. Wooden structure with fabric-covered wing and

*In kanji, Soto can also be read as gai.

uncovered fuselage structure.

50hp Gnome seven-cylinder air-cooled rotary engine, driving a two-bladed wooden propeller.

Span 10.30m (33ft 9½in); length 9.10m (29ft 10¼in).

Loaded weight 560kg (1,234lb).

One built in June 1912.

Shigeno
(Privately-built)

As with the majority of early private builders of aircraft in Japan, Kiyotake Shigeno was from an upper-class family, the third son of Baron Kiyoharu Shigeno, a Lt-Gen in the Imperial Japanese Army. Kiyotake lost his two older brothers through illnesses and therefore became the heir to his family position at an early age. He entered the Army Central Cadet School, but left it halfway through his training because of illness and finished his education at the Tokyo Ueno Conservatory, majoring in music.

At the age of 28, in July 1910, he left Japan for France, perhaps quite despondent after the death of his wife four months earlier. On arriving in Paris he went to an automobile driving school, and later to a flying school at Juvissy. Soon after, the school was closed and he transferred to the Caudron flying school and then the Issy-les-Moulineaux flying school, and acquired international pilot licence No.744 on 26 January, 1912.

Shigeno *Wakadori-go* Aeroplane

In 1912, Shigeno designed a single-seat tractor biplane and placed an order for its manufacture with Charles Roux, of France, who had already built a monoplane with the same structural principles. He named this aeroplane *Wakadori-go*, meaning *Young Bird*, after his late wife, Wakako. Powered at first by a 40–50hp Grégoire-Gyp four-cylinder water-cooled engine, it was soon replaced by a 50–60hp Anzani engine for its first flight on 26 April, 1912. The aeroplane was exhibited at the Fourth International Aviation Salon held in Paris that year.

During the flight-test period of the *Wakadori-go*, Shigeno was summoned by his family to return to Japan and left France in May 1912 by ship with his dismantled aeroplane. It was reassembled at Toko-

Shigeno Wakadori-go at Issy-les-Moulineaux, France, 29 January, 1912, when equipped with Grégoire-Gyp 50hp engine. (Museé de l'Air)

rozawa Flight Test Grounds the following September. On 9 September, when Shigeno banked too steeply at low altitude just after take off, the wingtip touched the ground, causing damage to the wings, propeller, and undercarriage. After repairs, the new wings were of greater span with consequent increase in wing area.

After these repairs and modifications, the *Wakadori-go* set a new civil aeroplane record in Japan on 20 April, 1913, reaching 300m (984ft) with a flight of 45min. The existence of flyable aircraft in Japan at this early date was quite an accomplishment. Later, the Anzani engine was installed in a Kaishiki aeroplane belonging to the Provisional Military Balloon Research Association.

Single-engine tractor biplane. Wooden structure with fabric covering. Pilot in open cockpit.

60hp Anzani six-cylinder air-cooled radial engine, driving a two-bladed wooden propeller.

Span, upper 10.07m (33ft 0¼in), lower 7.09m (23ft 3in), cord 1.54m (5ft); length 8.106m (26ft 7in); wing area 24.33sq m (261.89sq ft).*

Empty weight 370kg (815lb); loaded weight 500kg (1,102lb).

Maximum speed 62kt (71mph), endurance 3hr.

One built in April 1912.

In April 1914, Baron Shigeno returned to France to purchase a new aeroplane. After the start of the First World War that August he joined the French Army as a 2-Lt assigned to Pau aerodrome. During the war, he was awarded the Légion d'Honneur and Croix de Guerre while serving with one of the Escadrilles des Cigognes (Stork Squadrons). He attained the rank of Captain. In January 1920, Shigeno returned to Japan with his second wife, Jeanne, and their daughter, Ayako. He planned a career in aviation but died in Osaka in October 1924.

*Dimensions as originally built.

Sonoda
(Privately-built)

Takehiko Sonoda was one of the early civilian aviators who were typical in coming from distinguished and affluent Japanese families. He was born in London when his father, Kokichi Sonoda, was with the Japanese consulate in England. After he returned to Japan where he finished his secondary school education, he went back to Britain and later graduated from the Glasgow Polytechnic in mechanical engineering. He accepted several jobs in various factories and a shipyard, all the while developing an interest in aviation. Eventually he was employed by the Handley Page Aircraft Co.

Sonoda Aeroplane

The British pioneer Frederick Handley Page was always interested in new design ideas for his aeroplanes. As an employee in the summer of 1912, Takehiko Sonoda influenced Handley Page's aeroplanes with a significantly improved approach in aircraft design.

Sonoda had designed an advanced two-seat biplane and wanted Handley Page to build it. Apart from providing useful paid work for Handley Page, Sonoda's design was of great interest because he had incorporated ailerons in the upper wing in place of the Handley Page practice of using wing warping for

Sonoda Aeroplane.

lateral control. Handley Page was so impressed by their advantages that after exhibiting his own Yellow Peril monoplane at the 1913 Olympia show, he fitted it with wide-chord ailerons which gave it much improved handling qualities.

The Sonoda Aeroplane was a wood and fabric two-bay unequal-span biplane with marked stagger. The covered fuselage was mounted on short struts above the lower wing and in its nose was the 60hp Green water-cooled inline engine which Sonoda had bought with his father's financial assistance. The fuel tank was above the upper wing centre section, and there was a large radiator on each side of the fuselage near the centre of gravity. The undercarriage was conventional and had a central skid to prevent nosing-over. A deep tailskid held the Sonoda at about flying attitude while on the ground.

The aeroplane was finished in duck-egg blue, had the name Sonoda on the fuselage in large capital letters and the Japanese rising-sun flag was painted on the rudder.

The Sonoda biplane was built at Barking in Essex and taken to the London Aerodrome at Hendon for assembly. It was apparently rolled-out on 7 July and is reported as being first flown on 7 September, 1912, by Handley Page's pilot Cyril W. Meredith. The aeroplane was included in a line-up of types on the Naval and Military Aviation Day at Hendon on 28 September and soon after that was badly damaged in a forced landing following engine failure. Unfortunately no technical data are known to have survived.

Thus Sonoda's flying experience ended and he returned to Japan, keeping the promise that by having his father's financing of the engine, that this would be his only aeroplane and that he would not become an aviator. This engine was later installed in Einosuke Shirato's *Asahi-go* for flying demonstrations at various locations around Japan. Baron Takehiko Sonoda later became a member of the House of Peers.

Tachibana, also Japan Aeroplane Manufacturing Works (Nippon Hikoki Seisakusho)

In March 1915, a Gyro-engined Curtiss was purchased by Ryokan Tachibana just before his return to Japan from the United States. However, since he had not obtained a pilot's licence, he joined with aviator Shigeru Suzuki, who had also returned from the United States and became the exhibition pilot for Tachibana's Gyro-powered Curtiss at various places in Japan. Unfortunately, after a brief period while flying from the Asakura Military Grounds in Kouchi City, Shikoku Island, the aeroplane crashed on 25 May of that year, severely injuring Suzuki. The aeroplane was repaired but was again severely damaged in a landing accident at Zentsuji on Shikoku the following month.

In the meantime, the owner of the aeroplane, Tachibana, intended establishing a flying school and an aeroplane manufacturing company in Noda-cho, Kita-ku, Osaka. At that time he learned that Juichi Sakamoto had announced his intention of establishing an aviation school in Zasshonokuma, Tsukushi-gun, Fukuoka Prefecture, under the sponsorship of the chief editor of the *Kyushu Nippo* (*Daily Report*) newspaper. Rather than competing with one another, Tachibana and

Sakamoto joined partnership with the intention of forming the Oriental Aviation School (Toyo Hiko Gakko) in Zasshonokuma, at Fukuoka. This did not happen but the association of the two men continued.

Tachibana therefore went ahead with his plans to form the Japan Aeroplane Manufacturing Works (Nippon Hikoki Seisakusho) in Osaka. This facility came under the supervision of two Americans, aviator Barr Williams and engineer Harley Holms who accompanied Tachibana on his return to Japan with his aeroplane.

Suzuki Gyro No.2 Tractor

Using the wrecked components of Tachibana's Curtiss tractor, and incorporating design improvements made by Shigeru Suzuki, the aeroplane was rebuilt at the Nippon Hokoki Seisakusho (Japan Aeroplane Manufacturing Works), and called the Suzuki Gyro No.2 Tractor. An obvious difference from the original Curtiss design was that the rear part of the fuselage, formerly left uncovered and exposing its structure, was now completely covered. The former skids attached to the undercarriage were now eliminated. Once successfully test flown, it was entered in a competition at the Second Civil Flight Meet at Naruo Race Track near Osaka in December 1915. Flown by Ieyasu Nakazawa, it won the Second Prize for duration with a flight of 29min 35sec.

Although this was a two-seat aircraft, it was difficult to take off when carrying two, so it was used

Suzuki Gyro No.2 Tractor.

as a single-seater. Later this aeroplane became part of the Itoh Airfield organization.

Single-engine tractor biplane. Wooden structure with fabric covering. Two seats in open cockpits.

60hp Gyro J five-cylinder air-cooled rotary engine, driving a two-bladed wooden propeller.

Span 9.20m (30ft 2¼in); length 6.10m (20ft).

Empty weight 370kg (815lb); loaded weight 500kg (1,102 lb).

Maximum speed 60kt (69mph); endurance 1½hr.

One built in 1915.

Sakamoto No.6 Aeroplane

Brief mention has already been made of Juichi Sakamoto and his association with Tachibana. During his partnership, the Sakamoto No.6 Aeroplane was built at the Nippon Hikoki Seisakusho at his request. Having travelled to the United States in 1908, Sakamoto had built his previous aircraft there. While studying at a Los Angeles Techni-

Sakamoto No.6 Aeroplane with Japanese flags flying from the outer struts.

cal College, he built his first aeroplane which resembled a Blériot. The degree of success attained went unrecorded. After graduation he built and flew the Sakamoto No.2 Aeroplane which was of the Curtiss pusher type. Between May and November 1912, Sakamoto studied at the Shiller Aviation School and acquired pilot's licence No.192 on 8 January, 1913, from the Aero Club of America.

The next year he built and tested a Wright-type single-engined, twin-propeller tractor followed by a Curtiss-tractor as his No.3 and No.4. Sakamoto's No.5 combined Wright and Curtiss features. With this aeroplane, Sakamoto returned to Japan in April 1914. It was the success of this aeroplane in competitions and demonstrations that had interested Sakamoto in establishing an aviation school in Zasshonokuma with Tachibana although it did not happen.

Having worn out his No.5 aeroplane within one year with his flying activities, he required a replacement. The building of this aeroplane at the Nippon Hikoki Seisakusho was accomplished under the supervision of the Americans Barr Williams and Harley Holms in March 1915. The new aircraft was similar to the No.5, having two seats and tractor configuration but this time the ailerons were set within the planform of the upper wing, and the orthodox two-wheel undercarriage was without the usual skids. Sakamoto used the engine that had been installed in his No.5 aeroplane.

Sakamoto entered this aeroplane in the altitude category of the Second Civil Flying Meet held at Naruo Race Track in December 1915. He reached 600m (1,968ft) and won first prize, even though he was forced to make an emergency landing with engine trouble which resulted in an overturned aeroplane and some damage. After repairs and numerous exhibitions, Sakamoto took his aeroplane to Shantung in China in September 1916 to assist the Chinese revolution and established there the Revolutionary Army Aviation School. He and Ryokan Tachibana, the company owner, who was with him, were given major-general status and began pilot training for the Chinese. When their work was completed, Sakamoto sold the No.6 to the Chinese revolutionary army and returned to Japan in the spring of 1918. Sakamoto's later occupation is not known, but he died on 1 October, 1976, at the age of 87.

Single-engine tractor biplane. Wooden structure with fabric covering. Two seats in open cockpit.

80hp Curtiss OX eight-cylinder vee water-cooled engine, driving a two-bladed wooden propeller.

Span 11m (36ft 1in); length 8m (26ft 3in); height 2.30m (7ft 6½in).

Empty weight 490kg (1,080lb).

One built in 1915.

Umino Seaplane

In May 1914, aviator Ikunosuke Umino took with him from the United States to Japan, a Christofferson flying-boat. While taxi-ing this aeroplane on 1 July, 1914, before a test flight, the engine caught fire and burned the major components of the aeroplane. Umino escaped uninjured. The engine used in this flying-boat was the same 60hp Hall-Scott that had been used in the Curtiss in which Kouha Takeishi crashed and was killed at the Fukakusa Military Grounds in Kyoto on 4 May, 1913. The engine was then repaired for further use in the Christofferson and by Umino for his aircraft.

Umino Seaplane.

Using the remaining parts of the Christofferson flying-boat along with its engine, Umino designed a floatplane which he had built by Nippon Hikoki Seisakusho. This Umino Seaplane became the third and last aeroplane to come from this recently formed company. In the new aeroplane, the engine was in the tractor position instead of being a pusher as previously. The radiator was above the fuselage and behind the engine. There was a single main float with two wingtip pontoons. The cockpit was well aft at almost mid-fuselage.

This aeroplane was completed in May 1915 and tested at Nishinomiya Beach west of Osaka. Several attempts were made to get the seaplane airborne but none succeeded. Discouraged, Umino retired from aviation.

Single-engine single-float tractor biplane. Wooden structure with fabric covered wings, fuselage and tail unit. Wooden main float with tubular metal wingtip floats. Pilot in open cockpit.

60hp Hall-Scott eight-cylinder vee water-cooled engine, driving a two-bladed wooden propeller.

Span 10.30m (33ft 9½in); length 7m (22ft 11½in); height 3.60m (11ft 9¾in).

Empty weight 510kg (1,124lb).

One built in May 1915.

Because of a lack of further orders the Nippon Hikoki Seisakusho went out of business and Tachibana, the owner of the company, went into the film industry.

Takasou (Privately-built)

Takayuki Takasou built his own aircraft in order to obtain his objective, that of acquiring a pilot's licence. He was born in 1887 at Kobiki-cho, Kyobashi-ku, Tokyo, where he attended school at the Faculty of Commerce at Keio Gijuku (later a University), left at mid-term and began working at the Tokyo Automobile Manufacturing Works. In 1908, with the financial assistance of Horitoshi Ohmiya, Takasou went to the United States, seemingly with the express purpose of building an aeroplane there. In 1911 he built an aeroplane closely resembling a Curtiss pusher and called it the Takasou No.1 Aeroplane.

This aeroplane is recorded as having been destroyed while taxiing. Following this, he built his No.2 Aeroplane which was said to have been successful. In his No.3 Aeroplane, for which there is no description, he took his examination for an International Pilot Licence and was granted licence No.219.

Takasou No.4 Aeroplane

Takasou built another aeroplane, which he called the No.4, incorporating improvements over his earlier

Takasou No.4 Aeroplane.

designs. He returned to Japan with this aeroplane in April 1914. As with many of the earlier designs, this too was based upon the Curtiss pusher but with his own innovations, and powered with a 60hp Hall-Scott engine. His aeroplane had a unique control system which he called the 'three in one,' in which the fore and aft movement of the control wheel operated the elevator, and left and right rotation of the control wheel operated the ailerons which were interconnected with the rudder. The pilot's left foot operated the wheel brake, and the right foot operated the throttle.

This aeroplane made its first exhibition flight in May 1914 at Himeji Military Grounds in Hyogo Prefecture in central Honshu. In the following month Takasou entered his aeroplane in the First Civil Flying Meet, that was held at Naruo Race Track west of Osaka. He gained second place by staying airborne for 24min 5sec, but failed to win a prize for altitude, although he recorded 680m (2,230ft). He then participated in a memorial flight for Kouha Takeishi in July 1914 at the Kyoto Fukakusa Military Grounds where Takeishi had become the first victim of a civil aviation crash in Japan on 4 May the previous year. After that, Takasou took his No.4 Aeroplane for exhibition flights to Dairen (now Lüda) in China, Seoul in Korea, and then to Fukuyama and Tottori in October and November, finishing the tour at Tanba Sasayama in December 1914. By this

time the aeroplane was virtually worn out.

Single-engine pusher biplane. Wooden structure with fabric covering. Exposed tail and nose booms. Pilot in open structure.
60hp Hall-Scott eight-cylinder vee water-cooled engine, driving a two-bladed wooden propeller.
Span 11.20m (36ft 9in); length 11m (36ft 1in); height 2.30m (7ft 6½in).
Empty weight 230kg (507lb); loaded weight 545kg (1,201lb).
Maximum speed 33kt (38mph); endurance 1hr.
One built in 1914.

Takasou No.5 Aeroplane

In need of a replacement aeroplane for his No.4, Takayuki Takasou built an improved model at his home workshop at Bakuro-cho, Higashi-ku, Osaka. Known as the Takasou No.5 Aeroplane, it was powered by the same 60hp Hall-Scott engine as had been used in his No.4 Aeroplane.

After being assured of the new aeroplane's performance in flights at Osaka in March 1915, Takasou

Takasou No.5 Aeroplane.

took it to Taiwan and Okinawa for more demonstrations which further improved his reputation. He also entered the Second Civil Flying Meet held in December 1915 at Naruo, where he won First Prize for a flight of 35min 30sec, and Second Prize for altitude, having reached 360m (1,181ft).

On the following day he was making a return flight from Osaka to Naruo when the engine failed over the Muko River on which he made an emergency landing. After repairs he sold the airframe to a Chinese buyer and had the engine rebuilt for his next design, the Takasou TN-6 Aeroplane.

Single-engine pusher biplane. Wooden structure with fabric covered wings. Exposed tail and nose booms. Pilot in open structure.
60hp Hall-Scott eight-cylinder vee water-cooled engine, driving a two-bladed wooden propeller.
Span 11m (36ft 1in); length 9.62m (31ft 6¾in); wing area 27.5sq m (296sq ft).
Loaded weight 530kg (1,168lb).
Maximum speed 52kt (60mph).
One built in 1915.

Takasou TN-6 Aeroplane

The Hall-Scott engine, damaged while installed in the Takasou No.5 Aeroplane, was repaired by the Nakajima Machinery Manufacturing Works, managed by Ikusaburo Nakajima (no relation to the aeroplane manufacturer). After repairs, it was rated at 65hp and ran continuously for 8 hours in tests at the Oka Secondary School in Osaka.

Takasou built a new biplane of a tractor design in which he installed this rebuilt engine. He called this the TN-6, using the T of his name

Takasou TN-6 Aeroplane.

and N for Nakajima. With the help of his assistants, Yonezawa and Fukuda, and apprentice Harada, the aeroplane was completed in the autumn of 1917. Using features found in Morane-Saulnier and Martin-Wright designs, the fuselage could be separated at midpoint by four bolts for ease of transport by rail.

Takasou used this aeroplane for flying training at Osaka Joto Military Grounds but, because of a landing accident, this lasted only a month. After repairs, the aeroplane was sold to Soujiro Yasui of Kyoto in August 1918. Following this transaction, the aeroplane was frequently modified, so altering its appearance that it was renamed the Yasui TN-6 Kai Aeroplane. Takasou gave flying instruction to Yasui at Kagamigahara, after which Takasou returned to the United States, this time to buy automobiles and begin a new business venture. (*see* Yasui TN-6 Kai Aeroplane.)

Single-engine tractor biplane. Wooden structure with fabric covering and metal engine cowling. Pilot in open cockpit.

65hp Hall-Scott eight-cylinder vee water-cooled engine, driving a two-bladed wooden propeller.

Span 11.20m (36ft 9in); length 7.90m (25ft 11in); wing area 28.5sq m (306.78sq ft).

Empty weight 610kg (1,345lb).

Maximum speed 53kt (61mph).

One built in 1917.

Tamai (Privately-built) also Nippon Flying School (Nippon Hiko Gakko)

Seitaro Tamai was born in 1892, the eldest son of Tsunetaro Tamai who was a manager at the Hamada Iron Works in Yokkaichi City, south of Nagoya. At the age of 16, inspired by the work of the Wright brothers, he began building an aeroplane which when completed after years of work, was unsuccessful. In 1911, his father took him to Tokyo to visit Sanji Narahara, who had

Tamai No.1 Seaplane, reconfigured with wheels.

built his own aircraft, along with Army Captain Kumazo Hino, one of Japan's first pilots. On a later visit to Tokyo, when travelling by himself, he met Army Capt Yoshitoshi Tokugawa, Japan's first pilot, and received aeronautical instruction from him.

Returning home, Tamai built a taxi-ing vehicle which he ran at Chikko reclaimed ground at Yokkaichi City in February 1912. It was powered by a 25hp Cameron four-cylinder air-cooled inline engine borrowed from Sotoichi Saito, builder of the Saigai Aeroplane. With this experience and with the aid of his younger brother, Toichiro Tamai, the older Tamai started a business to build Tamai aeroplanes, and established an assembly shop at their father's factory in Yokkaichi City.

Tamai No.1 Seaplane

The so-called Tamai No.1 Seaplane was in fact originally completed as a floatplane and attempts to fly it were made on 12 October, 1912, but it would not leave the water. It was not only underpowered, but the floats were poorly designed and lacked steps. Not to be discouraged, Tamai took the aeroplane to Inage in Chiba Prefecture across the bay from Tokyo, where Itoh and other aircraft builders were located. He modified the machine and converted it to a landplane, with completion in November 1912. He used the 25hp Cameron engine borrowed from Saito, first used in his taxi-ing trainer. This unequal-span biplane had the typical wooden structure of that time and was covered with fabric treated

with gelatine and shibu (an astringent juice) for making the fabric airtight to produce lift. An unconventional feature was a small elevator at the nose even though this was a tractor-type aircraft. The undercarriage comprised two sets of dual wheels with skids between each pair and strangely the wheels were solid and without tyres. This aeroplane also failed to fly, but had it been able to do so, the Cameron engine would have overheated after a mere 10 minutes' running.

In December 1913, Tamai entered the Army and joined the Telegraphic Corps in Nakano, Tokyo. Although his manufacture of aeroplanes had to cease for the period of his mandatory Army service, he continued his study by visiting the Tokorozawa Flight Test Grounds on his off-duty days. With the outbreak of the First World War, he was transferred from the Army to the Navy Air Corps and engaged in the campaign to seize Tsingtao before being discharged from the service in January 1915.

Tamai 2 *Nippon-go* Seaplane

By the time of his discharge, Seitaro Tamai had already exhausted his funds for aeronautical research. With the help of Yoshihisa Kinoshita, an engine enthusiast, he arranged with Naoji Tomono, manager of Tomono Iron Works in Azabu, Tokyo, to assist with the building of a seaplane because this company also built light-weight engines. One of these was used for the new aeroplane that was com-

NFS Tamai No.1 Aeroplane.

pleted in 1916, and known as the Tamai 2 Seaplane, named *Nippon-go (Japanese-type)*.

This was an unequal-span two-bay biplane with a single main float, and auxiliary floats beneath the tail and each wingtip. The fuselage was left uncovered. It somewhat resembled early British Short seaplanes as well as the Umino Seaplane built the previous year.

Confident of success, Tamai took the aircraft to Yokkaichi City, where he intended to make the first flight to honour the residents of his home town. The event was to take place at the exhibition grounds of Umaokoshi Beach, where an admission charge was collected from the spectators. But at the start the engine failed to attain enough power to get the seaplane airborne and it only taxied. It was said that the seaplane would have flown if the engine had been running satisfactorily, but there is no record of later flights.

Single-engine single-float biplane. Wooden structure covered with fabric except for the fuselage which was uncovered. Pilot in open cockpit.

90hp Tomono six-cylinder water-cooled inline engine, driving a two-bladed wooden propeller.

Span 13.20m (43ft 3½in); length 10m (32ft 9½in).

Empty weight 350kg (771lb).

One built in 1916.

NFS Tamai No.1 Aeroplane

This was really the Tamai 3 Aeroplane in sequential order, but renumbering began because of this aeroplane's success. Financial support was again received from Naoji Tomono and his Iron Works, and the design was made by Aijiro Hara. With help from his brother Toichiro Tamai, the aeroplane was completed on 5 October, 1916, and flew for the first time on 4 November.

The Tamai No.1 was a small unequal-span two-bay biplane with two-wheel undercarriage and twin skids. Following this success, Tamai announced his intention of establishing the Tamai Flight Training Centre, but a reporter for a monthly magazine *Hikokai* (*Flight World*) Tamotsu Aiba, announced similar plans. With the continuing help of Naoji Tomono as a partner, the three together established the Nippon Flying School in August 1916 at Anamori, Shimo Haneda-cho, in Tokyo, thus the initials NFS used in the type name. At first the aircraft could only carry the pilot,

Tamai 2 Nippon-go *Seaplane.*

but modifications were made to carry pupil and instructor. Flights had to be limited to 10 minutes due to overheating of the engine.

The flying school opened on 4 January, 1917, and was located at the present site of Haneda International Airport, using buildings of the Nippon Hikoki Seisakusho (Nippon Aeroplane Manufacturing Works), situated where the airport parking lot now exists. This NFS Tamai No.1 Aeroplane was the first aeroplane to fly at what has become one of the busiest international airports in the world.

Single-engine biplane trainer. All-wooden construction covered with fabric, except for the forward part of fuselage which was ply-covered. Pupil and instructor in open cockpit.

35hp Cameron four-cylinder air-cooled inline engine, driving a two-bladed wooden propeller.

Span 10.20m (33ft 5½in); length 7.20m (23ft 7½in); height 2.82m (9ft 3in); wing area 32sq m (344sq ft).

Empty weight 290kg (639lb); loaded weight 448kg (987lb).

One built in 1916.

NFS Tamai No.2 Trainer

In January 1917, flying training began at the Nippon Flying School with the newly built NFS Tamai No.2 Trainer. This was again the design of Aijiro Hara, and manufactured at Haneda at the cost of 3,800 yen. The fuselage was shortened giving it more strength and the gap between upper and lower wings was increased. It was built from Japanese cypress (hinoki) and fastened with aluminium nails. Designed from the beginning as a

NFS Tamai No.2 Trainer.

NFS Tamai No.3 Trainer.

two-seat aircraft, it was powered by the Cameron engine taken from the Tamai 1. They carved their own propeller after laminating hinoki and katsura woods, and finished it with urushi (Japanese lacquer). The wings were slightly changed from the predecessor by having narrower chord, thus increasing the aspect ratio, and reducing the area to less than the NFS Tamai 1. The fabric covering was coated with waterproof varnish.

The school advertised its flying programme as using a 'Sopwith-type' two-seat tractor aeroplane, assuming that being associated with a foreign manufacturer's name might suggest greater reliability. However, the new Tamai aeroplane existed for less than a year, for on the night of 30 September, 1917, a tidal wave carried it into Tokyo Bay. The next morning, the wreckage of the Tamai 2 was caught in a fishing net off the coast of Urayasucho in Chiba Prefecture, but only the engine could be saved.

Single-engine two-bay biplane trainer. All-wooden construction with fabric covering. Two-seat in open cockpit.

35hp Cameron four-cylinder air-cooled inline engine, driving a two-bladed wooden propeller.

Span 10.50m (34ft 5½in); length 6m (19ft 8¼in); wing area 28sq m (301sq ft).

Empty weight 320kg (705lb)

One built in 1917.

NFS Tamai No.3 Trainer

The NFS Tamai No.3 Aeroplane was powered by a 50hp Gnome rotary engine which Director Tamotsu Aiba himself bought from Sotoichi Saito, the builder of Saigai Aeroplane, in the past. The fuselage was larger to provide better accommodation for the two occupants seated in tandem. It was completed after three months and made its first flight on 4 May, 1917, at Haneda.

The Nippon Flying School moved to a new site at Shibaura which was prepared on reclaimed land, a project that was sponsored by the *Tokyo Nichinichi* newspaper. On 20 May, the company began a large-scale advertising campaign coupled with exhibition flights from its new location. On the third flight of that day, Seitaro Tamai took off with press photographer Reizo Yuasa to fly over the centre of Tokyo but soon after take off, undetermined problems occurred with the aeroplane and he returned prematurely to the airstrip to land. While on the approach, however, the aeroplane was reported to break up in flight.

Tamai No.5 Trainer.

Tamai and Yuasa both died in the crash. This was the first fatality experienced by a civil flying school in Japan, and was also the first loss of a Japanese press photographer in flight on assignment.

This accident caused a serious problem: how to maintain a flying school after the loss of its primary equipment and the instructor. To help resolve the problem, Kazuhide Watanabe, chief editor of the monthly magazine, *Kokumin Hiko* (*Nation's Flight*), and four other people, took on the sponsorship of the Nippon Flying School. They invited Army Lt (Reserve) Mototaka Kawakami (graduate of the 3rd Army Aviation Cadet Class) to be the instructor, and re-started the flying school with the NFS Tamai No.2 Aeroplane.

As previously mentioned this aeroplane was lost in the tidal wave of 30 September, 1917. Nevertheless, the NFS, under the leadership of Terutaka Tamai (he had changed his first name from Toichiro) began construction of a new trainer for the continuance of the school.

Single-engine two-bay biplane trainer. Wooden construction with fabric covering. Three seats in open cockpit.

50hp Gnome seven-cylinder air-cooled rotary engine, driving a two-bladed wooden propeller.

Span 11.80m (38ft 8½in); length 8.40m (27ft 6½in); wing area 38sq m (409.04sq ft).

Empty weight 430kg (948lb).

One built in 1917.

Tamai No.5 Trainer

Retaining the name of the company founded by Seitaro Tamai, his brother Terutaka Tamai oversaw the building of a new aeroplane, the Tamai No.5 Trainer. To power the aeroplane, they used the Cameron engine recovered from the fishing nets that snagged the NFS Tamai No.2, and reconditioned it at the Tomono Iron Works. The new aeroplane was built to the drawings of the NFS Tamai No.2 and No.3 and incorporated remaining spare parts. The engine, fuselage and undercarriage were identical to the NFS Tamai No.2, and the wings and tail were the same as those on the NFS Tamai No.3. This aircraft was manufactured at the nearby Nippon Aeroplane Manufacturing Works owned by Terutaka Tamai beginning in February 1918, under the new name of Haneda Hikoki Kenkyusho (Haneda Aeroplane Research Studio).

(For details of dimensions see Tamai No.2 and 3 from which the components were derived)

Tamai No.24 Trainer

This was a reliable two-seat trainer designed and manufactured by Terutaka Tamai of Haneda Hikoki Kenkyusho in 1920. The design was similar to those of the Itoh Emi 16 *Fuji-go*, Shirato 31, 38, 39 and 40, all using the same type of engine, the 120hp Le Rhône rotary which Sale & Frazar Ltd imported from France. The types mentioned were the popular civil training aeroplanes before excess and obsolete military trainers came onto the civil market.

In May 1921, the Tamai 24 took part in the Second Prize-winning Flight Competition at Susaki Airfield on reclaimed ground in Tokyo. It was flown by Terutaka Tamai and was ranked as fourth in the speed category (89.47mph) and fifth in the distance category (87 miles). This was the last contest in which non-licensed pilots could take part.

Following the manufacture of the Awazu No.2 *Seicho-go* Aeroplane, this Tamai 24 was the second and the last aeroplane to be manufactured by Tamai. Operating from its new Tamai Airfield at Namamugi-cho, Yokohama City, in 1922, it was used for training and leaflet dropping advertising. Also operating from this airfield were Itoh Emi aeroplanes and Nieuport trainers. All this was ended, however, when in 1923 the Kanto area was severely struck by an earthquake, causing the airfield to be closed.

Single-engine two-bay biplane trainer. Wooden structure with fabric covering. Two seats in open cockpits.

120hp Le Rhône nine-cylinder air-

Tamai No.24 Trainer.

cooled rotary engine, driving a two-bladed wooden propeller.

Span 9.50m (31ft 2in); length 7.52m (24ft 8in); height 2.90m (9ft 6in); wing area 26.3sq m (283.1sq ft).

Empty weight 600kg (1,322lb); loaded weight 850kg (1,874lb).

Maximum speed 70kt (80mph); cruising speed 54kt (62.5mph); endurance 5hr.

One built in 1920.

Torigai
(Privately-built)

Shigesaburo Torigai was a manager of an imported automobile sales and repair business in Yuraku-cho, Tokyo. Because of his new-found interest in aviation as a hobby, he organized the Nihon Hiko Kenkyu-kai (Japan Flight Research Association). Under this name, and to satisfy his own interest in aviation, he voluntarily managed and promoted exhibition programmes for Einosuke Shirato who flew the Narahara No.4 *Ohtori-go* Aeroplane on tours throughout Japan, and his ambition was to have an aeroplane of his own. To achieve this, he asked Toyokichi Daiguchi, who was associated with Narahara, for technical assistance in the building of his own aeroplane.

Torigai *Hayabusa-go* Aeroplane

In 1913, to open the project, Torigai purchased a used 45hp

Torigai Hayabusa-go *Aeroplane.*

Tsuzuku No.1 Aeroplane with chain-driven twin-pusher propellers.

Grégoire Gyp engine from Shinzo Morita of Osaka after his flying accident. Torigai completed his aeroplane in April 1913 and called it the *Hayabusa-go* (*Falcon*). It was an equal-span three-bay biplane with uncovered fuselage, tractor engine, ailerons on the upper wing and undercarriage comprising two sets of twin wheels and two skids. He flew it for the first time on 3 May, 1913, at Inage, Chiba Prefecture, but at a height of about 20m the aeroplane stalled and crashed. Torigai survived, but the aeroplane was severely damaged.

After repairs by Daiguchi, Torigai took the aeroplane to Hokkaido. While preparing for a flying exhibition at the Tsukisappu Military Drill Grounds on 7 September, 1913, Torigai took off and, on the outskirts of Sapporo, soon crashed once again. Speculation about the cause of this and the earlier accident is that Torigai did not know how to fly, for there was no record of him having been given formal flying lessons. Torigai escaped serious injury but the aeroplane was badly damaged. The wreckage was saved and eventually transferred to Otojiro Itoh, to help

start his flying school at Inage the next year. Itoh made the necessary repairs along with his own modifications and made the aeroplane flyable.

Itoh eventually purchased the Grégoire Gyp engine from Torigai in August 1915 so that it could be installed in his first-built aircraft, the Emi 1 Aeroplane. This is the aeroplane that made the first flight to Tokyo from Inage on 8 January, 1916. (*see* Itoh Emi 1 Aeroplane.)

Tsuzuku
(Privately-built)

Tetsusaburo Tsuzuku of Koma-gome, Hongo-ku, Tokyo, began his direct involvement in aviation with scale models. Between 30 January and 19 February, 1911, he made experiments with a one-tenth scale model aeroplane towed behind a car at the Yoyogi Military Parade Grounds in Tokyo. It was at Yoyogi the month before, that the first manned flight took place in Japan. His efforts led to a patent he applied for on 15 November, 1910, and which was granted on 4 December, 1911, as No.21147. This patent and aeroplane concept interested a Tokyo businessman, Reizo Yamashina, in organizing an association for building a full-size Tsuzuku Aeroplane.

Tsuzuku No.1 Aeroplane

With this financial support, a 50hp Anzani engine was bought from France and construction of the aeroplane begun. It was a Blériot-type monoplane but with twin-pusher propellers having a drive system from the single engine much like that of the Wright brothers' aeroplane. The Tsuzuku aeroplane was completed in August 1911 and put on exhibition on 6 August at Takenodai, Ueno, Tokyo. Tsuzuku's theory was that a monoplane with pusher twin-propellers was the most efficient design for aeroplanes of the future.

The first attempts to fly this aeroplane took place at Tokorozawa on 13 March, 1912. However, because of the loss through the transmission system, insufficient power was available to sustain flight, and the aeroplane could only make repeated hops. After adjustments were made to the chain-drive system, the aeroplane became airborne on 5 May, 1912, at Tokorozawa Airfield, making two circuits on the first flight. On that same day, a second flight resulted in four circuits and a height of 20 to 30m (65 to 100ft). That afternoon, Tsuzuku took off once again to circle the airfield, but at approximately 40ft he encountered a strong wind and felt it prudent to make an immediate landing. Children were playing in the area, and in making a very low turn to avoid them, he collided with a fence. He was thrown out of the aeroplane with slight injuries but the aeroplane was destroyed.

Single-engine, twin-pusher-propeller high-wing monoplane. Wooden structure with fabric-covered wings and

Tsuzuku No.2 Aeroplane.

empennage. Pilot in open structure.

One 50hp Anzani five-cylinder air-cooled radial engine, driving two two-bladed wooden propellers.

Span 13m (42ft 8in); length 9.20m (30ft 2¼in); height 2.70m (8ft 10¼in); wing area 21sq m (226.04sq ft).

Empty weight 300kg (661lb); loaded weight 450kg (992lb).

One built in August 1911.

Tsuzuku No.2 Aeroplane

Recognizing the power loss with a chain-drive transmission system, Tsuzuku built a new aeroplane, this time with a single propeller attached directly to the engine in the front of the aeroplane. This aeroplane incorporated features of both the Rumpler Taube and the Blériot, and was completed in mid-June 1912. On 18 July of that year, during a training flight for Tsuzuku at Tokorozawa, a crash landing was made, flipping the aeroplane over and damaging the port wing. After repairs, the aeroplane was in the air again on 17 August at Tokorozawa. Four flights were made that day, all with increasing distances up to a maximum of more than three miles.

Tsuzuku No.3 Aeroplane.

Under sponsorship of the *Shinano Mainichi* newspaper, Tsuzuku took his aeroplane to Nagano Prefecture to make exhibition flights along the Sai River on 3 November, 1912. When preparing to land, in avoiding spectators, he had to land on unsuitable ground and badly damaged the airframe. A number of demonstration flights were made for military as well as civilian spectators by Tsuzuku with this aeroplane, many of which had similar endings followed by repeated repairs. Its ultimate fate is unrecorded.

Single-engine tractor monoplane. Wooden structure with fabric-covered wings and empennage. Pilot in open structure.

50hp Anzani five-cylinder air-cooled radial engine, driving a two-bladed wooden propeller.

Span 12m (39ft 4½in); length 10m (32ft 9½in).

Empty weight 300kg (661lb).

One built in June 1912.

Tsuzuku No.3 Aeroplane

Early in 1915, the Chinese Revolutionary Army placed an order with Tsuzuku for the manufacture of a monoplane resembling the Nieuport NG. To complete this order in the shortest time, work was begun at a factory building in Kikukawacho, Honjo, Tokyo, with Tsuzuku's assistant, Shuichi Yano, acting as chief engineer. Construction was begun on 10 January, 1915, under the supervision of Torajiro Nishijima, with six other workers. In charge of the metal work was Masao Ohta, later presi-

dent of Ohta Automobile Co, with three other sheet-metal workers. In record time, just 98 days, the aeroplane was completed on 28 April, 1915. The 50hp Gnome engine was taken from the Hoshino Aeroplane in which it was being used on loan.

The aeroplane was scheduled for flight testing at Inage on 5 May of that year, but this was delayed because of conflicting relationships between China and Japan. Delivery was made, however, to Chinese aviator Yun-Peng Jao, of the Aviation School of the Chinese Revolutionary Army, and engineer Rong-Jong Wu. A Japanese aviator, Yonezo Hoshino, was assigned to look after the aeroplane during shipment and while in China. (*see* Hoshino Aeroplane.) According to evaluations made by the Chinese pilot, the aeroplane was good in both flying qualities and speed, and a letter of appreciation was sent by the Chinese to Tsuzuku.

Single-engine shoulder-wing monoplane. Wooden structure (Japanese cypress) with ply-covered fuselage and fabric-covered wings and tail. Fuselage joined in the centre, with four bolts, for rail shipment. Pilot in open cockpit.

50hp Gnome seven-cylinder air-cooled rotary engine, driving a two-bladed wooden propeller.

Span 11.40m (37ft 5in); length 7.50m (24ft 7¼in); height 2.60m (8ft 6¼in).

Empty weight 350kg (771lb); loaded weight 550kg (1,212lb).

Maximum speed 49kt (56mph); endurance 4hr.

One built in April 1915.

Ueda
(Privately-built)

As a spare time project when not working as a shop assistant for a wholesale rice dealer, 22-year-old Shotaro Ueda built a biplane glider in 1908 in his temporary shop in Nagoya near Tsurumai Park. Such a project was most unusual for someone other than an upperclass Japanese. Helped by his 34-year-old friend, Kisaburo Sato, the two created an open framed fuselage of bamboo for their glider to which they mounted conventional biplane wings and a tail unit. It was then towed behind an automobile with unrecorded results.

Ueda *Hiryu-go* Aeroplane

Not satisfied with the results of a towed glider, but encouraged to pursue this project further, Ueda obtained a 25hp Anzani three-cylinder fan-type engine which was then mounted in the glider in addition to some modifications to the airframe. Ailerons were attached to the rear interplane struts between the two wings. The aeroplane had twin rudders to whose outer sides were attached short-span horizontal surfaces supplementing the eleva-

Ueda Hiryu-go *Aeroplane.*

tor which had balance tabs and was hinged at the rear of the fuselage frame well aft of the vertical surfaces. The undercarriage consisted of wooden cart wheels without tyres or shock absorbers. Ueda gave it the name *Hiryu-go* (*Flying Dragon*).

The aeroplane was completed as a powered aircraft towards the end of 1909, but there is no record that it actually flew. Had it done so, it would have been the first to fly in Japan. Unfortunately, Ueda's potential career was ended when he died in April 1912 at the age of 26.

Umeda
(Privately-built)

Umeda Aeroplane.

Around 1910, while working as manager of a kimono shop in Shiba-ku, Tokyo, Yuzo Umeda became an aviation enthusiast, and in his home workshop built a glider which he intended to tow with an automobile. Whether this was a success or a failure is not known, but it was followed by a powered aeroplane with a 25hp Anzani engine. When completed, it was tested at Inage, as well as Sambonyoshi at Haneda Beach, but these efforts ended in failure.

Believing that more power would solve most of his problems, Umeda purchased a 60hp Indian engine in the summer of 1914, and built a biplane. When completed, he assembled the major components in an Imperial Flight Association hangar located at the Yoyogi Military Parade Grounds. The aeroplane left the ground on its first attempt on 7 September, 1914, but crashed immediately and was destroyed.

Reverting to the use of the 25hp Anzani engine, Umeda built a sesquiplane at Inage in May 1916, assisted by Shuichi Yano, a graduate of the Department of Science and Technology at Waseda University, along with Kichinosuke Tsukamoto. This aeroplane was refer-

Umeda Aeroplane.

red to as a French Caudron design since it resembled that small single-seat aircraft. Umeda was disappointed again, for this aeroplane could only make short hops. Anticipating success, Umeda had erected a sign at Inage announcing the Umeda Aeroplane Co-operative Training Centre (Umeda Hikoki Kyodo Renshusho) on which he introduced his Anzani-powered sesquiplane as the trainer to be used, and called it the Umeda Tractor.

Desperate to achieve at least some success. Umeda lent his 60hp Indian engine to aircraft builder Einosuke Shirato who then produced the Shirato *Iwao-go* Aeroplane. This aeroplane was sent on flying tours accompanied by Umeda

Yasui TN-6 Kai Aeroplane.

as part of a team. Eventually the aeroplane was sold to Yukichi Goto, and Umeda gave up direct involvement in aviation. (*see* Shirato *Iwao-go* Aeroplane)

Yasui Flying Research Studio (Yasui Hiko Kenkyusho)

Soujiro Yasui of Uonotana-cho, Shimogyo-ku, Kyoto, was from a family famous for very high quality Nishijin Kimonos. He purchased

the TN-6 Tractor from Takayuki Takasou in August 1918, and began flying training with his friend and assistant Fukuda, while using the aeroplane at Kagamigahara, north of Nagoya, being instructed by Takayuki Takasou, the builder of the aeroplane.

Yasui TN-6 Kai Aeroplane

This was an attractive biplane but accidents were frequent with it to the point that with each repair changes were made to its design and appearance. Because of these changes which were generally innovated by Yasui, he renamed the aeroplane the Yasui TN-6 Kai Aeroplane (kai meaning modified).

Major modifications included entirely new wings with equal span, the addition of a second seat, and a newly designed vertical fin. A sheet aluminium cowling enclosed the original 65hp Hall-Scott engine.

For a civil aeroplane of the period, the TN-6 survived for a long time, mainly because of careful maintenance of the engine and airframe. On 3 January, 1920, Yasui made a New Year celebration flight over his home in Kyoto from the Fukakusa Military Parade Grounds, and over Osaka the following new

Yasui No.3 Aeroplane.

year, both major events for those that watched. During these years he gave flying lessons to several students with this aeroplane as well as with the Yasui No.3 Aeroplane that he later built.

Single-engine tractor biplane. Wooden structure with fabric covering. Pupil and instructor in open cockpits.

65hp Hall-Scott eight-cylinder vee water-cooled engine, driving a two-bladed wooden propeller.

Span 11.50m (37ft 8¾in); length 9.50m (31ft 2in).

Empty weight 590kg (1,300lb).

One built in 1917, modified in 1918–1919.

Yasui No.3 Aeroplane

Soujiro Yasui acquired his pilot 2/c licence by his diligent training in the TN-6 Kai Aeroplane. With this he established the Yasui Flying Research Studio in 1922 on the dry river bank in Suchi, Funai-gun, Kyoto. It was there that he built his next aircraft, the Yasui No.3 Aeroplane.

This aeroplane was smaller than the TN-6 and was of sturdy design. It was an equal-span two-bay biplane without dihedral and had ailerons in upper and lower wings. The engine was a 90hp Curtiss OX-5 with frontal car-type radiator.

At the beginning of January 1923, he again made a newsworthy flight over his home town of Kyoto, and he put the No.3 into service as a trainer for his newly formed Yasui Flying Research Studio. In addition, he used Army surplus aircraft as trainers along with and after his use of the Yasui No.3 Aeroplane. Yasui retained his business until he was killed in an aeroplane accident in 1928.

Single-engine tractor biplane trainer. Wooden structure with fabric covering. Pupil and instructor in open cockpits.

90hp Curtiss OX-5 eight-cylinder vee water-cooled engine, driving a two-bladed wooden propeller.

Span 8.55m (28ft 0¾in); length 5.80m (19ft 0¼in); height 2.90m (9ft 6in).

Empty weight 680kg (1,500lb); loaded weight 910kg (2,006lb).

Maximum speed 78kt (90mph); landing speed 40kt (46mph); climb to 1,000m (3,280ft) in 3min 30sec; endurance 4hr.

One built in 1922.

Aircraft Manufacturers

Although in the early days, before the First World War, some progressive individuals demonstrated their interest in aviation, it was that war that brought about the real beginning of aircraft manufacturing in Japan. This began in about 1917 when the first three major aircraft builders started. The Mitsubishi and Kawasaki aircraft works began as departments of the heavy industries of the same name, while Nakajima, independent of direct connection with other industry, was financed from the start with outside capital.

Japan turned primarily to European countries for aeronautical technology, sending its engineers to aircraft companies to study, and purchasing aircraft and engines, along with manufacturing rights for many of them. By the end of 1921, European engineers from Britain, France and Germany were invited to Japan to assist the various fledgling companies. In that same year, a wind tunnel of the Göttingen type was completed for Mitsubishi at Nagoya. Nakajima gained its foothold within the industry with the success of its aircraft in the Tokyo–Osaka Airmail Flying Contest, a proving ground for its product along with the development of a practical seaplane-scout aircraft. Kawasaki produced Army bombers designed around German BMW engines, built in Japan under licence. During these formative years Japanese technical missions visited Germany, England, France and the United States, many of whom later designed aircraft that fought against the Allied countries.

By 1930, the Japanese Army and Navy decided that the industry should stand on its own capabilities and established a policy of self-sufficiency, whereby only aircraft and engines of Japanese designs would be considered. Foreign engineers were no longer hired. This was intended mainly to increase Japanese national pride in their own accomplishments, but did not prevent their technical missions from continuing to buy the best foreign models as starting points for Japanese designs.

From 1937 the Japanese aircraft industry in general, and Mitsubishi in particular, were shrouded in purposeful secrecy. At a time when other countries were granting visas to Japanese technicians, most of the exchange visits were denied as the Japanese Government moved toward closer control of the aircraft industry. In August 1938 a new law required that all aircraft companies capitalized at three million yen or more be licensed by the government and controlled as to equipment, techniques, and production plans. The law encouraged and protected such companies by exempting them from income and business taxes, export duties and, in some cases, by monetary grants. Only licensed companies were permitted to engage in final assembly of aircraft.

Thus, for the period between the two wars, the military controlled the majority of aviation activities in Japan. Even the civil licensing of pilots and manufacture of civil-type aircraft was closely monitored by the military, particularly the Army. This control grew even stronger as Japan moved into the Pacific War period.

Army-built Aeroplanes by the Provisional Military Balloon Research Association (Rinji Gunyo Kikyu Kenkyu Kai), and Army Arsenals (Rikugun Kosho)

The formation and the background of this first source for Japanese built military aircraft, the Provisional Military Balloon Research Association (PMBRA), has been described in some detail at the beginning of this work. Its origin stemmed from the Imperial Order No.207 that was issued on 30 July, 1909, in that it was to develop new weapons systems, particularly those that pertained to balloons and aeroplanes for their military application along with associated air-to-ground communications.

Making up this organization were fourteen members from the Army, Navy, Tokyo Imperial University, and the Central Meteorological Observatory. While this was intended to be bipartisan between the two military services, it was determined by Army influence in that Army Lt-Gen Gaishi Nagaoka was appointed the first president, with Col Jiro Inoue as manager, and having their offices at the 7th Division Army Headquarters. These efforts resulted in aircraft that were developed or purchased of which some were put into Army service, while the Navy accepted none of the designs. This may well have been because of Army-Navy distrust, for each had its separate development groups that fed on findings made by the PMBRA.

The manufacture of these PMBRA aircraft that were identified as Kaishiki (Association Type) aeroplanes continued until 1916. During this period, officers of the PMBRA supervised modifications of imported Maurice Farmans and the manufacture of some of these took place at the Tokyo Army Artillery Arsenal. New designs that came from the PMBRA were normally built with the joint effort of the PMBRA's Tokorozawa Factory and the Tokyo Army Artillery Arsenal. As aeroplane manufacturing became more technologically orientated, the Nagoya Army Ordnance Arsenal was used for the repair and manufacture of the Type Mo-4 aircraft, and of later types.

In April 1919, the PMBRA was abolished and replaced by the Army Aviation School of the newly formed Army Department of Aviation. Aeroplanes emerging as a result of this organization were known as Koshiki (School Type) aircraft, instead of by their former designation of Kaishiki. The actual building of these aircraft that had been done by the Tokorozawa Factory was then taken over by the Tokorozawa Branch, Department of Supply, under the Army Department of Aviation. Simultaneously, the research and design of new aeroplanes was absorbed by the Department of Research of the Tokorozawa Army Aviation School.

During the Army's final phase of aircraft manufacture, the Chikusa Army Machinery & Equipment Manufacturing Works produced aero engines, while airframes were

Kaishiki No.1 Aeroplane.

manufactured at the Atsuta Army Weapon Manufacturing Works of the Nagoya Army Ordnance Arsenal. With the formation of the Army Air Headquarters on 1 May, 1925, the manufacture of aircraft by the Army was terminated. By this time the design and manufacture of new aeroplanes was undertaken through competition among civilian companies.

The descriptions of aircraft that follow will identify those that were built under the auspices of the Army production. Resources used in the development and building of aircraft were exclusively those of the Army that centred on the PMBRA facility at Tokorozawa, west of Tokyo, and Army arsenals in Tokyo and Nagoya.

Kaishiki No.1 Aeroplane

In 1911, Capt Yoshitoshi Tokugawa, an Army committee member of the PMBRA, designed and supervised the construction of the first Japanese-manufactured military aeroplane. This work took place at the Army Balloon Corps facility at Nakano Village, west of Shinjuku, Tokyo.

Using as a pattern, the Henri Farman of 1910 that had been imported, design began in April 1911 and construction was started the following July. Assistant Engineer Goichi Nakazato supervised the construction, while others assisting were Privates l/c Gisaburo Ohsh-

ima, Kichitaro Sugiyama and Jinzo Hirano, along with a carpenter and ten soldiers. Although the engine and the propeller were imported from France, all other materials were procured in Japan. The airframe was mainly constructed of hinoki (Japanese cypress) and covering was two layers of silk glued together by what was described as liquid rubber. Attachment fittings, bracing wires and turn buckles were specially procured from iron works companies or bought from local hardware shops.

While this was regarded as a Farman-type, it did have its unique differences. It was converted to a sesquiplane design, giving it reduced wing area and therefore increased speed. A change was made to the aerofoil by having a greater frontal curve in the hope of achieving better lift. Ailerons were on the upper wing only, and the tail was simplified by having a single horizontal tail surface. The engine and propeller were mounted higher than in the original design, and therefore the undercarriage could be shortened. A windshield was added for the pilot.

When completed, in October 1911, it was known as the Tokugawa Type aeroplane, but later was given the official identity Kaishiki No.1 Aeroplane. The aeroplane was moved to the Army facility and flying field at Tokorozawa where it made its first flight on 13 October, piloted by Capt Tokugawa.

The flight recorded on 25 October, 1911, indicated that the aeroplane reached an altitude of 50m (164ft) and attained a speed of 72km/h (45mph). Maximum height recorded was 85m (278ft) and distance covered was 1,600m (1 mile). As tests continued it was discovered that the propeller ground clearance was too small, causing the propeller blades to make contact with the grass and reducing its rotation speed and resultant power. After modifying this and other necessary changes, the aeroplane was known as the Kaizo Kaishiki No.1, Kaizo signifying modified.

Changes to the structure included lengthening the undercarriage, and fitting landing skids not integral with the airframe structure so that they could be more easily replaced when broken. The twin rudders were replaced by a single and larger-area rudder to take better advantage of the propeller slipstream for improved directional control. Longer interplane struts gave a greater spacing between the two wings, and the windshield was removed to give the student pilot a better sense of speed, thought at that time to be essential.

A controversy developed over which aeroplane was the first Japanese-made aeroplane to fly successfully: this Kaishiki No.1 or the civilian Narahara No.2. The problem was that after a straight

Kaishiki No.2 Aeroplane.

flight of 60m at a height of 4m, the undercarriage of the Narahara aircraft had failed on landing after its flight on 5 May, 1911, at Tokorozawa, five months before the Army-built craft was flown. Was the flight a failure or a success when the undercarriage broke upon landing? (*see* Narahara No.2 Aeroplane)

The following data are for the original Kaishiki No.1 aeroplane.

Single-engine pusher sesquiplane trainer. Wooden structure with fabric covering. Elevators at nose and tail. Skid-type undercarriage with dual wheels. Open tandem seating.

50hp Gnome Omega seven-cylinder air-cooled rotary engine, driving a Chauvière two-blade wooden propeller.

Span (upper) 10.50m (34ft 5½in), (lower) 8m (26ft 3in); length 11.50m (37ft 8½in); height 3.90m (12ft 9½in); wing area 41sq m (441.334sq ft).

Empty weight 450kg (992lb); loaded weight 550kg (1,212lb); wing loading 13.4kg/sq m (2.7lb/sq ft); power loading 11kg/hp (24.2lb/hp).

Maximum speed 39kt (45mph); endurance 3 hr.

One built in 1911, modified in 1912.

Kaishiki Nos. 2, 3 and 4 Aeroplanes

With confidence gained by the success of the Kaishiki No.1, the PMBRA began construction of the Kaishiki No.2 in March 1912. Like the first, this was designed by Capt Tokugawa. It was built in the

hangar at Tokorozawa Flight Test Grounds, and first flown in June 1912 by Tokugawa.

Similar designs completed in November 1912 were the No.3 and No.4. Basically, the No.2 was like the No.1 but had a longer undercarriage for better propeller ground clearance. Some changes were made in the interplane strut configuration, and the tailplane and rear elevator were enlarged to improve stability. Engines varied with these aeroplanes and they were often interchanged. Since they were pusher aeroplanes, the engine arrangement with a 50hp Gnome rotary had the propeller between the engine mounting and the engine; but the No.4 powered by a 50hp Anzani rotary engine had its propeller behind the engine.

In May 1912, with training aircraft now available, the Army selected five officers to become the first class of pilot officers. The next month, six officers were selected for the first reconnaissance-observer course. The importance of aviation within the Army was being recognized. To further demonstrate the capability of the aeroplane at this time, the first flight to visit Tokyo was made on 27 October, 1912, by the Kaishiki No.2. To make this long flight of about 18 miles, the removable windscreen nacelle was reinstalled, and Capt Tokugawa made this historic flight, starting at 05:58 and landing at the Yoyogi Parade Grounds at 07:45. It was

from here, twenty-two months before, that Tokugawa had made the first flight in Japan on 19 December, 1910, in an imported Farman. After refuelling, he circled the major boroughs of Tokyo and landed once again at Yoyogi for fuel. Returning to Tokorozawa, his starting point, he had covered 96.5km (60sm), a major accomplishment at that time.

These early 'Tokugawa-type' aircraft, as they were more popularly called, were entered in many exhibitions, both singly and together, receiving considerable press coverage. Since the military was the greatest motivator in developing the aeroplane in Japan, and with its intended use as a military weapon, it must be noted that the Army used the Kaishiki No.4 to demonstrate for the first time, in December 1913, the dropping of simulated bombs.

Single-engine pusher sesquiplane trainer. Wooden open structure with fabric-covered wings and control surfaces. Elevators at nose and tail. Skid-type undercarriage with two sets of dual wheels. Two seats in tandem.

50hp Gnome Omega seven-cylinder air-cooled rotary engine, driving a Chauvière two-bladed wooden propeller (No.2 and No.3). 60hp Anzani six-cylinder air-cooled rotary engine, driving a fixed-pitch two-bladed wooden propeller (No.3 after modification and No.4).

Span 11m (36ft); length 11m (36ft); height 3.90m (12ft 9½in); wing area 41sq m (441.334sq ft).

Army Type Mo (Maurice Farman Type) 1913 Aeroplane.

Empty weight 450kg (992lb); loaded weight 570kg (1,256lb); wing loading 13.4kg/sq m (2.74lb/sq ft); power loading 11kg/hp (24.2lb/hp).

Maximum speed 39kt (45mph); endurance 3hr.

Three built, No.2, No.3 and No.4, all in 1912.

Army Type Mo (Maurice Farman Type) 1913 Aeroplane

Army Lt Kenjiro Nagasawa and Lt Shigeru Sawada were sent to France to study aviation during the period July 1912 to Februry 1913. At the end of their stay in Europe, they bought a Maurice Farman 1912 aeroplane which arrived in Japan by ship in May 1913. This new aeroplane proved superior to all other imported aeroplanes and Japanese-made Kaishiki types in stability, control and reliability. This prompted the purchase of four more of this type, which by then, a year later, had been improved and were referred to as the Maurice Farman 1913 models.

When these disassembled parts arrived they were studied by the PMBRA with the idea of manufacturing them in Japan. Under the guidance of Nagasawa and Sawada of the PMBRA, the Tokyo Army Artillery Arsenal in Koishigawa, Tokyo, built the airframes and the 70hp Renault rotary engines under the supervision of Army Capt Haruhiko Uemura of the Arsenal. Aeroplane number five in this Type Mo 1913 series was completed in September 1913. Eight additional aircraft were built in 1914, and

beginning with No.7, steel spring heels were attached to the rear of the undercarriage skids. These could be made to dig-in and reduce the landing run. Also quite noticeable with the Type Mo 1913 was the raised seat behind the student, giving the instructor better visibility. When required, a third person could sit on the fuel tank behind the instructor. These became the first production aircraft in Japan.

In response to Japan's participation in the First World War with action against the Germans in Tsingtao, China, the Provisional Air Corps was organized and used the Mo Type 1913 aircraft as its primary equipment. Of the five aeroplanes sent to the Tsingtao campaign in September and October 1914, four were of this type, the other being a Nieuport NG. Of these four, three were imported, and the fourth Japanese-built. During this campaign, these aircraft undertook reconnaissance and bombing missions, dropping 15kg (33lb) from six bomb racks, and occasionally their crews firing pistols against rifle fire from a German Taube in air-to-air combat. This experience brought later improvements to what then became the Type Mo 1913 Armed Aeroplane with one automatic rifle and provision for six 10kg (22lb) bombs. By having a 'wirless' communication system on board one of the aerocraft, in July 1913 they effectively directed artillery fire from the air for evaluation purposes.

These Type Mo aeroplanes were continually used for distance records, connecting major cities on flights punctuated with frequent emergency landings along the way, and experiencing other delays due to weather. But they held the spotlight in news coverage and were popular topics of conversation. In March 1915, the most distinguished combat aircraft of the Tsingtao campaign, the third Type Mo 1913, was put on display in the Yushukan Military Museum in Kudan, Tokyo, perhaps the world's first exhibit of an aeroplane with a combat record.

Single-engine pusher sesquiplane trainer with crew nacelle. Wooden structure with fabric covering. Eleva-

tors at nose and tail. Skid-type under-carriage with dual wheels. Crew of two in open cockpit.

70–80hp Renault eight-cylinder vee air-cooled engine, driving a Chauvière two-bladed wooden propeller.

Span 15.54m (50ft 11¾in); length 11.28m (37ft); height 3.45m (11ft 3¾in); wing area 53.8sq m (589.117sq ft).*

Empty weight 580.6kg (1,280lb); loaded weight 855kg (1,885lb); wing loading 15.9kg/sq m (3.25lb/sq ft); power loading 12.21kg/hp (26.91lb/hp).

Maximum speed 51kt (59mph); cruising speed 38kt (44mph); service ceiling 3,000m (9,843ft); endurance 4hr.

Four imported, twenty-two built by Army Arsenal and four built by PMBRA and others.

Kaishiki No.5 and No.6 Aeroplanes

Following the arrival of the four Maurice Farman 1913 aircraft from France, the manufacture in Japan of No.5 and No.6 was put under the two officers who had studied in France and purchased the aero-planes, Lt Kenjiro Nagasawa and Lt Shigeru Sawada. The aircraft were built from the same drawings but one was constructed at the PMBRA at Tokorazawa and the other at the Artillery Arsenal in Tokyo. Both were powered by 70hp Gnome rotary engines, experi-mentally manufactured at the Artil-lery Arsenal, but they proved less reliable than the 70hp Renault engines, thus ending the production of the Gnome-type after only two engines had been built.

The two aeroplanes were a combination of designs for the Kaishiki No.3 and No.4 airframe and Maurice Farman 1913 wings. They were completed in the autumn of 1913 and entered operational service with the Type Mo 1913 Aeroplanes. Compared to the four preceding imported models, the two new aeroplanes had more powerful engines, making them faster by 2.7kt, larger fuel capacity for a duration of four hours, and the seats were located in a longer fuse-

*Dimensions for Japanese-built and modified model.

Converted Type Mo (Maurice Farman Type) Aeroplane.

lage nacelle to improve visibility for aerial reconnaissance. Within the PMBRA, the two aeroplanes were unofficially called Kaishiki Second Year Model (Second year of Taisho; 1913).

Single-engine pusher sesquiplane trainer with crew nacelle. Wooden structure with fabric covering. Eleva-tors at nose and tail. Skid-type under-carriage with dual wheels. Crew of two in open cockpit.

70hp Gnome seven-cylinder air-cooled rotary engine, driving a Rapid-santral two-bladed wooden propeller.

Span 15.50m (50ft 10¼in); length 11m (36ft 1in); height 3.66m (12ft); wing area 44.1sq m (474.7sq ft).

Empty weight 485kg(1,069lb); loaded weight 765kg (1,686lb); wing loading 12.7kg/sq m (2.6lb/sq ft); power loading 10.9kg/hp (24lb/hp).

Kaishiki No.6 Aeroplane.

Maximum speed 51kt (59mph); endurance 4hr.

One each of No.5 and No.6 built in 1913.

Converted Type Mo (Maurice Farman Type) Aeroplane

When originally built as the seventh aeroplane in May 1914 in the hangar of Tokorozawa Airfield this aeroplane was like all the other Type Mo 1913 aircraft. Flown by 2-Lt Jiro Takeda in the news-worthy flight to Tokyo on 22 May, 1914, it also established an altitude record of 2,200m on 9 June flown by 2-Lt Morikichi Saka-moto. It was then exhibited to the Crown Prince (later Emperor Showa) after landing at the Koma-zawa Parade Grounds. At the time Lt Sawada converted this aeroplane he had felt that it was a very lucky aeroplane, and since it was the seventh of the Type Mo, again the auspicious number, he painted number 7 on the tail.

However, on 26 July, 1914, the aeroplane ran out of luck, for it crashed and was badly damaged at Tokorozawa Airfield while being flown by Capt Tokugawa, and for a while, its remains sat idle in a hangar. At a time when much of the military strength at Tokorozawa was participating in the Tsingtao campaign in September 1914, Lt Sawada remained behind and was put in charge of pilot training and aircraft maintenance. Taking the initiative, he reassembled what he called the lucky aeroplane from its unbroken parts and replaced many others, only this time eliminating the front elevator. When completed on 19 January, 1915, this 7th Type Mo 1913 became known as the Sawada Type No.7, or more officially because of this radical modification, Kaishiki the 3rd Year Model. This change demonstrated improvements in reconnaissance capability, an increase in stability, improved maneouvrability and higher speed. By placing a machine-gun in the front-seat location no longer restricted by the front elevator, this became the first Japanese Army aircraft to be so armed.

This aeroplane was used extensively at Tokorozawaa for flight testing, until 26 May, 1915, when, being flown by Capt Naranosuke Oka, it crashed in a wheat field at Kitada, Tomioka Village, 4km north of the airfield, and the aeroplane was destroyed. However, because of the proven success of Sawada's modifications it introduced radical design changes in future Japanese aeroplanes.

Single-engined pusher sesquiplane trainer with crew nacelle. Wooden structure with fabric covering. Rear elevator only. Skid-type undercarriage with dual wheels. Crew of two in open cockpit.

70–80hp Renault eight-cylinder vee air-cooled engine, driving a Chauvière two-bladed wooden propeller.

One nose-mounted flexible machine-gun.

Span 15.50m (50ft 10¼in); length 9.35m (30ft 8in); height 3.66m (12ft); wing area 60sq m (645.85sq ft).

Empty weight 485kg (1,069lb); loaded weight 765kg (1,686lb); wing loading 12.7kg/sq m (2.6lb/sq ft); power loading 9.45kg/hp (20.8lb/hp).

Maximum speed 58kt (67mph); endurance 4hr.

One conversion in January 1915.

Kaishiki No.7 Aeroplane

Using the experience gained while studying in France, and the successful conversion of the Number 7 Type Mo aircraft, Lt Shigeru Sawada attempted a second modification, this time using a Henri Farman 1914 imported from France in November of that year. He began his conversion work in April 1915 at the Association's factory in Tokorozawa and completed the project the following July. Originally referred to as the Kaishiki A7, it became more commonly called the Kaishiki 7 Reconnaissance Aircraft since that was its designed mission.

Among the changes was a small amount of dihedral added to the wings as well as slight sweepback to both the upper and lower wings. The most apparent change was the replacement of the Gnome rotary engine for a Curtiss OX-5 with its increase of 30hp. This gave noticeably improved speed, increasing it to 54kt (62mph). Both Capt Oka and Lt Sawada liked the handling characteristics and were the only regular pilots of the No.7, since it

Kaishiki No.7 Aeroplane.

was disliked by the others who flew it. Flying came to an end on 25 September, 1915, however, when Lt Iwatomi was piloting the aeroplane and it crashed just north of Tokorozawa Airfield. The fire that followed partially destroyed the aeroplane and Lt Iwatomi was badly injured.

Single-engine pusher sesquiplane reconnaissance aircraft with crew nacelle. Wooden structure with fabric covering. Tail elevator only. Skid-type undercarriage with dual wheels. Crew of two in open cockpit.

90–100hp Curtiss OX-5 eight-cylinder vee water-cooled engine, driving a Curtiss two-bladed wooden propeller.

Span 14.50m (47ft 7in); length 7.80m (25ft 7in); height 3m (9ft 10in); wing area 46.8sq m (503.75sq ft).

Maximum speed 54kt (62mph).

One conversion in July 1915.

Kaishiki No.7 Small Aeroplane

Extending his aircraft design ingenuity, Lt Shigeru Sawada created the first Japanese-made aeroplane that could be classed as a fighter aircraft. This was a Curtiss-pusher design that used the rebuilt Curtiss OX-5 from the crashed Kaishiki No.7. Along with the more modern tricycle-type undercarriage and eliminating skids, this aeroplane featured a flexible forward-firing machine-gun.

Kaishiki No.7 Small Aeroplane.

Incorporating the aerobatic features of the Curtiss-built aeroplane, it was a small and nimble aircraft. The design was begun in the autumn of 1915 and the aeroplane completed on 11 June, 1916, making its first flight two days later. It was officially designated the Kaishiki 7 Small Aeroplane, but within the Association it was known as the Kaishiki Kaizo (Association-Type Modified) 3rd Year Model Aeroplane. Other names, for record purposes, included Kaishiki 7 Pursuit as well as the Sawada Curtiss Pursuit.

Because of the aircraft's apparent success, Lt Sawada was sent to Europe to study the latest developments being used in the war. On his return to Japan in February 1917, he continued further tests with his Kai-7 fighter. On 8 March, 1917, while making a dive from approximately 600m (2,000ft), he levelled at about 200m (656ft) at which

Army Henri Farman Type Model 4 Aeroplane.

point the structure failed and the aircraft crashed just north of Tokorozawa Airfield. Lt Sawada was killed, and his loss was severely felt by his associates and Japanese Army aviation in general, for he was regarded as a genius in aircraft design and a distinguished pilot.

Single-engine pusher biplane fighter aircraft with crew nacelle. Wooden structure with fabric covering. Tricycle undercarriage. Pilot in open cockpit.
90–100hp Curtiss OX-5 eight-cylinder vee water-cooled engine, driving a Curtiss two-bladed wooden propeller.
One nose-mounted flexible machine-gun.
Span 11m (36ft 1in); length 9m (29ft 6¼in); wing area 41.2sq m (443.487sq ft).
Loaded weight 734kg (1,618lb); wing loading 17.8kg/sq m (3.6lb/sq ft); power loading 7.34kg/hp (16.2lb/hp).
Maximum speed 60kt (69mph).
One built in June 1916.

Army Henri Farman Type Model 4 Aeroplane (Army Type Mo-4 Aeroplane)

The introduction of this aeroplane into Japanese military service, was the zenith of the Farman pusher biplanes in Japan. Earlier Farman types were already established, but one Henri Farman 1914 aeroplane which the Association imported from France in November 1914 would develop as a noteworthy type. The PMBRA decided to develop the aircraft further by making a new aeroplane using many of the changes perfected on the earlier converted Type Mo and Kaishiki No.7. Although Lt Shigeru Sawada was killed in the earlier Kaishiki No.7 Small Aeroplane, many development projects were being undertaken simultaneously, and Lt Sawada was in charge of this new design which used many of his earlier innovations. Noticeable differences with his redesign included the raising of the fuselage nacelle above the lower wing and providing a small triangular rudder and shorter undercarriage skids. It was completed in November 1915 three months after beginning the design. It was later discovered that similar conversions were being made in France without the knowledge of either user.

The Association called the new design the Sawada Type B 7, but it was officially designated Kaishiki 4th Year Model. These Association-built aircraft had a Japanese-made 70hp Renault engine installed which gave more power than the French-built aeroplane.

Participating in the military review held by the Emperor on 2 December, 1915, Lt Morikichi Sakamoto of the Association flew one of these new aeroplanes over the Komazawa Parade Grounds in winds gusting up to 45mph. Stability and performance were easily apparent when comparing the difficulties being experienced by the older Type Mo 1913s, and as a result the Type Mo 4th Year Model was regarded as revolutionary. Meeting with strong approval, the type was put into production at

the Association's factory at Tokorozawa, as well as the Tokyo Army Artillery Arsenal and the Atsuta Army Weapon Manufacturing Works of Nagoya Army Ordnance Arsenal.

The aeroplane had a number of designation changes, beginning as the Type Mo 1914, followed by the Type Mo 4th Year Model, and after 1918 becoming the Type Mo-4. They were used first as trainers at Tokorozawa for navigation, scouting and bombing, later to replace the Type Mo 1913s of the balloon company (squadron equivalent) and flight company that had been formed at Tokorozawa in December 1915 as part of an air battalion. When the Japanese Army deployed its 12th Division to Siberia in 1918, several air units were organized, one of which was sent to northern Manchuria, then to Siberia for patrol duties using eight Type Mo-4s, six Mo-6s and nine Sopwith 1A2 reconnaissance aircraft imported from England.

In time, a number of the Type Mo-4 aircraft passed into civil hands and were used as trainers with the Imperial Flying Association and Kishi Aeroplane Manufacturing Works (later Akabane Aeroplane Manufacturing Works). The former modified a Type Mo-4

Seishiki-1 Aeroplane.

with an additional fuel tank in the second crew position making it a single-seat aircraft. Called the *No.2 Mie-go*, it made a nonstop record flight between Tokyo and Osaka. Piloted by Masao Goto, it left Tokorozawa and landed at the Osaka Joto Parade Grounds, in 6hr 28min, on 1 April, 1918, a remarkable record for duration and distance in Japan for that period. The Type Mo-4s remained popular from when they were first manufactured in the autumn of 1915, and were put into production again in 1919 and 1920.

Single-engine pusher sesquiplane reconnaissance aircraft with crew nacelle. Wooden structure with fabric covering. Tail elevator only. Skid-type undercarriage with dual wheels. Crew of two in open cockpit.

70–80hp Renault eight-cylinder vee air-cooled engine, driving a Chauvière two-bladed wooden propeller.

One machine-gun when necessary.

Span 15.50m (50ft 10¼in); length 9.14m (29ft 11¾in); height 3.18m (10ft 51¼in); wing area 58sq m (624.327sq ft).

Empty weight 563kg (1,241lb); loaded weight 778kg (1,715lb); wing loading 13.4kg/sq m (2.7lb/sq ft); power loading 9.73kg/hp (21.4lb/hp).

Maximum speed 49kt (56mph); climb to 2,000m (6,562ft) in 25min; service ceiling 3,000m (9,843ft); endurance 4hr.

Eighty-four built: nine PMBRA, Fifty-one Army Arsenals (Tokyo and Nagoya), twenty Tokorozawa Branch, Supply Dept, three Imperial Flying Association (civil use), one Kishi Aeroplane (civil use).

Seishiki-1 Aeroplane

In May 1915, the PMBRA decided to experiment with the construction of a tractor-type aeroplane of more conventional design, powered by a 100hp engine. To undertake the design work, a committee was formed consisting of Engineer Shuhei Iwamoto, Capt Nobuhide Sakurai and Capt Akira Matsui, all recently returned from aviation research study in France. Joining them were Lt Shigeru Sawada and Lt Kenjiro Nagasawa, also from the PMBRA. The intention was to produce a general operational type aircraft to become standard equipment for the Army.

The design reflected many of the technical details found in the German L.V.G. D IX. The unequal-span two-bay wings folded to the rear for ease in railway transport. For this first aeroplane, the Association used the 100hp Mercedes Daimler engine that the Imperial Flying Association had imported from Germany for installation in the Rumpler Taube monoplane. This engine was later licence-built

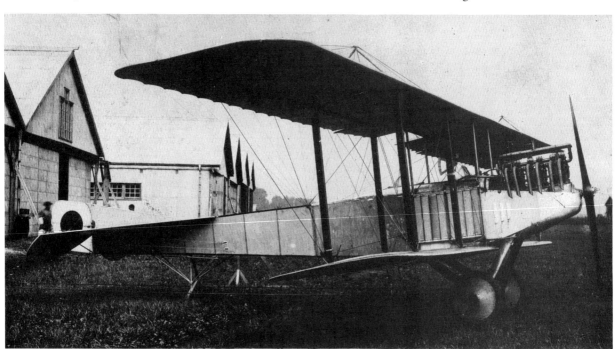

by the Army Tokyo Artillery Arsenal and the Chikusa Army Machinery & Equipment Manufacturing Works of the Nagoya Army Ordnance Arsenal for the Type Mo-6 Aeroplanes. Fuel capacity was 360 litres to enable non-stop flight between Tokyo and Osaka. This was the first Japanese-made aeroplane to have a loaded weight exceeding 1 ton.

When completed on 30 April, 1916, at Tokorozawa, it was designated the Seishiki-1 Aeroplane, Seishiki meaning official type, to mark the beginning of an all-new generation of military aircraft which came up to European military standards at that time. Ground tests made by Lt Morikichi Sakamoto on 1 May, 1916, were successful, and five days later, Lt Sawada made the first test flight. Unfortunately, immediately after take off, the fuel-tank pressurization was lost and the engine stopped, causing an emergency landing with serious damage to the aeroplane and slight injuries to Sawada.

Repairs were completed by December at the Nagoya Army Ordnance Arsenal and included installation of a gravity-feed fuel system with a fuel tank in the upper wing centre-section. Wing struts were added to support the outer extensions of the upper wing, aileron area was increased in chord, and the undercarriage skid was removed.

Once the aeroplane was flying again, its performance was found to be disappointing mainly because of poor stability, calling for a full redesign rather than modifications, so it was used only for experimental purposes. On 24 July, 1917, a Maurice Farman 1914 flown by Capt Nakanishi collided with the tail of the Seishiki-1 Aeroplane while on the ground, resulting in the dismantling of the aircraft for parts.

Single-engine tractor biplane tactical aircraft. All-wooden construction with fabric covering. Rearward folding wings for railway transport. Crew of two in open cockpits.

100–110hp Mercedes Daimler six-cylinder inline water-cooled engine,

Army Maurice Farman Type Model 6 Aeroplane.

driving a Heine two-bladed wooden propeller.

One dorsal flexible machine-gun. Unspecified bomb load.

Span 15.10m (49ft 6½in); length 9.35m (30ft 8in); height 3m (9ft 10in); wing area 40.5sq m (435.952sq ft).

Loaded weight 1,100kg (2,425lb); wing loading 27.2kg/sq m (5.57lb/sq ft); power loading 10kg/hp (22lb/hp).

Maximum speed 58kt (67mph); climb to 1,000m (3,280ft) in 10min; endurance 7hr.

One built in April 1916.

Army Maurice Farman Type Model 6 Aeroplane (Army Type Mo-6 Aeroplane)

Another stage of development came from advanced aero engines of 100hp or more, products of the First World War. To take advantage of these, Japan imported several liquid-cooled engines including the 90hp Curtiss OX-5 and the 100hp Daimler, each of which was tested by installing them in a Type Mo-4 Aeroplane. Impressed by the Daimler engine, the Army Artillery Arsenal began its manufacture in 1916, completing the first in the spring of 1917.

This Daimler-type engine was installed in an aeroplane that was newly designed for it. Since the aeroplane powered by this engine had had its start in May 1916, the PMBRA designated it the Type

Mo6-Year Model, but later the Army's official designation became the Type Mo 6th Year Model for the year of Taisho. In 1918 it was redesignated as the Type Mo Model 6, or the Type Mo-6 in short.

Outwardly, the Type Mo-6 was almost identical to the Type Mo-4, but was slightly larger and heavier and had coolant radiators on each side of the engine. Production models had shorter front skids and the front supporting diagonal strut to the skid was eliminated. On the production model there was an increase in fuel-tank capacity which made the loaded weight higher than that of the Mo-4, but the Mo-6 had a marked increase in speed from 49kt to 60kt. Production began in the autumn of 1917 at which time Mo-4 production was terminated. The Mo-6 became the Army's first Japanese-designed reconnaissance/trainer to be produced in quantity.

The new Army aeroplane made a good start when the first of the series, No.101, set a two-seat altitude record of 2,800m (9,186ft) on 25 May, 1917, while being flown by Lt Morikichi Sakamoto and Army Engineer Shuhei Iwamoto.

All did not continue well, however, for this new aeroplane. During the November 1917 Army Special Manoeuvres on the Ohmi Plain near Lake Biwa, of the fourteen newly built Type Mo-6 aircraft participating, twelve crashed or made emergency landings because of engine malfunctions among other things. As a result, the Army Department of Aviation organized an investigating committee of

Sole survivor of the Army Maurice Farman Type Model 6 Aeroplane is No.266 which is now in the Yasukuni Shrine.

twenty-five officers and specialist engineers with twenty-four pilot officers. Many problems became evident, among them the need to improve engine research and development, use of better materials, improve training for engineers, and better communications between PMBRA and the operational flying units. Many of the problems were corrected, thus extending the aircraft's operational life long past their practicality as combat aircraft.

However during their service life, these Type Mo-6 Aeroplanes became the Army's last biplane pusher aircraft. When the 2nd Army Air Battalion was being organized, in December 1917, Type Mo-6s from Tokorozawa became its initial equipment.* This unit was formed at the Army's newly activated airfield at Kagamigahara in Gifu Prefecture, better known after the Pacific War as Gifu

*The first air battalion was organized in December 1915 at Tokorozawa and named the Tokorozawa Army Air Battalion. When the 2nd was organized, it was re-named the 1st Army Air Battalion.

Air Base, north of Nagoya. Air battalions at Tokorozawa and Kagamigahara used their Type Mo-6s for reconnaissance and training until around 1923. When the Army sent units to Siberia and northern Manchuria in August 1918, four of the twelve aeroplanes of the 2nd Army Air Battalion were Type Mo-6s. However, because of the severe cold of the ensuing winter, they could not be used because the engine coolant froze.

One of the Type Mo-6 Aeroplanes, No.266, survived for many years by having been dismantled and stored in the rafters of what had been the Nukiyama Laboratory, of the Department of Engineering, Tohoku University, where it escaped destruction during the Second World War. It was later restored and is now preserved in the Yasukuni Shrine in Tokyo.

Single-engine pusher reconnaissance-biplane with crew nacelle. All-wooden

The Standard H-3 Trainer was a Japanese-built copy of a United States Army trainer.

construction with fabric covering. Crew of two in open cockpit.

100–110hp Daimler six-cylinder in-line water-cooled engine, driving a two-bladed wooden propeller.

One nose mounted Hotchkiss flexible 7.7mm machine-gun.

Span 16.13m (52ft 11in); length 9.33m (30ft 7½in); height 3.10m (10ft 2in); wing area 62sq m (667.364sq ft).

Empty weight 758kg (1,671lb); loaded weight 1,060kg (2,336lb); wing loading 17.1kg/sq m (3.5lb/sq ft); power loading 9.64kg/hp (21.2lb/hp).

Maximum speed 60kt (69mph); cruising speed 49kt (56mph); climb to 2,000m (6,562ft) in 25min; service ceiling 3,500m (11,482ft).

134 built 1917–1921: PMBRA thirty-five; Army Arsenals forty-seven; Tokorozawa Branch, Supply Dept forty-eight; Akabane Aeroplane Manufacturing Works four.

Standard H-3 Trainer

In search of proven trainer aircraft, the PMBRA purchased two Standard H-3 Trainers from the US Army in May 1917. The H-3 was a two-bay biplane with large gap and 10-degree sweep back to the wings, and powered by 125hp Hall-Scott A-5 engines. Only nine were built, and the type had been carried over from the former Sloan Aircraft Co Inc that became the Standard Aero Corporation.

Three more of these aeroplanes were built in Japan, with the higher powered 150hp Hall-Scott engine. Production was limited because the

Seishiki-2 Aeroplane.

aeroplane was considered dangerous. They were used for flying training from May 1917 to March 1918, beginning at Tokorozawa and later at the newly opened Kagamigahara Airfield. Fifteen pilot officers received training in them.

Single-engine tractor biplane trainer. All-wooden construction with fabric covering. Pupil and instructor in open cockpit.

150hp Hall-Scott L-4 six-cylinder in-line water-cooled engine, driving a two-bladed wooden propeller.

Span 12.25m (40ft 1in); length 8.22m (27ft).

Loaded weight 1,225kg (2,700lb).

Maximum speed 71kt (82mph); endurance 6hr.

Three or more built.

Seishiki-2 Aeroplane

Making a sharp break away from the Farman pushers, the PMBRA began the design in July 1917 for what would be the Seishiki-2. It was designed by Lt Morikichi Sakamoto with the help of Assistant Engineer Shiro Yoshihara who had just returned from aircraft design studies in Europe. In charge of construction was Lt Nakazawa at the Association's factory at Tokorozawa.

This aeroplane was only intended as an experimental high-speed tractor design to help the development of other types, and was to be powered by a 100hp Daimler water-cooled engine produced by the Tokyo Army Artillery Arsenal. The fuselage was fairly large, being constructed of wood and having a

contoured plywood covering. Radiators were mounted close to the fuselage sides like those of the Seishiki-1. Completed in December 1917, it made its first flight on 11 January, 1918, piloted by Lt Sakamoto. When making the second flight on 17 January, at a height of about 50m after take off, it was reported that the engine emitted heavy black smoke and lost power. Sakamoto attempted a tight turn back, which resulted in a spin and the aeroplane crashed on the north side of the Tokorozawa Airfield, killing Lt Sakamoto. Like its predecessor the Seishiki-1, the Seishiki-2 was the sole example. Although the PMBRA began design work on a Seishiki-3 in March 1918, it was taken over by the Department of Research at Tokorozawa Aviation School because of Army reorganization but the aircraft was not completed.

Designers and engineers believed that the maximum speed of the Seishiki-2 could have been 70kt (80mph) but for the continuing problems with the Japanese-built Daimler engine. Others felt that the design was too advanced for Japanese manufacture, and as a result the twin boom pusher Type Mo-4 and Type Mo-6 Farmans remained the standard Army equipment until the French Aviation Mission visited Japan in 1919.

Single-engine high-speed tractor biplane. All wooden construction with ply-covered fuselage and fabric-covered wings and tail. Two seats in open cockpits.

100–110hp Daimler six-cylinder in-line water-cooled engine, driving a two-bladed wooden propeller.

Span 9.86m (32ft 4in); length 6.7m (21ft 11¾in); height 2.60m (8ft 6¼in); wing area 31sq m (333.692sq ft).

One built in December 1917.

Army Maurice Farman 5 Aeroplane

This aeroplane was identical to the Army Maurice Farman 1914, Type Mo-4 Aeroplane, but was equipped with dual controls for primary pilot training. With the exception of the length being extended from 9.14m to 9.38m it hardly warranted a re-

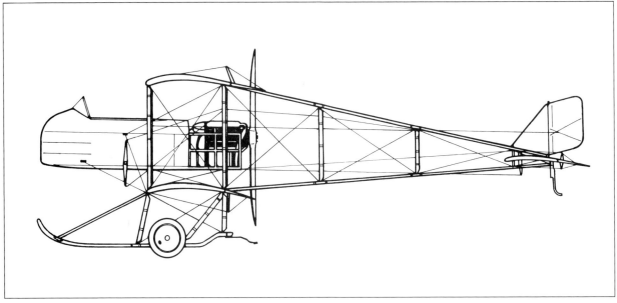

Army Maurice Farman 5 Aeroplanes (*Shorzoe Abe*)

designation. This became the Army's first primary trainer to be built expressly for this purpose.

Production became the responsibility of the Army Artillery Arsenal. Six were manufactured in 1919 and the Tokorozawa Branch of the Department of Supply built an additional five in 1920. However, in that year, licence rights for manufacturing the Nieuport 81E2 primary trainer came into effect and with this the Army organized a new system of flying training and, as a result, there was no further need for the Farman trainers. A few were retained at the Tokorozawa Aviation School until about 1923.

Single-engine pusher biplane primary trainer with crew nacelle. Wooden construction with fabric covering. Crew

Army Model 2 Ground Taxi-ing Trainer.

of two in open cockpit.

70–80hp Renault eight-cylinder vee air-cooled engine, or 100hp Daimler six-cylinder inline water-cooled engine, driving a two-bladed wooden propeller.

Span 15.52m (50ft 11in); length 9.38m (30ft 9¼in); height 3.17m (10ft 5in); wing area 58sq m (624.327sq ft).

Loaded weight 778kg (1,715lb); wing loading 13.4kg/sq m (2.74lb/sq ft); power loading 9.73kg/hp (21.4lb/hp).

Maximum speed 49kt (56mph); climb to 2,000m (6,562ft) in 35min; endurance 4hr.

Data for Renault-powered version.

Eleven built 1919–1920: Army Artillery Arsenal six; Tokorozawa Branch, Dept of Supply five.

Army Model 2 Ground Taxi-ing Trainer

Based on the experience gained from the French Aviation Mission that assisted Army aviation training in 1919, the Army decided to use non-flying taxi-ing trainers for the first phase of training. Initially, the Army used three Morane-Saulnier ground-taxi-ing monoplanes and two of their older Nieuport monoplanes which had shortened wing spans. Following the use of these, the Army adopted the Type Ni Ground Taxi-ing Aircraft that was designed and manufactured by the Tokorozawa Branch, Department of Supply, Army Department of Aviation. The designation, Type Ni, stood for Nieuport since it was designed along the lines of the flyable Nieuport 81 Trainer, later designated Type Ko 1 Trainer. The design was converted into a monoplane with shortened wings and reduced engine power.

The Tokorozawa Branch of Army Supply built three of these trainers in 1919 and powered them with 50hp Gnome rotary engines. After operational tests at the Tokorozawa Flying School, they were designated the Army Model 2 Ground Taxi-ing Trainer, and seven more were manufactured at Tokorozawa in 1920. Nakajima followed by manufacturing five more. At this time, they cost 3,720yen as compared to a flyable Nieuport 81 Trainer costing 6,228yen, making the ground trainer a rather costly machine. It was soon discovered that cheaper ground taxi-ing training was possible with other types of aircraft.

Single-engine monoplane ground-taxi-ing trainer. Wooden structure with fabric covering. Single seat in open cockpit.

Gnome Omega seven-cylinder air-cooled rotary engine, rated at 50hp at 1,200rpm, driving a two-bladed wooden propeller.

Wing area 12.5sq m (134.553sq ft).

Empty weight 388kg (855lb); loaded weight 502kg (1,106lb); wing loading 40.2kg/sq m (8.23lb/sq ft); power loading 10kg/hp (22.0lb)hp).

Fifteen built 1919–1920: Tokorozawa Branch ten; Nakajima five.

Army Model 3 Ground Taxi-ing Trainer

Following the Model 2 Ground Taxi-ing Trainer, the Tokorozawa Branch of the Department of Supply designed and built an original trainer in 1920. It was a smaller and lighter-weight trainer that closely resembled the Blériot Monoplane and was fitted with a front skid to prevent inadvertent nosing-over, but the skid was not fitted to later production trainers.

All Model 3s were built at Tokorozawa and used as the standard ground taxi-ing trainer until about 1926. After the introduction of the stable Type Ki 1 Trainer (Hanriot HD-14) in large numbers beginning in 1925, replacing the Type Ko 1 Trainer, the need for an exclusive ground taxi-ing trainer was eliminated.

Single-engine shoulder-wing monoplane ground taxi-ing trainer. Wooden

Army Model 3 Ground Taxi-ing Trainer.

structure with fabric-covered wings and tail. Ply-covered forward section of fuselage. Pupil in open cockpit.

30hp Anzani three-cylinder air-cooled radial, driving a Ratmanoff two-bladed wooden propeller.

Thirty built 1921–1923.

Koshiki-1 Experimental Reconnaissance Aircraft

Following the development of the Seishiki-2 Aeroplane of 1917, the PMBRA designed the Seishiki-3, but the work was taken over by the Department of Research at the Tokorozawa Aviation School when the PMBRA was dissolved in April 1919. Some design changes were made and the aeroplane was completed, in 1921, with the new designation of Koshiki-1, meaning School Type. This was an advanced high-speed reconnaissance aircraft, much of it based upon the Standard Trainer powered by a 150hp Hall-Scott engine, an aircraft that the Tokorozawa Branch of the Department of Supply manufactured in 1919. During flight testing, the aeroplane sustained heavy damage and for unknown reasons the entire project was terminated.

Single-engine biplane reconnaissance aircraft. Crew of two in open cockpits.

150–165hp Hall-Scott six-cylinder inline water-cooled engine, driving a Regy two-bladed wooden propeller.

Wing area 30.7sq m (330.462sq ft).

Loaded weight 1,000kg (2,204lb); wing loading 32.6kg/sq m (6.6lb/sq ft); power loading 6.06kg/hp (13.3lb/hp).

Maximum speed 87kt (100mph) at sea

level; climb to 2,000m (6,562ft) in 12 min; service ceiling 3,700m (12,139ft).

One built in 1921.

Koshiki-2 Experimental Fighter

In 1920 the Department of Research of the Army Tokorozawa Aviation School undertook a new project that was to be a fighter of all-Japanese design. While this was indeed a Japanese design, it incorporated the best features of existing foreign-types, which resulted in its appearing to be a cross between a Salmson 2-A.2 and a SPAD XIII.

On the design staff at Tokorozawa were Maj (Eng) Akira Matsui of the Aeroplane Section; a graduate from a polytechnic school in France, Maj Shujiro Itoh of the Equipment Section; Maj Shigeo Shibuya of the Engine Section; and Engineer Shuhei Iwamoto from the Experimental Section. Their design for this fighter used an engine installation very similar to that of the Salmson 2-A.2, and the wings, fuselage and undercarriage closely resembled those of the SPAD XIII. The single I interplane struts were similar to those of the SPAD-Herbemont racing aeroplanes. The horizontal tail surface was of the one-piece all-flying type used by Salmson.

The first prototype was complete in 1922 and flown by Lt Kawaida, an instructor at the Tokorozawa Aviation School. The aeroplane showed great promise initially by achieving a maximum speed of 111kt (128mph) in addition to being regarded quite highly for its flying characteristics except for poor longitudinal stability. It was found to be unstable during take offs and landings which was attributed to the type of horizontal stabilizer being used. Upon completing its fourth test flight, the aeroplane landed long and was destroyed when it struck obstacles at the far end of the landing ground.

The design was considered good enough to warrant the construction of a second prototype and that was built in 1923 by the Tokorozawa Branch of the Department of Supply, but nothing further was recorded about it.

Koshiki-2 Experimental Fighter.

Single-engine biplane fighter. Wooden structure with fabric covering. Pilot in open cockpit.

230–260hp Salmson 9Z nine-cylinder water-cooled radial engine, driving a two-bladed wooden propeller.

Two fixed fuselage-mounted forward-firing 7.7mm machine-guns.

Span 10m (32ft 9½in); length 6.60m (21ft 8in); height 2.40m (7ft 10½in); wing area 20sq m (215.285sq ft).

Empty weight 650kg (1,433lb); loaded weight 950kg (2,094lb); wing loading 47.5kg/sq m (9.7lb/sq ft); power loading 4.13kg/hp (9.1lb/hp).

Maximum speed 111kt (128mph) at 3,000m (9,843ft); climb to 2,000m (6,562ft) in 9min; service ceiling 6,200m (20,341ft); endurance 2hr.

Two built 1922–1923.

Koshiki A-3 Experimental Long-range Reconnaissance Aircraft

This aeroplane became the first

The very unusual Army Koshiki A-3 Experimental Long-range Reconnaissance Aircraft.

strategic reconnaissance project undertaken by the Japanese Army, a project that became the responsibility of the Department of Research at the Tokorozawa Aviation School. The design was by six French engineers who arrived in Japan in early 1922. The team was led by Captain Antoine de Boysson, Army Artillery, who had designed a reconnaissance-aircraft for Farman. Assisting were Japanese engineers headed by Maj Akira Matsui, Aeroplane Section Manager of the Department of Research, Tokorozawa Aviation School. Their demanding work on this major project began in April 1922.

The design that resulted was unique in many ways for this early period. It was a sesquiplane with the upper wing mounted very high above the fuselage, featuring very marked sweepback, and containing the fuel tanks. The aeroplane was of all-metal construction with fabric covering. Most of the aluminium used was imported from France but some was made by Sumitomo Copper Co Ltd. Two 300hp Hispano-Suiza engines were mounted ahead of the lower wings, and there were plans to equip them later with

turbo-superchargers. Had the superchargers materialized, it was estimated that the aeroplane would have had a maximum speed of 133kt (152mph) at 5,000m (16,404ft) and a service ceiling of 9,500m (31,167ft).

The construction of the prototype was delayed by the heavy earthquake that occurred in the Kanto area in September 1923 but work was completed in February 1924. Lt Kawaida of the Flight Section, Department of Research at the School, flight tested the new aeroplane. During one of these flights an undercarriage shock absorber failed, and since replacement parts were not available, the single large wheel on each side was changed to a dual-wheel configuration with smaller wheels.

A number of other problems became apparent. The method used for mounting the engines caused severe vibration and the aeroplane was found to be underpowered for the over-weight condition that developed. Hoping to correct these problems, the aeroplane was dismantled and taken by rail to Kagamigahara for further test flights and modifications but few improvements could be made. As a result, the project ended with this one prototype.

Twin-engined sesquiplane long-range reconnaissance aircraft. Metal structure with fabric covering. Crew of three in open cockpits.

Two 300–320hp Mitsubishi Hispano-Suiza water-cooled engines, driving Koshiki AT two-bladed wooden propellers.

Span 21m (68ft 10¾in); length 16m (52ft 6in); height 5.27m (17ft 3½in); wing area 85sq m (914.962sq ft).

Empty weight 2,000kg (4,409lb); loaded weight 3,000kg (6,613lb); wing loading 35.3kg/sq m (7.2lb/sq ft); power loading 4.69hg/hp (10.3lb/hp).

Maximum speed 109kt (125mph) at 5,000 (16,404ft); service ceiling 7,500m (24,606ft); endurance 5hr.

One built in February 1924.

Kaibo Gikai KB Experimental Flying-boat

In September 1922, a patriotic or-

ganization known as the Teikoku Kaibo Gikai (Imperial Maritime Defence Volunteer Association) recognized that an all-metal aeroplane of the quality being demonstrated by other countries, had not been manufactured in Japan, and therefore undertook such a project. For the design they organized the All Metal Aeroplane Design Committee which consisted of leading authorities of the Aeronautical Research Institute of Tokyo Imperial University, the Army, and the Navy. Although this was a joint effort, the design was identified with the PMBRA since the main component, the hull, was built by the Army Arsenal.

The committee was led by Dr Sc Aikichi Tanakadate, with other members being Narihisa Yokota who became the chief designer, Yuzo Hishida, Matsutaro Honda, Shuhei Iwamoto, Yoshitake Ueda, Haruhiko Uemura, Hisakichi Akaishi, Masayuki Hori, Fumio Murase and Kyohei Arisaka. Joining the committee at a later date were two engineers, Keikichi Satake and Jun Okamura. The basic design for what was first called the All Metal Seaplane was undertaken at the Aeronautical Research Institute, Tokyo Imperial University. Detail design, tooling and manufacturing of components and airframe were provided by the Army Tokyo Artillery Arsenal, Army Ordnance Arsenal. Wind-tunnel model testing, powerplant and control system installations became the responsibility of the Aeroplane Factory,

Kaibo Gikai KB Experimental Flying-boat.

Department of Ordnance, Yokosuka Naval Arsenal.

The planned performance was a 3,000m (9,843ft) operational altitude with a maximum speed of 108kt (125mph) provided by two 200hp engines, giving a range of more than 1,080nm (1,250sm). A unique feature of this parasol-wing design was that the wing was supported by two massive wide-chord outward sloping structures in place of the more normal pylon connecting the hull to the wing. This feature was later patented, along with the type of metal propellers developed, as well as the all-metal hull. A spare hull was built for additional test purposes.

Although the work was suspended temporarily by the severe Kanto earthquake in September 1923, the airframe was nearly completed by March 1924, with the exception of the engine installation and other systems. In July of that year, the airframe was transported to the Department of Ordnance Yokosuka Naval Arsenal, where the engines and other systems were installed. Because of development delays with the Japanese engine which was to deliver 200hp at 3,000m, it was decided to use two 185hp BMW IIIa high-altitude engines instead. With these installed, the KB Flying-boat (KB for Kai Bo) as it was now called, was completed in December 1924.

After the aeroplane was donated to the Navy by the Kaibo Gikai, flying trials began at Taura Beach, Yokosuka, with Navy test pilot Lieut-Cdr Hisakichi Akaishi. As a result of minor modifications, the aeroplane showed excellent take off and alighting performance under light load conditions. The preliminary performance in speed and range gave strong indications that the desired performance would be met at the intended operational altitude. However, on 22 March, 1926, during its seventh test flight, the aeroplane was seen in a glide with both engines stopped, its gliding angle continued to steepen and it crashed into the water nearly vertical, killing all four on board. The cause of the crash was attributed to a malfunction of the flight control system.

With this loss, further development of the design was ended; however tests did continue with the second hull that was built for structural analysis. Considerable experience was gained through the design of this aeroplane and it greatly influenced the 1928 Giyu No.3 flying-boat sponsored by the Kaibo Gikai and built by Kawasaki.

Twin-engined parasol-wing flying-boat with two-step hull and sponsons. All-metal construction with metal stressed skin and some fabric covering on the wings and control surfaces. Four crew.

Two 185–230hp BMW IIIa six-cylinder water-cooled inline engines, driving two-bladed metal propellers later changed to wooden units.

Span 21.78m (71ft 5½in); length 13.95m (45ft 9in); height 4m (13ft 1½in).

Empty weight 2,012kg (4,435lb); loaded weight 3,086kg (6,803lb); power loading 6.7kg/hp (14.7lb/hp).

Maximum speed 109kt (125mph); minimum speed 50kt (58mph); climb to 3,000m (9,843ft) in 15 min; service ceiling 6,500m (21,325ft).

One built in 1924.

Army Experimental Model 3 Fighter

At the time this fighter-type biplane was being designed, work was undertaken by the newly organized Department of Engineering, Army Air Headquarters, which was formed in May 1925. Up until this time, research and design projects for new aircraft had been handled by the Department of Research, Army Tokorozawa Aviation School, since April 1919. Because of this change, the name of

Army Experimental Model 3 Fighter with undercarriage mounted Lamblin radiators.

Koshiki meaning School Type was eliminated from the title, beginning with this aircraft.

Under the guidance of the Department of Engineering, this aeroplane was manufactured by the Army Artillery Arsenal, with work beginning in 1926 and being completed in June 1927. The primary purpose of this fighter-type aircraft was to test the efficiency of the Rateau turbo-supercharger that was to be used on the A-3 Long-range Reconnaissance-aircraft to improve engine performance. Aircraft development was suspended early, but the results of the tests made with this aeroplane would have future value.

This aircraft design was based upon the Type Ko 4 Fighter (Nieuport 29-C.1) but differed in having two seats and two very awkwardly placed Lamblin radiators mounted in front of the main undercarriage legs. Tests with the turbine continued while using this aeroplane until 1928 at which time

Army Experimental Three-seat Light Bomber.

it was determined that the desired results could not be achieved. The project was then ended with this one prototype aircraft.

Single-engine fighter-type biplane. Wooden structure with ply covering and some fabric on the wings. Crew of two in open cockpits.

300–320hp Hispano-Suiza eight-cylinder vee water-cooled engine with Rateau turbo-supercharger, driving a two-bladed wooden propeller with specially notched trailing edge.

Span 9.70m (31ft 10in); length 6.725m (22ft 0¾in); height 2.55m (8ft 4½in); wing area 26.84sq m (288.912sq ft).

Empty weight 940kg (2,072lb); loaded weight 1,277kg (2,815lb); wing loading 47.5kg/sq m (9.7lb/sq ft); power loading 9.39kg/hp (20.7lb/hp).

Maximum speed 104kt (120mph) at sea level; climb to 3,000m (9,843ft) in 12min 40sec; service ceiling 6,500m (21,325ft).

One built in June 1927.

Army Experimental Three-seat Light Bomber

Early in 1925, the Army placed orders with Mitsubishi, Kawasaki and Nakajima to design and build a new-category Light Bomber. At the same time, and independent of the set specifications, the Army was designing an all-metal light-bomber, at the Army Department of Aviation's Department of Supply.

For those within the competition, Mitsubishi submitted a wooden-framed light bomber modified from its Navy Type 13 Carrier Attack Aircraft for Army use along with its Washi-Type, metal structure bomber designed by Dr Baumann

from Germany. Kawasaki entered a modified version of the all-metal Dornier Do C imported from Germany. Nakajima submitted the all-metal Breguet 19B.2 which had been imported from France.

During the course of this competition, the Army Department of Supply obtained the assistance of Dr Richard Vogt of Germany between March and December 1927 who was in Japan at the invitation of Kawasaki to help with yet another design of an all-new metal light bomber. The manufacture of the Army's entry was undertaken by the Department of Engineering, Army Air Headquarters, but the actual construction was accomplished at the Tokyo Army Artillery Arsenal.

Commonly called the Kawasaki-type 3-seat Light Bomber, because of its Kawasaki/Vogt design appearance, this all-metal sesquiplane was recognized as the most advanced of all the contenders, a tribute traced to Dr Vogt's innovative ideas. However, the scheduled evaluation was made in October 1926, before the completion of the Army's entry, and Mitsubishi's Type 13 was accepted as the Army Type 87 Light Bomber because of the good reputation it had achieved in Navy service even though its wooden structure was obsolete by current standards.

Continuing with the Army project, two examples were completed in 1927, as recorded by one source, and 1928, by another. Engineer Nario Ando of the Department of Engineering continued with research and improvements but, in 1929, the Army decided to accept Kawasaki's Army Type 88 Light Bomber as its standard, which was a direct descendant of the well

proven Army Type 88 Reconnaissance type. With this decision, further refinements to the Army's design were suspended. Although rather large and costly, this aeroplane had the highest payload for a single-engined aeroplane at that time.

Single-engine sesquiplane bomber. Metal construction with semi-stressed metal skin on the fuselage and fabric-covered wings. Crew of three in open cockpits.

500–600hp BMW VI twelve-cylinder vee water-cooled engine, driving a Kawasaki two-bladed wooden propeller.

One nose mounted fixed forward-firing 7.7mm machine-gun and one dorsal flexible 7.7mm machine-gun. Maximum bomb load 500kg (1,102lb).

Empty weight 2,221kg (4,896lb); loaded weight 3,676kg (8,104lb); power loading 6.13kg/hp (13.5lb/hp).

Service ceiling 6,000m (19,685ft).

Two built in 1927.

By this stage in Japan's aircraft design and manufacture, the private aviation industry had become well established and the Army temporarily ended further projects of this type, depending instead upon competition among these companies to provide the Army with new types. Close monitoring was maintained by the Army through the Department of Engineering, Army Air Headquarters, to ensure high quality. This function was moved from Tokorozawa to Tachikawa in November 1928. In March 1934, the Department of Supply of the Army Air Headquarters changed its name to the Army Air Supply Arsenal Headquarters, and also moved from Tokorozawa to Tachikawa. Both facilities were located on the west side of Tachikawa Airfield. In 1936, the Department of Engineering of the Army Air Headquarters was re-organized as the Army Air Technical Research Institute (Rikugun Kokugijutsu Kenkyusho), or Rikugun in shortened form. It was not until the Pacific War that the Rikugun produced other aircraft designs under this name in its effort to keep up with the Navy's Yokosho.

Aichi Watch and Electric Machinery Company, Ltd (Aichi Tokei Denki Kabushiki Kaisha)

This company was better known as the Aichi Aircraft Company Ltd, but during the time of this coverage it was the Aichi Watch and Electric Machinery Company Ltd. In addition to producing aeroplanes, as its name implies, the company also produced marine-type explosive mines, torpedo tubes and ordnance fuses for the Navy before it started producing aircraft at its Funakata plant in Nagoya in 1920. Captain Umitani, an ex-Navy air officer was the first director and chief engineer of the Aircraft Department of the company. Early Aichi presidents were S Suzuki, followed by K Aoki.

Water-based aircraft became the initial speciality of the company, beginning with the Navy Yokosho Ro-go Ko-gata Reconnaissance Seaplane. (*see* Yokosho.) This was a sub-contract for the Navy as the design was complete and production techniques were used that were already employed at the Aeroplane Factory of the Naval Arsenal. Other aircraft built for the Japanese Navy by Aichi included the Avro 504K trainer and the Type Hansa Reconnaissance Seaplane (*see* Yokosho for both), samples of the latter having been acquired by Japan as part of its war reparations. Aichi was also the largest producer of the Navy F.5 Flying-boat in the 1920s, building a total of 40 of these large twin-engined all-wooden flying-boats; this was the licence-built Felixstowe F.5 which had been produced in Britain by Short Brothers. (*see* Hirosho for aircraft details.) The award of these Navy contracts to Aichi firmly established the company in the aircraft manufacturing business.

In the mid-1920s, it was custom-

ary for major Japanese aircraft companies to obtain manufacturing licence agreements from foreign companies to enhance their ability to match their design and manufacturing skills with the rest of the world. In Aichi's case, it aligned itself with Heinkel in Germany and sent engineers to study at the Heinkel factory. Aichi invited Dr Ernst Heinkel, president of that company, along with chief engineer Karl Schwärzler and Lt Bücker to assist in Japan.

With its successful design of the Navy Type 94 Carrier Bomber in 1934, Aichi became the exclusive builder of dive-bombers for the Japanese Navy. This was initially accomplished with the aid of Heinkel, and this in turn assisted that fledgling German company to become more soundly established. By the early 1930s, direct foreign assistance with Aichi designs was being shunned in favour of its own designs.

In addition to the manufacture of aircraft, Aichi began building engines in 1927. The first of these were Lorraine liquid-cooled engines built under licence from the French Société Générale Aéronautique. Aichi later developed its own air-cooled engines as well as other licence manufacturing such as producing the German Daimler-Benz engines. By 1938, engine production was transferred to a newly completed Atsuta plant across the street from the Funakata plant in south central Nagoya, leaving more space for expanding the manufacture of airframes.

Another Aichi factory, in south-western Nagoya, known as the Eitoku plant was acquired in February 1940. The first buildings were completed in May 1941 and once the new plant was established, Aichi's head office was moved to this location. The company's further growth and accomplishments are summarized at the end of this chapter.

Experimental Type 15-Ko Reconnaissance Seaplane (Mi-go)

In 1924, the Imperial Japanese Navy wished to replace its war-

Aichi Experimental Type 15-Ko Reconnaissance Seaplane (Mi-go).

vintage Type Hansa Reconnaissance Seaplanes. Three aircraft companies, Aichi, Nakajima and Yokosho, made proposals since all three had experience with the German-designed Type Hansa seaplane for the Navy.

Under the supervision of Narihisa Yokota, and aircraft designer Tetsuo Miki, the Aichi company completed four prototypes in 1925 and 1926. There was a close similarity to the earlier low-wing twin-float Hansa monoplane, but Aichi's entry had noticeable refinements. The wing and float designs were completely changed, and there was a different strut arrangement for attaching the floats to the wing instead of the fuselage. A Dornier bench-type aileron balance was tried, but was not as effective as was expected. When flight tested for the first time by Lieut-Cdr Hisakichi Akaishi, he reported that the aircraft had poor stability.

Modifications were made in the hope of correcting this and other problems, which included adjusting the centre of gravity, raising the pilot's seat, and lowering the rear observer's seat for better access to interior equipment. Despite numerous modifications, the instability of the aircraft could not be rectified to the satisfaction of the Navy. As a consequence, the Nakajima Navy Type 15 Reconnaissance Seaplane won the competition.

Single-engine twin-float low-wing monoplane. Wooden structure with fabric covered wing and tail, ply-covered fuselage. Crew of two in open cockpits.

300hp Mitsubishi Type Hi (Hispano)

vee water-cooled engine, driving a two-blade wooden propeller.

One dorsal flexible 7.7mm machine-gun.

Span 13.63m (44ft 9in); length 9.485m (31ft 1½in); height 3.28m (10ft 9in); wing area 32.45sq m (349.3sq ft).

Empty weight 1,200kg (2,645.5lb); loaded weight 1,700kg (3,748lb); wing loading 25.4kg/sq m (5.2lb/sq ft); power loading 5.67kg/hp (12.5lb/hp).

Maximum speed 97.5kt (112mph) at sea level; minimum speed 52kt (60mph); climb to 3,000m (9,843ft) in 18min 10sec; service ceiling 4,800m (15,748ft).

Approximately four built in 1925–26.

Navy Type 2 Two-seat Reconnaissance Seaplane
(Company designation HD 25)

During the mid-1920s, while Germany was still forbidden to build military aircraft, Heinkel had designed and manufactured a number of high-performance civil aircraft that obviously had military potential. These aeroplanes were primarily mailplanes, cargo/passenger

transports and trainers as well as some military aircraft for export. Heinkel float-equipped aircraft were regarded as among the best in the world.

At the request of the Japanese Navy, Aichi imported a selection of Heinkel aircraft such as the HD 25, HD 26 and HD 28* reconnaissance seaplanes and later the HD 23 carrier fighter, all intended for research and testing by the Navy. While the Navy was developing in parallel its own Yokosho Type 14 Reconnaissance Seaplane it also accepted the HD 25 design for manufacture in Japan. This aeroplane was to take off from a very short ramp (before catapults were introduced) aboard a warship and be recovered after alighting alongside on the water.

Unofficially the HD 25 was called the Heinkel Large Reconnaissance Seaplane or Heinkel-type Warship Seaplane. When it was officially accepted by the Navy in March 1928, the designation became Type 2 Two-seat Reconnaissance Seaplane. Design changes required of Heinkel under this licence agreement were for shortening the rear portion of the fuselage to provide sufficient clearance while the aircraft was on the take off ramp which was to be on top of one of the ship's gun turrets. Wing loading had to be reduced in order to shorten the take off run. Structurally, its ply-covered fuselage and

*Up to about 1933 HD stood for Heinkel Doppeldecker (biplane), HE stood for Heinkel Eindecker (monoplane).

Aichi Navy Type 2 Two-seat Reconnaissance Seaplane adapted from the Heinkel HD 25.

semi-cantilever thick-section wings were quite advanced when compared with its counterpart, the Yokosho Type 14, with fabric covered fuselage, four interplane struts on each side and the usual bracing wires. Other innovations on the Heinkel design were simple hook-type wing fittings for ease in handling.

The prototypes of which there were two (Heinkel Mfg Nos.222 and 223) were built by Heinkel in Germany. The first flight took place in 1926 at Warnemünde with Heinkel's test pilot, Lt Bücker, and engineer Blomssie occupying the rear seat. Test data were recorded by Japanese Navy engineers Okamura and Yonezawa and engineer Schwärzler of Heinkel, monitored by Dr Heinkel. The aeroplane was said to have good stability with excellent take off capability. A land-based ramp similar to that which would be mounted on top of one of the ship's gun turrets was used for these tests. Once the aircraft reached Japan, similar take off tests were made from a turret-mounted ramp constructed aboard the battleship *Nagato*. These Heinkel seaplanes were considered superior to Type 14 and Type 15 reconnaissance seaplanes in climb, speed, durability, and especially in take offs under their own power from ramps.

Aichi assumed production of the Type 2 Two-seat Reconnaissance Seaplane. The port of Nagoya was the site of the first test flight which was made by Aichi's test pilot Kanekichi Yokoyama, under the close scrutiny of the Navy's representatives for the project, Lieut Makoto Awaya and Lieut-Cdr Ichitaro Yonezawa. Once the Navy was satisfied with the aeroplane's performance, some were used aboard heavy cruisers, but, with the advent of shipboard catapults, these early ship-based seaplanes became obsolete in favour of higher performance seaplanes designed for catapult launching. As a result, some of them were released for civil use and production terminated after a small number was built.

Navy Type 2 Single-seat Reconnaissance Seaplane
(Company designation HD 26)

The prototype of this aircraft, the HD 26, was imported in 1926 at the same time as other Heinkel aircraft. It was intended that it should be used as a basis upon which to design a reconnaissance seaplane capable of taking off under its own power from on top of a warship gun turret. The aeroplane was basically the same as the HD 25 but was scaled-down as a single-seat aircraft. In Germany it was referred to as a fighter seaplane, but in Japan it was unofficially called the Heinkel Small Reconnaissance Seaplane or Heinkel-go Reconnaissance Seaplane.

Tests were made with the one imported HD 26 and one built by Aichi in operating from the gun turrets of the battleship *Nagato* and the cruiser *Furutaka*. As with its predecessor, catapult use rendered the aircraft obsolete in favour of more suitable designs.

Single-engine twin float biplane. Wooden structure with fabric covering except for fuselage and floats which were ply-covered. Rearward folding wings for stowage. Crew of two in open cockpits.

450–500hp Napier Lion twelve-cylinder W-type water-cooled engine, driving a two-blade wooden propeller.

One dorsal flexible 7.7mm machine-gun. Bomb load: 300kg (66lb) bombs. Maximum speed 110kt (127mph) at sea level; alighting speed 48.5 kt (56mph); climb to 3,000m (9,843ft) in 15min 14sec; range 495nm (568sm).

Sixteen built between 1926 and 1928.

	Prototype	*Production models*
Span	14.856m (48ft 9in)	14.878m (48ft 10in)
Length	9.684m (31ft 9in)	9.695m (31ft 9½in)
Height	4.268m (14ft)	4.269m (14ft)
Empty weight	1,601kg (3,529lb)	1,700kg (3,747lb)
Ship take off weight	2,343kg (5,165lb)	2,350kg (5,180lb)
Water take off weight	–	2,565kg (5,654lb)

An Aichi Navy Type 2 in civil use as J-BCOH.

Aichi Navy Type 2 Single-seat Reconnaissance Seaplane based on the HD 26.

Single-engine twin-float biplane. Wooden structure with fabric covering except for fuselage and floats which were ply-covered. Rearward folding wings for stowage. Pilot in open cockpit.

300hp Hispano-Suiza eight-cylinder vee water-cooled engine (HD 26); 420hp Bristol Jupiter VI nine-cylinder air-cooled radial engine (Aichi-built example), driving a two-blade wooden propeller.

One forward firing 7.7mm machine-gun.

	HD 26	Aichi-built
Span	11.80m (38ft 8½in)	11.80m (38ft 8½in)
Length	8.30m (27ft 3in)	8.438m (27ft 8¼in)
Height	3.60m (11ft 10in)	3.593m (11ft 9½in)
Wing area	37.8sq m (406.889sq ft)	37.8sqm (406.889sq ft)
Empty weight	1,146kg (2,526.5lb)	1,150kg (2,535.3lb)
Loaded weight	1,526kg (3,364.2lb)	1,500kg (3,306.9lb)
Wing loading	40.3kg/sq m (8.254lb/sq ft)	39.7kg/sq m (8.131lb/sq ft)
Power loading	5.08kg/hp (11.2lb/hp)	3.57kg hp (7.8lb/hp)
Maximum speed	99kt (114mph) sea level	114kt (132mph)
Alighting speed	43kt (50mph)	—
Climb to	3,000m (9,843ft)	3,000m (9,843ft)
in	14min	7min 30sec
Service ceiling	7,200m (23,622ft)	

Two built in 1926.

Aichi Experimental Three-seat Reconnaissance Seaplane imported as the HD 28.

Experimental Three-seat Reconnaissance Seaplane
(Company designation HD 28)

In 1926, at the time of acquiring the HD 25 and HD 26, Aichi imported from Heinkel an HD 28 three-seat long-range reconnaissance seaplane. This HD 28 was referred to as the Heinkel Three-seat Reconnaissance Seaplane or Heinkel-2 Reconnaissance Seaplane.

This aeroplane was of very strong construction for seaworthiness and had more than nine hours endurance when cruising at 80 knots, and was Heinkel's most ambitious design at that time. Structurally, it was very different to the earlier HD 25 in that it had a welded steel-tube fuselage with fabric covering, and wire-braced wings. These features were adopted for Aichi's later designs which became the AB-5 and AB-6.*

Much was expected of this aeroplane but it failed to achieve its anticipated performance due to engine problems, and it did not provide the crew with a good view. These deficiencies caused the Navy to withdraw its interest by 1928. Determined to resolve the problems, however, Tetsuo Miki, acting as project engineer, modified the design to use the Japanese built, but less powerful 450hp Nakajima Jupiter engine. This re-design made the aeroplane slightly smaller in overall dimensions in order to compensate for the less powerful engine. The fuel tank was moved from the fuselage to the upper wing centre section, allowing the three seats to be moved further forward. Unfortunately, these modifications were not effective, and further design changes included a shorter span lower wing, and stagger by moving the upper wing forward of the lower wing, all to no avail. Calculations revealed that the intended reduction in weight could not

*Aichi assigned a two-letter prefix and a consecutive number to each of its aircraft designs. The first letter was always A for Aichi, and the second was B for biplane or M for monoplane. These model designations applied only within the factory, for in the case of military aircraft the military designation was dominant.

Aichi Experimental Type-H Carrier Fighter, one of two imported HD 23s (H Ando).

be met and as a result further development ended in 1929. Although this redesigned aeroplane was not built following the import of the one HD 28, it had a strong influence upon later Aichi designs of three-seat reconnaissance seaplanes.

Single-engine twin-float biplane. Wood and metal structure with fabric covering. Rearward folding wings for stowage. Crew of three in tandem open cockpits.

650–710hp Lorraine-Dietrich 18-III eighteen-cylinder W-type water-cooled engine, driving a four-bladed wooden propeller.

Two forward-firing 7.7mm machine-guns, one flexible rear-firing 7.7mm machine-gun. Bomb load: two 110kg (242lb) bombs (with 220kg [485lb] of fuel reduction).

Span 15m (49ft 2½in); length 10.95m (35ft 11in); height 4.17m (13ft 8¼in); wing area 59.5sq m (640.473sq ft).

Empty weight 2,365kg (5,214lb); loaded weight 3,850kg (8,488lb); wing loading 64.7kg/sq m (13.2lb/sq ft); power loading 5.9kg/hp (13lb/hp).

Maximum speed 108kt (125mph) at sea level; cruising speed 81kt (93mph); alighting speed 52kt (60mph); climb to 3,000m (9,843ft) in 19min 24sec; service ceiling 4,500m (14,763ft).

One built in 1926.

Experimental Type-H Carrier Fighter
(Company designation HD 23)

In April 1926, the Navy asked for design proposals from Mitsubishi, Nakajima and Aichi for the development of a new carrier-based fighter to replace the Mitsubishi Type 10 Carrier Fighters. These had been the world's first carrier-type aircraft built for that purpose and were first used aboard the *Hosho*. In turn, Aichi asked Heinkel to design and build two prototypes to meet this requirement. These became the HD 23. One aircraft was powered by a 500hp BMW VIA while the other had a 450hp Hispano-Suiza engine. By the summer of 1927 the two aircraft were shipped to Japan and flight tested at Kagamigahara (Gifu AB north of Nagoya) beginning that December by Aichi's test pilot Kanekichi Yokoyama. The Navy also made its tests which led to some modifications. These recommended changes were incorporated into the design by engineer Tetsuo Miki who was assigned to the development project.

The final design had a number of interesting features. Among them were provision for safer emergency landing at sea made possible by jettisoning the undercarriage and a device which stopped the propeller in a horizontal position. This allowed for a relatively unhindered alighting on the hull-type under fuselage. The fuselage and wing leading edges were relatively watertight for buoyancy. Movable wing slats were incorporated which reduced landing distances from 160m (525ft) to 130m (426ft) when used.

Perhaps more emphasis was placed on ditching features than the aircraft itself, because the HD 23 was overweight and had poor stability when landing due particularly to being nose heavy. This made it difficult to make a three-point landing on a carrier. The general manoeuvrability of this fighter was poor. With a multitude of problems, further development was terminated. Mitsubishi also lost in the competition, and the winning entry was the light-weight Nakajima Type G, which was a modified version of the British Gloster Gambet. This became the Type 3 Carrier Fighter, but without the elaborate safety features of the HD 23.

Single-engine biplane fighter with fixed (jettisonable) undercarriage for land and carrier operation. Wooden structure with metal frame tail. Mixed fabric and plywood covering. Pilot in open cockpit.

500–700hp BMW VIA twelve-cylinder vee water-cooled engine, driving a two-bladed wooden propeller, or

450hp Hispano-Suiza 12Ha twelve-cylinder vee water-cooled engine, driving a two-bladed wooden propeller.

Two forward-firing 7.7mm machine-guns. Bomb load: two 30kg (66lb) bombs.

Span 10.80m (35ft 5¼in); length 7.64m (25ft 1in); height 3.40m (11ft 2 in); wing area 35.32sq m (380.193sq ft).

Empty weight 1,275kg (2,810lb) with Hispano-Suiza, 1,467kg (3,234lb) with BMW: loaded weight 1,830kg (4,034lb) with Hispano-Suiza, 2,010kg (4,431lb) with BMW; wing loading 51.9kg/sq m (10.630lb/sq ft); power loading 4.06kg/hp (8.9lb/hp).

Maximum speed 135kt (155mph) at sea level; cruising speed 90kt (104mph) at 1,000m (3,280ft); minimum speed 35kt (40mph) at 1,000m (3,280ft); climb to 3,000m (9,843ft) in 7min 36sec; service ceiling 6,250m (20,505ft).

Two built in 1927.

Navy Type 15-2 Flying-boat (H1H3)

Recognizing the end of the service life of the F.5 Flying-boats, the Navy developed a replacement at the Hiro Naval Arsenal in 1927. This design, known as the Type 15, went through a number of changes from that of an all wooden flying-boat as was the F.5, to newly designed wings and all-metal

Aichi AB-1 Transport.

hull. It underwent numerous configuration changes for its twin engines and propellers at both production locations, Hirosho and Yokosho. By the time production was assigned to Aichi, the design had developed into the Type 15-2 Flying-boat, with the short designation H1H3, and Aichi produced this model exclusively, with a total of 45. (*see* Hirosho Navy Type 15 Flying-boat.)

AB-1 Transport

In February 1926, the Aviation Bureau of the Department of Communications sponsored a competition for a 'made in Japan' passenger transport. Aichi entered the competition, and, like the other competitors, was given a grant-in-aid for the project.

Using the HD 25 as the basic design, Aichi's design for the AB-1 was begun by its designer Tokuichiro Gomei under the supervision of Tetsuo Miki. While the structure resembled that of the HD 25, the overall dimensions were larger. The interplane struts of the single-bay wings were changed from V to N configuration. The four passenger seats were positioned near the centre of gravity, with the two pilots' open cockpits in tandem behind the passenger cabin. To facilitate potential production in Japan, the engine was Aichi's

licence-built Lorraine W-12 replacing the imported Napier Lion used on the HD 25. The undercarriage was interchangeable with either wheels or floats to meet a requirement of the Aviation Bureau.

Also entered in the competition were such aeroplanes as the Mitsubishi MC-1 derived from the Type 13 Carrier Attack Aircraft, and the Nakajima N-36, a version of the Breguet 36. The N-36 crashed during a test flight, and both the AB-1 and the MC-1 completed the Aviation Bureau's qualifying tests but were graded poorly for pilot visibility. This brought about the transition from biplane to monoplane for air transport. This was apparent when Nihon Koku Yuso KK (Japan Air Transport Co Ltd), which was established in 1929, imported the Fokker Super Universal as standard equipment instead of adopting either of the Japanese types. Despite shortcomings with all three Japanese entries, the top award went to the Aichi design, receiving first prize for the seaplane, and second prize for landplane competitions.

The sole AB-1 was used for a short time in 1929 by Nihon Koku Yuso KK as a landplane until the arrival of the Fokker Super Universal. Later, the AB-1 was used for many years by the Tokyo Koku KK, owned by Tamotsu Aiba, on the Haneda (Tokyo)–Shimoda route as a floatplane.

Single-engine biplane, interchangeable as landplane and seaplane. Wooden structure covered with a mixture of fabric and plywood. Rearward folding wings for stowage. Crew of two in tanden open cockpits with cabin for four passengers.

450–485hp Aichi-Lorraine twelve-cylinder W-type water-cooled engine, driving a two-bladed wooden propeller.

	Landplane	Seaplane
Span	15.11m (49ft 7in)	15.11m (49ft 7in)
Length	9.90m (32ft 6in)	11.26m (36ft 11½in)
Height	3.73m (12ft 3in)	4.65m (15ft 3in)
Wing area	59.2sq m (637.244sq ft)	59.2sq m (637.244sq ft)
Empty weight	1,680kg (3,704lb)	2,030kg (4,475lb)
Loaded weight	2,710kg (5,974lb)	3,060kg (6,746lb)
Wing loading	45.7kg/sq m (9.36lb/sq ft)	51.7kg/sq m (10.587lb/sq ft)
Power loading	6kg/hp (13.2lb/hp)	6.80kg/hp (14.9lb/hp)
Maximum speed	106kt (122mph)	97.5kt (112mph)
Cruising speed	75.5kt (87mph)	70kt (81mph)
Climb to	3,000m (9,843ft)	3,000m (9,843ft)
in	24min	33min 43 sec
Service ceiling	4,000m (13,123ft)	3,500m (11,483ft)

One built in 1928.

Aichi Type 2 Transport, one of two operated by Nippon Koku Yuso Kenkyusho.

Type 2 Transport
(Company designation HD 25)

When the aircraft catapult was introduced aboard Navy ships, it rendered obsolete the Type 2 Reconnaissance Seaplanes built by Aichi. These aircraft were derived from the Heinkel HD 25 and designed specifically with a low wing loading to give them short take-off ability under their own power from ramps on the gun turrets of large ships. Once replaced by aircraft designed for catapult launching, three of these Type 2 Reconnaissance Seaplanes were declared surplus to Navy needs and made available for civil use.

These aeroplanes were converted to transports in 1930, and given the designation Type 2 Transport. One of these used as a courier aircraft by the *Kouchi Shimbun* (Newspaper) was modified by having a third seat added behind the original two. The other two aircraft were released to Nippon Koku Yuso Kenkyusho (Japan Air Transport Research Association), which in turn converted them to transports by putting two seats in the fuselage behind the normal rear open cockpit seat which was then used for a third passenger. These modifications took place in the NKYK's hangar at Sakai City, just south of Osaka, under the engineering guidance of Seiji Nakamae. They were given the

registrations J-BBEI and J-BBFI.

The low wing loading of these aircraft provided good climb and stability even with the addition of the passenger accommodation, but the short fuselage restricted their load carrying capability. Consequently these passenger aircraft were uneconomic and used only for a short time.

Single-engine twin-float transport biplane. Wooden structure with fabric covering except for fuselage and floats which were ply-covered. Pilot and two or three passengers.

450–500hp Napier Lion twelve-cylinder W-type water-cooled engine, driving a two-bladed wooden propeller.

Span 14.89m (48ft 10¼in); length 9.60m (31ft 6in); height 4.26m (13ft 11½in); wing area 56.1sq m (603.875sq ft).

Empty weight 1,650kg (3,637.5lb); loaded weight 2,636kg (5,811.3lb); wing loading 42kg/sq m (8.6lb/sq ft); power loading 5.22kg/hp (11.5lb/hp).

Maximum speed 108kt (124mph) at sea level; cruising speed 81kt (94mph); climb to 3,000m (9,843ft) in 13min; service ceiling 6,000m (19,685ft).

Three converted from Type 2 Reconnaissance Seaplanes in 1930.

Navy Type 90-1 Reconnaissance Seaplane (E3A1)
(Company designation HD 56)

In 1928, the Navy sought interest from Aichi and Nakajima in developing a shipboard reconnaissance seaplane for catapult launching. Again, Aichi turned to Heinkel for the design, and imported the HD 56 that, when accepted, became the Type 90-1 Reconnaissance Seaplane. Nakajima's similar entries became the Type 90-2-1 and -2 Reconnaissance Seaplanes, and the joint Yokosho/Kawanishi aircraft became the Type 90-3 Reconnaissance Seaplane. The Navy accepted the Aichi/Heinkel HD 56 design in 1931 as the best example of a catapult launch aeroplane, being particularly impressed by its Wright Whirlwind engine. The overall structure was well built, having simple interplane struts without bracing wires, and a sound mixture of wood and metal throughout the structure. What the Navy did not like about this Heinkel design was that it had too short a range, and lacked the desired speed. Despite these shortcomings, it was accepted by the Navy in December 1931, but with the stipulation that corrective modifications were made.

To satisfy the Navy, Aichi's engineer Tetsuo Miki set about making the desired improvements. The much liked 200hp Wright Whirlwind engine was replaced by a Japanese-built 300hp Type 90 Tempu to avoid import problems and to improve performance with the higher power. The wing span was reduced by 60cm (23¾in), which in turn reduced the wing area by 2.04sq m (21.959sq ft). The interplane struts and the struts from the lower wing to the floats were moved inward by 30cm (1ft) and the empennage span and the height were reduced by 40cm (15¾in) and 5cm (2in) respectively. Other changes were made in the ailerons, floats, and cockpit combing, all in an attempt to improve performance.

Aichi's test pilots Kanekichi Yokoyama and Tamizo Amagai made the first test flight with the Aichi-built (3rd Type 90-1 Reconnaissance Seaplane) in August 1931 from the port at Nagoya. Follow-on aircraft were delivered to Naval operational units beginning in 1932. Type 90-1s were used in the early stage of the Sino-Japanese conflict aboard the *Jintsu*-class light cruisers. Others were used in various tests related to catapult-launching.

Because of the inferior speed and climb of these aeroplanes, operational service life was short, and their existence is hardly known, having been overshadowed by the more manoeuvrable Nakajima Type 90-2-2 Reconnaissance Seaplane. Only twelve Type 90-1 aircraft were built, and they were soon transferred to training units. Some were released for civil flying.

Single-engine twin-float reconnaissance biplane. Steel tube fuselage and wooden wings with fabric covering. Rearward folding wings for stowage. Crew of two in open cockpits.

200–220hp Wright Whirlwind J-6 nine-cylinder air-cooled radial engine, driving a two-bladed wooden propeller (prototype). 300–340hp Type 90 (Gasuden Tempu) nine-cylinder radial air-cooled engine, driving a two-bladed wooden propeller (Type 90-1).

One fixed forward-firing 7.7mm machine-gun and one dorsal flexible 7.7mm machine-gun. Bomb load: Two 30kg (66lb) bombs.

	Prototype HD 56	Type 90-1
Span	11.70m (38ft 4½in)	11.10m (36ft 5in)
Length	8.50m (27ft 10½in)	8.45 (27ft 8¾in)
Height	3.50m (11ft 6in)	3.67m (12ft)
Wing area	38sq m (409.041sq ft)	34.5sq m (371.367sq ft)
Empty weight	993kg (2,189lb)	1,118kg (2,464lb)
Loaded weight	1,500kg (3,307lb)	1,600kg (3,527lb)
Wing loading	39.5kg/sq m (8.09lb/sq ft)	46.3kg/sq m (9.483lb/sq ft)
Power loading	7.5kg/hp (16.5lb/hp)	5.33kg/hp (11.7lb/hp)
Maximum speed	90kt (104mph) at sea level	107kt (123mph) at sea level
Cruising speed at	63kt (72.5mph) 500m (1,640ft)	67.5kt (77.6mph) 500m (1,640ft)
Minimum speed	37kt (42.5mph)	41kt (47mph)
Climb to in	3,000m (9,843ft) 24min 30sec	3,000m (9,843ft) 18min 18sec
Service ceiling	3,270m (10,728ft)	4,710m (15,452ft)
Range	296nm (340sm)	407nm (468sm)
Endurance	4.7hr	6hr

Twelve built from 1929 to 1932.

Aichi Navy Type 90-1 Reconnaissance Seaplane (E3A1).

Experimental AB-2 Catapult-Launched Reconnaissance Seaplane

Although the Navy accepted the Aichi-built Type 90-1 Reconnaissance Seaplane in 1931 in spite of its lacking the desired performance, Aichi's designer Tetsuo Miki had already begun a design in 1929 for a new catapult-launched reconnaissance seaplane. This became the AB-2 and is noted as having been the first shipboard reconnaissance seaplane designed without foreign assistance and to be manufactured

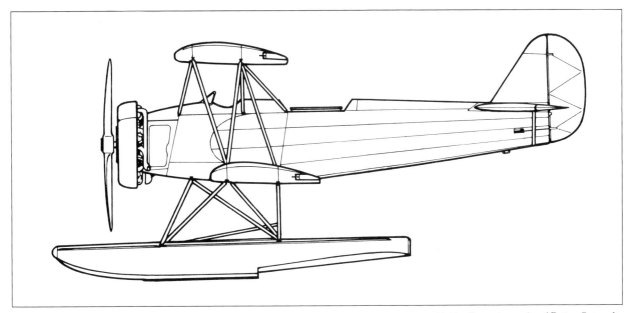

Aichi Experimental AB-2 Catapult-Launched Reconnaissance Seaplane. (Shorzoe Abe).

entirely in Japan. This marked a major turning point, not only for Aichi, but the other Japanese aircraft manufacturers which could now keep pace and improve upon foreign influence.

This AB-2 was a small two-seat floatplane, powered by Aichi's own experimental 300hp AC-1 nine-cylinder radial air-cooled engine. With this combination of airframe and engine, Aichi expected superior performance to that of the Nakajima Type 15 Reconnaissance Seaplane, E2N1, accepted as the Navy's standard just two years before, in 1927.

The engine proved to be a disappointment by not performing as expected. It also became obvious during construction of the airframe that numerous modifications were also necessary. While testing was still underway, an exhaust fire spread to the airframe of one prototype and the aeroplane was lost, and, soon after, the project was ended with only two prototypes having been built, although experience gained with the AB-2 was useful in the next design, the AB-3, which was completed two years later.

Single-engine, twin-float reconnaissance biplane. Welded steel tube fuselage and wooden wings, fabric covered. Rearward folding wings for stowage. Crew of two in open cockpits.

300–330hp Aichi AC-1 nine-cylinder air-cooled radial engine, driving a two-bladed wooden propeller.

One forward-firing fixed 7.7mm machine-gun, one dorsal flexible 7.7mm machine-gun. Bomb load: Two 30kg (66lb) bombs.

Span 11m (36ft 1in); length 8.24m (27ft 0½in); height 3.44m (11ft 3½in); wing area 36sq m (387.513sq ft).

Empty weight 1,115kg (2,458lb); loaded weight 1,656kg (3,648lb); wing loading 45kg/sq m (9.216lb/sq ft); power loading 5.31kg/hp (11.7lb/hp).

Maximum speed 97.4kt (112mph) at sea level; cruising speed 70kt (81mph); minimum speed 38.8kt (44.7mph); climb to 3,000m (9,843ft) in 20min; endurance 5.9hr at cruising speed, 3.8hr at maximum speed.

Two built in 1930.

Experimental AB-3 Single-seat Reconnaissance Seaplane

While the AB-2 was still under development in 1928, the Chinese Navy requested from the Japanese Navy a small warship that was eventually built by Japan's Harima Shipyard. Included in its equipment was to be a small single-seat biplane reconnaissance seaplane with quickly detachable wings for ease in shipboard stowage. The Navy selected Aichi for this seaplane project.

Other specifications for this seaplane called for a 130hp Gasuden Jimpu engine. The airframe when dismantled was to fit into an area 3.20m (10ft 6in) by 3.3m (10ft 10in) wide. It was to be of conventional construction, carrying a pilot and enough fuel and oil to fly for 3 hours at maximum speed with a payload of 30kg (66lb). Performance specifications were modest, a maximum speed of 100kt (115mph), climb to 3,000m (9,843ft) in 20 minutes, service ceiling of 4,000m (13,123ft) and alight at a speed of 43kt (49.5mph).

Drawing from experience in designing the closely related AB-2, Aichi's aircraft designer Tetsuo Miki completed the prototype in January 1932. It was a petite looking aeroplane with well proportioned lines. Test flights were made by Aichi's test pilots, Kanekichi Yokoyama and Tamizo Amagai, from the port of Nagoya, beginning in February of that year. In comparison with the AB-2, they reported that the AB-3 was a much better performer, especially in control response. This became the first aeroplane originally designed by Aichi to show great promise from the very first flight, with all performance figures exceeding the specified requirements.

The Chinese accepted this one prototype, but the aeroplane was never put into production. Instead, the Chinese Naval Arsenal built the

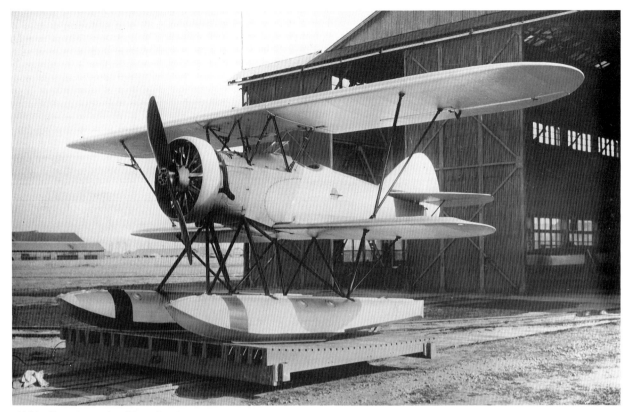

Aichi Experimental AB-3 Single-seat Reconnaissance Seaplane.

Ning Hai shipboard single-seat reconnaissance seaplane designed by Lieut T T Mar of the Chinese Navy, and powered it with the Japanese built 130hp Gasuden Jimpu engine.

Single-engine twin-float reconnaissance biplane. Detachable wood and metal wings with fabric covering. Fuselage of welded steel tube, fabric covered. Pilot in open cockpit.

One 130–150hp Gasuden Jimpu seven-cylinder air-cooled radial engine, driving a two-bladed wooden propeller.

No armament, but capable of carrying 20kg (44lb).

Span 9m (29ft 6in); length 6.6m (21ft 8in); height 2.88m (9ft 5½in); wing area 19.5sq m (209.896sq ft).

Empty weight 575kg (1,267lb); loaded weight 790kg (1,741lb); wing loading 40.5kg/sq m (9.216lb/sq ft); power loading 6.08kg/hp (13.4lb/hp).

Maximum speed 105kt (121mph) at sea level; cruising speed 74kt (85mph) at 500m (1,640ft); minimum speed 35kt (40.5mph); climb to 3,000m (9,843ft) in 15min 40sec; service ceiling 4,300m (14,107ft).

One built in 1932.

Navy Type 89 Flying Boat (H2H1)

Aichi was now established as a builder of water-based aircraft and continued to obtain Navy orders, and among them was a contract to build the Navy Type 89 Flying-boat, H2H1. This was a Navy adaptation of the British-designed and built Supermarine Southampton of which one was imported into Japan in 1929. The Hiro Arsenal was given the task of designing a flying-boat which would incorporate the better features of this twin-engine all-metal biplane flying-boat. This became the Type 89 Flying-boat of which production began at Hiro and Kawanishi, with thirteen built. In 1931 production was moved to Aichi where four were built. (*see* Hirosho for aircraft details.)

Experimental 6-Shi Night Reconnaissance Flying-boat (Company designation AB-4)

Aichi began developing a catapult-launched small flying-boat in 1931

Aichi Experimental 6-Shi Night Reconnaissance Flying-boat.

Aichi AB-4 Transport Flying-boat.

at the request of the Navy. This aeroplane was intended for a different mission to the previous conventional reconnaissance aircraft. It was to be used to direct gunfire during sea engagements at night, to observe enemy ship movements at night, and to maintain communications with friendly submarines. Apart from having good seaworthiness, it was to be capable of flying at low speed and have long endurance. Good stability was required in order to reduce pilot fatigue on long night flights.

Like previous Aichi aircraft, this flying-boat was designed under the supervision of Tetsuo Miki, assisted by Morishige Mori as the designer. The first prototype was completed and test flown in May 1932 by Kanekichi Yokoyama, with later test flights by Tamizo Amagai. In general appearance it resembled the Heinkel HD 55 flying-boat, but this Aichi design is said to have been original. During the test period, various changes were made to the fin and rudder.

For the official Navy tests, Lieut Terai did most of the evaluation. He graded the aircraft as good in most aspects, but questionable in

control on take offs and alightings. Visibility for the pilot was poor, as was the seating arrangement for the rest of the crew.

As the Navy's first night-reconnaissance aircraft the type was accepted as the Experimental 6-Shi Night Reconnaissance Flying-boat. Because of prolonged tests for operational suitability, the Navy decided to abandon further production after the sixth prototype, but these flying-boats did serve as effective reference for later designs that became the Type 96 and Type 98 night-reconnaissance aircraft. Eventually three of these AB-4s were released for civil use, and, after some conversion, they were used for a long period as passenger transports. (*see* AB-4 Transport Flying-boat that follows).

Single-engine pusher biplane flying-boat with rearward folding wings mounted above the hull. All-metal structure with light alloy and fabric covering. Crew of three in open cockpits.

300-330hp Gasuden Urakaze six-cylinder water-cooled inverted inline engine, driving a two-bladed wooden propeller.

One forward-firing flexible 7.7mm

machine-gun. Bomb load: Flare bombs up to 33.7kg (74.3lb).

Span 13.50m (44ft 3½in); length 9.75m (32ft); height 3.94m (12ft 11in); wing area 47.1sq m (507sq ft).

Empty weight 1,610kg (3,549lb); loaded weight 2,350kg (5,180lb); maximum weight 2,600kg (5,732lb) when catapult launched; wing loading 50kg/sq m (10.2lb/sq ft); power loading 7.83kg /hp (17.2lb/hp).

Maximum speed 89kt (102mph) at sea level; cruising speed 61kt (70 mph); minimum speed 45kt (52mph) at 1,000m (3,280ft); climb to 2,800m (9,186ft) in 60min 50 sec.

Six built from 1932 to 1934.

AB-4 Transport Flying-boat

With the Navy's abandonment of the 6-Shi Night Reconnaissance Flying-boat project in 1935, three of the six aircraft were released to Nippon Koku Yuso Kenkyusho (Japan Air Transport Research Association) at Sakai City, the organization set up to advance development of civil air transport.

Under the supervision of NKYK's engineer, Seiji Nakamae, each of these three flying-boats was con-

One of the Aichi AB-4s converted for civil use.

verted into a transport at the NKYK maintenance hangar at Sakai. The first aircraft, registered J-BBHI, carried the name *Kuroshio-go* (a warm sea current flowing near Japan). It had all military equipment removed from the forward portion of the hull and was converted into a cargo-transport. It remained the most original of the three. The second aircraft was J-BBQI, *Urakaze-go* (*Bay Breeze*). Its pilot's position was moved to the previous gunner's position in the extreme forward part of the bow, making room for a five-passenger cabin, with side windows, in the main part of the hull. Aircraft number three was J-BAIC, and was not named. Its pilot's seat was also relocated to the forward position, seating was provided for six passengers, and there were much larger windows in the hull. Its original Gasuden Urakaze engine was replaced by the more powerful 450hp Napier Lion by Nippi (Nihon Hikoki KK) at Yokohama.

Once these changes were made, the three flying-boats were used on the company's regular routes connecting Osaka with Takamatsu, Matsuyama and Beppu, as well as from Osaka to Shirahama. Begin-

ning in 1935, service was extended to the islands of the Inland Sea and the boats were also used for sightseeing flights. They won a good reputation for their stability and slow-flying capability; but tragedy struck on 27 May, 1937, when the second aircraft was alighting in bad weather after a test flight and struck a chimney of the Dai Nippon Celluloid Co in Sakai. All five NKYK staff members on board were killed.

Single-engine pusher biplane flying-boat with rearward folding wings mounted above the hull. All-metal structure with light alloy and fabric covering. Pilot and five or six passengers.

300–330hp Gasuden Urakaze six-cylinder water-cooled inverted inline engine, driving a two-bladed wooden propeller (first and second aircraft). 450hp Napier Lion twelve-cylinder W-type water cooled engine, driving a two-bladed wooden propeller (third aircraft).

Span 14m (45ft 11¼in); length 9.70m (31ft 10in); height 3.90m (12ft 9½in); wing area 46.02sq m (495.371sq ft).

Empty weight 1,740kg (3,836lb) [1,770kg (3,902lb)]; loaded 2,550kg (5,621lb) [2,550kg (5,621lb)]; wing

loading 49.2kg/sq m (10.077lb/sq ft); power loading 7.28kg/hp (16lb/hp).

Maximum speed 81kt (93.5mph) [84kt (97mph)] at sea level; cruising speed 70kt (81mph); climb to 2,000m (6,561ft) in 23min 20sec; service ceiling 3,500m (11,483ft).

Three converted from Navy aircraft from 1935 to 1937.

Data for 3rd aircraft within square brackets.

Experimental AB-5 Three-seat Reconnaissance Seaplane (Company designation HD 62)

In 1931, at the Navy's request, Aichi placed an order with Heinkel to design and build a high-performance long-range reconnaissance seaplane. This became the HD 62, a development of the HD 28, also a twin-float aircraft. In 1932 this one example reached Japan and was delivered to the Navy under Aichi's designation AB-5.

This high-speed catapult-launched aircraft was a single-bay biplane with a Clark Y aerofoil, having an all-metal structure covered with fabric. The crew consisted of pilot, observer and radio operator/gunner. The AB-5 showed superior performance to that of the Yokosho-designed Type 14-2 Reconnaissance Seaplane it was to replace. However, only the one AB-5 was built. Recognizing the potential of the design, this aeroplane was further developed into the 7-Shi Reconnaissance Seaplane and completed by the two companies, Aichi and Kawanishi. The following data pertain to the one AB-5 aircraft.

Single-engine twin-float reconnaissance seaplane. Metal structure with fabric covering. Rearward folding wings for stowage. Crew of three in open cockpits.

600–660hp Lorraine Courlis twelve-cylinder W-type water-cooled engine, driving a two-bladed wooden propeller.

One forward-firing fixed 7.7mm machine-gun and one dorsal flexible 7.7mm machine-gun. Bomb load: Four 30kg (66lb) bombs.

Aichi AB-5 Three-seat Reconnaissance Seaplane (HD 62).

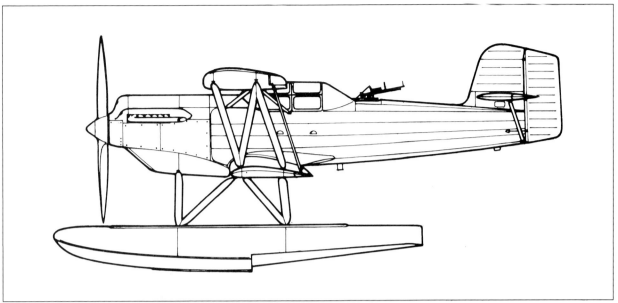

Aichi Experimental 7-Shi Reconnaissance Seaplane. (Shorzoe Abe).

Span 13.50m (44ft 3½in); length 10.60m (34ft 9½in); height 4.35m (14ft 3¼in); wing area 52.22sq m (562.109sq ft).

Empty weight 1,845kg (4,067lb); loaded weight 3,200kg (7,054lb); wing loading 61.5kg/sq m (12.596lb/sq ft); power loading 5.33kg/hp (11.7lb/hp).

Maximum speed 130kt (150mph) at sea level; cruising speed 82kt (95mph); alighting speed 51kt (59mph) climb to 3,000m (9,843ft) in 13min 36sec; service ceiling 4,800m (15,748ft); endurance 14hr.

One built in 1932.

Experimental 7-Shi Reconnaissance Seaplane
(Company designation AB-6)

In 1932 the Navy still required a new long-range reconnaissance seaplane to replace the Yokosho Type 14 and Type 90-3 Reconnaissance Seaplanes, and looked to Aichi and Kawanishi to develop it. The newly accepted 500hp Type 91 Engine for Naval aircraft was specified. Aichi's designer for the project, Tetsuo Miki, completed the design in May 1932, using as reference the Heinkel HD 62 (AB-5). When the prototype was completed in February 1933, its lines emphasized the trend towards a more modern design. It had an enclosed cockpit and the wings were smoothly faired to the fuselage.

The first flight was made by Kanekichi Yokoyama from the port of Nagoya, with later evaluation flights made by Tamizo Amagai, also of Aichi, and Lieut-Cdr Nakajima and Lieut Terai for the Navy. Disappointingly, these tests showed that the aeroplane failed to achieve the desired performance, and a number of changes were necessary, particularly to the wings. When evaluated against the competing Kawanishi 7-Shi entry, (which was to become the Type 94 Reconnaissance Seaplane), the AB-6 failed the test, and only the one prototype was built.

The AB-6 had many sound features, good stability, control and rate of climb, but with respect to speed and take off and alighting, the aeroplane did not meet the Navy specifications. The armament was also considered to be below acceptable standards. A number of modifications were made to the AB-6 in the hope of achieving Navy acceptance, including a change in the bottom contour of both wings which had originally been of Clark Y aerofoil section. Full-span leading-edge slats were also added, but the Kawanishi 7-Shi remained the superior aircraft.

Single-engine twin-float reconnaissance seaplane. All-metal structure with fabric covering. Wings folded rearward for stowage. Crew of three in closed cockpit.

500–630hp Type 91 twelve-cylinder W-type water-cooled engine, driving a Hamilton two-position variable-pitch two-bladed metal propeller. After modifications the propeller was a wooden two-blade unit and still later a four-blade propeller was fitted.

One forward-firing fixed 7.7mm machine-gun, one dorsal flexible 7.7mm machine-gun, one rear under fuselage flexible 7.7mm machine-gun.

	Prototype	*After Modification*
Span	13.60m (44ft 7½in)	12.98m (42ft 7in)
Length	10.39m (34ft 1in)	10.44m (34ft 3in)
Height	4.80m (15ft 9in)	4.80m (15ft 9in)
Wing area	43.2sq m (465.016sq ft)	40.61sq m (437.136sq ft)
Empty weight	2,080kg (4,585lb)	1,920kg (4,232lb)
Loaded weight	3.061kg (6,748lb)	3,020kg (6,657lb)
Maximum weight	3,300kg (7,275lb)	3,300kg (7,275lb)
Wing loading	70.9kg/sq m (14.5lb/sq ft)	74.4kg/sq m (15.238lb/sq ft)

Power loading	6.12kg/hp (13.5lb/hp)	6.04kg/hp (13.3lb/hp)
Maximum speed at sea level	119.4kt (137.4mph)	121.7kt (140mph)
Cruising speed at 1,000m (3,280ft)	80kt (92mph)	80kt (92mph)
Minimum speed at 1,000m (3,280ft)	44kt (51mph)	51kt (59mph)
Alighting speed	57.4kt (66mph)	58kt (67mph)
Climb to	3,000m (9,843ft)	3,000m (9,843ft)
in	13min 5sec	14min 54sec
Service ceiling	—	4,850m (15,912ft)
Endurance at 3,300kg (7,275lb)	—	6.9hr
Maximum endurance	—	11.9hr

One built in 1933.

Experimental 8-Shi Reconnaissance Seaplane (E8A1) (Company designation AB-7)

In 1933, the Navy asked Aichi, Kawanishi, and Nakajima, to submit development proposals for a new reconnaissance seaplane as a replacement for the E4N2 Nakajima Type 90-2 Reconnaissance Seaplane. This aeroplane had been based upon the imported American Vought O2U-1 Corsair developed under licence with Vought. This aeroplane had an easily interchangeable undercarriage, with a single float or conventional wheels configuration. Aichi's chief designer

Aichi Experimental 8-Shi Reconnaissance Seaplane (E8A1). (Shorzoe Abe).

for the new project, Yoshishiro Matsuo, had been studying the United States example of the Corsair since 1932 and had been working on an improved design over that of the Type 90-2. This became the Aichi AB-7.

Designated the 8-Shi Reconnaissance Seaplane project by the Navy, design requirements included the capability of being catapult launched and to be highly manoeuvrable as a fighter. Both the Aichi and Nakajima entries were similar in appearance, speed and climb capability, but the Nakajima entrant was superior in manoeuvrability and stability. In September 1935 the Nakajima aeroplane was accepted by the Navy as the Type 95 Reconnaissance Seaplane, E8N1, winning the competition over the AB-7. The E8N1 served early in the Pacific War under the Allied code name Dave.

As a separate venture in 1933, while the AB-7 was under development along proven design concepts, Aichi was planning a twin-float low-wing reconnaissance seaplane which it designated AM-7. This was similar to the Kawanishi 8-Shi under this same design competition except in float arrangement. The engine was to be the 520–570hp Bristol Mercury, designed for high-altitude fighter use, and would be enclosed in a NACA cowling. It, too, was rejected because its performance was not better than that of the Type 90-2-2, for which it was to have been a replacement. As a result the design was abandoned early in development, possibly in favour of the more traditional concepts. The following data pertain to the AB-7.

Single-engine reconnaissance seaplane with interchangeable wheels and single-float undercarriage. Wood and metal structure with fabric covering. Wings folded rearward for stowage. Pilot in open cockpit and gunner/observer in semi-enclosed cockpit.

460–580hp Nakajima Kotobuki 2-kai 1 nine-cylinder air-cooled radial engine, driving a fixed-pitch two-bladed metal propeller.

One forward-firing fixed 7.7mm machine-gun. One dorsal flexible 7.7mm machine-gun.

Span 10.50m (34ft 5½in); length 8.85m (29ft); height 3.57m (11ft 8½in).

Two built in 1933.

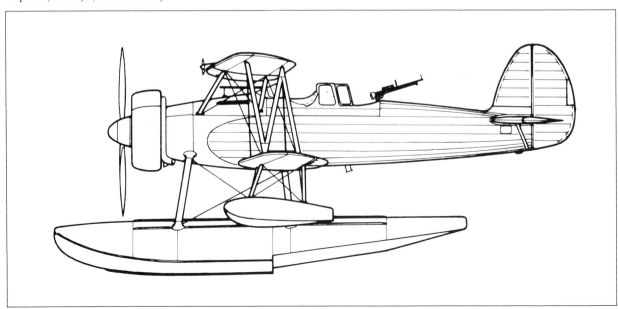

Aichi Experimental 7-Shi Carrier Attack Aircraft.

Experimental 7-Shi Carrier Attack Aircraft*
(Company designation AB-8)

Because of the bad reputation of the B2M1 and B2M2 Mitsubishi Type 89 Carrier Attack Aircraft, the Navy requested Mitsubishi and Nakajima to submit design proposals in 1932 for a replacement aircraft. Separately, Naval Kusho, formerly Yokosho, began a parallel project in further development of its Type 13 Carrier Attack Aircraft which was to be powered by a 600hp Type 91 engine. Also in parallel and as a private venture, Aichi designed a three-seat carrier attack aircraft it designated AB-8. This design was completed in September 1932 and the prototype was finished in 1933.

Much of the success for the 7-Shi competition depended upon the engine selected for these aeroplanes. Aichi imported the 600hp Lorraine engine from France for its AB-8. Other possibilities were the 600hp Mitsubishi Type Hi (Hispano-Suiza) which at that time had a poor reputation for reliability, and the 600hp Hiro Type 91 engine which had not yet reached production. As a result, Mitsubishi, Nakajima and Kusho, laboured through the project with little confidence of success in replacing the Type 89 with a better aircraft.

The most practical design was a modified version of another Kusho

*Attack Aircraft (Kogekiki) was the Japanese Navy's term for aeroplanes that were used for horizontal bombing and torpedo dropping. Bomber (Bakugekiki) was the term for aeroplanes with dive bombing capability.

design, almost outside the realm of the competition, the modified Kusho Type 13, re-engineered by Aichi's designer of the AB-8, Tokuichiro Gomei. The Navy declared that the best choice and it was put into production by Aichi, Hiro and Watanabe as the Kusho Type 92 Carrier Attack Aircraft, B3Y1.

The losing and sole AB-8 was later given the civil registration J-BESL and used by the company as an air-test vehicle at Kagamigahara. This was the only biplane three-seat carrier attack aircraft ever designed by Aichi.

Single-engine biplane carrier attack aircraft. Metal and wood structure with fabric covering. Wings folded rearward for stowage. Crew of three in open cockpits.

600hp Lorraine Courlis twelve-cylinder W-type water-cooled engine, driving a fixed-pitch three-bladed metal propeller.

One forward-firing fixed 7.7mm machine-gun. One dorsal flexible 7.7mm machine-gun. Bomb load: 800kg (1,763lb) torpedo or bomb.

Span 14m (45ft 11¼in); length 9.55m (31ft 4in); height 3.67m (12ft 0½in);

wing area 48.3sq m (519.913sq ft).

Empty weight 1,770kg (3,902lb); loaded weight 3,200kg (7,054lb); wing loading 66.2kg/sq m (13.5lb/sq ft); power loading 5.33kg/hp (11.75lb/hp).

Maximum speed 128kt (147mph); landing speed 50kt (57.5mph); minimum speed 45kt (52mph).

One built in 1933.

Navy Type 92 Carrier Attack Aircraft (B3Y1)

As already related, the Aichi AB-8 design was not accepted as the new carrier attack aircraft for the Navy. However, during 1933, Aichi designer Tokuichiro Gomei modified a Kusho Type 13 Carrier Attack Aircraft to meet the requirement and it proved to be the best replacement for the Type 89 Carrier Attack Aircraft and was put into production with Aichi, followed by Watanabe and the Hiro Arsenal. Aichi built seventy-five of these aircraft, a number of which served in the Sino-Japanese Conflict. (*see* Kusho Navy Type 92 Carrier Attack Aircraft)

Experimental 8-Shi Special Bomber
(Company designation AB-9)

Neither the 6-Shi nor the 7-Shi dive-bomber projects for which Kusho and Nakajima entered jointly were accepted by the Navy because they had poor stability during the dive. For the 8-Shi carrier

Aichi Navy Type 94 Carrier Bomber.

dive-bomber competition in 1933, the Navy asked for new designs from Aichi and Nakajima. Under licence agreement with Heinkel, Aichi decided to use that company's design of the He 50 (single and two-seat) dive-bomber which were then equipping Luftwaffe dive-bomber units as a new concept of aerial warfare. An order was placed with Heinkel to build one example of the He 50 for Aichi, which, as an export model, became the He 66.

The He 66 looked obsolete by the standards of the time because of its numerous interplane struts and bracing wires, but it could have a land or twin-float undercarriage, and the concept for this sound design remained practical. The production He 66 was equipped with a wooden four-bladed propeller and the undercarriage shock absorbers were attached to the fuselage, but the Aichi-acquired aeroplane had modifications to include a two-bladed wooden propeller and the shock-absorber struts attached to the underside of the wing. Beneath the fuselage was a bomb displacement arm which was a release mechanism that positioned the bomb outside the propeller arc during the drive. In 1934, chief designer Tokuichiro Gomei and his assistant on the project, Yoshimichi Kobayashi, had the original Siemens engine replaced with a Nakajima Kotobuki 2-kai-1 and a metal two-bladed propeller, along with some minor changes. The aeroplane was submitted to the Navy for its consideration as Aichi's 8-Shi Special Bomber, no mention of dive-bomber being carried in the title because of security classification.

Compared to the competing Nakajima prototype, the Aichi aircraft had better control and stability. Because of these qualities, along with other considerations, the Navy accepted the aeroplane in December 1934 as the Type 94 Carrier Light Bomber, soon changed to Type 94 Carrier Bomber, with the short designation D1A1. This would become Aichi's first mass-produced aeroplane and establish the company as the exclusive builder of carrier-based dive-bombers for the Japanese Navy throughout the Pacific War. At the beginning of

the Sino-Japanese conflict, Type 94s were Japan's sole operational dive-bomber, giving good results in precision bombing against specific targets. Because the Allies expected to meet it in combat in the early stages of the Pacific War they gave it the code-name Susie, but by that time, few were in service.

The following data pertain to the AB-9, the He 66 after being modified by Aichi.

Single-engine biplane dive-bomber. Wood and metal structure with fabric covering. Wings folded rearward for stowage. Crew of two in open cockpits.
520-715hp Siemens SAM 22B nine-cylinder air-cooled radial engine, driving a four-bladed wooden propeller (He 66). 580hp Nakajima Kotobuki 2-kai-1 nine-cylinder air-cooled radial engine, driving a fixed-pitch two-bladed metal propeller (AB-9).
Two fixed forward-firing 7.7mm machine-guns. One flexible rear-firing 7.7mm machine-gun. Bomb load: One 250kg (551lb) bomb under the fuselage and two 30kg (66lb) bombs under the wings.
Span 11.50m (37ft 8½in); length 9.76m (32ft 0¼in); height 4.15m (13ft 7½in); wing area 34.8sq m (374.596sq ft).
Empty weight 1,600kg (3,527lb); loaded weight 2,600kg (5,732lb); wing loading 74.7kg/sq m (15.3lb/sq ft); power loading 5kg/hp (11lb/hp).
Maximum speed 127kt (146mph); landing speed 51.5kt (59mph); climb to 1,000m (3,280ft) in 3min; service ceiling 6,400m (21,000ft).
One built in 1934.

Aichi Navy Type 96 Reconnaissance Seaplane (E10A1).

Navy Type 96 Reconnaissance Seaplane* (E10A1) (Company designation AB-12)

Aichi was destined to remain closely tied to the development of seaplanes and flying-boats throughout its years of aircraft production. In 1934, the Navy arranged with Aichi and Kawanishi to develop the 9-Shi Night Reconnaissance Seaplane with a 500hp engine as the successor to the 6-Shi Small Night Reconnaissance Flying-boat. The 6-Shi had not received Navy acceptance despite the prolonged time in its research and development.

By June 1934, chief designer for the project, Morishige Mori, had completed the new design and the first prototype was finished in December that same year. This aeroplane bore a close resemblance to the Supermarine Seagull V which had flown a year before. Both were biplane flying-boats with the lower wing set high on the hull and a pusher engine mounted between the wings. Improvements hoped for over the 6-Shi were a better designed structure and improved control and stability. Like the 6-Shi and the Seagull, this aeroplane had catapult-launch capability.

The competing Kawanishi design used a tractor arrangement with an air-cooled Kotobuki engine, while the Aichi entry was powered by a 500hp pusher Type 91 water-cooled

*Although this was a flying-boat the literal translation of its Japanese designation was seaplane.

Aichi Experimental 10-Shi Observation Aircraft in landplane configuration. (J W Underwood).

engine. Initial flight tests were made by Aichi's test pilot Tamizo Amagai. The Aichi AB-12 proved to have better stability than the Kawanishi and this brought Aichi the order with production beginning in May 1935.

The Navy officially accepted the aeroplane as a service type in August 1936 designating it Type 96 Reconnaissance Seaplane. Night-reconnaissance operations would be its primary mission, one of the unique missions developed by the Japanese Navy. The Navy saw the advantage of having night surveillance of enemy fleet activities and the consequent ability to put its fleet in an advantageous position for the next engagements. For these all-black flying-boats, it was essential that they have low speed capability and be able to remain aloft for many hours. Good stability was necessary to reduce pilot fatigue on their long missions.

Production continued until 1937, with fifteen aircraft being built, but they were phased out of service just before the Pacific War.

Single-engine pusher biplane flying-boat. All-metal structure with stressed metal skin and fabric covering. Rearward folding wings for stowage. Crew of three in enclosed cabin.

500–650hp Aichi Type 91 twelve-cylinder W-type water-cooled engine, driving a four-bladed wooden propeller.

One nose-mounted flexible 7.7mm machine-gun.

Span 15.50m (50ft 10¼in); length 11.219m (36ft 9½in); height 4.50m (14ft 9in); wing area 52.10sq m (560.818sq ft).

Empty weight 2,100kg (4,629lb); loaded weight 3,300kg (7,275lb); wing loading 63.2kg/sq m (12.944lb/sq ft); power loading 6.6kg/hp (14.5lb/hp).

Maximum speed 111kt (128mph) at sea level; cruising speed 57kt (66mph) at 1,000m (3,280ft); climb to 3,000m (9,843ft) in 17min 42sec; service ceiling 4,120m (13,517ft); range 1,000nm (1,150sm).

Fifteen built between 1934 and 1937.

Experimental 10-Shi Observation Aircraft (F1A1)
(Company designation AB-13)

With dependency upon ship- and sea-based reconnaissance seaplanes, the Japanese Navy was always in search of improved designs. A number of projects were considered with Aichi as the leader in seaplane designs and modern concepts and the company initiated a low-wing tapered-wing monoplane as an 8-Shi Reconnaissance Seaplane design designated AM-10. This showed considerable Heinkel influence but was a creation of Yoshishiro Matsuo of Aichi. It embodied the new feature of large-area wing flaps and could be equipped with either a conventional retractable wheel undercarriage, or a single main float. The AM-10 was a very advanced seaplane design, and perhaps for that reason, it never got beyond the drawing board.

The requirement remained, however, for an improved design to replace the two-seat reconnaissance floatplanes then in service. In 1934 the Navy requested Aichi, Kawanishi and Mitsubishi to submit proposals for a floatplane having sufficient manoeuvrability for aerial combat in addition to the observation role. Aichi was given the requirement by the Navy in March 1935, and Tetsuo Miki was assigned design responsibility for the project. Two versions of this prototype biplane were to be built: one with wheels and the other with a central float so that both could be tested simultaneously. The prototype float-equipped aircraft was completed first, in June 1936, and the landplane the following September.

To achieve high performance, wing design was critical and two different structures were studied, both with a Koken No 1 aerofoil, a development of the Aeronautical Research Institute at Tokyo Imperial University. In order to keep this aerofoil section constant across the wings, a requirement difficult to achieve with fabric covering, a plywood skin was used with celluloid at the leading edge, and coated with a special paint to give a very smooth surface. These watertight stress-skin wings were constructed with less than normal components as a weight saving measure, but resulted in very complicated structure within the wing. The previously developed, yet seldom applied, combat flaps were incorporated in the wing design. These were operated in conjunction with elevator movement.

The fuselage was equally as advanced in structural concept in that the metal skin thickness was increased and formed in larger panels than normal to reduce the number of formers and seam lines. Considerable attention was given to the interplane and float struts for their streamlining and juncture fittings. The undercarriage of the landplane version consisted of a single cantilever member, with the wheels neatly faired with spats. Every detail was studied and refined in order to reduce drag. Results of test flights brought about changes in the engine cowling, main and wingtip floats, rudder, and rear cockpit enclosure. After much work, the float-configured aeroplane was accepted by the Navy in September 1936 following tests by Navy Lieut-Cdr Minematsu and Lieut-Cdr (Ordnance) Honjuku. Sixty-one flights had been made, accumulating 38hr and 47min of flight-test time.

The land-based version was shipped to Kagamigahara when completed in June 1936 and made its first flight the next month. After thirty-seven test flights by Aichi's Tamizo Amagai, amounting to 19hr and 21min, the resultant changes included one engine replacement, modifications to the cowling, change in the vertical tail, and strengthening of the undercarriage.

After months of work in perfecting these two aeroplanes in competition with the Mitsubishi contender, the Navy made the decision to accept the Mitsubishi F1M1 which had better control and stability, while the Aichi, now referred to by the shortened designation F1A1, was unacceptable for other reasons. In 1940, Mitsubishi's F1M1 was officially adopted by the Navy after a number of modifications, and became known during the Pacific War by the Allied code-name Pete. Data pertaining to the Aichi F1A1 follow.

Single-engine biplane observation land and seaplane. Wooden wings covered with plywood and celluloid. All-metal fuselage, with rear half of monocoque construction. Wings fold rearward for stowage. Crew of two in open and canopied cockpits.
600–820hp Nakajima Hikari 1 nine-cylinder air-cooled radial engine, driving a two-position variable-pitch two-bladed metal propeller.
Two forward-firing fixed 7.7mm machine-guns. One dorsal flexible 7.7mm machine-gun.

	Floatplane	*Landplane*
Span	11m (36ft 1in)	11m (36ft 1in)
Length	9.30m (30ft 6in)	8.15m (26ft 9in)
Height	4.10m (13ft 5in)	3.40m (11ft 2in)
Wing area	28sq m (301.399sq ft)	28sq m (301.399sq ft)
Empty weight	1,400kg (3,086lb)	1,290kg (2,844lb)
Loaded weight	2,100kg (4,629lb)	2,003kg (4,415lb)
Maximum weight	2,380kg (5,247lb)	2,283kg (5,033lb)
Wing loading	75.0kg/sq m (15.361lb/sq ft)	71.5kg/sq m (14.644lb/sq ft)
Power loading	3.18kg/hp (7lb/hp)	3.03kg/hp (6.6lb/hp)

(Floatplane only)
Maximum speed 177.3kt (204mph) at sea level, 207.8kt (240mph) at 3,000m (9,843ft); minimum speed 51.5kt (59.5mph); climb to 3,000m (9,843ft) in 4min 26sec; service ceiling 9,275m (30,430ft); range 783nm (900sm) at 100kt (115mph) at 3,000m (9,843ft); endurance 8hr 30min at 85kt (98mph) at 3,000m (9,843ft).
Two built in 1936.

Experimental 12-Shi Two-seat Reconnaissance Seaplane (E12A1)

In June 1937, the Navy placed orders with Nakajima, Kawanishi and Aichi to develop an Experimental 12-Shi Two-seat Reconnaissance Seaplane with the capability of being catapult-launched from warships. For the Aichi project, Yoshishiro Matsuo became chief designer, assisted by Morishige Mori and Yasunori Ozawa. The development of this all-new design began in September 1937 and continued through to February the following year, with two prototypes emerging by the end of 1938.

This aeroplane was modern by world standards of the time in that it was an all-metal cantilever low-wing monoplane, a departure from biplane designs for this mission. It had an elliptical tapered wing fitted with slotted flaps. The floats were carried by a pair of struts with sway-brace wires. Power was the newly developed double-row 850hp Mitsubishi Zuisei radial engine with a constant-speed metal propeller.

Although this aeroplane contained a number of innovative features as well as having good performance, it lacked inflight stability and control. As a result of the competition between the designs, the Aichi E12A1, as it was designated, was not accepted, nor were the Nakajima E12N1 entries. Kawanishi declined the competition before the basic configuration was finalized. However, the Aichi design concept was applied to the 12-Shi Three-seat Reconnaissance Seaplane that became accepted as the Type 0

Aichi Experimental 12-Shi Two-seat Reconnaissance Seaplane (E12A1).

Three-seat Reconnaissance Seaplane used during the Pacific War and known to the Allies by the code-name Jake.

Single-engine low-wing twin-float reconnaissance seaplane. All-metal construction with fabric-covered control surfaces. Wings folded upward for stowage. Crew of two in tandem enclosed cockpits.

850–870hp Mitsubishi Zuisei fourteen-cylinder air-cooled radial engine, driving a constant-speed two-bladed metal propeller.

Two forward-firing fixed 7.7mm machine-guns, one dorsal flexible 7.7mm machine-gun. Bombs: one 250kg (551lb) bomb or two 60kg (133lb) bombs under fuselage.

Span 13m (42ft 8in); length 10.45m (34ft 3¼in); height 3.45m (11ft 3¾in); wing area 30.8sq m (331.539sq ft).

Empty weight 2,100kg (4,630lb); loaded weight 2,850kg (6,283lb); wing loading 92.5kg/sq m (18.9lb/sq ft); power loading 3.35kg/hp (7.3lb/hp).

Maximum speed 195kt (225mph) at 1,900m (6,233ft); cruising speed 150kt (172mph); climb to 3,000m (9,843ft) in 5min; service ceiling 8,150m (26,738ft); range 575nm (662sm); endurance 3.8hr.

Two built in 1938.

New designs and engineering de-velopments in the mid-1930s continued to come from the expanding Aircraft Department of the Aichi Watch and Electric Machinery Company Ltd. The Experimental AB-11 dive-bomber, for instance, was a further development of the AB-9. This was a very streamlined version of such bulky biplanes as the Grumman XFF-1 or Curtiss XSBC-1 Helldiver under development at that time and which featured the same type of retractable undercarriage having the wheels flush with the fuselage sides. For 1934, this was too radical in the eyes of Navy planners and the project was dropped.

That same year brought the preliminary design of the Experimental AB-12G Night Reconnaissance Seaplane. This was a shoulder-wing monoplane with its strut-mounted tractor engine placed high above the hull similar to the Heinkel He 57, a practice common at the time. The Navy showed more interest in the more proven design concepts of the AB-12 (E10A1). As a consequence, the monoplane feature was dropped for a time. What did develop, however, was a refinement in the biplane design which resulted in the AB-14 (E11A1), Allied code named Laura, of which some were used during the Pacific War.

As a new project, Aichi developed a design for an Experimental AM-16 which was a twin-engined flying-boat, with American-made Menasco Super Buccaneer engines, which would have been comparable to the Grumman Goose and Widgeon at that time. Only the hull of the AM-16 had been completed when the Navy ordered abandonment of the project in favour of production of the Aichi D3A, Navy Type 99 Carrier Bomber, Allied code-name Val, that played a major role in the opening stages of the Pacific War. Aichi's AM-20 proposal was to be a Navy Experimental 13-Shi High-speed Land-based Reconnaissance Aircraft for which the mock-up was completed in March 1939. Instead, the Navy accepted a modified version of the Army's Ki-15 as the Type 98 Land-based Reconnaissance Aircraft. The proposed AM-15 small fighter, and the reissue of the number AM-15 for a sports-plane, were abandoned early in their development.

Aichi became a major manufacturer of Navy aircraft from the 1930s to the end of the Pacific War, and ranked fourth in the industry. The Aircraft Department of the Aichi Watch and Electric Machinery Co Ltd (Aichi Tokei Denki KK) became independent in February 1943 and at that time took the more appropriate name Aichi Aircraft Co Ltd.

Akabane Aeroplane Manufacturing Works (Akabane Hikoki Seisakusho) (Kishi)

Kishi No.2 Tsurugi-go *Aeroplane.*

This company was founded by Doctor Kazuta Kishi, MD, an extraordinary man with numerous diverse interests which included aviation. In 1914, he served as the director of the ear hospital (ENT) at Akashi-cho, Tsukiji, Tokyo, and was in addition known for his interests as an inventor of various machines, and an enthusiast for automobiles and swords. Achieving success in discovering a molybdenum vein in Tsurugigadake (Sword Mountain), Toyama Prefecture, he managed a refinery and undertook the manufacturing of the 70hp Renault engine using his molybdenum steel alloy. Assisting him in the technical aspects of these major undertakings were Aijiro Hara BSc and Rikichi Sasaki BSc, both graduates of Tokyo Imperial University, Department of Engineering.

At about this time, Tsunejiro Obata, the oldest son of Iwajiro Obata, a noted civil contractor of Fushimi, Kyoto, built the airframe of a Maurice Farman 1913, financed by his father. The aircraft needed an engine, and a Kishi-Renault engine was soon mated to it. In December 1915, the aeroplane was successfully flown by Army Lt (Reserve) Takesaburo Inoue at Okinohara, Yokaichi City, near Lake Biwa. In March 1916, flown by Ieyasu Nakazawa, it was used in Japan's first motion picture in which an aeroplane was part of the plot. With this, the success of the aeroplane, although punctuated by the unreliability of the Kishi-built engine, was confirmed.

Kishi No.1 *Tsurugi-go* Aeroplane

Involving himself more deeply in aviation, Doctor Kishi established an aeroplane manufacturing shop in his hospital grounds, and hired Etsutaro Munesato to be in charge. The shop produced a Maurice Farman 1913 in May 1916 and Kishi named it the *Tsurugi-go,* later to be known as the No.1 *Tsurugi-go,* meaning Sword-type.* Taking

*This name may have been derived from his lucrative mine at Tsurugigadake.

the finished aeroplane to the Susaki reclaimed ground in eastern Tokyo, the aeroplane, piloted by Lt Inoue, flew for 1hr and 12min on 2 July of that year. With its success proven, it was taken on an exhibition tour of parts of northern central Honshu, Kyushu and Shikoku to promote aviation knowledge and to demonstrate the reliability of the Kishi-Renault engine.

Kishi No.2 *Tsurugi-go* Aeroplane

To introduce improvements, a second aeroplane was built by Kishi, again using his 70hp Renault engine. This aeroplane was designed by Aijiro Hara along with T Naganuma and E Munesato from Kishi's staff. Being fully original, it differed from the previous aeroplane by having no forward elevator but having slight sweepback to the wings, and was a pusher-type aeroplane with a cockpit pod to which was attached a nosewheel thus giving it a tricycle undercarriage.

Lt Inoue made the first, and last flight of this aeroplane at Inage on 12 December, 1916. Immediately after take off, the craft banked sharply to the left, allowing the wingtip to contact the ground, causing it to cartwheel and end the flight with considerable damage to the aeroplane. It was assumed that the cause of the accident was the sweptback wing design. Aspects of the design were therefore never

Kishi No.1 Tsurugi-go *Aeroplane.*

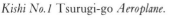

tested but it was expected to have a maximum speed of 57kt (65mph) as opposed to that of 49kt (56mph) of the Maurice Farman 1913. It had the structural strength for aerobatics and the range to fly nonstop from Tokyo to Osaka, a major feat for 1916.

Single-engine pusher biplane. Wooden structure with fabric covered wings, empennage and fuselage pod. V-shaped twin open-structure tail-booms with orthodox tail unit. Two seats in open cockpit.

70hp Kishi-Renault eight-cylinder vee air-cooled engine, driving a two-bladed wooden propeller.

Span 12.50m (41ft); length 8.55m (28ft 0¾ in); height 2.80m (9ft 2¼in); wing area 40sq m (430.57 sq ft).

Empty weight 480kg (1,058lb); loaded weight 730kg (1,609lb).

One built in 1916.

Kishi No.4 Tsurugi-go *Aeroplane.*

Kishi No.3 *Tsurugi-go* Aeroplane

Suspecting the unsafe design of the sweptback wing used on the No.2 *Tsurugi-go,* this new aeroplane used the conventional straight wing, very much like that of the Army Maurice Farman Type Mo–4. Al-

Kishi No.3 Tsurugi-go *Aeroplane.*

though the centre cockpit nacelle was original in design structure, other parts of the airframe were identical to the Type Mo–4.

After its first public flying demonstration on 11 February, 1917, Japan's National Foundation Day known as Kigensetsu, Kishi designated the aeroplane as the No.3 *Tsurugi-go.* Acting as flying instructor, Lt Inoue used it to introduce many people to the experience of flying an aeroplane. Because of its activity at the Susaki Airfield on reclaimed ground, the site became known as Kishi Airfield. Eventually, this aeroplane went to Itoh Airfield.

Kishi No.4 *Tsurugi-go* Aeroplane

Although based on the No.3 *Tsurugi-go,* various changes were incorporated into the airframe of this new aeroplane. The lower wing was shortened and the diagonal struts near the wingtips were dispensed with. With overall weight and size less than that of the Maurice Farman Type Mo–4, this No.3 *Tsurugi-go* Aeroplane was more commonly called the Small Mo-type aeroplane.

Following successful flights, it joined others at Susaki to celebrate

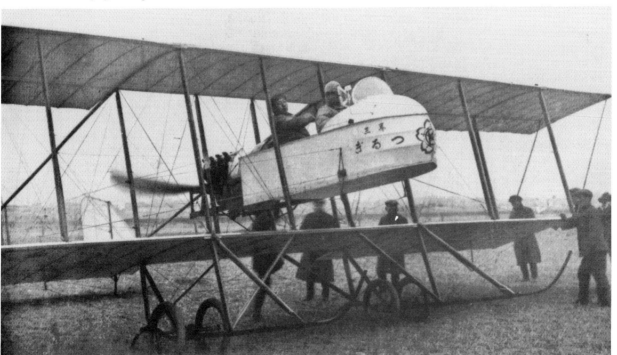

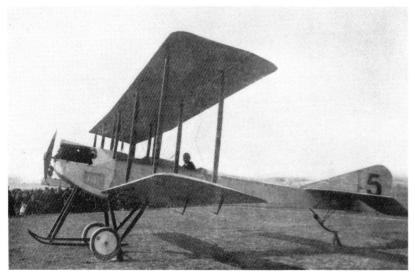

Kishi No.5 Tsurugi-go *Aeroplane.*

the 50th Anniversary of Metropolitan Tokyo. Also present were the Itoh Tsurubane No.2, Nakajima Type 3, and the Maurice Farman Type Mo–4 of the Imperial Flying Association. They all made circuits of Ueno Park in Tokyo where the ceremony was held.

Single-engine pusher biplane. Wooden structure with fabric covered wings, empennage and fuselage pod. V-shaped twin open-structure tail-booms. Two seats in open cockpit.

70hp Kishi-Renault eight-cylinder vee air-cooled engine, driving a two-bladed wooden propeller.

Span upper 15.50m (50ft 10¼in), lower 9.8m (32ft 2in); length 8m (26ft 3in); height 2.80m (9ft 2¼in).

Empty weight 450kg (992lb).

Maximum speed 54kt (62mph).

One built in 1917.

Kishi No.5 *Tsurugi-go* Aeroplane

In 1917, Dr Kishi made a major personal investment by creating a true aviation business enterprise. He purchased 165,000sq m of land at Akabane, across the Arakawa River from Kawaguchi on the northern edge of Tokyo. Creating an airfield there, he built a hangar, an aircraft factory, a flying school and student dormitories. The first phase was completed in December 1917. Employing his original staff, he assigned Etsutaro Munesato as manager of the airframe shop,

Rikichi Sasaki to manage the machine shop, Aijiro Hara as design superintendent, Lt Inoue as chief flying instructor, and Takehiko Satokata, a former reporter of *Jiji Shimpo* newspaper, as chief of administration. With these appointments the Akabane Aeroplane Manufacturing Works (Akabane Hikoki Seisakusho) was established. By January 1918 students were enrolled in the first pilot training course at Akabane and were using the No. 4 *Tsurugi-go* as their trainer.

Manufacture and sales expanded, with an improved engine magneto, experimental manufacture of the 130hp Benz engine, and a new aeroplane, the No.5 *Tsurugi-go*. The No.5 was a new design in that it was a fuselage-type tractor aeroplane, closely resembling the British B.E.2c reconnaissance biplane. Using the same 70hp Renault engine as earlier Kishi aeroplanes but now forward-facing, the cooling fan was eliminated and air baffles used instead. When needed, an additional fuel tank could be installed in the front cockpit to give an endurance of 8 hours.

After its completion in November 1917, Lt Inoue made a few ground taxi-ing tests but soon he left the company and the aeroplane then sat idle in a hangar. After three years it went to aviator Kinzo Negishi, a graduate from the Akabane Flying School. Negishi worked on the aeroplane over the next six months to gain an airworthiness certificate from the Aviation

Bureau that had begun to set standards in the summer of 1921. He named his rejuvenated aeroplane the *Hagoromo-go* (*Robe of Feathers*), and hangared it at the Nakajima Airfield at Ojima. On the night of 18 August that year, a fire destroyed the hangar containing three SPAD XIIIs, three Nakajima aeroplanes and the *Hagoromo-go*.

Single-engine two-bay biplane trainer. Wooden structure with fabric covering. Nose-mounted roll-over skids. Two seats in open cockpits.

70hp Kishi-Renault engine, driving a two-bladed wooden propeller.

Span 13m (42ft 8in); length 9m (29ft 6¼in); height 2.70m (8ft 10¼in).

Empty weight 500kg (1,102lb).

Maximum speed (calculated) 60kt (69mph).

One built in November 1917.

Kishi No. 6 *Tsurugi-go* Aeroplane

In the autumn of 1918, the Akabane Aeroplane Manufacturing Works was awarded an initial Army contract for four Maurice Farman Type Mo–6s. At about that time, through the influence of Viscount Shimpei Goto, Dr Kishi received the support of a noted businessman, Soichiro Asano, and they reorganized and expanded the company, undertook the manufacture of automobiles, and established a flying-cadet programme for school-age boys at the aerodrome.

Less attention was given to the production order for the new No.6 *Tsurugi-go* Aeroplane, and therefore the design reverted to the earlier Maurice Farman Type Mo–4 so as to use existing parts. At this time, the Kishi iron ore mining business at Osore-yama in Aomori Prefecture, had failed, and Kishi became heavily in debt. The popular period of the Farman biplanes had passed and the Army cancelled further orders, forcing the Akabane Aeroplane Manufacturing Works and its flying activities to be closed in March 1921. Dr Kishi abandoned aviation and became a director of the Electricity Bureau of Tokyo, thus ending the name of Kishi in aviation.

Fukuda Light Aeroplane Manufacturing Works (Fukuda Kei Hikoki Seisakusho)

Fukuda/Hitachi HT-3 Research Glider.

Located in Amagasaki City, Hyogo Prefecture, on the western edge of Osaka, this company was established, in about 1939 or 1940, for the building of gliders and wooden sub-assemblies for Army trainers. Very few designs of its own were developed. Sometime during the Pacific War, Fukuda joined with the San-in Aeroplane Co Ltd, also a manufacturer of wooden components for aircraft.

Fukuda Hikari Research-2 Motor Glider

At the request of the Aviation Bureau in 1940, Keicho Yo of the Fukuda Light Aeroplane Manufacturing Works designed a motorized glider powered by the same type of Scott 16–28hp engine installed in the Tachikawa TS–1 lightplane. The Fukuda aeroplane was completed in July 1941 and was the second motorized glider built in Japan, preceded only by the Nippon Hachi Motor Glider.

It was a low-wing monoplane

Fukuda Hikari Research-2 Motor Glider.

having a slightly inverted gull configuration at the roots making possible a shorter undercarriage. The wing had an aspect ratio of 13.75, which was equivalent to that used on sailplanes, and was equipped with spoilers.

The first flight was made at Osaka No.2 Airfield on 5 August, 1941, piloted by Isamu Oda, a holder of a first-class licence for both powered aircraft and sailplanes. Test flights exceeded expectations. Calculated data as a glider indicated a minimum sink-rate of 1.03m/sec, minimum level-flight speed of 36.5kt producing a glide ratio of 18.3. Optimum glide ratio was to be 18.6. Sinking speed at a best gliding speed of 38.3kt was 1.06m/sec. With the propeller stationary, a horizontal positioning would produce the best results. It carried the registration J-BFHN.

Single-engine monoplane powered-glider. Wooden structure covered with fabric and plywood. Pilot in closed cockpit.

16–28hp Scott Flying Squirrel two-cylinder two-stroke air-cooled inverted inline engine, driving a two-bladed wooden propeller.

Span 13m (42ft 8in); length 6.95m (22ft 9½in); height 1.70m (5ft 7in); wing area 12.3sq m (132.4sq ft).

Empty weight 210kg (463lb); loaded weight 300kg (661lb).

Maximum speed 67.5kt (78mph); cruising speed 48kt (55mph); landing speed 32.5kt (37.5mph); climb to

1,000m (3,280ft) in 10min 30sec; absolute ceiling 3,100m (10,170ft).

One built in 1941.

Fukuda/Hitachi HT-3 Research Glider

This aeroplane was a 60 percent scaled-down version of the Hitachi HT–3 Medium Passenger Transport that was to be flown as a towed research glider. It was manufactured by Fukuda at the request of the Aviation Bureau that sponsored the development of a domestic service type transport. It was felt that better performance data could be acquired from this glider version than from a wind-tunnel model. The wing aspect ratio was 8.78. As a glider, it had simulated engine nacelles as well as having the undercarriage in the retracted position.

The glider was first flown on 17 December, 1940, piloted by Isamu Oda, a noted glider pilot, at Osaka No.2 Airfield. This glider carried only the pilot but the actual HT–3 transport was to have a crew of two and accommodation for eight passengers. It was at this time, however, that priority was directed to military aircraft, causing the HT–3 to be terminated at the mock-up stage.

Low-wing monoplane glider. Wooden structure with fabric and plywood covering. Pilot in enclosed cockpit.

Span 12.21m (40ft); length 9.42m (30ft 11in); height 1.25m (4ft 1¼in); wing area 16.4sq m (176.533sq ft).

Empty weight 250kg (551lb); loaded weight 350kg (771lb).

Gliding speed 41–49kt (47–56.5mph); towing speed 70kt (81mph); landing speed 33kt (38mph); sink rate 1.46–1.71m/sec; gliding ratio 14.3–14.7.

One built in 1940.

Fukunaga Aeroplane Manufacturing Works (Fukunaga Hikoki Seisakusho)

Fukunaga Tenryu 6 Long-range Racing Aeroplane.

One of few privately financed companies to be classed as a manufacturer of aircraft was founded by Asao Fukunaga from Ikeda-cho, Osaka. He was first associated with aviation when in 1917 he imported a Blériot 25 which he called the Tenryu 1. He then built an imitation of a Caudron-type tractor biplane in the hangar of the former Sempu Flying School in Yokkaichi, southeast of Lake Biwa. Designated Tenryu 2, it failed to fly because it was underpowered with a 25hp Anzani engine. It was used instead as a ground taxiing trainer. Recognizing his need for further knowledge and experience in aviation, Fukunaga attended the Itoh Flying School in April 1918 at Tsudanuma and acquired a graduate certificate within two months of starting his training.

Fukunaga Tenryu 3 Trainer

To help Fukunaga establish a flying school of his own, Itoh released the Emi 2 Aeroplane to him and took it to Osaka. Using numerous fields in trying to find a suitable place for his flying school, the aeroplane was

Fukunaga Tenryu 3 Trainer.

frequently damaged and repaired. Eventually Fukunaga settled on the dry river bed of Tenryu River in Kakezuka-cho, Iwata-gun, Shizuoka Prefecture, near his family's place of origin, where he established in November 1919 what was at first the Fukunaga Aeroplane Research Studio. Because of the many repairs and modifications, his aeroplane was so unlike the original Emi 2 Aeroplane that he renamed it the Tenryu 3 Aeroplane, a name he applied in retrospect to the two previous aircraft and continued to use, numerically sequenced, to those that followed.

The Tenryu 3 was used to provide flying training for his younger brothers, Shiro and Goro, followed by other students who were merely allowed to taxi the aeroplane since the 1911 Grégoire Gyp engine was all but worn out and difficult to adjust. (*see* Itoh Emi 2).

Single-engine tractor biplane trainer. Wooden structure with fabric covering. Student and instructor in open cockpit.

45hp Grégoire Gyp four-cylinder inline water-cooled engine, driving a two-bladed wooden propeller.

Span, upper 9.75m (32ft); lower

7.92m (26ft); length 5.93m (19ft 5½in); wing area 20.8sq m (223.896sq ft).
   Maximum speed 48kt (55mph).
   One built in 1917.

Fukunaga Tenryu 6 Long-range Racing Aeroplane

Two aeroplanes that followed the Tenryu 3 Trainer were the 70hp Renault-powered Tenryu 4 Trainer, an aeroplane very difficult to fly, and the Tenryu 5 ground taxi-ing monoplane trainer that was powered by a converted 8hp Deluxe automobile engine. Little else is known about these aeroplanes.

Fukunaga's next design was the Tenryu 6 Long-range Racing Aeroplane, his first successful and practical design. Tomizo Asami, chief editor of the monthly magazine *Hikokai (Flight World)*, assisted with the design. They followed the American trend in design, producing an aeroplane very much like the Curtiss JN-4. The two-bay strut- and wire-braced wings were without dihedral and of RAF 15 aerofoil section. The engine was a 180hp Hispano-Suiza purchased from the British import firm, Sale & Frazar Ltd. In the hope of achieving greater success with this aeroplane, its construction was supervised by Kihachiro Ohta from the Itoh Airfield.

Completed in July 1921, and tested, it was entered in the Third Prize-winning Airmail Flying Contest in August 1921, flown by Asao Fukunaga's younger brother

Fukunaga Tenryu 7 Trainer.

Shiro. The competition flight course was from Yoyogi Parade Grounds in Tokyo to Morioka, 325 statute air-miles to the north. Covering the distance in 4hr 18min including an emergency landing at Ohkawara, Miyagi Prefecture, because of engine problems, the Tenryu 6 was disqualified as were the other three participants because of making unscheduled landings or becoming lost.

That same year, in November, Fukunaga entered the Tenryu 6 in the Fourth Prize-winning Airmail Flying Contest, between Kanazawa on the coastline of the Sea of Japan and Hiroshima in southern Honshu. This time, an emergency landing at Okayama was caused by bad weather, and therefore after recording 5hr 4min of flying time to reach the destination, the aircraft's capability was firmly established. It carried Japanese registration: J-TARS.

Single-engine long-range racing biplane. Two in open cockpits, one when extra fuel tank was installed in front cockpit.

180hp Hispano-Suiza eight-cylinder vee water-cooled engine, driving a two-bladed wooden propeller.

Span 11.37m (37ft 3½in); length 7.785m (25ft 6½in); wing area 32.5sq m (349.83sq ft).

Empty weight 814kg (1,794lb); loaded weight 1,200kg (2,645lb).

Maximum speed 84kt (97mph); landing speed 43kt (50mph); service ceiling 3,000m (9,843ft); endurance 3hr, with added fuel tank in front seat 9hr.

One built in July 1921.

Fukunaga Tenryu 7 Trainer

This was a small two-seat trainer closely resembling Sopwith types, designed by Tomizo Asami in 1921. It was powered by an 80hp Le Rhône engine imported by Sale & Frazar Ltd. Dimensions for the fuselage were determined by limitations imposed for railway transport to and from flying competition locations. Its two-bay wings were strut- and wire-braced and there was only dihedral on the lower wing, USA–1 foil-section was used. Completed in November 1921, it was used as a trainer for a short period.

Single-engine biplane trainer. Wooden structure with fabric covering. Pupil and instructor in open cockpits.

80hp Le Rhône nine-cylinder air-cooled rotary engine, driving a two-bladed wooden propeller.

Span 9.149m (30ft); length 6.17m (20ft 3in); wing area 24sq m (258.342sq ft).

Empty weight 685kg (1,510lb); loaded weight 922kg (2,032lb).

Maximum speed 79kt (91mph); landing speed 33kt (38mph); service ceiling 5,000m (16,404ft); endurance 2hr.

One built in November 1921.

Fukunaga Tenryu 8 Trainer

The Fukunaga Aeroplane Research Studio acquired as company president, Tetsuo Hasegawa, a prosperous landowner in Hamamatsu, who reorganized the company and gave it the new name Fukunaga Aeroplane Manufacturing Works, effective from 10 October, 1921. Asao Fukunaga remained exclusively the business manager, leaving all flying activities as the responsibility of Shiro Fukunaga.

In January 1922, Tomizo Asami began the design of a new aeroplane at the request of Pilot Third-class Shiro Yoshida of Kouchi Prefecture. It was basically a two-seat trainer but with provision for a long-range fuel tank to be installed in the front cockpit as with the Tenryu 6. It was completed in April 1921 and called the Tenryu 8.

One of the worst of the early aviation related accidents in Japan occurred with this aeroplane on 18 June, 1921, attracting considerable news coverage. While landing at Hata-gun, Kouchi Prefecture, after making demonstration flights over the city, Yoshida lost control of the aeroplane and it flew into the spectators, killing four and injuring four others. This was not only the worst civil aviation accident in the Taisho era, but it happened four days after the crash of the Tenryu 9 about to be described. Because of this tragedy, pilot Yoshida had no further involvement with aviation.

Single-engine two-bay biplane trainer. Wooden structure with fabric covering. Pupil and instructor in open cockpits.

Fukunaga Tenryu 8 Trainer.

125hp Hall-Scott six-cylinder inline water-cooled engine, driving a two-bladed wooden propeller.

Span 11.71m (38ft 5in); length 7.65m (25ft 1in); height 2.81m (9ft 2½in); wing area 34sq m (366sq ft).

Empty weight 611kg (1,347lb); loaded weight 820kg (1,807lb).

Maximum speed 70kt (81mph) at sea level; service ceiling 4,000m (13,123ft); endurance 2hr.

One built in April 1921.

Fukunaga Tenryu 9 Trainer

To provide newer equipment for the Training Department of the Fukunaga Airfield, a trainer was designed by Tomizo Asami using a 70hp Renault engine previously used on a Maurice Farman Type Mo–4 pusher aeroplane. It was completed in June 1922 and is said to have been stable and ideal as a primary trainer.

On 14 June, 1922, the aeroplane was submitted for Aviation Bureau evaluation which included typical instructor/pupil training flights. Immediately after one of the take offs, the engine failed, and the aeroplane entered a right turn back towards the field during which the aeroplane stalled, entered a spin and crashed. The pupil, Ryoichi Kaneko, later died from his injuries, while Shiro Fukunaga, the instruc-tor, was only slightly injured. The aeroplane was extensively damaged.

Single-engine biplane trainer. Wooden structure covered with fabric. Pupil and instructor in open cockpits.

70hp Renault eight-cylinder vee air-cooled engine, driving a two-bladed wooden propeller.

Span 10m (32ft 9½in); length 7.017m (23ft 0¼in); height 2.70m (8ft 10¼in); wing area 30sq m (322.927sq ft).

Empty weight 376kg (829lb); loaded weight 531kg (1,170lb).

Maximum speed 59kt (68mph); service ceiling 3,000m (9,843ft); endurance 2hr.

One built in June 1922.

Fukunaga Tenryu 10 Passenger Transport

The Fukunaga Aeroplane Manufacturing Works built a long-range aeroplane to participate in the Prize Winning Flight Competition to Shanghai sponsored by the Imperial Flying Association to be held in the spring of 1921. The design by Tomizo Asami was undertaken with the assistance of Yoshihisa Kinoshita, an engineer in charge of aeroplane parts manufacture for the Japanese Navy at the Aeroplane Department of Nihon Jidosha KK (Japan Automobile Co Ltd) at Tameike, Akasaka, Tokyo.

To compete with the 400hp Liberty-powered Itoh 22 *Yamagat-akinen-go* that was to be the Itoh Airfield's entry, they purchased a stock 300hp Fiat engine from a Yokohama dealer. The Tenryu 10 was a large two-bay equal-span biplane with the fuselage filling the gap. The long engine and large frontal radiator gave the aeroplane a very nose-heavy appearance.

The cross-axle undercarriage was quite short and the V struts had triangular fairings. The horn-balanced rudder was attached to a large vertical fin to relieve control loads, a new feature in Japan at that time. The cabin was between the wings and the pilot's open cockpit was behind the cabin.

Before the aeroplane was completed, the competition flight to Shanghai was cancelled, and the design was modified by eliminating the large fuselage fuel tank and converting the cabin to accommodate four passengers. The open cockpit had side-by-side seats for two occupants. The Tenryu 10 was then the largest passenger-carrying aeroplane in Japan. It was completed in late October 1922 and first test flown by the brothers Shiro and Goro Fukunaga for 38 minutes on 26 October, 1922.

The aeroplane received its type certification by the Aviation Bureau

Fukunaga Tenryu 10 Passenger Transport.

and the following month participated in the Tokyo–Osaka Round-
robin Airmail Flight Competition.
While enroute, because of engine
trouble, an emergency landing was
made on the dry bed of the
Kizugawa River in Nara Prefecture
and the aeroplane was therefore disqualified. Upon entering the Fourth
Prize-winning Flight Competition
held at Shimoshizu Airfield, in
June 1923, Shiro Fukunaga flew
this aeroplane for 3hr 48min in the
duration category but ranked only
fourth. For this event, the 200-litre
fuel tanks in the upper wing were
replaced by a 500-litre tank in the
cabin. The aircraft's poor showing
was attributed to its being underpowered, the 300hp Fiat engine
actually produced only 250hp.

Single-engine cabin biplane. Ply-
covered wooden fuselage, wing structure of wood covered with fabric. Crew
of two in open cockpit, cabin for four
passengers.
300hp Fiat six-cylinder inline water-
cooled engine, driving a two-bladed
wooden propeller.
Span 12.95m (42ft 5¾in); length
9.40m (30ft 10in); wing area 37.4sq m
(402.583sq ft).
Empty weight 1,100kg (2,425lb);
loaded weight 1,818kg (4,007lb).
Maximum speed 97kt (112mph).
One built in 1922.

In the later years of the Taisho
reign (ending in 1926), Japanese
civil aviation gained in popularity,
yet the Fukunaga Airfield activities
failed to prosper. This was attributed to their being isolated from
the Osaka and Tokyo centres of
aviation where other companies
continued to grow. Furthermore,
following the devastating earthquake in the Kanto Planes area
(Tokyo), the government control
over aviation became stronger, and
the three brothers of the Fukunaga
organization gradually and separately withdrew. The main business of the company became the
repair and conversion of surplus
military aircraft. In 1929, the
company moved to Mikatagahara,
a suburb of Hamamatsu, and
changed its name to the Hamamatsu Hikoki Seisakusho (Hamamatsu Aeroplane Manufacturing
Works), closing finally in 1936.

Gasuden (Tokyo Gas & Electrical Industry Co Ltd) (Tokyo Gasu Denki Kogyo KK)

This company entered aircraft
manufacturing in 1933 as a private
venture to build small transport
aircraft. Known initially as the
Tokyo Gasu Kogyo KK (Tokyo
Gas Industry Co Ltd), the company was actually formed in 1910
and was a builder of electrical parts
and glass-lined hardware. It was
located at Narihira-cho, Honjo-ku,
Tokyo, with Goro Matsukata as
president and Isamu Hoshiko as
director. In 1913, the name was
changed to Tokyo Gasu Denki
Kogyo KK (Tokyo Gas and
Electrical Industry Co Ltd), better
known by its acronym Gasuden.
The company produced shell fuses,
marine fittings, marine auxiliary
engines, and other types of engines
before the outbreak of the First
World War. By the time the war
ended, the expanding company had
moved its head office to Ohte-
machi, Koujimachi-ku, Tokyo, with
its main factory at Ebara-gun, also
in Tokyo. It was there that it manufactured aero-engines as the first
Japanese civil company to do so,
along with military cars, machine-
guns and similar items. Head office
moved once again, when it was
relocated in 1922 at Ohmori,
Tokyo.

Aircraft engines became the first
focal point for the company within
the aero industry. Under the leadership of Isamu Hoshiko it became a
sub-contractor for the 100hp Daimler under the supervision of the
Army Tokyo Artillery Arsenal.
Other engines that soon followed
were the 80hp and 120hp Le
Rhône and 230hp Salmson under
licences from France, and the
130hp Benz engine under contract
for the Navy. By 1929, the
company had developed its own
130hp Jimpu seven-cylinder air-
cooled radial, and a year later, the
larger 300hp Tempu. After each
had passed a 50hr continuous running test, these engines became
Gasuden's main products.

Wishing to branch into the building of aircraft, Sei-ichi Yamashita,
formerly a Navy Commander assigned to the Provisional Military
Balloon Research Association, joined the newly formed Department
of Airframes in 1932 at the Ohmori
factory. Chief aircraft designer for
the company was Shozo Kawaguchi, formerly with Kawasaki,
and production superintendent was
Tomiji Kudo. Kudo had gained his
earlier aircraft experience when
working with Dewoitine in France.
With this nucleus of engineers and
designers established, the company
embarked upon aircraft designs of
its own.

Gasuden KR-1 Small Passenger Transport

As an initial aircraft design in 1932,
the company embarked on a project
to build a small passenger aeroplane

*Gasuden KR-1 Small Passenger
Transport.*

suitable for the route between Tokyo and Osaka. The plan was for it to have a top speed of 200km/h (108kt) and be easy to manufacture and maintain with a low operating cost, and, with one pilot and three passengers, was to be able to operate from small, relatively unimproved airfields.

What developed was a near copy of the de Havilland Fox Moth, but powered by the company's own Gasuden Jimpu 150hp radial engine. An opportunity to closely examine the type came when the Machinery Department of Mitsui & Co imported three Fox Moths for resale in Japan. Two became the Army's *Aikoku-go* small ambulance aeroplane, while the other was delivered to a pre-committed buyer after first being examined by Gasuden. The Fox Moth was a well liked light passenger aeroplane of which 98 were manufactured in Britain, with others built in Canada and Australia.

The KR-1, which stands for Kogata Ryokaku-ki (Small Passenger Aircraft), was of the typical de Havilland design, with wooden airframe of spruce, faired with plywood and covered with fabric, and required skilled craftsmen for this type of woodworking. The undercarriage was interchangeable with twin metal-floats manufactured by Deruta (Delta) Shipyard of Chiba City.

The first prototype was test flown by Mansaku Akaike from the Tachikawa Airfield on 23 December, 1933, with predicted and satisfactory results. Its first public demonstration flight took place at Tokyo's Haneda Airport on 27 January, 1934. Much attention was given to the aeroplane when it was mounted on twin floats for a second public demonstration from Tokyo Bay near Haneda on 15 March, 1934. It was given the appropriately illustrative name *Chidori-go* (Plover) the shore bird with a short tail and long pointed wings. As a floatplane the *Chidori-go* was confined to operation from reasonably calm water and its payload was reduced.

Seven aeroplanes were built in all. Three KR-1s, including the prototype, J-BBJI, J-BBMI, J-BBNI,

with wooden twin-floats, were operated by Nippon Koku Yuso Kenkyusho of Sakai City, near Osaka, on the regular routes Osaka–Shikoku and Osaka–Shirahama, as well as on air taxi services. Two

others were delivered to Taiwan Kokubo Gaikai (Taiwan National Defence Volunteer Association) and an additional two to the Manchurian Coast Guard at Eikou (now Yingkou, China).

Single-engine passenger-carrying single-bay biplane, twin wheel or twin-float undercarriage. Wooden structure with fabric covering. Pilot and three passengers (floatplane: two passengers).

150–160hp Gasuden Jimpu 3 seven-cylinder air-cooled radial engine, driving a fixed-pitch Mitsubishi-Reed two-bladed metal propeller.

	Landplane	*Seaplane*
Span	9.20m (30ft 2¼in)	9.20m (30ft 2¼in)
Length	7.60m (24ft 11¼in)	7.88m (25ft 10¼in)
Height	2.70m (8ft 10¼in)	3.40m (11ft 2in)
Wing area	22sq m (236.813sq ft)	22sq m (236.813sq ft)
Empty weight	576kg (1,270lb)	680kg (1,499lb)
Loaded weight	964kg (2,125lb)	988kg (2,178lb)
Wing loading	43.8kg/sq m (8,971lb/sq ft)	45.5kg/sq m (9,319lb/sq ft)
Power loading	6.48kg/hp (14.2lb/hp)	6.66kg/hp (14.6lb/hp)
Maximum speed at sea level	107kg (123mph)	102kt (117mph)
Cruising speed	86kt (99mph)	81kt (93mph)
Climb to	3,000m (9,843ft)	3,000m (9,843ft)
in	15min 50sec	17min 6sec
Service ceiling	4,200m (13,779ft)	3,800m (12,467ft)
Range	351nm (404sm)	324nm (373sm)
Endurance	4hr	4hr

Seven built from 1933 to 1934.

Gasuden KR-2 Small Passenger Transport

Gasuden KR-2 Small Passenger Transport.

The KR-2 was a redesign of the KR-1 with the intention of improving the speed and range of the KR-1 with the same engine and aircraft weight. In an attempt to achieve this, the lower wings were reduced in span by 2.4m and upper and lower wings were given curved tips. These changes reduced the wing area from the KR-1's 22sq m

(236sq ft) to 17.68sq m (190sq ft). The top wing no longer had the 3-degree sweepback of the KR-1, and the trailing-edge cutout above the cockpit was eliminated. Ailerons were fitted to both wings and interconnected. As a result of the changes cruising speed was increased by 11kt (13mph), and range extended by approximately 100km

(62sm) and there was a slight increase in payload. Originally, the KR–2 was equipped with a side-opening canopy for the pilot, but this was changed later to an open cockpit like that of the KR–1.

The prototype KR–2 was first flown at Haneda on 17 November, 1934. As expected, the take off and landing distances were greater and the rate of climb not as good as the earlier aeroplane's. While in production the Navy showed an interest in the aeroplane as a liaison transport after certain modifications were made in the flying control surfaces.

The KR–2 was an excellent 150hp class light passenger aeroplane in general performance. It won a good reputation because of economy of operation and suitability for its intended task. The first prototype, J-BLIB, with the name Teikoku Hiko Kyokai No.12 (Imperial Flying Association No.12) with individual name *Kaigai-Doho-go (Japanese in Overseas)* was leased to Tokyo Koku Yuso-sha on 2 March, 1935, for passenger service. Another, Teikoku Hiko Kyokai No.14, and named *Chosen Doho-go (Japanese in Korea)* was leased to Chosen Koku Jigyo-sha on 19 May, 1936. Both aircraft were used primarily for air-taxi work and sightseeing flights. An additional KR–2 was delivered to Tokyo Koku and one other to the Manchurian Coast Guard in Eikou (Yingkou, China). Two others were purchased by the *Yomiuri Shimbun* newspaper, and later production aircraft were delivered to the Navy for liaison/transport duty. The Navy used the aeroplanes for transport between land bases and aircraft carriers. In all, nineteen KR–1s and KR–2s were built.

Single-engine unequal-span passenger biplane, wheel or twin-float undercarriage. Wooden structure with fabric covering. Pilot and three passengers (floatplane; two passengers).

150–160hp Gasuden Jimpu 3 seven-cylinder air-cooled radial engine, driving a Mitsubishi-Reed fixed-pitch two-bladed metal propeller.

	Landplane	Seaplane
Span	9.20m (30ft 2¼in)	9.20m (30ft 2¼in)
Length	7.71m (25ft 3½in)	7.90m (25ft 11in)
Height	2.70m (8ft 10¼in)	3.40m (11ft 2in)
Wing area	17.68sq m (190.312sq ft)	17.68sq m (190.312sq ft)
Empty weight	570kg (1,256lb)	680kg (1,499lb)
Loaded weight	980kg (2,160lb)	1,070kg (2,358lb)
Wing loading	55.4k/sq m (11.347lb/sq ft)	60.5kg/sq m (12.391lb/sq ft)
Power loading	6.53kg/hp (14.4lb/hp)	7.13kg/hp (15.7lb/hp)
Maximum speed at sea level	117kt (134mph)	108kt (125mph)
Cruising speed	97kt (112mph)	89kt (102mph)
Climb to in	3,000m (9,843ft) 20min 10sec	3,000m (9,843ft) 24min
Service ceiling	4,500m (14,763ft)	4,000m (13,123ft)
Range	405nm (466sm)	378nm (435sm)
Endurance	4.33hr	4.33hr

Twelve built from 1934 to 1939.

Gasuden Model 1, 2 and 3 Trainers

At its Ohmori factory in 1936, Gasuden designed a new trainer. This aeroplane used the same engine and undercarriage as the KR–2, but differed by having three interchangeable wings to be used for the three different grades of pilot training. Model 1 was the primary trainer biplane with equal-span wings, Model 2 was a sesquiplane intermediate trainer, and Model 3 was the advanced trainer, a high-wing monoplane. All other components were common to all three aircraft.

The first prototype of Model 1 was completed in April 1937. Although the engine remained the 150hp Jimpu 3, it was fitted with a wide-chord NACA cowling. The upper wings were interesting in that they were of gull-wing design with their roots on the centre line of the fuselage. This design was later changed to a straight wing supported by cabane struts. Dual controls were provided in tandem open cockpits. Although this was a primary trainer, it was much faster than its contemporaries. The Navy

Gasuden Model 1 Trainer before the gull-wing was changed to a straight-wing.

Gasuden Model 2 Trainer sesquiplane.

evaluated the aeroplane but showed no further interest.

The Model 2, with its sesquiplane configuration, had a straight-through top wing instead of the gull wing. The Model 2 was first shown to the public in 1940 as the only intermediate type trainer available to the civil market as an aerobatic sportsplane. The sole Model 2 aircraft was registered J-BBFK. The Model 3 was not built because there was no interest in the project.

Model 2

Single-engine biplane trainer. Welded steel-tube fuselage and wooden wings with fabric covering. Crew of two in open cockpits. Could be converted to single-seat layout.

150–180hp Gasuden Jimpu 3 seven-cylinder air-cooled radial engine, driving a Mitsubishi-Reed fixed-pitch two-bladed metal propeller.

Span 9.291m (30ft 5¾in), lower wing

Gasuden Koken Long-range Research Aircraft.

5.768m (18ft 11¼in); length 6.687m (21ft 11¼in); height 2.859m (9ft 4½in); wing area 15.3sq m (164.693sq ft); upper wing 10.46sq m (112sq ft), lower wing 4.85sq m (52sq ft).

Empty weight 650kg (1,433lb); loaded weight 906kg (1,997lb); wing loading 59.2kg/sq m (12.125lb/sq ft); power loading 5.03kg/hp (11lb/hp).

Maximum speed 119kt (137mph) at sea level; cruising speed 87kt (100mph); climb to 3,000m (9,843ft) in 14min 15 sec; service ceiling 4,900m (16,076ft); range 270nm (310sm); endurance 3.1hr.

One Model 1 built in 1937 and one Model 2 in 1940.

Gasuden Koken Long-range Research Aircraft

During the 1920s and 1930s, aviation records were constantly being set in all categories throughout the world; distance, duration, speed, and altitude. It was appropriate that Japan should make its mark in one or more of these events. In 1931 a plan was initiated by the Aeronautical Research Institute for a flight to achieve the greatest nonstop closed-course distance. Because the Institute retained a close alliance with Tokyo Imperial University, although formally separated from it in 1921, the plan was submitted to the Ministry of Education which led to approval by the Diet for a grant to finance the project.

Study and specifications for the aeroplane began in December 1932, with many staff members of the University being involved in the design and engineering of this major undertaking. Committees were formed under skilled leadership for the engineering of specific systems. Heading the project was Dr Koroku Wada, assisted by the Department Manager of Powerplants, Professor Keikichi Tanaka. A stronger incentive for the programme while still in the design stage came when the French claimed a new world distance record of 10,601km (6.587sm) with the Blériot Zappata 110 in March 1932, a distance far short of the projected 13,000km (8.078sm) that the Japanese were aiming for.

Upon completion of the basic design in August 1934, Tokyo Gasu Denki Kogyo KK was selected as the airframe manufacturer. The engine was to be a modified version of the BMW VIII built under licence by Kawasaki Kokuki KK.

The most important aspect of the project centred on the aerofoil. Those selected were known as the Koken Model 4 to be used at the root (17.5 percent thickness) tapering to Model 11 at the wingtip (4 percent thickness) having an overall aspect ratio of 8.7. Fuel was carried in fourteen tanks within the wing, all interconnected as one system in order to maintain a constant centre of gravity. A very advanced feature at that time was a fully-retractable undercarriage with sliding fairings, the first of its kind. The slender fuselage was of semi-monocoque design, having the open cockpit set to port that could be faired over flush with the surface to reduce drag while in flight.

Construction of the aeroplane was slow in starting because final design was not begun until August 1934 and tooling began the follow-

Gasuden TR-1 Medium Passenger Transport.

ing year. Due to new concepts in metal fabrication incorporated into this design and lack of Japanese experience, production was slow and not completed until 31 March, 1937. The components of the aircraft were moved to a hangar of Kaibo Gikai at Haneda Airport where its assembly was completed on 8 April. The long awaited first flight of the Koken finally took place on 25 May, 1937, with Major Yuzo Fujita as the pilot. He, and the other two crew members, Master Sergeant Fukujiro Takahashi as co-pilot, and assistant engineer Chika-kichi Sekine as flight engineer, were all from the Army Air Technical Research Institute at Tachikawa. This Army air crew remained fully involved with the project from the start, and preparation for the long-distance flight continued for another year.

Just a month later, between 17 and 20 June, 1937, the Russians in an ANT–25 made their famous first nonstop flight over the North Pole from Moscow to Vancouver in Washington State on the United States west coast. The Japanese Koken and the Russian ANT–25 were strikingly similar in layout. Although the Russian flight covered 5,288 straight-course miles, the distance planned for the Japanese flight would far exceed this.

At 0455hr on the morning of 13 May, 1938, the Koken took off from Kisarazu Naval Air Base on the east side of Tokyo Bay to begin its record breaking flight. It was monitored by Navy Lieut-Cdr Tomokazu Kajiki who was the FAI's representative in Japan. The route was a four-sided course of 401.759km (249sm) from Kisarazu to Choshi, Ohta, Hiratsuka and back to Kisarazu. After 29 laps, the aeroplane landed at Kisarazu at 1921 hr after establishing a closed-course record of 11,651.011km (7,239.58sm).This record stood for 15 months but was broken by the Italian Savoia Marchetti SM.82 in August 1939 with 12,936km (8,038sm) flown. However, the Koken's flight remains the only record to be established by the Japanese with FAI recognition.

After the flight, the Koken was put into the Kaibo Gikai hangar at Haneda and was used occasionally for tests by the Aeronautical Research Institute. Reportedly, the last flight of this aeroplane was on 14 June, 1939, when flown on a memorial flight at the funeral of Major Fujita, the pilot who had established the record, but who had been killed when flying in combat in China. It has been reported that the Koken survived the Pacific War, only to be burned with other Japanese aeroplanes at Haneda Airport after the war.

Single-engine low-wing cantilever monoplane with retractable undercarriage. All metal construction with fabric covered flying controls and outer wing panels. Crew of three.
700–715hp Kawasaki twelve-cylinder vee water-cooled engine, driving a Sumitomo SW-4 two-bladed metal-covered wooden propeller.
Span 27.93m (91ft 7¾in); length 15.06m (49ft 5in); height 3.60m (11ft 9¾in); wing area 87.3sq m (939.720sq ft).
Empty weight 4,225kg (9,314lb); loaded weight 9,216kg (20,317lb) for record flight; wing loading 105.9kg/sq m (21.690lb/sq ft); power loading 11.5kg/hp (25.3lb/hp).
Maximum speed 135kt (155mph) at sea level, 132kt (152mph) at 2,000m (6,562ft); cruising speed 114kt (131-mph) at 2,000m (6,562ft); service ceiling 3,410m (11,187ft). Performance figures at 9,000kg (19,841lb) all-up weight.
One built in 1937.

Gasuden TR–1 Medium Passenger Transport

Gasuden undertook another private venture in 1937, the development of a high-performance medium passenger transport as a feeder liner. According to unofficial Aviation Bureau information, it was intended as a replacement for the Mitsubishi Hinazuru medium passenger transport that was developed from the Airspeed Envoy. This was the TR–1, TR standing for Chugata (Tyu-gata) Ryokaku-ki, meaning medium passenger transport. The company was able to produce this all-metal aircraft because it had gained experience with the manufacture of the Koken Long-range Research Aircraft, and Gasuden's chief designer Akira Murayama applied his Koken experience to the TR–1.

Design features were quite advanced for that period in Japanese aircraft development. Specification for the new design was:

1. To have similar power and payload to that of the Airspeed Envoy, more than 162kt (186mph) maximum speed, and 810nm (930sm) range.

2. Two 240hp Gasuden Jimpu 5A engines. Wing flaps were to have large area and simple operating mechanism. Ailerons were also to operate as flaps. The retractable undercarriage was to be manually operated to ensure reliability.

3. Flaps, wheel brakes and fuel dump valve were to be pneumatically operated.

4. Because the fuselage had a narrow elliptical cross-section to reduce drag, the two pilots' seats were to be in tandem with dual control. Navigation and radio equipment were to be located in the rear co-pilot's position.

5. Passenger seats were staggered to allow maximum seat width in the narrow fuselage. Standard seating was four but could be increased to six. Large windows provided good cabin lighting and visibility for passengers. A lavatory was located in the rear of the cabin.

6. Conversion capability to be offered for aerial survey/observation, ambulance and crew training.

7. Cargo stowage in the nose, under the wing centre section of the fuselage and in the rear fuselage, for 30kg (66lb), 60kg (132lb) and 60kg respectively.

Uichi Suwa flew the first prototype, J-DAAH, for the first time at Haneda on 8 April, 1938. The aeroplane was found to have stability and control problems but these were corrected by increasing the area of the vertical tail surfaces. While under test, an agreement was reached whereby this aircraft would be delivered to the Taiwan Kokubo Gikai (Taiwan National Defence

Volunteer Association) and it was called Taiwan Giyu Gakko *Niitata-go*, meaning Taiwan Volunteers School, *Niitata*, *Niitata* being the highest mountain in Taiwan.

While being flight tested by Muramatsu on 22 June, 1938, the port undercarriage failed to lower. After burning off fuel for about two hours, an emergency landing was made with the port undercarriage still retracted. After repairs to the damaged structure, the aeroplane was shipped from Kobe to Taiwan. While en route an accident on board the ship caused further damage and the aeroplane was returned to the Gasuden Factory where it lingered indefinitely.

Twin-engined low-wing light transport. All-metal construction with fabric covered control surfaces. Retractable undercarriage. Crew of two with four-six passengers.

Two 240–280hp Gasuden Jimpu 5A nine-cylinder air-cooled radial engines, driving Sumitomo fixed-pitch two-bladed metal propellers.

Span 14.10m (46ft 3in); length 10.60m (34ft 9¼in); height 3.50m (11ft 5¾in) to top of radio mast; wing area 24.5sq m (263.724sq ft).

Empty weight 1,910kg (4,210lb); loaded weight 3,000kg (6,613lb); wing loading 122.4kg/sq m (25.069lb/sq ft); power loading 5.36kg/hp (11.8lb/hp).

Maximum speed at 2,800kg (6,172lb) 163kt (188mph) at sea level; cruising speed 135kt (156mph); climb to 3,000m (9,843ft) in 14min 47sec; service ceiling 4,380m 14,370ft); range 820m (942sm); endurance 6hr.

One built in 1938.

Gasuden TR-2 Medium Passenger Transport.

Gasuden TR-2 Medium Passenger Transport

The TR–2 was built to replace the TR–1 which had been badly damaged while being shipped to Taiwan. It was completed in October 1940, registered J-DAAJ, and named Taiwan Giyu Gakko No.2.

Compared to the TR–1, its wing span was slightly longer, giving it greater wing area. The helmeted cowling used on the TR–1 was replaced by a smooth contoured NACA cowling. The mainwheels protruded slightly from the nacelle when retracted to permit a safer landing in the event of undercarriage failure, as had happened with the TR–1.

In late November 1940, the completed aircraft was fitted with ferry tanks, and flown from Haneda to Taiwan by pilot Muramatsu for safe delivery. Although there were some shortcomings with the aeroplane, it was considered a practical medium-size passenger transport. With increase in weight due to design changes, performance was somewhat inferior to that of the TR–1.

Twin-engined low-wing light transport. All-metal construction with fabric-covered control surfaces. Retractable undercarriage. Crew of two and four-six passengers.

Two 240–280hp Gasuden Jimpu 5A nine-cylinder air-cooled radial engines, driving Sumitomo fixed-pitch two-bladed metal propellers.

Span 14.387m (47ft 2½in); length 10.984m (36ft 0¼in); height 4.193m (13ft 9in); wing area 25.6sq m (275.565 sq ft).

Empty weight 2,175kg (4,795lb); loaded weight 3,200kg (7,054lb); wing loading 125kg/sq m (25.6lb/sq ft); power loading 6.66kg/hp (14.6lb/hp).

Maximum speed 156kt (180mph) at 725m (2,378ft); cruising speed 136kt (156mph); climb to 2,000m (6,562ft) in 12min 26sec; service ceiling 3,150m (10,334ft).

One built in October 1940.

In May 1939, the Tokyo Gasu Denki Kogyo KK was dissolved by a merger with Hitachi Manufacturing Co Ltd, making this the Hitachi Aircraft Company Ltd, (Hitachi Kokuki KK) with its three plants at Ohmori, Tachikawa, and Haneda, all within the Tokyo suburbs. The Haneda plant remained primarily concerned with airframes, while the other two started engine production. The president of the new aircraft organization was Rohei Kohira, with managing director Senshu Yokota.

The company began design work in 1939 on the Hitachi HT-3 Medium Passenger Transport. This was sponsored through a grant made by the Aviation Bureau to advance the development of passenger aircraft in Japan. The concept was a very slender and graceful design that resembled the later twin-engined de Havilland Dove. However, as the aeroplane entered the mock-up stage, the project was suspended because of the more urgent need for military aircraft.

By this time, all three plants were manufacturing equipment for the Army. In July 1939, however, the Ministry of Navy requested the services of the Haneda plant, which was then assigned to it. Aircraft construction consisted primarily of the Navy designed Type 3 Primary Trainer (K2Y2) and the Type 93 Intermediate Trainer (K5Y1) later known as Willow by the Allies. Also in July 1939, the company started a new plant at Kawasaki, between Tokyo and Yokohama, which was devoted to the production of engine castings, and production began there in August of that year.

In February 1941 the Japanese Government ordered Hitachi to expand, and a site was selected across Tokyo Bay, and operation began the following year. In October 1941 the Ohmori plant came under Navy supervision and the Chiba plant from its inception produced equipment only for the Navy. The Tachikawa plant, the company's largest engine factory, remained under Army contract. From this time, no aircraft of Hitachi design were produced under that name.

Hirosho (Hiro Naval Arsenal) (Hiro Kaigun Kosho)

The Hiro Arsenal was established on 1 August, 1920, under the name of the Aircraft Department, Hiro Branch Arsenal, Kure Naval Arsenal, as the Navy's first real aircraft repair and manufacturing factory. At that time, two Naval aircraft factories were operating at Yokosuka and Sasebo, but space was very limited. To increase production capability for the Navy, the Kure Naval Arsenal expanded by establishing the Hiro Branch Arsenal three miles southeast of Kure on flat ground between the mouths of two rivers, the Hiro Ohkawa on the west and the Misakaiji-gawa on the east. This new factory, known by its acronym Hirosho, was completed in October 1921, and licence-production of the F.5 Flying-boats was begun. On 1 April, 1923, the Hiro Branch Arsenal was upgraded to the Hiro Naval Arsenal to which the Aircraft Department belonged.

Navy F.5 Flying-boat

As a result of the British Aviation Mission that helped train the Japanese Naval air force during 1921 and 1922, approximately ten types of British aircraft were taken to Japan by sea for instruction purposes. Among these was the Felixstowe F.5 built by Short Brothers, the aeroplane reputed to be the best of the large flying-boats. At that time, the Navy intended to build these aircraft for its own use, and had invited to Japan twenty-one engineers from Short Brothers for that purpose. This group, led by Shorts' engineer Dodds who arrived in Japan in April 1921, began work at the Ordnance Department of the Yokosuka Arsenal where the flying-boats were to be built. The Japanese contingent under British leadership were Capt (Ordnance) Ryuzo Tanaka, Capt (Ordnance) Tomasu Koyama, Lieut Kishichi Umakoshi, Lieut Misao Wada, Engineer Masasuke Hashimoto and others. The manufacture of the F.5 was the start of many years of large flying-boat construction in Japan.

In addition to the licensed manufacturing rights, Short Brothers supplied partially built assemblies to complete the first six* of the F.5, in addition to assembly tooling and instruction in the manufacturing process. These F.5s were assembled at Yokosuka Arsenal, with the first one completed in April 1921. Since the F.5 was already renowned throughout the world as an excellent twin-engined all-wood flying-boat, it was no surprise that those assembled in Japan had excellent performance. When the first of them visited Tokyo, with a fly past in October 1921, there was impressed public reaction to their, then, enormous size.

*According to British sources, Shorts exported seven Rolls-Royce Eagle powered and three Napier Lion powered flying-boats to Japan.

Hiro Navy F.5 Flying-boat.

Following these imported and Japanese-assembled aircraft, the flying-boat was put into full production at the Aircraft Department of the Hiro Naval Arsenal in the Kure area, beginning in October 1921. An additional forty F.5s were built by Aichi up until 1929.

The engines initially used in these aeroplanes were the imported Rolls-Royce Eagle, which developed 360hp. As work developed, the Engine Factory of the Hiro Arsenal manufactured their first licence-built 400hp Lorraine engines in August 1924. In 1925, the Hiro Arsenal experimentally installed these new engines in one of the flying-boats and designated it the F.1. As the power rating of the Lorraine was increased to 450hp, another flying-boat was equipped with them, to become the F.2. Although the Hiro Arsenal expected that both the F.1 and F.2 would be adopted as standard equipment, the prototype aircraft were never put into production because the design of the airframe was already considered obsolete as it was based on First World War construction concepts. In addition to the prototypes, there were modifications of others, primarily in

Hiro Experimental R-3 Flying-boat.

engine configurations, one version being powered by two 360hp Eagle direct-drive engines with faired nacelles, two-bladed propellers and Lamblin-type radiators.

Only the F.5 version was taken into Japanese Naval air service. They were used as long-range patrol aircraft from 1922 to 1930, from bases at Yokosuka and Sasebo. They gave impressive service during their operational life, and numerous newspaper accounts covered their long-range over-water flights; but also during this time there were numerous accidents with deaths and injuries, the result of engine problems, improper maintenance, and bad weather. Nevertheless, the F.5 made its mark in Japanese aviation history.

Experimental R-3 Flying-boat

All-metal flying-boat technology and experience having become available in Europe, the Navy decided that both Mitsubishi and the Hiro Naval Arsenal should manufacture aircraft of this type. Thus in the spring of 1923, the Navy sent Lieut Misao Wada and engineer Junichiro Nagahata of the Yokosuka Naval Arsenal to Germany and the Rohrbach company to study the new techniques, and Hiro sent Lieut (Ordnance) Jun Okamura to Rohrbach for the same purpose.

By 1925, components for one Rohrbach R 1 flying-boat manufactured in Copenhagen, and powered by two 360hp Rolls-Royce engines, reached Japan and the president of Rohrbach and an engineer, Paul Ludwig, went to assist with the assembly which was done at the Yokosuka Naval Arsenal where it was evaluated. Mitsubishi took the opportunity to establish the Mitsubishi-Rohrbach GmbH in Berlin where parts and components of flying-boats were manufactured, apparently to control the market in Japan. Not to be outdone, the Hiro Arsenal built a follow-on with sufficient changes to avoid infringements. This was called the R-3, differing from the R 1 and R-2 by having the 450hp Hiro-built Lorraine 2 engines mounted on newly configured struts. The squared-off wingtips were changed to rounded configuration, and a wing centre section without dihedral was added. The wings and hull were slightly larger, which accounted for an increase in weight. A change was made in the wing-mounted floats in that they were

Twin-engined biplane flying-boat. All wooden construction with ply covered hull and fabric-covered wings, tail and control surfaces. Originally crewed by four; two pilots, observer/bow gunner and flight engineer/rear gunner. Later crewed by six, adding navigator and radio operator.

Two 360hp Rolls-Royce Eagle twelve-cylinder vee water-cooled engines, driving four-bladed wooden propellers.

Two flexible 7.7mm machine-guns.

	Aircraft Technical Order	Japanese Navy Data
Span	31.59m (103ft 8in)	31.59m (103ft 8in)
Length	15.03m (49ft 4in)	15.16m (49ft 8¾in)
Height	5.75m (18ft 10¼in)	5.75m (18ft 10¼in)
Wing area	131.3sq m (1,413.347sq ft)	—
Empty weight	3,720kg (8,201lb)	3,784kg (8,342lb)
Loaded weight	5,627kg (12,405lb)	5,800kg (12,786lb)
Wing loading	42.7kg/sq m (8.7lb/sq ft)	44.1kg/sq m (9lb/sq ft)
Power loading	8.04kg/hp (17.7lb/hp)	8.05kg/hp (17.7lb/hp)
Maximum speed	89kt (102mph)	78kt (90mph)
Climb to	2,000m (6,562ft)	1,000m (3,280ft)
in	16min 06sec	15min
Service ceiling		3,550m (11,646ft)
Range	620nm (712sm)	
Endurance	7hr	8hr

Ten built by Yokosuka Arsenal (including six imported unassembled, ten (approx) by Hiro Arsenal, forty by Aichi.

This view of the R-3 more clearly shows the hull shape and marked dihedral.

square-sectioned to improve take off ability. In all, there was a slight increase in speed, but a reduction in rate of climb because of the greater weight. The most noticeable change was in the slight V-shape of the planing bottom.

Because of its excessive weight, the R-3 was not put into production, but aerodynamically the design had numerous innovations. Its cantilever wing with thick-section aerofoil and Wagner diagnonal tension-field structure, high wing loading and high aspect ratio were advancements in the state of the art. Square sections of the hull eased production adding strength but also bringing about skin distortion. The R-3's shortcomings, in addition to weight, were its poor ability to cope with waves of any size and its high power loading. Therefore, it was never accepted as an operational aeroplane but, like the Mitsubishi-built R-2 which influenced later designs for that company, so the R-3 influenced later Hiro designs. The contribution to design technology of these Type-R flying-boats was held in high regard by the Japanese aeronautical community.

Twin-engined shoulder-wing monoplane flying-boat. All-metal construction with cantilever wing and stressed skin throughout. Crew of six.

Two 450-485hp Hiro Lorraine 2 twelve-cylinder W-type water-cooled engines, driving two-bladed wooden propellers.

One nose-mounted flexible 7.7mm machine-gun, one dorsal flexible 7.7mm machine-gun.

Span 29.10m (95ft 5¾in); length 17.67m (57ft 11¾in); height 5.20m (17ft 0¾in).

Empty weight 4,676kg (10,308lb); loaded weight 6,690kg (14,749lb); power loading 7.43kg/hp (16.3lb/hp).

Maximum speed 100kt (115mph); climb to 3,000m (9,843ft) in 30min; endurance 12hr.

One built in 1927.

Navy Type 15 Flying-boat (H1H1 to 3)

In 1926, five years after the F.5 flying-boats entered service, the Navy decided to develop a replacement aeroplane to be built at the Hiro Naval Arsenal. Lieut (Ordnance) Yoshio Hashiguchi was assigned as chief designer for the project that was to be based upon the experience gained from the F.5 and from new technology acquired from Short Brothers in Britain.

The hull design of the new type closely resembled the successful F.5 design with its all-wooden structure, but the wings were completely new, giving emphasis on greater

Hiro Navy Type 15-1 Flying-boat (H1H1).

speed. Retreating from the monoplane design of the Type-R flying-boats, the new design was a simple single-bay biplane.

The first prototype was completed at the Hiro Arsenal in the autumn of 1927. Although some minor modifications were required, the aeroplane proved to have good performance, stability and control. It was officially adopted as the Navy Type 15 Flying-boat and was put into production as soon as F.5 production ended in February 1929. At the same time, it was also put into production at Aichi in 1927 at the end of its F.5 contract.

The Type 15 Flying-boat appeared in several versions. The first were the 1927 prototypes each powered by two 400hp Lorraine 1 engines of which several were built by Hiro.

The Type 15-1 Flying-boat with the short designation H1H1, was accepted by the Navy in February 1929, and was powered by the 450hp Lorraine engines driving two-bladed wooden propellers. Early production models were fitted with bench-type aileron balance surfaces, but later horn-balanced ailerons were fitted. Additional vertical fins were attached near the tips of the tailplane, and the wingtip floats were then made of metal. These were built by the Hiro Arsenal as well as Aichi.

The Type 15-kai-1 Flying-boat, the H1H2, was an experimental project undertaken by Yokosho. This had an all-metal hull of the same shape as the H1H1, but with Dornier-type longitudinal external stiffeners added. There were no changes in the engine arrangement

from that of the H1H1, but the additional stabilizing fins were discontinued because the rudder horn-balance tab was increased in area. This version was not delivered to the Navy until 1930, which was the mid-point of the production period.

While in process of experimentation with flying-boats, the Yokosuka Arsenal built another aircraft of this type but with many design changes including the use of two BMW VII engines with four-bladed propellers. Although the hull and the wingtip floats were all-metal as on the H1H2, their contours differed substantially. The equal-span wings were of wood with fabric covering. An all-up weight increase of approximately 10 percent caused termination of further development of this concept.

The Type 15-2 Flying-boat, H1H3, was adopted by the Navy at the same time as the H1H1 but its completion was delayed two years due to late acceptance of new engines. This Type 15-2 version was powered by the Lorraine 3 twelve-cylinder vee water-cooled engine, rated at 450hp at 1,850rpm at sea level, driving four-bladed wooden propellers. The wings and tail were identical to later production H1H1s. There were two versions, differing mostly by the change from bench-type aileron balances to horn-balanced ailerons. A weight reduction was achieved in this model, and it was 600kg lighter than the H1H1. Aichi was the builder of this last model of the Type 15 Flying-boat.

These flying-boats, successors to the F.5s, were the main naval flying-boats until about 1938, making them the first successful Japanese-designed flying-boats in production in Japan. They were superior in all respects to the other types already described. As a demonstration of their high quality, Lieut Yoshiaki Itoh and Lieut Iwao Minematsu jointly commanded four of them (Yo-56, 57, 58 and 59) on a flight from Yokosuka, to Chichi Jima in the Bonin Islands, to Maug, North Mariana Islands, to Saipan, south-central Mariana Islands, and return, covering 2,544nm from 20 May to 25 May, 1929.

Twin-engined biplane flying-boat. Hull of wooden construction covered with plywood, wooden wing and tail structure covered with fabric. Crew of six, two pilots, observer/bow gunner, navigator, radio operator and engineer/rear gunner.

Two 450hp Lorraine 2 twelve-cylinder W-type water-cooled engines, driving two-bladed wooden propellers (H1H1), two 500hp BMW VII twelve-cylinder vee water-cooled engines, driving four-bladed wooden propellers (H1H2).

One bow-mounted flexible 7.7mm machine-gun, one dorsal flexible 7.7mm machine-gun.

	H1H1	H1H2
Span	22.973m (75ft 4¼in)	22m (72ft 2in)
Length	15.11m (49ft 7in)	15.912m (52ft 2½in)
Height	5.192m (17ft)	5.468m (17ft 11¼in)
Wing area	125sq m (1,345.5sq ft)	—
Empty weight	4,020kg (8,862lb)	4,450kg (9,810lb)
Loaded weight	6,100kg (13,448lb)	6,500kg (14,330lb)
Wing loading	52kg/sq m (10.6lb/sq ft)	—
Power loading	6.78kg/hp (14.9lb/hp)	6.5kg/hp (14.3lb/hp)
Maximum speed	92kt (106mph)	90.5kt (104mph)
Climb to	3,000m (9,843ft)	3,000m (9,843ft)
in	33min 50sec	34min 15sec
Endurance	14½hr	—

Approximately twenty built by Hirosho and Yokosho in 1927-32 and forty-five by Aichi in 1927-34.

Hiro Navy Type 15-2 Flying-boat (H1H3).

Navy Type 89 Flying-boat (H2H1)

Near the end of 1928, the Navy imported from Britain an all-metal Supermarine Southampton biplane flying-boat. This Napier Lion-powered aeroplane was straightforward in design, unlike the radical and more advanced German flying-boats. It revealed many innovations in all-metal hull design, features which the Japanese Navy hoped to incorporate in an aeroplane as a replacement for the Type 15 Flying-boat.

After performance testing at Yokosuka, the Southampton was ferried to the Hiro Arsenal for further study before the design was begun of a new Japanese aircraft.

Lieut-Cdr (Ordnance) Jun Okamura was assigned as chief designer for the project that began in 1929. For obvious reasons this aeroplane bore a striking resemblance to the Southampton, the most noticeable difference being a single fin and rudder in place of the Southampton's three. Compared to the Type 15 Flying-boat, which was then in production at Hiro, this hull was an all-metal semi-monocoque structure instead of wooden, with a rounded contour upper surface to meet the hull bottom instead of flared chines beyond the straight sides of the earlier hulls. This was an aerodynamic improvement that was incorporated in all Japanese flying-boats from that time. The wings were also all-metal structures

Hiro Navy Type 89 Flying-boat (H2H1).

with fabric covering. By the autumn of 1930, the first prototype was completed and submitted for Navy testing.

A serious incident occurred while test flying the second prototype when a fuel line ruptured and the aeroplane caught fire. Lieut Saburo Wada hastily alighted near the beaching ramp at the Hiro Arsenal where the crew safely evacuated but the aeroplane was lost.

After further development, the aeroplane was officially adopted by the Navy as the Type 89 Flying-boat in March 1932. Production was begun not only by Hiro, but by Aichi and Kawanishi. In the case of Kawanishi, it produced major sub-assemblies for Hiro produced Type 89 Flying-boats.

The H2H1 (the short designation for the Type 89 Flying-boat) was regarded as a very functional aeroplane and remained in service for a long time, together with the Type 15 Flying-boats, although production was relatively small. In practical terms, the Type 89 was really an all-metal structured version of the Type 15, with similar dimensions and only a slight increase in weight, and served the Navy from the time of the Shanghai Incident to the early stage of the Sino-Japanese Conflict. These were the last of the Japanese twin-engined biplane flying-boats.

Twin-engined biplane flying-boat. Hull of all-metal semi-monocoque construction, metal structured wings and tail surfaces with fabric covering. Crew of six, later version carried seven.

Two 550hp Hiro Type 14 or 600-750hp Hiro Type 90 twelve cylinder W-type water-cooled engines, driving four-bladed wooden propellers.

Twin bow-mounted flexible 7.7mm machine-guns, one mid-ship flexible 7.7mm machine-gun each side. Bomb load: Two 250kg (551lb) bombs.

	Early version	Later version
Span	22.14m (72ft 7¾in)	22.12m (72ft 7in)
Length	16.283m (53ft 5¼in)	16.25m (53ft 3¾in)
Height	6.13m (20ft 1¼in)	5.96m (19ft 6¾in)
Wing area	120.5sq m (1,297.093sq ft)	120.5sq m (1,297.093sq ft)
Empty weight	4,368kg (9,629lb)	4,370kg (9,634lb)
Loaded weight	6,500kg (14,330lb)	6,500kg (14,330lb)
Wing loading	53.9kg/sq m (11lb/sq ft)	53.9kg/sq m (11lb/sq ft)
Power loading	5.415kg/hp (11.9lb/hp)	—
Maximum speed	103.6kt (119mph)	106kt (122mph)
Cruising speed	70kt (80.5mph) at 1,000m (3,280ft)	—
Alighting speed	52.6kt (60.5mph)	—
Climb to in	3,000m (9,843ft) 19min	—
Service ceiling	4,320m (14,173ft)	4,000m (13,123ft)
Endurance at 68kt	14½hr	13hr

Approximately thirteen built from 1930 by Hirosho and Kawanishi, and four from 1931 by Aichi.

Navy Type 90-1 Flying-boat (H3H1)

With the knowledge gained in manufacturing and developing the F.5, R-3, Type 15 and Type 89 Flying-boats, Hiro was the most experienced producer of large flying-boats in Japan. Because of this, plans were developed by the Hiro Arsenal in 1930 to build a large three-engined flying-boat, the first large all-metal aeroplane entirely of Japanese design. General manager for the project was Cdr Misao Wada, with as his chief designer, Lieut-Cdr (Ordnance) Jun Okamura.

The new flying-boat was a cantilever monoplane embodying the proven Wagner box-spar acquired from Rohrbach, and hull features used in the Supermarine Southampton and the previously built Hiro Type 89 Flying-boats. To aid in determining the hull contours, water-tank tests were made at the Naval Technical Research Institution under the supervision of Rear Admiral (Naval Architect) Yuzuru Hiraga. Main requirements were that it was to be capable of flying on two engines and that it must have good water characteristics. This would be the first Japanese Navy aircraft capable of carrying a one-ton bomb load.

The test aeroplane was completed at the Hiro Naval Arsenal in 1931 and given the designation Type 90-1 Flying-boat. (Another aircraft that year, the Type 90-2 Flying-boat, was built by Kawanishi.) The H3H1, its short designation, was then flown to Yokosuka where exhaustive flight testing was undertaken by Lieut-Cdr Daizo Nakajima. Many problems were encountered which brought about modifications, including moving the radiators further aft under the engine nacelles, and experimenting with different propellers. To improve flying control, auxiliary vertical fins were added to the tailplane, and struts to the horizontal surfaces were relocated so that the angle of incidence could be adjusted. With each modification, a new dash-number was assigned so the final configuration became the

*Hiro Navy Type 90-1 Flying-boat
(H3H1).*

Type 90-1-4 Flying-boat.

By 1933, without proving satisfactory, the aeroplane was relegated to use as a flying testbed for the 950hp Mitsubishi Shinten air-cooled double-row fourteen-cylinder engine before it was retired from service. It was regarded as being inferior in stability to the Kawanishi Type 90-2 Flying-boat (H3K1) of the same period regardless of the revolutionary monoplane design features for a large flying-boat. As a result, only the one aeroplane was built, but the design and fabricating experience gained proved very useful in developing later all-metal large aircraft.

Three-engined monoplane flying-boat. All-metal stressed skin construction. Crew of nine.

Three 650-790hp Mitsubishi Hispano-Suiza twelve-cylinder vee water-cooled engines, driving four-bladed wooden propellers.

Twin bow-mounted flexible 7.7mm machine-guns, twin flexible 7.7mm machine-guns amidship on each side, and twin tail-mounted flexible 7.7mm machine-guns. Bomb load: two 500kg (1,102lb) or four 250kg (551lb) bombs.

Span 31.047m (101ft 10½in); length 22.705m (74ft 6in); height 7.518m (24ft 8in); wing area 137sq m (1,474.703 sq ft).

Empty weight 7,900kg (17,416lb); loaded weight 11,900kg (26,245lb); wing loading 86.7kg/sq m (17.7lb/sq ft); power loading 6.1kg/hp (13.4lb/hp).

Maximum speed 123kt (142mph) at sea level; cruising speed 85kt (98mph); alighting speed 60.4kt (69.5mph); climb to 3,000m (9,843ft) in 17min; service ceiling 4,500m (14,763ft); range 1,105nm (1,273sm); endurance 13hr.

One built in 1931.

Navy Type 91 Flying-boat (H4H1 and 2)

In 1931, the Hiro Arsenal began the design of a modern twin-engined monoplane flying-boat as a replacement for its biplane Type 15 and Type 89 Flying-boats. The new aircraft was a scaled-down version of the Type 90-1 Flying-boat, with more emphasis on a practical design for an aircraft of this type. Chief designer for the project was Lieut-Cdr (Ordnance) Jun Okamura.

Originally, this all-metal aeroplane was powered by two 500hp water-cooled Type 91-1 or 600hp Type 91-2 engines mounted on struts well above the wing. After repeated tests and modifications over a long period, they were replaced by a set of 760hp Myojo engines. These Myojos were licence-built Pratt & Whitney Hornets of US design. Other changes in an effort to improve the design involved moving the shoulder-mounted wing to the top of the hull and repositioning the empennage. There were other subtle changes. Nearly each prototype differed from the previous one in some way in efforts to improve upon the design. This consumed much time, and, by 1937, further efforts to improve the design and production were terminated because the design was becoming obsolete.

The many variations in these flying-boats were responsible for two distinct designations for this type. Beginning in July 1933, the earliest configuration of the series to be accepted by the Navy was the Type 91-1 Flying-boat with the short designation H4H1. These had water-cooled engines. After such changes as repositioning the two hull steps, replacing two-bladed propellers with four-bladed types, and changes in the tail configuration, a redesignation for the type was in order. More advanced models with the air-cooled Myojo engines and three-bladed propellers became the Type 91-2 Flying-boat (H4H2). Both models varied, however, some had shoulder-mounted wings and others were high-wing monoplanes. They also differed within each type designation by having either a straight or tapered trailing edge, and the later versions had the Junkers double-wing type flaps. The design was never cured of instability while on the water or of its poor ability to cope with waves. Also, general performance never reached projected figures for the design; however, lessons learned helped in the development of the Kusho Type 99 Flying-boat, H5Y1, that carried the Allied code-name Cherry during the Pacific War.

Production of the H4H series was undertaken by Kawanishi as well, even though experimentation on design changes continued at Hirosho. This caused uncertainties and slowed production. Within the Kawanishi company, the flying-boat was known as the Type L, the first of which made its maiden flight on 16 June, 1933.

During the entire Sino-Japanese Conflict, these flying-boats were very active although used in small numbers. They patrolled along the coast of China, and served as transports for mail and cargo between the home islands of Japan and across the East China Sea to the mainland. This brought about the claim that the Type 91 Flying-boats were the first Japanese flying-boats to be used in a war zone.

Twin-engined monoplane flying-boat with two-step hull. All-metal stressed skin construction with wing having a Wagner/Rohrbach box-spar. Crew of six to eight.

Two 600hp Type 91-2 twelve-cylinder W-type water-cooled engines, driving four-bladed wooden propellers (H4H1), two 760hp Myojo 1 or 2 nine-cylinder air-cooled radial engines (H4H2).

One bow-mounted flexible 7.7mm machine-gun, twin dorsal flexible 7.7mm machine-guns. Bomb load: Two 250kg (551lb) bombs.

	H4H1	H4H2
Span	23.55m (77ft 3in)	23.46m (76ft 11in)
Length	16.675m (54ft 8½in)	16.57m (54ft 4½in)
Height	5.81m (19ft 0¾in)	6.22m (20ft 5in)
Wing area	82.7sq m (890.204sq ft)	82.7sq m (890.204sq ft)
Empty weight	4,924kg (10,855lb)	4,663kg (10,280lb)
Loaded weight	7,500kg (16,534lb)	7,500kg (16,534lb)
Wing loading	90.7kg/sq m (18.5lb/sq ft)	90.7kg/sq m (18.5lb/sq ft)
Power loading	6.25kg/hp (13.7lb/hp)	4.93kg/hp (10.8lb/hp)
Maximum speed	112kt (129mph)	126kt (145mph)
Cruising speed	85kt (98mph)	—
Climb to	3,000m (9,843ft)	—
in	18min	—
Service ceiling	4,970m (16,305ft)	3,620m (11,876ft)
Range	1,080nm (1,243sm)	1,260nm (1,450sm)

Dimensions, weights and performance from Japanese Navy Technical Orders.

Hiro built about thirty from 1932, Kawanishi built five in 1933, four in 1934, one in 1935, four in 1936 and three in 1937. Approximate total forty-seven.

Hiro Navy Type 91-1 Flying-boat (H4H1).

Navy Type 92 Carrier Attack Aircraft (B3Y1)

To replace the unpopular Type 89 Carrier Attack Aircraft, the Naval Air Arsenal developed a new single-engined biplane carrier-borne attack bomber in 1932. Once the prototype was modified to the satisfaction of Navy engineers, it was put into production by Aichi and Watanabe, as well as by the Hiro Arsenal, the Hiro aircraft being readily identified by having a four-bladed propeller. These aeroplanes saw service in the early stage of the Sino-Japanese Conflict with recognized success in level bombing. Approximately thirty of these three-seat bombers were built by the Hiro Arsenal. (*see* Kusho Navy Type 92 Carrier Attack Aircraft.)

Hiro Navy Type 95 Land-based Attack Aircraft (G2H1), also known as the Navy Experimental 7-Shi Special Attack Aircraft.

Navy Type 95 Land-based Attack Aircraft (G2H1) (Navy Experimental 7-Shi Attack Aircraft)

As the Washington (Disarmament) Treaty of 1922 limited the tonnage for capital ships for the US Navy, the Royal Navy and the Japanese Navy, so did the London (Disarmament) Treaty of 1930 limit the number of smaller ships including aircraft carriers and cruisers. Japanese Navy planners recognized the capability of Navy land-based bombers that could be used to supplement and reinforce fleet activities and thus were responsible for the development of the Hiro Navy Type 95 Land-based Attack Aircraft.

To meet this new requirement for air power starting in 1932, Rear Admiral Isoroku Yamamoto, Chief of Engineering Department, Naval Air Headquarters, called for a land-based long-range attack bomber that could fly more than 2,000nm and carry two tons of bombs. The Hiro Arsenal was selected for the project, for at that time it was the most experienced in the design of all-metal large aircraft. Chief designer was Lieut-Cdr (Ordnance) Jun Okamura who had served in this capacity for the preceding Type 91 Flying-boat project. This land-based bomber became the primary concern at the Hiro Arsenal, diverting attention from the development of the flying-boats previously described.

At the start of the project, the prototype's designation was the Hirosho 7-Shi Special Attack Aircraft, with the short designation G2H1. Structurally, it was a combination of a large wing of traditional Wagner diagonal tension-field structure and a slender fuselage of monocoque construction. The twin fins and rudders were similar to those of the final design of the Type 90-1 Flying-boats, and the ailerons were of the Junkers double-wing variety. One of the innovative features of the armament installation was a cylindrical belly gun turret which retracted into the fuselage. This feature was carried over into early versions of the Mitsubishi Navy Type 96 Land-based Attack Aircraft, that were code-named Nell by the Allies during the Pacific War.

To power the new bomber, two 900-1,180hp Type 94 water-cooled engines were selected, the most powerful aircraft engines available at that time. They were being developed by the Hiro Arsenal as a scaled-up version of the 600hp Type 90 Engine. It was felt that with these new engines, the aeroplane would be equivalent to a three- or four-engined aircraft of the time. Although the airframe dimension, wing area, and empty weight were almost identical to the Type 90-1 Flying-boat, aircraft range and payload were increased by nearly 50 percent. This was the largest land-based aeroplane in the Navy at that time, second only to the Army's Type 92 Heavy Bomber (Ki.20) of the Junkers-G 38 design, yet it was the first of such a large size to be designed from the beginning as a land-based attack bomber. With two engines, its wing span was 103ft 11¼in, marginally bigger than the four-engined Boeing B-17 Flying Fortress with 103ft 9in wingspan.

The first prototype was completed on 29 April, 1933, at the Hiro Arsenal and moved by ship to Yokosuka. There it made its first flight in mid-May 1933 in the presence of Rear Admiral Yamamoto who had originated this bomber concept for the Navy. Making the first flight were Lieut-Cdr Shinnosuke Muneyuki and Lieut-Cdr Toshihiko Odahara, both of the Flight Experiment Group of the Yokosuka Kokutai. After taking off, Muneyuki made one pass over the field for the spectators and proceeded to Kasumigaura Air Base where testing was to take place.

As flight evaluations continued, it was found that the aeroplane possessed outstanding performance as the Navy's largest land-based aeroplane at that time. But shortcomings became evident, including tail vibrations caused by the light structure of the fuselage, aileron flutter, and unreliable engines. One aircraft was lost during test flying because of aileron and tail flutter, causing it to ditch in Tokyo Bay. Corrections were made to the design enough to justify production.

In June 1936, the aeroplane was officially accepted by the Navy as the Type 95 Land-based Attack Aircraft, at the same time as the Navy accepted the Type 96 Land-based Attack Aircraft (G3M1), Nell. To avoid identity confusion between the two, the G3M1 was referred to as the Type 96 Chu-ko (Medium Attack) or simply 'Chu-ko,' while the G2H was called the Type 95 Dai-ko (Large Attack) or 'Dai-ko.'

After six of the G2H bombers had been produced at Hiro Arsenal, production was transferred to Mitsubishi. Before long, however, the Navy asked that production be concentrated on the smaller G3M, curtailing the G2H because of maintenance difficulties with the Type 94 Engines and the aeroplane's low-speed flying characteristics. Consequently, production ended with only two having been manufactured by Mitsubishi.

With the activation of the Kisarazu Kokutai on 1 April, 1936, all remaining G2H1s (a total of eight were built) were assigned to this unit but were regarded as second-line aircraft because of the better performance of the G3Ms.

Heavy losses were experienced by G3Ms over Nanjing in August 1937, resulting in the deployment of the G2Hs to an airfield on Saishuto Island (now Cheju Do, off the southern coast of South Korea), and while en route, and for unexplained reasons, one G2H dropped out of formation and crashed near the coast of Sagami Bay southwest of Tokyo. Once in place, and established as the 1st Combined Kokutai with other forces from Kanoya, they made their first mission into China in support of ground forces in the Shanghai area on 30 September, 1937, under the command of Lt Motokazu Mihara. They made further attacks against nine major combat areas and received considerable damage from AA fire but no aeroplanes were lost.

Disaster did catch up with these G2Hs on 24 October, 1937, when one aircraft caught fire while its engines were being started and soon exploded. The fire spread to the other G2Hs, each loaded with three 250kg, five 60kg and five 50kg bombs, exploding successively until four aircraft were destroyed and the fifth badly damaged.

Twin-engined land-based mid-wing monoplane bomber. All-metal stressed skin construction. Crew of seven.

Two 900-1,180hp Hiro Type 94-1 eighteen-cylinder W-type water-cooled engines, driving four-bladed wooden propellers.

One nose-mounted flexible 7.7mm machine-gun, twin dorsal 7.7mm machine-guns retractable turret-mounted, one retractable turret-mounted ventral 7.7mm machine-gun. Bomb load: six 250kg (551lb) bombs or four 400kg (881lb) bombs.

Span 31.68m (103ft 11¼in); length 20.15m (66ft 1¼in); height 6.28m (20ft 7¼in); wing area 140sq m (1,506.996sq ft).

Empty weight 7,567kg (16,682lb); loaded weight 11,000kg (24,250lb); wing loading 78.5kg/sq m (16lb/sq ft); power loading 6.11kg/hp (13.4lb/hp).

Maximum speed 132kt (152mph) at 1,000m (3,280ft); cruising speed 90kt (104mph); climb to 3,000m (9,843ft) in 9min 30sec; service ceiling 5,130m (16,830ft); range 1,080 to 1,557nm (1,245 to 1,800sm).

Hirosho built six from 1933 and Mitsubishi built two from 1936.

Thus, Hirosho closed its impressive history of all-metal aircraft development. Its refinement of the technology, with improvements over the imported Rohrbach designs, was passed to Mitsubishi which led to its success with the 9-Shi Single-seat Fighter (later A5M Claude) and the 8-Shi Special Reconnaissance Aircraft (that developed into the G3M Nell), and brought Japanese aeronautical engineering capability to Western levels. Once this success was recognized, the new technology spread to all other Japanese aircraft manufacturers, for both the Army and the Navy.

From 1935, the Navy continued to expand its aircraft repair and supply facilities. At Hirosho, new ground was added by cutting down mountains and reclaiming coastal land, and ultimately branch arsenals of Hirosho were established at Ohita and Maizuru. From 1 October, 1941, all aircraft departments of Naval arsenals became Naval Air Arsenals. These were different to the former Air Arsenals which had already been renamed Naval Air Technical Arsenals. With this reorganization, Hirosho became the 11th Naval Air Arsenal.

Hirosho began augmenting production of aircraft types developed by other manufacturers in an effort to supplement the build up of the war effort. Among these principal types were the Nakajima Navy Type 97 Carrier Attack Aircraft (Kate) and Aichi Navy Type 0 Three-seat Reconnaissance Seaplane (Jake) followed by the Aichi Navy Carrier Bomber Suisei (Judy) and various Navy engines from commercial manufacturers. No other aircraft after the Type 95 Attack Aircraft (G2H) of the mid-1930s was identified as a Hirosho designed aircraft, since the function of new aircraft development was transferred to Kugisho.*

*The last aircraft with Hiro code H was the H10H1, 14-Shi Medium Flying-boat, but this was not completed because of higher wartime priorities.

Ishikawajima Aeroplane Manufacturing Co Ltd (KK Ishikawajima Hikoki Seisakusho)

This company was founded in November 1924 as a branch of the Ishikawajima Shipbuilding Company Limited, one of the largest industries of this type in Japan. For the construction of aircraft the company established a factory at the Ishikawajima Shipyard in Tsukishima, Kyobashi-ku, in Tokyo.

In order to begin on a sound technical footing, the Ishikawajima company invited Dr Gustav Lachmann to become its technical advisor. Lachmann was well known in Germany for the development of high-lift devices he devised after an aircraft accident which hospitalized him while serving as a pilot during the First World War. He later held a joint patent with Handley Page Ltd for the slotted wing. Before joining Ishikawajima in May 1926, he was chief designer at the Albatros-Gesellschaft für Flugzeug-unternehmungen mbH near Berlin. He remained with Ishikawajima until 1929, at which time he moved to England and joined Handley Page Ltd to serve as director of scientific research.

In December 1926, Ishikawajima purchased an area at the northeast corner of Tachikawa Airfield, located in a western suburb of Tokyo, for its aeroplane assembly plant. A hangar and an office building were completed in June 1927, followed by an assembly factory the following February. It was here that aeroplanes manufactured at its Tsukishima location were assembled, along with those of Kawasaki Type 88 Reconnaissance Aircraft under contract with the Army. By March 1930, the company's entire aeroplane manufacturing capability was moved from Tsukishima to Tachikawa.

Ishikawajima's first efforts with aircraft began with an experimental reconnaissance biplane in 1926, followed by a series of trainers and civil liaison types. Production of its later aeroplanes reached a rate that varied from one to ten aircraft a month until mid-1932. At that time, production rate increased further when the Nakajima Army Type 91-1 Fighter was put into production with Ishikawajima. Production terminated by 1934, with 101 of these fighters built, according to Tachikawa records, supplementing the 350 built by Nakajima.

In addition to airframes, Ishikawajima also built aircraft engines under licence agreement with A D C Aircraft Ltd, of England, beginning in 1927. These particular A D C Cirrus engines were the first of the light four-cylinder inline air-cooled type.

Ishikawajima T-2 Experimental Reconnaissance Aircraft

In November 1925, the Japanese Army issued a letter of intent to Mitsubishi, Kawasaki, Nakajima and Ishikawajima for an experimental reconnaissance aircraft that was to be exclusively a Japanese design. According to the plan, these four companies were to submit their basic design proposal to the Army in January of the following year.

Ishikawajima assigned Shiro Yoshihara to be the chief designer for the new project. Before joining the company, Yoshihara had been with the Tokorozawa Army Aviation School's Department of Research. As previously related, in May 1926, Dr Gustav Lachmann joined the company and the project as technical advisor. By August of that year, the design was completed and received the Army's initial approval. After evaluating the other proposals, the Army ordered two prototypes from three of the companies, excluding Nakajima.

The first Ishikawajima prototype, powered by a 450hp Hispano-Suiza engine, was completed in

July 1927. The Ishikawajima designation was T-2, the T standing for Teisatsuki, meaning reconnaissance aircraft. An earlier design called the T-1 had been planned but not built.

Initial test flights of the T-2 were made by Dr Lachmann who was a qualified pilot. Further testing was done by Zenjiro Kamata who had been transferred from the Army to Ishikawajima. When the company was satisfied with the aeroplane, two prototypes were delivered to the Army's flight-test team of the Department of Engineering at the Army Air Headquarters at Tokorozawa in December 1927.

In November 1927, the second T-2 prototype was completed. It was powered by an imported 500hp BMW VI. This higher powered version had a slightly larger fuselage than the first prototype. In keeping with the requirements made by the Army, only the Ishikawajima aeroplanes were to be

Ishikawajima T-2 Experimental Reconnaissance Aircraft.

of all-wooden construction, and tests proved structural weaknesses in this aircraft.

The Mitsubishi and Kawasaki prototypes were to be of metal-frame construction. Ishikawajima's wooden structure had the advantage of easier construction and lower cost, but during evaluation, one aileron was damaged which resulted in further damage to the airframe. From this experience, it was decided to adopt a light metal structured wing and steel-tube fuselage in subsequent designs.

Only the two T-2 prototypes were constructed, as were the two examples of the Mitsubishi Experimental Tobi-Type Reconnaissance Aircraft. Kawasaki's was the winning entry, and it was adopted by the Army as the Type 88 Reconnaissance Aircraft.

Single-engine two-seat reconnaissance single-bay biplane. All-wood construction with fabric covering. Crew of two in open cockpits.

450-500hp Hispano-Suiza twelve-cylinder vee water-cooled engine, driving a Reed fixed-pitch two-bladed metal propeller (1st prototype), 500-600hp BMW VI twelve-cylinder vee water-cooled engine, driving a two-bladed wooden propeller (2nd prototype).

Two forward-firing fixed 7.7mm machine-guns, twin dorsal flexible 7.7mm machine-guns.

	First prototype	*Second prototype*
Span: upper	—	14.01m (45ft 11½in)
lower	—	12.246m (40ft 2in)
Length	9.817m (32ft 2½in)	10.293m (37ft 9in)
Height	3.725m (12ft 2¾in)	3.853m (12ft 8in)
Wing area	—	49sq m (527.448sq ft)

The following data are for the second prototype:

Empty weight 1,733.8kg (3,820lb); loaded weight 2,816.6kg (6,209lb); wing loading 57.5kg/sq m (11.7lb/sq ft); power loading 4.69kg/hp (10.3lb/hp).

Maximum speed 126kt (145mph); landing speed 48.7kt (56mph); climb to 5,000m (16,404ft) in 29 min 9sec; service ceiling 7,150m (23,458ft).

Two built in 1927.

Ishikawajima CM-1 (R-1) Experimental Trainer.

Ishikawajima CM-1 (R-1) Experimental Trainer

While the design of the Army T-2 Reconnaissance Aircraft was under way in 1926, Ishikawajima started the design of a trainer as a private venture. Chief designer for the project was Shiro Yoshihara with the assistance and supervision of Dr Lachmann.

The aeroplane was ideally suited for the 80hp Cirrus Mk I engine being built under licence by Ishikawajima. The designation for the aeroplane was CM-1, reflecting the name Cirrus Motor. This designation was later changed to R-1, in this case, the R stood for Renshuki or trainer.

The R-1 was considered to be the first modern Japanese built trainer to be evaluated by the Army. In comparison with the Mitsubishi Type Ki 1 Trainer (Hanriot HD-14) which the Army used extensively at that time, the R-1 was a greatly advanced structural design. However, the aeroplane was considered too unstable, and

performance was less than expected. As a result, it was not adopted by the Army.

Single-engine single-bay biplane basic trainer. Wooden structure with fabric covering. Pupil and instructor in open cockpits.

75-80hp Cirrus Mk I four-cylinder air-cooled inline engine, driving a two-bladed wooden propeller.

Span 9.60m (31ft 6in); length 7m (22ft 11½in); height 2.85m (9ft 4¼in); wing area 23.4sq m (251.883sq ft).

Empty weight 493kg (1,086lb); loaded weight 683kg (1,505lb); wing loading 29.2 kg/sq m (5.9lb/sq ft); power loading 8.54kg/hp (18.8lb/hp).

Maximum speed 65kt (75mph); cruising speed 54kt (62mph); landing speed 32kt (37mph); service ceiling 4,000m (13,123 ft); endurance 2hr.

One built in July 1927.

Ishikawajima R-2 Experimental Trainer

Recognizing the potential of the CM-1 (R-1) trainer if improve-

Ishikawajima R-2 Experimental Trainer.

ments were made, Ishikawajima engineers set to work in July 1927 on a major redesign. The fuselage was made of welded steel tubing, to overcome a shortcoming of the all-wooden T-2 that was recognized at an early stage. The wings remained of wooden construction but with metal tube ailerons to resolve another early structural problem. Noticeable changes were made in the outline of the tail surfaces and the N interplane struts were also changed to two parallel struts with bracing wires. A much more streamlined engine cowling was used to house the lower-mounted and later model 90hp Cirrus II engine.

The first of two of these trainers ordered by the Army was completed in March 1928 and delivered to the Army for evaluation. The R-2 was found to be lighter in weight and stronger in construction than the CM-1. Stability improved, but the Army assessed the aeroplane as still being inferior in stability to the Mitsubishi Type Ki 1 Trainer (Hanriot HD-14). It regarded the Ishikawajima-built Cirrus engine as lacking reliability, and therefore concluded that the R-2 was unacceptable as a military trainer.

With this adverse finding, only the two prototypes were built, and in time, the Army released the two aeroplanes back to Ishikawajima for its own use which lasted until around 1935.

Single-engine single-bay biplane basic trainer. Welded steel tube fuselage frame and wooden wing structure with fabric covering. Pupil and instructor in open cockpits.

80-90hp Cirrus Mk II four-cylinder air-cooled inline engine, driving a Y-27 two-bladed wooden propeller.

Span 9.72m (31ft 10¾in); length 6.78m (22ft 3in); height 2.80m (9ft 2¼in); wing area 23sq m (247.578sq ft).

Empty weight 430kg (948lb); loaded weight 630kg (1,388lb); wing loading 31.5kg/sq m (6.4lb/sq ft); power loading 7kg/hp (15.4lb/hp).

Maximum speed 79kt (92mph); cruising speed 65kt (75mph); landing speed 35kt (40.5mph); service ceiling 5,000m (16,404ft); range 230nm (265 sm); endurance 3½hr.

Two built in 1927.

Ishikawajima T-3 Experimental Reconnaissance Aircraft.

Ishikawajima T-3 Experimental Reconnaissance Aircraft

In an attempt to recover from the failure of the T-2 reconnaissance aircraft to achieve Army acceptance, Ishikawajima made refinements to this earlier design. Correcting the failings of the earlier all-wooden structure of the T-2, the new aeroplane had a welded steel tube fuselage structure which was closely patterned after that of the Fokker C.V. The new wings and tail structures were aluminium framed and fabric-covered. This form of construction made the newer aeroplane much stronger than the T-2, lack of strength being the former's major shortcoming. In outward appearance, the T-3 closely matched that of the second prototype T-2. During construction of the T-3, the design of the ailerons with bench-type balance surfaces was changed to inset hinges.

The sole example of the T-3 was delivered to the Army after the January 1928 competition with three other entries. As a consequence of the competition the declared winner was the Kawasaki KDA-2 (later the Type 88 Reconnaissance Aircraft). The other two competitors were the Mitsubishi

Tobi-Type, badly damaged when its undercarriage failed upon landing and the Nakajima N-35 that was nearly destroyed during a forced landing due to engine problems.

Not having a military buyer for this aeroplane, Ishikawajima obtained its release from the Army and modified it into a civil communications type. It was sold to the *Asahi Shimbun* in 1932. This became the Asahi No.53 (J-BBCA) and remained in service until about 1939. To Ishikawajima, the aeroplane was a failure in its intended role but the company gained much experience from it in the manufacture of metal airframes for future use.

Single-engine two-seat reconnaissance single-bay biplane. All-metal construction with fabric covering. Crew of two in open cockpits.

500-600hp Kawasaki BMW VI twelve-cylinder vee water-cooled engine, driving a two-bladed wooden propeller.

Two nose-mounted fixed 7.7mm machine-guns and twin dorsal flexible 7.7mm machine-guns with 2,000 rounds each. Bomb load: 200kg (440lb).

Span 14.01m (45ft 11½in); length 10.293m (33ft 9in); height 3.856m (12ft 8in); wing area 49sq m (527.436 sq ft).

Empty weight 1,580kg (3,483lb); loaded weight 2,780kg (6,128lb); wing loading 56.7kg/sq m (11.6lb/sq ft); power loading 4.63kg/hp (10.2lb/hp).

Maximum speed 127kt (146mph) at sea level; landing speed 49kt (56mph); climb to 5,000m (16,404ft) in 25min 24sec; service ceiling 7,150m (23,459ft); endurance 7hr without armament.

One built in 1928.

The Ishikawajima T-3 in service with Asahi Shimbun.

Ishikawajima R-3 Trainer Seinen Nihon-go *at Croydon in 1931.*
(J W Underwood).

Ishikawajima R-3 Trainer

Drawing on the experience gained with the R-2 trainer, the R-3 was designed by Shiro Yoshihara under the supervision of Dr Lachmann. The first prototype was completed in September 1929, and considered to be the first practical trainer designed by Japanese. Improvements over the R-2 included a much stronger airframe, better control and an engine with sufficient power.

In all, five of these aeroplanes were built by 1931. Four of them were equipped with experimentally installed automatic wing slots, an innovation with which Lachmann was closely associated. As co-holder with Lachmann to patent rights for automatic slots of this type, Handley Page had to release its share of the rights for manufacture and sale of the aeroplanes in October 1929. A Göttingen 591 aerofoil was chosen for the wings.

The R-3 trainer was stressed for aerobatics, and was very much the equivalent of the de Havilland Gipsy Moth, one of the world's best known light aircraft. However, the Army was still not satisfied with the aeroplane, stating that the airframe was not suitable as a military trainer, and there were continuing problems with the troublesome Japanese-built Cirrus engine.

Of the five aircraft, the first two were delivered to the Army which later released them to the Nihon Gakusei Koku Remmei (Japan Students' Aviation League) with registrations J-BDEA and J-BDEB. The third was retained for company use as a test vehicle and registered J-BDED, while the fourth, J-BDUB, was sold to *Asahi Shimbun* as a communications aeroplane, its title being Asahi No.52. The last of the five was purchased by the Kaibo Gikai and donated to the Students' League with the registration J-BEPB.

This last was to become the best known. Named *Seinen Nihon-go, (Youthful Japan)* it made a series of visits to European countries in 1931. It was piloted by a Hosei University student who was also a member of the Students' Aviation League, Moritaka Kurimura, and flying instructor for the league, Ryotaro Kumagawa. This was the aeroplane formerly known as No.10 Giyu, one of the Giyu series of aeroplanes donated by the Kaibo Gikai. Leaving Haneda on 29 May, 1931, the R-3 flew to Europe via Siberia. Crossing the Sea of Japan in such a small lightplane was considered by some at that time as being a brave undertaking. The aeroplane and crew visited Harbin, Moscow, Berlin, Brussels, London, Paris, Marseilles, and reached Rome on 31 August as its final port of call. The distance covered was 13,926km (8,653sm) with a flying time of 126hr 53min over the 95-day period. The aeroplane was shipped back to Japan from Rome. It had been specially configured for this long flight with the addition of fuel tanks in the wing. Its normal loaded weight of 680kg was increased to 930kg with this extra fuel, giving it an endurance of 10hr at cruising speed.

In July and August 1932, two R-3s of the League were also flown by students of Waseda University and Meiji University, visiting Manchuria on a good-will flight. On the return flight, Waseda's aircraft made an emergency landing on the beach of Nishi Tozaki, in Fukuoka Prefecture on Kyushu. The other aircraft, however, covered the round trip from Tokyo to Hsinking (now Chang-chun, China), successfully. This round-trip was a distance of 5,400km (3,355sm).

Single-engine basic trainer single-bay biplane. Welded steel tube fuselage frame, wooden wing structure and aluminium frame ailerons, all with fabric covering. Two seats in open cockpits.

105-115hp Ishikawajima Cirrus Hermes Mk II four-cylinder air-cooled in-line engine, driving a Y-32 two-bladed wooden propeller.

Span 9.80m (32ft 2in); length 7.50m (24ft 7½in); height 2.98m (9ft 9¼in); wing area 24.5sq m (263.724sq ft).

Empty weight 455kg (1,003lb); loaded weight 680kg (1,500lb); wing loading 27.7kg/sq m (5.6lb/sq ft); power loading 5.91kg/hp (13lb/hp).

Maximum speed 92kt (106mph); cruising speed 76kt (87mph); climb to 2,000m (6,562ft) in 12min; service ceiling 6,000m (19,685ft).

Five built from 1929 to 1931.

Ishikawajima R-5 Experimental Trainer

The designer of the R-3 trainer, Shiro Yoshihara, took a two-year absence from the company from September 1930 to February 1932 to study aeronautical engineering in England. Upon his return, he assumed the position of design supervisor. Chief engineer for Ishikawajima was Moriyuki Nakagawa. As a team, the two men designed a new trainer known as the R-5. Its lines were far more compatible with contemporary designs than earlier efforts. An inverted inline engine was used which provided better forward visibility for the pilot, and made possible a shorter undercarriage because of the higher position of the propeller. Clark Y aerofoil was used for the wings. The good aerobatic qualities of the R-3 were retained in the new aeroplane.

The first prototype was completed in August 1933, and the flight trials confirmed the expected excellent performance. However, during flight evaluation by the Army, the Cirrus Hermes engine revealed its inherent shortcomings, causing the Army to withdraw its interest while admitting to the aeroplane's excellent flying characteristics.

The first Ishikawajima R-5 Experimental Trainer.

The second Ishikawajima R-5.

A second prototype was completed before the Army lost interest, and both aeroplanes joined those belonging to the Students' League, carrying registrations J-BAAG and J-BISB. They were used for higher grade pilot qualifications within the League for a long period, primarily for advanced aerobatic training. Both these aircraft were highly regarded at Haneda Airfield along with the Avro 504K trainers that were the primary training equipment at that time.

From September to October 1936, members of the Students' League made a second good-will flight to Manchuria in recognition of the establishment of the Manchurian Aviation Association. Students from Kwansei Gakuin and Keio Gijuku Universities flew the two R-5s on this round-trip flight between Tokyo and Hsinking. En route they made demonstration flights at stop-over points.

Single-engine basic trainer biplane. Welded steel tube fuselage frame, wooden wing structure and aluminium empennage structure. Fabric-covered. Two seats in open cockpits.

120-135hp Cirrus Hermes Mk IV four-cylinder air-cooled inverted inline engine, driving a fixed-pitch two-bladed propeller; one wooden and one metal for the two prototypes.

Span 9.55m (31ft 4in); length 7.17m (23ft 6in); height 2.54m (8ft 4in); wing area 19sq m (204.52sq ft).

Empty weight 537kg (1,183lb); loaded weight 777kg (1,173lb); wing loading 40.9kg/sq m (8.3lb/sq ft); power loading 5.75kg/hp (12.6lb/hp).

Maximum speed 100kt (115mph) at sea level; cruising speed 80kt (92mph); landing speed 40kt (46mph); climb to 3,000m (9,843ft) in 18min 18sec; service ceiling 4,000m (13,123ft); range 260nm (300sm); endurance 3½hr.

Two built in 1933.

Army Type 91 Fighter

As a replacement for the Type Ko 4 Fighter, Nakajima produced the winning design in May 1928, and obtained a production contract from the Army. This was a parasol-wing monoplane of all-metal construction with metal-covered fuselage and fabric-covered wings. Powered by the Jupiter VII air-cooled radial engine, it was well received by Army pilots because of its ease of handling in the air and excellent manoeuvrability. At the outbreak of the Shanghai Incident, production was accelerated by placing additional orders with Ishikawajima for the Type 91-1 Fighter model. According to company figures 101 were built, the first in September 1932 and the last by March 1934. (*see* Nakajima Army Type 91 Fighter).

Army Type 94 Reconnaissance Aircraft (Ki-4)

Nakajima was given a contract by the Army to develop a reconnaissance aircraft to replace the ageing Mitsubishi Army Type 92 Reconnaissance Aircraft. Patterning much of the construction technique on that of its Army Type 91 Fighter, the first prototype was completed in March 1934 and delivered to the Army. Accepted the following July, this became the Army Type 94 Reconnaissance Aircraft. They were used in the close air support role in China from the beginning to the middle stage of the Sino-Japanese Conflict. Because of this need for combat aircraft, production was extended to Ishikawajima/Tachikawa, which produced fifty-seven aircraft in co-operation with Manshu and Nakajima. (see Nakajima Army Type 94 Reconnaissance Aircraft).

While Ishikawajima trainers may have been classed as only marginally successful in the early years of the company, especially because none was accepted as a standard trainer for the Army for whom they were designed, this lack of success for the company soon ended. Recognizing that the engines were the major problem, officials of the company were persuaded by personnel of the Tokorozawa Army Flying School to submit a new design for a trainer with more powerful engines and greater reliability. From this request developed the very successful Army Type 95-1 and 95-3 Trainers, also known as the Ki-9 and Ki-17, with Allied code-names Spruce and Cedar respectively. These served in large quantities from 1935 throughout the Pacific War.

Production of aircraft continued with this company under the new name Tachikawa Hikoki KK (Tachikawa Aeroplane Co Ltd) which became effective in July 1936. For descriptions of these later aircraft, see the Tachikawa section of this book.

Itoh Aeroplane Research Studio (Itoh Hikoki Kenkyusho)

The Itoh Aeroplane Works came into being on 30 January, 1915. It was his enthusiasm for and love of flying that prompted Otojiro Itoh to become involved with aviation and eventually to create his own aircraft manufacturing company. This is in sharp contrast to other aircraft companies in Japan whereby the more prominent ones had their beginnings with military contracts that assured success. Never a large company or builder of aircraft in quantity, Itoh was one of the earliest prominent companies and the first established aircraft manufacturer in Japan.

While employed as a young man by the Sadoshima Copper and Iron Company in his hometown of Osaka, Otojiro Itoh became inspired with flight when seeing the Wright brothers' success in a film. He wrote to the Japanese aviation pioneer Sanji Narahara, asking him what was needed to get into the field of aviation. He was advised that he should have schooling in mechanical engineering and Itoh diligently obeyed by attending night school.

At the age of 19, in 1910, Itoh left home and moved to Tokyo where he worked as a mechanic at the Narahara aeroplane company.* Impressed with his eagerness and interest in aviation, Narahara made Itoh an assistant to Einosuke Shirato, who had worked exclusively for Narahara as a pilot. This association was interrupted when Itoh reached the age of 20 because, like all other young Japanese men, he was conscripted for a one year term of service in the military. Upon returning to Narahara in

*This was a private group, not a registered company.

1912, he assisted in the manufacture of the aeroplanes and accompanied demonstration flights around Japan as a ground crewman.

As spare-time employment, Itoh assisted Shigesaburo Torigai with the manufacture of the Torigai *Hayabusa-go* Aeroplane which eventually crashed in September 1913. Itoh borrowed this aeroplane, quit his job and moved with the aeroplane to Inage, on Tokyo Bay just north of Chiba City. There he made repairs and modifications to the aeroplane, and began to learn to fly with the help of two others. The sandy beach there proved an excellent runway, but its availability was dependent upon the height of the tide. After three months of flying training, maintaining and repairing his own aircraft, he had accumulated a total of a mere 3 hours of flying.

Pilot licences, or, for that matter, any regulations concerning flying and aeroplanes were yet to come. Therefore, Itoh established a flying school on the beach at Inage in February 1915, and called it the Itoh Kyodo Hiko Renshusho (Itoh Co-operative Flight Training Ground). The Itoh Aeroplane Research Studio and Training Ground were both known to the public as Itoh Airfield. For flying training, he used the Torigai *Hayabusa-go* Aeroplane after it had been modified. To supplement his income, Itoh joined part time with Shirato, formerly with the Narahara company, who now was building his own aeroplanes. This added income allowed Itoh to begin his commercial construction of aircraft and by the autumn of 1915 he completed his first; the Itoh Emi 1.

Itoh Emi 1 Aeroplane

This was the first aeroplane built by the young aviator Otojiro Itoh, assisted by Toyokichi Daiguchi, Toyotaro Yamagata, and a hired carpenter. The work was begun in September 1915 and the aeroplane was flown for the first time on 11 November that year at Inage Beach. The engine was the French-designed 45hp Grégoire Gyp purchased in August 1914 from Shigesaburo Torigai.

Itoh Emi 1 Aeroplane.

The aeroplane was a three-bay biplane with fabric-covered wooden structure and four-wheel undercarriage. Since today's common dope was not then available, primer paint was mixed with gelatine and Formalin,* and external 'paint' was paraffin dissolved in petrol. The cost of building this aeroplane was about 400 yen, plus 1,200 yen for the engine, extremely cheap when compared to equivalent imported aeroplanes then costing over 10,000 yen.

This was a time when there were few prepared airfields other than Tokorozawa Army Base. Aviation events normally took place on Army parade grounds, racecourses and dry river beds. Undercarriages had to be designed with sufficient strength for take off and landings from rough surfaces, and normally consisted of twin dual wheels and skids. Ground transport between events was normally by rail, and therefore the airframes were designed for ease of assembly and disassembly as well as repair.

Overcoming these difficulties, Itoh made a daring flight on 8 January, 1916, from his base at Inage Beach to Tokyo, a distance requiring 55 minutes' flying, making this event the first flight by a civil aeroplane to Tokyo. This was the first of fifty-eight cities which he visited to demonstrate his aeroplane and create air mindedness in Japan. This was the second successful Japanese-made civil aeroplane, following the Narahara 4 *Ohtori-go* Aeroplane.

*TM A solution of formaldehyde in water.

The success of the Emi 1 was not only due to Itoh's excellent design but also to his own flying ability. To express his appreciation to sponsors in Ebisu-cho, Osaka, where he was born, he named his aeroplane *Emi-go* (Emi and Ebi are the same when written in Kanji) and continued to use this name for his aircraft. Later the Emi 1 was used by Masaaki Fujiwara who replaced the engine with a 50hp Hino Type engine and used it for flying training at Inage.

Single-engine tractor biplane. Wooden structure with fabric covering. Pilot in open cockpit.

35-45hp Grégoire Gyp four-cylinder water-cooled inline engine, driving a two-bladed wooden propeller.

Span 11.50m (37ft 8¾in); length 6.65m (21ft 9¾in); height 2.50m (8ft 2½in); wing area 33sq m (355.22sq ft).

Empty weight 350kg (771lb).

Maximum speed 41kt (47mph).

One built in 1915.

Itoh Emi 2 Aeroplane

These early aircraft were noted for their short life span, so, early in 1917, Otojiro Itoh designed and built what he called the Emi 2 Aeroplane as a replacement for the ageing Emi 1. The engine and the propeller were those removed from the Emi 1. The new aeroplane was smaller than the earlier craft in the hope of increasing general performance. The wings were changed from three-bay to two-bay configuration, and an aerofoil with less drag was used. The undercarriage was changed from twin dual-wheels to a single wheel each side, and bungee cords were used for shock absorbers. The aeroplane was completed in April 1917 and on its first flight climbed to an altitude of 5,000m in 3min 40sec.

After making flying demonstrations at many locations around Japan beginning at Tsuyama in May 1917, Itoh made a triumphal flight over Osaka, visiting his home town in September 1917. While there, the coast of Tokyo Bay was hit by a typhoon and a tidal wave on the night of 30 September–1 October, 1917, destroying his hangar on the east side of the bay at Inage Beach. Fortunately for Itoh, the Emi 2 Aeroplane and his staff, normally based there, were safe in Osaka. (*see* fate of NFS Tamai 2 Trainer).

After many demonstrations, the aeroplane was used as a trainer at Itoh Airfield which had by then been moved to nearby Tsudanuma Beach from Inage on 12 April, 1918. Eventually, the aeroplane

Itoh Emi 2 Aeroplane.

passed into the hands of new operators at faraway Fukunaga Airfield at Kakezuka-cho, Iwata-gun, just east of Hamamatsu. After training in the Emi 2, aviator Asao Fukunaga took the aeroplane to the Osaka area for demonstrations in August 1919. Misfortune plagued this inexperienced aviator. On one occasion, after taking off from Ikeda City to fly over his hometown of adjacent Toyonaka, the aircraft nosed over and turned onto its back after landing on the parade grounds. (This is thought to be the site of the present Osaka International Airport.) Although badly damaged, the Emi 2 was soon repaired. In the following May, soon after taking off from Osaka's Joto Army Parade Grounds, the aeroplane levelled off too soon and struck the roof of a private house, bringing a sudden end to the Emi 2.

Single-engine two-bay biplane. Wooden structure with fabric covering. Pilot in open cockpit.

35-45hp Grégoire Gyp four-cylinder water-cooled inline engine, driving a two-bladed wooden propeller.

Span 9m (29ft 6¼in); height 2.25m (7ft 4½in); wing area 25sq m (269.106 sq ft).

Empty weight 250kg (551lb)

Maximum speed 46kt (53mph).

One built in 1917.

Itoh Emi 3 Seaplane

In 1916, with the failure of Ikunosuke Umino to provide aerial demonstrations with his Christofferson Flying-boat because of its unreliable Hall-Scott engine, newspaper re-

Itoh Tsurubane No.1 Aeroplane.

porter Kokutempu Koyama of the *Asahi Shimbun* urged Itoh while performing at Iida-cho, Nagano Prefecture, to equip his Emi 1 Aeroplane with floats for water operations. While touring, he purchased the Hall-Scott engine from Umino, despite the problems it caused while installed in the Christofferson Flying-boat including an inflight fire.

Using his experience of land-based aircraft, Otojiro Itoh designed a seaplane with twin wooden floats and built it at Inage Beach. Assisted by Toyokichi Daiguchi and Toyotaro Yamagata, and with the help of student pilots, the aeroplane was completed in August 1917 and proved to have excellent flying characteristics. It was then dismantled and transported to Osaka by rail.

In preparation for demonstration flights, the Emi 3 Seaplane was assembled and maintained in a hangar located on the beach at Nishinomiya, just west of Osaka. It proved a successful venture for Itoh with frequent visitors paying to see this

Itoh Emi 3 Seaplane.

seaplane in operation. This became known as Japan's first civil float aircraft, and it had a reputation for good stability and flying performance. Itoh named the Emi 3, *Kamome-go*, meaning seagull.

Single-engine twin-float biplane. Wooden structure with fabric covering. Pilot and one passenger in open cockpit.

80hp Hall-Scott eight-cylinder vee water-cooled engine, driving a two-bladed wooden propeller.

Span 15.41m (50ft 6½in); length 7.27m (23ft 10¼in); height 4.51m (14ft 9½in); wing area 46.5sq m (500.53sq ft).

Empty weight 580kg (1,278lb).

Maximum speed 43kt (50mph).

One built in 1917.

Itoh Tsurubane No.1 Aeroplane

Following the move of the company from Inage to nearby Tsudanuma after the tidal wave of 1 October, 1917, the next aeroplane was the Tsurubane No.1 Aeroplane. The aeroplane was to be flown by Toyotaro Yamagata, Itoh's assistant, who showed good qualities as an aviator and was well suited to the task.

The design evolved around the 50hp Gnome engine from the Tamai No.3 Aeroplane that crashed at Shibaura, Tokyo, in May 1917. This engine was obtained by Yamagata's uncle, Shigesaburo Torigai, with the intention of letting Yamagata design his own aeroplane around it. Eventually, Otojiro Itoh was asked to take over the project, using Yamagata's sketches of the intended design. It was a very simple single-seat two-bay tractor biplane, having as an important feature a very rugged undercarriage. It also had the inherently stable flying qualities which made Itoh's aircraft acknowledged as successful trainers. The name of the aeroplane *Tsurubane* (Crane's wing) came from Tsurubane Shrine to which Yamagata belonged in his hometown of Hiroshima. This name was painted on the rudder, and No.1 was painted on the sides of the fuselage.

When the aeroplane was completed on 8 May, 1918, Yamagata took the aeroplane to Hiroshima for early flying demonstrations. From there, after arrangements were made by *Asahi Shimbun* reporter, Soten Abe, Yamagata visited Korea for nearly the full month of November and made exhibition flights at various locations at the request of the Governor-General in Korea, also named Yamagata. After the tour, exhibition flights were made over Osaka City for an extended period in the spring of 1919. On one occasion another person straddled the fuselage behind the pilot for a low flight over the spectators.

In its later service life the Tsurubane No.1 Aeroplane served as a trainer for the Itoh flying school. Eventually it was bought by Hisayasu Sakae and donated to Aki-Itsukushima Shrine near Hiroshima.

Single-engine two-bay biplane. Wooden structure with fabric covering. Pilot in open cockpit.

50hp Gnome seven-cylinder aircooled rotary engine, driving a two-bladed wooden propeller.

Span 10m (32ft 9½in); length 6.5m

Itoh Emi 5 Aeroplane.

(21ft 4in); height 2.6m (8ft 6½in); wing area 30sq m (322.927sq ft).

Empty weight 380kg (837lb); loaded weight 520kg (1,146lb).

Maximum speed 43kt (50mph).

One built in 1918.

Itoh Emi 5 Aeroplane

An internationally known showman, Yumito Kushibiki, the man who had invited Art Smith and Katherine Stinson to give flying displays throughout Japan, had been looking for an opportunity to manufacture aero engines, when his friend, William Gorham, suggested that he manufacture airframes as well as aero engines in Japan. The two agreed to a partnership. At the start, in 1918, an American aviator, E. H. Patterson, arrived in Japan bringing a second-hand Gorham 125hp biplane and a new 150hp Gorham engine. The aeroplane closely resembled a Curtiss Jenny and may have been one. It was powered by a 125hp Gorham engine, and was therefore called by the Japanese the Gorham Biplane.

Patterson announced a plan to begin air mail services between Tokyo and Osaka, but this was met by strong opposition in Japan. Discouraged, he returned to the United States, leaving the aeroplane and engine in the hands of Kush-

Itoh Emi 6 Aeroplane, also known as the Fujiwara Tsubame-go.

ibiki after a final exhibition at Tokorozawa in August 1918.

The aeroplane was later purchased by Itoh, and with minor modifications it now became the Itoh Emi 5 Aeroplane. Consequently, the Emi 5 was not an aeroplane designed or built by Itoh but was useful to him in later aeroplane designs.

On 23 October, 1919, the aeroplane participated in the First Tokyo–Osaka Airmail Flying Contest, piloted by Toyotaro Yamagata, but did not win a place in the competition. In 1920, the aeroplane was entered in the First Prize-winning Flight Competition, this time piloted by Taiwanese Wen-Ta Shie. It won third-place in the altitude (1,400m) and speed (120 km/h) categories.

Single-engine two-bay biplane. Wooden structure with fabric covering. Pilot and passenger in open cockpits.

125hp Gorham six-cylinder watercooled inline engine, driving a two-bladed wooden propeller.

Maximum speed 65kt (75mph); service ceiling 1,400m (4,593ft).

One modified in 1918.

Dimensions and weights not known.

Itoh Emi 6 Aeroplane) (Fujiwara *Tsubame-go*)

This was a typical two-bay sports biplane of the period, having a simple, light-weight wooden structure with fabric covering. Completed in May 1918 with a 40hp Elbridge four-cylinder inline watercooled engine, it was built at the request of Masaaki Fujiwara, from Tsuyama-cho, Okayama Prefecture. Fujiwara (who later changed his first name to Noburu) was one

of the top bicycle racers in Japan, and had won the cycle racing championship in the Far East Olympic Games in Shanghai in 1916. Early in 1917, he decided to be an aviator, and took his training at the Itoh Airfield.

With the help of sponsors in Kobe, Fujiwara purchased this Itoh Emi 6 which he named Fujiwara *Tsubame-go (Swallow),* after the brand name of his favourite bicycle. Fujiwara moved to Kobe, taking his aircraft with him. While test flying this aeroplane from the Naruo Horse Racing Track west of Osaka on 13 November, 1918, he overshot on landing and badly damaged it. After major repairs and following a safe test flight on 14 December, he decided on a new name for his aeroplane, the *Kobe-go.*

Flying mishaps continued for Fujiwara. On 5 January, 1919, immediately after taking off from Naruo en route to Kobe, the aeroplane stalled and crashed. Fujiwara survived, but the aeroplane did not; yet it is said that the misfortunes of Fujiwara in flying this and other aircraft established a new record of continuous air accidents for any one person. (*see* Ichimori Monocoque Aeroplane).

These misfortunes did not dampen Fujiwara's spirits, for he continued to fly with second-hand aircraft such as other Itoh Emi aeroplanes, Nakajima Type 5, converted Navy Type 10 Carrier Fighter, Type 14 Reconnaissance Seaplane and others, with repeated accidents and damage to the aeroplanes. To satisfy his mounting debts, he sold the six bath-houses he owned and withdrew from active participation in aviation. According to his own account, after 1,040 flying hours, he was involved in three total crashes, twelve over-turning on take off or landing, and four emergency landings. This became a classic case of 'quitting while still ahead' (and alive).

Technical data are not available.

Itoh Emi 9 Trainer

A number of new student pilots arrived at the Itoh Aeroplane Research Studio after it relocated to Tsudanuma Beach following the tidal

Itoh Emi 9 Trainer.

wave. A new two-seat trainer became a necessity. A frequent visitor to Itoh Airfield, Tomotari Inagaki involved himself with this project and, while still not employed by the company, he created a stable and practical two-seat trainer powered by an 80hp Hall-Scott engine which had been installed in the Emi 3 Seaplane. This was designated the Emi 9, and became the first authentic trainer aircraft at the Itoh Airfield.

The design was started in the summer of 1918. To ease manufacture, the two-bay wings were without taper, dihedral, and stagger. Ailerons were on the upper wing only. The fuselage was also of simple design, to a large extent based on the Emi 5 with similar nose configuration and side radiator arrangement.

To obtain more effective control, horn-balances were used on the rudder and elevators, the first on a Japanese-built civil aeroplane.

Single-engine two-bay biplane. Wooden structure with fabric covering. Pupil and instructor in open cockpit.

80hp Hall-Scott eight-cylinder vee water-cooled engine, driving a two-

This view of the Emi 9 shows the side radiator.

bladed wooden propeller.

Span 9.80m (32ft 2in); length 7.45m (24ft 5¼in); height 2.30m (7ft 6½in).
Empty weight 350kg (771lb).
Maximum speed 60kt (69mph).
One built in 1918.

Itoh Tsurubane No.2 Aerobatic Aeroplane

In 1918, the Japanese Army purchased from France some of the most highly regarded military aeroplanes of the First World War, among them Nieuport 24 fighter. This and others were evaluated at the newly established Kagamigahara Army Airfield. At that time, 27 October, 1918, Tomotari Inagaki, a long-time friend of the company, and still studying in Tokyo Polytechnical School, became engineer of Itoh Aeroplane Research Studio. By chance, he had an opportunity to visit Kagamigahara and was able to rationalize the design and manufacture of a small aerobatic aircraft similar to the designs he had just seen. Beginning on 8 January, 1919, Inagaki started his first design as a company employee. It was to be a single-seat single bay biplane, light in weight, rugged, and easy to fly.

Logically, the design followed that of the Nieuport, but to obtain sufficient lift with the low powered

Itoh Tsurubane No.2 Aerobatic Aeroplane.

50hp Gnome engine Inagaki increased the total wing area, yet retained the same overall wing span and chord of the upper wing, by enlarging the lower wing to conform to that of an equal-span biplane rather than the sesquiplane arrangement of the Nieuport. The appearance of this aeroplane was considered radical when compared to other Japanese aircraft at that time.

The front half of the fuselage was ply-covered. To enhance the aeroplane's appearance and resemble a fighter aircraft after which it was patterned, Itoh himself painted a white crane like a unit insignia on the sides of the fuselage similar to those often used by the French Air Force. This aeroplane was completed on 21 April, 1919, and made its first flight on 25 April.

Although Yamagata began teaching himself the skills of aerobatic flying, much had to be learned from an English-language book he had bought. His efforts included being suspended upside down while strapped in a chair to visualize control movements while in inverted flight, which must be considered a rather drastic measure by today's standards of teaching. On 5 May, using this aeroplane, he became the first civil pilot in Japan to complete a loop.

Single-engine single-bay biplane. Wooden structure with fabric covering. Pilot in open cockpit.

50hp Gnome seven-cylinder air-cooled rotary engine, driving a two-bladed wooden propeller.

Span 7.21m (23ft 8in); length 5.77m (18ft 11¼in); height 2.38m (7ft 9½in); wing area 14.58sq m (156.942sq ft).

Empty weight 204kg (450lb); loaded weight 340kg (749lb).

Maximum speed 74kt (85mph); climb to 1,000m (3,280ft) in 4min 30 sec.

One built in 1919.

Itoh Emi 11 Ground Taxi-ing Trainer

Flying students at the Itoh flying school, around 1918, received instruction that began with ground taxi-ing. After this came short hops, then longer flights straight ahead before landing and taxi-ing back for another try. Turns in flight were made with an instructor, then the student was ready for solo flight.

The creation of the Emi 11 Taxi-ing Trainer stems from the availability of a 30hp Hino two-cycle engine that had powered the Hino No.2 Aeroplane. This engine had been purchased by Shigesaburo Torigai from an antique dealer who had not known its worth. Torigai in turn made it available to Otojiro Itoh who spent many hours reconditioning the engine. This so-called 30hp inline two-cylinder two-stroke engine, that actually developed about 25hp, was built by Army Capt Kumazo Hino in his spare time during military service. The engine looked like a four-cylinder engine but two of its cylinders were suction pumps. The carburettor was from a 25hp Anzani engine, with automobile magneto and distributor.

In February 1920, Itoh began the design of a ground taxi-ing trainer to be powered by this engine and it was completed the following May. The fuselage of this single-seat biplane trainer closely resembled that of the Tsurabane No.1 aeroplane. Students were first trained in a 16hp Franklin powered trainer that stayed firmly, yet often unpredictably on the ground. The next phase was in the Itoh Emi 11 which could lift its tail and make short hops into the air. One pupil, 21-year old Miss Tadashi Hyodo, happened to fly this aeroplane un-

Itoh Emi 11 Ground Taxi-ing Trainer.

Itoh Emi 11 Ground Taxi-ing Trainer after undercarriage collapse.

intentionally, presumably because of her light weight. The trainer reached about 7m or 8m before she calmly landed it without previous instruction, only having the knowledge she had from reading about flying. It landed on soft sand which resulted in a broken undercarriage. She later qualified as a pilot 3/c on March 1922 as the first woman pilot in Japan.

Single-engine two-bay tractor biplane. Wooden structure with fabric covering. Pilot in open cockpit.

30hp Hino-Type two-cylinder water-cooled inline engine, driving a two-bladed wooden propeller.

Span 9.70m (31ft 10in); length 7.30m (23ft 11in).

Empty weight 230kg (507lb).

One built in 1920.

Itoh Emi 12 Trainer

To overcome its shortage of two-seat trainers, the Itoh flying school received a surplus Type Mo-4 (Kishi No.3 *Tsurugi-go*) pusher aeroplane from Kishi Airfield. From this, Itoh built a tractor training biplane, using the wings and undercarriage from the Kishi aircraft mated to another fuselage, with appropriate modifications. Itoh used an 80hp Shimazu-Le Rhône rotary engine which had received first prize for a Japanese-made engine in 1916. (*see* Ozaki Tractor Biplane).

While Motoharu Itoh, a nephew of Otojiro Itoh, was practising ground taxi-ing, he suddenly gave the aeroplane full power and took

off, only to stall immediately and crash, badly damaging the aeroplane although the young Itoh escaped serious injury. This was an aeroplane with a very low wing-loading, and pupils disliked it because it was difficult to control.

Single-engine biplane. Wooden structure with fabric covering. Two seats in open cockpit.

80hp Shimazu-Le Rhône nine-cylinder air-cooled rotary engine, driving a two-bladed wooden propeller.

Span 15.50m (50ft 10¼in); length 11m (36ft 1in).

Empty weight 570kg (1,256lb).

Maximum speed 33kt (38mph).

One built in 1919.

Itoh Emi 13 No.1 and No.2 Trainers

This was a two-seat trainer built between the summer of 1919 and the spring of 1920. The design by Tomotari Inagaki was based on

Itoh Emi 12 Trainer.

experience gained with the Emi 9, and was powered by the 80hp Hall-Scott that had been used in that aircraft. The two aeroplanes looked very similar except that the later design had a single oval cockpit for student and instructor for better communication. The practicality of this aeroplane was recognized when Komayoshi Yasuoka won fourth prize in both altitude (1,370m) and speed (59kt) with this aeroplane at the First Prize-winning Flight Competition sponsored by the Imperial Flying Association held at Susaki Airfield, Fukagawa, in Tokyo, in August 1920.

Itoh built a second Emi 13 Trainer in 1921 when the engine on the first began to deteriorate. The second aircraft was powered by a 90hp Curtiss OX-5 engine. It was called the Emi 13 No.2, and was used as the main trainer at the Itoh Airfield.

Single-engine two-bay biplane. Wooden structure with fabric covering. Pupil and instructor in large open cockpit.

80hp Hall-Scott eight-cylinder vee water-cooled engine (No.1), one 90hp Curtiss OX-5 eight-cylinder vee water-cooled engine (No.2), driving a two-bladed wooden propeller.

Span 10.37m (34ft 0¼in); length 6.40m (21ft); height 2.50m (8ft 2½in); wing area 29sq m (312.163sq ft).

Empty weight 450kg (992lb); loaded weight 600kg (1,322lb).

Maximum speed 57kt (66mph); climb to 1,000m (3,280ft) in 7min; endurance 2hr.

Two built 1920-21.

Itoh Emi 13 No.2 Trainer.

Itoh Emi 14 Long-range Aeroplane

The report in 1920 that a formation of Italian aeroplanes would fly from Europe to Japan for the first time caused considerable enthusiasm for aviation events in Japan. In addition to a visit to Seoul, Korea, by Army aircraft and to Chinhae, Korea, by Naval aircraft, the Imperial Flying Association devised a long-range flight competition as a civil event for nonstop flights from Tokyo to Osaka and return. Competing aircraft manufacturers were Nakajima, Oguri, Kawasaki and Itoh, all preparing specially modified aircraft for the event.

Chief designer for the Itoh aircraft was Tomotari Inagaki, with two assistants, Yano and Sato. The aeroplane was to be powered by a 150hp Gorham engine which had been purchased from the United States the year before. In order to have a seven-hour endurance for the flight, the most serious problem was for the aeroplane to become airborne with sufficient fuel from the 600m runway at Susaki Airfield in Tokyo. To achieve this, they designed the wing with the very high aspect ratio of 8, which was unusual at that time. The aerofoil was USA-1. This was expected to be the heaviest civil aircraft built in Japan.

Special modifications were the conversion of this two-seat aircraft to allow extra fuel tankage in the front cockpit. An auxiliary wheel was added to the tailskid but this would drop off after take off. A spinner was added to streamline the nose as was customary on European high-speed aeroplanes at that time.

At the set date of the competition, 21 April, 1920, only two entries were on hand, the Emi 14 and Nakajima Type 7; the other two entries, sponsored by manufacturers, and one Kishi Modified Maurice Farman were therefore disqualified. The two competing heavily-loaded aircraft took off successfully from Susaki Airfield, but on the outbound leg of the flight, while in dense fog, the Nakajima aeroplane crashed into Mt Tanzawa, the pilot, Kintaro Iinuma, being badly injured and his aircraft destroyed. The Emi 14, flown by Toyotaro Yamagata, covered the 1,013.67km in 6hr 43min nonstop round trip successfully, and this was a remarkable achievement in Japan's aviation history. Yamagata was awarded the prize of 5,000 yen and 50 yen monthly for three years. Itoh Aeroplane Research Studio also received an award of 5,000 yen.

On 2 and 3 August of that year, the Emi 14, again flown by

Itoh Emi 14 Long-range Aeroplane.

Yamagata, participated in the First Prize-winning Flight Competition sponsored by the Imperial Flying Association. Over the route between Funabashi and Chiba they won first prize in the speed category of 74kt and second prize in altitude by reaching 11,072ft, thereby receiving an award of 8,000 yen.

On 27 August, while Yamagata was practising loops in the vicinity of the factory at Tsudanuma in preparation for an exhibition over Kanagawa City soon after, a starboard wing inner strut socket failed, and the wing separated at about 2,000ft. The fatal crash ended the life of the 23-year-old Yamagata and destroyed what was considered an outstanding aeroplane.

Single-engine two-bay biplane. Wooden structure with fabric covering. Crew of two in open cockpits (one for record flight).

150hp Gorham six-cylinder water-cooled inline engine, driving a two-bladed wooden propeller.

Span 11m (36ft 1in); length 7.17m (23ft 6¼in); height 2.74m (9ft); wing area 32sq m (344.456sq ft).

Empty weight 760kg (1,675lb); loaded weight 1,150kg (2,535lb); wing loading 36kg/sq m (7.3lb/sq ft).

Maximum speed 79kt (91mph); climb to 1,000m (3,280ft) in 4min 30sec; endurance 8hr.

One built in 1920.

Itoh Emi 16 *Fuji-go* Racing Aeroplane

To fulfil a requirement for a special aircraft defined by former Nakajima partner Shun-ichi Bando and aviator Yukichi Goto, the Itoh

Itoh Emi 16 Fuji-go *Racing Aeroplane.*

company began a new design by Tomotari Inagaki beginning in May 1920. This was the Itoh 16 *Fuji-go*, intended as a multi-purpose aeroplane of interest to the civil market. Simplicity in design was featured for economy. Wings would have no dihedral or sweep-back. The now readily available Le Rhône rotary engines, imported from war surplus stocks, would be used, and an additional fuel tank could be installed in the front cockpit on the centre of gravity. First test flights began on 22 July, 1922.

When the First Prize-winning Flight Competition was held at Susaki Airfield in August 1920, Goto flew the Itoh 16 *Fuji-go* as an entry, taking first prize in the altitude category. In the speed race between Funabashi and Chiba, he won second prize for a speed of 69kt over the route. After this competition, Bando sent the *Fuji-go* to Kyoto to advertise his intended flying exhibition and to perform exhibition flights over the city of Osaka.

When the announcement was made of the Second Airmail Flying Contest between Osaka and Kurume, sponsored by the Imperial Flying Association, to be held on 20 November, 1920, Goto registered himself and the *Fuji-go* for the event. Other entries included French SPAD XIII fighters powered by the much larger 220hp Hispano-Suiza engines. Another participant was the Shirato 25, powered by a 180hp Hispano-Suiza. With this strong competition against Goto's 120hp *Fuji-go*, the outer bay of the wings was removed to reduce wing area and

associated drag, reducing the wingspan by 2.3m. As a result speed was increased from 90kt to 109kt.

As expected, the competition was won by a SPAD XIII, flown by Katsunami Ishibashi, but Goto's *Fuji-go* flew the route in 4hr 25min and won the second prize of 8,000 yen. Used mostly after that for promotional purposes, the aeroplane was entered again in the Second Prize-winning Flight Competition in May 1921. This time, while flown by Komayoshi Yasuoka, it maintained an average speed of 94kt over the 389km course and won third place. Such achievements kept the Itoh name in front of the public for the duration of the company's existence.

Single-engine biplane. Wooden structure with fabric covering. Crew of two in open cockpits.

120hp Le Rhône nine-cylinder air-cooled rotary engine, driving a two-bladed wooden propeller.

Span 9.34m (30ft 7¾in); length 6.05m (19ft 10in); height 2.52m (8ft 3in); wing area 23.5sq m (252.96sq ft). Loaded weight 740kg (1,631lb).

Maximum speed 90kt (104mph); climb to 1,000m (3,280ft) in 3min 30sec.

One built in 1920.

Data for original configuration.

Itoh Emi 17 Tsurubane No.3 Aerobatic Aeroplane

This aeroplane was designed by Tomotari Inagaki to be used by Yamagata for aerobatic demonstrations at about the same time as the Itoh *Fuji-go* aeroplane was being developed. It was intended to participate in the First Prize-winning Flight Competition in August 1920; however, the 80hp Gyro rotary engine gave problems from the start, even during its ferry flight from Tsudanuma to Susaki Airfield for the competition. It was therefore withdrawn from the competition.

About two weeks later, Yamagata was killed in the Emi 14 accident, and the Emi 17 never served its intended purpose. Very little was recorded about this aeroplane, and it was the last of Itoh's Tsurubane-go aeroplanes. The troublesome rotary had been purchased as a used engine by Kiyoshi Nishiide while studying in the United States, and was installed in Nishiide's aircraft when he was killed in a crash with a US-made Gage Tractor Biplane at Osaka in April 1919. After repairs by Shigesaburo Torigai, who figured prominently in the early years of Itoh as a source for engines, it was taken to Itoh Airfield and eventually used in this aircraft with never-ending problems.

Itoh Emi 17 Tsurubane No.3 Aerobatic Aeroplane.

Single-engine single-bay biplane. Wooden structure with fabric covering. Pilot in open cockpit.

80hp Gyro nine-cylinder air-cooled rotary engine, driving a two-bladed wooden propeller.

Span 9.15m (30ft); length 6.30m (20ft 8in); height 2.45m (8ft 0¼in); wing area 27.8sq m (299.246sq ft).

Empty weight 590kg (1,300lb); loaded weight 740kg (1,631lb).

Maximum speed 65kt (75mph).

One built in 1920.

Itoh Emi 18 Private Aeroplane

The three best Itoh designed aircraft after the *Fuji-go* were the Emi 18, 19 and 20. Although there were differences in each, basically the structures were the same, featuring straight lines and simple construction. The Itoh Emi 18 was built to order for the Taiwanese aviator, Wen-Ta Shie, and was powered by a 120hp Clerget engine.

This aircraft was entered in the Second Prize-winning Flight Competition at Susaki Airfield in May 1921, but became eighth among the nine participants in the speed category and sixth in the endurance category. The aeroplane was later destroyed when it overturned during an emergency landing.

Single-engine biplane. Wooden structure with fabric covering. Crew of two in open cockpits.

120hp Clerget nine-cylinder air-cooled rotary engine, driving a two-bladed propeller.

Span 9.50m (31ft 2in); length 6m (19ft 8¼in); wing area 24sq m (258.342sq ft).

Empty weight 750kg (1,653lb).

Maximum speed 89kt (103mph).

One built in 1921.

Itoh Emi 19 *Akira-go* Private Aeroplane

This aeroplane was built to order for aviator Yozo Sato, a graduate of the second cadet class of the Imperial Flying Association. After his air tour of Shikoku Island and the western part of Honshu, he resigned from the Association in 1917. He then became a pilot for the Japan Aeroplane Works Company Ltd. As company pilot for the Nakajima Type 4, he took first prize at the First Tokyo-Osaka Airmail Flying Contest in 1919. He later returned home to Akita, in northern Honshu, and announced the start of an aviation business there, appointing Kyohaku Yoshida, a news reporter for the *Tokyo Nichinichi* newspaper, and Totaro Takagi, of the Imperial Flying Association, as advisors.

He placed an order with Itoh for a new aircraft, this being the Itoh Emi 19, and one of the Inagaki series of aircraft. It was almost identical to the very practical *Fuji-go*, but differed in being powered by a 120hp Turrin engine from Switzerland, and was completed in March 1921. Showing confidence in his new aeroplane, he looped it on his first flight at the factory, astonishing all the onlookers with his bravery.

Itoh Emi 19 Akira-go *Private Aeroplane.*

Around this time, Sato changed his first name from Yozo to Akira, and called his aeroplane the *Akira-go*. With his new aeroplane and the newly formed company, he covered the Hokuriku-Shinetsu area, facing the Sea of Japan, where no aircraft had been seen or demonstrated before. Experiencing success in the aviation business he was looking forward to receiving the *Akita-go* Long-range Aeroplane which he had on order with the Itoh company following the delivery of his first *Akira-go*. But on 3 November, 1921, while on a practice aerobatic flight in another aircraft over the factory area, he lost control during a spin and crashed on a nearby railway and the aeroplane caught fire. Both Akira Sato and aviator Shinzo Takeishi died in the crash. Sato was long remembered as the poet-aviator, always cheerful and very popular with the public. After Akira Sato's death at the age of 28, the *Akira-go* aircraft remained at Itoh Airfield and was never flown again.

Single-engine biplane. Wooden structure with fabric covering. Crew of two in open cockpits.

120hp Turrin nine-cylinder air-cooled rotary engine, driving a two-bladed wooden propeller.

Span 9.34m (30ft 7¾in); length 6.05m (19ft 10in); wing area 23.5sq m (252.96sq ft).

Empty weight 740kg (1,631lb); loaded weight 990kg (2,182lb).

Maximum speed 87kt (100mph).

One built in 1921.

Itoh Emi 20 *Oguri-go* Private Aeroplane

After a lengthy stay in the United States studying aviation, aviator Tsunetaro Oguri returned to Japan in 1919 and established the Oguri Flying School at Susaki Airfield in Tokyo. He was a flamboyant person, often exhibiting his flying skills in his Oguri-Curtiss JN-4. (*see* Oguri Aircraft).

So that he could participate in the Second Prize-winning Flight Competition to be held from 21 to 25 May, 1921, he placed an order for a new aircraft with the Itoh com-

pany. This was the Itoh Emi 20 which was named *Oguri-go*. Its airframe was almost identical to the Itoh 18 and 19, but differed in being powered by a 80hp Le Rhône engine. Special attention was given to making this a light-weight airframe.

Although Oguri took part in the competition, he was poorly placed because of unfamiliarity with the aircraft due to its delay in completion. He came seventh in the speed category. Later the aeroplane was used as a trainer by the Oguri Flying School.

Single-engine two-bay biplane. Wooden structure with fabric covering. Crew of two in open cockpit.

80hp Le Rhône air-cooled rotary engine, driving a two-bladed wooden propeller.

Span 9m (29ft 6¼in); length 6m (19ft 8¼in); height 2.50m (8ft 2½in); wing area 23sq m (247.578sq ft).

Maximum speed 65kt (75mph).

One built in 1921.

Itoh Emi 20 Oguri-go *Private Aeroplane.*

Itoh Emi 22 Yamagatakinen-go *Long-range Aeroplane, with* Yamagatakinen-go *painted on the fuselage.*

Itoh Emi 22 *Yamagatakinen-go* Long-range Aeroplane

In April 1921 when Itoh Aeroplane Research Studio was reorganized as a limited company, the Imperial Flying Association was planning the Visiting Shanghai Prize-winning Flight Contest. Stimulated by this news, aviator Katsumami Ishibashi placed an order in France for a SPAD Herbemont seaplane. To compete against this aeroplane, Yozo Sato placed his order with Itoh for the *Akita-go* Long-range Aeroplane to be powered by a Japanese Army surplus 230hp Maybach engine. In anticipation of this same competition, the Itoh company had purchased a surplus 400hp Liberty engine from the United States and had begun an Inagaki-design for an ambitious high-speed long-range aeroplane which was to be the Itoh Emi 22. However, the Shanghai flight was

cancelled early in the planning stage.

It was around this time that the Beppu Land Holding & Trust Co was planning a regular air service between northeast Kyushu and Osaka with intermediate stopovers along the Seto Inland Sea route. To work this route the company asked for the design and manufacture of a transport aircraft from Itoh. As a result, the design of the Itoh 22 was changed from a long-range aircraft to a passenger transport and powered by the Liberty engine. Before long the Bappu plan was also cancelled. Itoh then decided to continue building the 22 as a two-seat long-range aeroplane as originally planned, and to be named the *Yamagatakinen-go*, meaning in memory of Toyotaro Yamagata who had been killed in the Itoh Emi 14.

The design of this aircraft was strongly influenced by the de Havilland D.H.4 which was also powered by the 400hp Liberty engine and produced in both Britain and the United States during the First World War. This Liberty was the most powerful engine in Japan. The two-bay wings were of high aspect ratio. The fuselage was of plywood stressed-skin construction which increased its weight. A unique feature was the off-set pilot's seat to port, with the rear seat to starboard in close proximity for better visibility and ease in communication in a common open cockpit. To achieve good control on the ground the tail-skid was linked to the rudder. The entire aircraft was painted a flat black and carried the inscription in large white kanji characters on the sides of the fuselage, which read *Yamagata Kinen-go*.

The aeroplane was completed in the spring of 1922, but with elimination of two possible tasks for it, it was put to little use. However, it did participate in the Fourth Prize-winning Flight Competition sponsored by the Imperial Flying Association which was held at Shimoshizu, Chiba Prefecture, in June 1923, when, flown by pilot 3/c Shinzo Sugimoto, it was entered in the distance category for this competition. After flying for 1hr 12min, the aeroplane caught

Itoh Emi 23 Bulldog Trainer.

fire because of engine problems and had to make an emergency landing which disqualified it. For this same reason, the competing Nakajima-Breguet 14 and the Fukunaga Tenryu-go were also disqualified.

Following its mishap, the Itoh Emi 22 was used for the Visiting Metropolitan Tokyo demonstration flights, but it was mostly stored in the hangar at Itoh Airfield.

Single-engine two-bay biplane. Wooden fuselage covered with plywood. Wings and empennage of wooden structure with fabric covering. Crew of two in single open cockpit.

400hp Liberty twelve-cylinder vee water-cooled engine, driving a two-bladed wooden propeller.

Span 13.50m (44ft 3½in); length 9.25m (30ft 4in); wing area 41sq m (441.334sq ft).

Empty weight 1,100kg (2,425lb); loaded weight 1,700kg (3,747lb).

Maximum speed 119kt (137mph).

One built in 1922.

Itoh Emi 23 Bulldog Trainer

This aeroplane was originally a United States built Standard Bulldog, one of the aircraft left by members of the Burt Barr Flying Circus after visiting Japan from the United States in 1921. After some modification it was renamed the Itoh Emi 23. It was distinctive in having deep-cut cockpit openings which allowed the occupants better sideways visibility as they sat low in the cockpit to avoid the slipstream. Other features included a steel-tube engine mounting, an all-plywood monocoque fuselage, and flying wires only from the N interplane struts.

Modifications were completed in the spring of 1922. By June of that year, the aeroplane won second prize in the speed category at the Third Prize-winning Flight Competition held at Shimoshizu, recording 148.32km/h while being flown by pilot 3/c Takamoto Yoshikawa of the Itoh Airfield. After the competition, it was used as a trainer.

On 6 August, that same year, while Yoshikawa was flying with his friend, Taizo Tashiro, the aircraft stalled during a low turn and crashed into the sea. Yoshikawa died in the accident and Tashiro badly injured, and the aeroplane was destroyed.

Single-engine single-bay biplane. Wooden fuselage with ply covering, wooden wings and empennage with fabric covering. Crew of two in open cockpits.

90hp Curtiss OX-5 eight-cylinder vee water-cooled engine, driving a two-bladed wooden propeller.

Span 8.828m (28ft 11½in); length 6.45m (21ft 2in); height 2.57m (8ft 5¼in); wing area 23sq m (247.578sq ft).

Empty weight 500kg (1,102lb); loaded weight 720kg (1,587lb).

Maximum speed 70kt (80mph); climb to 1,000m (3,280ft) in 5min; endurance 2½hr.

One modified in 1922.

Itoh Emi 24 *Akita-go* Long-range Aeroplane

For a proposed flying contest from Fukouka to Shanghai by Imperial Flying Association in 1921, three long-range aeroplanes were developed in Japan, Fukunaga's *Tenryu-go* and Itoh's *Yamagatakinen-go* and *Akita-go*. The Itoh Emi 24 No. 1 *Akita-go* was ordered by Yozo Sato with funds from sponsors in Akita Prefecture, but he was killed in a crash before testing the aircraft which was completed in October 1921. The aircraft was then converted to a private transport aeroplane as No.2. Several flights were made by Komayoshi Yasuoka and other pilots around the Tsudanuma factory area, and the aeroplane was then put in a hangar there for the remainder of its existence.

The aeroplane was designed by Tomotari Inagaki, using the monocoque structure of the Bulldog as a pattern, with scaled-down wings of the *Yamagatakinen-go*. It used a German 320hp Maybach airship engine, and as a result was nose heavy in spite of the large fuel tank and the pilot being located well to the rear, with consequent poor view. To improve this deficiency, the radiators were removed from the sides of the fuselage and a single

Itoh Emi 24 Akita-go *Long-range Aeroplane.*

The Emi 24 after being fitted with a frontal radiator.

radiator was put beneath the fuselage. There was a rugged steel-tube undercarriage with large diameter tyres. Ailerons were on the lower wing only, and plywood fairings were used throughout.

Although advanced in design for the purpose for which it was built, the absence of a requirement left it a useless aeroplane.

Single-engine single-bay biplane. Wooden fuselage with ply covering. Wings and empennage of wood with fabric covering. Pilot in open cockpit.

320hp Maybach six-cylinder inline water-cooled engine, driving a two-bladed wooden propeller.

Span 10.60m (34ft 9¼in); length 7.712m (25ft 3½in); height 2.80m (9ft 1¾in); wing area 28.8sq m (310sq ft).

Empty weight 970kg (2,138lb); loaded weight 1,573kg (3,467lb).

Maximum speed 97kt (112mph).

One built in 1921.

Itoh Emi 25 Trainer.

Itoh Emi 25 Trainer

In the spring of 1921, the defunct Burt Barr Flying Circus returned home to the United States, leaving its aircraft behind because of a customs restraining order. Choichi Inoue, a manager of an automobile business in Osaka, and a former student of the Itoh Flying School, purchased the four American aircraft and spare engines from the Kobe Customs House and donated them to the Itoh school. Among them were two Curtiss JN-4 Jennys, one Standard R-1 and one Canadian-built Curtiss-Reid. After some repairs, they were put into much needed service as trainers.

The smallest of the aircraft was the Curtiss-Reid which was modified by Inagaki and renamed the Itoh Emi 25 and called the Baby Curtiss. At the Third Prize-winning Flight Competition held at Shimoshizu in June 1922, this aircraft was flown by pilot 3/c Masatoki Kato, who was also a reporter for an aviation magazine. He misjudged his landing, overturned and was disqualified from further competition. The aircraft was badly damaged.

Single-engine two-bay biplane. Wooden structure with fabric covering. Crew of two in open cockpits.

90hp Curtiss OX-5 eight-cylinder vee water-cooled engine, driving a two-bladed wooden propeller.

Span 8.828m (28ft 11½in); length 6.45m (21ft 2in); height 2.56m (8ft 4¾in); wing area 23sq m (247.578sq ft).

Empty weight 500kg (1,102lb); loaded weight 750kg (1,653lb).

Maximum speed 76kt (87mph).

One modified in 1922.

Itoh Emi 29 *Taihoku-go* Passenger Transport

Built in 1923, this was the first limousine passenger aeroplane to be built in Japan. This design by Tomotari Inagaki followed that of the widely used European limousine passenger aircraft converted from single-engine military types. The Emi 29 was built for pilot 2/c Wen-Ta Shie of Taiwan.

Beginning with an all-new design, the aeroplane had two passenger seats in a high cabin with windows that could be opened in flight. The interior looked as though a limousine body had been inserted into the fuselage, with separation from the pilot, but outwardly, the aircraft had a rugged and somewhat rustic appearance. There was no room in the fuselage for the fuel tank so it was placed within and above the upper wing. The wing and the empennage were similar to those of the *Yamagatakinen-go* and the *Akita-go*. After designing this aircraft, Inagaki left Japan on 28 January of that year to study light aircraft in France and Britain.

This *Taikoku-go* Passenger Aeroplane was put into service on the Tokyo–Osaka route of Tozai Teiki Kokukai, together with Nakajima 5s and the Shirato 25, but saw limited service.

Single-engine two-bay cabin biplane. Wooden fuselage with ply-covered forward half and fabric rear of the cabin. Wooden wings and empennage with fabric covering. Pilot in open cockpit and two passengers in cabin.

220hp Hispano-Suiza eight-cylinder vee water-cooled engine, driving a two-bladed wooden propeller.

Itoh Emi 29 Taihoku-go *Passenger Transport.*

Span 10.50m (34ft 5¼in); length 7.25m (23ft 9¼in); height 3.15m (10ft 4in); wing area 31sq m (333.692sq ft).

Empty weight 870kg (1,918lb); loaded weight 1,710kg (3,770lb).

Maximum speed 76kt (87mph).

One built in 1923.

Itoh Emi 28 and 31 Flying-boats

In June 1922, Shun-ichi Bando and Yukichi Goto combined their assets to establish the Nippon Koku Yuso Kenkyukai (Japan Air Transport Research Society) to open an air service between Tokyo and Yokohama. Bando was formerly with Nakajima and now seeking his own way in aviation, and Goto had previously tried his hand at the manufacture of aircraft and had pilot training and technical knowledge. They had previously purchased the Itoh Emi 16 *Fuji-go*

This view of the Emi 29 clearly shows the cabin profile.

Racing Aeroplane, and now for their first passenger aircraft they bought a Curtiss MF Seagull flying-boat from Sale & Frazar Ltd. However, the Seagull was badly damaged before delivery in an alighting mishap on Tokyo Bay near Tsudanuma on 10 July, 1922. Based on this flying-boat, Itoh-designer Tomotari Inagaki created a new flying-boat, the Itoh Emi 28, to meet an order for its replacement. This aircraft was to have a 150hp Hispano-Suiza engine, but was never built.

In the meantime, Choichi Inoue of Osaka established Nippon Koku Yuso Kenkyusho (Japan Air Transport Research Association) at O-hama, Sakai City, in Osaka Prefecture, in June 1922, and operated Japan's first regular air transport service between Sakai and Takamatsu, as well as Sakai and Tokushima. He operated float aircraft released from the Japanese Navy, but planned to use passenger transport flying-boats and therefore ordered one from the Itoh company. This flying-boat became the Itoh Emi 31 based upon the previously designed Itoh Emi 28, and was also

designed by Tomotari Inagaki.

The hull section was identical to the Curtiss Seagull. Contrary to other small flying-boats of the time which had an up-sweep aft section to position the tail high above the water, the top of this hull was straight, but the tailplane was high on the fin. The crew's seats were side-by-side in an open cockpit with the pilot on the left and the flight engineer on the right. The two passengers were seated side by side behind the pilot also in an open cockpit. Eventually the engineer's seat was used for a third passenger.

The aeroplane was completed in the summer of 1922, followed by flight tests at Tsudanuma, then sent to the purchaser in Sakai by rail. While in service it was also used by *Asahi Shimbun* during Army manoeuvres in Kagawa Prefecture. During this time it was seen by the Prince Regent (Emperor Showa [Hirohito]) who asked his chamberlain about the aircraft's unusual shape, and he was informed that it was an Itoh-type Japanese-made flying-boat engaged in regular air transport service. As a result the Regent remained very interested in this particular aircraft.

The flying-boat was modified several times, being redesignated Itoh Emi 31 No.3 on 28 October, 1922. Nippon Koku Yuso Kenkyusho operated it for a time, and it remained operational until around 1924. When its flying days were over it was further modified as a water-taxi sightseeing boat.

Single-engine pusher biplane flying-boat. Plywood hull with wooden stiffeners, wooden wings and tail with fabric covering. Pilot and three passengers in open cockpits.

220hp Hispano-Suiza eight-cylinder vee water-cooled engine, driving a two-bladed wooden propeller.

Span 14.66m (48ft 1in); length 7.65m (25ft 1in); height 3m (9ft 10in); wing area 26sq m (279.87sq ft).

Empty weight 780kg (1,719lb); loaded weight 1,350kg (2,976lb).

Maximum speed 65kt (75mph); endurance 2½hr.

One built in 1922.

Itoh Emi 30 Sport Aeroplane

For a Peace Rally held in Tokyo at Ueno Park in 1922, aircraft were flown as part of the entertainment. In addition to Army aircraft from Kagamigahara that gathered at Yoyogi Parade Grounds, the Kawanishi-K3 was flown from Osaka to participate. The Itoh company had on exhibition for the first time a very small light sporting aeroplane which was unusual in Japan at that time. This

Itoh Emi 31 Flying-boat operated by Japan Air Transport Research Association.

aircraft resulted from the company's interest in the development of sporting aviation in the United States and Europe after the First World War.

This small biplane was Japan's first light-weight sports plane and was powered by a 40-45hp Itoh-type 11 five-cylinder air-cooled radial engine. The engine was manufactured by Itoh using cylinders from a Japanese-made 70hp Renault engine formerly installed in the Type Mo-4 aeroplane, and the crankshaft and crankcase were designed by Itoh. The engine weighed 50kg and could run at 1,200rpm.

This aeroplane had the smallest dimensions of any aircraft in Japan.

Itoh Emi 30 Sport Aeroplane. (S Nicolaou).

A thick, high-lift aerofoil was used, and the lower wing was slightly longer than the top wing. Its slender fuselage had a streamlined headrest behind the single-seat cockpit. An exhibition committee in July 1922 awarded the Itoh company a silver plaque for the aeroplane's originality. Later the aircraft was test flown by Seizo Ohkura and after modifications used as a trainer at Itoh Hikoki Seisakusho (Itoh Aeroplane Manufacturing Works, formerly the Itoh Aeroplane Research Studio which was renamed in November 1924 following its reorganization as a

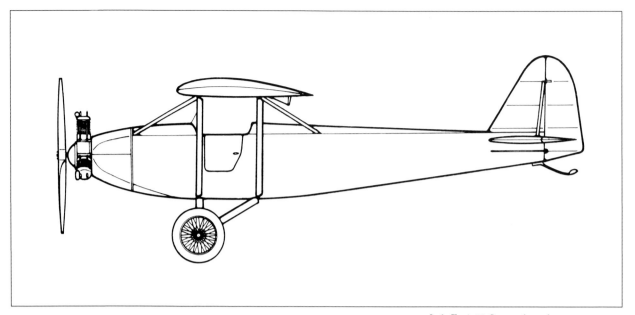

Itoh Emi 50 Sport Aeroplane.
(Shorzoe Abe)

private company) and Toa Hiko Semmon Gakko (East Asia Professional Flying School). In March 1924, an aviation exhibition was held at Tokyo's Mitsukoshi Department Store, and the aeroplane was displayed on the roof, with sales price of 5,000 yen.

Single-engine single-bay biplane. Wooden structure with fabric covering. Pilot in open cockpit.

45hp Itoh 11 five-cylinder air-cooled radial engine, driving a two-bladed wooden propeller.

Span 5.80m (19ft); length 5.11m (16ft 9in); height 2.10m (6ft 10¾in); wing area 13sq m (140sq ft).

Empty weight 295kg (650lb); loaded weight 605kg (1,333lb).

Maximum speed 70kt (80mph); endurance 2hr.

Possibly only one built in 1922.

Note: There is a reference made to an Itoh Emi 49 Sports-aircraft toward the end of the Taisho reign (1926), but details are not known.

Itoh Emi 50 Sport Aeroplane

Around 1931, Itoh planned the design and manufacture of a sport aeroplane for his own Nihon Kei Hikoki Kurabu (Japan Light Aeroplane Club) using a 35hp Anzani three-cylinder air-cooled engine of the type used in the surplus Army Type 3 Ground Taxi-ing Trainer. This was to be a parasol-wing

monoplane with two side-by-side seats. This design was intended for the private pilot market.

However, the intended Anzani engines were already old and worn out; they vibrated badly and could not produce their rated power. Lacking a suitable engine, manufacture of the Itoh Emi 50 Sport Aeroplane was ended in 1933. The Emi 50 was the last of the Itoh company's own designs of powered aircraft.

Single-engine parasol-wing monoplane. Two seated side-by-side in open cockpit.

30hp Anzani three-cylinder air-cooled engine, driving two-bladed wooden propeller.

Span 11.50m (37ft 8¾in); length 6.90m (22ft 7¾in); height 2.27m (7ft 5¼in); wing area 20sq m (215.285sq ft).

Empty weight 300kg (661lb); loaded weight 500kg (1,102lb); service ceiling 4,000m (13,123ft).

Maximum speed 65kt (75mph); service ceiling 4,000m (13,123ft); endurance 3½hr.

Unknown quantity built between 1931 and 1933.

Early in the Showa reign (which began in 1927), the Itoh company became more involved in aircraft overhaul, and in conversions of surplus military aircraft for civil use. These aircraft were given the Emi name followed by a number. One example was the Emi 53 which was a converted Navy Type 15 Recon-

naissance Seaplane completed in 1938, intended for use in fishery spotting, aerial survey and sightseeing. Other conversions included those made from Navy Type 10 Carrier Reconnaissance Aircraft, Navy Type 13 Carrier Attack Aircraft, Navy Type 14 Reconnaissance Seaplanes, Type Hansa Reconnaissance Seaplanes. Some ex-military trainers were modified by Itoh to tow gliders. Gliders were also a speciality of the company, it having designed and built fifteen to sixteen different types by 1939. In time, as greater emphasis was placed on procuring military aircraft, the Itoh company became a subcontractor for many of these larger firms, and continued to do such work until the end of the Pacific War.

In December 1937, the company name was again changed, this time to Itoh Hikoki KK (Itoh Aeroplane Co Ltd) and developed as the sponsored factory of the Aviation Bureau, Department of Communications. Itoh aircraft were noted for being those most used for the training of Japanese civil pilots during the prewar years.

Japan Small Aeroplane Co Ltd (Nippon Kogata Hikoki KK)

The predecessor of this company was the Japan Small Aeroplane Research Studio (Nippon Kogata Hikoki Kenkyusho) which was established in 1937 by Kiyoharu Yoshihara* at Kamata, Tokyo. In March 1939, this organization became the Japan Small Aeroplane Co Ltd with the intention of building gliders. Akira Miyahara was appointed as the chief engineer.

Nippon Hachi Motor Glider

Beginning in 1940, the company developed the Nippon Hachi (Bee) which was Japan's first modern motor-glider. Designed by Akira Miyahara, it was completed in February 1941. Since the Aviation Bureau did not have set standards

*Yoshihara was a pilot known for his flight from Berlin to Japan in 1930 and the aborted trans-Pacific flight sponsored by *Hochi Shimbun* in 1931–1932.

for aircraft of this type, it was registered as an aeroplane and given the registration J-BBEA. On 7 February, it was flown for the first time, by Kiyoharu Yoshihara, a holder of both a pilot 1/c licence and licence for sailplanes. The Hachi's sailplane qualities with shut down engine exceeded expectations.

The Hachi was powered by a 28hp AVA engine, produced by L'Agence Générale des Moteurs AVA of Paris. This was the same type of engine that powered the prototype Nippi NH-1 Hibari (Pou du Ciel), although the Hachi was more refined in design. This single-seat aeroplane had a higher aspect ratio mid-positioned wing, slim fuselage and orthodox tail surfaces. The single-seat cockpit was enclosed and the single-wheel undercarriage was on the fuselage centreline beneath the cockpit.

After flight testing at Haneda, it was used by the Japan Students' Aviation League which was expected to arouse general interest and produce production orders. The company did receive orders for three from the Manchurian Flying Association, but the war prevented production. Engine production in Japan of the AVA to power the Hachi was undertaken by the Japan Internal Combustion Engine Co Ltd (Nihon Nainenki KK) and given the name Semi, meaning cicada. Production of these engines was diverted to power the Navy

Type 1 Target Aircraft (MXY3).

Single-engine mid-wing monoplane powered-glider. Wooden monocoque fuselage with fabric-covered wooden wing. Pilot in covered cockpit.

28hp AVA-4H four-cylinder two-cycle horizontally-opposed air-cooled engine, driving a two-bladed wooden propeller.

Span 15m (49ft 2½in); length 7.56m (24ft 10in); height 1.60m (5ft 3in); wing area 15.5sq m (166.8sq ft).

Empty weight 257kg (566lb); loaded weight 341kg (751lb); wing loading 20.8kg/sq m (4.26lb/sq ft); power loading 11.4kg/hp (25.1lb/hp).

Maximum speed 73kt (84mph); landing speed 34kt (39mph); climb to 3,000m (9,843ft) in 59min 18sec; service ceiling 3,000m (9,843ft); endurance 1hr.

One built in February 1941.

In September 1941, the company received an order from the Navy Kugisho to develop a new pilot-training glider which became the K-12 Chikara, and the first to be mass produced by the company. Because of the success of the German commando operations with troop-carrying gliders, military orders were given to the company to design and develop a combat glider capable of carrying 12 soldiers. This became the Army Ku-11.

Nippon Hachi Motor Glider.

Kawanishi Aircraft Company Ltd (Kawanishi Kokuki KK)

This aircraft manufacturing company really began in 1921 with the completion of its first aeroplane when part of the Kawanishi Machinery Manufacturing Works. However its origins go back further, to May 1918 when Seibei Kawanishi, owner-president of the Nihon Woollen Co Ltd entered into partnership with Chikuhei Nakajima of the Nakajima Aeroplane Manufacturing Works. Together they established the Japan Aeroplane Works Co Ltd. After just over a year of partnership, a bitter dispute caused Kawanishi to withdraw his assets and break his association with the company in December 1919. As part of his share, he took numerous precision machine tools he had purchased from the United States.

In February 1920, Kawanishi established the Kawanishi Kikai Seisakusho (Kawanishi Machinery

Kawanishi K-1 Mail-carrying Aircraft.

Manufacturing Works) at Hyogo, Kobe, where he installed his machinery for the purpose of manufacturing textile spinning machines, and made his second son, Ryuzo, president of the company.

Pressure was soon placed upon the elder Kawanishi to re-enter the aircraft manufacturing business, not only by Shun-ichi Bando, the general manager representing Kawanishi in the previous joint-venture, but designer Eiji Sekiguchi, engineers Fujio Togawa and Konoshin Tamaki, and pilot Yukichi Goto, all of whom had also left Nakajima. Seibei's son Ryuzo also joined in the persuasion, and the elder Kawanishi reluctantly granted permission to build an aeroplane in the company's warehouse and to use the 200hp Hall-Scott engine taken as part of the settlement with Nakajima.

Yukichi Goto had purchased the Itoh Emi 16 *Fuji-go* Racing Aeroplane (*see* Itoh aircraft by this name) and participated in prizewinning flying competitions and provincial flying tours to raise money for the construction of aeroplanes. In the spring of 1921, the Kawanishi team completed its first aircraft, the K-1, which was a contemporary biplane design. Because of the success achieved by this aeroplane in the Second Prize-winning Flight Competition, Seibei Kawanishi approved further investment

and the Aeroplane Department of the Kawanishi Machinery Co Ltd was established. Work began on the K-2 Racing Aircraft along with other designs. Rather then concentrating on securing military contracts, Kawanishi directed its initial designs toward the civil market for air mail and passenger carrying.

In April 1923, an additional Kawanishi company was registered as the Nippon Koku KK (Japan Aviation Co Ltd) as an air transport business. This began on 10 July, 1923, from its own airport* on reclaimed land with a hangar located at the mouth of the Kizu River, south of Osaka. Ryuzo Kawanishi was president, and Shun-ichi Bando was general manager. Business was started with regular flights between Osaka and Beppu, Kyushu, flying Navy-surplus Yokosho Ro-go Kogata seaplanes until some of its own manufacture became available. The air route was extended to Fukuoka, to Seoul in Korea, and Dairen (now Lüda) (near Port Arthur) in China. Kawanishi aircraft also made flights to Shanghai.

Since the Kawanishi owned and operated airline with its Kawanishi aeroplanes could not legally monopolize all civil air transport throughout Japan, it soon had to be dissolv-

*This airport later became known as Osaka International Airport until 17 January, 1939, when replaced by a new Osaka International Airport which was also Itami Air Base.

ed and a new government-owned company, Nihon Koku Yuso KK (Japan Air Transport Co Ltd) took its place. Being without a substantial civil market for its aircraft, the Aeroplane Department separated from the Kawanishi Machinery Company and became the Kawanishi Kokuki KK (Kawanishi Aircraft Company Ltd) in November 1928. It gained recognition as a Navy-sponsored factory under the continued presidency of Ryuzo Kawanishi with Ryohei Arisaka, a former Navy Commander as director for engineering. Many former Naval officers, engineers and mechanics were employed within the company. In December 1930 the company moved to Naruo Village, midway between Kobe and Osaka on Osaka Bay, and established a newer plant there.

In co-operation with Short Brothers in Britain, the Kawanishi Company started to build all-metal, three-engined flying-boats in 1931. Most Kawanishi designs were flying-boats and seaplanes, thus retaining a kinship with the Navy for which it produced Navy aircraft exclusively up to and during the Pacific War.

K-1 Mail-carrying Aircraft

This first aeroplane to be manufactured by the Aeroplane Department of Kawanishi Machinery Works was designed by chief designer, Eiji Sekiguchi, beginning in February 1920. It was powered by a 200hp Hall-Scott L-6 engine imported from the United States while Seibei Kawanishi was associated with Nakajima and the Nihon Hikoki Seisakusho (Japan Aeroplane Works Co Ltd). In its design considerable reliance was made on the American L W F Engineering Company design features which made the K-1 fairly advanced for its time. It had a bullet-shaped nose above which was placed a very pronounced radiator, and the two-bay wings had USA 1 aerofoil section. It was completed in December of that same year, and was expected to create interest as a mail-carrying aircraft.

At the Second Prize-winning

Kawanishi K-2 Racing Aircraft.

Flight Competition sponsored by Imperial Flying Association in May 1921, Kawanishi pilot Yukichi Goto won the distance competition by flying 370nm (427sm) in 4hr 50min. He was also awarded the second prize in the speed category, being timed at 103kt (119mph). Nevertheless, the aeroplane was never accepted as a commercial type, and therefore was only flown by Goto occasionally at the factory. The K-1 holds the honour of being the first aeroplane in Japan to be issued an airworthiness certificate by the Aviation Bureau. The issue of certificates of airworthiness began on 11 May, 1921.

During its limited operational life the K-1 was fitted with a modified and larger fin for improved directional stability. It also had its engine changed to that of a German-built 180hp Daimler.

Single-engine two-bay biplane. All wooden structure with fabric covering. Crew of two in open cockpits.

200-244hp Hall-Scott L-6 six-cylinder water-cooled inline engine; later 180-200hp Austro-Daimler six-cylinder water-cooled inline engine, both driving a two-bladed wooden propeller.

Span 10m (32ft 9¾in); length 7.50m (24ft 7¼in); height 2.55m (8ft 4¼in); wing area 28.5sq m (306.781sq ft).

Empty weight 775kg (1,708lb); loaded weight 1,159kg (2,555lb); wing loading 40.7kg/sq m (8.3lb/sq ft); power loading 6.44kg/hp (14.2lb/hp).

Maximum speed 108kt (125mph) at sea level; landing speed 46kt (53mph); service ceiling 6,000m (19,685ft); endurance 5hr.

One built in 1920.

Performance with Daimler engine.

K-2 Racing Aircraft

Recognizing that there was competitive interest in speed-racing categories at aviation exhibitions sponsored by the Imperial Flying Association, Kawanishi produced the first aircraft of Japanese origin designed exclusively as a high-speed racing aircraft, at the suggestion of Yukichi Goto. The design that became the K-2 was begun in January 1921 and was the creation of Eiji Sekiguchi.

This design was extremely radical for Japan at this time. A Junkers-type cantilever low-wing layout was used for the first time in Japan and the Durand 52 aerofoil was chosen. Later, at the sugges-

This view of the K-2 shows the unusual rear fuselage.

tion of Goto, bracing wires were added to the wings, and eventually struts replaced the bracing-wires connecting the wing to the upper fuselage. The K-2 had no vertical fin for directional stability, relying only on the shape of its aft fuselage to which the rudder was attached. For this obvious reason, it was noted for the lack of directional control, particularly on take off. The cockpit was placed low into the fuselage and was without a windshield. Every possible effort was made to reduce drag, yet strangely the radiator was installed clumsily high above the engine as was the case with the K-1 from which the Hall-Scott L-6 engine was obtained. The only example was completed in August 1921.

On flight tests, the K-2 attained a maximum speed of 127kt (146mph) showing great promise for competition flying. However, propeller damage and other accidents plagued the aircraft from the start, denying it its chance of competing for the speed title. On 31 July, 1921, the aeroplane recorded a speed of 139kt (160mph) at low altitude over Kagamigahara, but no official speed records were claimed.

The K-3B Communication Aircraft modified with 230hp Benz engine.

Single-engine semi-cantilever low-wing monoplane racing aircraft. All-wooden structure with fabric covering. Pilot in open cockpit.

200-244hp Hall Scott L-6 six-cylinder water-cooled inline engine, driving a two-bladed wooden propeller.

Span 9.67m (31ft 8½in); length 6.57m (21ft 6½in); height 2.35m (7ft 8½in); wing area 13.2sq m (142.088sq ft).

Empty weight 680kg (1,499lb); loaded weight 860kg (1,896lb); wing loading 65.1kg/sq m (13.3lb/sq ft); power loading 4.3kg/hp (9.4lb/hp).

Maximum speed 139kt (160mph) at sea level; landing speed 57kt (65mph); service ceiling 7,600m (24,934ft).

One built in 1921.

K-3 Communication Aircraft

In March 1921 Eiji Sekiguchi began the design of the K-3 high-speed communication aircraft. This was the first Japanese aircraft to be powered by a Maybach airship engine of which many were delivered to Japan from Germany as war reparations.

The K-3 was evolved from the K-1 biplane but with many refinements. Wing struts were simplified, and the wing aerofoil was RAF 15. Instead of the previously upright mounted radiator, this design had the radiator flat within the upper wing section. Two cockpits pro-

Kawanishi K-3 Communication Aircraft with 260hp Maybach engine.

vided seating for three, with two passengers side by side in the front cockpit. Although termed a communication aircraft, it could be used for sightseeing, advertising, mail-carrying and other purposes. Completed in October 1921, it had the highest performance of any civil Japanese aeroplane at that time, having the speed equivalent to fighter aircraft, and a payload matching that of light bombers.

The factory had great hopes for this design, but it was out-matched by the lower-powered Nakajima 5 which had been previously produced for the Army and then becoming available as surplus. As a result, only one K-3 was built. The aeroplane was re-engined in 1926 with a 200-230hp Benz IIIaV water-cooled inline unit and the airframe was partially modified. This became known as the Kawanishi K-3B.

Single-engine single-bay communications biplane. All-wooden structure with fabric covering. Pilot and two passengers in two open cockpits.

260-305hp Maybach MIV a six-cylinder water-cooled inline engine, driving a two-bladed wooden propeller.

Span 10.03m (32ft 11in); length 8.86m (29ft); height 2.60m (8ft 6¼in); wing area 30.5sq m (328.3sq ft).

Empty weight 970kg (2,138lb); loaded weight 1,400kg (3,086lb); wing loading 45.9kg/sqm (9.4lbsq ft); power loading 5.38kg/hp (11.8lb/hp).

Maximum speed 121kt (140mph) at sea level; landing speed 52kt (60mph); climb to 3,000m (9,843ft) in 10min; service ceiling, 8,500m (27,88ft); endurance 5hr.

One built in 1921.

K-5 Mail-carrying Seaplane

In November 1921 the design of the K-5 was started by Eiji Sekiguchi. Hopes were high that this would be the first truly successful large Japanese seaplane transport. The concept provided a spacious cabin, aft of the pilots' side-by-side cockpit, for mail or cargo and with an option for two-by-two seating for four passengers. The wings, of USA 27 section, were of unequal span, the lower wing had marked

Kawanishi K-5 Mail-carrying Seaplane.

dihedral, and the interplane struts were of unusual arrangement forming unequal Vs in front view.

The aeroplane was completed in October 1922, but tests proved disappointing. Underpowered with its 260-305hp Maybach engine, the seaplane was unable to take off with any reasonable payload. As a result, and having no foreseeable engine of greater power, only one aircraft was built.

Single-engine twin-float transport biplane. All-wooden structure with fabric covering. Two pilots in open cockpit, cabin for four passengers.

260-305hp Maybach MIV a six cylinder water-cooled inline engine, driving a two-bladed wooden propeller.

Span 18.70m (61ft 4¼in); length 12.635m (41ft 5¼in); height 4.60m (15ft 1in); wing area 68.5sq m (737.351 sq ft).

The cabin and cockpit of the K-5 are better shown in this view.

Empty weight 1,750kg (3,858lb); loaded weight 2,700kg (5,952lb); wing loading 39.4kg/sq m (8lb/sq ft); power loading 10.4kg/hp (22.9lb/hp).

Maximum speed 81kt (93mph) at sea level; alighting speed 49kt (56mph); service ceiling 4,000m (13,123ft).

One built in 1922.

K-6 Transport Seaplane

Learning from the failure of the K-5, Eiji Sekiguchi began the design of a more practical seaplane transport in late 1922. The basic points of the design were for improved stability and easier flying control based on Göttingen reports obtained from Germany.

Although this was an entirely new design, the main external differences were in having equal span two-bay wings with RAF 15 aerofoil, and no vertical fin, and the rudder only extending below the fuselage. The passenger compartment for two was an open cockpit, later to be enclosed. This one aeroplane was completed in November 1923.

Kawanishi K-6 Transport Seaplane.

The K-6 was built for the use of Nippon Koku KK (Japan Aviation Co Ltd), an airline owned by Kawanishi, as a seaplane transport. However, soon after the completion of the aeroplane, it was decided to use it for the Around-Japan Flight sponsored jointly by Nippon Koku KK and *Daimai Tonichi Shimbun*. Modifications were made to enhance this seaplane for the event by installing additional fuel tanks, repositioning the radiator, adding outrigger floats, and small fins to the lower surface of the tailplane.

Given the name *Harukaze (Spring Wind)* by His Imperial Highness Prince Takehiko Yamashina, it was referred to by the press as the 'Harukaze-go around-Japan aeroplane.' The course began at Osaka and continued to Kagoshima, Hakata, Kanazawa, Akita, Minato, Kasumigaura, Yokaichi and back to Osaka. Piloted by Yukichi Goto with flight engineer Minezo Yonezawa, this flight took from 23 July to 31 July, 1924, covering a distance of 2,370nm (2.727sm) with an actual flying time of 33hr 48min, averaging 74kt (85mph). Later that same year, on 2 December, the K-6

was entered in the Around Ise Bay Prize-winning Flight Competition, being declared the best of seaplanes by making three circuits totalling 460nm (530sm) in 6hr 30min.

The modified K-6 performed very well, but construction of additional aircraft was not undertaken because the more refined K-7 seaplane was already being planned. Following the Around-Japan Flight, the K-6 was converted to its original purpose as a transport, with the rear passenger seats re-installed.

Single-engine twin-float transport biplane. All-wooden structure with fabric covering. Pilot in open cockpit, two passengers in cabin.

260-305hp Maybach M IVa six-cylinder water-cooled inline engine, driving a two-bladed wooden propeller.

Span 13.60m (44ft 7½in); length 9.895m (32ft 5½in) [10.375m (34ft)]; height 3.95m (12ft 11¼in), [3.785m (12ft 5in)]; wing area 43.6sq m (469.321 sq ft).

Empty weight 1,150kg (2,535lb); loaded weight 1,890kg (4,166lb); wing loading 43.3kg/sq m (8.8lb/sq ft); power loading 7.27kg/hp (16lb/hp).

Maximum speed 90kt (104mph), [84kt (97mph)] at sea level; alighting speed 51kt (59mph) [49kt (56mph)];

climb to 3,000m (9,843ft) in 17min; service ceiling 7,000m (22,965ft), [6,500m (21,325ft)]; endurance 4hr.

One built in 1923.

Figures for modified version in square brackets.

K-7A Transport Seaplane

High performance combined with practicality was the objective of Eiji Sekiguchi when he began design of the K-7A transport seaplane in December 1923, one month after the completion of the K-6. The new aeroplane was a semi-cantilever sesquiplane with thick Göttingen 420 aerofoil and simplified interplane struts. It was markedly German in appearance. After the first one was completed in November 1924, it proved to have excellent stability, control, and general performance. Ten of these Maybach-powered seaplanes were built by 1927, making this the first Kawanishi aeroplane to be produced in numbers and they were used as the initial main equipment for the Nippon Koku KK of the Kawanishi Group.

In comparison with the failed K-5 aeroplane, the K-7 had the wing

Kawanishi K-7A Transport Seaplane.

area reduced by about 50 percent. Passenger seats were located at the centre of gravity in a cabin forward of the two tandem open cockpits. In appearance, this aircraft was more refined than previous designs and was considered very advanced for Japan.

By January 1925, the K-7A was put into operation on the regular route of Nippon Koku KK between Osaka and Fukuoka on Kyushu, carrying mostly mail and very few passengers. This service continued until around 1929 when Nihon Koku Yuso KK replaced the Kawanishi-owned service.

During the service life of the K-7s they were entered in numerous flying events and achieved high praise. In November 1925, for instance, the type won the Around Lake Biwa Flight Competition, and in May 1926 one successfully carried mail between Fukuoka and Shanghai, a distance of more than 600 miles. In October 1926 three K-7As set out for a round trip from Osaka, to Fukuoka, Mokpo (Korea), with the ultimate destination being Shanghai. One aborted at Mokpo but the other two reached

Shanghai from Mokpo in 3hr 40min. On the return one reached Osaka, leaving the second with an emergency water alighting near the Goto Islands. Despite these mishaps, these were heroic attempts in those early days, with extended overwater flights in single-engined aircraft.

Single-engine twin-float sesquiplane transport. All-wooden structure with fabric covering. Two pilots in open cockpits, four passengers in cabin.

260-305hp Maybach MIVa six-cylinder water-cooled inline engine, driving a two-bladed wooden propeller.

Span 12m (39ft 4¼in); length 11m (36ft 1in); height 4.08m (13ft 4½in); wing area 34sq m (365.984sq ft).

Empty weight 1,250kg (2,755lb); loaded weight 2,000kg (4,409lb); wing loading 58.8kg/sq m (12lb/sq ft); power loading 7.69kg/hp (16.9lb/hp).

Maximum speed 106kt (122mph) at sea level; alighting speed 54kt (62mph); service ceiling 6,000m (19,685ft); endurance 6hr.

Ten built, one in 1924, three in 1925, four in 1926 and two in 1927.

K-7B Mail-carrying Aircraft

The sole example of the K-7B was completed in November 1925 as a modified version of the K-7A seaplane, and it could be equipped with either floats or wheels. It was powered by a 400hp Lorraine engine.

Initially, the aeroplane was fitted with wheels to demonstrate its capability as a mailplane. In this configuration the undercarriage spreader bar was in the form of a wing which added to the overall lift. Bench-type ailerons were fitted temporarily to the upper wing, while the lower wing had landing flaps. The normal payload of 300kg (661lb) was considerably reduced when the K-7B was equipped with the heavier floats.

In September 1926, this aeroplane successfully completed the first mail-carrying flight between Osaka and Dairen in conjunction with the later Kawanishi K-10 aircraft.

Single-engine mail-carrying sesquiplane with wheel or float undercarriage. All-wooden structure with fabric covering. Two pilots in open cockpits.

400-440hp Lorraine 1 twelve-cylinder vee water-cooled engine, driving a

Kawanishi K-7B Mail-carrying Aircraft.

The K-7B as a Transport Seaplane.

two-bladed wooden propeller.

Span 12m (39ft 4½in); length 9.45m (31ft) [11m (36ft 1in)]; height 3.80m (12ft 5½in) [4.08m (13ft 4½in)]; wing area 34sq m (365.984sq ft).

Empty weight 1,150kg (2,535lb) [1,282kg (2,826lb)]; loaded weight 2,330kg (5,136lb) [2,082kg (4,590lb)]; wing loading 68.5kg/sq m (14lb/sq ft); power loading 5.75kg/hp (12.6llb/hp).

Maximum speed 119kt (137mph) [115kt (132mph)] at sea level; cruising speed 91kt (105mph); landing speed 43kt (50mph); service ceiling 7,000m (22,965ft); endurance 10hr.

One built in 1925.

Data for seaplane in square brackets.

K-8A Transport Seaplane

The need for long-range seaplanes became more apparent as Japanese aviation continued to develop. As a result of the success of its K-7A, Kawanishi embarked upon a new design in early 1925, the K-8A long-range twin-float transport monoplane. Designed by Eiji Seki-

Kawanishi K-8A Transport Seaplane.

guchi, this aeroplane was intended as a mail transport, but consideration was also given to the possibility of interesting the Navy in its use as a long-range reconnaissance aircraft.

The first of the type completed in January 1926 had a shoulder-mounted wing, with the two open cockpits above the wing. Those that followed had parasol-type wings, all strut braced from the twin-floats. The wing aerofoil was the Göttingen 420, the same as that of the K-7A. In appearance, the fuselage, especially in the area of the engine cowling, was nearly identical to that of the K-7A. These modern lines were deceiving, however, because this aeroplane was a slow performer due to its low power and excessive wing area. But this combination contributed to its good stability and control, making it highly regarded for long-distance flights. Five of these aircraft were built, each having differing details.

All the K-8As were used by Nippon Koku KK for regular mail flights between Osaka and Fukuoka.

Single-engine twin-float parasol-wing

monoplane transport. All-wooden construction with fabric covering. Crew of two in open cockpit.

260-305hp Maybach M IVa six-cylinder water-cooled inline engine, driving a two-bladed wooden propeller.

Span 17.6m (57ft 9in); length 10.935 m (35ft 10½in); height 3.68m (12ft 1in); wing area 39sq m (419.806sq ft).

Empty weight 1,320kg (2,910lb); loaded weight 1,930kg (4,255lb); wing loading 49.5kg/sq m (10.1lb/sq ft); power loading 7.42kg/hp (16.3lb/hp).

Maximum speed 89kt (103mph) at sea level; alighting speed 49kt (56mph); service ceiling 6,500m (21,325ft); endurance 7hr.

Five built in 1926.

K-8B Transport Seaplane

In September 1926, the Teikoku Kaibo Gikai (Imperial Maritime Defence Volunteer Association) contracted with Kawanishi for two K-8B seaplanes. These were a modified version of the K-8A, with reduced wing area as a result of shortened wing span, and rounded wingtips. The fuselage was slimmer and the two cockpits were moved

Kawanishi K-8B Transport Seaplane.

rearward, resulting in aerodynamic improvements. Both were completed in March 1927.

These two aircraft were given the identities Giyu No.1 (J-TUST) and Giyu No.2 (J-TUTU) by the Kaibo Gikai, which in turn leased them without charge to the Nippon Koku KK on condition that they be turned over to the Navy if requested. These two aeroplanes were built to make a formation flight round Japan for public demonstration. The crews selected were pilot Uichi Suwa and flight engineer Shigezo Fujita for Giyu No.1, and pilot Nobutake Umieda and flight engineer Masatake Yasuda for Giyu No.2. The demonstration was made in two sections, the first leaving Osaka for Kouchi, Kagoshima, Fukuoka, Beppu and back to Osaka from 10 to 24 April, 1927. Actual flying time for the 1,590km circuit was 14hr 12min. The second flight left Osaka for Tsu, Shimizu, Kasumigaura, Otaru, Niigata, Kanazawa, Matsue, Tsuruga and Osaka from 7 to 25 May,

1927. The 3,059km were covered in 31hr 15min. During these flights, the seaplane alighted at sixteen harbours and bays at major cities where they were put on exhibition in conjunction with lectures to promote aviation.

After these much publicized flights, the two aeroplanes were re-registered J-BDAE and J-BDAF respectively. They were used on the regular service of Nippon Koku KK between Osaka and Fukuoka, eventually being retired in April 1929 through extensive use, despite the fact they were merely two years old. During their operational lifetimes, Giyu No.1 recorded 394 flying hours, carrying a total of 70 tons of mail, while Giyu No.2 logged 447 hours, having carried 80 tons. This was considered a major achievement in Japanese civil aviation.

Single-engine twin-float parasol-wing monoplane transport. All-wooden construction with fabric covering. Crew of two in open cockpits.

260-305hp Maybach M IVa six-cylinder water-cooled inline engine, driv-

ing a two-bladed wooden propeller.

Span 16m (52ft 6in); length 11.80m (38ft 8½in); height 3.8m (12ft 5½in); wing area 34sq m (365.984sq ft).

Empty weight 1,345kg (2,965lb); loaded weight 1,955kg (4,310lb); wing loading 57.5kb/sq m (11.7lb/sq ft); power loading 7.52kg/hp (16.5lb/hp).

Maximum speed 100kt (115mph) at sea level; cruising speed 80kt (92mph); alighting speed 45kt (52mph); service ceiling 5,000m (16,404ft); endurance 9hr.

Two built in 1927.

K-10 Transport

The K-10 transport was designed in 1925 by Eiji Sekiguchi for use on the route between Seoul and Dairen, by the Nippon Koku KK. The design reverted to the proven biplane concept, with special attention given to stability and control. This aeroplane was unique in that it carried a radio telegraph, the first installed in a Japanese civil aircraft although at the time not a new technology, and it provided progress reports to ground stations.

The first aeroplane was completed in August 1926, initially power-ed by a 400hp Lorraine engine with a four-bladed propeller. Two passengers were seated side by side in an open cockpit in front of the pilot. The aeroplane was soon modified with a 260hp Maybach engine with a two-bladed propeller. Seating capacity was increased to four passengers in an enclosed cabin. In September 1926, the first of two K-10s carried mail on the Osaka–Seoul–Dairen route along with the Kawanishi K-7B already in service. This was a long and perilous route with these early aeroplanes but essential for the airline because it was excluded from operating domestic routes. This K-10 made a total of six round trips before being withdrawn from the route for unexplained reasons.

Later, on 2 October, 1926, on Kansai Aviation Day, this aero-plane participated by demonstrating its passenger carrying capability to promote aviation awareness in Japan.

Single-engine single-bay biplane trans-port. All-wooden structure with fabric covering. Pilot in open cockpit, four passengers in cabin.

260-305hp Maybach six-cylinder water-cooled inline engine, driving a two-bladed wooden propeller.

Span 13m (42ft 8in); length 8.90m

(29ft 2½in); height 3.55m (11ft 7¾in); wing area 44.85sq m (482.777sq ft).

Empty weight 1,057kg (2,330lb); loaded weight 1,762kg (3,884lb); wing loading 39.3kg/sq m (8lb/sq ft); power loading 6.77kg/hp (14.9lb/hp).

Maximum speed 93kt (107mph) at sea level; landing speed 43kt (49mph); service ceiling 6,000m (19,685ft); en-durance 7hr.

Two built in 1926.

K-11 Experimental Carrier Fighter

In April 1926, Mitsubishi, Naka-jima and Aichi, received orders from the Navy for a carrier-based fighter to replace the Mitsubishi Type 10 Carrier Fighter. Kawani-shi, in seeking Naval recognition for such contracts, proceeded with its own design as a private venture.

Eiji Sekiguchi used the Göttingen 420 aerofoil on the upper wing and 416 on the lower and neither wing had dihedral. Manually-operated re-tractable radiators were incorpor-ated on each side of the fuselage aft of the lower wing for cooling the 500hp BMW VI. Prominent features were the unusually high fin and rudder, and long-span ailerons on the upper wing only, also serving as landing flaps. The newly avail-able Oleo shock struts were used in combination with bungee cords within the undercarriage.

Completed in July 1927, the K-

11 was tested at Kagamigahara along with the other three fighters built at the Navy's request. The Kawanishi aeroplane showed such promise that a second example was built in 1928 in order to incorp-orate desired changes in the fuse-lage and empennage. However, these aeroplanes and two other entries failed to win Naval approval and the Nakajima Type 3 Carrier Fighter was declared the winner.

Following the competition, the two K-11s were put into service with Kawanishi's Nippon Koku KK and used experimentally for carrying mail on three trips along its Osaka–Seoul–Dairen route.

Single-engine single-bay biplane carrier-based fighter. Fuselage of light metal structure with fabric covering, wooden structure wing with upper wing fabric-covered, lower wing ply-covered. Pilot in open cockpit.

500-630hp BMW VI twelve-cyl-inder vee water-cooled engine, driving a two-bladed wooden propeller.

Two forward-firing fixed 7.7mm machine-guns.

Span 10.8m (35ft 5¼in); length 7.88m (25ft 10¼in); height 3.28m (10ft 9in); wing area 33.8sq m (363.832 sq ft).

Empty weight 1,170kg (2,579lb); loaded weight 1,750kg (3,858lb); wing loading 51.8kg/sq m (10.6lb/sq ft); power loading 3.8kg/hp (8.3lb/hp).

Maximum speed 140kt (161mph); landing speed 44kt (51mph); climb to

Kawanishi K-10 Transport.

Kawanishi K-11 Experimental Carrier Fighter.

3,000m (9,843ft) in 5min 30sec; service ceiling 9,000m (29,527ft); endurance 3½hr.

Two built in 1927.

K-12 Long-range Monoplane

Inspired by Lindbergh's transatlantic flight of May 1927, in the *Spirit of St Louis*, the Imperial Flying Association decided in August that year to sponsor a trans-Pacific flight with a wholly Japanese-built aeroplane and that Japan would be the first to make the nonstop crossing. This was to be a joint effort by the Army, Navy, Imperial University and Central Meteorological Observatory, along with the Imperial Flying Association. The task of building the aeroplane would be given to Kawanishi, using the design skills of Eiji Sekiguchi so aptly demonstrated on previous aircraft.

Two aeroplanes were built for the project, which began in October 1927. Sekiguchi drew heavily upon his earlier design of the K-9 Transport which had been terminated before completion. The K-12s were semi-cantilever high-wing monoplanes without dihedral. The design was similar in appearance to the *Spirit of St Louis*, although much larger. Unlike Lindbergh's aeroplane, the K-12 had its cabin under the wing leading edge with forward view for its two-man crew. Although not confirmed, it has been said that the concept of the design was to make the aeroplane proportionally larger than the *Spirit of St Louis* in relation to the greater distance to be flown.

The first aeroplane was completed in June 1928 and was to serve as the stand-by and training aircraft. Flight tests were made at Kagamigahara. While the tests were underway, complications developed between the Aviation Bureau and the project committee whereby the project became deadlocked. The Bureau contended that the aircraft structure was not strong enough for such a heavy take-off load, and that the K-12's range was not sufficient to make the crossing. The project committee disagreed. In the end, the Bureau's views prevailed and flight testing was suspended in September 1928, and the project officially cancelled the following November.

During construction of the two aircraft, the second of which was completed in August 1928, crews for the two aircraft were selected from pilots of Nippon Koku KK. They were Yukichi Goto, Nobutake Umieda, Teruo Fujimoto and Uichi Suwa, all of whom underwent rigorous training for the flight. Before cancellation of the project, Goto was killed in a flying accident while in training in a Type 13 Carrier Attack Aircraft. The second aircraft, the one intended to make the crossing, was referred to as the Nichi-Bei-Go, or The Japan-US Model, and named *Sakura*, (Cherry Blossom). Early in its

Kawanishi K-12 Long-range Monoplane.

flight-testing phase it was damaged in an accident, raising further suspicions of unsuitable design for the task.

With the project terminated, Kawanishi had planned to repair and modify *Sakura* as a transport for its airline company, with provision for passengers and fuel capacity reduced to five hours, but repairs to the aeroplane were never made. The other aircraft was hung up in the Kawanishi factory with a sign below it that read; 'How not to design and build a Special-Purpose Aeroplane.' The K-12 was the last civil aircraft manufactured by Kawanishi Machinery Work's Aeroplane Department.

Single-engine high-wing monoplane long-range aircraft. Metal fuselage structure with fabric covering, wings of wooden structure covered with fabric on the upper surface, plywood on the lower surface. Crew of two in closed cockpit.

500-550hp Kawasaki BMW VI twelve-cylinder vee water-cooled engine, driving a two-bladed wooden propeller.

Span 19.05m (62ft 6in); length 11.60m (38ft 0½in); height 3.40m (11ft 2in) [first aircraft], 3.60m (11ft 9¾in) [second aircraft]; wing area 57sq m (613.562sq ft).

Empty weight 1,920kg (4,232lb); loaded weight 5,500kg (12,125lb); wing loading 96.5kg/sq m (19.7lb/sq ft); power loading 11kg/hp (24lb/hp).

Maximum speed 114kt (131mph); landing speed 66kt (76mph); climb to 1,500m (4,921ft) in 20min; range 2,985nm (3,435sm).

[Predicted calculations before Aviation Bureau restrictions: Range 3,930 nm (4,522sm) with take off weight 5,500kg (12,125lb), or 3,370sm (3,878 sm) with take off weight 5,000kg (11,023lb).]

Two built in 1927.

Navy Type 13 Seaplane Trainer (K1Y2)

No sooner had Kawanishi expanded its aircraft manufacturing capability than civil production requirements diminished, caused by the loss of its subsidiary company's domestic air route. As a result, Kawanishi sought Navy contracts, a potential enhanced by the staff which included many former Naval officers, engineers and mechanics. When Kawanishi Aircraft Co Ltd was reorganized in November 1928, it became a designated aircraft manufacturer for the Navy. In recognition, the company was awarded a Navy contract to build the Yokosho-designed Navy Type 13 Seaplane Trainer, which Kawanishi identified as its Type 0. This was a conventional-looking biplane trainer that could be equipped with wheels or floats. Kawanishi built forty-eight of the float-equipped version between 1928 and 1932. Having the short designation K1Y2 it was the first mass-produced aeroplane by Kawanishi, and the last of the tail-float equipped seaplanes. (*see* Yokosho Navy Type 13 Seaplane Trainer.)

Navy Type 15 Reconnaissance Seaplane (E2N1 and 2)

A competition held in 1925 resulted in a Nakajima design for a reconnaissance seaplane for the Navy. This was a conventional sesquiplane with a crew of two, known as the Navy Type 15 Reconnaissance Seaplane. This was Japan's first originally designed shipboard reconnaissance seaplane. By 1929, Nakajima discontinued production, and the Navy transferred production to Kawanishi. Kawanishi had built thirty of this type by 1930 when production terminated. (*see* Nakajima Navy Type 15 Reconnaissance Seaplane).

Navy Type 3 Land-based Primary Trainer (K2Y1 and 2)

In 1928, the Yokosuka Arsenal designed the Navy Type 3 Primary Trainer as a replacement for the Avro 504 trainer which had then been in service for a considerable time. Also referred to by its short designation, K2Y1 and 2, production was eventually transferred to Kawanishi which completed its first example in June 1930. By 1932, Kawanishi had built sixty-six of these trainers of the following models and quantities: twenty-five K2Y1 in 1930, fifteen K2Y1 in 1931 and twenty-six K2Y2 in 1933. All were referred to within the company as the Type E. (*see* Yokosho Navy Type 3 Land-based Primary Trainer).

Navy Type 90-2 Flying-boat (H3K1) (Company designation Type F)

The Army's introduction of the very large Junkers G 38 into Japan in 1928 strongly influenced the Navy to manufacture a very large flying-boat. Planning began in 1929, and the Navy contracted with Kawanishi to work with Short Brothers in the United Kingdom, regarded as the world-authority on large flying-boats.

Representing Kawanishi, Yoshio Hashiguchi was sent to Shorts to assist in the design of a new three-engined biplane flying-boat that was based on the Short Singapore and Calcutta. The new aeroplane was powered by three 825hp Rolls-Royce Buzzard engines, strut mounted between the two wings. The entire project, known as the KF Flying-boat, was kept very confidential during design and manufacture. When completed, it was sent by ship to Japan in the spring of 1930 where it was assembled at the Experimental Department of the Yokosuka Kokutai, then assigned to Tateyama Kokutai for operational testing. Flight tests revealed that it had good performance and good endurance, an essential for an aircraft of this type.

While service testing was under way, licence manufacturing rights were secured by Kawanishi, and production began with the use of drawings, documents and imported components from Shorts. Under the continued supervision of Yoshio Hashiguchi, the first Kawanishi-built flying-boat was completed in March 1931 and a second aircraft one-year later. Tests were delayed because of unfamiliarity with the imported engines, but in October 1932, the Navy completed its evaluation of the one imported and

*Kawanishi Navy Type 90-2 Flying-boat
(H3K1).*

two Kawanishi-built aircraft in
service with the Tateyama Kokutai.
They were then accepted for Navy
service as the Type 90-2 Flying-
boat, with the short designation
H3K1. Two more examples followed in November 1932 and
February 1933.

The four aircraft built by Kawanishi had distinctive features of their
own, but all had the same type
engines and performance. Significant features of the design of these
large metal flying-boats were that
the lower part of the hull was made
of sheet stainless steel which formed
a monocoque structure, a servo-
rudder to reduce manual control
forces, and the addition of a tail gun
turret, the first in Japan.

These were recognized as the
largest flying-boats in the Pacific.
One H3K1 commanded by Lieut
Sukemitsu Itoh made a 1,300nm
(1,496sm) long-range demonstration flight between the Tateyama
Naval Air Base, on Tokyo Bay,
and Saipan in the summer of 1932.
Unfortunately, on 8 January 1933,
one of these flying-boats crashed
while alighting at night near Tateyama on a training flight. A slow-
reading altimeter was given as the
cause of the accident that killed
the noted naval pilot Lieut-Cdr
Shinzo Shin, and two more of the
crew of nine.

These large flying-boats established Kawanishi as a manufacturer
of flying-boats throughout the
Pacific War years and after.

Three-engined biplane flying-boat. All-metal two-step hull with stainless
steel stressed-skin below water-line. Wings of metal structure covered with
fabric. Crew of six to nine.

Three 825-955hp Rolls-Royce H-10 Buzzard twelve-cylinder vee
water-cooled engines, driving two-bladed wooden propellers.

One nose twin-flexible 7.7mm machine-gun, two dorsal twin-flexible
7.7mm machine-guns, one tail twin-flexible 7.7mm machine-gun. Bomb
load: two 500kg (1,102lb) or four 250kg (551lb) bombs.

Data source:	Kawanishi	Yokosho
Span	31.05m (101ft 10½in)	31.09m (102ft)
Length	22.55m (73ft 11¾in)	22.047m (72ft 4in)
Height	8.77m (28ft 9in)	8.128m (26ft 8in)
Wing area	214sq m	214sq m
	(2,303.5sq ft)	(2,303.5sq ft)
Empty weight	10,030kg (22,111lb)	10,129kg (22,330lb)
Loaded weight	15,000kg (33,069lb)	17,200kg (37,919lb)
Wing loading	70.1kg/sq m	80.4kg/sq m
	(14.3lb/sq ft)	(16.4lb/sq ft)
Power loading	6.46kg/hp (14.21lb/hp)	6.95kg/hp (15.3lb/hp)
Maximum speed	121.6kg (140mph)	120.8kt (139mph)
Cruising speed	91kt (105mph)	—
Climb to	3,000m (9,845ft)	3,000m (9,845ft)
in	19min 40sec	23min 36sec
Service ceiling	4,040m (13,254ft)	4,950m (16,240ft)
Endurance	9hr	13.36hr

One built by Short Bros in 1930, four by Kawanishi 1932–33.

Navy Type 90-3 Reconnaissance Seaplane (E5K1)

To bring its reconnaissance sea-planes up to world standards, the Navy accepted a highly modified version of the Yokosho Navy Type 14 Reconnaissance Seaplane. Welded steel-tube fuselage construction was introduced, and the wings were completely redesigned. A more reliable 450hp Jupiter radial engine replaced the Lorraine inline engine of the same power. After Yokosho had produced about three of these aircraft, known then as the Type 14 Kai-1, the design with further changes was passed to Kawanishi which manufactured two pre-production models in 1931 as its Type G. After testing by the Navy, the type was accepted as the Navy Type 90-3 Reconnaissance Seaplane, with the short designation E5Y1. This advanced three-seat seaplane was put into production with modifications that were uniquely Kawanishi's. These included a change from the Jupiter air-cooled radial to the 500hp Type 91 water-cooled engine, with which they had the designation E5K1. In all, Kawanishi built 17 of these reconnaissance seaplanes by the end of 1932. (*see* Yokosho Navy Type 90-3 Reconnaissance Seaplane).

Navy Type 90-2-2 Reconnaissance Seaplane (E4N2)

Under a licence agreement with The Chance Vought Corporation in the United States, in 1930 Nakajima began the manufacture of the 02U Corsair with slight modifications including the use of the Jupiter engine. In Japan, they were designated the Navy Type 90-2-2 Reconnaissance Seaplane. This single-float biplane was a much more nimble aeroplane than its twin-float predecessors, being described as being as manoeuvrable as a fighter, a duty which they were expected to perform when needed. They gained a high reputation as reconnaissance seaplanes for catapulting from battleships and cruisers. From 1932 to 1934 Kawanishi supplemented Naka-jima production by building sixty-seven of these floatplanes which it called Type K. (*see* Nakajima Navy Type 90-2-2 Reconnaissance Sea-plane.)

Navy Type 91 Flying-boat (H4H1 and 2)

In an attempt to keep pace with aviation technology, the Hiro Arsenal began a design in 1931 of a twin-engined all-metal monoplane flying-boat as a replacement for its Type 15 and Type 89 Flying-boats. Development was slow and while it continued, Kawanishi as well as Hiro began production, with each incorporating new changes. Among the major differences was the choice of Type 91 water-cooled engines for the H4H1s while H4H2s were powered by Myojo radial air-cooled engines. The first of these Kawanishi-produced aircraft was flown on 16 June, 1933, followed by a total of seventeen Type 91 Flying-boats built by the company, and Hiro produced approximately thirty. (*see* Hirosho Navy Type 91 Flying-boat.)

Navy Type 91 Reconnaissance Seaplane (E6Y1)

Based upon a programme begun in 1929 to improve upon the submarine-borne reconnaissance seaplane concept, the Yokosuka Naval Arsenal (Yokosho) produced the Navy Type 91 Reconnaissance Seaplane. This was a very small, foldable, single-seat biplane on quickly-detachable twin-floats. Yokosho built two prototypes and, when satisfied with flying characteristics and related modifications, production was transferred to Kawanishi as its Type N. Kawanishi produced eight of these seaplanes. (*see* Yoko-sho Navy Type 91 Reconnaissance Seaplane).

Experimental 8-Shi Reconnaissance Seaplane (E8K1) (Company designation Type P)

Continually trying to improve its aircraft, in 1933 the Navy placed orders with Aichi, Nakajima and Kawanishi for an 8-Shi Experimental Reconnaissance Seaplane that would have better manoeuvrability and higher performance than the Nakajima Navy Type 90-2 Reconnaissance Seaplane, the E4N2, that it was to replace. The newly-formed Kawanishi team of young design engineers under the supervision of Eiji Sekiguchi began the task in May 1933. Their project was known within Kawanishi as the Type P.

The team undertook an entirely new concept for single-float reconnaissance seaplanes, designing a low-wing monoplane instead of the usual biplane it was intended to replace. This was five years in advance of the US Navy's OS2U-1 Kingfisher and SO2C-1 Seagull monoplanes for the same mission. Through concentrated work, the aeroplane was designed and completed by December 1933. It made

Kawanishi Experimental 8-Shi Reconnaissance Seaplane (E8 K1).

Kawanishi Experimental 9-Shi Night Reconnaissance Seaplane (E10K1), later converted to the Navy Type 94 Transport.

its first flight on 8 January, 1934, and was delivered to the Navy the following month as the E8K1.

Navy evaluation showed that its handling qualities on take off and alighting were inferior to those of the Type 90-2. It also lacked manoeuvrability for dog-fighting as compared to its biplane predecessor. In short, the Kawanishi E8K1 monoplane and the Aichi E8A1 biplane entries in this competition revealed no appreciable improvements over the Type 90-2, and therefore were declared unacceptable. Instead, the Navy accepted Nakajima's orthodox E8N1 biplane, which was a development of the Type 90-2 and became the Type 95 Reconnaissance Seaplane (Dave) that saw service in the Pacific War. Kawanishi undertook production of the E8N1, assisting Nakajima by building forty-eight of these aircraft. Consequently, a suitable two-seat reconnaissance monoplane for shipboard catapult service was never satisfactorily developed in Japan.

Single-engine single-float low-wing monoplane reconnaissance seaplane. Fuselage of wood and metal structure covered with fabric, wings of metal with fabric covering. Rearward folding wings for stowage. Crew of two in open cockpits.

460–580hp Kotobuki 2-kai-1 nine-cylinder air-cooled radial engine, driving a fixed-pitch two-bladed metal propeller.

Two forward-firing fixed 7.7mm machine-guns, one dorsal flexible 7.7 mm machine-gun. Bomb load: two 30kg (66lb) bombs.

Span 11.95m (39ft 2½in); length 9.23m (30ft 3¼in); height 3.87m (12ft 8½in); wing area 23.34sq m (251.237sq ft).

Empty weight 1,326kg (2,923lb); loaded weight 1,900kg (4,188lb); wing loading 81.6kg/sq m (16.7lb/sq ft); power loading 4.1kg/hp (9lb/hp).

Maximum speed 158kt (182mph) at 2,000m (6,562ft); alighting speed 65.5kt (75.5mph); climb to 3,000m (9,843ft) in 7min 56sec; service ceiling 7,300m (2,395ft); endurance 3.3hr.

One built in 1933.

Experimental 9-Shi Night Reconnaissance Seaplane (E10K1) and Navy Type 94 Transport

(Company designation Type T)

Early in 1934, the Navy contracted with Aichi and Kawanishi to design and build an Experimental 9-Shi Night Reconnaissance Seaplane that was to be powered by a 500hp class engine. This was to be a further development of the 6-Shi Experimental Small Night Reconnaissance Flying-boat built by Aichi which, after prolonged evaluation, was still not acceptable for

service. The aircraft's mission was to be the eyes of the fleet at night: directing friendly gunfire and launching torpedoes on the distant enemy ships and to inform submarines of enemy ship movements at night.

Desired qualities for such an aeroplane were that it should fly slowly, have good endurance and be suitable for catapulting from warships. This would be a small flying-boat, with good water-handling capability and ability to cope well in open seas. To reduce crew fatigue while on long night missions it had to have good control and stability while in low-speed flight. Thus the design requirements for this aircraft were considerably different to those of previous Kawanishi aircraft.

The design was started in January 1934 and became known as the Kawanishi Type T: the first flying-boat to be purely of Kawanishi design from the very beginning. Design work was eased somewhat by using the wing design of Kawanishi's own E7K, Navy Type 94 Reconnaissance Seaplane (Allied code-name Alf). Its radial air-cooled engine was mounted forward of the top wing, contrary to the Aichi AB-12 which used a water-cooled pusher engine layout.

The first flight of the Type T

was made on 10 September, 1934, and the aircraft was delivered to the Navy the following month as the E10K1. Although changes were made in the engine and airframe, the Navy found the aeroplane unacceptable for the night reconnaissance role because of stability problems, both on the water and in the air. In its place, the Aichi AB-12 was accepted as the Type 96 Reconnaissance Seaplane.

In the hope of salvaging the Type T design, the flying-boat was modified into a utility transport by installing a beaching gear that would simply be rotated out of the water when afloat and in the air. In this transport configuration, it was accepted as the Navy Type 94 Transport, but only the one prototype was ever built.

Single-engine tractor single-bay equal-span biplane small flying-boat. All-metal stressed skin two-step hull, metal structured wing with fabric covering. Rearward folding wings for stowage. Crew of three; pilot, co-pilot and observer/gunner.

480-600hp Kotobuki 1 nine-cylinder air-cooled radial engine (E10K1), 610-710hp Kotobuki 4-kai nine-cylinder air-cooled radial engine (Type 94 Transport), both driving fixed-pitch three-bladed metal propellers.

One nose flexible 7.7mm machine-gun.

	9-Shi Reconnaissance Seaplane	Type 94 Transport
Span	14.55m (47ft 8¾in)	15m (49ft 2¾in)
Length	11.337m (37ft 2¼in)	11m (36ft 1in)
Height	4.40m (14ft 5¼in)	4.40m (14ft 5¼in)
Wing area	50.5sq m (543.595sq ft)	52sq m (559.741sq ft)
Empty weight	1,670kg (3,681lb)	2,300kg (5,070lb)
Loaded weight	2,870kg (6,327lb)	3,380kg (7,451lb)
Wing loading	56.8kg/sq m (11.6lb/sq ft)	65kg/sq ft (13.3lb/sq ft)
Power loading	5.98kg/hp (13.2lb/hp)	5.54kg/hp (12.2lb/hp)
Maximum speed	111kt (128mph)	102kt (118mph)
Cruising speed	—	60kt (69mph)
Alighting speed	53.2kt (61mph)	—
Service ceiling	—	3,460m (11,351ft)
Range	—	640nm (737sm)

One built in 1934.

Kawanishi Experimental 11-Shi Special Reconnaissance Seaplane (E11K1), which later became the Navy Type 96 Transport.

Experimental 11-Shi Special Reconnaissance Seaplane (E11K1) and Navy Type 96 Transport

In 1936, with hopes of achieving a more suitable small flying-boat as a replacement for the Aichi Navy Type 96 Reconnaissance Seaplane the Navy again placed contracts with Aichi and Kawanishi to design and build an Experimental 11-Shi Special Reconnaissance Seaplane. Kawanishi engineers began their design in October 1936. This was of a cantilever monoplane, having a gull-wing with wingtip floats which when retracted became the wingtips. The pylon mounted engine was a water-cooled pusher type, with its radiator placed high above the rear deck of the hull to position it within the propeller wash for cooling air while the aircraft was flying at low speed or on the water. The structure was stressed for catapult launching, and the wing had a unique method of folding for storage.

The prototype made its first flight on 11 June, 1937, and was delivered to the Navy on 27 June. Results of the Navy's evaluation were very similar to those of the E10K1, in that it lacked stability, both in the air and on the water. There were chronic problems with the retracting mechanism for the wingtip floats, and problems developed in the engine installation system. The aircraft was heavier than expected, and was generally inferior to its competitor, the Aichi AB-14. These shortcomings resulted in the Navy's conclusion that the aeroplane showed little prospect of fulfilling the night reconnaissance role for which it was designed.

As a result, the more orthodox Aichi AB-14 biplane was accepted and designated the Navy Type 98 Reconnaissance Seaplane. Kawanishi then added retractable beaching gear to its two prototypes of the E11K1 as it had done with E10K1, and the Navy accepted them as the Navy Type 96 Transport. These served as command aircraft for reconnaissance seaplane squadrons and remained in service for a considerable period.

Single-engine pusher monoplane flying-boat. All-metal stressed skin two-step hull, metal structure shoulder-mounted gull-wing with metal stressed skin. Rearward folding wings for stowage. Crew of three; pilot, co-pilot and observer/gunner.

520-620hp Type 91-1 twelve-cylinder W water-cooled engine (11-Shi), or 600-750hp Type 91-2 twelve-cylinder W water-cooled engine (Type 96), both driving four-bladed wooden propellers.

One nose flexible 7.7mm machine-gun.

	11-Shi Special Reconnaissance	Type 96 Transport
Span	16.19m (53ft 1½in)	16m (52ft 6in)
Length	11.90m (39ft 0½in)	11.80m (38ft 8½in)
Height	4.504m (14ft 9¼in)	4.40m (14ft 5¼in)
Wing area	38sq m (409.041sq ft) with floats retracted.	
Empty weight	2,170kg (4,784lb)	2,720kg (5,996lb)
Loaded weight	3,300kg (7,275lb)	3,860kg (8,509lb)
Wing loading	86.9kg/sq m (17.8lb/sq ft)	101.6kg/sq m (20.8lb/sq ft)
Power loading	6.34kg/hp(13.9lb/hp)	6.43kg/hp (14.1lb/hp)
Maximum speed	125kt (144mph)	112kt (129mph)
Cruising speed	70kt (81mph)	70kt (81mph)
Alighting speed	55.3kt (64mph)	—
Climb to	3,000m (9,843ft)	—
in	22min	—
Service ceiling	3,795m (12,450ft)	4,200m (13,779ft)
Range	820nm (943sm)	—
Endurance	8.4hr	—

Two built in 1937.

Experimental 11-Shi Intermediate Seaplane Trainer (K6K1)

On 12 February, 1937, the Navy placed orders with Watanabe and Kawanishi to develop a high-performance intermediate-level seaplane trainer, to be specifically powered by a Kotobuki engine. Kawanishi engineers planned their new design on experience accumulated with the Type 93 Intermediate Seaplane Trainer (K5Y2) and the

Kawanishi Experimental 11-Shi Intermediate Trainer Seaplane (K6K1).

Type 94 Reconnaissance Seaplane (E7K2), both then under production. The first of three prototypes was flown on 30 April, 1938, and delivered to the Navy the following July. All three were delivered by October but were unacceptable because of poor alighting characteristics. Major modifications were made until January 1940, when the Navy abandoned both the Kawanishi K6K1 and the Watanabe K6W1.

Instead the higher-powered version of Yokosho's Navy Type 93 Intermediate Seaplane Trainer-kai was evaluated and found acceptable. However, this was not put into production; instead, the original models of the K5Y1 and 2 were kept in production until the end of the Pacific war.

Single-engine twin-float biplane intermediate-level trainer. All-metal structure with fabric covering. Twin-floats of metal construction. Pupil and instructor in open cockpits.

460-580hp Kotobuki 2-kai-1 nine-cylinder radial air-cooled engine, driving a fixed-pitch two-bladed metal propeller.

Span 12.20m (40ft 0¼in); length 9.30m (30ft 6in); height 4m (13ft 1½in); wing area 30sq m (322.927sq ft).

Empty weight 1,300kg (2,866lb); loaded weight 1,800kg (3,968lb); wing loading 60kg/sq m (12.2lb/sq ft); power loading 3.95kg/hp (8.7lb/hp).

Maximum speed 125kt (144mph) at sea level; climb to 3,000m (9,843ft) in 11min; endurance 6hr.

Three built in 1938.

Experimental 12-Shi Three-seat Reconnaissance Seaplane (E13K1)

In 1937, hoping to obtain a suitable replacement for the Navy Type 94 Reconnaissance Seaplane, the Navy placed orders with Aichi and Kawanishi for a high-performance long-range three-seat aircraft suitable for catapult launching and shore-based operations.

Kawanishi began work in March 1937 on a very slim low-wing monoplane mounted on two well-contoured single-step floats. The first of two prototypes flew on 28 September, 1938, and was delivered to the Navy the following month as the E13K1. Performance was superior to Aichi's E13A1 except for maximum speed, but the Kawanishi example had more difficult maintenance and deck handling and was considered less practical. As a result, it did not gain the Navy's acceptance, and the project was terminated when the Aichi E13A1 (Jake) was accepted.

During flight testing, the first Kawanishi prototype developed excessive vibration which resulted in an accident, and the second prototype mysteriously disappeared while being flown by a Navy test pilot.

Kawanishi Experimental 12-Shi Three-seat Reconnaissance Seaplane (E13K1).

Single-engine twin-float low-wing monoplane reconnaissance seaplane. All-metal construction with fabric-covered control surfaces. Outer wing panels folded upward for stowage. Crew of three in tandem enclosed cockpits.

910-1,030hp Mitsubishi Kinsei 3 kai, fourteen-cylinder double-row air-cooled radial engine, driving a constant-speed three-bladed metal propeller.

One dorsal flexible 7.7mm machine-gun. Bomb load: One 250kg (551lb) or four 60kg (132lb) bombs.

Span 14.49m (47ft 6½in); length 11.725m (38ft 5½in); height 4.453m (14ft 7¼in); wing area 34sq m (365.984 sq ft).

Empty weight 2,170kg (4,784lb); loaded weight 3,550kg (7,826lb); wing loading 104.4kg/sq m (21.3lb/sq ft); power loading 3.9kg/hp (8.6lb/hp).

Maximum speed 189kt (218mph) at 1,100m (3,608ft); cruising speed 120kt (138mph); alighting speed 58kt (67 mph); climb to 4,000m (13,123ft) in 9min 14sec; service ceiling 6,690m (21,948ft); endurance 16hr.

Two built in 1938.

Navy Type 0 Primary Seaplane Trainer (K8K1)

In 1937, the Navy placed orders with Nippi, Watanabe and Kawanishi for a 12-Shi Primary Seaplane Trainer to be powered by a 130hp Jimpu engine as replacement for the Navy Type 90 Primary Seaplane Trainer. There was little latitude in design concept, therefore all three entries were almost the same in appearance and performance.

The design of the Kawanishi model was begun in May 1937 having been given the short designation K8K1. The first of three prototypes was flown on 6 July, 1938, and delivered to the Navy the following month. After operational testing and evaluation by the Navy against both the Nippi K8Ni1 and Watanabe K8W1, the Kawanishi aircraft was accepted in June 1940 as the Navy Type 0-1-1 Primary Seaplane Trainer, later shortened to Type 0, and was superior in flying stability and control, and a vast improvement over the Navy Type 90 Primary Seaplane Trainer then in service. The only aerodynamic modification was reduction of the area of the rudder horn balance. The aeroplane was put into production at the beginning of 1940, but production ended after fifteen aircraft, when a change was made and seaplane pilots' training began on the Type 93 Intermediate Seaplane Trainer.

Single-engine twin-float biplane seaplane trainer. Fuselage of welded steel tubing with fabric covering, wooden wing structure covered with fabric.

Metal floats. Student and instructor in open cockpits.

130-160hp Gasuden Jimpu 2 seven-cylinder air-cooled radial engine, driving a two-bladed wooden propeller.

Span 9.50m (31ft 2in); length 8.80m (28ft 10½in); wing area 24sq m (258.342sq ft).

Empty weight 719kg (1,585lb); loaded weight 991kg (2,184lb); wing loading 42kg/sq m (8.6lb/sq ft); power loading 7.6kg/hp (16.7lb/hp).

Maximum speed 100kt (115mph) at sea level; cruising speed 65kt (75mph); alighting speed 40kt (46mph); climb to 3,000m (9,843ft) in 5min 40sec; service ceiling 3,490m (11,450ft); range 277nm (319sm); endurance 4.6hr.

Three prototypes built in 1938 and twelve production aircraft in 1940.

Several designs created before the Pacific War continued in service during the war. These included the Navy Type 94 Reconnaissance Seaplane (Alf) E7K1 and 2, as well as the widely used, very large, four-engine flying-boats, the Navy Type 97 Flying-boat (Mavis) H6K2 to H6K5, and the Navy Type 2 Flying-boat (Emily) H8K1 and 2. Other marine aircraft projects were also underway, such as the E15K1 (Norm) reconnaissance seaplane and N1K1 (Rex) single-float fighter that was later developed into the N1K2-J (George) land-based fighter. Thus Kawanishi remained a prominent manufacturer throughout the period of the Pacific War.

Kawanishi Navy Type 0 Primary Seaplane Trainer (K8K1).

Kawasaki Aircraft Company Ltd (Kawasaki Kokuki Kabushiki Kaisha)

As part of the large Kawasaki Dockyard Company (KK Kawasaki Zosensho), an Aeroplane Section was formed in April 1919 at its Hyogo Factory in Kobe for the purpose of building foreign-designed aircraft for the Army. For the next eighteen years, aircraft were manufactured within the shipbuilding site in this heavily industrialized area of the steel and ship producing part of Kobe. There was no direct access to an aerodrome, but this was of no importance because the newly manufactured aircraft needed only to be delivered to the Army in disassembled form.

In 1922, the Aeroplane Section was upgraded to the Aeroplane Department. A small landing area was constructed the following year as Kagamigahara Airfield near Gifu, 18 miles north of Nagoya, on flat, unobstructed ground, with mountains at a safe distance on three sides. The already established

trans-Honshu railway provided a 190km (118 miles) surface link between the aircraft department at the Kagamigahara Airfield and the Kobe factory and headquarters. By May 1927, it was recognized as the Aeroplane Factory of the Kawasaki Dockyard Co Ltd and the following December moved its airframe manufacturing activities to its expanding facility on the northern edge of what was now the Kagamigahara Army Air Field. It was not until November 1937 that the factory separated completely from the parent company and became the Kawasaki Aircraft Co Ltd (Kawasaki Kokuki KK).

As with other Japanese aircraft in the early days, there was considerable evidence of foreign influence on the design of Kawasaki products. In August 1919 the company purchased the licence to manufacture the French Salmson 2-A.2 two-seat reconnaissance aeroplane, complete with engine. When Kawasaki established its Aeroplane Department, former Navy Captain (Engineering) Tomokichi Takezaki was assigned as the first general manager. The company aligned itself with Dornier in Germany and obtained numerous manufacturing rights for Dornier aircraft. As part of this licence agreement, Dornier's Dr Richard Vogt was transferred to Kawasaki in 1924 as its chief advisor and designer. That same

year, the company began building BMW aero-engines under a licence agreement with the Bayerische Motoren-Werke of Munich. Advancing towards the building of bigger aircraft, in 1927 the company began manufacture of the Type 87 Heavy Bomber, and built twenty-eight of these twin-engined all-metal land-based bombers that closely resembled the Dornier Wal flying-boat, all within the restricted area of the Kobe shipbuilding facilities.

The company's early manufacture of aircraft engines took place at the Kawasaki Dockyard until early in 1939. A new plant was erected in 1940 at Akashi, just west of Kobe on the Inland Sea. At the same time, a subsidiary unit of airframe division was formed at Akashi, but operated under the Kagamigahara management. This continual expansion led to the establishment of the main office at Akashi, which exercised control over all airframe and aero-engine manufacture by Kawasaki. An airfield was constructed at Akashi in September 1941.

Through the late 1920s and early 1930s the company received sizable Army orders, brought about by the impending Chinese war. By 1935,

Kawasaki Army Type Otsu 1 Reconnaissance Aircraft, adapted from the French Salmson 2-A.2. (H Ando).

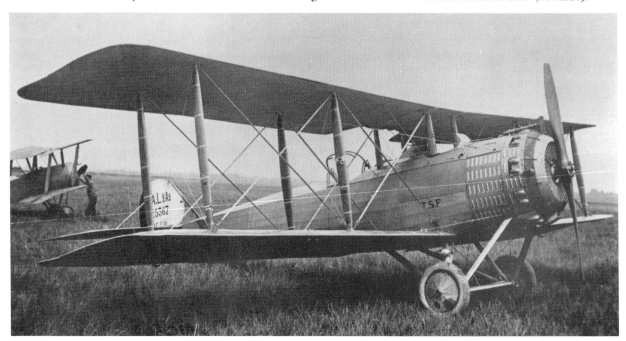

this prompted a 1,000-unit order for the Kawasaki Army Type 98 Light Bomber (Ki-32), many of which remained in service in China until after the start of the Pacific War. This large order further cemented a lasting alliance with the Army in the exclusive manufacture of army aircraft types apart from a few civil models in the earlier years of the company.

An Army Type Otsu 1 with Japanese markings.

Army Type Otsu 1 Reconnaissance Aircraft (Kawasaki-Salmson 2-A.2)

At the end of the First World War, the president of Kawasaki Dockyard, Kojiro Matsugata, received a strong indication that the Army intended acquiring a number of Salmson 2-A.2 aircraft. The Army was impressed by this aeroplane of which several were taken to Japan by the Mission Française d'Aéronautique in January 1919 and in which Japanese pilots and crews were trained by the French. Wishing to enter the aircraft manufacturing market, Matsugata went to Paris and acquired the manufacturing rights for the Salmson 2-A.2 reconnaissance aeroplane along with its engine. He also shipped two of these aircraft and one Salmson 7-A.2 to Japan, arriving there in August 1919.

Before their arrival, Kawasaki secured a contract from the Army for the manufacture of the Salmson. In 1920, in order to study the Salmson manufacturing process, the company sent to the Salmson factory in France, Engineer Suzuki, and senior mechanics of the automobile section, Kasahara and Nishida along with Engineer Miwa and chief mechanic Hayashi of the head office, and they returned with the knowledge and materials needed for Salmson production. At the same time, the Army wanted to begin its own manufacture of this aircraft but only had a licence to build the engine. Army aircraft production began however, under the guise of 'aircraft repair.' Salmson filed a protest, and mediation by the manager of Kawasaki's Aeroplane Department, Tomokichi Takezaki,

cleared the way for continued Army production.

The two production sources worked in collaboration. The Army completed its first Salmson 2-A.2 in late 1920 at Tokorozawa and officially accepted it in December 1921 as the Type Otsu 1 Reconnaissance Aircraft. Kawasaki sent engineers Suzuki and Arai to Tokorozawa to learn ways of speeding its own production and this enabled Kawasaki to complete its first two prototypes in November 1922. One, assembled from Army parts, the other built solely by Kawasaki, received serial numbers 1001 and 1002 respectively. When flight tests were successfully accomplished, the Army placed an order for 45 with Kawasaki, followed by further orders reaching 300 aircraft before production terminated in August 1927. These Japanese aircraft were identical to the French Salmson 2-A.2 with the exception of some with modifications around the engine cowling and seats. Kawasaki imported fifty-six engines from Salmson for installation in early production aircraft, but after 1923 all airframes were equipped with Kawasaki-built engines. In time, the Army fitted some with dual controls to use them as trainers. Some variants had a forward-firing fixed machine-gun, or wing-mounted shackles for six small bombs or small flare bombs.

In April 1923, when production of the Type Otsu 1 was well underway, Kawasaki began a performance-improvement project calling for modification of existing aircraft. Withdrawing two Type Otsu 1 aircraft from production

and the imported Salmson 7-A.2, which was the French improved version of their 2-A.2, modifications were made on them, including the use of the more powerful 300hp Salmson AZ-9 engine, and a radiator change to the Lamblin type. Dimensions remained the same but the modified aircraft were 100kg heavier in empty weight. However, with the added power, an increase in performance was expected, but engine overheating problems brought a decision to retain the original 230hp Z-9 engines.

As the Army reorganized its air units according to the French system, the Type Otsu 1s were assigned to bomber units as interim light bombers. The first combat from the Army Type Otsu 1 took place in October 1922 while operating in Siberia. In the Manchurian and Shanghai Incidents, the Type Otsu 1s were also very active, not only in their original reconnaissance role, but for bombing, liaison, light cargo transport, message pick-up and dropping, smoke-screen laying and ration re-supply. Because of their large numbers they remained in service as the Army's primary aircraft until replaced by the Type 88 Reconnaissance Aircraft around 1933. Those released to civilians as surplus aircraft were popular during the biplane era together with Avro 504Ks and Hanriots.

Single-engine two-bay reconnaissance biplane. All-wood structure with fabric covering. Crew of two in open cockpits.

230-260hp Kawasaki Salmson Z.9 nine-cylinder water-cooled radial engine, driving a two-bladed wooden propeller.

Single or twin dorsal flexible 7.7mm machine-guns, with optional forward-firing fixed 7.7mm machine-gun.

Span 11.767m (38ft 7¼in); length 8.624m (28ft 3in); height 2.90m (9ft 6in); wing area 37.27sq m (401.174sq ft).

Empty weight 930kg (2,050lb); loaded weight 1,500kg (3,306lb); wing loading 40.2kg/sq m (8.2lb/sq ft); power loading 6.51kg/hp (14.35lb/hp).

Maximum speed 101kt (116mph) at 2,000m (6,562ft); climb to 3,000m (9,843ft) in 11min 42sec; service ceiling 5,800m (19,028ft); endurance 3½-7hr.

300 built by Kawasaki from November 1922 to August 1927 and approximately 300 built by Tokorozawa Branch of Army Supply Dept.

Army Type 87 Heavy Bomber (Kawasaki- Dornier Do N)

In early 1924, the Army placed an order with Kawasaki for a new all-metal monoplane heavy night bomber to replace the Type Tei 1 (Farman F.50) and Type Tei 2 (Farman F.60 Goliath) Heavy Bombers. Kawasaki asked for Dornier's assistance to design and build the prototype. Manager of the Aeroplane Department, Tomokichi Takezaki, went to Dornier and BMW in March 1924, taking with him engineer Hisashi Tojo and four other engineers. Once the licence agreements were concluded, Kawa-

saki then obtained the assistance of seven Dornier engineers led by Dr Richard Vogt, and was later visited by Dr Claude Dornier to co-ordinate matters between the two companies.

By Army order, the new bomber, known originally as the Do N Heavy Bomber, was a top secret project both by Kawasaki and by Dornier at its factory in Switzerland where it was designed. Two prototypes were built by Kawasaki, the first of which was completed in January 1926 and the second by the spring of the same year. Because of the delay in Kawasaki's production of BMW VI engines, the prototypes were powered by 450hp Napier Lion engines imported from Britain.

The bomber looked like a landplane version of the Wal all-metal flying-boat which Dornier had recently launched, and which was to prove such an outstanding success. Tests continued for nearly a year until the type was officially adopted by the Army in the spring of 1927 as the Army Type 87 Heavy Bomber. Production continued until 1932, with twenty-eight aircraft (including two prototypes) delivered to the Army. This was the first Japanese bomber to be able to carry a one-ton bomb load.

In the early period of its operational service, problems became evident with its power, structural strength and stability. Despite shortcomings however, it was the main

equipment for the heavy bomber force and served without any significant changes being made. These were the first bombers to be part of regiment strength assigned to Hamamatsu, beginning in 1927, at which time this became the Japanese Army's main bomber base and remained so until the end of the Pacific War. These bombers initially consisted of one chutai (four aircraft) of Army Type 87 Heavy Bombers and one chutai (consisting of nine aircraft) of Army Type 87 Light Bombers. A small number of these heavy bombers were based at Kagamigahara and Tachikawa. During the Manchurian Incident, one chutai of these bombers participated experimentally in the campaign for a short period. Although a technical breakthrough as a large all-metal aeroplane for the Army, it was excessively slow, and not greatly appreciated by its crews.

Twin-engined parasol-monoplane. Metal construction throughout with Dornier stressed skin. Crew of six, pilot, co-pilot, bombardier/nose gunner, navigator, radio operator, and engineer/rear gunner.

Two 450-600hp Kawasaki BMW VI twelve-cylinder vee water-cooled engines mounted in tandem and driving two-bladed wooden propellers.

Kawasaki Army Type 87 Heavy Bomber, also referred to as the Kawasaki-Dornier Do N.

One nose flexible twin 7.7mm machine-gun, one dorsal flexible twin 7.7mm machine-gun, and one rear ventral flexible 7.7mm machine-gun. Bomb load: Maximum 1,000kg (2,204lb).

Span 26.80m (87ft 11in); length 18m (59ft 0½in); height 5.85m (19ft 2½in); wing area 121sq m (1,302.475sq ft).

Empty weight 4,400–5,100kg (9,700–11,243lb); loaded weight 7,650–7,700 kg (16,865–16,975lb); wing loading 64.1kg/sq m (13.1lb/sq ft); power loading 8.55kg/hp (18.8lb/hp).

Maximum speed 97.5kt (112.5mph) at sea level; cruising speed 92kt (106mph); climb to 3,000m (9,843ft) in 44min; service ceiling 5,000m (16,404ft).

Two prototypes built in 1926, twenty-six production aircraft 1928–32. (Six to nine built by Army Artillery Arsenal in Atsuta, Nagoya.)

Army Type 88 Reconnaissance Aircraft

(Company Designation KDA-2)

In the spring of 1926, the Army placed orders with Kawasaki, Mitsubishi, Ishikawajima, and later with Nakajima, to compete in designing a new reconnaissance aircraft. Nakajima chose to design for long-range missions rather than close air support, (see Nakajima N-35), but the remaining three were to be for a replacement for the Type Otsu 1 Salmson 2-A.2. Since this was a new venture for the three companies, each invited designers from Germany. Dr Richard Vogt was obtained for the Kawasaki project, to be assisted by Hisashi Tojo. Initially, the project went under the designation KDA-2 Reconnaissance Aircraft, the letters standing for Kawasaki Dockyard Army-type.

The Army's specification called for a maximum speed of more than 200km/h, range of more than 1,000km, and armament consisting of one forward-firing fixed 7.7mm machine-gun and one dorsal flexible twin machine-guns of the same type. Extra equipment was to be a large aerial camera and radio. Design work was begun in April 1926.

The first aircraft was completed as a company aircraft at Kawasaki's Kobe Factory in February 1927. Flight tests of the first prototype showed that the Army specifications were exceeded and that the maximum speed was 240km/h. The second and third prototypes for delivery to the Army were completed in July of that year. Although heavier, with a weight increase of approximately 250kg because of added Army equipment, flight specifications were still met. After the ferrying of the two Army prototypes to Tokorozawa for testing, they were accepted as the Army Type 88 Reconnaissance Aircraft on Kigensetsu day (Nat-

ional Foundation), 11 February, 1928, with Kawasaki declared the winner with the prize of 200,000 yen. Factors in this success were the excellent basic airframe design and the very powerful BMW VI engine.

The prototypes went through a number of modifications during the test phase, some of which included successful air-to-air refuelling trials, incorporation of a Sperry autopilot, seaplane conversion, the Army's first testing of a three-bladed propeller, and special equipment for long-range flights. Leading-edge wing slats on the upper wing were tried but not retained.

After introduction of some of these refinements, later models became the Type 88-2, the earlier models becoming Type 88-1. The later model had a more streamlined nose, with a faired radiator below the nose rather than a flat frontal radiator. It had a propeller spinner and a taller and tapered fin and rudder. Ailerons were added to the lower wing as well, and connected with an external push rod. Other changes during production were mainly in the propeller and radiator.

Two specially modified Type 88-1 aircraft having a total fuel capacity of 1,600 litres made a remarkable flight from Tachiarai, Kyushu, to Pingtung, Taiwan, on 21 October, 1929, covering the

Kawasaki Army Type 88-1 Reconnaissance Aircraft.

The Type 88-2 had cleaner lines.

650nm (750sm) overwater flight in just over 8hr. This not only demonstrated the tactical capability of these aircraft, but confirmed the reliability of the Kawasaki BMW VI engine.

As the successor to the Type Otsu 1, many Type 88s were used in first-line service from 1929 to 1940 for reconnaissance and as a multi-purpose aircraft in such incidents as Chinan, Manchuria and Shanghai as well as in the early stage of the Sino-Japanese Conflict. Type 88 Reconnaissance Aircraft were the first aircraft of all-metal structure in Japan, and the large number produced confirmed Kawasaki's position as an Army aircraft manufacturer until the end of the Pacific War.

Single-engine reconnaissance biplane. All-metal construction with stressed metal skin on forward fuselage. Remainder of aircraft was fabric covered. Crew of two in open cockpits.

450-600hp Kawasaki BMW VI twelve-cylinder vee water-cooled engine, driving a two-bladed wooden propeller.

One forward-firing fixed 7.7mm machine-gun, twin dorsal flexible 7.7mm machine-guns.

	Type 88-1	Type 88-2
Span	15m (49ft 2¾in)	15m (49ft 2¾in)
Length	12.8m (42ft)	12.8m (42ft)
Height	3.40m (11ft 2in)	3.40m (11ft 2in)
Wing area	48sq m (516.684sq ft)	48sq m (516.684sq ft)
Empty weight	1,750kg (3,858lb)	1,800kg (3,968lb)
Loaded weight	2,800kg (6,172lb)	2,850kg (6,283lb)
Wing loading	58.5kg/sq m (11.9lb/sq ft)	58.6kg/sq m (12lb/sq ft)
Power loading	6.22kg/hp (13.7lb/hp)	6.33kg/hp (13.9lb/hp)
Maximum speed	108kt (125mph)	119kt (137mph)
Climb to	—	3,000m (9,843ft)
in	—	16min
Service ceiling	6,500m (21,325ft)	6,200m (20,341ft)
Endurance	—	6hr

710 built: three prototypes February–July 1927; 520 Type 88-1 and 88-2 February 1928–December 1931; and 187 Type 88-2 by Tachikawa February 1928–December 1931.

Army Type 88 Light Bomber (Company designation KDA-2)

By the late 1920s, only a small number of Mitsubishi Type 87 light bombers were operating in the Army, still focusing most of its attention on reconnaissance aircraft. However, the need for a light bomber was evident, and these wood and fabric bombers had reached their limit of development. It was expected that they would be replaced by the all-metal sesquiplane light bomber built by the Army's Department of Supply at Tokorozawa but these did not perform as expected. (*see* Army-Built Experimental-Three-seat Light Bomber). Thus, the Army planned to use the newly-adopted Type 88-2 Reconnaissance Aircraft as an interim light bomber. Equipped with bomb racks beneath the fuselage and the strengthened lower wing, and with a bomb sight, this aircraft served very well in its new role and was adopted by the Army as the Type 88 Light Bomber.

In addition to production by Kawasaki, Tachikawa produced thirty-seven. The external differences in appearance between the Type 88 Reconnaissance and Light Bomber aircraft were the two additional centre-section struts which formed a W when viewed from the front. The underwing bomb racks were removable and therefore could

Kawasaki Army Type 88 Light Bomber.

not be used to identify the model.

These light bombers served the Army well from 1930 to around 1938. Along with the Type 88 Reconnaissance Aircraft, they were very active in tactical bombing, reconnaissance liaison roles in the Chinan, Manchurian and Shanghai Incidents, as well as in the early stage of the Sino-Japanese Conflict. A few Type 88s were fitted with weather-observation equipment as well as chemical spray equipment. Recognized as being very slow, they were still regarded as excellent operational aircraft, retaining this reputation even while being augmented by the newer Kawasaki Type 93 Single-engine Light-Bomber (Ki-3).

Single-engine biplane light bomber. All-metal construction with stressed metal skin on forward fuselage. Remainder of aircraft was fabric covered. Crew of two in open cockpits.

450-600hp Kawasaki BMW VI twelve-cylinder vee water-cooled engine, driving a two-bladed wooden propeller.

One forward-firing fixed 7.7mm machine-gun, twin dorsal flexible 7.7 mm machine-guns.

Span 15m (49ft 2¾in); length 12.8m (42ft); height 3.40m (11ft 2in); wing area 48sq m (516.684sq ft).

Empty weight 1,850kg (4,078lb); loaded weight 3,100kg (6,834lb); wing loading 64.5kg/sq m (13.2lb/sq ft);

power loading 6.88kg/hp (15.1lb/hp).

Maximum speed 114kt (132mph) at sea level; climb to 3,000m (9,843ft) in 18min; service ceiling 5,500m (18,044 ft); endurance 6hr.

407 built: 370 by Kawasaki June 1929–December 1933; and thirty-seven by Tachikawa.

Experimental KDC-2 Transport
(Company designation KDC-2)

In October 1927, the Teikoku Kaibo Gikai (Imperial Maritime Defence Volunteer Association) decided to order two aircraft, and in turn to lend them to the *Asahi Shimbun* which was sponsoring a regular air route between Tokyo and Osaka, as part of the Tozai Teiki Kokukai (East-West Regular Air Transport Association) that would eventually begin in December 1928.

Orders for the two aircraft were placed with Kawasaki, and would be a version of the Army Type 88 Reconnaissance Aircraft, having passenger accommodation and the ability to operate on floats. This redesign was made by Dr Richard Vogt and Hisashi Tojo. The two aircraft were completed in October 1928 and identified as Giyu No.4 (J-BAKH) and Giyu No.5 (J-BALH) respectively.

Major structural changes included a shortened upper wing, an increase in span and chord on the lower wing and N interplane struts. The four-seat passenger cabin, aft of the cockpit, could be converted for aerial photography and mail carrying. When equipped with floats, an enlarged rudder was used and it extended below the fuselage.

Their use on the Tokyo-Osaka run was short-lived, with the activation of Nihon Koku Yuso K K on the same route. *Asahi* suspended its operation and planned an All Japan City-Visiting Flight with the two aeroplanes. Beginning in July 1929, they made formation flights covering cities in eastern Japan, and then western Japan beginning that October. Many cities were visited, and lectures were given by those flying on the KDC-2s to further promote the potential of aviation.

When the tours ended, the aeroplanes were used by *Asahi Shimbun* for courier work, aerial photography and transport duties. They were also used for regular mail flights between Tokyo and Niigata, and for courier flights to Manchuria during the Manchurian Incident. In September 1930, Giyu No.4 was badly damaged during a take off on the Kizu River in Osaka and required a year for repairs. When back in service in June 1932 and on a courier flight to Manchuria, an emergency landing had to be made on the Fukuyama Army Parade Grounds and the

Kawasaki Experimental KDC-2 Transport.

aeroplane was again badly damaged and then scrapped after 229 flying hours.

Following the Manchurian Incident, Giyu No.5 continued its regular service between Tokyo and Toyama, or Tokyo and Sendai. It was retired in April 1935 with 723 flying hours, to become training equipment for the Students' Aviation League.

Single-engine transport biplane. All-metal construction with Dornier stressed metal skin on fuselage, wings and tail fabric covered. Pilot in open cockpit, four passengers in closed cabin.

500-630hp BMW VI twelve-cylinder vee water-cooled engine, driving a two-bladed wooden propeller.

Span 14.30m (46ft 11in); length 11.185m (36ft 8¼in); height 3.39m (11ft 1½in); wing area 48sq m (516.684 sq ft).

Empty weight 1,747kg (3,851lb); loaded weight 2,972kg (6,552lb); wing loading 61.9kg/sq m (12.6lb/sq ft); power loading 5.88kg/hp (12.9lb/hp).

Maximum speed 120kt (138mph); cruising speed 81kt (93mph); climb to 1,000m (3,280ft) in 4min; service ceiling 5,000m (16,404 ft); range 600nm (689sm); endurance 6hr.

Two built in October 1928.

Army Experimental KDA-3 Fighter

As a replacement for the 1923 Type Ko 4, Nakajima Nieuport 29-C-1 Fighter, the Army placed orders in March 1927 with Mitsubishi, Nakajima and Kawasaki for new fighter designs to be completed by the end of April 1928. All three entries, designed by German and French engineers, had the Army's favoured parasol wings and Dr Vogt from Germany designed the KDA-3 entry for Kawasaki.

Of the three Kawasaki prototypes, the first, as a company aircraft, was powered by a 450hp BMW VI engine and completed in March 1928, but met with misfortune in a landing accident at Kagamigahara on 1 April, damaging its undercarriage. The second and third prototypes were powered by 450hp Hispano-Suiza engines

Kawasaki Army Experimental KDA-3 Fighter.

with changes in the cowling and tailplane. Both were completed in May 1928. After satisfactory test flights, they were flown to Tokorozawa to participate in the Army's evaluation.

First to be tested was the Mitsubishi Hayabusa-type but it disintegrated during a 215kt dive and this terminated further testing of these parasol-wing concepts for fighters. The Kawasaki, Nakajima and remaining Mitsubishi prototypes were used for structural strength ground testing only. As a result of these tests, it was determined that Nakajima's was the best, followed by Kawasaki, then Mitsubishi, but all were below specification and therefore disqualified.

The Kawasaki KDA-3 design was based upon the Dornier Do H Falke fighter with its 300hp Hispano-Suiza engine which Kawasaki had previously imported from Dornier, and the sesquiplane light bomber which Dr Vogt had designed for the Japanese Army. Although

the KDA-3 clearly showed Dornier influence in its design, there were a number of major differences. The all-metal structures and fuselages with external longitudinal stiffeners were similar but whereas the Dornier Falke had a cantilever wing mounted on four centre-section struts, the KDA-3 had two sets of N centre-section struts inclined to form an inverted V in front view and rear-parallel diagonal bracing struts to a point near mid-span. The undercarriage designs were similar but the KDA-3 had a cleaner tail unit with horn-balanced control surfaces instead of the severe lines of the Falke's tail unit. When the KDA-3 was disqualified by the Army, Kawasaki used its prototype for further experiments. One of the other prototypes was eventually given to the Ajiya Kokukikan Gakko (Asian Aero-engine School) for educational use.

Single-engine parasol-wing monoplane single-seat fighter. Metal fuselage structure with Dornier stressed skin, wing of metal and wood construction with fabric covering. Pilot in open cockpit.

500-630hp BMW VI twelve-cylinder vee water-cooled engine, driving two-bladed wooden propeller.

Two forward-firing fixed 7.7mm machine-guns.

Span 12.60m (41ft 4in); length 8.85m (29ft 0½in); height 3m (9ft 10in); wing area 25sq m (269.106sq ft).

Empty weight 1,350kg (2,976lb); loaded weight 1,950kg (4,299lb); wing loading 78kg/sq m (15.9lb/sq ft); power loading 3.9kg/hp (8.6lb/hp).

Maximum speed 153kt (176mph); climb to 5,000m (16,404ft) in 12min; service ceiling 9,000m (29,527ft).

Three built from March to May 1928.

Kawasaki-Dornier Merkur Transport.

Kawasaki-Dornier Komet Transport

Towards the end of 1924, Kawasaki imported seven all-metal aircraft from Dornier. Among them were the Do C landplane and the Do D seaplane, both military aircraft, but disqualified by the Japanese for military service. The design of the Do C was used in 1926, however, when the *Asahi Shimbun Sha* placed an order with Kawasaki for three Komet passenger transports. Making a number of design changes in the Komet was Kawasaki engineer Goroku Moro who remained in charge of the project throughout its duration. Additional requirements by *Asahi* were that these transports be equipped with a dark room and film processing facilities.

The first was delivered to *Asahi Shimbun* after test flights at Kagamigahara. The first of these aeroplanes was powered by a 300hp Rolls-Royce Eagle engine. The second and third were powered by the 450hp Napier Lion and for a short time, one had a 400hp Lorraine engine. Eventually all Komets were fitted with the BMW VI engine. The success of this aeroplane brought an additional

Kawasaki-Dornier Komet Transport.

order for a fourth Komet when these were to be used for the Tozai Teiki Kokukai (East-West Regular Air Transport Association), an airline venture sponsored by the *Asahi Shimbun*. All these aircraft were assembled by Kawasaki from imported components and completed between January and August 1927.

Put into airline service before the Junkers F-13s were imported by Mitsubishi, the Komet was the first all-metal passenger transport used on regular Japanese passenger service. Once the Nihon Koku Yuso K K began to operate on this same route between Tokyo and Osaka in 1929 with Fokker Super Universals, Tozai Teiki Kokukai ended this service and the Komets were then used in regular service between Tokyo and Niigata. Eventually, *Asahi Shimbun* used them for a long time and for their original purpose as flying editorial offices and express news delivery.

A close relative to the Komet was the Merkur, one of which was imported by Kawasaki in 1928. Registered J-BAFH, it was soon leased to *Asahi Shimbun* and used by them for a short period as a six-passenger and cargo transport. This last of the Komet series aircraft (serial No.162) was structurally the same as the earlier models, the most noticeable differences being the unbraced horizontal tailplane and cutout in the wing inboard trailing edge.

In 1931, after the outbreak of the Manchurian Incident, the Army ordered Kawasaki to convert the Merkur for ambulance service to carry war casualties. It contained two litter beds and folding seats for

two ambulatory patients, a medical attendant and a doctor. This aeroplane was donated as *Aikoku No.2* on 10 January, 1932, and immediately flown to Manchuria. The Merkur remained very active in air evacuation service between Harbin and Mukden (now Shen-yang), China. When retired, it was used as a memorial until deliberately burned by the Japanese after the Russian invasion in 1945.

Single-engine parasol-monoplane transport. All metal construction with Dornier semi-stressed skin. Two pilots in open cockpit and four passengers in cabin.

500-630hp BMW VI twelve-cylinder vee water-cooled engine, driving a two-bladed wooden propeller.

	Modified prototype	Third aircraft
Span	19.60m (64ft 3½in)	19.60m (64ft 3½in)
Length	12.10m (39ft 8in)	12.42m (40ft 9in)
Height	—	3.48m (11ft 5in)
Wing area	62sq m (667.3sq ft)	62sq m (667.3sq ft)
Empty weight	2,154kg (4,748lb)	2,286kg (5,039lb)
Loaded weight	3,526kg (7,774lb)	3,700kg (8,157lb)
Wing loading	56.8kg/sq m (11.6lb/sq ft)	59.9kg/sq m (12.1lb/sq ft)
Power loading	7.05kg/hp (15.5lb/hp)	7.4kg/hp (16.3lb/hp) hp)
Maximum speed	98kt (113mph)	106kt (122mph)
Climb to	—	2,000m (6,562ft)
in	—	15min 30sec
Range	—	600nm (690sm)
Endurance	—	5½hr

Four built from January to August 1927: Asahi No. 46 (J-BAEA), Asahi No.101 (J-COFH/J-BAN), Asahi No.102 (J-COHJ/J-BAMA), Asahi No.103 (J-BADA/J-BAHA).

Experimental Giyu No.3 Flying-boat

After the fatal crash of the KB Flying-boat (*see* Kaibo Gikai KB Experimental Flying-boat) the Kaibo Gikai (Maritime Defence Volunteer Association) decided in September 1926 to construct another large flying-boat of entirely new design. A committee was established to study metal flying-boat design, with the co-operation of the Navy and civilian engineers, led by Dr Sc Aikichi Tanakadate together with Narihisa Yokota who was to be chief designer, Shuhei Iwamoto, Yoshitake Ueda, Haruhiko Uemura, Navy Lieut (Ordnance) Yoshio Hashiguchi as engineering supervisor, Katsuharu Kondo, and Keikichi Satake.

Using as reference the previously built KB Flying-boat by the Army Arsenal, the Wal flying-boat imported from Dornier by Kawasaki, and the Rohrbach flying-boat, the new aeroplane was to incorporate the committee's more advanced concepts and, powered by two 500hp Kawasaki-BMW VI engines, it was to be the largest Japanese-made aircraft at that time. It was given the designation Giyu No.3 Flying-boat.

Construction was undertaken at the Aeroplane Factory at Kawasaki Dockyard in Kobe. Design began in April 1927 and tooling started the following October. Detail design was finished in August 1928, and the aeroplane was completed three months later. After centre of gravity checks were made while the flying-boat was suspended under a Kawasaki dockyard crane, it was test flown over a period of a month from the harbour at Kobe and then delivered to the Navy at Yokosuka for six months' further testing.

The aeroplane was given good marks in general performance but had shortcomings in roughish water. Initially, wooden propellers were fitted but were later replaced with metal propellers manufactured by Kawanishi Aircraft as originally planned. These improved performance but, following an accident to a Navy fighter caused by its metal propeller, the Navy reverted to wooden propellers. Vibration developed around the engine nacelle causing other related problems and a decrease in performance, and greatly hampered further test flying.

As a result, in May 1931, the aeroplane was dismantled at Hiro Arsenal and the components were used for research and testing of materials for metal aircraft. Before dismantling, the Hiro Arsenal conducted vibration tests by installing wooden and metal propellers for ground testing and low altitude flying.

Twin engined parasol monoplane flying-boat. All metal construction with stressed skin. Crew of five to ten with pilots in open cockpit.

Two 500-750hp Kawasaki-BMW VI twelve-cylinder vee water-cooled

Kawasaki Experimental Giyu No.3 Flying-boat.

engines, mounted in tandem and driving two-bladed wooden or fixed-pitch metal propellers.

One nose flexible 7.7mm machine-gun, one dorsal flexible 7.7mm machine-gun, one ventral flexible 7.7mm machine-gun. Bomb load: two 250kg (551lb) bombs.

Span 29.50m (96ft 9½in); length 19.972m (65ft 6¼in); height 5.272m (17ft 3½in); wing area 141sq m (1,517.761sq ft).

Empty weight 5,400kg (11,904lb); loaded weight 8,600kg (18,959lb); wing loading 60.99kg/sq m (12.5lb/sq ft); power loading 5.73kg/hp (12.6lb/hp), normal 8.6kg/hp (18.9lb/hp).

Maximum speed 108kt (125mph) at sea level; minimum speed 50kt (58mph); climb to 3,000m (9,843ft) in 20min 25sec; service ceiling 4,500m (14,763ft); range 1,620nm (1,864sm); endurance 20hr.

One built in November 1928.

Experimental Carrier Reconnaissance Aircraft

In March 1927, the Navy decided to manufacture an experimental aeroplane funded by a programme sponsored by the Kaibo Gikai (Maritime Defence Volunteer Association), and named the project: 'Research of Material for All-metal Aircraft'. Kawasaki was awarded the project by the Navy.

The aeroplane was to be a single-engined carrier reconnaissance aircraft having an all-metal structure with fabric covering. It had a fully cantilever parasol wing with marked sweepback, and large area slotted flaps, the first in Japan and probably the first in the world. At that time, no monoplane existed for carrier-based aircraft and there were certainly none with cantilever wings and slotted flaps. The fuselage was unusual in that it was almost triangular in cross section. The structure of the aeroplane was heavily influenced by Dornier design practices.

Design was begun in March 1927 and completed in June 1928 under the leadership of Jun-ichiro Nagahata and his assistant Hiroshi Sato. Both engineers had been in

Kawasaki Experimental Carrier Reconnaissance Aircraft.

charge of aircraft design at the Aviation Research Department, Naval Technical Research Institute. Built during the same time as the Giyu No.3 Flying-boat, both aircraft were constructed at the Kawasaki Dockyard, with the construction of the reconnaissance type being completed in September 1928, one month after the flying-boat.

Flight tests began in March 1929 at Kasumigaura under the control of Navy Cdr Sakae Yamamoto. However, tests were suspended after very few flights because of problems with flap operation. The flaps were considered to be a major feature of this aeroplane and their use at such an early date deserves to be recorded in aeronautical engineering history. But early suspension of the tests without further refinements to the flaps, coupled with top-secret security, resulted in the lack of public awareness and has deprived that aeroplane of its rightful place in history. With this aeroplane Kawasaki's affiliation with the Japanese Navy ended, and the company became solely a manufacturer of Army aircraft and a few civil types.

Single-engine cantilever parasol-monoplane with slotted flap system. All-metal construction with fabric covering. Crew of two in open cockpits.
450-600hp Mitsubishi-Hispano-Suiza twelve-cylinder vee water-cooled engine, driving a two-bladed wooden propeller.
Span 16.60m (54ft 5½in); length 10.65m (34ft 11½in); height 3.18m (10ft 5¼in); wing area 43.70sq m (470.398sq ft).
Empty weight 1,200kg (2,645lb); loaded weight 1,800kg (3,968lb); wing loading 41.2kg/sq m (8.4lb/sq ft); power loading 4kg/hp (8.8lb/hp).

Maximum speed 142kt (164mph) at sea level; minimum speed 37kt (43mph) at sea level; service ceiling 10,000m (32,808ft); endurance 3hr.

One built in September 1928.

Kawasaki-Dornier Wal Transport Flying-boat

Because Kawasaki had already imported one example of the Dornier Do J Wal the Aviation Bureau of the Department of Communications placed an order with the company in August 1929 to develop a passenger-carrying flying-boat. Using this aircraft to meet the order, the two 360hp Rolls-Royce Eagle engines were replaced by 500hp Kawasaki-BMW VIs, and the cabin was modified to accommodate six passengers and there was a cargo compartment in the rear. Except for the change of engines and the passenger cabin windows, there was little difference in outward appearance.

Conversion was completed in January 1930 under the supervision of Goroku Moro of Kawasaki, and after inspection by the Aviation Bureau to ensure that improvements in the carriage of passengers had been achieved, it was delivered to Nihon Koku Yuso KK. (Another company, Nippon Koku KK (Japan Aviation Co Ltd) of the Kawanishi Group had already put a Dornier Wal into service, one that has been imported from Italy and unassociated with Kawasaki.) Once in operational service, the new Kawasaki-built aeroplane gave excellent performance on the Seto Island route, making nine trips

Kawasaki-Dornier Wal Transport Flying-boat.

between Osaka and Fukuoka in January and February 1930, and four trips between Fukuoka and Shanghai in March and April that year.

Based on this success, NKYKK placed an order with Kawasaki for two additional Wals for commercial service. Major components of the Wal were imported from Dornier and Kawasaki completed the first in October and the second in November 1930. The two Wals differed, one having open cockpits for the pilots behind the passenger compartment, while the other had the cockpits at the bow forward of the passenger cabin. Performance of the two was much better than the prototype's, giving high hopes for the successful operation of passen-

ger services between Fukuoka and Shanghai. But this hope dwindled when relations between Japan and China deteriorated, and the service was suspended.

As a result, the flying-boats were used on the Inland Sea route between Osaka and Fukuoka, but for this shorter-range service they were inferior to the Fokker Super Universals or even the three engined Fokker F. VII in operational economy. The Wal's popularity ended in February 1932 when one of them, the *Shirohato-go*, disintegrated over Yawata City, Kyushu, killing Capt Teruo Fujimoto and four other crew members, and no more were built in Japan.

Twin-engined parasol-monoplane transport flying-boat. All-metal construction with Dornier stressed skin. Crew of four with six to ten passengers.

Two 450-600hp Kawasaki-BMW VI twelve-cylinder vee water-cooled engines, driving four-bladed wooden propellers.

	Prototype	*Production*
Span	22.50m (73ft 9½in)	22.50m (73ft 9½in)
Length	16.80m (55ft 1½in)	17.845m (58ft 6½in)
Height	4.265m (14ft)	4.857m (15ft 11¼in)
Wing area	96sq m (1,033.369sq ft)	96sq m (1,033.369sq ft)
Empty weight	5,070kg (11,177lb)	5,222kg (11,512lb)
Loaded weight	7,400kg (16,314lb)	7,500kg (16,534lb)
Wing loading	77.1kg/sq m (15.8lb/sq ft)	78.1kg/sq m (16lb/sq ft)
Power loading	7.4kg/hp (16.3lb/hp)	7.5kg/hp (16.53lb/hp)
Maximum speed	129kt (148mph)	125kt (144mph)
Cruising speed	103kt (119mph)	95kt (109mph)
Climb to	—	2,000m (6,562ft)
in	—	12min 30sec
Service ceiling	4,000m (13,123ft)	3,700m (12,139ft)
Range	—	760nm (875sm)
Endurance	8hr	

One conversion in January 1930, two built October–November 1930.

Army Type 92 Fighter (Company designation KDA-5)

After the Army's rejection of the KDA-3 parasol-wing fighter, Kawasaki continued its interest in fighters and in June 1929 began design for a light-weight metal structured fighter biplane. This was to be the KDA-5 powered by a BMW VI Engine.*

The design for this fighter was completed in April 1930 by chief designer Richard Vogt, assisted by Takeo Doi (Doi would later become the designer of such Kawasaki aircraft as became known as Tony, Nick, Lily and others). Numerous structural tests were made to ensure that this light-weight fighter would have sufficient strength. The first prototype was completed in July 1930. Unique structural features introduced by Dr Vogt were Kawasaki's use of M-12 aerofoil for the first time, a simplified interplane strut configuration and a different type of metal and fabric skin combination. In appearance, there was a marked difference between this apparently rugged fighter biplane and the previous year's competition winner, the Nakajima Army Type 91 Fighter with parasol-wing and clean lines.

The first prototype was tested by Kawasaki's chief test pilot Kambei Tanaka at Kagamigahara beginning in July 1930. During the tests, the aeroplane recorded Japan's

*A KDA-4 design probably did not exist because the number four (shi) has the same pronunciation as the word for death.

fastest speed at 173kt (200mph), ranking with the Hawker Fury and the Boeing P-12 fighters of the same period. On 4 November, the aeroplane also reached the greatest height in Japan at 10,000m (32,808 ft), which was also considered the highest in the world for any fighter. However, during one of the test flights, the aeroplane caught fire and Tanaka had to bale out.

The second and third prototypes were completed in January and March 1931, with modifications found necessary from the first aircraft. In the quest for greater speeds, the second prototype recorded 181kt (208mph) on 22 January, 1931. The Army concentrated on testing the third prototype between April and June 1931, discovering in the process that the front interplane strut would bend during a high-speed dive and this had to be corrected. Extensive testing was curtailed with the outbreak of the conflict in Manchuria, and the Army decided to accept the KDA-5 as its Type 92 Fighter, placing the order in January 1932, with production to begin immediately.

Two more prototypes were already underway, each differing in engine, radiator type and contour, control surfaces and undercarriage details. Although the Type 92 proved to have superior climb and speed, making it a better interceptor than the Nakajima Army Type 91,

pilots disliked its unstable take off and landing characteristics. It proved difficult to maintain, particularly in northern bases during cold weather. Army Type 92 Fighters were assigned to the interceptor role in Manchuria and northern China from 1932 to 1935, making them even more unpopular with crews. However, this aeroplane provided the foundation for the very similar Kawasaki Army Type 95 Fighter that became the Ki-10, which was known as Perry by the Allies at the start of the Pacific War.

Beginning in January 1933, the newer Kawasaki-BMW VII engine was installed in production aircraft. This engine differed in detail to the German-built BMW VII, but dimensions and weight were nearly the same. This new Kawasaki model delivered 600 rated hp, and 750 to 800hp maximum output but a record of improved aircraft performance is not available. Kawasaki distinguished between the two aircraft as Type 92-1 and Type 92-2 Fighter, but the Army did not adopt this classification.

Single-engine single-seat fighter biplane. All-metal construction with the light alloy and fabric covering. Pilot in open cockpit.

500hp Kawasaki-BMW VI twelve-cylinder vee water-cooled engine, driving a two-bladed wooden propeller. Production after January 1933: 600-750hp Kawasaki-BMW VII twelve-cylinder vee water-cooled engine, driving a two-bladed wooden propeller.

Two fuselage mounted forward-firing 7.7mm machine-guns.

	KDA-5	Type 92 Fighter
Span	9.55m (31ft 4in)	9.55m (31ft 4in)
Length	7.20m (23ft 7½in)	7.05m (23ft 1½in)
Height	3.10m (10ft 2in)	3.10m (10ft 2in)
Wing area	24sq m (258.342sq ft)	24sq m (258.342sq ft)
Empty weight	1,220kg (2,689lb)	1,280kg (2,822lb)
Loaded weight	1,640kg (3,615lb)	1,700kg (3,747lb)
Wing loading	68.3kg/sq m (13.9lb/sq ft)	70.8kg/sq m (14.5lb/sq ft)
Power loading	3.28kg/hp (7.2lb/hp)	3.4kg/hp (7.5lb/hp)
Maximum speed	173kt (200mph)	173kt (200mph)
Climb to	5,000m (16,404ft)	5,000m (16,404ft)
in	8min 10 sec	8min
Service ceiling	9,500m (31,168ft)	9,500m (31,168ft)

385 built. Five in 1930-31, 180 in 1932 and 200 in 1933.

Kawasaki Army Type 92 Fighter.

Kawasaki Experimental KDA-6 Reconnaissance Aircraft.

Experimental KDA-6 Reconnaissance Aircraft and Kawasaki A-6 Communication Aircraft
(Company designation KDA-6, later A-6)

In November 1930, Kawasaki undertook the design of a high-speed reconnaissance aircraft based on the experience gained with the KDA-5, and expected to secure Army interest in the project. This new aircraft, the KDA-6, was to have improved performance, range and manoeuvrability, equal to two-seat fighters being developed at that time by the western powers. Structurally, it was to be based upon Kawasaki's KDA-5 fighter just accepted as the Army Type 92 Fighter.

Designed by Dr Richard Vogt and assisted by designer Takeo Doi, tooling was started in February 1931 and completed in the following August. One prototype was finished in October 1931, and flight tests began immediately at

Kagamigahara, with the success expected. It was then flown to Tachikawa and evaluated there by the Army under the designation Improved Type 88 Reconnaissance Aircraft, referring to Kawasaki's KDA-2. The Army found this aeroplane to have very satisfactory performance, but a decision had previously been made that the Army would decide its needs and then assign certain manufacturers to produce specific types. Therefore, under this ruling, Kawasaki had no market for this military aeroplane, but, when the company was awarded a contract to develop the Army Type 93 Single-engine Light Bomber beginning in September 1932, the KDA-6 became the basis for the design that became the Ki-3.

In the meantime, the sole prototype KDA-6 was sold to *Asahi Shimbun* and used as a news communications aircraft. When a landing accident prompted extensive

Kawasaki A-6 Communication Aircraft converted from the KDA-6.

structural repairs, modifications were made at the same time to make it a long-range liaison aeroplane. Changes included replacement of the 450hp BMW VI with a 600hp BMW VIII, the open cockpit was given a canopy, a cargo compartment was added, and fuel capacity was increased to 1,085 litres. To compensate for this increase in weight, a stronger undercarriage was fitted, and the tail unit was entirely redesigned.

With completion of these modifications, the aeroplane was redesignated Kawasaki A-6 Communication Aircraft. It made its first flight at Kagamigahara in late August 1934, then was delivered to *Asahi* as Asahi No.111. As part of the 10th Anniversary Flight Programme to commemorate the first Visiting Europe Flight, the aeroplane was used for the Visiting North China Liaison Flight between Osaka and Peking (Beijing). Flown by Masaaki Iinuma and flight engineer Kiyoshi Shimazaki, it left Osaka on 6 September, 1934, and flew the 1,070nm (1,230sm) in 9hr 47min, making one stop at Seoul. Actual flying time was 8hr 26min. Following this notable flight, the aeroplane remained active with *Asahi Shimbun* along with the monoplane C-5 as a high-speed communications aeroplane.

Single-engine communications biplane. All-metal construction with light alloy and fabric covering. Crew of two in open cockpits, later enclosed.

500-700hp Kawasaki-BMW VI twelve-cylinder vee water-cooled engine, driving a two-bladed wooden propeller (KDA-6), 600-800hp Kawasaki-BMW VIII twelve-cylinder vee water-cooled engine, driving a two-bladed wooden propeller (A-6).

Two fuselage mounted forward-firing 7.7mm machine-guns, one dorsal flexible 7.7mm machine-gun (KDA-6).

Span, upper 12.40m (40ft 8in), lower 10.30m (33ft 9in); length 9.20m (30ft 2¼in); height 3.05m (10ft); wing area 34.5sq m (371.367sq ft).

Empty weight 1,460kg (3,218lb); loaded weight 2,310kg (5,092lb); wing loading 67kg/sq m (13.7lb/sq ft); power loading 4.6kg/hp (10.1lb/hp).

Maximum speed 160kt (184mph).

One built in 1931.

Kawasaki Army Type 93 Single-engine Light Bomber (Ki-3).

Army Type 93 Single-engine Light Bomber (Ki-3)

Under the new ruling by which the Army all but eliminated competition in designs between aircraft manufacturers, Kawasaki was awarded a contract to develop a single-engine light bomber in September 1932. This was to have good manoeuvrability as a tactical bomber in support of ground troops. Dr Richard Vogt and Takeo Doi began design work immediately, using their experience gained with the A-6 high-speed communications aircraft.

The first prototype was completed in April 1933. This aeroplane was powered by the new supercharged BMW IX which was put into licensed production by Kawasaki in September 1933. An elliptical radiator with controllable shutters was positioned forward of the engine, but this functioned poorly and was soon moved to the more conventional position below the engine.

Two additional prototypes were built, and after evaluation the Army adopted this design as the Type 93 Single-engine Light Bomber in August 1933, with the short designation Ki-3. Production began in January 1934 and later some production was undertaken by Tachikawa. However, production was terminated in March 1935 because the aeroplane lacked operational

suitability due to continuing supercharger problems.

Ki-3s were assigned mainly to operational units in mid- and northern China, and Manchuria, beginning in 1935 as replacements for the Kawasaki Type 88 Light Bomber. The new bombers performed the tactical mission quite well in bombing, reconnaissance and light cargo carriage, but were continually plagued with engine problems that were never solved. As a consequence, their operational life was relatively short. Many had been donated to the Army as *Aikoku-go* aircraft.

Single-engine biplane light bomber. All-metal construction with light alloy and fabric covering. Crew of two in open cockpits.

755–800hp Kawasaki-BMW IX twelve-cylinder vee water-cooled engine, driving a two-bladed wooden propeller.

One fuselage mounted forward-firing 7.7mm machine-gun, one single or twin dorsal flexible 7.7mm machine-guns. Bomb load: 500kg (1,102lb).

Span 13m (42ft 8in); length 10m (32ft 9½in); height 3m (9ft 10in); wing area 38sq m (409.041sq ft).

Empty weight 1,650kg (3,637lb); loaded weight 3,100kg (6,834lb); wing loading 81.6kg/sq m (16.7lb/sq ft); power loading 4.1kg/hp (9lb/hp).

Maximum speed 141kt (162mph); climb to 3,000m (9,843ft) in 12min; service ceiling 7,000m (22,965ft).

243 built. Three prototypes from April 1933, 200 built by Kawasaki January 1934–March 1935, and forty built by Tachikawa.

Experimental Ki-5 Fighter

As a replacement for the Kawasaki Army Type 92 Fighter, in June 1933 the Army instructed Kawasaki to begin work on a new fighter. This was to be a radical change in design and was to be a fully cantilever low-wing monoplane which the Army designated Ki-5. The design was initially supervised by Dr Richard Vogt with chief designer Takeo Doi and the company completed the first prototype in February 1934. (In 1933, before the aeroplane was completed, Vogt returned to Germany as chief designer, general manager, and part owner of the Hamburger Flugzeugbau.) The Ki-5 had an inverted gull-wing to provide better downward visibility for the pilot and make possible a shorter undercarriage. It was powered by an Ha-9 I water-cooled engine, a development of the Kawasaki-BMW IX, with a three-bladed metal propeller.

In all, four prototypes were built, each having differences in centre-section anhedral, outer wing dihedral, fuselage shape, undercarriage configuration, radiator, seat positioning and other refinements. These failed to produce a good aeroplane with desired visibility for the pilot, or good stability at low speeds. Progressive designs reduced and finally eliminated the inverted-gull wing concept.

Efforts continued for more than half a year to improve the Ki-5's performance, but in September

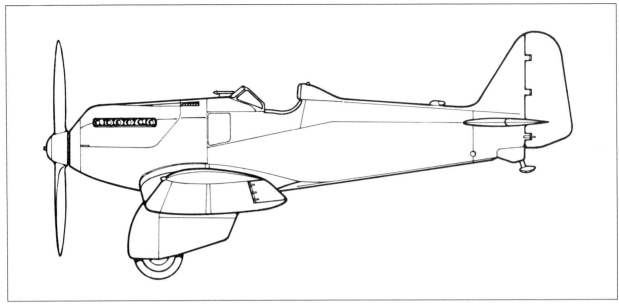

Kawasaki Experimental Ki-5 Fighter.
(Shorzoe Abe).

1934 the Army decided that the aeroplane showed little promise of achieving the desired manoeuvrability and cancelled the project. In general, test results showed that it had poor lateral stability at low speed and suffered from engine vibration and engine cooling system problems. By now, with the passing of much time, Kawasaki had an alternative, reverting to biplane layout, and the Army then turned its attention to developing this later aeroplane which became the Ki-10 fighter (Perry).

Single-engine low-wing monoplane fighter with inverted gull-wing. All-metal construction with light alloy and fabric covering. Pilot in open cockpit.

720-800hp Kawasaki Ha-9 I twelve-cylinder vee water-cooled engine, driving a fixed-pitch three-bladed metal propeller, or two-bladed wooden propeller.

Two fuselage mounted forward-firing 7.7mm machine-guns.

Span 10.60m (34ft 9¼in); length 7.78m (25ft 6¼in); height 2.60m (8ft 6½in); wing area 18sq m (193.756sq ft).

Empty weight 1,500kg (3,306lb); loaded weight 1,870kg (4,122lb); wing loading 103.9kg/sq m (21.3lb/sq ft); power loading 2.33kg/hp (5.1lb/hp).

Maximum speed 195kt (224mph); climb to 5,000m (16,404ft) in 8min; service ceiling 9,000m (29,527ft); range 540nm (622sm).

Four built in 1934.

Kawasaki C-5 Communication Aircraft
(Company designation KDC-5)

In June 1933, *Asahi Shimbun* placed an order with Kawasaki for a modern high-speed communication aeroplane with long range, strong structure and easy to fly and maintain. Initially supervised by Dr Richard Vogt, and having as chief designer Shigeki Naito, Kawasaki began the design, parallel to that of the Ki-5 Fighter. This was a scaled-up version of the Ki-5 and had the appearance of being a high-speed reconnaissance aircraft. Instead of having the high-altitude Ha-9 engine like that of the Ki-5, this aeroplane

Kawasaki C-5 Communication Aircraft.

was powered by a BMW VIII for better reliability and long endurance. The new aeroplane was designated C-5, a derivative of the KDC-5 factory designation, the C indicating civil-type.

Features of this advanced design included the double cambered M-12 aerofoil with a notch at the rear of the wing centre section for better downward visibility, wheel brakes (which were just being introduced), undercarriage trouser-fairings that split at their rear to act as air-brakes when opened on the landing run (but never developed), and an oversized wing-fuselage fairing to reduce turbulence drag. The space between the two canopy-enclosed seats could be used for a third person or payload.

When completed in February 1934, flight tests were made at Kagamigahara from 17 to 20 February, and the aeroplane was accepted

by *Asahi Shimbun* as J-BBEA Asahi No.110. The C-5 was the fastest civil aeroplane in Japan, with a maximum speed equal to that of the Army Type 92 Fighter. Range was also the greatest of any Japanese-designed civil aircraft up to that time.

To take advantage of the range, *Asahi* planned a nonstop flight from Osaka to Hsinking, Manchuria (now Chang-chun, China), in March 1934 to carry news-drafts of the Commemoration Day of Establishment of Manchuria. The flight was unsuccessful because the C-5 was forced to make an emergency landing near Hsinking when the 20 per cent Benzol mixed with the fuel began to freeze. To give a more positive demonstration of this aeroplane, on 10 September, 1934, pilot Mosaburo Niino and flight engineer Kenji Tsukagoshi of *Asahi Shimbun* flew from Beijing to Tokyo, with a stop at Osaka, covering the 1,420nm (1,634sm) in 9hr 34min. This was but one of several spectacular distance and speed records set by this aeroplane for Japan and the *Asahi Shimbun*. Kawasaki planned a follow-on aircraft, the C-6, as a passenger transport with retractable undercarriage, but this was never built.

Single-engine low-wing communications monoplane. All-metal construction with light alloy and fabric covering. Crew of two in enclosed cockpits with provisions for a third person.

600-800hp Kawasaki BMW VIII twelve-cylinder vee water-cooled engine, driving a two-bladed wooden propeller.

Span 13.42m (44ft 0½in); length 9.13m (29ft 11½in); height 2.60m (8ft 6½in) tail down, 4m (13ft 1½in) tail up; wing area 30sq m (322.927sq ft).

Empty weight 1,725kg (3,803lb); loaded weight 2,860kg (6,305lb); wing loading 95.4kg/sq m (19.5lb/sq ft); power loading 4.7kg/hp (10.5lb/hp).

Maximum speed 181kt (209mph) at sea level; cruising speed 136kt (156 mph); landing speed 68kt (78mph), climb to 3,000m (9,843ft) in 7min 30sec; service ceiling 7,000m (22,965 ft), range 1,070nm (1,230sm), endurance 7hr.

One built in February 1934.

Experimental Ki-28 Fighter

For various reasons, the Army did not accept any of the low-wing monoplane fighter proposals submitted in 1934 by three major aircraft manufacturers; these were the Kawasaki Ki-5, Nakajima Ki-11 and the Mitsubishi Ki-18. Instead, until an acceptable monoplane design was available, the Army chose the classic biplane and more manoeuvrable Kawasaki Ki-10 fighter for production beginning in December 1935, hoping its troublesome engine problems would be solved. Recognizing that the next generation of fighters would be monoplanes, in April 1936 the Army announced a new competition.

Nakajima and Mitsubishi selected air-cooled engines for their designs, but Kawasaki chose the traditional water-cooled engine for its entry. There was considerable controversy at this time as to which engine would be the better choice. Retractable undercarriages were being adopted for United States and European fighters, but Japanese designers decided to retain the lighter and less troublesome non-retractable undercarriage, and to concentrate their attention on better streamlining.

For Kawasaki, Takeo Doi was chief designer for the project designated the Ki-28 fighter. Using his previous experience with the Ki-5 as a starting point, his major differences included a manually-retractable radiator for the engine coolant, a straight wing centre section with slight taper on the outer panels, and an aspect ratio greater than seven to enhance speed, climb and manoeuvrability. A semi-enclosed cockpit was faired into the fuselage, and Kawasaki adopted for the first time manually-operated split flaps.

The design of the Ki-28 was begun in November 1935, and a year later the first prototype was completed and the second in December 1936. After company testing at Kagamigahara, the two prototypes were flown to the Army for evaluation at Tachikawa. Tested against the other contenders, Nakajima's Ki-27 and Mitsubishi's Ki-33, all three were fairly evenly matched.

The Ki-28 recorded the highest speed at 262kt (302mph) and was superior to the others above 5,000m (16,404ft) in climb and acceleration. The Ki-28 was really a 'heavy fighter' when compared with the other two entries. Its turning radius was greater, but able to fly faster than the two other competitors, the time taken to make a turn was the same. Therefore, in this aerial combat test, it was difficult to conclude which was the best fighter. The Army's steadfast policy in demanding the best in close-in dog fighting capability prevailed; thus, in March 1937 the Ki-28 was regarded as unacceptable. Had the Army recognized the advantage of high-speed in hit-and-run tactics sooner, the Ki-28 would have been much more highly regarded. Later, the Army reversed this policy, which made possible its acceptance of the Kawasaki Ki-60 and Ki-61 fighters.

Single-engine low-wing monoplane fighter. All-metal structure with light alloy and fabric covering. Pilot in semi-closed cockpit.

Kawasaki Experimental Ki-28 Fighter.

720-800hp Kawasaki Ha-9 II Ko twelve-cylinder vee water-cooled engine driving a fixed-pitch two-bladed metal propeller.

Two fuselage mounted forward-firing 7.7mm machine guns.

Span 12m (39ft 4½in); length 7.90m (25ft 11in); height 2.60m (8ft 6½in); wing area 19sq m (204.521sq ft).

Empty weight 1,420kg (3,130lb); loaded weight 1,760kg (3,880lb); wing loading 92.6kg/sq m (18.9lb/sq ft); power loading 2.2kg/hp (4.8lb/hp).

Maximum speed 252kt (302mph) at 3,500m (11.482ft); climb to 5,000m (16,404ft) in 5min 10sec; service ceiling 11,000m (36,089ft); range 541nm (623sm).

Two built in November and December 1936.

Kawasaki continued into the Pacific War years as a major producer of Army aircraft exclusively. These included not only the Ki-10 (Perry) biplane fighter, of which a few remained in service early in the war, but also major types that fought throughout the war. Among those on which design work began during this prewar period were the Ki-45 Two-seat Fighter (Nick), Ki-48 Light Bomber (Lily), and Ki-61 Fighter (Tony). In addition, it is remarkable that a comparatively small company like Kawasaki could have been experimenting with such advanced designs as the Ki-64, Ki-78, Ki-88, Ki-96/102, before and during the **Pacific War.**

Manko/Man-pi (Manchurian Airways Co Ltd/Manchurian Aeroplane Manufacturing Co Ltd) (Manshu Koku KK/Manshu Hikoki Seizo KK)

Six months after the setting up of the puppet state of Manchukuo in March 1932, the Manshu Koku KK airline was established in joint partnership between the Japanese and Manchukuo governments. The airline began service with British de Havilland Puss Moths and Naka-jima-Fokker Super Universals but when replacement aircraft became necessary, in 1934 it began to produce Fokkers at its factory in Mukden (now Shen-yang, China).

As experience was gained, it developed the MT-1 Hayabusa passenger transport of its own design. Manko continued to grow

Manko MT-1 Hayabusa Passenger Transport.

as its airline expanded, and so did its aircraft manufacturing capability. Therefore, it signed a contract with the Japanese Army in 1936 to build the Nakajima-designed Type 94 Reconnaissance Aircraft (Ki-4), and the 550hp Type 94-1 Engine that powered it, thus making Manko Manchukuo's sole aircraft producer.

This led to the formation of a new company, the Manshu Hikoki Seizo KK, better known as Man-pi, where small-scale production of the MT-1 continued. Greater importance was placed on production of Army aircraft, primarily the Kawasaki Type 95 Fighter (Ki-10) and the Nakajima Type 97 Fighter (Ki-27), totalling 1,395 aircraft in all.

Manko MT-1 Hayabusa Passenger Transport

Early in 1935, Manchurian Airways Co. Ltd (Manshu Koku KK), wanted to replace its Fokker Super Universals with aircraft of its own design. Leading this project were company vice-president Tsuneo Kodama, company depot manager Saburo Nagafuchi and engineering manager Yoshizo Takeishi. Design was started in 1934 by chief designer Hajime Hayashi under the supervision of Goro Tominaga. The Aeronautical Research Institute of Tokyo Imperial University provided wind-tunnel test analysis. Once the general design was established, detail design began in April

1935 and the first prototype completed in December 1936.

In appearance it closely resembled the 1931 Lockheed Orion passenger transport. This was the first Japanese-designed low-wing monoplane transport with a retractable undercarriage and flaps. The engine was a 450hp Nakajima Kotobuki 2-kai-1 under helmeted-cowling. The main wing and tail were of all wooden construction with ply and fabric covering, and the fuselage was of welded steel tube construction with aluminium skin on the forward section and fabric at the rear.

The first flight of the prototype was made in April 1937 by Minoru Kunieda at Dong-Ta Airfield (East Airfield) in Mukden. Flight tests showed the need for a number of changes. The first was removal of the undercarriage retraction mechanism which was chain-driven from a hand-wheel and which proved difficult to operate and did not function smoothly. On the modified prototype and production aircraft, the undercarriage was non-retractable but had streamlined fairings, although these fairings were generally removed when operating from muddy fields. The engine cowling was changed to a smooth contour type, and modifications were made to the location of the exhaust pipe, and the pilot's canopy. Accommodation originally provided was for a pilot, flight engineer and five passengers but this was changed to pilot and six passengers.

Although modifications continued to be made during the early operations, the MT-1s (MT stood for Manshu Transport) gradually developed into practical short-range transports suited to the operations in Manchukuo and China, and replacing the Fokker Super Universals. Those manufactured by Manshu Koku KK (sometimes referred to as its air arsenal) were used by its own company, and those built at the Hiratsuka Factory of Nihon Kokusai Koku Kogyo KK (Japan International Aviation Industry Co Ltd), were used by China Airways Co Ltd (Chuka Koku KK). Many remained operational until the end of the Pacific War.

Single-engine low-wing transport monoplane. Welded steel tube fuselage, metal and fabric covered, wooden wing and empennage with ply and fabric covering. One pilot and six passengers.

460-570hp Nakajima Kotobuki 2-kai-1, nine-cylinder air-cooled radial engine, driving a fixed-pitch two-bladed metal propeller.

	1st and 2nd Prototypes	Production
Span	13.60m (44ft 7½in)	13.60m (44ft 7½in)
Length	8.88m (29ft 1¾in)	9.38m (30ft 9¼in)
Height	3.65m (11ft 11½in)	3.60m (11ft 9¾in)
Wing area	27.3sq m (293.864sq ft)	27.3sq m (293.864sq ft)
Empty weight	1,700kg (3,747lb)	1,700kg (3,747lb)
Loaded weight	2,640kg (5,820lb)	2,700kg (5,952lb)
Wing loading	96.7kg/sq m	98.9kg/sq m
	(19.8lb/sq ft)	(20.2lb/sq ft)
Power loading	5.75kg/hp (12.67lb/hp)	4.65kg/hp (10.25lb/hp)

Maximum speed 130kt (150mph) at 2,000m (6,562ft); cruising speed 108kt (124mph) at 3,000m (9,843ft); service ceiling 6,000m (19,685ft); range 353 to 487nm (405 to 560sm).

Thirty-five Manshu-built from 1936 and fifteen to twenty built by Nihon Kokusai Koku Kogyo KK.

Manko MT-2 Light Passenger Transport

When commercial operations with the MT-1 Hayabusa began in 1938, Manko proposed the design of a light passenger transport to replace the de Havilland Puss Moth which was used in that role. For this new project, Hajime Hayashi was in charge of the design as he had been for the MT-1. This was a well proportioned low-wing monoplane with a cantilever non-retractable undercarriage, and powered by a 250hp Menasco C6S Super Buccaneer six-cylinder air-cooled inverted inline engine with a metal propeller imported from the United States. Except for its elliptical planform wing, the aeroplane bore a striking resemblance to the 1934 French Caudron C.620 Simoun. The wing was built up round a box spar and fitted with split flaps. The MT-2 had accommodation for

Manko MT-2 Light Passenger Transport.

pilot and four passengers. This was the first low-wing light passenger monoplane transport in Japan.

In July 1938, the manufacturing section of Manko and its facilities became the Manchurian Aeroplane Manufacturing Co Ltd (Manshu Hikoki Seizo KK), and it was at that time that the first test flights of the MT-2 were made. Very little development followed, for Manko decided to use the Messerschmitt Bf 108 Taifun imported from Germany for liaison transport duties, and only the prototype MT-2 was built. No technical data are available.

In 1941 Man-pi established its design department at Kunitachi-cho, Tokyo, near Tachikawa, and then organized a special team within the Army Air Technical Research Institute at Tachikawa. This allowed a closer co-operation with the Army Air Technical engineers in developing new aircraft in Manchukuo, which it did throughout the war.

Mitsubishi Aircraft Co Ltd (Mitsubishi Kokuki KK)

From the early days of the Japanese aircraft industry until the end of the Pacific War the name Mitsubishi was the best known, ranking only with that of Nakajima. Mitsubishi became associated with aircraft manufacture in May 1920 when the Mitsubishi Nainenki Seizo KK (Mitsubishi Internal Combustion Engine Manufacturing Co Ltd) was registered as an aeroplane manufacturing company with its plant in Oh-e-machi,* Minami-ku, facing the Port of Nagoya in the southern outskirts of the city. As early as 1916, the company started producing the 70hp Renault aero-engine at its Nainenki-ka, Zokisho (Internal Combustion Engine Section, Machinery Works). In December 1917, Mitsubishi obtained from France the licence to build water-cooled Hispano-Suiza engines.

Success for Mitsubishi's aviation activity was almost assured from the start, when the company secured a contract from the Navy to develop and produce three types of carrier-borne aircraft: fighter, reconnaissance, and torpedo-dropper, all without competition. These would equip Japan's first purpose-built aircraft carrier, the *Hosho*, completed in late 1922. A design team headed by British engineer Herbert Smith, formerly with the Sopwith Aviation Company, produced the three air-craft that became standard equipment for the Navy. For years to come, the design of Mitsubishi aircraft retained this British influence although supplemented by the arrival of German Professor Alexander Baumann in April 1925, former head of the Riesen Flugzeug design department of Zeppelin-Werke at Staaken, and later a professor at Stuttgart University.

Mitsubishi also received Army orders and started production of the Type Ko 1 (Nieuport 81-E2) trainers in 1922, and two years later the Ki 1 (Hanriot HD-14) trainers. Thus, with Nakajima, these two companies remained the only producers of aircraft for both military services.

Manufacturing activities grew, and on 1 May, 1928, the company changed its name to Mitsubishi Kokuki KK (Mitsubishi Aircraft Co Ltd). Soon afterwards a branch of the company was established in Tokyo as the Tokyo Kikai Seisakusho (Tokyo Engineering Works), but in June 1934 a change in policy regrouped and amalgamated all Mitsubishi industrial activities under a single company, Mitsubishi Heavy Industries Ltd. Each phase of its activities, shipbuilding, aircraft, surface vehicles, etc, was organized as separate works divisions. All aircraft activities were grouped under the name of the Nagoya Kokuki Seisakusho (Nagoya Aircraft Works) at Oh-e-machi, Nagoya, although manufacture of a few parts for engines was still undertaken by its general engineering works in Tokyo and Nagoya. By July 1934, the Nagoya Aircraft Works comprised an airframe department (kitai bu) and an engine department (hatsudoki bu).

In 1928 the Army required Mitsubishi to build a bomber version of the Junkers G 38 which brought an influx of German technology into the Mitsubishi company. This Junkers technology in particular formed an entirely new design/manufacturing concept for the company, making Mitsubishi the leading aircraft manufacturer in Japan.

Early in 1938 Mitsubishi, with considerable secrecy at the insistence of the Japanese Government, began to expand its activities. The company was still directly dependent upon United States steel companies for steel billets and forgings for engines such as the fourteen-cylinder air-cooled Kinsei, but the Government directed that all deliveries of these special steels were to be made directly to its air arsenals, where the military allotted supplies to manufacturers.

During this period the Japanese press was permitted on only one occasion to refer directly to Mitsubishi in terms of aircraft manufacturing. The press then claimed that the Nagoya Works at Oh-e-machi was 'the second largest aeroplane factory in the world.' By this time, in July 1938, new and improved facilities had been built at Daikocho, Higashi-ku, Nagoya, for the manufacture of radial engines, with much of its modern machinery having been purchased from the United States. Aero-engine production was then consolidated at this new plant, at which time the airframe and engine works came under separate management.

In an endeavour to be free of foreign sources for special machinery during this expansion period, Mitsubishi opened a special aircraft machine tools plant at Hiroshima in January 1939.

Between 1936 and 1939, research and development activities of Mitsubishi were at a peak. Prototypes of aircraft that would be major types throughout the approaching Pacific War were under rapid development. Most of these would be acclaimed some of the best combat aircraft in the world, their background and success stemming from the early aircraft of Mitsubishi. To accommodate this development, the Oh-e-machi research facilities were expanded, and new land, dredged from Nagoya harbour, expanded the property.

Both the Oh-e-machi and Daikocho works in Nagoya continued to grow through 1940. With the attack on Pearl Harbor, expansion continued at an even faster pace. By the time the war ended, after twenty-four years of aircraft production Mitsubishi ranked first among Japanese industries in weight of aeroplanes produced because of the large number of relatively heavy

---

*This was on reclaimed land purchased by Mitsubishi Shipbuilding and Engineering Co Ltd in 1919 for a new submarine shipyard, moving its existing shipyard from Kobe. Since this location was found to be unsatisfactory, its marine enterprise remained in Kobe, and a new company was established on this ground in May 1920 as the Mitsubishi Nainenki Seizo KK (Mitsubishi Internal Combustion Engine Manufacturing Co Ltd) for the manufacture of aircraft and automobiles. Finding limited demand for automobiles, Mitsubishi used it for aircraft production only, retaining half of the property as an aerodrome.

bombers it assembled, but ranked second in number of aeroplanes produced.

Mitsubishi aircraft are described here, first as Navy, Army, then Civil since each was manufactured by separate divisions of the company.

Navy Aircraft by Mitsubishi

Navy Type 10 Carrier Fighter
(Company designation 1MF1-5)

In February 1921, the Nagoya Factory of Mitsubishi Internal Combustion Engine Manufacturing Co hired British engineer Herbert Smith, who was an engineer with Sopwith, to assist the company to design and manufacture military aircraft, and Smith brought with him a team of seven other British engineers. Mitsubishi had just been awarded a Navy contract to design and build a carrier-borne

Mitsubishi Navy Type 10 Carrier Fighter.

fighter, a reconnaissance aircraft and a torpedo dropper, its first efforts in original designs.

Mitsubishi's work with carrier-based fighters produced the first prototype in October 1921, the same year as the British engineers arrived in Japan. The aeroplane was delivered to the Provisional Naval Aeronautics Institution at Kasumigaura the next month. After flight testing, the aeroplane was adopted as Japan's first Naval standard fighter. Variations of this fighter were all reflected by a slight change in designation: the basic types were the Type 10-1 (1MF1) for models with the honeycomb radiator, and the Type 10-2 (1MF3) for those with the Lamblin radiator. Other variations within these two designations included the 1MF1A having increased wing area, and 1MF2 with two-bay wings and increased tail area, all for Type 10-1 series. Within the Type 10-2 series were the Mitsubishi model 1MF3 with honeycomb radiator changed to the Lamblin radiator fitted to the fuselage underside, and 1MF4 with the cockpit moved forward. Some of these models had a larger wing cut-out over the pilot's head for ease of egress and better visibility.

The 1MF5A also of the Type 10-2 series had an even larger wing for use as a carrier fighter trainer. This model had torpedo-shaped floats beneath the lower wing along with a jettisonable undercarriage for alighting on the water in an emergency.

In October 1921, the first flight of the Type 10 Fighter was made by William Jordan, a former Flight Lieutenant with the Royal Naval Air Service, who joined Mitsubishi with the Smith team. Jordan made nine take offs from and landings on the deck with the new fighter in December 1923. With satisfactory tests of the aircraft completed, carrier operations were begun. These took place on Japan's first aircraft carrier, the Imperial Japanese Navy's *Hosho*. The first operational flights of the Type 10 from the *Hosho* were made by Lieut Shunichi Kira on 16 March, 1923. Until then Sopwith Pups and Gloster Sparrowhawks imported from Britain had served as deck fighters; the Type 10 was the world's first fighter designed specifically for carrier operations. They served with operational units from 1923 to 1930. Some were later released for civilian service.

Single engine biplane carrier-borne fighter. Wooden construction with fabric covering. Pilot in open cockpit.

300hp Mitsubishi Type Hi eight-cylinder vee water-cooled engine, driving a two-bladed wooden propeller.

Two forward-firing fixed 7.7mm machine-guns.

	1MF1 (Prototype)	*1MF3* (Type 10-2 Carrier Fighter)
Span	9.296m (30ft 6in)	8.50m (27ft 10½in)
Length	6.706m (22ft)	6.90m (22ft 7½in)
Height	2.946m (9ft 8in)	3.10m (10ft 2in)
Wing area	27.68sq m (297.954sq ft)	—
Empty weight	790kg (1,741lb)	940kg (2,073lb)
Loaded weight	1,140kg (2,513lb)	1,280kg (2,821lb)
Wing loading	41.2kg/sq m (8.438lb/sq ft)	—
Power loading	3.8kg/hp (8.3lb/hp)	4.27kg/hp (9.4lb/hp)
Maximum speed	128kt (147mph)	115kt (132mph)
Climb to in	3,000m (9,843ft) 10min	3,000m (9,843ft) 10min
Service ceiling	—	7,000m (22,965ft)
Endurance	2½hr	2½hr

128 built October 1921 to December 1928.

Navy Type 10 Carrier Reconnaissance Aircraft

(Company designation 2MR1-2MR4, 2MRT1-2MRT3A)

Mitsubishi received a non-competitive request from the Navy to design and build a carrier-borne reconnaissance aircraft, the first of this type to be built in Japan for its new aircraft-carrier. Herbert Smith was to be the designer. His Type 10 Fighter, then in the design stage,

Mitsubishi Navy Type 10 Carrier Reconnaissance Aircraft.

was showing so much promise, that the reconnaissance aircraft was to be of similar design, but scaled-up to be a two-seat version. The first prototype was completed on 12 January, 1922, and was flown for the first time by William Jordan from the airfield in front of the Nagoya factory. The success of this aeroplane was immediately apparent and led the Navy to officially adopt this new design as the Navy Type 10 Carrier Reconnaissance Aircraft. Production began at once in 1922 and continued until 1930, the type serving operational units for this entire period.

The aeroplane was produced in a number of configurations to meet certain specific needs. Of these, two

basic designs evolved: the Type 10-1 (2MR1) identified those with the honeycomb radiator in front of the engine, while the Type 10-2 (2MR-2) had the more pointed nose and Lamblin radiators placed in other locations. Other variations included having the pilot's seat further forward on the 2MR2 than on the 2MR1, and replacing the car-type honeycomb radiator in front of the engine with that of a Lamblin radiator beneath the fuselage. This change improved pilot visibility. The 2MR3 had an increase in tail area, and the Lamblin radiator moved further forward. The 2MR4 was the last production version of this aircraft for carrier duty. Wingtips were more rounded, and the pilot's seat was returned to the original rearward position for better communication with the rear-seat occupant.

A later version of the Type 10 Carrier Reconnaissance Aircraft built around 1928 was called the Karigane-type. This had improved performance, and the Lamblin radiators were moved from beneath the fuselage to under the wings outside the propeller arc. This model also had a taller vertical tail, but with all these refinements at this late stage of development, neither the Navy nor the Army accepted the version.

Pushing the design even further, the 2MRT1 became an intermediate trainer with dual controls fitted to the 2MR1. The 2MRT1A was as

the previous model but with the horizontal tail of the 2MR2. The change from the frontal honeycomb radiator to that of the under fuselage located Lamblin created the 2MRT2. The rudder and vertical fin were identical to those of the later version (from the 93rd aircraft) of the 2MR2, ie larger rudder, smaller fin. The horizontal tail remained the same as that of the 2MR2. The 2MRT2A became the trainer version of the 2MR3, except that the Lamblin radiator was relocated to beneath the lower wing and the pilot's cockpit moved rearward. The wings were no longer staggered. The 2MRT3 model had the radiator of the 2MRT2 moved underneath the lower wings, and the final version, the 2MRT3A had emergency water alighting flotation bags installed inside the rear of the fuselage. External and internal lighting was also installed for night flying.

Until the Kusho Type 93 Intermediate Trainer became operational in 1933 as the K5Y, this converted reconnaissance aeroplane was the sole intermediate trainer for the Navy. Most of them were assigned at Kasumigaura Air Base for Navy pilot training. Many were eventually released for civilian service, used mostly by the press for communication, liaison and other duties.

Single-engine carrier-borne reconnaissance biplane. Wooden construction with fabric covering. Crew of two in open cockpits.

300hp Mitsubishi Type Hi eight-cylinder vee water-cooled engine, driving a two-bladed wooden propeller.

Two forward-firing fixed 7.7mm machine-guns and twin dorsal flexible 7.7mm machine-guns. Bomb load: Three 30kg (66lb) bombs.

Span 12.039m (39ft 6in); length 7.925m (26ft); height 2.895m (9ft 6in); wing area 37.69sq m (405.695sq ft).

Empty weight 980kg (2,160lb); loaded weight 1,320kg (2,910lb); wing loading 35kg/sq m (7.168lb/sq ft); power loading 4.4kg/hp (9.7lb/hp).

Maximum speed 110kt (127mph); climb to 3,000m (9,843ft) in 17min; endurance 3½hr.

159 built from 1922 to 1930.

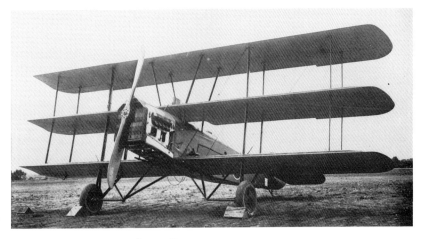

Mitsubishi Navy Type 10 Carrier Torpedo Aircraft.

Navy Type 10 Carrier Torpedo Aircraft
(Company designation 1MT1N)

It is interesting to note, yet confusing to some, that this and the two previously described Mitsubishi aircraft for the Navy have all been Type 10 aircraft. As a reminder, this number ten refers to the 10th year of Taisho, 1921, the year that all these aircraft were accepted as design concepts by the Navy yet differentiated by function titles. This acceptance was before the introduction of competition between manufacturers, and the contract to this single source was expected to produce acceptable aeroplanes.

At the request of the Navy, Herbert Smith was to design a single-seat torpedo aircraft, based upon the anticipated success of the previous fighter and reconnaissance aircraft designs. The prototype was completed the following year, on 9 August, 1922, and test flown by pilot William Jordan at the factory airfield. In November, the first and second prototypes were test flown by Navy pilots at Kasumigaura. This brought about the acceptance of the design as the Type 10 Carrier Torpedo Aircraft, which became the first of this category in Japan.

In order to carry the prescribed payload of a torpedo as well as possessing good manoeuvrability, the aeroplane was configured as an equal-span two-bay triplane, an adoption of the layout foreign designs demonstrated earlier by Sopwith, Fokker, and Caproni. However, the aeroplane's performance failed to meet expectations and it was difficult to handle on the ground because of its height, although pilots liked its flying characteristics and general performance. However, production was suspended after only twenty aircraft had been built, in favour of the newer Mitsubishi-designed three-seat biplane, the Type 13 Carrier Attack Aircraft. The Type 10 Carrier Torpedo Aircraft was the only triplane design for an aeroplane made in Japan. One of these aeroplanes was converted into a seaplane by Ando Aeroplane Research Studio at Shin-Maiko beach, Chita Peninsula, Aichi Prefecture, in 1926 and was used as a passenger transport and pilot trainer.

Single-engine triplane carrier-borne torpedo carrier. Wooden structure with fabric covering. Non-folding wings. Pilot in open cockpit.

450hp Napier Lion twelve-cylinder W water-cooled engine, driving a two-bladed wooden propeller.

One 18in torpedo.

Span 13.259m (43ft 6in); length 9.779m (32ft 1in); height 4.457m (14ft 7½in); wing area 43sq m (462.863sq ft).

Empty weight 1,370kg (3,020lb); loaded weight 2,500kg (5,511lb); wing loading 36.1kg/sq m (7.3lb/sq ft); power loading 5.56kg/hp (12.2lb/hp).

Maximum speed 113kt (130mph); cruising speed 70kt (81mph); climb to 3,050m (10,000ft) in 13min 30sec; service ceiling 6,000m (19,685ft).

Twenty built in 1922-23.

Mitsubishi Navy Type 13-1 Carrier Attack Aircraft (B1M1), equipped with 450hp Napier Lion engine.
(H Ando)

Navy Type 13 Carrier Attack Aircraft (B1M1 to 3)
(Company designations 2MT1-3MT2)

Based upon experience in satisfying the needs of the Japanese Navy, Herbert Smith undertook a new design for a carrier attack bomber, reverting to the biplane configuration. The first of this type was completed in 1923, and a year later it was accepted as the Navy Type 13 Carrier Attack Aircraft, of which several variations were produced.

Because of this aircraft's superior performance it was further developed as the Army Type 87 Light Bomber, and versions were used as civil passenger transports. The first production version was powered by a Napier Lion engine, and designated Type 13-1 Carrier Attack Aircraft (B1M1). All could be equipped with either wheel undercarriage or twin floats to meet different mission requirements.

Within the Navy Type 13 Carrier Attack Aircraft series was the model 2MT4 known as the Ohtori (Large Wild Goose) Type Reconnaissance Seaplane. This was a twin-float long-range reconnaissance aircraft completed in 1925. It

was evaluated by the Navy at Kasumigaura along with the Nakajima-Breguet 19A.2B and the Kawasaki-Dornier Do D, but none of the three was accepted by the Navy.

As an experiment the 2MT5 Tora (Tiger) Type Carrier Attack Aircraft was fitted with the 450hp Type Hi engine instead of the 450hp Napier Lion. Completed on 4 February, 1926, it recorded a maximum airspeed of 122kt and a rate of climb of 17 minutes to 3,000m during test flights at Kagamigahara. On a closed-course distance test from Kagamigahara to Ohmura, Morioka, Kasumigaura and return with stop-overs, Mitsubishi pilot Sumitoshi Nakao flew this aeroplane 3,108km from 25 May to 31 May, 1926. This model became the prototype of the Type 13-2 Carrier Attack Aircraft (B1M2) although production aircraft were three-seaters.

The model 3MT2 also powered by the Type Hi engine had a Farman reduction gear to improve take off and climb performance. The propeller was either as a four-blade or a larger diameter two-blade unit to absorb the added power. This model was officially accepted by

the Navy as the Type 13-3 Carrier Attack Aircraft (B1M3) in January 1931 and served as an all-round combat aircraft for the Navy except in the fighter role. It was relied upon as the main strike force aircraft until the early stage of the Sino-Japanese conflict. It was never considered inferior to its Western counterparts and was therefore highly respected within the operational units. Many remained operational until 1938, some having been donated as *Hokoku-go* aircraft.

On 22 February, 1932, Japan experienced its first air-to-air combat which occurred over Suchou in China. Involved were a Chinese Boeing P-12 fighter flown by American pilot Robert Short, and six Japanese Naval aircraft, three Type 13-3 Carrier Attack Aircraft and three Nakajima Type 3-2 Carrier Fighters (A1N2). The P-12 was shot down by the combined fire from the six Japanese aircraft, which ended the engagement. The Japanese unit commander, Lieut Susumu Kotani, was killed and his gunner/radio operator, Airman 1/c Setsuro Sasaki, was badly injured. However, Sub-Lt Yoshiro Sakinaga flew the aircraft back to its base at Shanghai.

Single-engine three-bay biplane carrier attack bomber with wide-track undercarriage. Rearward folding wings for stowage. Wooden structure with fabric covering. Crew of two and/or three in open cockpits.

450hp Napier Lion twelve-cylinder W water-cooled engine with reduction gearing, driving a two-bladed wooden propeller (Type 13-1). 450hp Type Hi twelve-cylinder vee water-cooled direct drive engine, driving a two-bladed wooden propeller (Type 13-2).

Twin dorsal flexible 7.7mm machine-guns (Type 13-1). Two forward-firing fixed 7.7mm machine-guns and twin dorsal flexible 7.7mm machine-guns (Type 13-2). Bomb load: One 18in torpedo or two 240kg (529lb) bombs.

	Type 13-1	Type 13-2
Span	14.766m (48ft 5½in)	14.766m (48ft 5½in)
Length	9.773m (32ft 1in)	10.06m (33ft)
Height	3.505m (11ft 6in)	3.52m (11ft 6½in)
Wing area	59sq m (635sq ft)	57sq m (613.5sq ft)
Empty weight	1,442kg (3,179lb)	1,765kg (3,891.1lb)
Loaded weight	2,697kg (5,945.7lb)	2,850kg (6,283lb)
Wing loading	45.6kg/sq m (9.339lb/sq ft)	50kg/sq m (10.241lb/sq ft)
Power loading	6kg/hp (13.227lb/hp)	6.33kg/hp (13.955lb/hp)
Maximum speed	113kt (130mph)	105kt (121mph)
Landing speed	—	75kt (86mph)
Climb to	—	3,000m (9,843ft)
in	—	20min
Service ceiling	4,500m (14,763ft) (2MT4)	—
Endurance	2.6hr	5hr

402 built by Mitsubishi: 197 2MT1-3 (Type 13-1) from 1923; one 2MT4 Ohtori (1925); one 2MT5 Tora (1926); 115 2MT5 (Type 13-2) from 1926; eighty-eight 3MT2 (Type 13-3) from 1930. Approximately forty Type 13-3 built by Hiro Naval Arsenal.

Experimental Taka-type Carrier Fighter
(Company designation 1MF9)

In April 1926, the Navy called upon Mitsubishi, Nakajima and Aichi to develop a new carrier fighter to replace the Type 10 Carrier Fighter. Mitsubishi's entry, called the Taka-Type (Falcon) fighter, was the design of Joji Hattori from experience gained through working with Herbert Smith on design of the Type 10 fighter.

The first two prototypes were delivered to the Navy in July and September 1927 respectively. These aeroplanes embodied Navy requirements in having a watertight fuselage with boat-shaped bottom and a watertight lower wing leading-edge to enable them to remain afloat in the event of alighting on water. A jettisonable undercarriage and fuel dumping system were incorporated for this eventuality. The first prototype was equipped with flaps to reduce landing speed.

Evaluation by the Navy of the three contenders proved that the light-weight Nakajima-modified Gloster Gambet best met the Navy standard. The Mitsubishi entry and the Heinkel-designed Aichi HD 23 failed in this competition and it was resented that the winner had failed to comply with the provisions for an emergency descent onto water. The Mitsubishi Taka-Type remains significant, however, in that it was the first carrier fighter designed by a Japanese, and it is further noteworthy in that it was the first Japanese fighter equipped with split-flaps.

Mitsubishi Experimental Taka-type Carrier Fighter.

Single-engine single-seat single-bay biplane fighter. Wooden structure with fabric covering. Pilot in open cockpit.

450-600hp Mitsubishi Type Hi twelve-cylinder vee water-cooled engine, driving a Mitsubishi Reed-type fixed-pitch two-bladed metal propeller.

Two fixed forward-firing 7.7mm machine-guns.

Span 10.80m (35ft 5¼in); length 8.443m (27ft 8½in); height 3.403m (11ft 2in); wing area 41.50sq m (446.716 sq ft).

Empty weight 1,200kg (2,645lb); loaded weight 1,855kg (4,090lb); wing loading 44.69kg/sq m (9.15lb/sq ft); power loading 3.8kg/hp (8.3lb/hp).

Maximum speed 132kt (152mph); climb to 3,000m (9,843ft) in 6min 10sec; service ceiling 7,000m (22,965 ft).

Two built in 1927.

Experimental Type-R Flying-boat
(Company designation R-2)

As already mentioned, Rohrbach in Germany was one of the pioneers of metal aircraft design and construction, and because of the Japanese Navy's interest as applicable to large flying-boats, Mitsubishi was asked to study the methods for future use. To do so, Mitsubishi sent its engineer Keisuke Ohtsuka to Germany in December 1921, followed by engineer Joji Hattori the next July. Together, the companies established Mitsubishi-Rohrbach GmbH in Berlin in June 1925.*

*At that time, the manufacture of aircraft parts was allowed in Germany. Thus parts were made in Berlin but assembled in Copenhagen in a new factory built with the assistance of the Japanese Navy.

Mitsubishi Experimental Type-R Flying-boat (Mitsubishi-Rohrbach R-2)
(H Ando)

Mitsubishi also acquired the services of Rohrbach engineer Paul Ludwig to act as Manufacturing Supervisor.

By this time, the Navy had imported one example of a Rohrbach flying-boat, and it was assembled by the Yokosuka Naval Arsenal as the R-1. Following this, Mitsubishi imported yet another example from Rohrbach in semi-finished condition and completed its assembly in 1927 as the R-2, and the Hiro Naval Arsenal modified and assembled a third and last example. These machines became known as the Experimental Type-R Flying-boats, the R standing for Rohrbach. Some of the internal components for these aircraft were manufactured in Japan, as were two 450hp Mitsubishi Type Hi engines.

The outstanding feature of this type of flying-boat was its high aspect ratio thick-section wing which had marked dihedral and, for its time, a high wing loading. The two-step hull was of almost square cross section.

Although the structure was very advanced for its time, the design was not fully accepted by the Navy because of poor performance during take off and alighting. It was unable to cope with waves of any size.

This problem arose through ignoring a known fundamental, that of avoiding a combination of high wing-loading and high power loading.

However, the aeroplane provided exceptional experience in the manufacture of all-metal aeroplanes, especially with the Wagner diagonal tension-field structure, or stressed skin construction. These features were studied closely and developed further at the Hiro Naval Arsenal, contributed to the immediate success for Mitsubishi designs of two 9-Shi aircraft, the Type 96 Attack Aircraft (Nell) and the Type 96 Carrier Fighter (Claude), and spread throughout the Japanese aeronautical industry.

Hiro modified and assembled R-3.
(H Ando)

Twin-engine shoulder-wing cantilever monoplane flying-boat. All-metal stressed-skin construction. Two-step hull with square box cross-section. Wing aspect ratio 10.5. Crew of five to six.

Two 450-600hp Mitsubishi Type Hi twelve-cylinder vee water-cooled engines, driving two-bladed wooden propellers.

Two or three flexible 7.7mm machine-guns.

Span 28.586m (93ft 9½in); length 17.425m (57ft 2in); height 5m (16ft 5in); wing area 74.20sq m (798.708sq ft).

Empty weight 4,068kg (8,968lb); loaded weight 5,940kg (13,095lb); wing loading 80kg/sq m (16.3lb/sq ft); power loading 6.6kg/hp (14.5lb/hp).

Maximum speed 86.5kt (99mph); climb to 1,000m (3,280ft) in 20min; service ceiling 2,200m (7,217ft).

One built in 1927.

Experimental Special-purpose Carrier Reconnaissance Aircraft
(Company designation 2MR5)

Many innovations in construction techniques were incorporated into this new project. It was not a further development of the Type 10 Carrier Reconnaissance Aircraft but was one of Baumann's original experimental series as were his designs for the Washi-, Tobi- and Hayabusa-Type aircraft. Assisting him in 1927 with this Mitsubishi private venture were engineers Nobushiro Nakata and Takao Tokunaga.

Incorporated into the biplane's lower wing, which was all duralumin, was a hollow tubular-spar known by its German term oval Röhre. This provided a watertight section within the lower wing to give buoyancy in the event of an emergency alighting on water. Landing flaps were of the slotted-type, a relatively new innovation in aerodynamic engineering. Also of interest were slotted ailerons that also functioned as flaps.

Little else is known about this small biplane except that it was designed for light-weight construction, a goal that was more than

Mitsubishi Experimental Special-purpose Carrier Reconnaissance Aircraft.

adequately achieved. It seemed to fail acceptance, however, because it was heavy on the controls and generally ineffective for its intended mission. As a result, only two examples were built.

Single-engine carrier reconnaissance single-bay biplane. Metal and wood fuselage and upper wing with fabric covering. All-metal lower wing of watertight construction. Crew of two in open cockpit.

300hp Mitsubishi-Hispano-Suiza eight-cylinder vee water-cooled engine, driving a two-bladed wooden propeller.

Span 10.20m (33ft 5½in); length 7.15m (23ft 5½in); height 3.129m (10ft 3in).

Empty weight 900kg (1,984lb); loaded weight 1,400kg (3,086lb); power loading 6.7kg/hp (14.7lb/hp).

Maximum speed 104.2kt (120mph); climb to 3,000m (9,843ft) in 14min 30sec; endurance 5hr.

Two built in 1927.

Navy Type 89 Carrier Attack Aircraft (B2M1 and 2)
(Company designation 3MR4)

In a competition that began in February 1928, the Navy asked for proposals from Mitsubishi, Nakajima, Aichi and Kawanishi, for a design for a new carrier attack bomber to replace the Mitsubishi Type 13 Carrier Attack Aircraft, B1M3. The Navy stipulated a crew of three, the 600hp Hispano-Suiza, 450-600hp BMW or 600-650hp Lorraine engine and that the struc-

ture was to be of mixed wood and metal construction. The span was to be less than 15m, length less than 10m, and height less than 3.8m.

Performance asked for was reasonable for that time, with a maximum speed of more than 110kt at sea level, climb to 3,000m in 15 minutes, and a ceiling of over 6,000m. Endurance was to be more than three hours with a load of bombs, or more than eight hours without bombs. The deck landing speed was to be less than 45kt, and take-off distance less than 45m with a surface wind of 20kt.

Mitsubishi sub-contracted each different design study to three parties. The first design termed 3MR3 was engineered by Herbert Smith, who had returned to England in June 1924. Mitsubishi decided to use an even newer engine, an Armstrong Siddeley Leopard with 650hp. The company sub-contracted a second design study they termed 3MR4 to Blackburn in Britain, powered by a 600hp Hispano-Suiza. The third design study, the 3MR5, was sub-contracted to Handley Page. This was to have a 600hp Hispano Suiza engine like that of the 3MR4. Of the three designs proposals, Mitsubishi selected the Blackburn-designed 3MR4 as the best and submitted it for the competition. The Navy declared this aircraft to be the design winner in December 1928, and Mitsubishi therefore directed Blackburn to manufacture the first prototype.

Before the order was placed, Mitsubishi sent engineer Hajime Matsuhara to England to gain technical knowledge on aircraft engineering planning and design. Following him, three additional engineers, Arikawa, Yui and Fukui, were also sent to Blackburn to learn the fundamentals that were to be incorporated into the 3MR4.

After preliminary flight tests in England, the first prototype was shipped to Japan, arriving there in February 1930. Accompanying the aircraft was its chief British designer, G E Petty, who was to assemble the aeroplane on arrival and supervise the building of additional aircraft in Japan. A second prototype, completed on 31 October, 1930, was powered by a 650hp Type Hi engine, but was lost in an accident due to a pilot error. The third prototype, completed on 2 February, 1931, was delivered to the Navy but suffered shortcomings, such as engine oil overheating, difficulty in making a three-point landing which was so essential for carrier operations, and poor stability. The fourth prototype, with modifications to overcome the failings of its predecessors, performed well and was officially accepted as the Type 89 Carrier Attack Aircraft in March 1932 and put into production.

As the new aeroplane entered service (with the short designation B2M1), engine problems and other shortcomings were discovered and frequently encountered during this transitional period. In addition, it was said to have poor performance and high operating cost. To correct these deficiencies, engineers Ohgi and Matsufuji made changes in the materials used and manufacturing technique. As a result, this aeroplane became the Type 89-2 Carrier Attack Aircraft (B2M2), which remained in production until 1935.

In spite of the high expectations for the new aeroplane as a replacement for the Mitsubishi Type 13 Carrier Attack Aircraft, the Type 89 had a bad reputation with operational units even after improvements which resulted in the Type 89-2. However, with the structure of steel and aluminium, the excellent characteristics of the Blackburn B-9 aerofoil, and use of Handley Page slots, these features were valuable for future designs. Small numbers of Type 89 Carrier Attack Aircraft participated in campaigns during the Shanghai Incident, as did earlier Type 13 Carrier Attack Aircraft. Some of these Type 89s were

Mitsubishi Navy Type 89 Carrier Attack Aircraft (B2M1).

donated to the Navy through the *Hokoku-go* programme, and, later, the Type 89 design was released by the Navy as a civilian conversion. (*see* Mitsubishi Type 89 General Purpose Aircraft).

Single-engine two-bay biplane carrier attack bomber. Steel and aluminium construction with fabric covering. Rearward folding wings for stowage. Aerofoil: Mitsubishi 27 (Modified Blackburn B-9). Crew of three in open cockpits.

650hp Mitsubishi Type Hi twelve-cylinder vee water-cooled engine, driving a two-bladed wooden propeller.

One forward-firing (from fuselage side) 7.7mm machine-gun, one dorsal flexible 7.7mm machine-gun. Bomb load: One Type 91 or Type 94 torpedo, or one 800kg (1,763lb) bomb.

	Type 89-1, B2M1	*Type 89-2, B2M2*
Span	15.22m (49ft 11¼in)	14.98m (49ft 1¾in)
Length	10.27m (33ft 8½in)	10.18m (33ft 4¾in)
Height	3.712m (12ft 2in)	3.60m (11ft 9½in)
Wing area	55sq m (592.034sq ft)	49sq m (527.448sq ft)
Empty weight	2,260kg (4,982lb)	2,180kg (4,806lb)
Loaded weight	3,600kg (7,936lb)	3,600kg (7,936lb)
Wing loading	65.5kg/sq m (13.4lb/sq ft)	73.5kg/sq m (15lb/sq ft)
Power loading	4.87kg/hp (10.7lb/hp)	4.55kg/hp (10lb/hp)
Maximum speed	115kt (132mph)	123kt (142mph)
Climb to	3,000m (9,843ft)	3,000m (9,843ft)
in	18min	12min
Range	960nm (1,105sm)	950nm (1,094sm)

205 built 1930-35.

Navy Type 93 Land-based Attack Aircraft
(Company designation 3MT5A first to fourth, 3MT5 fifth to eleventh)

In February 1929, the Navy issued to Mitsubishi a design requirement for a new, large, carrier attack bomber capable of carrying one torpedo or one ton of bombs. Departing from conventional designs, this was to be a twin-engined carrier-based aeroplane, powered by two 400-500hp engines. By January 1930, the official Navy specifications were concluded, and Mitsubishi accepted the order. The design of the new twin-engined bomber became the responsibility of Mitsubishi engineers Hajime Matsuhara, Naoichi Yui, and Akira Miyahara,

Mitsubishi Navy Type 93 Land-based Attack Aircraft.

under the supervision of G E Petty, who was overseeing the manufacture of the earlier Mitsubishi Type 89 Carrier Attack Aircraft.

This new aeroplane became the 7-Shi Twin-engine Carrier Aircraft, and ultimately the only twin-engined biplane landplane in the Japanese Navy. Its outward appearance resembled to some extent the Boulton Paul Sidestrand and Overstrand of the RAF. During the prolonged design phase, alterations were continually made in order to comply with the Navy's changing requirements. The first of these aircraft was completed in September 1932 and test flights were begun on 19 October, 1932, at Kagamigahara by test pilot Yoshitaka Kajima and others under his supervision. The first four of the prototypes were identical, but the fifth and following aircraft up to the total of eleven incorporated changes that were recommended by the Navy through test results. Some of the changes included the use of four-bladed propellers as well as the original single vertical tail being changed to twin fins and rudders.

During the test flights in March 1934, one of the prototypes developed severe vibration, resulting in the ailerons of both the upper and lower wings being torn off. Without this lateral control, the pilot was still able to bring the aeroplane back for an emergency landing. Following this close call, other shortcomings of design were voiced by the test pilots, particularly the poor controllability, and vibration in the aft fuselage section; major defects that were never resolved. In addition, the aeroplanes were by now obsolete because of the long development period, and therefore were never considered suitable for their intended carrier operations. Consequently, the type was never put into full production.

After the first four prototypes, subsequent aircraft had twin fins and rudders, increased wing area, and additional interplane struts. After the bombers were considered to be unsuitable for carrier, or any tactical operations, they carried the designation Navy Type 93 Land-based Attack Aircraft, but were used almost exclusively for training air crews for large land-based bombers at the Tateyama Kokutai.

Twin-engined biplane carrier-based bomber. Wooden and metal fuselage structure and metal frame wing with fabric covering. Rearward folding wings for stowage. Crew of three for attack missions, five for scouting missions.

Two 600-800hp Mitsubishi A4 fourteen-cylinder double-row radial air-cooled engines, driving two-bladed wooden propellers (3MT5A), four-bladed wooden propellers (3MT5).

Twin nose mounted flexible 7.7mm machine-guns and one dorsal flexible 7.7mm machine-gun. Bomb load: One 800kg (1,763lb) torpedo, or 1,000kg (2,204lb) bombs.

	3MT5A	3MT5
Span	19.20m (63ft)	20.70m (67ft 11in)
Length	12.80m (42ft)	12.05m (39ft 6¼in)
Height	4.43m (14ft 6¼in)	4.70m (15ft 5in)
Wing area	92.40sq m	102.3 sq m
	(994.617sq ft)	(1,101.184sq ft)
Empty weight	3,600kg (7,936lb)	3,940kg (8,686lb)
Loaded weight	6,350kg (13,999lb)	6,400kg (14,109lb)
Wing loading	68.8kg/sq m	62.5kg/sq m
	(14lb/sq ft)	(12.8lb/sq ft)
Power loading	4.18kg/hp (9.2lb/hp)	4.21kg/hp (9.2lb/hp)
Maximum speed	130kt (150mph)	127kt (146mph)
Landing speed	48kt (55mph)	50kt (57.5mph)
Climb to	3,000m (9,843ft)	3,000m (9,843ft)
in	13min 45sec	13min
Range: Attack	768nm (884sm)	535nm (615sm)
Scout	1,170nm (1,346sm)	1,245nm (1,432sm)

Four 3MT5A built in 1932, seven 3MT5 built in 1933.

Mitsubishi Experimental 7-Shi Carrier Attack Aircraft.

Experimental 7-Shi Carrier Attack Aircraft
(Company designation 3MT10)

In April 1932, the Navy asked Mitsubishi and Nakajima to design a more advanced experimental carrier attack bomber to supplement or replace the Type 89 Carrier Attack Aircraft. Mitsubishi's chief designer Hajime Matsuhara undertook the project, using the experience gained from the Type 89. This new aeroplane was to be powered by the 835hp Rolls-Royce Buzzard engine.

The prototype was completed in October 1932, and delivered to the Navy with two different types of wings, 57sq m area and 48.8sq m respectively, and it was typical of the three-seat biplane carrier attack bombers produced by Mitsubishi, based upon earlier Blackburn designs.

During one of the flight tests of the first aircraft at Yokosuka in February 1934, the aircraft lost power on take off and was destroyed. Thus, the aeroplane was never accepted by the Navy.

Single-engine biplane carrier attack bomber. Wood and metal structure with fabric covering. Rearward folding wings for stowage. Crew of three in open cockpits.

835-955hp Rolls-Royce Buzzard II-MS twelve-cylinder vee water-cooled engine, driving a two-bladed wooden propeller.

One forward-firing 7.7mm machine-gun, twin dorsal flexible 7.7mm machine-gun. Bomb load: one Type 91 torpedo or one 900kg (1,984lb) bomb.

Span 14.723m (48ft 3½in); length 10.08m (33ft 1in); height 3.885m (12ft 8¾in); wing area 57sq m (613.562sq ft).

Empty weight 2,600kg (5,732lb); loaded weight 4,400kg (9,700lb); wing loading 77kg/sq m (15.7lb/sq ft); power loading 5.26kg/hp (11.6lb/hp).

Maximum speed 115kt (132mph); climb to 3,000m (9,843ft) in 12min; endurance 12hr.

One built in 1932.

Experimental 7-Shi Carrier Fighter
(Company designation 1MF10)

As a replacement for the Nakajima Type 90 Carrier Fighter, in April 1932 the Navy ordered a new carrier fighter through competition between Mitsubishi and Nakajima. This was part of a programme to encourage new designs, with production to be developed in Japan rather than abroad. For this project Mitsubishi assigned Jiro Horikoshi as chief designer (a name closely associated with the Zero Fighter), who had just returned from Europe and the United States to observe aeronautical engineering in foreign countries, in particular to get new concepts in fighter design from Curtiss in the USA. Eitaro Sano (future designer of Pete), Takano-suke Nakamura and Tomio Kubo (future designer of Dinah) were assigned to assist him.

The first prototype was completed near the end of February 1933 and flight tested the following March by Mitsubishi pilot, Yoshitaka Kajima, at Kagamigahara. Structural failure of the vertical fin caused the aeroplane to crash during a test dive in July of that year, but Kajima baled out safely.

A similar fate befell the second prototype in June 1934. This was the result of a flat spin from which recovery was impossible. Like Kajima, test pilot Lieut Motoharu Okamura baled out and survived but was injured.*

The design, although not accepted by the Navy because of poor controllability and poor forward visibility, was considered quite advanced. The competing Nakajima aircraft, which was a modified version of the Army Type 91 parasol-wing fighter, also failed to gain Navy acceptance.

The 1MF10 was the first low-wing monoplane carrier fighter designed for the Japanese Navy. An interesting feature was the box-spar structure for the front and rear wing spars, connected by similar members to form a girder to resist torsion. This was the development made by Hiro Naval Arsenal based on Rohrbach flying-boat construc-

*Okamura lost four fingers in this incident, ending his career as a fighter pilot. As a Navy Capt, he later commanded the 341st (Tateyama) Kokutai for kamikaze attacks in June 1944.

Mitsubishi Experimental 7-Shi Carrier Fighter.

tion. This feature was further improved upon and led to the success of the 9-Shi Single-seat Carrier Based Fighter, A5M1, with the Allied code-name Claude. Other Mitsubishi aircraft which profited from this type of wing spar were the 8-Shi Special Reconnaissance Aircraft (forerunner of the G3M1 Nell), Type 97 Carrier Attack Aircraft (Mabel) and the Type 96 Land-based Attack Aircraft (Nell). Because of the success of these aircraft, other Japanese manufacturers adopted this spar design.

Single-engine low-wing cantilever monoplane carrier-based fighter. Metal wing structure with fabric, covering and all-metal monocoque fuselage. Non-retractable undercarriage. Pilot in open cockpit.

580-780hp Mitsubishi A4 fourteen-cylinder double-row air-cooled radial engine, driving a Nakajima Hamilton Standard fixed-pitch two-bladed metal propeller or two-blade wooden unit.

Two forward-firing fixed 7.7mm machine-guns.

Span 10m (32ft 9½in); length 6.925m (22ft 8½in); height 3.31m (10ft 10¼in); wing area 17.70sq m (190.527sq ft).

Empty weight 1,225kg (2,700lb); loaded weight 1,578kg (3,478lb); wing loading 89kg/sq m (18.2lb/sq ft); power loading 2.02kg/hp (4.4lb/hp).

Maximum speed 173kt (200mph) at 3,000m (9,843ft); landing speed 56.9kt (65mph); endurance 3hr.

Two built in 1933.

Experimental 8-Shi Two-seat Fighter
(Company designation Ka-8)

In Europe and the United States the concept and practicality of two-seat fighters were being seriously considered. This brought about in 1933 a Navy competition for designs to be submitted by Mitsubishi and Nakajima. Mitsubishi's design group was managed by Joji Hattori, with Eitaro Sano and Takanosuke Nakamura in charge. By June 1933 the mock-up was ready for evaluation, and construction of the first prototype was completed in January

Mitsubishi Experimental 8-Shi Two-seat Fighter.

1934 and flown by Yoshitaka Kajima at Kagamigahara.

As a result of evaluation from the first prototype, modifications were made to the second prototype before both were delivered to the Navy. While the second prototype was being tested at Yokosuka, it disintegrated when pulling out of a dive on 16 September, 1934. The pilot successfully baled out, but the observer in the rear seat was killed in the crash. Further tests of the design were discontinued because of this accident.

The Navy did not have great enthusiasm for the two-seat fighter concept, and therefore neither the Mitsubishi nor the Nakajima designs were accepted, but experience gained with the Mitsubishi aeroplane was later incorporated into the Mitsubishi Navy Type 0 Observation Aircraft, Allied code-name Pete.

Single-engine single-bay biplane two-seater fighter with twin fins and rudders. Duralumin spar with wooden ribs. Welded steel tube fuselage construction with the entire structure fabric covered. Wing aerofoil NACA M-12. Crew of two in open cockpits.

460-580hp Nakajima Kotobuki 2 nine-cylinder air-cooled radial engine, driving a fixed-pitch two-bladed metal propeller.

Two forward-firing fixed 7.7mm machine-guns and one dorsal flexible 7.7mm machine-gun.

Span 10m (32ft 9½in); length 7.39m (24ft 3in); height 3.35m (11ft); wing area 26sq m (279.87sq ft).

Empty weight 1,153kg (2,541lb);

loaded weight 1,700kg (3,747lb); wing loading 65.3kg/sq m (13.3lb/sq ft); power loading 3.6kg/hp (7.9lb/hp).

Maximum speed 154.7kt (178mph) at 3,000m (9,843ft).

Two built in 1934.

Experimental 8-Shi Special Reconnaissance Aircraft (G1M1)
(Company designation Ka-9)

In 1933 the Navy asked Mitsubishi to design a very demanding aircraft, not only in a new category but one with performance that would outmatch all other similar aircraft anywhere at that time. This became the Experimental 8-Shi Special Reconnaissance Aircraft. Its purpose was to meet a requirement for aerial surveillance over the Pacific to ascertain current fleet movements of the US Navy, particularly at home ports such as Pearl Harbor and in the Philippines.

Aerial reconnaissance was felt to be so important that an early requirement was for a range of 4,000nm; if not possible, a range of 2,000nm would be acceptable provided that on the return flight the aircraft must be ditched and its crew recovered by submarine. The need to know the whereabouts of the US fleet was responsible for such extreme measures.

The design of the Mitsubishi aircraft was begun with Kiro Honjo as chief designer, assisted by Tomio Kubo in charge of structural design and Nobuhiko Hisakabe responsible for systems. Apart from

Mitsubishi Experimental 8-Shi Special Reconnaissance Aircraft (G1M1).

this young engineer, there were no other Mitsubishi engineers with experience in design of large all-metal aircraft. Some engineers on the Army staff of Mitsubishi had had experience with such aircraft as the Type 93 Heavy Bomber and the Type 93 Twin-engined Light Bomber, but these were based upon the Junkers K 37 design and limited engineering work had been required of Mitsubishi.

The new Mitsubishi design was to have two engines. Only a slender fuselage would be required because the aircraft was intended only for reconnaissance missions, with no need for internal payload. A retractable undercarriage was to be provided; the first in Japan, and designed by Sadahiko Kato, it was manually retracted and the wheels housed within the engine nacelles. Armament was not an initial requirement because of the high speed expected, but this was added later to the nose and dorsal positions. As the design developed and mission requirements expanded, the designation also changed in February 1934 to become the Experimental 8-Shi Land-based Medium Attack Aircraft.

The aeroplane was completed in April 1934 and made its maiden flight on 7 May of that year, with Yoshitaka Kajima as pilot. In com-

parison with the unsatisfactory stability and control of the earlier Mitsubishi twin-engined Type 93 Land-based Attack Aircraft, this aircraft showed excellent flying qualities. Furthermore, it developed maximum speed of 143.4kt (165mph), far in excess of the required specification of 120kt. Rear Admiral Yamamoto, the originator of this aircraft, visited Kagamigahara to fly in the aeroplane and to thank Mitsubishi for its achievement.

However, this aircraft had many problems and only one was built. Designed originally as a research aircraft and now with the addition of operational equipment, located well behind the designed centre of gravity, it was very tail heavy, requiring considerable ballast in the nose. To achieve adequate development, a new design was started, the 9-Shi Land-based Medium Attack Aircraft, later to be known as the Type 96 Land-based Attack Aircraft, G3M1. Taking advantage of the successful features of the 8-Shi Special Reconnaissance Aircraft, the 9-Shi was certain of the success which it achieved over China and from its participation in the early phase of the Pacific War. It was known to the Allies by its codename Nell.

Twin-engine mid-wing monoplane with retractable undercarriage. All-

metal fuselage of monocoque construction. High aspect ratio metal wing with metal skin and Junkers 'double wing'. Twin fins and rudders. Crew of five.

Two 500-650hp Type 91 twelve-cylinder W water-cooled engines, driving four-bladed wooden propellers.

One nose flexible 7.7mm machine-gun and one dorsal flexible 7.7mm machine-gun.

Span 25m (82ft); length 15.83m (51ft 11¼in); height 4.532m (14ft 10¼in); wing area 75sq m (807.319sq ft).

Empty weight 4,775kg (10,527lb); loaded weight 7,003kg (15,439lb); wing loading 93.3kg/sq m (19.1lb/sq ft); power loading 7kg/hp (15.4lb/hp).

Maximum speed 143.4kt (165mph); climb to 3,000m (9,843ft) in 16min 54sec; service ceiling 4,600m (15,091ft); range 2,380m (2,739sm).

One built in April 1934.

Experimental 9-Shi Carrier Attack Aircraft (B4M1) (Company designation Ka-12)

Although unsuccessful with the 7-Shi Carrier Attack Aircraft, the Navy again requested Mitsubishi and Nakajima to compete for a 9-Shi version in February 1934. As with the 7-Shi, Hajime Matsuhara was assigned chief designer, assisted by Sadahiko Kato and Minoru Hasegawa, which resulted in an aeroplane that was completed in August of that year, and made its first flight at Kagamigahara on 25 August.

Since the failure of the 7-Shi was in part due to the heavy Buzzard water-cooled engine, the new concept was to have an air-cooled engine in an attempt to reduce weight. The wings were metal structures with fabric covering based upon the Boulton Paul design. The remainder of the airframe closely resembled that of the 7-Shi Carrier Attack Aircraft, therefore the design and manu-facture of the aeroplane were completed in a very short time.

Tests showed that the wings were not sufficiently rigid, causing control problems and both it and the Nakajima type failed to achieve Navy acceptance. Instead, the Kusho-designed aeroplane was adopted as the Type 96 Carrier Attack Aircraft and approximately two hundred were manufactured by Nakajima, Mitsubishi and Hiro Naval Arsenal. These carried the designation B4Y1 and were known as Jean in the Allied code-name system.

The 9-Shi Carrier Attack Aircraft were the last biplane designs for Japanese service, excluding seaplanes and trainers. Their appearance and structures resembled the Blackburn Shark and Fairey Swordfish, the latter serving with the Royal Navy throughout the Second World War. Despite their obsolescence, one of these Mitsubishi aircraft was a valuable test vehicle for the improvement of the A4 engine which later became the much used Mitsubishi Kinsei during the war.

Single-engine biplane carrier attack bomber. Metal structure with fabric covering. Rearward folding wings for stowage. Crew of three in open cockpits.

650-800hp Mitsubishi 8-Shi fourteen-cylinder radial air-cooled engine, driving a two-bladed wooden propeller, or fixed-pitch three-bladed metal propeller.

Three 7.7mm machine-guns. Bomb load: Bombs or torpedo up to 800kg (1,763lb).

Span 14.80m (48ft 6½in); length 9.96m (32ft 8in); height 3.94m (12ft 11in); wing area 54sq m (581.270sq ft).

Empty weight 2,000kg (4,409lb); loaded weight 3,827kg (8,437lb); wing loading 70.9kg/sq m (14.5lb/sq ft); power loading 5.88kg/hp (12.9lb/hp).

Mitsubishi Experimental 9-Shi Carrier Attack Aircraft.

Maximum speed 130kt (150mph); climb to 3,000m (9,843ft) in 14min 33sec; endurance 6.17hr.

One built in August 1934.

Experimental 9-Shi Single-seat Fighter
(Company designation Ka-14)

Although the 7-Shi Carrier Fighter had failed the competition, the Navy asked Mitsubishi and Nakajima to submit proposals for a 9-Shi Single-seat Fighter in February 1934. The outcome of this design would result in the next, and very similar, model to become the world's first operational monoplane Navy carrier-based fighter and to be noted for its superior performance. It would be known to the Allies as Claude (A5M1 to A6M5).

The initial specifications for the aeroplane were simple and direct in all categories, well within the state of the art, and they were prepared by Lieut-Cdr Hideo Sawai of the Department of Engineering, Naval Air Headquarters. In response, Mitsubishi assigned Jiro Horikoshi

Mitsubishi Experimental 9-Shi Single-seat Fighter.

as chief designer assisted by Tomio Kubo, Yoshitoshi Sone, Masakichi Mizuno, Yoshimi Hatanaka, Yoshio Yoshikawa, and Takefusa Mori. The design was optimized for high speed, low weight and excellent control, qualities deemed essential after the bitter experience with the earlier 7-Shi Carrier Fighter.

The fuselage was of all-metal monocoque construction with a very slim cross section in order to keep drag to a minimum. Horikoshi paid close attention to reducing friction drag by having a smooth surface on the airframe. Flush riveting was used throughout the airframe for the first time in Japan, only a few months behind this being used on the German Heinkel He 70. Flush type fasteners for removable panels were also used.

A retractable undercarriage was being introduced in foreign designed fighters, but Horikoshi was confident that careful design and using smooth contouring would avoid the increased weight and complicated mechanism of the retraction system. Giving consideration to propeller efficiency, Horikoshi selected an engine with reduction gearing, which was rather unusual for installation on a fighter.

The prototype was completed in January 1935 and test flying was begun the following month at Kagamigahara by Mitsubishi test pilot Yoshitaka Kajima and the Navy's Lieut-Cdr Sueto Kobayashi. During flight tests it recorded a speed of 243kt, much faster than the Navy requirement and also exceeded the expectations of those involved in the project. It was far superior to the Nakajima competitor, a modified version of its K-11, an aircraft that resembled the Boeing P-26 in both design and flying performance.

The first prototype of the 9-Shi fighter was found to be unsuitable for short-field landings because of the high-lift-to-drag ratio that often made the touchdown point an uncertainty. To counteract this, the second prototype was fitted with split-flaps which gave the pilot more precise control. The split flap had been invented by engineer Tetsuo Noda of Mitsubishi in 1927. A patent was granted for this invention in 1928 but only in Japan, and not applied for elsewhere; consequently it was put to practical use several years later in the United States without restriction. It had not been used in Japan before because Japan had had no aerodynamic need for such flaps.

The success of the 9-Shi fighter ruled out once and for all the misconception that a cantilever wing was structurally impossible for the high wing loadings imposed upon a fighter aeroplane. It was Mitsubishi's undaunted courage that retained the cantilever structure despite previous failures, and also to pursue the development of a thinner wing of elliptical planform to minimize induced drag. To reduce interference drag between the wing and the fuselage and to improve forward and downward visibility with a shortened undercarriage, an inverted gull wing was tried; since there was concern that the gull wing would induce turbulence and create control response problems, a second prototype was designed with a straight centre section for comparative trials.

The second prototype was tested and evaluated by the Flight Experiment Department of Kusho and the Yokosuka Kokutai for operational suitability. Modifications were made to determine the optimum size of the movable tailplane. It was determined that the best ratio of the elevator tailplane area was approximately 26 percent which was a compromise between control in landing and that needed in combat manoeuvres. This ratio was extremely small when compared with existing ratios, and became a good line of reference for high-speed aircraft.

In order to delay the occurrence

This view of the 9-Shi fighter shows the wing planform to advantage.

of the stall around the wingtips at high angles of attack, Horikoshi provided wash-out to the outer portion of the wing. From an angle of attack of 2 degrees at the wing roots, this decreased by 40min at the wingtips, manoeuvrability at a high angle of attack was remarkably improved and this wash-out was introduced from the 37th aircraft. Up to that point, the Navy evaluations had concluded that the Mitsubishi 9-Shi fighter was inferior to the Nakajima Type 95 biplane fighter in combat manoeuvres, but with these refinements, the 9-Shi fighter was considered to be capable of dog-fighting against biplane fighters in general. This also established the Japanese Navy's future fighter development policy to make manoeuvrability compatible with speed.

The engine used was the 600hp Kotobuki 5, with reduction gear, a combination that lacked durability. The second prototype was powered by the 715hp Kotobuki 3, with the more conventional direct-drive to the propeller, but this also lacked reliability. The third, fourth and fifth prototypes were powered by the 800hp Hikari 1 Engine, but these had inefficient cooling and increased the frontal area and weight which gave adverse results. Thus it seemed impractical to proceed with production. In time, the Naval Air Headquarters decided to select the Kotobuki 2-kai-1 which was already operational and proved to be reliable.

The Mitsubishi 9-Shi Single-seat Fighter was technically on a level with the rest of the world's operational aircraft. It set the pattern for future Japanese aeroplanes in basic design and structure, giving the needed confidence for Japanese aeronautical engineers to meet world standards. It is natural that this aeroplane was the most memorable aeroplane in Japanese aeronautical engineering history together with the Type 96 Land-based Attack Aircraft (Nell) also built by Mitsubishi. Even Lieut Minoru Genda, considered the most talented and experienced Naval fighter pilot through his long biplane career, admitted that the aeroplane was superior to the Type 95 Carrier Fighter, not only in speed, climb and range, but also in manoeuvrability. It developed into the Type 96 Carrier Fighter, acclaimed as the best all-around fighter in the world and, in Genda's opinion, was fully proved in combat against foreign fighters in the Sino-Japanese Conflict.

After the outbreak of the Sino-Japanese Conflict, first-line fighters such as the Seversky 2PA-B3, Vought V-143 and Heinkel He 112 were still imported to supplement production shortage or for research purposes. But these imported aircraft lost their importance once the A5M became operational.

Single-seat low-wing cantilever monoplane carrier-borne fighter with non-retractable undercarriage. All-metal construction with fabric covered control surfaces. Pilot in open cockpit.

Span 11m (36ft 1¼in); length 7.67m (25ft 2in); height 3.265m (10ft 6in); wing area 17.8sq m (191.597sq ft).

Prototype	No. 1	No. 2	No. 3	No. 4	Company Fighter
Engine:	Kotobuki 5 Geared	Kotobuki 3 Geared	Hikari 1 Direct drive	Hikari 1 Direct drive	A9
Type:	Air-cooled radial 9-Cyl	Air-cooled radial 9-Cyl	Air-cooled radial 9-Cyl	Air-cooled radial 9-Cyl	Air-cooled radial 9-Cyl
Rated hp:	600	715	800	800	610
Rated altitude:	3,100m (10,170ft)	2,800m (9,186ft)	3,500m (11,482ft)	3,500m (11,482ft)	3,500m (11,482ft)
Propeller:	Metal fixed-pitch 2-bld	Metal fixed-pitch 2-bld	Metal fixed-pitch 2-bld	Metal fixed-pitch 2-bld	Metal fixed-pitch 2-bld
Aircraft loaded weight:	1,373kg (3,026lb)	1,470kg (3,240lb)	1,500kg (3,306lb)	1,630kg (3,593lb)	1,525kg (3,362lb)
Wing loading	77.13 kg/sq m (18.72) (lb/sq ft)	82.6 (16.9)	84.3 (17.2)	91.6 (18.7)	85.7 (17.5)
Power loading:	2.25 kg/hp (4.9) lb/hp	2.06 (4.5)	1.88 (4.1)	2.04 (4.4)	2.5 (5.5)
Fuel:	200 litres (44 Imp gal)	200 litres (44 Imp gal)	200 litres (44 Imp gal)	330 litres (72 Imp gal)	330 litres (72 Imp gal)
Max Speed at: kt/m (mph/ft)	243.5/3,200 (280/10,498)	243.5/3,740 (280/12,270)	244.5/3,500 (281/11,482)	233/2,685 (268/8,809)	231/3,630 (266/11,909)
Climb (min-sec) to 5000m (16,685ft)	5' 54"	5' 59"	5' 03"	6' 04"	7' 25"
Take off run m (ft)	189 (620)	145 (475)	147 (482)	148 (485)	195 (639)

Six prototypes built in 1935.

Navy Type 3 Land-based Primary Trainer (K2Y1 and 2)

The Navy found that its Type 3 Primary Trainer was a sound replacement in 1930 for the Avro 504K that had been introduced into Japan in 1921 and used by both the Army and Navy. Production of this Type 3, known as the K2Y1 was initially undertaken by the Yokosuka Arsenal and later shared with other manufacturers. Mitsubishi was among these, beginning production in 1934 and producing forty-five of them. (*see* Yokosho Type 3 Land-based Primary Trainer.)

Navy Type 95 Land-based Attack Aircraft (G2H1)

When the Japanese Navy issued the specification for the 7-Shi Special Attack Aircraft it made it the largest naval land aircraft it had attempted,

and its original design was based on a land-based bomber.

Japanese Naval planners recognised the capability of land-based bombers to supplement and reinforce fleet activities and it was to meet this role that the new aeroplane was designed. The Hiro Arsenal created this twin-engined aeroplane based upon its experience in designing and building large all-metal monoplane flying-boats. The first prototype was completed in March 1933 and shipped to Yokosuka for testing. Because of its anticipated potential, the bomber was put into production at Hiro and a production contract was also given to Mitsubishi. By now, Mitsubishi also had experience with large bombers through its Army Type 92 and 93 Heavy bomber (Ki-20 and Ki-1 respectively). When awarded the contract to build the Type 95 Land-based Attack Aircraft in 1935, Mitsubishi was well advanced in the development stages of the Type 96 Land-based Attack Aircraft, G3M (Nell), which soon proved

more practical. As a result, production by Mitsubishi terminated after completing two of the Navy Type 95 Attack Aircraft. Hiro had produced six. Aircraft from both manufacturers were known as the G2H1. (*see* Hirosho for aircraft details.)

The success of the G1M1 led Mitsubishi to produce further innovative Navy designs and all that followed were involved in the Pacific War. The G3M series were engaged in the first over-water bombing missions of any war, operating from Japan with strikes in China. The bomber that followed became the G4M, better known throughout the war as Betty. The A5M and A6M were advanced designs for their time, being respectively the first low-wing monoplane carrier-based fighter and the famous Zero that formed the backbone of Japan's naval fighter force throughout the Pacific War. A variety of other types came from the Mitsubishi drawing boards but these are outside the scope of this volume.

Army Aircraft by Mitsubishi

Army Type Ko 1 Trainer (Nieuport 81-E2)

French influence on the Japanese Army resulted in an influx of imported French aircraft for training, starting in January 1919. Among these were 40 Nieuport-81-E2s and as their numbers diminished the Japanese Army decided to supplement them with others built in Japan.

Nieuport 81-E2s and 83-E2s were the standard Army trainers and they were initially manufactured under licence in Japan by the Army at Tokorozawa. But recognizing that manufacturing aircraft was not a function of the military, the production of the Nieuport 81-E2 was transferred to Mitsubishi which had recently begun building Navy aircraft, and production of the Nieuport 83-E2 went to Nakajima, a newly formed aircraft manufacturer. All drawings and specifications were furnished by the Army and both aeroplanes remained identical to the French-built aircraft. The first of the Mitsubishi-built aircraft was completed in May 1922.

Mitsubishi Army Type Ko 1 Trainer, a Japanese manufactured Nieuport 81-E2

The identity of these two aircraft changed from the French system beginning in November 1921 when the Army established a new designation system, giving a separate identity symbol to each foreign manufacturer's name: Type Ko for Nieuport, followed by a sequential number for each separate type. The Nieuport 81-E2 therefore became the Ko 1 and the Type 83-E2 became the Ko 2.

These Army trainers served at Tokorozawa from the time the Tokorozawa Army Flying School was opened in 1922. Others served at the Kagamigahara Airfield and with some Air Regiments, some remaining operational until around 1926. These two types, with the Nakajima Ko 3, were the main trainers for the Japanese Army during its initial expansion period. After service with the Army, many were released to civil flying schools.

Single-engine sesquiplane trainer. Wooden structure with fabric covering and some plywood and metal. Crew of two in open cockpits.

80-100hp Le Rhône nine-cylinder air-cooled rotary engine, driving a Regy-type two-bladed wooden propeller.

Span 9.20m (30ft 2¼in); length 7.20m (23ft 7½in); height 2.60m (8ft 6¼in) tail down; wing area 23sq m (247.578sq ft).

Empty weight 490kg (1,080lb); loaded weight 760kg (1,675lb); wing loading 33kg/sq m (6.759lb/sq ft); power loading 7.6kg/hp (16.7lb/hp).

Maximum speed 70kt (81mph) at sea level; service ceiling 4,000m (13,123ft).

Fifty-seven built.

Army Type Ki 1 Trainer (Hanriot HD-14)

Having purchased one or more examples of the French Hanriot HD-14, the Japanese Army considered these to be more suitable as primary trainers than the existing Ko 1. Because of this, Mitsubishi acquired the manufacturing rights for the HD-14 in February 1923. Mitsubishi sent Toshinori Sakurai and four other engineers to France to learn first-hand about the construction of the aeroplane.

The first Mitsubishi-built aeroplane was completed in March 1924. Fully satisfied with the result, the Army adapted it as its standard trainer, with the designation of Ki 1.* The aeroplane was an exact copy of the HD-14 with the exception of the powerplant and certain internal systems. It had good flying characteristics and was stable with power on and power off. As a replacement for the Type Ko 1 in 1924, it remained in service until replaced by the Tachikawa Type 93-3 (Allied code-name Cedar) in 1935. In time, a number of Ki 1s were released to civil flying schools which referred to them as Hanriot 28s. This was the last trainer aircraft to be powered with a rotary engine.

Single-engine two-bay biplane trainer with four-wheel undercarriage. Wooden structure with fabric covering and some plywood and metal. Crew of two in open cockpits.

80-100hp Le Rhône nine-cylinder air-cooled rotary engine, driving a Merville-type two-bladed wooden propeller.

Span 10.26m (33ft 8in); length 7.13m (23ft 4¾in); height 3.05m (10ft); wing area 34.50sq m (371.367sq ft).

Empty weight 550kg (1,212lb); loaded weight 800kg (1,763lb); wing loading 23.1kg/sq m (4.731lb/sq ft); power loading 8kg/hp (17.6lb/hp).

Maximum speed 63kt (72mph) at 2,000m (6,561ft); cruising speed 44kt (50mph); climb to 2,000m (6,561ft) in 15min; service ceiling 4,000m (13,123

*This is not a Kitai number but a kanji letter, *i.e.* Ko, Otsu, Hei, Tei, Bo, Ki, etc. Ki was assigned to Hanriot aircraft.

Mitsubishi Army Type Ki 1 Trainer, the Japanese-built Hanriot HD-14.

ft); range 240km (150sm).

145 built: forty March 1924–March 1925, thirty-five April 1925–March 1926, forty-five April 1926–March 1927 and twenty-five from April 1927.

Experimental Washi-type Light Bomber
(Company designation 2MB2)

In 1925, the Japanese Army made a request to Nakajima, Kawasaki and Mitsubishi to develop a Japanese-built light bomber. For its entry, Mitsubishi requested the services of Dr Alexander Baumann, a professor at Stuttgart University, to supervise the project. Nobushiro Nakata was the chief designer, assisted by Satsuo Tokunaga. The aeroplane designed by Mitsubishi was a sesquiplane with high aspect ratio and unusual appearance. It was of mixed wood and metal construction.

The aeroplane, called the Experimental Washi-type (Eagle) Light Bomber, was completed in December 1925. It recorded an impressive 210km/h (114kt) during its test flights at Kagamigahara. Evaluated by the Army in the summer of 1926, the overall performance of the bomber was regarded as better than that of the Nakajima and Kawasaki entries which were then rejected. However, the Washi-type was also graded as unacceptable because of its complicated structure resulting in a high unit cost. As a

result, Mitsubishi submitted to the Army what was termed its 2MB1, which was a modified version of the Mitsubishi Navy Type 13 Carrier Attack Aircraft, the first of which had been completed two years before. Although this design was obsolete by that time, it was a practical aeroplane and was accepted by the Army as the Type 87 Light Bomber. The following figures pertain to the Washi-type Light Bomber

Single-engine sesquiplane with a marked W wing strut arrangement. Metal fuselage structure with wood and metal wings, fabric covered with some light metal on the forward fuselage. Crew of two in open cockpits.

450-600hp Mitsubishi-Hispano-Suiza twelve-cylinder vee water-cooled engine, driving a Reed-type fixed-pitch two-bladed metal propeller.

Two forward-firing fixed 7.7mm machine-guns, one dorsal flexible 7.7mm machine-gun, and one ventral flexible 7.7mm machine-gun. Bomb-load: 800kg (1,763lb).

Mitsubishi Experimental Washi-type Light Bomber.

Span 20m (65ft 7½in); length 9.85m (32ft 3¾in); height 4.10m (13ft 5½in); wing area 64sq m (688.912sq ft), upper 44sq m (473.627sq ft), lower 20sq m (215.285sq ft).

Empty weight 2,100kg (4,629lb); loaded weight 3,640kg (8,024lb); wing loading 56.2kg/sq m (11.510lb/sq ft); power loading 6.06kg/hp (13.3lb/hp).

Maximum speed 114kt (131mph) at sea level; service ceiling 6,000m (19,685 ft); endurance 3hr.

One built in 1925.

Army Type 87 Light Bomber
(Company designation 2MB1)

In a 1925 attempt to fill the requirements for which the Washi-type Light Bomber was not acceptable, Mitsubishi modified one of its Navy Type 13 Carrier Attack Aircraft of 1923 to meet the Army specifications. For this parallel project to the Washi-type, Hajime Matsuhara was assigned as chief designer.

Changes to the Type 13 were having the 450hp Napier Lion engine replaced by the 450hp Hispano-Suiza, with a honeycomb type radiator in front of the engine rather than at the sides of the fuselage. The dihedral on the upper wing was eliminated as well as the folding capability formerly used for stowage. The three-seat configuration was changed to two, with dual controls.

While neither the Nakajima nor Kawasaki, nor Mitsubishi Washi-type entrants in the bomber competition were acceptable, the Mitsubishi 2MB1, although obsolete by then current standards, obtained Army approval because of its

Mitsubishi Army Type 87 Light Bomber.

practicality and good flying control characteristics. Consequently, this was accepted as the Army Type 87 Light Bomber. Initial deliveries equipped two chutais at Hamamatsu (nine light bombers per chutai).

When hostilities developed in Manchuria, these Type 87 Light Bombers participated in early ground support roles. However, production was suspended when the Kawasaki Type 88 Light Bomber and Reconnaissance Aircraft were adopted by the Army. In a remarkable long-range experimental flight, one of these Type 87 Light Bombers flew nonstop from Kagoshima on southern Kyushu, to Taihoku (now Taipei in Taiwan) with the aid of an 800 litres (176 Imp gal) belly tank and a 110 litres (24 Imp gal) fuselage tank.

Single-engine three-bay biplane light bomber. Wooden structure with fabric covering. Crew of two in open cockpits.

450-600hp Mitsubishi-Hispano-Suiza twelve-cylinder vee water-cooled engine, driving a Reed-type fixed-pitch two-bladed metal propeller.

Two forward-firing fixed 7.7mm machine-guns, one dorsal flexible 7.7 mm machine-gun, and one ventral flexible 7.7mm machine-gun. Bomb load: 500kg (1,102lb).

Span 14.80m (48ft 6½in); length 10m (32ft 9½in); height 3.63m (11ft 11in); wing area 60sq m (645.855sq ft).

Empty weight 1,800kg (3,968lb); loaded weight 3,300kg (7,275lb); wing loading 55kg/sq m (11.265lb/sq ft); power loading 5.5kg/hp (12.1lb/hp).

Maximum speed 100kt (115mph) at sea level; cruising speed 76kt (87mph); climb to 1,000m (3,280ft) in 9min 10sec; service ceiling 4,275m (14,025 ft); endurance 3hr.

Forty-eight built: four March 1926–March 1927, ten April 1927–March 1928, twenty-five April 1928–March 1929 and nine from April 1926.

Experimental Tobi-type Reconnaissance Aircraft
(Company designation 2MR1)

To replace the Type Otsu 1 Reconnaissance Aircraft which were Salmson 2-A.2s in 1926, the Army asked for competitive designs from Nakajima, Kawasaki, Ishikawajima and Mitsubishi. Mitsubishi, again with the assistance of Professor Baumann, assigned Nobushiro Nakata as chief designer and Satsuo Tokunaga as his assistant. The result was a radical design for a sesquiplane, having the upper wing set unusually high above the slender fuselage, connected with a unique type of centre-section and interplane struts. As one of the Mitsubishi bird series projects in 1925–27, this aircraft was given the name Tobi which is a bird of the Hawk family.

The first prototype was completed in July 1927. In the hands of test pilot Jiro Itoh the aircraft achieved speed of 227km/h (123kt) faster than the Army's specified 200km/h (108kt). Mitsubishi had high expectations for the new aeroplane, but during an official qualifying test flight by the Army at Tokorozawa, an undercarriage shock strut failed and during the landing the aeroplane was badly damaged and eliminated from the competition. The Nakajima and Ishikawajima entries also failed, but the Kawasaki aircraft met the requirements and was accepted as the Type 88 Reconnaissance Aircraft.

Single-engine sesquiplane with large gap. Metal fuselage structure with wood and metal wings, fabric covered with some plywood and thin metal on the forward fuselage. Crew of two in open cockpits.

450-600hp Mitsubishi-Hispano-Suiza twelve-cylinder vee water-cooled engine, driving a Mitsubishi-Reed fixed-pitch two-bladed metal propeller.

Two forward-firing fixed 7.7mm machine-guns and twin dorsal flexible 7.7mm machine-guns.

Span 17.40m (57ft); length 9.55m (31ft 4in); height 4.35m (14ft 3½in); wing area 50sq m (538.213sq ft), upper 34.50sq m (371.367sq ft), lower 15.50sq m (166.846sq ft).

Empty weight 1,350kg (2,976lb); loaded weight 2,500kg (5,511lb); wing loading 50kg/sq m (10.241lb/sq ft); power loading 3.5kg/hp (7.7lb/hp).

Mitsubishi Experimental Tobi-type Reconnaissance Aircraft.

Maximum speed 123kt (142mph) at 5,000m (16,404ft); landing speed 48kt (55mph); service ceiling 8,280m (27,165 ft), endurance 6hr.

Two built in 1927.

Experimental Hayabusa-type Fighter
(Company designation 1MF2)

To replace the Nakajima Type Ko 4 fighter, which was already obsolete, the Army arranged a competition in 1927 for an interceptor fighter for the defence of metropolitan areas. Among the contenders were Nakajima, Kawasaki, Ishikawajima and Mitsubishi. The Ishikawajima proposal was terminated early in the design stage when declared unsuited to Army requirements. The Mitsubishi entry was supervised again by Professor Baumann and Nobushiro Nakata was chief designer, assisted by Jiro Horikoshi and Jiro Tanaka. The name Horikoshi will be recognized as the famous designer of the much later Zero fighter.

In the initial phase of this design, the aeroplane was a low-wing monoplane with a swept-forward wing uniquely strut braced. However, at the Army's request, it was changed to a parasol monoplane with the cockpit placed well to the rear and clear of the wing for better visibility. To evaluate these design concepts, a mock-up was built, which was unusual for this time. Other features included a jettisonable fuel tank, wing struts which did not require bracing wires, and simplified assembly and maintenance along with other innovations. This was a very advanced design compared with that of its competitors.

The first of two aeroplanes called the Hayabusa-Type (Falcon) was completed in May 1928 and success-

Mitsubishi Experimental Hayabusa-type Fighter.

fully test flown at Kagamigahara Airfield. During the Army's official tests at Tokorozawa, the aeroplane attained a maximum level-flight speed of 147kt (169mph) at 3,000m, the best of the three entries. However, during the diving test to reach the specified 400km/h (216kt) the aeroplane disintegrated. Fortunately, pilot Sumitoshi Nakao was able to bale out and was uninjured. He became the first in Japan to rely upon a parachute for survival.

Because of the accident, further flight evaluations were suspended with the other aircraft, and the aircraft was used for static structural tests to destruction. As a result, all three companies failed in the competition, although Nakajima continued with modifications and improvements in the design which eventually developed into the Type 91 Fighter.

Single-engine strut-braced parasol-wing fighter. Metal frame fuselage and wooden wing structure with fabric covering. Pilot in open cockpit.

450-600hp Mitsubishi-Hispano-Suiza twelve-cylinder vee water-cooled engine, driving a Reed-type fixed-pitch two-bladed metal propeller.

Two forward-firing fixed 7.7mm machine-guns.

Span 12.62m (41ft 5in); length 8.20m (26ft 11in); height 3.35m (11ft); wing area 23sq m (247.578sq ft).

Empty weight 1,265kg (2,789lb); loaded weight 1,800kg (3,968lb); wing loading 78.26kg/sq m (16.02lb/sq ft); power loading 3kg/hp (6.6lb/hp).

Maximum speed 145kt (169mph) at 3,000m (9,843ft); climb to 5,000m (16,404ft) in 11min 18sec; service ceiling 8,500m (27,887ft).

Two built in 1928.

Experimental Short Range Reconnaissance Aircraft
(Company designation 2MR7)

In 1929, as a private venture, Mitsubishi undertook a design project for a short-range reconnaissance aircraft at the same time as it was developing the 2MR8 for the Army. Chief designer was Joji Hattori.

The basic design came from Mitsubishi's own Navy Type 10 Carrier Reconnaissance Aircraft, with the modified structure incorporating features developed by Blackburn. In appearance it was a scaled-down, lighter-weight model of the Navy Type 89 Carrier Attack Aircraft. The Army did give consideration to this aeroplane as a replacement for the Type Otsu 1 Reconnaissance Aircraft but it was never accepted because a modified version of the 2MR8 received Army approval. Only one prototype was built, and this was used as Mitsubishi's company aircraft.

Single-engine biplane with marked stagger. Structure of metal and wood, with fabric covering. Crew of two in open cockpits.

300-320hp Mitsubishi-Hispano-Suiza eight-cylinder vee water-cooled engine, driving a Reed-type fixed-pitch two-bladed metal propeller.

One forward-firing fixed 7.7mm machine-gun and one dorsal flexible 7.7mm machine-gun.

One built in 1929.

Dimensions and performance not available.

Army Type 92 Reconnaissance Aircraft
(Company designation 2MR8)

In 1930, Mitsubishi submitted two proposals to meet the Army's requirement for a short-range reconnaissance aeroplane. These were the 2MR7 biplane design just described and a high-wing parasol monoplane. Only the latter achieved Army acceptance. For this project, Mitsubishi used the services of French engineer and technical advisor Henri Vernisse as design leader, assisted by Mitsubishi engineers Fumihiko Kawano, Minojiro Takahashi and Masakichi Mizuno. For its time the configuration was of

Mitsubishi Experimental Short Range Reconnaissance Aircraft.

advanced design, and its performance confirmed this. Unlike the Kawasaki Type 88 Reconnaissance Aircraft which was a large and heavy biplane for long-range duties, the 2MR8 had comparatively short range, light weight and was manoeuvrable. This was the Army's first light reconnaissance aeroplane and it introduced the class of 'direct co-operation reconnaissance aircraft'.

The first prototype was powered by a 320hp Mitsubishi A2 engine but more powerful engines were used as development continued. Its wing had a modified Clark-Y aerofoil and the original area of 32sq m was eventually reduced to 26sq m.

The aircraft made its first flight on 28 March, 1931, at the Kagamigahara Airfield piloted by Mitsubishi's pilot, Sumitoshi Nakao. The second prototype, which was also flown, was subject to severe structural testing as was the first prototype, the results of which led to the reduction in wing area and a shorter fuselage on the third prototype. This version also had the improved 345hp Mitsubishi A2 kai 3 engine. Total weight was reduced by more than 100kg. In this configuration it became the first prototype to have the appearance of what was developing into the Type 92

Mitsubishi Army Type 92 Reconnaissance Aircraft.

Reconnaissance Aircraft. Although handling qualities met Army expectations, its maximum speed was only 194km/h whereas 215 km/h had been specified. To improve upon this, the fourth prototype was powered by the experimental Mitsubishi A5 engine which was completed in June 1931. It produced 475hp and later became the 400hp Type 92 Engine. With this engine, the fourth prototype attained a speed of 220km/h at 1,000m during tests and the Army's acceptance as the Type 92 Reconnaissance Aircraft.

In 1934, one of these aeroplanes was tested as a 'High Performance Reconnaissance Aircraft' powered by a 760hp Mitsubishi A4 engine, but the project was unsuccessful because of problems with the new engine. Other tests were made, including the use of a larger diameter wooden propeller driven by a 400hp Type 92 Engine with reduction gear. An undercarriage with a caterpillar-type tread was also tried.

Nothing further was gained through these tests, and although the Army was disappointed with overall performance, production models of the Type 92 Reconnaissance Aircraft were used from 1932 as the Army's standard short-range reconnaissance aeroplane, mainly for close support of ground troops in campaigns in Manchuria and

northern China. Many were later donated to the Army as *Aikoku-go,* or patriotic gifts purchased with funds solicited from private and commercial groups as part of the re-armament programme. These aircraft became the first military aeroplanes powered by an engine exclusively designed and manufactured in Japan.

Single-engine parasol-wing monoplane. Metal structure throughout, mainly fabric covered but with metal-covered forward fuselage. Crew of two in open cockpits.

400-475hp Type 92 (Mitsubishi A5) nine-cylinder air-cooled radial engine, driving a Reed-type fixed-pitch two-bladed metal propeller.

Two forward-firing fixed 7.7mm machine-guns and twin dorsal flexible 7.7mm machine-guns.

Span 12.75m (41ft 10in); length 8,515m (27ft 11¼in); height 3.48m (11ft 5in); wing area 26sq m (279.87sq ft).

Empty weight 1,060kg (2,336lb); loaded weight 1,770kg (3,902lb); wing loading 68.1kg/sq m (13.948lb/sq ft); power loading 4.2kg/hp (9.2lb/hp).

Maximum speed 119kt (137mph); climb to 3,000m (9,843ft) in 10min 30sec; service ceiling 5,700m (18,700ft), endurance 4 to 5hr.

130 built by Mitsubishi from April 1930 to March 1934 and 100 built by Army Arsenal.

Mitsubishi Army Type 92 Heavy Bomber (Ki-20).

Army Type 92 Heavy Bomber (Ki-20)

In order to meet an Army order to manufacture a bomber version of the, then, very large Junkers G 38 passenger aircraft, Mitsubishi entered into a contract with Junkers in September 1928 to obtain design data, working drawings, manufacturing techniques and production rights. Germany at that time was forbidden to build military aircraft, but, as the K 51, the G 38 could be converted into a bomber for export. Features could be designed into the basic aircraft for the purchaser, such as armament and internal systems to meet Japanese Army requirements. Accordingly, the Junkers K 51 design became in Japan the Ki-20, a retroactive designation made long after its existence. The intended, but very secret, purpose was for the bomber to be capable of attacking the fortified Corregidor Island at the entrance to Manila Bay from the Japanese airfield at Pingtung in Taiwan, a need that did not materialize until thirteen years later. This Junkers technology introduced Mitsubishi to entirely new design and manufacturing methods.

Nobushiro Nakata, to be the chief designer for this project, and Kyonosuke Ohki were sent by Mitsubishi to Germany in 1928 to study the design and prepare for manufacture in Japan. In December of that year, engineer Yonezo Mitsunawa and chief mechanic Tsunetaro Ishihama went to Junkers to study manufacturing techniques, while engineer Keisuke Ohtsuka purchased the necessary machines, tools, jigs and materials in Germany in April 1930. From Germany came a team of engineers led by Eugene Harbard Schade to assist with manufacture. Representatives of the Japanese Army's interest, were Col Kozumi as chief, with engineers Kuranishi, Ando, Lt Matsumura and others to assist.

When production was begun, the first and second aircraft were built with the main components imported from Junkers. For the third to the sixth aircraft Mitsubishi relied more on the use of components made in Japan and less on imports from Germany. Basically, the airframes of the Ki-20s were almost identical to the Junkers K 51, but gun turrets, both upper and lower, were added at the wing trailing-edge, the upper turrets blending into the rear portions of the two outboard engine nacelles. These were enormous aircraft for their day, with a huge bat-like wing which spanned nearly one-metre more than the Boeing B-29 Superfortress. The wing area was almost double that of the B-29. Its non-retractable undercarriage consisted of dual tandem wheels on each side. Because the design was based on a transport aeroplane, bombs were carried externally.

The first aircraft was completed in 1931 and flown from Kagamigahara under extreme secrecy which prevailed for nearly the entire life of the aircraft. Engines powering the first four aircraft were the 800hp Junkers 88 until the Junkers Jumo 204 diesel engine of 750hp became available and was installed in the fifth and sixth aircraft. Power arrangements varied from time to time, such as installing two Junkers 88s inboard and two Junkers Jumo 204s outboard. Later Kawasaki Ha-9 engines were installed for

This view of the Ki-20 shows the form of its bat-like wing.

Mitsubishi Army Type 93-1 Heavy Bomber (Ki-1-I).

trials to further develop the aeroplane for long-range bomber missions. But by the time these tests and manufacture were concluded, the Army realized that the aeroplanes were now obsolete for any military operations. They were heavy, slow, and had chronic engine problems.

In terms of wing area the Ki-20 was the largest aircraft ever built in Japan. It was one of the world's largest landplanes at that time, and because of this caused considerable problems especially if assigned to operational units in unprepared forward areas. Although conflicts involving Japan were in progress during the time of the Ki-20s, they were never used in combat; instead, they were used for research in Manchuria and Japan. Their first public demonstration was not until three appeared over Tokyo for a parade in January 1940, having taken off from Tachikawa Airfield. When taken out of service soon after, they were displayed at various defence exhibitions and amusement parks. The last was stored in the Aviation Memorial Hall at Tokorozawa where it survived with other rare types until the end of the Pacific War.

Four-engined mid-wing monoplane bomber with non-retractable undercarriage with tandem wheels and biplane tail unit. Construction was Junkers all-metal structure with corrugated stressed skin. Crew of ten (Capt, two pilots, bombar-

dier/nose gunner, flight engineer/top gunner, radio operator/top gunner and four wing gunners).

Four 800hp Junkers L 88 twelve-cylinder vee liquid-cooled engines, or four 750hp Type Ju (Jumo 204) twelve-cylinder vertically-opposed liquid-cooled diesel engines, driving four-bladed wooden propellers.

Twin nose 7.7mm machine-guns, one 20mm cannon on top of fuselage, twin 7.7mm machine-guns in each upper wing turret and one 7.7mm machine-gun in each lower wing turret. Bomb load: normal 2,000kg (4,409lb), maximum 5,000kg (11,023lb).

Span 44m (144ft 4¼in); length 23.20m (76ft 1½in); height 7m (22ft 11¾in); wing area 294sq m (3,164.693 sq ft).

Empty weight 14,912kg (32,875lb); loaded weight 25,448kg) 56,103lb); wing loading 86.6kg/sq m (17.7lb/sq ft); power loading 7.96kg/hp (17.5 lb/hp).

Maximum speed 108kt (125mph).

Six built: No.1 April 1931–March 1932, Nos.2 and 3 April 1932–March 1933, No.4 April 1933–March 1934 and Nos.5 and 6 April 1934–March 1935.

Army Type 93 Heavy Bomber (Ki-1)

In February 1931, a Junkers K 37 was imported from Swedish-Junkers and donated to the Army by sponsors as *Aikoku No.1* (patriotic gift).

Pressed into Army service, it was flown in combat in Manchuria where it showed a remarkable performance. Impressed with the aeroplane's capability, the Army issued specifications in April 1932 exclusively to Mitsubishi for a new heavy bomber on similar lines to the K 37 to replace the ageing Kawasaki Type 87 (Do N) Heavy Bomber. The Army was becoming more specific through experience with successes and failures. The new aeroplane, to be the Type 93 Heavy Bomber, was to be a twin-engined monoplane with 800hp engines, and able to have inflight single-engine capability. Bomb load was to be 1,000kg or 1,500kg with reduced fuel load, and gross weight to be less than 7,500kg. Operational altitude was to be between 2,000m and 4,000m with a maximum speed in level flight of more than 240km/h (130kt) at 3,000m. Armament was to consist of three 7.7mm machine-guns, flexibly mounted, and each with 1,000 rounds. Two prototypes were to be built, with completion date by the end of March 1933.

After considering these factors, Mitsubishi engineers and advisors felt the requirements could be met by designing an enlarged version of the K 37, using the experience gained from the very large Ki-20 four-engined bomber. The new aeroplane would provide close proximity for

Mitsubishi Army Type 93-2 Heavy Bomber (Ki-1-II).

the crew so that they could be in visual and voice contact. For further convenience, a Gosport tube could be used between the bombardier and pilot. A special feature for this design would be the dispersal of fuel tanks throughout the airframe so that any one enemy bullet would not affect the entire fuel system. Also to be incorporated was simplicity in disassembly so that the aeroplane could be easily transported by rail. To facilitate this, the Junkers-type ball joint connectors were to be used.

As with the Ki-20, Nobushiro Nakata was chief designer for this project. Assisting him were Kiro Honjo, Hisanojo Ozawa* and Jiro Tanaka. Capt Komamura was the Army representative assigned to Mitsubishi to oversee the design, manufacture, delivery and acceptance of the new bomber.

The mock-up was evaluated in August 1932 and the first prototype completed in record time by the following March. All was not as planned, however, for the aeroplane had to be powered by two imported 800hp Rolls-Royce Buzzard engines because the intended Mitsubishi 700hp Type 93 water-cooled engine was delayed in development. Even with this added horsepower, flight tests with the first two prototypes showed that the maximum level speed fell short of the intended mark by 20km/h (11kt). However, the Army decided to adopt the aeroplane as Type

*Honjo would later be the chief designer for the G3M Nell and G4M Betty bombers, while Ozawa would be chief designer for the Ki-67 Peggy bomber.

93 (later Type 93-1) Heavy Bomber (Ki-1-I) and production began immediately. Deliveries replaced the Type 87 Heavy Bombers at the operational units.

Problems with the engines continued, however, the most severe being that the aeroplane would not maintain level flight with one engine inoperative. Control was very difficult to maintain under these conditions. In the hope of rectifying the problem, the 71st aircraft was assigned for extensive modification which resulted in later aircraft being designated Type 93-2 Heavy Bomber (Ki-1-II). Major changes included placing the engines lower on the wing and as a result the undercarriage had to be extended and streamlined with a trouser-type fairing. The cockpit canopy was extended to include the rear gunner's position. Smooth skin replaced some of the corrugated panels on the outer wings, and a landing light was installed in an fairing which added streamlining for the externally-mounted bombs.

These modifications improved the aeroplane to some extent; however it retained its reputation of being heavy and slow and was not well liked by its crews in Manchuria and northern China. They preferred the Mitsubishi Type 93 Twin-engine Light Bomber, even though that aeroplane had shortcomings which the Type 93 Heavy Bomber had been designed to resolve. The aeroplane remained in production until the Ki-21, Type 97 Heavy Bomber (later given the Allied code-name Sally) was conceived in 1936. As an interim aircraft until the Ki-21s were in sufficient quantity, the Army purchased about 100

Fiat BR.20s, known as the Type I Heavy Bomber.

Twin-engined low-wing monoplane heavy bomber with non-retractable undercarriage and twin fins and rudders. Construction was Junkers all-metal structure with corrugated stressed skin. Crew of four, two pilots, bombardier/nose gunner and dorsal gunner.

Two 750-940hp Type 93 (Ha-2II) twelve-cylinder vee water-cooled engines, driving two-bladed wooden propellers.

One nose flexible 7.7mm machine-gun, one dorsal flexible 7.7mm machine-gun and one ventral flexible 7.7mm machine-gun. Bomb load: 1,000kg (2,204.5lb), maximum 1,500kg (3,306.8lb).

Span 26.50m (86ft 11½in); length 14.80m (48ft 6½in); height 4.923m (16ft 2in); wing area 90.74sq m (976.725sq ft).

Empty weight 4,880kg (10,758lb); loaded weight 8,100kg (17,857lb); wing loading 89.2kg/sq m (18.2lb/sq ft); power loading 4.35kg/hp (9.5lb/hp).

Maximum speed 119kt (137mph); climb to 3,000m (9,843ft) in 14min; service ceiling 5,000m (16,404ft).

118 built: seventeen March 1933–March 1934, thirty-seven April 1934–March 1935, thirty-seven April 1935–March 1936 and twenty-seven from April 1936.

Army Type 93 Twin-engine Light Bomber (Ki-2)

In close association with the Type 93 Heavy Bomber, the Army was interested in developing a twin-engined light bomber that was also based upon the qualities observed in the imported Swedish-built Junkers K 37. During the K 37's participation in combat in Manchuria in support of ground troops, its performance proved superior to that of the Mitsubishi Type 87 and the Kawasaki Type 88 Light Bombers. To replace these older aeroplanes, in September 1932 the Army asked Mitsubishi to redesign the K 37 to meet specific requirements for a new bomber that would become the Type 93 Twin-engine Light Bomber, the Ki-2 in the new Kitai numbering system. The Army recognized Mitsubishi's experience in working with Junkers designs from having built the corrugated skinned Type 92 Heavy Bomber, and from the work that was in progress on the Type 93 Heavy Bomber.

The design team remained that of the Ki-1 project, Nobushiro Nakata as chief designer, assisted by Kiro Honjo, Hisanojo Ozawa, and Jiro Tanaka. Capt Komabayashi continued his liaison for the Army. This new light bomber was to have a crew of three or four and be very manoeuvrable, especially in making tight turns. With one engine inoperative, it was not only to be able to maintain straight and level flight but be turned into the operative engine, a manoeuvre not easily made with asymmetrical power during this early period of twin-engine aeroplanes. Ease of handling in night landings and take offs as well as daytime operations would be a strong consideration. Maximum speed should be 260km/h (140kt) at 3,000m. Fuel capacity should allow for a 4½h flight at 240km/h (130kt) at 3,000m with a 300 to 500kg bomb load, or 6hr at the same speed without a bomb load. Normal operating altitude would be from 2,000m to 3,000m, with a service ceiling of 7,000m. The engines were to be the 450hp Jupiter. Two prototypes of the new bomber were asked for, the first to be completed by July 1933.

After reviewing the specifications, Mitsubishi responded with its proposal to meet them. The K 37 fuselage would be completely redesigned, leaving the wing basically the same except for a redesign of the ailerons. If the Mitsubishi A4 engine would be acceptable, a speed of 270km/h (146kt) could be expected. In any case, the engines would have the newly developed Townend cowlings. Armament would include a fully-enclosed nose turret and a better downward firing angle for the lower gun position. The bungee-cord shock absorbers on the undercarriage would be replaced with the newly introduced Oleo shock struts.

The Army reviewed this proposal, and in November 1932 Mitsubishi received a commitment

Mitsubishi Army Type 93-1 Twin-engine Light Bomber (Ki-2-1).

from the Army for the new aeroplane with the following exceptions to the Mitsubishi proposal. The so-called nose ball turret was not approved, instead it was to be an open position with some wind protection, and a wider angle of fire for the upper gun position was necessary. The open cockpit for the pilot should have a means whereby a covering could be attached, and the engines should be equipped with shutter-covers for cold weather operations. The proposal for a retractable undercarriage was considered but would be deferred to a later time.

The design was changed accordingly. A mock-up was built, and the first prototype was completed in May 1933, two months ahead of schedule. The aeroplane when tested at Kagamigahara achieved 255km/h (137kt) at 3,000m, a mere 5km/h short of the specification. It received good marks in handling qualities. However, during the tests when making a landing, the aircraft stalled, breaking the fuselage aft of the wing and killing the crew. Modifications to the fuselage altered the taper and gave it greater strength. The aeroplane then entered production as the Army Type 93-1 Twin-engine Light Bomber (Ki-2-I), and 113

were built before production ended in 1936.

A revised version designated the Type 93-2 (Ki-2-II) began coming off the production line in 1936, replacing the earlier model. These had the superior 550hp Type 94 Engines, replacing the 450hp Jupiter engines. The undercarriage was now retractable, folding forward into the engine nacelles. The pilot's cockpit was fitted with a rearward sliding canopy, and some of the airframes had a ball-turret-like cover over the nose gunner's position for aircraft assigned to cold weather areas. Some corrugated panels on the wing were replaced with smooth skin, and a landing light was fitted in a fairing under the fuselage. Twenty 15kg bombs could be carried internally installed vertically in the bomb bay. With these modifications, the maximum speed of the aircraft was increased by about 30km/h.

During the Sino-Japanese conflict, the bomber was used mainly in the northern China and Manchurian campaigns. Performance of this new type was considered far

Mitsubishi Army Type 93-2 Twin-engine Light Bomber (Ki-2-II)

superior to that of the Ki-1 and Ki-3. In time, many were relegated to the role of trainer and remained in service for a long time. This became the last Japanese aeroplane to have corrugated skinning.

Twin-engined low-wing monoplane light bomber with fixed (later retractable) undercarriage. Construction was Junkers all-metal structure with corrugated stressed skin. Crew of three, pilot, bombardier/nose gunner, and dorsal gunner.

Two 450-570hp Nakajima Jupiter nine-cylinder air-cooled radial engines, driving two-bladed wooden propellers (Ki-2-I). Two 500-750hp Type 94 (Ha-8) nine-cylinder air-cooled radial engines, driving fixed pitch two-bladed metal propellers (Ki-2-II).

One nose flexible 7.7mm machine-gun and one dorsal flexible 7.7mm machine-gun (Ki-2-I). Bomb load: normal 300kg (661lb), maximum 500kg (1,102lb).

	Ki-2-I	Ki-2-II
Span	19.962m (65ft 6in)	19.962m (65ft 6in)
Length	12.60m (41ft 4in)	12.70m (41ft 8in)
Height	4.635m (15ft 2½in)	4.635m (15ft 2½in)
Wing area	56.20sq m	56.20sq m
	(604.951sq ft)	(604.951sq ft)
Empty weight	2,800kg (6,172lb)	—
Loaded weight	4,550kg (10,031lb)	4,700kg (10,361lb)
Maximum weight	4,645kg (10,240lb)	—
Wing loading	80.9kg/sq m	83.6kg/sq m
	(16.5lb/sq ft)	(17.1lb/sq ft)
Power loading	3.99kg/hp (8.8lb/hp)	3.13kg/hp (6.9lb/hp)
Maximum speed	138kt (159mph)	153kt (176mph)
Climb to	3,000m (9,843ft)	—
in	10min	—
Service ceiling	7,000m (22,965ft)	—
Range	900nm (1,036sm)	—

Ki-2-I: 113 built May 1933–1936; Ki-2-II: 61 built April 1937–1938. Total 174. (Additional 13 Ki-2-I by Kawasaki November 1934–August 1935.)

Experimental Ki-7 Crew Trainer

In 1933 the Army expressed a need for a crew trainer. In May of that year, Mitsubishi was given a contract by the Army to build two prototypes of a high-wing cabin monoplane trainer based on very broad requirements. This was not solely a pilot trainer but also to be used for training navigators, gunners, and other air crew. The company converted one of its own Navy Type 90 Crew Trainers, a type which had already been accepted by the Navy, but with changes to satisfy Army specifications. In charge of the project as chief designer was Masakichi Mizuno, and to make the flying evaluation for the Army was Capt Onda from the Army Air Technical Research Institute.

Basic changes to be made in converting the Navy model to Army uses was replacement of the 300hp Tempu engine with a 400hp Type 92 having a reinforced engine mounting and forward fuselage. The second prototype was powered by the 450hp Nakajima Kotobuki. Aircraft equipment and systems were to be changed to

Mitsubishi Experimental Ki-7 Crew Trainer seen after release to Aviation Bureau.

Army types, such as the propeller used on the Type 92 Reconnaissance Aircraft.

The first prototype was completed in December 1933, but it was badly damaged in an emergency landing accident while undergoing flight evaluation at Hamamatsu Army Flying School. For unexplained reasons, the trainer was not put into production, and the second prototype was later released from the Army as a civil aircraft.

Single-engine high-wing cabin monoplane trainer. Welded steel tube fuselage and wooden frame wing with fabric covering. Pilot in open cockpit and instructor and three students in cabin.

400-475hp Type 92 (A5-AS) nine-cylinder air-cooled radial engine, driving a Mitsubishi-Reed fixed-pitch two-bladed metal propeller.

One dorsal flexible 7.7mm machine-gun. Bomb load: six 4kg bombs.

Span 15.78m (51ft 9¼in); length 9.65m (31ft 8in); height 3.85m (12ft 7½in) approx; wing area 34.5sq m (371.367sq ft).

Empty weight 1,345kg (2,965lb); loaded weight 2,000kg (4,409lb); wing loading 57.6kg/sq m (11.797lb/sq ft); power loading 4.21kg/hp (9.2lb/hp).

Maximum speed 100kt (115mph) at 1,000m (3,280ft); climb to 2,000m (6,562ft) in 5min.

Two built in 1933–34.

Experimental Ki-18 Fighter

In a new fighter competition organized by the Army in 1934, in which Mitsubishi was not initially involved, Nakajima submitted a low-wing monoplane with non-retractable undercarriage, which looked similar to the Boeing P-26, and it

Mitsubishi Experimental Ki-18 Fighter

became the Ki-11. Kawasaki's entry was a sesquiplane fighter, to be known as the Ki-10. The Ki-11 was slightly superior to the Ki-10 in speed, yet the Ki-10 was more manoeuvrable. The latter aeroplane, however, was accepted by the Army as the Type 95 Fighter, but without much enthusiasm.

At this time Mitsubishi's Navy 9-Shi Fighter was showing outstanding performance and not only captured the respect of the Navy, but of the Army as well. With the Navy's consent, the Army ordered an example of the 9-Shi Fighter (which developed into the A5M1, Allied code-name Claude) for evaluation. It was to have Army equipment and systems to replace those of the Navy. This became the Ki-18. Changes from the Navy model were in the direction of the throttle movement (in the Army forward was idle) and substituting Army standard machine-guns. The reverse movement of the throttle probably resulted from French influence.

The new aeroplane was completed in August 1935 and evaluated until the following spring at the Air Technical Research Institute at Tachikawa and later at the Akeno Army Flying School. In the early part of 1936 the Kotobuki 5 engine was changed to the Kotobuki 3 at the suggestion of Capt Oujiro Matsumura, an instructor at Akeno. The direct-drive Kotobuki 3 seemed to be an Army preference. During these tests, flown primarily by Capt Akita, a maximum speed of 240kt at 3,050m was recorded, and the aeroplane was able to climb to 5,000m in 6min 25.8scc – an exceptional rate. These remarkable tests

continued until the Ki-18 was badly damaged in a landing accident.

Opinions by those who flew the aeroplane were that stability and control could be improved but no changes were made. However, while the Ki-18 was being evaluated at the Akeno Flying School, it gained excellent marks in every respect and it was requested that further models be produced. These Akeno recommendations were countered by the Air Technical Research Institute expressing dissatisfaction with the engine which it termed unreliable. Supporting this claim, the senior organization, Army Air Headquarters, concluded that the Ki-18 had insufficient performance for acceptance as an Army fighter. Therefore, a new competition would be staged, inviting three aircraft companies to participate. Thus, the Ki-18 ended with only the one aircraft, to the astonishment of Mitsubishi, because of the dissatisfaction expressed by the Air Headquarters, while this same aeroplane was considered a revolutionary fighter for the Japanese Navy. One might speculate that the never-ending rivalry and jealousy between the Army and the Navy had much to do with this decision.

Single-engine low-wing monoplane fighter. All-metal construction with fabric-covered control surfaces. Pilot in open cockpit.

600hp Nakajima Kotobuki 5 nine-cylinder air cooled radial engine, driving a fixed-pitch two-bladed metal propeller.

Two forward-firing fixed 7.7mm machine-guns.

Span 11m (36ft 1in); length 7.655m (25ft 1¼in); height 3.15m (10ft 4in); wing area 17.80sq m (191.603sq ft).

Empty weight 1,110kg (2,447lb); loaded weight 1,422kg (3,135lb); wing loading 79.9kg/sq m (16.3lb/sq ft); power loading 2.37kg/hp (5.2lb/hp).

Maximum speed 240kt (276mph) at 3,050m (10,000ft); landing speed 61kt (70mph); climb to 5,000m (16,404ft) in 6min 26sec.

One built in 1935.

Experimental Ki-33 Fighter

After the failure of the Ki-11 and the non-acceptance of the Ki-18, the Army informed three of the major aircraft manufacturers in December 1935 that a competition would be held for a new fighter the following April. This date was based upon the expected availability of the new Army Ha-1 Ko engine. Features asked for in the competition closely followed those of the rejected Ki-18 (A5M1).

In response, Mitsubishi engineers felt that the company was too involved with two 9-Shi aircraft, the A5M fighter and the G3M bomber, both of which had recently been accepted by the Navy. There was no advantage in diluting manpower resources with separate projects for both the Army and the

Mitsubishi Experimental Ki-33 Fighter

Navy. In addition, the rejection by the Army of the Ki-18 in light of its outstanding capability was considered to be a second rejection on principles rather than quality.

An internal debate between Mitsubishi's marketing division and its engineers brought about a compromise that the Army's purchase order would be honoured provided it did not cause a noticeable drain upon engineering resources unless such design work was absolutely necessary.

The new fighter was designated Ki-33. Chief designer was Jiro Horikoshi, who had designed the 9-Shi Fighter. By August 1936, the first prototype was completed, far earlier than the other companies' prototypes. This was understandable because Mitsubishi had current fighter designs and fabrication experience with its existing models. When the second prototype was completed, both aircraft were delivered to the Army after intercompany flight tests at Kagamigahara.

In appearance, the Ki-33 closely resembled the Navy A5M1 Fighter, as did the Ki-18 which had been rejected. What made this aeroplane significant, aside from the Ha-1 engine replacing the Kotobuki 5 engine, was the wash-out of the wing that Horikoshi introduced into the design of the second prototype for comparison with the first prototype which had a conventional wing. This wash-out reduced wingtip stall at high angles of attack, which is so essential for improved manoeuvrability when dog-fighting.

Mitsubishi's competitors were much later with their test aircraft. By the time they produced their second prototypes, they too had the wash-out feature incorporated into the wingtips. The results of the evaluation concluded that the Ki-33 was superior to the Nakajima Ki-27 both in speed and control. However, the prolonged evaluation of the two designs resulted in modifications made by Nakajima to the Ki-27, some of which included three newer wing designs with different wing area and wash-out. Mitsubishi made few if any changes to its Ki-33, recognizing a pattern,

either real or imagined, of the rejection cycle that had occurred with its Ki-18.

As a consequence, the Nakajima Ki-27 was determined to be the superior fighter and was accepted by the Army as the Type 97 Fighter. Kawasaki's Ki-28 with its water-cooled Ha-9 II Ko recorded the maximum speed of 261kt during the winter season (speed would have decreased by 5½kt during the heat of summer). The fighter failed in the competition because Kawasaki ignored the importance placed by the Army on manoeuvrability for dog-fighting rather than pure speed.

Single-engine low-wing monoplane fighter. All-metal construction with fabric-covered control surfaces. Pilot in semi-enclosed cockpit.

620-745hp Ha-1 Ko nine-cylinder air-cooled radial engine, driving a fixed-pitch two-bladed metal propeller.

Two forward-firing fixed 7.7mm machine-guns, 800 rounds each.

Span 11m (36ft 1in); length 7.545m (24ft 9in); height 3.19m (10ft5½in); wing area 17.80sq m (191.603sq ft).

Empty weight 1,132kg (2,495lb); loaded weight 1,462kg (3,223lb); wing loading 82.2kg/sq m (16.8lb/sq ft); power loading 1.97kg/hp (4.3lb/hp).

Maximum speed 256kt (294.6mph) at 3,000m (9,843ft); climb to 5,000m (16,404ft) in 5min 56sec.

Two built in 1936.

Mitsubishi suffered a number of failures during this period with Army aircraft, while development of Navy aircraft was flourishing. But this rash of failures did not continue. The Army aircraft designs that immediately followed these attempts were the Army Type 97 Command Reconnaissance Aircraft, Ki-15 (code-name Babs); the Army Type 97 Heavy Bomber, Ki-21 (Sally) both in many versions; the Army Type 97 Light-Bomber, Ki-30 (Ann) and others. All these types figured prominently in China as well as the opening stages of the Pacific War.

Civil Aircraft by Mitsubishi

Mitsubishi-Hanriot 28 Trainer

For a civilian trainer, Mitsubishi created a version of the Army Type Ki 1, a design that originated from the Hanriot HD-14. It was described as being extremely slow, creating the appearance of a kite, but being very stable. Even with an engine failure, its glide equated to that of a sailplane. Having these qualities, it gained a good reputation as a primary trainer. It was used in small numbers mainly by civilian flying schools and student aviation clubs over a long period, from 1925 to about 1937.

Single-engine two-bay biplane trainer with four-wheel undercarriage. Wooden structure covered with fabric and some plywood and metal. Crew of two in open cockpits.

80-100hp Le Rhône nine-cylinder air-cooled rotary engine, driving a Merville-type two-bladed wooden propeller.

Span 10.26m (33ft 8in); length 7.13m (23ft 4¾in); height 3.05m (10ft); wing area 34sq m (365.984sq ft). Empty weight 565kg (1,246lb); loaded weight 800kg (1,763lb); wing loading 23.5kg/sq m (4.8lb/sq ft); power loading 10kg/hp (22lb/hp).

Maximum speed 60kt (69mph); cruising speed 44kt (50mph); landing speed 19kt (22mph); climb to 2,000m (6,561ft) in 15min; service ceiling 4,000m (13,123ft); range 240km (150sm); endurance 3hr.

Mitsubishi R-1.2 Trainer

For the development of a civilian intermediate trainer, Mitsubishi used as a basis its Navy Type 10-1 Carrier Reconnaissance Aircraft. There were other conversions made from this design for multi-purpose use such as communications/liaison for newspaper companies. These conversions were made by the Itoh Aeroplane Manufacturing Works and the Hamamatsu Aeroplane Manufacturing Works. Some of these biplanes were used as late as 1930.

Single-engine two-bay biplane trainer. Wooden construction with fabric covering. Crew of two in open cockpits.

300hp Mitsubishi Type Hi eight-cylinder vee water-cooled engine, driving a two-bladed wooden propeller.

Span 12.039m (39ft 6in); length 7.925m (26ft); height 2.896m (9ft 6in); wing area 37.69sq m (405.695sq ft).

Empty weight 900kg (1,984lb); loaded weight 1,450kg (3,196lb); wing loading 38.5kg/sq m (7.8lb/sq ft); power loading 4.85kg/hp (10.6lb/hp).

Maximum speed 103kt (118.5mph); climb to 2,000m (6,562ft) in 6min; service ceiling 6,500m (21,325ft); endurance 3½hr.

Mitsubishi Trainer R-2.2

Another conversion of a military aircraft for civilian training was a modification of the Navy Type 10-2 Carrier Reconnaissance Aircraft. In addition, direct use was made of surplus Navy Type 10-2 Intermediate Trainers of the same basic design, which were operated in

Mitsubishi R-1.2 Trainer.

Mitsubishi-Hanriot 28 Trainer.

several variations by the press for communications/liaison, and for sight-seeing because they were able to carry two passengers. The aeroplane used by the *Osaka Maini-chi Shimbun* had the designation RT3A2, while another aircraft,

Mitsubishi R-2.2 Trainer converted with a cabin for three passengers.

registered J-BEGG, had the rear cockpit converted into a cabin for two passengers seated in tandem. A small number of these aircraft, generally called Type 10th year, denoting their design year of Taisho 10 (1921), were in use up to 1938.

Single-engine two-bay biplane trainer. Wooden construction with fabric covering. Crew of two to four in open or enclosed cockpits.

300hp Mitsubishi Type Hi eight-cylinder vee water-cooled engine driving a two-bladed wooden propeller.

Span 12.039m (39ft 6in); length 7.925m (26ft); height 2.895m (9ft 6in); wing area 37.69sq m (405.695sq ft).

Empty weight 915kg (2,017lb); loaded weight 1,455kg (3,207lb); wing loading 38.5kg/sq m (7.8lb/sq ft); power loading 4.85kg/hp (10.6lb/hp).

Maximum speed 103kt (118mph); service ceiling 6,500m (21,325ft); endurance 3½hr.

Mitsubishi R-4 Survey Aircraft

To supply the need for a civil aeroplane for aerial survey, surplus Navy Type 10-2 Carrier Reconnaissance Aircraft (2MR4) were acquired for modification. Most noticeable changes were the cockpits which were enclosed into a single unit, and the radiator changed from a Lamblin to box-type. Two aeroplanes received these particular modifications, which were given the

Mitsubishi R-4 Survey Aircraft.

Mitsubishi Tora-type Long-range Aircraft.

name *Ohji-Ki* and *Dai-Ni Hakuryu-ki* respectively. Originally built by Mitsubishi, these were converted by the Itoh Aeroplane Manufacturing Works at Tsudanuma in Chiba Prefecture.

Single-engine two-bay biplane. Wooden construction with fabric covering. Crew of two in enclosed cockpit.

300hp Mitsubishi Type Hi eight-cylinder vee water-cooled engine, driving a two-bladed wooden propeller.

Span 12.039m (39ft 6in); length 7.925m (26ft); height 2.896m (9ft 6in); wing area 37.69sq m (405.695sq ft).

Two conversions.

Mitsubishi F3B1 Trainer

Little was recorded about this aeroplane other than that it was a civilian aerobatic trainer converted from a Navy Type 10-2 Carrier Fighter.

Single-engine biplane. Wooden construction with fabric covering. Pilot in open cockpit.

300hp Mitsubishi Type Hi eight-cylinder vee water-cooled engine, driving a two-bladed wooden propeller.

Span 8.84m (29ft); length 6.88m (22ft 7in); height 2.997m (9ft 10in); wing area 28.89sq m (310.979sq ft).

Empty weight 772kg (1,701lb); loaded weight 1,135kg (2,502lb); wing loading 39.287kg/sq m (8.04lb/sq ft); power loading 3.85kg/hp (8.4lb/hp).

Maximum speed 122kt (140mph); climb to 2,000m (6,562ft) in 4min 36sec; service ceiling 6,100m (20,013ft); endurance 2.6hr.

One conversion.

Mitsubishi Tora-type Long-range Aircraft

Mitsubishi built this aeroplane as a private venture in 1926, in order to demonstrate the efficiency of the company's 450hp Hispano-Suiza engine for which it had just acquired licence rights. Many of the components and design features of the aeroplane were those of the Navy Type 13-1 Carrier Attack Aircraft and led to the prototype for the Type 13-2.

During the period 25 to 31 May 1926, this Tora-Type (Tiger) aeroplane flew from Kagamigahara, north of Nagoya, to Ohmura on Kyushu, covering 725km (450sm) in 4hr 39min, and from Ohmura to Morioka in northern Honshu, in 8hr 21min over a distance of 1,530km (950sm). While making these demonstration flights, the familiar three-diamond trademark of Mitsubishi was painted on the tail. The pilot on these flights was

Mitsubishi T-1.2 Converted Aeroplane J-BAHC.

the civilian company pilot Sumitoshi Nakao.

Single-engine three-bay long-range biplane. Wooden structure with fabric covering. Crew of two in open cockpits.

450-640hp Mitsubishi-Hispano-Suiza twelve-cylinder vee water-cooled engine, driving a Mitsubishi-Reed fixed-pitch two-bladed metal propeller.

Span 14.80m (48ft 6½in); length 10m (32ft 9½in); height 3.55m (11ft 7¾in); wing area 57sq m (613.562sq ft).

Empty weight 1,550kg (3,417lb); loaded weight 2,900kg (6,393lb); wing loading 50.9kg/sq m (10.4lb/sq ft); power loading 4.53-6.44kg/hp (9.9-14.1lb/hp).

Maximum speed 124kt (142.6mph); cruising speed 95kt (109mph); landing speed 40.5kt (47mph); climb to 3,000m (9,843ft) in 20min; endurance 6hr, with added tanks 12hr.

One built in 1926.

Mitsubishi T-1.2 Converted Aeroplane

Japanese newspapers were continual users of aircraft for communication and liaison duties, and most of these were conversions of previous designs of surplus military types. In the case of the T-1.2 Converted Aeroplane this was originally a Navy Type 13 Carrier Attack Aircraft. The accommodation was increased to provide two side-by-side seats in an enclosed cockpit above the leading edge of the upper wing and a cabin for two passengers and 30kg of cargo. Beginning in

1929, these aeroplanes were used by newspapers such as the *Daimai Tonichi* (Osaka Mainichi and Tokyo Nichinichi syndicate) and the *Osaka/ Tokyo Asahi Shimbun.*

Another user of two of these aeroplanes was the Central Meteorological Observatory. One, registered J-AAMC *Umikaze* (*Sea Wind*), had a Nakajima Jupiter engine, and J-BAFF was powered by a Mitsubishi-Hispano-Suiza. The latter aeroplane was used for observing the solar eclipse in Hokkaido in June 1936, marking the beginning in Japan of astrological observations made from aeroplanes.

Although the official Aviation Bureau designation for this aeroplane was Mitsubishi T-1.2 Converted Aeroplane, most were more commonly called the Type 13th Year Converted Aeroplane, referring partially to the Navy designation which used the 13th year of Taisho (1924) when the original aircraft was officially adopted.

There were variations on this type. Some were powered by the 450-hp Mitsubishi-Hispano-Suiza while others were equipped with the 420hp Nakajima Jupiter VI and in earlier models the 450hp Napier Lion. Most of the conversions were made by the Itoh Aeroplane Manufacturing Works, yet they remained known as Mitsubishi aircraft.

Single-engine cabin biplane. Rearward folding wings for stowage. Wooden structure with fabric covering. Pilot and two or three passengers.

450hp Napier Lion twelve-cylinder W water-cooled engine, driving a two-bladed wooden propeller; one 450hp Mitsubishi-Hispano-Suiza twelve-cylinder vee water-cooled engine, driving a Reed fixed-pitch two-bladed metal propeller; or one 420hp Nakajima Jupiter VIA nine-cylinder air-cooled radial, driving a two-bladed wooden propeller.

(Following data for Lion-powered version.)

Span 14.783m (48ft 6in); length 9.804m (32ft 2in); height 3.507m (11ft 6in); wing area 59sq m (635.091sq ft).

Empty weight 1,465kg (3,229lb); loaded weight 2,600kg (5,732lb); wing loading 44.1kg/sq m (9.03lb/sq ft); power loading 5.78kg/hp (12.74lb/hp).

Maximum speed 107kt (123mph); landing speed 43.5kt (50mph); climb to 3,000m (9,843ft) in 10min; service ceiling 6,000m (19,685ft); endurance 6hr.

Mitsubishi T-1.2 Converted Aeroplane of a different configuration and equipped with skis.

Mitsubishi Hibari-type Trainer

Using the basic design of its 1921 Navy Type 10 Carrier Reconnaissance Aircraft, Mitsubishi engineers developed the Hibari (Skylark)-Type Trainer. The prototype of this civilian model was completed in June 1925, and registered by the Aviation Bureau as the Type FT-1.2, but the aeroplane was never put into production. As a consequence, only one was built and it was retained by Mitsubishi as its company aircraft for research, but primarily as an experimental aircraft for training and liaison between the factory at Nagoya and flight test facility at Kagamigahara.

Single-engine biplane. Wooden construction with fabric covering. Crew of two in open cockpits.

300hp Mitsubishi-Hispano-Suiza eight-cylinder vee water-cooled engine, driving a two-bladed wooden propeller.

Span 11.13m (36ft 6in); length 7.55m (24ft 9¼in); height 3.34m (10ft 11½in).

Empty weight 930kg (2,050lb); loaded weight 1,220kg (2,689lb); power loading 4.07kg/hp (8.9lb/hp).

Maximum speed 87kt (100mph); endurance 1½hr.

One built in June 1925.

Mitsubishi Tombo-type Trainer

(Company designation 2MS1)

This trainer, based on the Army Type Ki 1 Trainer (Hanriot 28)

Mitsubishi Type-R Transport Flying-boat J-BHAE.

that was manufactured by Mitsubishi, was redesigned to accommodate the Armstrong Siddeley Mongoose engine. The first flight was made in June 1927 by Sumitoshi Nakao at the Nagoya Factory airfield. This was a private venture undertaken by Mitsubishi, and even though performance was recorded as good, neither the Army nor the Navy was interested in the aeroplane. As a result, Mitsubishi retained the aeroplane it called Tombo (Dragonfly) and used it for research, training and liaison duties.

Single-engine two-bay biplane trainer. Wooden structure with fabric covering. Crew of two in open cockpits.

125-144hp Armstrong Siddeley Mongoose five-cylinder air-cooled radial engine, driving a fixed-pitch two-bladed metal propeller.

Span 9.20m (30ft 2¼in); length 7.30m (23ft 11½in); height 3.08m (10ft 1¼in); wing area 31.3sq m (336.921sq ft).

Empty weight 590kg (1,300lb); loaded weight 850kg (1,873lb); wing loading 27.2kg/sq m (5.5lb/sq ft); power loading 5.9kg/hp (13lb/hp).

Maximum speed 80kt (92.12mph) at 3,000m (9,843ft); minimum speed 30kt (34.5mph); climb to 3,000m (9,843ft) in 23min 48sec; service ceiling 5,000m (16,404ft); endurance 3hr.

One built in 1927.

Mitsubishi Tombo-type Trainer.

Mitsubishi Type-R Transport Flying-boat

The Type-R Flying-boat built by Mitsubishi for the Navy in 1927 was a poor performer and was therefore unacceptable particularly because of its poor take off and alighting characteristics. This was one of three Type-R Flying-boats that appeared in Japan. The first of these, the R1, had been imported as parts from Rohrbach in Copenhagen and assembled by the Yokosuka Naval Arsenal. The R-2 was built by Mitsubishi, and the R-3 by the Hiro Naval Arsenal, and all served the Navy for experimental purposes only.

In September 1927, the R-1 and R-2 were released to Nippon Koku KK (Japan Aviation Co Ltd) in Osaka, a subsidiary of Kawanishi. At that time, Nippon Koku KK was planning an air route between Osaka, Fukuoka and Shanghai with a Dornier Wal flying-boat. By adding the two Type-R flying-boats, Nippon Koku KK could schedule more frequent services to Shanghai.

Originally the R-2 was powered by two 450hp Mitsubishi-Hispano-Suiza engines, but after being registered J-BHAE as a civil aircraft, the engines were replaced by the more familiar 360hp Rolls-Royce Eagles, but no changes were made to the airframe. However, operations along the mouth of the Kizu River in Osaka were disappointing because of the relatively high alighting speed and what was determined to be a weak hull design. As a result, there were no services to Shanghai with these aircraft. (*see* Mitsubishi Experimental Type-R Flying-boat).

Mitsubishi MC-1 Passenger Transport

In November 1927, the Aviation Bureau of the Department of Communications announced a competition to improve the quality of Japanese-made passenger transports. The companies qualified to compete, including Mitsubishi, were given a grant-in-aid from the Aviation Bureau to design and manufacture a passenger transport wholly free from foreign influence. Mitsubishi based its design on its successful Navy Type 13 Carrier Attack Aircraft. This aeroplane was completed in April 1928 and announced as ready for the competition.

The MC-1 used the wings from the Type 13 Carrier Attack Aircraft without changes, because these were efficient and well designed. The fuselage was a new design to accommodate four passengers. Mitsubishi replaced the Hispano-Suiza with an imported 385hp Armstrong Siddeley Jaguar, for which Mitsubishi acquired a licence.

The evaluation of the aeroplane took place along with the Aichi AB-1, which relied heavily on Heinkel ideas, and the Nakajima N-36, having Breguet influence. During the evaluation flights, the Nakajima N-36 crashed. The Mitsubishi MC-1 and the Aichi AB-1 reached qualifying performance standards but neither was termed acceptable because of poor visibility from the cockpit. Another reason for not declaring a winner was that, by the time of the competition, the biplane configuration was considered obsolete. Consequently, none of the types went into production. As a result when Nihon Koku Yuso KK required transports it bought Fokker Super Universals from the United States.

The MC-1 was used experimentally on the scheduled service of the East-West Regular Aviation Association between Tokyo and Osaka, a project established by the *Asahi Shimbun* in June 1928 and lasting until April 1929. After that, the MC-1 was used by Nihon Koku Yuso KK for its regular service connecting Fukuoka and Ulsan in Korea from June 1929

Mitsubishi MC-1 Passenger Transport J-BAKG.

until May 1930. Beginning about August 1931, the MC-1 was relegated to sight-seeing flights as a seaplane, as the first aeroplane of Nihonkai Koku Kaisha based at Kinosaki, Hyogo Prefecture, on the north coast of Honshu. It survived with this company and continued this type of work until 1938, an amazingly long time for an experimental wood structured aeroplane.

When the Mitsubishi MC-1 was being designed, the MC-2 was also being planned as a biplane passenger transport with three 215hp Armstrong Siddeley Lynx radials manufactured by Mitsubishi. There was a six-seat cabin and aft of that an open cockpit with two side-by-side seats. Predicted maximum speed was 114kt (131mph), but no other details are known.

Single-engine commercial transport cabin biplane, wheel or twin-float equipped. Wood structure with fabric covering. Rearward folding wings for stowage. Crew of two in open cockpit and cabin for four passengers.

385hp Mitsubishi-Armstrong Siddeley Jaguar fourteen-cylinder double-row air-cooled radial engine, driving a Mitsubishi-Reed fixed-pitch two-bladed metal propeller.

	Landplane	Seaplane
Span	14.75m (48ft 4¾in)	14.75m (48ft 4¾in)
Length	10.945m (35ft 11in)	11.528m (37ft 10in)
Height	3.80m (12ft 5¾in)	4.238m (13ft 11in)
Wing area	59sq m (635.091sq ft)	59sq m (635.091sq ft)
Empty weight	1,550kg (3,417lb)	1,903kg (4,195lb)
Loaded weight	2,600kg (5,732lb)	2,600kg (5,732lb)
Wing loading	44.1kg/sq m (9lb/sq ft)	44.1kg/sq m (9lb/sq ft)
Power loading	6.76kg/hp (14.9lb/hp)	6.76kg/hp (14.9lb/hp)
Maximum speed	103kt (118.5mph)	97.5kt (112.2mph)
Cruising speed	—	83kt (95.57mph)
Climb to	3,000m (9,843ft)	1,000m (3,280ft)
in	20min 36sec	4min 20sec
Endurance	6hr	4hr

One built in April 1929

Another view of J-BAKG. On the right is a Japanese-registered Junkers F 13.

Mitsubishi Type 89 General Purpose Aircraft

This is believed to have been a civil adaptation of the 1929 Type 89 Carrier Attack Aircraft, some examples of which were released for civil use when they became surplus to the Navy inventory. Little has been recorded about this aeroplane.

Single-engine biplane. Steel and aluminium construction, with fabric covering. Rearward folding wings for stowage. Aerofoil: Mitsubishi 27. Crew of three in open cockpits.

650hp Mitsubishi Type Hi twelve-cylinder vee water-cooled engine, driving a two-bladed wooden propeller.

Span 14.98m (49ft 1¼in); length 10.33m (33ft 10¾in); height 3.67m (12ft 0¾in); wing area 49sq m (527.448 sq ft).

Loaded weight 3,600kg (7,936lb); wing loading 73.6kg/sq m (15lb/sq ft); power loading 5.6kg/hp (12.3lb/ hp).

Maximum speed 120kt (138mph); cruising speed 85kt (98mph); climb to 3,000m (9,843ft) in 14min; service ceiling 4,620m (15,157ft); maximum range 1,050nm (1,208sm) in 13hr with additional fuel tank.

Mitsubishi 2MR8 Trainer

This parasol monoplane which Mitsubishi registered as a civilian trainer was actually one of the earlier prototypes of the Army Type 92 Reconnaissance Aircraft. Mitsubishi put it to good use as a company aircraft for research and training.

Single-engine parasol monoplane. Metal structure throughout with fabric covering and metal-covered forward fuselage. Pilot in open cockpit and one additional crew member.

580hp Mitsubishi AWCS-1 fourteen-cylinder double-row air-cooled radial engine, driving a Reed-type fixed-pitch two-bladed metal propeller.

Span 12.795m (41ft 11¾in); length 8.92m (29ft 3in); height 3.22m (10ft 6¾in); wing area 26sq m (279.87sq ft).

Empty weight 1,350kg (2,976lb); loaded weight 2,140kg (4,717lb); wing loading 82.3kg/sq m (16.8lb/sq ft); power loading 3.69kg/hp (8.1lb/hp).

Maximum speed 146kt (168mph) at 3,000m (9,845ft); cruising speed 109kt (125mph); landing speed 65kt (75mph); climb to 3,000m (9,845ft) in 7min 22sec; service ceiling 7,200m (23,622 ft); range 433nm (500sm); endurance 4hr.

One built.

Mitsubishi Type 90 General Purpose Aircraft

Aircraft with this civil designation were in fact Navy Type 90 Crew Trainers of 1930, with the short designation K3M, that found their way into civil operations after becoming surplus to Navy requirements. One is known to have been registered J-AFTB and used as a general purpose aircraft and as a trainer at the Pilot Training Centre of the Aviation Bureau. They are

Mitsubishi Type 90 General Purpose Aircraft J-BAEI.

known to have had two types of engines, the 300hp Tempu and the 450hp Kotobuki 2. Some of the higher-powered versions were used as glider tugs.

Single-engine light civil transport high-wing strut-braced monoplane. Welded steel tube fuselage and wooden wings with fabric covering. Pilot in open cockpit and four-seat cabin.

450hp Nakajima Kotobuki 2-kai-2 nine-cylinder air-cooled radial engine, driving a fixed-pitch two-bladed metal propeller.

Span 15.78m (51ft 9¼in); length 9.534m (31ft 3¼in); height 3.97m (13ft 0¼in); wing area 34.5sq m (371.367sq ft).

Empty weight 1,354kt (2,985lb); loaded weight 2,200kg (4,850lb); wing loading 63.8kg/sq m (13.2lb/sq ft); power loading 4.78kg/hp (10.5lb/hp).

Maximum speed 115kt (132mph); cruising speed 95kt (109mph); climb to 2,500m (8,202ft) in 15min 35sec.

Mitsubishi MS-1 Passenger Transport

The design of this transport was based on the conventional Navy 90-2 Crew Trainer high-wing monoplane. In the civil model, the engine was a 420hp Nakajima Jupiter VI, replacing the 340hp Gasuden Tempu of the military version. The MS-1 could be fitted with either conventional undercarriage or twin-floats. When declared ready for service, Tokyo Koku KK used it as an air taxi for charter work as a landplane. When needed for the shore-line route between Tokyo and Shimoda, it was equipped with floats.

Single-engine high-wing strut-braced monoplane. Optional wheel or float undercarriage. Welded steel tube fuselage with wood structured wing, fabric covered. Pilot in open cockpit and cabin for four passengers.

420hp Nakajima Jupiter VI nine-cylinder air-cooled radial engine, driving a two-bladed wooden propeller.

(Following data for Seaplane.)

Span 15.78m (51ft 9¼in); length

Mitsubishi MS-1 Passenger Transport J-BABG.

10.33m (33ft 10¾in); height 4.26m (13ft 11¾in); wing area 34.5sq m (371.367sq ft).

Empty weight 1,461kg (3,220lb); loaded weight 2,100kg (4,629lb); wing loading 60.9kg/sq m (12.4lb/sq ft); power loading 5kg/hp (11lb/hp).

Maximum speed 125kt (144mph) at 500m (1,640ft); cruising speed 103kt (119mph); climb to 1,500m (4,921ft) in 13min 33sec.

One built.

Mitsubishi MS-1 Passenger Transport J-BABG as a twin-float seaplane.

Mitsubishi Hato-type Survey Aircraft

In 1935, the Ministry of Railways had a requirement for two survey aircraft and ordered one each from Mitsubishi and Nakajima. Mitsubishi used the design of the Army Type 92 Reconnaissance Aircraft and delivered the finished product in May 1936. This, too, was a parasol monoplane. The most marked exterior difference from the Army version was the rear cockpit large fore and aft windshields which supported a canopy when desired.

Mitsubishi named the aircraft Hato-Type (Pigeon) Survey Aircraft. It was given the civil registration J-AARA and assigned to the Bureau of Railway Construction. After Nakajima delivered its survey aeroplane, which was a modified Super Universal, the Mitsubishi aircraft bore the title of Ministry or Railroads No.1 in Japanese on its fuselage. The Nakajima aircraft became Ministry of Railroads No.2. Both aircraft were used to monitor new railway construction and for geographical survey for future railway tracks. In times of emergency, they were used to survey damage caused by storms and flooding as well as railway accidents.

Single-engine strut-braced parasol monoplane. Metal structure throughout, with fabric covering and metal-covered forward fuselage. Pilot in open cockpit and one or two additional crew in enclosed cockpit.

400hp Mitsubishi A5 nine-cylinder air-cooled radial engine, driving a Reed-type fixed-pitch two-bladed metal propeller.

Span 12.70m (41ft 8in); length 8.51m (27ft 11in); height 2.975m (9ft 9in); wing area 26sq m (279.870sq ft).

Empty weight 1,130kg (2,491lb); loaded weight 1,900kg (4,188lb); wing loading 73.1kg/sq m (14.9lb/sq ft); power loading 4.75kg/hp (10.4lb/hp).

Maximum speed 119kt (137mph); cruising speed 103kt (118mph); service ceiling 6,000m (19,685ft); range 487nm (560sm), endurance 5hr; range 900km (560sm).

One built in 1936.

Mitsubishi Hato-type Survey Aircraft.

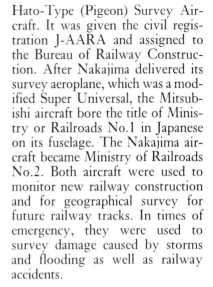

Mitsubishi Hinazuru-type Passenger Transport derived from the Airspeed Envoy.

Hinazuru-type Passenger Transport (Mitsubishi-Airspeed Envoy)

From 1929 the Fokker Super Universal was used by Nihon Koku Yuso KK as its main type of aircraft, for which Mitsubishi wished to build a replacement. In its attempt to do so, it imported two Airspeed Envoy twin-engine short-range passenger aircraft from Britain for evaluation. Japan Air Transport Co Ltd (NKYKK) was to evaluate one, while the Navy would test the other under the short designation LXM1. Mitsubishi acquired the licence production rights in June 1935. Both Envoys were assembled at Mitsubishi's Nagoya Works, and the first was flown on 20 July that year. The Envoy was acclaimed as being superior to the Super Universal in having twin-engined safety, better performance, lower operating costs and easier maintenance.

The first Envoy manufactured by Mitsubishi, which it called the Hinazuru-type (Young Crane), was powered by two Gasuden Jimpu engines. It was also equipped with flaps which the original British model did not have. Completed in about November 1936, it began a series of flight tests which lasted until 27 October, 1937, when it crashed on take off at Kagamigahara. The pilot, Iwahori, was badly injured, and engineer Sakakibara was killed. Sakakibara was the first to be killed in flight-test work for Mitsubishi, a remarkable record for the seventeen years since Mitsubishi had begun aircraft manufacture.

The cause of the crash was recorded as being due to a stall caused by the added drag of the enlarged nacelles to accommodate the Gasuden engines. Thus, production aircraft were powered by either licence-built Armstrong Siddeley Lynx, or Wolseley Aries Mk III engines as were installed in the two imported British aircraft. The flaps were also deleted.

Production aircraft were used on domestic services of Nihon Koku Yuso KK (later to become Greater Japan Airways) mainly on its routes from Tokyo to Fukuoka, and Tokyo to Sapporo. Licence-produced Envoys were used only for domestic routes in Taiwan and Japan, but their service was limited because of unreliability of the Japanese-built British engines, production of which terminated after a short time.

Twin-engined low-wing monoplane transport with retractable undercarriage. Wood construction throughout with fabric and plywood covering. Crew of two, with six passengers.

Two 215-240hp Armstrong Siddeley Lynx IV C seven-cylinder air-cooled engines, or two 205-225hp Wolseley Aries Mk III nine-cylinder air-cooled radial engines, driving two-bladed wooden propellers.

Span 15.903m (52ft 2in); length 10.516m (34ft 6in); height 3.165m (10ft 4¾in); wing area 31.50sq m (339.074sq ft).

Empty weight 1,776kg (3,915lb); loaded weight 2,664kg (5,873lb); wing loading 84.6kg/sq m (17.3lb/sq ft); power loading 6.58kg/hp (14.5lb/hp).

Maximum speed 152kt (175mph) at sea level; cruising speed 133kt (153 mph); landing speed 56kt (64mph); rate of climb 1,063ft/min; service ceiling 5,020m (16,470ft); range 558nm (642sm); endurance 5hr.

Eleven built from 1936 to 1938.

Ohtori-type Long-range Communications Aircraft

In 1936, the *Asahi Shimbun* placed an order with Mitsubishi for a long-range communications aircraft. Mitsubishi assigned Jiro Tanaka as chief designer for converting a twin-engined Ki-2-II Army light bomber to meet this order. Modifications called for the removal of all armament and other military equipment and the canopy was extended to enclose the rear cockpit as well, a co-pilot's position with dual controls being installed behind the first pilot. Fuel capacity was increased by having a tank of approximately 1,500 litres installed in the fuselage. The absence of protruding armament gave the aeroplane a more modern appearance with refined lines.

This conversion made from a Ki-2-II became an excellent long-range communications aircraft, giving it a range of 1,620 nautical miles with an endurance of 13hr. Known in this form as the Ohtori (Phoenix)-type, it was claimed to be the most advanced twin-engined liaison aircraft used by any newspaper.

(There were other similar conversions. For instance, there was a modified Army Type 93-2 Twin-engine Light Bomber, which was an earlier version of the Ki-2-II that had a non-retractable undercarriage. This conversion consisted only of removing the armament to gain civil registry and for this purpose the Aviation Bureau assigned the designation 93SKB).

The *Asahi Shimbun* named its Ohtori-type aeroplane *Nanshin-go* (*March to the Pacific*). It was used on a number of long distance flights, attracting publicity for the newspaper itself. Among these was a flight in September 1936 from Haneda to Hsinking, Manchuria (now Changchun, China) a distance of 2,000km (1,242sm) in 9hr 10min, having as its three-man crew, Nagatomo, Nagata and Kawachi. On a good will flight, the Ohtori-type left Tachikawa in December that year for Bangkok, a distance of 4,930km (3,063sm), which it covered in 21hr 30min actual flying time with one stop. Japanese readers also followed with interest the flight of the Ohtori-type in February 1939, when it flew round the perimeter of Japanese-occupied territory in China, covering 9,300km (5,778sm).

Twin-engined low-wing monoplane with retractable undercarriage and twin fins and rudders. Construction was Junkers all-metal structure with corrugated stressed skin. Two pilots and radio operator and two additional seats in enclosed cockpits.

Two 550-690hp Nakajima Kotobuki 3 engines, driving Sumitomo Standard fixed-pitch two-bladed propellers.

Span 19.95m (65ft 5½in); length 12.41m (40ft 8½in); height 4.60m (15ft 1in); wing area 56.2sq m (604.951 sq ft).

Empty weight 2,800kg (6,173lb); loaded weight 4,512kg (9,947lb); maximum weight 5,200kg (11,464lb); maximum wing loading 92.5kg/sq m (18.9 lb/sq ft); power loading 5.5kg/hp (12.1lb/hp).

Maximum speed 155kt (178mph) at 2,500m (8,202ft); cruising speed 130kt (150mph); climb to 2,000m (6,562ft) in 5min 17sec; service ceiling 4,500m (14,763ft).

One built in 1936.

Although military production took priority over civil aircraft, Mitsubishi continued to create some remarkable civil-registered designs.

Mitsubishi Ohtori-type Long-range Communication Aircraft used by Asahi Shimbun.

At this late period just before the Pacific War, all follow-on civilian aircraft were limited in quantity and all were adaptations of military types. Although these aircraft are covered in greater detail in publications dealing with Japanese military aircraft of the Pacific War, mention here of these types is warranted because of their significance.

World attention was drawn to the flight of the *Kamikaze* (*Divine Wind*) in April 1937, when this Mitsubishi aircraft generally known as a Karigane I (Wild Goose I) made a goodwill flight to London on the occasion of the Coronation of HM King George VI. This aeroplane was actually the second prototype of the Army Ki-15 for which the *Asahi Shimbun* obtained permission from the Army to purchase from Mitsubishi. The flight proved an excellent testing ground for the aeroplane. The distance of 9,542 miles was covered in an actual flying time of 51hr 19min 23sec, establishing a new international record officially recognized by the FAI. The *Kamikaze*, J-BAAI, also visited Brussels, Berlin, Paris, and Rome, before returning to Tokyo Airport on 21 May, 1937.

A small number of additional aircraft of this type also served in the civil role. Among them were J-BAAM known as the *Sachikaze* (*Providential Wind*) and J-BAAL, the *Asakaze* (*Morning Breeze*). Because of the wide publicity they were easily identified, and they were given the Allied code-name Babs

when reconnaissance aircraft of this type were encountered in the Pacific War.

Another civil aircraft by Mitsubishi, known as *Nippon*, gained prominence when it succeeded in a round-the-world goodwill flight for the first time in Japan's civil aviation history. This took place between 28 August and 20 October, 1939, when a converted twin-engined Type 96 Attack Aircraft (G3M2) was operated as a civil aircraft, J-BACI, under joint sponsorship of the *Tokyo Nichinichi* and the *Osaka Mainichi Shimbun*. In fifty-six days, *Nippon* visited 20 countries on five continents in 194hr actual flying time. The accomplishment and advanced technology of this Japanese aeroplane received wide press attention, but its capability as a bomber was overlooked. Aeroplanes of this type also served as transports for Dai Nihon Koku KK (Greater Japan Airways Co Ltd). Both the transport version and the Navy bombers of this design served prominently in the Pacific War as the G3M, Allied code-name Nell.

The Mitsubishi MC-20 twin-engined transport was first manufactured in 1940 as a medium-range commercial transport although it was an Army sponsord design and developed for their use as the Type 100 (Ki-57) Transport. In commercial service they were used by the Greater Japan Airways. Another version of the MC-series was the MC-21 cargo aircraft also used by by Greater Japan Airways. They were converted from the Army Type 97 Heavy Bomber, better known as the Ki-21 Sally.

These civil aircraft were limited in number compared to the military aircraft types produced by Mitsubishi. However, they were regarded as aircraft of high quality, confirmed by the many records they set. As with other Japanese aircraft manufacturers, production, by necessity, was devoted almost exclusively to combat aircraft.

Nakajima Aeroplane Company Ltd (Nakajima Hikoki KK)

The name Nakajima ranks equally with Mitsubishi in being among the best known and largest aviation companies in Japan up to the end of the Second World War. Originally founded on 6 December, 1917, it also became the oldest aircraft company as well. Known initially as the Hikoki Kenkyusho, or Aeroplane Research Institute, it was established on 20 December of that year on the east side of the Daikoin Temple, better known as the Donryu-sama, in northwest Ohtacho, Gumma Prefecture, about 50 miles north of Tokyo on the wide expanse of the fertile Kanto Plains. The company was also unique in that it was formed as a private venture without predetermined military contracts for aircraft. Its initial designs were original and relied very little on foreign influence. This changed, however, as a matter of necessity when the military market demanded certain types of aircraft.

The founder of the new company was Chikuhei Nakajima, a former Imperial Japanese Navy Lieut (Reserve, Engineering), who was involved with Japanese Naval aviation from the start, including designing and building aeroplanes with the Provisional Military Balloon Research Association that had been established in 1909.

From July 1912, while still in the Navy, Chikuhei Nakajima spent six months in the United States as a naval observer of aviation activities. He studied manufacturing techniques and aircraft maintenance at the Curtiss school and, although not on assignment, he learned to fly at the Curtiss Exhibition Company flying school at Hammondsport, New York. After he returned to Japan, he left the Navy on 1 December, 1917, and concentrated on forming his own aircraft company.*

Other principals within the company were Sadajiro Okui, Jingo Kurihara, Ichiro Sakuma, all of whom had experience of aircraft manufacture while in the Navy. Also included, but joining later, were Genzo Sasaki and Teruji Ishikawa. The company's single building originally covered 80 tsubo, equivalent to a room measuring 15ft by 19ft, hardly ample for the ten-man staff. This was the beginning of what was first referred to as the Donryu Factory of what became the Nakajima Aeroplane Company. When the time came to begin actual fabrication of aeroplane parts in January 1918, they occupied an additional building of 100 tsubo floor space, or approximately 15ft by 22ft.

A name change became necessary in April 1918 when the Koku Kenkyusho, or Aeronautical Research Institute, was established as part of the very well-known Tokyo Imperial University. To avoid confusion between the two similar names, the company's founder, Nakajima, changed the name to Nakajima Hikoki Seisakusho, or Nakajima Aeroplane Manufacturing Works, on 1 April, 1918. The start-up capital diminished rapidly and Nakajima needed financial assistance. The following month, he obtained backing from Seibei Kawanishi of Kobe, the owner of the Nihon Woollen Co Ltd, who joined with Nakajima in a partnership arrangement. This co-ownership prompted the renaming of the

*Nakajima was challenged by his superiors about learning to fly in the United States without authorization. Being a shrewd debater, tactful in sidestepping issues, he convinced them that aircraft design engineers should have a knowledge of flying in order to improve their technology. The review board agreed that his logic was reasonable and therefore cleared his record of any wrongdoing. However, after six months he asked to resign and this was approved and he reverted to reserve status on 1 December, 1917, with a hearing impairment noted. He became an activist, proclaiming that 3,000 torpedo-carrying aeroplanes could be built at the cost of one battleship and be far more effective. Because of military budget handling bureaucracy, Japan's aircraft development could not keep pace with America and European countries; therefore, he advocated that aircraft development should be placed with civilian companies.

company to Goushikaisha Nihon Hikoki Seisakusho, meaning Japan Aeroplane Works Co Ltd.

The success of the new business was largely assured because of Nakajima's personal association with Major General Ikutaro Inoue, a member of the PMBRA at that time and later the Chief of the Army Air Headquarters. Through this association, Inoue released two Hall-Scott engines to Nakajima, provided trained test pilots and to some extent assured the purchase of successful aeroplanes. This connection undoubtedly played a major role in Nakajima's rise to become Japan's dominant aircraft producer. Nakajima's business future was further strengthened in April 1918 when General Inoue arranged for Mitsui Bassan KK (Mitsui & Co), the most powerful trading company in Japan, to be appointed as the company's sole agent.

A year later, in April 1919, after trials and problems with aircraft of its own design, the company received an order from the Army to produce twenty Nakajima Type 5 two-seat trainer biplanes. In October of the same year, two Nakajima aircraft achieved publicity by winning the first and second places in the Tokyo–Osaka Airmail Flying Contest. This early success brought Nakajima additional orders for the Type 5 aircraft.

The first of the initial order for the Type 5 was delivered to the Army in December 1919. Confident of continuing orders, Chikuhei Nakajima placed an order with Mitsui for 100 Hall-Scott engines. Astonished at such a large order, Mitsui questioned Gen Inoue about Army commitments for aircraft purchases and learned that they were verbal only. His partner Kawanishi learned of the incident and found that Nakajima had used his han (seal) in connection with this purchase without his knowledge. The entire matter infuriated Kawanishi, since such a large financial commitment could, if the order for aircraft failed to materialize, cause the collapse of the aircraft company and his own Nihon Woollen Co. Kawanishi therefore severed his relationship with Nakajima in 1920 and he eventually founded the independent Kawanishi Aircraft Company (Kawanishi Kokuki KK) in Kobe. Nakajima readopted the earlier name Nakajima Hikoki Seisakusho (Nakajima Aeroplane Manufacturing Works) in December 1919.

Beginning in April 1920 Nakajima received an order from the Navy to manufacture the Navy Yokosho Ro-go Ko-gata Reconnaissance Seaplane which was a design created by the Navy. Contrary to other major Japanese aircraft manufacturers Nakajima from the beginning avoided hiring foreign engineers and designers and instead built existing designs or purchased foreign design rights.

With a background of success in manufacture of airframes, Nakajima decided in 1924 to begin the manufacture of aero-engines. There was no government financial support for this venture but the Japanese Government had encouraged it and had given Nakajima to understand that it would support the factory with government orders if the engines proved satisfactory. Accordingly, the rights to the French water-cooled Lorraine engine were purchased and four technical engineers from Lorraine were contracted to assist in the establishment of an engine-assembly plant.

This engine plant was completed in March 1925 in Ogikubo, a western suburb of Tokyo, and was largely equipped with American machine tools. Manufacture of 450hp Lorraine 450 Engines began in 1926. In the following year, the British air-cooled Bristol Jupiter was imported, from which developed the Model VI engines that were produced for the first time in 1928. On 15 December, 1931, the company became the Nakajima Hikoki KK with the retirement of Chikuhei Nakajima, and his younger brother, Kiyoichi Nakajima, was appointed president.*

The success of the Nakajima company was based upon the acceptance of its aircraft and engines. The first of these was a civil venture, and therefore the civil aircraft of Nakajima are described first even

*Chikuhei Nakajima became involved in politics, and by the end of the Pacific War he was the Minister of Munitions.

though it was early military sales that firmly established the company's success.

Nakajima Type 1 Biplane

A sign of Chikuhei Nakajima's independence in manufacture and design of aircraft was his intention that the company's first aeroplane design be directed toward sale to the Army. This aeroplane was designated Nakajima Type 1 Landplane. Design and draughting were mostly accomplished by Sakuma and Okui under Nakajima's close supervision. Tooling responsibility for aeroplane fittings was that of Kurihara. When fabrication was begun an additional fifteen to sixteen new craftsmen were hired for the project.

The Army showed early interest in the aeroplane by releasing to Nakajima two of its US-built 125hp Hall-Scott engines. When this first aircraft was completed in July 1918, it was described as the Nakajima Type 1-1, meaning Type 1, No.1. In configuration, it had a strong resemblance to the first Boeing aeroplane, the B & W of 1916. The Type 1-1 was flown for the first time by Yozo Sato from the Tone river-bed near Ohta which eventually became the Ojima Airfield. However, on that first flight, poor control caused it to crash immediately after take off. Sato survived, but the airframe was badly damaged.

Nakajima Type 1 Biplane.

In the meantime, design work had begun on the Nakajima Type 2. This was to be a seaplane intended to interest the Japanese Navy. Materials were on hand for the first Type 2 but the aeroplane was never completed because they were diverted to repairing the damaged Type 1-1. After repair taking about twenty days, the aeroplane emerged as the Type 1-2. The second flight was made, again from Ojima Airfield, on 25 August, 1918, this time piloted by Army Cavalry Capt Naranosuke Oka, and three flights, each of several minutes, were made that day. Upon landing the third time, however, a wingtip touched the bank of the river-bed and the aeroplane was damaged once again.

This time, repairs took about a week. In making the repairs some changes were made in the design, as recommended by Capt Oka. This also called for a change in designation to Type 1-3. To avoid repeating the mishap because of the narrow take-off strip at Ojima, further flights were transferred to the Army's test base at Kagamigahara Airfield, north of Nagoya, a considerable distance away. On 13 September the aeroplane flew again, piloted by Capt Oka. After approximately 17 minutes in the air, the Nakajima Type 1-3 made a safe landing. However, while taxi-ing to the starting point, one of the wheels skidded into a ditch near the corner of the flying field, and yet again the airframe was damaged. The aeroplane was returned to the factory.

Again repairs, including more modifications suggested by Capt

Oka, were made, making it necessary to change the designation to Type 1-4. For the next test flights, the long trip back to Kagamigahara was avoided by using the nearby Ojima Airfield. Becoming airborne on 9 November, once again at the hands of Nakajima's pilot Yozo Sato, structural failure occurred and the aeroplane crashed into the rushing waters of the river, destroying the aeroplane and severely injuring Sato.

It was later learned that centre of gravity problems plagued the aircraft from the very beginning, it being tail-heavy. Coupled with this, tractor-type aircraft were thought to be extremely difficult to control, since at that time most of the Army and Naval aircraft were pusher types. In truth, the failings of the Type 1 were due to inexperience on the part of those who designed it. Although built to serve Army needs, it was never delivered because of its total destruction. Thus came the unhappy ending to the first Nakajima aircraft.

Single-engine unequal-span biplane. Wooden structure with fabric covering. Crew of two in open cockpits.

125-130hp Hall-Scott A-5 six-cylinder water-cooled inline engine, driving a two-bladed wooden propeller.

Span 14m (45ft 11½in); length 8m (26ft 3in); height 3m (9ft 10in); wing area 40sq m (430.57sq ft).

Empty weight 800kg (1,763lb); loaded weight 1,200kg (2,645lb); wing loading 30kg/sq m (6.1lb/sq ft); power loading 9.6kg/hp (21.1lb/hp).

Maximum speed 65kt (75mph) at sea level; landing speed 32.5kt (37.5mph); service ceiling 3,000m (9,843ft); endurance 4hr.

One built in July 1918.

Nakajima Type 3 Biplane

With the failure of the Type 1, design of the Type 3 was approached in a more practical way to gain experience in aircraft design, using the proven design of the wings and tail of the Yokosho Ro-go Ko-gata Reconnaissance Seaplane with which Lieut Nakajima had been closely involved just before leaving the

Nakajima Type 3 Biplane.

Navy. As a tractor-type it was a successful aeroplane and was used extensively as a proficiency trainer. The fuselage of the Type 3 was the same as that of the Type 1-4 with only minor changes.

The new aeroplane, powered by the second of the two 125hp Hall-Scott engines released by the Army, was completed in December 1918. This time, careful attention was given to calculation and adjustment of the centre of gravity. It had a very light wing loading, and in calm air was quite stable. In the hands of Katota Mizuta, a pilot hired by Nakajima to test fly the Type 3, this became Nakajima's first successful aeroplane.

Mizuta was formerly an Army Lt and a pilot instructor at Tokorozawa. He established the Mizuta Flying School, which was sponsored by Nakajima, and then used this Type 3 aeroplane as the school's trainer. It was also used in a number of celebrations by giving flying demonstrations. As part of the celebration of the 50th Anniversary of Metropolitan Tokyo, demonstrations were made from Susaki Airfield in Tokyo by Yozo Sato, who by now had recovered from his injuries in the crash of the Type 1-4. In March 1921 a rope ladder was attached to the aeroplane for aerial demonstrations at the 50th

Anniversary of Kobe Port when it was flown by Mizuta with student pilot Toshio Hino in the rear seat. The next month, over Takasaki City in Gumma Prefecture flying demonstrations were given by Gyozo Imaizumi, further proving the qualities of this successful aeroplane which led the way to later successful Nakajima aeroplanes.

However, its demise came when, making a landing on the Notsuke Army Parade Grounds in Takasaki City, a man ran from the crowd in front of the aeroplane. In avoiding him a wheel and strut were broken causing the aeroplane to nose-over with resultant extensive damage to the port wing.

Single-engine unequal-span biplane. Wooden structure with fabric covering. Crew of two in open cockpits.

125-130hp Hall-Scott A-5 six-cylinder water-cooled inline engine, driving a two-bladed wooden propeller.

Span 15.50m (50ft 10¼in); length 8m (26ft 3in); height 3.30m (10ft 10in); wing area 59.5sq m (640.473sq ft).

Empty weight 800kg (1,763lb); loaded weight 1,100kg (2,425lb); wing loading 18.4kg/sq m (3.7lb/sq ft);

This view of the Nakajima Type 3 Biplane shows the wide span and deep gap.

power loading 8.8kg/hp (19.4lb/hp).

Maximum speed 54kt (62mph) at sea level; minimum speed 27kt (31mph); service ceiling 3,000m (9,843ft); endurance 3hr.

One built in December 1918.

Nakajima Type 4 Biplane

The design of the Type 4 biplane was made very cautiously, relying heavily on the experience gained with the Type 3. The company's intention was to gain Army acceptance of the aeroplane and to eliminate the reputation for failure that lingered after the Type 1 mishap.

For this new and better streamlined aeroplane, the fuselage had minor modifications from that of the Type 3, and the area of the wings and horizontal tail surfaces was reduced. In planform, the shape of the new wing was reminiscent of the German Albatros reconnaissance aeroplanes. Jiro Sakuma was the chief designer under the close supervision of managing director Chikuhei Nakajima. Design calculations and experiment and test phases of the project were checked by Eiji Sekiguchi and Tatsuo Miyazaki respectively. Jingo Kurihara oversaw the general management of manufacture and final assembly. Like the earlier aeroplanes, this too used a Hall-Scott A-5 engine, but this was later replaced by a Hall-Scott A-5a rated at 150hp.

The new aeroplane was completed in February 1919 and Army evaluation gave genuine approval of its excellent performance and inflight stability. The Army agreed immediately to order a large number. Following the issuance of its letter of intent, the Army requirement was changed to twenty prototypes and production models with minor changes to that of the Type 4. The aeroplanes built to this order became the Nakajima Type 5, the first civilian-built military standard aeroplane made in Japan. Following the Army's evaluation of the Type 4 it was used by Nakajima for test purposes.

Fame for the Type 4 had not ended. Participating in the First

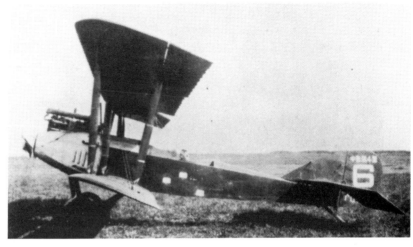

Nakajima Type 4 Biplane.

Tokyo–Osaka Airmail Flying Contest in October 1919, sponsored by the Imperial Flying Association, the Type 4, flown by Yozo Sato, took first prize after making the round-trip flight in 6hr 58min (to Osaka in 3hr 40min, to Tokyo in 3hr 18min). Second prize was won by an American-built Graham biplane flown by Toyotaro Yamagata, requiring 8hr 28min to make the trip. This decided advantage by the Japanese-built aeroplane firmly established Nakajima in the aviation market.

Single-engine two-bay biplane. Wooden structure with fabric covering. Crew of two in open cockpits.

150-165hp Hall-Scott A-5a six-cylinder water-cooled inline engine, driving a two-bladed wooden propeller.

Span 13m (42ft 8in); length 7.50m (24ft 7¼in); height 2.90m (9ft 6in); wing area 35sq m (376.749sq ft).

Empty weight 700kg (1,543lb); loaded weight 1,200kg (2,645lb); wing loading 34.3kg/sq m (7lb/sq ft); power loading 8kg/hp (17.6lb/hp).

Maximum speed 70kt (80.6mph) at sea level; minimum speed 32.5kt (37.5mph); service ceiling 3,500m (11,482ft); endurance 5hr.

One built in February 1919.

Nakajima Type 5 Biplane

The success of the Type 5 was almost assured because of the successful demonstrations made its the forerunner, the Type 4, and the new aeroplane went into immediate production. Approximately one hun-

dred were manufactured for the Army, one for the Government House in Taiwan, and a small number was built to fill civilian orders. After a time, several of the aeroplanes manufactured for the Army were released because of design shortcomings, but with modifications they served well in a civil capacity. Total production was 118.

In original production aeroplanes and those modified into civil aircraft, there were numerous differences that were made at the request of the purchasers. Paint schemes and markings also varied widely. The most widely-known user of the Type 5 was the Mizuta Flying School.

In one aviation event after another the Type 5 performed remarkably well. In May 1921 student pilot Toshio Hino displayed remarkable aerobatic proficiency in a Type 5, taking second prize in the Second Prize-winning Flight Competition held at Susaki Airfield in Tokyo, giving the Type 5 an even greater reputation. At the Second Airmail Flying Contest, this time between Osaka and Kurume, Kyushu, in November 1920, Mizuta entered with a Type 5 powered by a 220hp Sturdevant engine, but dropped out of the race because of radiator problems. He entered the third of these competitions with a Type 5; this time the route was between Tokyo and Morioka, in northern Honshu, but without awards. When the course was once again between Tokyo and Osaka, five of the fourteen entries were the 150hp Hall-Scott Nakajima Type

Nakajima Type 5 Biplane.

5s and there was one that had a 160hp Daimler engine.

The Type 5s remained very popular in these events. In the Tozai Teiki Kokukai (East-West Regular Air Transport Association) event sponsored by the *Asahi Shimbun* in January 1923, six of the eight entries were Type 5s. At the Fourth Flight Competition in June 1923, Army-released Type 5s were the majority of the entries. In December 1924 at the Ise Bay Flight Competition, four Type 5s participated and achieved high scores.

Single-engine two-bay biplane. Wooden construction with fabric covering. Crew of two in open cockpits.

150-165hp Hall-Scott A-5a six-cylinder water-cooled inline engine, driving a two-bladed wooden propeller.

Span 12.606m (41ft 4¼in); length 7.046m (23ft 1½in); height 2.882m (9ft 5½in); wing area 34sq m (365.984sq ft).

Empty weight 780kg (1,719lb); loaded weight 1,130kg (2,491lb); wing loading 33.2kg/sq m (7lb/sq ft); power loading 7.53kg/hp (16.6lb/hp).

Maximum speed 70kt (80.6mph) at sea level; minimum speed 32.5kt (37.5mph); service ceiling 3,400m (11,155ft); endurance 4hr.

118 built including civil production of seventeen from April 1919 to May 1921.

Nakajima Type 6 Biplane

As was to be expected the Type 6 Biplane was a version of the Type 5 with improved performance. It was built in August 1919 during the production run of the first twenty Type 5s for the Army. The major difference in the Type 6 was that the airframe was designed to take the heavier and more powerful 200hp Liberty Hall-Scott L-6 engine. The L-6 was a faster-running engine, and required a smaller diameter fighter-type propeller. It could be compared with first-line military aircraft of other major countries at that time.

The Type 6 was in existence by the time Nakajima entered the first Tokyo to Osaka Prize-Winning Flight Competition on 22 and 23 October, 1919. The Type 4 piloted by Yozo Sato was the winner. The Type 6 piloted by Katota Mizuta had been expected to win because of its greater power but Mizuta became disoriented on his way from Tokyo to Osaka and made an emergency landing near the Kinokawa River in Wakayama City, south of his destination, and was disqualified. On his return from Osaka to Tokyo, Mizuta took off from the Joto Military Parade Grounds in Osaka, with engineer Kurihara in the rear seat, and flew to Susaki Airfield in Tokyo in 2hr 10min, taking advantage of a strong tailwind. This established a new speed record between the two cities.

Single-engine biplane. Wooden structure with fabric covering. Crew of two in open cockpits.

200-244hp Liberty Hall-Scott L-6 six-cylinder water-cooled inline engine, driving a two-bladed wooden propeller.

Span 12m (39ft 4½in); length 7m (22ft 11½in); height 2.80m (9ft 2¼in); wing area 32sq m (344.456sq ft).

Empty weight 850kg (1,873lb); loaded weight 1,300kg (2,866lb); wing loading 40.6kg/sq m (8.3lb/sq ft); power loading 6.5kg/hp (14.3lb/hp).

Maximum speed 76kt (87.5mph) at sea level; minimum speed 35kt (40mph); service ceiling 3,500m (11,482ft); endurance 5hr.

One built in August 1919.

Nakajima Type 7 Biplane

The Nakajima Type 7 was the result of an order placed by the Imperial Flying Association, using funds that were donated in 1919 by Japanese living in the United States, and known as *Zaibei Doho Go* (Japanese in USA). Incorporating features of the Type 5 and Type 6, the new aeroplane was basically a modified version of the Type 6, but powered by the new 210hp Sturdevant 5A V-8 engine, which had a circular nose radiator.

The Type 7 was completed in February 1920 and test flown by Yozo Sato who proclaimed that the

Nakajima Type 6 Biplane.

new aeroplane had good flying characteristics, but that the engine had a tendency to over-heat in prolonged flight. Succeeding test pilot Kintaro Iinuma even experienced a faceful of hot water as a result of the over-heating problem.

The fuel tank was enlarged in order to increase the endurance of the Type 7 to ten hours in preparation for the coming round-trip competition between Tokyo and Osaka. The aeroplane was painted entirely dark green and bore the insignia of the Imperial Flying Association on the side of the fuselage and the inscription of *Zaibei Doho Go* in Japanese across the rudder.

For the competition that took place on 21 April, 1920, the aeroplane was flown by Kintaro Iinuma. This was a very challenging race of 730km round-trip, from the starting point of Susaki Airfield in Tokyo, round the turning point over Joto Military Parade Grounds in Osaka, and returning to Susaki. There was only one other competitor against the Type 7, an Itoh Emi aeroplane flown by Toyotaro Yamagata. En route to Osaka, Iinuma made a navigational error and crashed into Mt Tanzawa approximately 30 minutes after taking off from Susaki. He was badly injured. Yamagata made the circuit successfully in the Emi 14 in 6hr 43min (3hr 48min to Osaka, and 2hr 55min to Tokyo).

The wreckage of the one and only Type 7 was donated to a nearby primary school, and the slightly damaged engine was bought by Tamotsu Aiba, the superintendent of the Nippon Hiko Gakko (Nippon Flying School) for instructional use. This was the last civil aircraft for some time to be designed by Naka-

Nakajima Type 7 Biplane.

jima because military contracts absorbed its production capacity.

Single-engine two-bay biplane. Wooden construction with fabric covering. Crew of two in open cockpits, changed to one when extra fuel tank was added. 210-240hp Sturdevant 5A eight-cylinder vee water-cooled engine, driving a two-bladed wooden propeller.

Span 12.60m (41ft 4in); length 7.05m (23ft 1½in); height 2.90m (9ft 6in); wing area 34sq m (365.984sq ft).

Empty weight 850kg (1,873lb); loaded weight 1,300kg (2,866lb); wing loading 38.2kg/sq m (7.8lb/sq ft); power loading 6.2kg/hp (13.6lb/hp).

Maximum speed 81kt (93.2mph) at sea level; minimum speed 35kt (40.3 mph); service ceiling 3,500m (11,482ft); endurance 10hr.

One built in February 1920.

Nakajima B-6 Biplane

Directing its efforts toward the new technology of all-metal aeroplane structures in 1921, Nakajima completed an experimental B-6 Biplane in April 1922, using Sumitomo Metal Industry Co Ltd's experimental duralumin; Sumitomo Kei Gin (Kei Gin meaning 'light silver'). Although the new aeroplane was built from materials procured in Japan, the design was that of the

Nakajima B-6 Biplane.

Breguet 14B.2 light bomber for which Nakajima purchased the manufacturing-licence from France. The engine was an imported 360hp Rolls-Royce Eagle, making this Nakajima's first aeroplane with more than 300hp.

To assist construction Nakajima used the actual Breguet 14B.2 that the French Aviation Mission had taken with them for instructional purposes when invited by the Japanese Army in 1919. It differed in that it was powered by a 400hp Liberty engine and was equipped as a light bomber. This Breguet was used by the Army's Mikatagahara Bombing Team for bombing research.

Nakajima called its B-6 biplane the *Keigin-go*, (Light Silver Model) and, because it was never delivered to the Army, the company used it for a long time as a test aircraft. This was the first duralumin framework aeroplane built in Japan, and it was displayed at the Peace Memorial Exhibition at Uneo Park in Tokyo soon after its completion.

In November 1922, Kan-ichiro Kato, Nakajima's test pilot, participated in the Fifth Tokyo–Osaka Airmail Round-robin Flight Competition as an extra entry and set a new record of 4hr 49min for the round-trip. At the Ise Bay Trophy-winning Flight in December 1924, Kato flew a modified Nakajima B-6 and won Second Prize among fourteen other landplanes. The winner of this competition was Tatsugoro Endo who flew a modified version of a Salmson 2-A.2 Reconnaissance Aircraft. The B-6 was intended to be an Army light bomber, but the Army failed to develop a firm policy on metal-framed aircraft, so this remained in the hands of Nakajima and was the only aircraft of the type.

Single-engine two-bay biplane. All-metal framework with fabric covering. Crew of two in open cockpits.

360hp Rolls-Royce Eagle VIII twelve-cylinder vee water-cooled engine, driving a two-bladed wooden propeller.

Span, upper 14.76m (48ft 5in); lower 13.12m (43ft 0½in); length 8.985m (29ft 5¾in); height 3m (9ft 10¼in); wing area 51sq m (548.977sq ft).

Empty weight 1,171kg (2,581lb); loaded weight 1,950kg (4,299lb); wing loading 38.2kg/sq m (7.8lb/sq ft); power loading 5.42kg/hp (11.9lb/hp).

Maximum speed 103kt (118.5mph); cruising speed 92kt (106mph); climb to 5,000m (16,404ft) in 46min; endurance 4hr.

One built in March 1922.

Nakajima N-36 Transport

In the late 1920s Japan's Department of Communications sponsored a competition for 'Made in Japan' transport aircraft. Nakajima was one of the contenders and, like the others that qualified to compete, was given a grant-in-aid to design and manufacture such an aeroplane. This project came under the design supervision of Kimihei Nakajima who had just returned to Japan in April 1927 from his stay in France in connection with importation of technologies and procurement of materials.

For the Nakajima entry, the Breguet 26 and 28 transports were favoured for their design concepts. These aircraft were highly regarded

Nakajima N-36 Transport.

single-engined passenger transports in France at that time. Nakajima's earlier experience with the Breguet B-6 and Breguet 19 was also helpful. To power the new aeroplane, the licence-built Bristol Jupiter was selected, an engine that was widely used in Europe because of its reliability.

The two examples of these aeroplanes, J-BAKB and J-BAYO, were completed in May 1928 and April 1929 and Kan-ichiro Kato took the aeroplane on its first flight on 3 May, 1928, a flight which gave high expectations for the success of the new transport. On the next day a flight was made with seven mechanics to test full-cabin occupancy and to reward them for their efforts in building the aeroplane. Without warning when about 100m in the air after take off, the aeroplane suddenly nosed over and plummeted to the ground, killing everyone on board. The cause of the accident was never fully determined.

Various modifications were made to the second aeroplane, and it was used as the experimental aeroplane of Nihon Koku Yuso KK at Tachikawa and Haneda Airfield, mainly as a cargo transport and crew trainer. In this service it showed that it out-performed the other contenders, the Aichi AB-1 and the Mitsubishi MC-1, as well as a Junkers F 13 in both climb and payload, according to evaluations made by the Aviation Bureau. The Aichi entry was declared the winner, but all were deemed unsatisfactory by the Bureau because biplane designs were considered obsolete by European standards.

Single-engine biplane of unequal span. Metal construction with fabric

covering. Crew of two and cabin for six passengers.

450-520hp Nakajima Jupiter VI nine-cylinder air-cooled radial engine, driving a two-bladed wooden propeller.

Span, upper 17.42m (57ft 2in), lower 11.736m (38ft 6in); length 11.73m (38ft 5¾in); height 3.909m (12ft 10in); wing area 53sq m (570.505 sq ft).

Empty weight 1,350kg (2,976lb); loaded weight 2,800kg (6,172lb); wing loading 52.8kg/sq m (10.8lb/sq ft); power loading 5.28kg/hp (11.6lb/hp).

Maximum speed 109kt (125.4mph) at sea level; cruising speed 86kt (99mph); climb to 3,000m (9,843ft) in 17min 10sec; service ceiling 5,000m (16,404ft).

Two built in 1928-29.

Nakajima Fishery Seaplane

In April 1930, Nakajima received an order from the Teikoku Kaibo Gikai (Imperial Maritime Defence Volunteer Association) for two seaplanes for use in spotting fish from the air. At the request of the Kaibo Gikai, these were adaptations of the two-seat Navy Type 15 Reconnaissance Seaplane. Normally, the Type 15 carried a pilot and observer, but for the fishery version, a third seat was added so that it could carry a radio operator as well as a fishery observer. Because of this, the aeroplanes were normally referred to as the Nakajima 3-seater Seaplane.

The seaplanes were completed in July 1930 and named *Giyu-8* and *Giyu-9* respectively. They were assigned to Shizuoka Prefecture on a loan basis during peacetime for observing the shoals of fish; however, during wartime, they were to be returned to the Navy when requested. The two aeroplanes worked from the beach at Miho-no-Matsubara, and operated over Suruga Bay which it faced, to Hachijo Island, 180 miles south of Tokyo, reporting fish locations along the shoals of the Izu Islands by radio or dropping messages in tube containers to fishing boats in the areas.

The aeroplanes earned a good

reputation for the work that they did in vastly improving the fishing industry. In November 1930, when a heavy earthquake occurred in the Izu area, these aeroplanes made aerial surveys of the affected area. During this work *Giyu-8* was lost in a crash caused by engine trouble. To replace the loss, the Navy had one of its Type 15 Reconnaissance Seaplanes converted in June 1933 to the same specification as the previous two. Like the one it replaced, it, too, was given the name *Giyu-8*.

The two aeroplanes continued in the fish-spotting role until 1937, but during that time they were also used for commercial advertising and aerial survey work. They ended their service as the best of Japan's civil seaplanes.

Single-engine twin-float sesquiplane. Wooden structure with fabric covering. Rearward folding wings for stowage. Crew of three in open cockpits.

300-330hp Mitsubishi-Hispano-Suiza eight-cylinder vee water-cooled engine, driving a two-bladed wooden propeller. Span, upper 13.558m (44ft 5½in), lower 9.50m (31ft 2in); length 9.59m (31ft 5½in); height 3.58m (11ft 9in); wing area 44sq m (473.627sq ft).

Empty weight 1,465kg (3,230lb); loaded weight 2,013kg (4,437lb); wing loading 45.75kg/sq m (9.36lb/sq ft); power loading 7.1kg/hp (15.6lb/hp).

Maximum speed 90kt (103.6mph); cruising speed 70kt (80.6mph); climb to 2,000m (6,562ft) in 27min 20sec; service ceiling 3,500m (11,482ft).

Two built in July 1930 and one conversion in June 1933.

Nakajima Fishery Seaplane.

Nakajima-Fokker Super Universal Transport.

Nakajima-Fokker Super Universal Transport

Nihon Koku Yuso KK (Japan Air Transport Co Ltd) was established on 20 October, 1928, and began operations the following July. As its primary equipment it acquired six Fokker Super Universals from the Atlantic Aircraft Co, the United States Fokker subsidiary. The Aviation Bureau had hoped to introduce a Japanese-built transport into the country's airline service, and therefore sponsored a competition among Japanese aircraft designers and builders, namely, Aichi, Mitsubishi, and Nakajima. All, however, failed to surpass the Super Universal. As a result, a continuing need for more of these aircraft was apparent, so Nakajima secured components for four additional aircraft which it assembled. By direction of the Aviation Bureau, Nakajima obtained a licence from Atlantic Aircraft to fully manufacture these aeroplanes in Japan, and production began in September 1930.

The Super Universal soon gained a reputation for being a reliable and practical aeroplane. The all-wooden wing was of typical Fokker design, with a deep aerofoil section and ply covering.

The first of these Nakajima-built aircraft was completed on 18 March, 1931, and it and a few that followed were assembled from imported parts and had Nakajima Jupiter VI engines. The production models that followed continued to be improved with minor modifications including a change from the Jupiter engine to the slightly more powerful Kotobuki. Some of the earlier aircraft were modified to take the latter engine.

The majority of these aircraft were used on domestic routes of Nikon Koku Yuso KK, but some were delivered to Manshu Koku KK (Manchurian Airways Co Ltd) for its operations. This was Japan's first type for regular scheduled passenger transport, and was also the first passenger aircraft mass produced in Japan.

Production of Super Universals was undertaken at the Ohta Works of Nakajima until October 1936, when the work was transferred to the Manshu Koku, with a total of forty-seven aeroplanes including a small number for the Army and Navy.

Japan's Super Universal gained the reputation of being an excellent transport and remained in domestic service for more than ten years. A disadvantage was the wooden wing which often warped because of the high humidity in Japan, but a bigger problem was the unreliability of the Nakajima-built Jupiter engine. Frequent problems with this engine caused the Aviation Bureau to issue strict compliance requirements for its overhaul. Finally, in July 1939, the Bureau ordered the complete suspension of operations with Jupiter-powered Super Universals.

Nakajima-Fokker Super Universal Transport as a seaplane.

After the availability of twin-engined all-metal passenger trans-ports as standard equipment for Nihon Koku Yuso KK, the Super Universals continued with the com-pany as pilot and crew trainers for a long period.

Single-engine high-wing cantilever monoplane. Welded steel tube fuselage with fabric covering, wooden wing with ply covering. Crew of two and six passengers.

420hp Nakajima Jupiter VI nine-cylinder air-cooled radial engine (early models), and 460hp Nakajima Kotobuki 2-kai-1 nine-cylinder air-cooled radial engine (later and modified models), driving fixed-pitch two-bladed metal propellers.

	Early production	Kotobuki-powered
Span	15.43m (50ft 7½in)	15.43m (50ft 7½in)
Length	11.09m (36ft 4½in)	11.09m (36ft 4½in)
Height	2.819m (9ft 3in)	2.819m (9ft 3in)
Wing area	34.37sq m	34.37sq m
	(369.967sq ft)	(369.967sq ft)
Empty weight	1,640kg (3,615lb)	1,720kg (3,792lb)
Loaded weight	2,700kg (5,952lb)	2,700kg (5,952lb)
Wing loading	78.6kg/sq m	78.6kg/sq m
	(16.1lb/sq ft)	(16.1lb/sq ft)
Power loading	5.2kg/hp (11.4lb/hp)	6.43kg/hp (14.1lb/hp)
Maximum speed	125kt (144mph)	134kt (154mph)
Cruising speed	92kt (106mph)	117kt (135mph)
Climb to	1,000m (3,280ft)	1,000m (3,280ft)
in	4min 16sec	7min 18sec
Service ceiling	—	6,000m (19,685ft)
Range	1,045nm (1,202sm)	900nm (1,035sm)
Endurance	5½hr	5hr

Forty-seven built from March 1931 to October 1936 (including thirty-five by Manchurian Airways Co Ltd).

Nakajima P-1 Mail-carrying Aircraft

In January 1933, the Nihon Koku Yuso KK made plans to operate a night mail service with the use of a specialized aeroplane. Nakajima was given a contract to build eight of these mailplanes for the company.

The new aeroplanes were based on the design of the Navy Type 90-2-3 Reconnaissance Seaplane. The design was converted into a single-seat mailplane with land undercarriage and equipment spec-ified by Nihon Koku for night flying. Two large landing lights were installed beneath the lower wings. It also had a radio trans-ceiver, radio beacon and parachute flares. The first of these attractive biplanes was completed in May 1933. At first, these aircraft had a single open cockpit but later were changed by adding a canopy over the cockpit with a turtle-back fairing into the fuselage. The wings were of two different aerofoils, the N-22 was used on the upper, while the lower wing was of Clark Y section.

Although the Type 90-2-3 recon-naissance aircraft was powered by the Kotobuki 2-kai-1 engine, Ni-hon Koku specified the Jupiter engine in order to standardize with those used on its Super Universals. Later they were to learn that the Kotobuki was the more reliable of the two and re-engined the Super Universals as well as some of the mailplanes with the Kotobuki.

The night airmail route connec-ted Tokyo, Osaka, and Fukuoka, and was opened in August 1933. It was soon determined that a single-seat aircraft was unsafe for this type of strenuous night flying, often in adverse weather conditions. Mail loads increased also, and soon this type of operation was taken over by the twin-engined Douglas DC-2, Nakajima AT-2s and Mitsubishi Hinazuru-Type Transports. Thus, the P-1 Mailplanes were gradually phased out of service after about two years of operation.

In addition to Nihon Koku's aircraft, one P-1 was used as a special communications aircraft by the Ministry of Communications. It was named *Giyu Kyushu Teishin Go*.

Single-engine single-seat single-bay biplane. Structure of wood and metal with fabric covering. Pilot in open cockpit, later changed to enclosed cockpit.

420-450hp Nakajima Jupiter VI, nine-cylinder air-cooled engine, driving a Hamilton Standard fixed-pitch two-bladed metal propeller.

Span 10.97m (36ft); length 7.66m (25ft 1½in); height 3.70m (12ft 1½in); wing area 32.57sq m (350.592sq ft). Empty weight 1,225kg (2,700lb);

Nakajima P-1 Mail-carrying Aircraft with enclosed cockpit.

loaded weight 1,992kg (4,391lb); wing loading 62kg/sq m (12.7lb/sq ft); power loading 4.6kg/hp (10.1lb/hp).

Maximum speed 131kt (150.75mph); cruising speed 105kt (120.8mph); climb to 3,000m (9,843ft) in 9min 27sec; range 1,000km (621sm); endurance 5hr.

Nine built beginning in May 1933.

Nakajima-Douglas DC-2 Transport

The beginning of Japan's association with Douglas transports dates to the 1930s when Nakajima worked closely with the Douglas Company in California, sending several of its engineers there for training. When the fourteen-passenger DC-2 went on the market in 1934, Nakajima was immediately interested and secured production rights for the new aeroplane.

In the meantime, one of the Douglas-built DC-2s was purchased by Great Northern Airways in Canada, serving as an agent for Mitsui Bussan KK (Mitsui & Co), one of Japan's largest industrial trading companies, and the aeroplane was immediately shipped to Japan. It arrived at Yokohama on 22 November, 1934, was assembled at Tokyo's Haneda Airport, and was put on public display there on 1 December that year. When it departed, it flew to Tachikawa Airfield and was taken inside Nakajima's hangar where the Army studied it for the latest developments in aeronautical technology. It retained its US registration NC14284 (s/n1323) for some time before the airframe was camouflaged after purchase by the Army. The Army used it on the serviceability test flights between Japan and Manchuria, using Nihon Koku flight crews.*

The aircraft proved quite satisfactory, and Nihon Koku decided to acquire DC-2s for its airline opera-

tions to replace the three-engined Fokkers and Super Universals. Nakajima was to produce the aircraft after concluding a licence manufacturing agreement with Douglas. Once this was agreed, Nakajima engineers Kiyoshi Akegawa, Setsuro Nishimura and Katsuji Nakamura, began adapting the Douglas drawings to Japanese manufacturing techniques early in 1935.

To get DC-2 production started, major airframe components of five DC-2s (Douglas s/ns 1418/1422) were purchased from Douglas the same year that the DC-2 (Douglas s/n 1323) arrived in Japan. At Nakajima's Koizumi plant, 45 miles northwest of Tokyo, these components were assembled and completed with Japanese flight and engine instruments along with other indigenous accessories. The

*While this is believed to be correct and supported by several records, other sources have indicated that this first aircraft was retained continuously by Nihon Koku Yuso KK and that the first Nakajima produced aircraft is the one that entered Japanese Army service.

engines were the US-produced and imported Wright Cyclone SGR-1820-F2s with Hamilton Standard controllable-pitch propellers. Other US-made components were imported as well.

The first Nakajima-built/assembled DC-2 was completed in February 1936. Production continued and Nihon Koku Yuso KK used them on its Fukuoka to Taiwan route beginning that same year. They were given names of famous Japanese mountains including *Niitaka*, *Fuji* and *Atago*. In comparison to the original imported DC-2, the Japanese-built aircraft was lighter by 120kg (264lb) empty and 187kg (412lb) loaded. But performance was slightly lower than that of the Douglas-built model when comparing figures from two different sources. The Nakajima aircraft had a maximum speed of 172kt and a service ceiling of 5,400m, while figures for the Douglas-built DC-2 were 182kt and 7,100m. The difference was believed to have been caused by the Cyclone F-2 engine of the Nakajima aircraft, while the American

aircraft used the Cyclone F-3 engine. Later, the engines used on the DC-2s built by Nakajima were changed to Cyclone F-52 series for improved reliability.

The DC-2 was expected to be the mainstay of Nihon Koku's high-speed airliners, but production was suspended with only the five aircraft because the DC-3 entered the market, a decidedly better aircraft for future airline use. In September 1938, all civil air carriers came under Army control and the DC-2s were used as far away as mainland China. Seen with Japanese markings by Allied aircrews, they gave it the code-name Tess, as production of DC-2s was expected to have been high and that they would therefore be met in large numbers. The DC-2 was a noteworthy aeroplane in Japan, for it modernized Japanese commercial airline equipment standards and was the source for the Nakajima AT-2 of similar design.

Twin-engined low-wing monoplane transport with retractable undercarriage. All-metal construction with fabric-

covered control surfaces. Crew of four and fourteen passengers.

Two 730hp Wright Cyclone SGR-1820-F52 nine-cylinder air-cooled radial engines, driving Hamilton Standard three-blade metal propellers.

Span 25.91m (85ft); length 18.89m (61ft 11¾in); height 4.97m (16ft 3¾in); wing area 87.236sq m (939sq ft).

Empty weight 5,585kg (12,313lb); loaded weight 8,160kg (17,990lb); wing loading 93.54kg/sq m (19.16lb/sq ft); power loading 5.58kg/hp (12.3lb/hp).

Maximum speed 174kt (200mph) at 760m (2,493ft); cruising speed 156kt (179.5mph) at 1,000m (3,280ft); climb to 3,000m (9,843ft) in 8min 54sec; service ceiling 5,400m (17,716ft).

Five assembled/built from February 1936 to 1937.

Nakajima-Douglas DC-2 Transport J-BBOQ.

Army Aircraft Built by Nakajima

Nakajima Type 5 Trainer.

Nakajima Type 5 Trainer

In May 1919, while the Nakajima company was still in its infancy and known as the Nihon Hikoki Seisakusho, it was informed by the Army of the acceptance of its newly designed and built Type 4 trainer. After failures of previous designs, it was the Type 4 that achieved the success Nakajima needed in attaining Army recognition of its aeroplanes. With minor changes to this aeroplane, the Army requested another prototype which became the Type 5 and this was followed by an order for twenty aircraft, a figure that was later increased to one hundred. This was an astonishingly large order, as well as the first order of this type placed with a civil company. Up to that time, almost all aeroplanes used by the Army were imported or licence-manufactured. Japanese-designed aeroplanes were looked upon as only experimental and not to be considered for acceptance as standard military equipment. For these experimental aircraft and small production runs, the Army had relied upon its own Tokorozawa Branch of Army Supply Dept.

The design of the earlier Type 4 was based largely on the successful designs of the United States Standard H-3 and the German Albatros C II. The engine for the new aeroplane was to be the imported 125hp Hall-Scott from the USA. Under the direction of the company founder, Chikuhei Nakajima, engineers adapted these design concepts into a Nakajima product. The drawings were by Jiro Sakuma and structural analysis was undertaken by Eiji Sekiguchi. Tatsuo Miyazaki and Jingo Kurihara supervised production tool making and product manufacturing respectively.

When the first aeroplane was completed, it was delivered to the Army by surface transport to Tokorozawa Airfield where it was closely examined and assembled, making its first flight towards the end of April 1920. It showed excellent performance. The pilot was Katota Mizuta, a former Army cavalry lieutenant, and flying instructor at the Tokorozawa Army Flying School. Production aircraft were equipped with the 150hp Hall-Scott engine of greater power than the prototype. Variations included one that was tested with a 130hp Benz and a modified engine cowling.

As the Type 5 Trainers were delivered to the Army, they were assigned to various flight regiments and flying schools. In service, a number of defects were encountered which resulted in serious accidents. Stalls were prematurely induced because of wing ribs having been manufactured to incorrect drawings. Inflight fires were not uncommon, caused by a build-up of engine oil in the bottom of the engine cowling. On 14 October, 1920, the 60th

This view of the Nakajima Type 5 Trainer shows the tail more clearly.

aircraft of this type, flown by Capt Saburo Iniwa, caught fire in flight and the ensuing crash killed the pilot and the mechanic. These and other defects brought an end to the Army's use of the Type 5 as standard equipment in favour of the Type Ko 1, Type Ko 2, and Type Otsu 1.

After 1921 and approximately a year of service, many of the Type 5s were released by the military and used as civil aircraft. As a consequence the aircraft was better known as a civil aeroplane than a military trainer. It was this initial military order, however, that placed the Nakajima company on a sound financial footing, as well as instigating the disagreements that brought about the separation of Seibei Kawanishi from the company.

Single-engine two-bay biplane. Wooden construction with fabric covering. Crew of two in open cockpits.

150-165hp Hall-Scott A-5a six-cylinder water-cooled inline engine, driving a two-bladed wooden propeller.

Span 12.606m (41ft 4¼in); length 7.046m (23ft 1½in); height 2.882m (9ft 5½in); wing area 34sq m (365.984 sq ft).

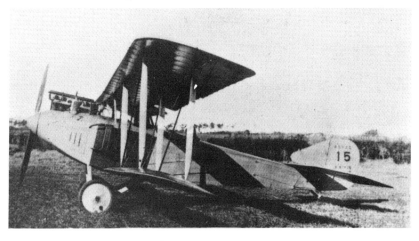

Empty weight 780kg (1,719lb); loaded weight 1,130kg (2,491lb); wing loading 33.2kg/sq m (7lb/sq ft); power loading 7.53kg/hp (16.6lb/hp).

Maximum speed 70kt (80.6mph) at sea level; minimum speed 32.5kt (37.4 mph); climb to 1,000m (3,280ft) in 7min; service ceiling 3,400m (11,155ft); endurance 4hr.

101 built from April 1919 to May 1921 (military purchase only).

Army Model 2 Ground Taxi-ing Trainer

In many respects, the early aeroplanes were more difficult to handle on the ground than in the air. To assist in ground handling, ground-taxi-ing trainers were devised and used in Japan as well in as other countries. In 1921, two variations were designed by the Tokorozawa Branch, Department of Supply, Army Department of Aviation, the Model 3 which was manufactured at the Tokorozawa Army Supply Depot and the tractor-engined Model 2 produced by Nakajima. These trainers did have wings and tail control surfaces, which helped in taxi-ing, since they had no brakes or steering capabilities other than the skilful deflection of the controls in conjunction with engine operation, a technique much like sailing a boat. Some were used for training with skis.

The Model 3 built by Tokorozawa resembled a Blériot monoplane powered by an Anzani engine. The Model 2, also designed and built at Tokorozawa and later by Nakajima, was similar to a Nieuport 81 trainer converted to a shoulder-wing monoplane and powered by a Gnome engine. The first of these was completed in June 1921. It was soon realized that the expected training was not all that effective, and that the obsolete Type Ki 1 Trainer (Hanriot HD-14) served equally well.

Thus, production ended with the five being built and delivered to the Army. A few were released for civil use, one being used by a circus as late as 1938-39. At first it thrilled spectators to see this aeroplane swing in orbit around the circus tent, suspended by cables from a

rotating arm. But once the engine was started, the exhaust gas and engine noise filled the tent, sending spectators fleeing with tears streaming and violent coughing.

Single-engine monoplane ground taxi-ing trainer. Wooden structure with fabric covering. One or two in open cockpits.

50hp Gnome Omega seven-cylinder air-cooled rotary engine, driving a two-bladed wooden propeller.

Five built in 1921.

Note: This aeroplane is illustrated under PMBRA Army Model 2 Ground Taxi-ing Trainer.

Army Type Ko 3 Fighter/Trainer

Following the First World War, the Japanese Army imported a number of aircraft that had proved themselves in combat. Among these was the SPAD S. VII, imported in 1918, the (100) SPAD S. XIIIs in 1919,

Nakajima Army Type Ko 3 Fighter/ Trainer of the Nieuport 24.C 1 design.

(50) Sopwith Pups in 1919, and the Morane-Saulnier A.1 in 1922. Additionally, there were French Nieuport 24.C 1 and 27.C 1 fighters, imported in 1917. These were found to be the most manoeuvrable, and as a result the Army adopted the Nieuport 24.C 1 as its standard fighter.

This brought the need for additional aircraft of this type for Army service. They were built under licence agreement at the Tokorozawa Branch of the Army Supply Depot beginning in March 1919, but, later, production of these fighters was transferred to Nakajima. Le Rhône engines to power the aircraft were licence-manufac-

Nakajima Army Type Ko 3 Fighter converted for civil use with fuel tank under the upper wing for the November 1922 Tokyo–Osaka mail flight competition.

tured by Tokyo Gasuden.

There were actually two missions assigned to these Nieuport designed fighters. The Nieuport 24.C 1 was used as a single-seat trainer powered by an 80hp Le Rhône engine; the other, the Nieuport 27.C 1, equipped with a 120hp Le Rhône, was used as a fighter. Both were so identified by markings on their tails. The Japanese Army referred to both as the Type Ni-24; the Ni being the first kana in the word Nieuport. In November 1921, a new designation system for Army aircraft was enacted, and both became the Ko 3.

The first of the Nakajima-built aircraft was completed in July 1921. Structurally it was identical to the Nieuport 24.C 1. These were assigned to fighter units beginning in June 1922 to replace the Type Hei 1 (SPAD XIII) Fighters and remained operational until the later years of the Taisho reign which ended in 1926, replaced then by the Type Ko 4; Nakajima Nieuport 29-C-1 fighters.

As the Ko 3 was phased out of Army service, some were released to the civil market and used as single-seat sports aircraft until around 1933.

facture was planned for these aircraft as well. In keeping with the usual practice, production was started at Tokorozawa, but by this time aircraft manufacturing was being shifted to civil companies. The Army remained responsible for the licence agreement with Nieuport and transferred all production materials to respective companies. In doing this, the Army contracted with Mitsubishi to build the Nieuport 81 E.2 as the Type Ko 1, and with Nakajima to build the Nieuport 83 E.2 as the Type Ko 2 in addition to the Type Ko 3.

The first of the Nakajima-built Type Ko 2s was completed in March 1922, and was identical to the Nieuport 83 E.2.* Subsequent trainers of both the Type Ko 1 and 2 types were delivered and assigned to Army Flying Schools at Tokorozawa and Kagamigahara, and some Flight Regiments beginning in 1922. They remained in service until around 1926. After that a number was released to civil flying schools.

Single-engine single-bay biplane fighter. Wooden structure with fabric covering. Pilot in open cockpit.

80-93hp Le Rhône or 120-130hp Le Rhône nine-cylinder air-cooled rotary engines, driving two-bladed wooden propellers.

One fixed forward-firing 7.7mm machine-gun.

Span 8.22m (26ft 11½in); length 5.67m (18ft 7¼in); height 2.40m (7ft 10½in); wing area 15sq m (161.463sq ft).

	With 80hp Le Rhône	With 120hp Le Rhône
Empty weight	415kg (915lb)	450kg (992lb)
Loaded weight	595kg (1,311lb)	630kg (1,389lb)
Wing loading	39.7kg/sq m (8.1lb/sq ft)	42kg/sq m (8.6lb/sq ft)
Power loading	7.44kg/hp (16.4lb/hp)	5.25kg/hp (11.5lb/hp)
Maximum speed	74kt (85mph)	88kt (101mph)

Nakajima production only: thirty in 1921, forty-seven in 1922, twenty-five in 1923.

Army Type Ko 2 Trainer

In November 1921 the Army developed and used a new identifying system for its standard equipment. In the case of Nieuport aircraft, they were all given the designator Type Ko, making the Nieuport 81 E.2 the Ko 1, and the Nieuport 83 E.2 the Type Ko 2. As with the Nakajima-built Type Ko 3, already described, the Type Ko 1 and 2 were needed in greater numbers than could be imported, so licence-manu-

Nakajima Army Type Ko 2 Trainer, a Japanese-produced Nieuport 83 E.2.

Single-engine sesquiplane fighter. Wooden structure with fabric covering. Pupil and instructor in open cockpit.

80-100hp Le Rhône nine-cylinder air-cooled rotary engine, driving a Regy fixed-pitch wooden propeller.

Span 8.11m (26ft 7¼in); length 7.035m (23ft 1in); height 2.9m (9ft 6in); wing area 18.40sq m (198.062sq ft).

Empty weight 440kg (970lb); loaded weight 710kg (1,565lb); wing loading 38.5kg/sq m (8lb/sq ft); power loading 8.8kg/hp (19.4lb/hp).

Maximum speed 76kt (87.5mph) at sea level; service ceiling 5,000m (16,404 ft); endurance 2hr.

Forty built from March to July 1922.

Army Type Ko 4 Fighter

Immediately after the First World War, the Nieuport company introduced its new fighter, the Nieuport 29-C-1, then acclaimed the best fighter in the world, and it became

*These had single-controls only but the pupil and instructor sat in tandem in a single cockpit. These were used as intermediate trainers after initial training in the Ko 1.

Nakajima Army Type Ko 4 Fighter, a licence-produced Nieuport 29-C-1.

the standard equipment of the Armée de l'Air. The Japanese Army imported some of these fighters in 1923 to replace the Type Hei 1 and Type Ko 3 Fighters as its standard equipment. To provide the additional aircraft necessary, Nakajima procured the licence to manufacture them in Japan, as the Type Ko 4 Fighter.

These aircraft were markedly different in structure from previous Army fighters in that the Nieuport 29-C-1 had a very advanced well streamlined wooden monocoque fuselage.

The first was assembled from imported components in December 1923. Production began with some Japanese modifications and continued until January 1932, 608 being delivered to the Army. It was the Army's first mass-produced fighter, and the lack of changes in its outward appearance from that of the original Nieuport 29-C-1 confirmed its excellent design. The

A rare inflight view of a Nakajima Army Type Ko 4 Fighter.

slim fighter had a very smooth skinned fuselage, Lamblin radiator, and dihedral on the upper wing only. Armament consisted of two Vickers 7.7mm machine-guns on top of the forward fuselage. The type entered operational service with Japanese Army units in 1925 and remained as standard equipment until about 1933, being replaced by the Nakajima-built Army Type 91 Fighter.

The Ko 4 was excellent in general performance, but it had peculiarities such as a tendency to slide-slip and stall at speeds greater than normal stalling speed. Many pilots experienced emergency landings because of engine problems and they preferred the earlier Type Ko 3 with the better flying qualities. The wooden monocoque fuselage caused new difficulties when requiring repair.

Type Ko 4 Fighters participated in the Manchurian and Shanghai Incidents, making them the first Japanese fighters to be sent overseas for combat; however, they did not engage the enemy because there was no air opposition. Following their military service life, some were released to civil operators and

remained in flying schools until as late as 1937.

Single-engine single-seat single-bay biplane fighter. Wooden monocoque fuselage with fabric-covered wooden wing. Pilot in open cockpit.

300-320hp Mitsubishi-Hispano-Suiza eight-cylinder vee water-cooled engine, driving a two-bladed wooden propeller.

Two forward-firing fixed 7.7mm machine-guns.

Span 9.70m (31ft 9¾in); length 6.44m (21ft 1½in); height 2.64m (8ft 8in); wing area 26.80sq m (288.482sq ft).

Empty weight 825kg (1,818lb); loaded weight 1,160kg (2,557lb); wing loading 43.3kg/sq m (8.8lb/sq ft); power loading 3.84kg/hp (48.4lb/hp).

Maximum speed 126kt (145mph); cruising speed 92kt (106mph); landing speed 50kt (59mph); climb to 4,000m (13,123ft) in 13min 30sec; service ceiling 8,000m (26,246ft); endurance 2hr.

608 built from December 1923 to January 1932.

Experimental Nakajima N-35 Reconnaissance Aircraft

In 1926, the Army had a requirement for a reconnaissance aeroplane to replace the Type Otsu 1 which was a First World War type, the French-designed Salmson 2-A.2. Asked to participate in this design competition were Kawasaki, Ishikawajima and Mitsubishi. Nakajima was not invited because its heavy involvement in production of the Ko 4 Fighter. Chikuhei Nakajima, president of the company; did not take this decision kindly, and therefore undertook the design of a reconnaissance aeroplane as a private venture in order to compete.

Chief designer for the new aircraft was Shinobu Mitsutake, who relied heavily upon the imported Potez 25 for wing and undercarriage design, and on the Breguet 19 for fuselage details. Further French influence came from two French engineers hired by the company, André Marie, overall supervisor of the project, and Maxime Robin. Originally, the aeroplane

Experimental Nakajima N-35 Reconnaissance Aircraft.

was intended to be powered by a 450hp Lorraine, but, when completed in October 1927, it had the later 600hp Lorraine in the hope of even better performance. This aeroplane was referred to by Nakajima personnel as the Potez-type Reconnaissance Aircraft. Some sources state that two of these N-35s were built, but in fact only one was completed.

Competing aircraft for the new Army reconnaissance aircraft were the Mitsubishi Tobi-Type, Kawasaki KDA-2, and the Ishikawajima T-2, and the design of all of them had been strongly influenced by foreign designers and engineers, i.e. Alexander Baumann, Richard Vogt and Gustav Lachmann respectively, all from Germany. The Kawasaki KDA-2 was declared the winner. The Nakajima N-35 failed to compete against the others because of an engine failure during its first flight on 17 November, 1927. Pilot Kan-ichiro Kato and flight engineer Yoshitaro Ogino were only slightly injured, but the aircraft was badly damaged. It remained in this condition for a

long time in a corner of a hangar at Ojima Airfield.

Single-engine reconnaissance sesquiplane. Wood and metal structure with fabric covering. Crew of two in open cockpits.

650-710hp Lorraine 18W eighteen-cylinder W-type water-cooled engine, driving a Reed fixed-pitch two-bladed metal propeller.

Two forward-firing fixed 7.7mm machine-guns and one dorsal lexible 7.7mm machine-gun and 500kg (1,102 lb) of bombs.

Span 16.45m (53ft 11⅓in); length 9.65m (31ft 7¾in); wing area 54sq m (581sq ft).

Empty weight 1,704kg (3,756lb); loaded weight 2,720-2,970kg (5,396-6,548lb).

Maximum speed 238km/h (148mph) at sea level, 217km/h (135mph) at 3,000m (9,843ft), 194km/h (120.5 mph) at 5,000m (16,404ft); climb to 1,000m (3,280ft) in 2min 40sec, to 3,000m (9,843ft) in 10min 5sec, to 5,000m (16,404ft) 22min 34sec; service ceiling 7,400m (24,278ft).

One built in 1927.

Nakajima Bulldog Fighter.

Nakajima Bulldog Fighter

Nakajima's design for a parasol-wing fighter, along with those of other companies competing for the Army's requirement for a new fighter, met with early uncertainties. Eventually, Nakajima's design was further developed and became the successful Army Type 91 Fighter, but in the interim, Nakajima, in 1930, bought the licence-manufacturing rights for the Bristol Bulldog. This aircraft was thought by Nakajima to be an ideal replacement for the ageing Type Ko 4 Fighters.

Like the earlier N-35 Reconnaissance Aircraft, this project was supervised by the same French team headed by André Marie, assisted by Maxime Robin and others. Because this was a British-designed aircraft, Leslie G. Frise of the Bristol Aeroplane Co and his assistant H.W. Dunn were invited to Japan to assist. The first prototype was completed in June 1930, followed soon after by the second prototype.

The design was based upon the Bristol Bulldog Mk. II of four variants, but differed by having each engine cylinder covered by separate fairings, the interplane struts were changed to the N type as used on the Bristol Bullpup, and struts were used to brace the tailplane. The Nakajima Jupiter engine was substituted for the Bristol-built Jupiter. After two prototypes were built, some of the parts were found to have insufficient strength for safe flight, therefore Chikuhei Nakajima grounded them. As a consequence, they were never submitted to the Army for evaluation; however, Nakajima's design for the parasol-wing Type 91 Fighter had by now achieved success. The two Bulldogs were eventually donated to the Navy, at the outbreak of the Shanghai Incident, for structural research purposes.

Single-engine single-seat fighter biplane. Metal structure with fabric covering. Pilot in open cockpit.

450-520hp Nakajima Jupiter VII nine-cylinder air-cooled radial engine,

Nakajima Army Type 91 Fighter.

driving a two-bladed wooden propeller.

Two forward-firing 7.7mm machineguns.

Span 10.36m (34ft); length 7.54m (24ft 9in); height 2.99m (9ft 9½in); wing area 28.5sq m (306.781sq ft).

Empty weight 1,000kg (2,204lb); loaded weight 1,600kg (3,527lb); wing loading 56.1kg/sq m (11.5lb/sq ft); power loading 3.55kg/hp (7.8lb/hp).

Maximum speed 148kt (170.3mph) at 3,000m (9,843ft); climb to 5,000m (16,404ft) in 11min; service ceiling 7,650m (25,098ft). Estimated figures.

Two built in 1931.

Army Type 91 Fighter
(Company designation NC)

To replace the Type Ko 4 Fighter of the French Nieuport design, in 1927 the Army asked Nakajima, along with Kawasaki and Mitsubishi, to submit design proposals for a new fighter. This became the Army's first open competition for a Japanese-designed fighter.

Nakajima appointed Shigejiro Ohwada and Yasushi Koyama as chief designers for this project, under the supervision of André Marie assisted by Maxime Robin. While Mitsubishi and Kawasaki followed the conservative German designs and used water-cooled engines, Nakajima departed from this tradition and drew from the design of the more graceful French Nieuport-Delage fighter with a parasol-wing and an air-cooled radial engine. The first prototype was completed in May 1928, followed by the second prototype a month later. Its smooth contoured lines gave the impression of nimble performance.

All three companies' entries were ambitious designs when compared to world standards; but when the Mitsubishi Hayabusa-type Fighter disintegrated at Tokorozawa in a test dive, the evaluation of all competitors was ended, and the remaining aircraft were used for static structural testing to destruction. All these aircraft were found to have insufficient strength to meet the rigours required of fighter aircraft.

The Army was not ready to dismiss these fighter designs entirely. Nakajima was asked to refine its design in order to explore further the advantages of the parasol-wing layout. With structural modifications, Nakajima built five additional prototypes in 1929-1931 in parallel with the Bristol Bulldog project previously described. These parasol-wing fighters were found to have stability problems because the centre of gravity was too far aft. After modifications the prototypes resumed flight testing. By the autumn of 1931, the aeroplane was accepted by the Army as the Type 91 Fighter, identified by the Japanese year 2591. It was put into production at the outbreak of the Manchurian Incident, and declared the Army's standard fighter, replacing the Ko 4. This was a year after the Navy had accepted Nakajima's entry, the Naval Type 90 Carrier Fighter, as its standard fighter aircraft. The Army Type 91 was in service for only a year before the later Kawasaki aeroplane was accepted as the Type 92 Fighter for air defence. Nakajima's Army Type 91 Fighter was regarded as an air-superiority fighter and eventually set many records, particularly during long-range operational flying training.

Pilots assigned to operational units liked these fighters, especially their ease of handling in the air. With the outbreak of the Shanghai Incident, production was accelerated and the Type 91 fighters were hurried to the front, but, in this early stage of operation, an aircraft disintegrated near Shanghai raising the question once again about structural integrity. However, unless the aeroplane was flown in violent manoeuvres, it was found to be safe, and few later accidents were attributed to structural failure.

There were two distinguishable models of this fighter. The Army Type 91-1 Fighter was adopted after the seven prototype and pre-production aircraft and was made known to the Japanese public in February 1932. The Type 91-1 Fighter was powered by the 450hp Nakajima Jupiter VII which proved to be much more trouble-free than the water-cooled engines of its competitors.

The Army Type 91-2 Fighter was basically a result of an engine change to that of the more powerful and more reliable Nakajima Kotobuki 2. This engine change altered the shape of the nose significantly with the replacement of the individual cylinder head fairings by a Townend ring cowling. Soon after the first of this series was completed in July 1934, the Kawasaki Army Type 95 Fighter, Ki-10, Allied code-name Perry, was accepted as a replacement, and production of the Type 91-2 was limited to twenty-two aircraft. This aeroplane was regarded as one of the more successful Japanese-designed fighters up to that time and had a relatively long service life.

Single-engine parasol-monoplane single-seat fighter. All-metal monocoque fuselage with metal structured wing with fabric covering. Pilot in open cockpit.

450-520hp Nakajima Jupiter VII nine-cylinder air-cooled radial engine, driving a two-bladed wooden propeller (Type 91-1); 460–580hp Nakajima Kotobuki 2 nine-cylinder air-cooled radial engine, driving a controllable-pitch two-bladed metal propeller (Type 91-2).

Two fixed forward-firing 7.7mm machine-guns.

	Type 91-1	*Type 91-2*
Span	11m (36ft 1in)	11m (36ft 1in)
Length	7.27m (23ft 10¼in)	7.30m (23ft 11¼in)
Height	2.79m (9ft 2in)	3m (9ft 10in)
Wing area	20sq m (215.285sq ft)	20sq m (215.285sq ft)
Empty weight	1,075kg (2,370lb)	—
Loaded weight	1,530kg (3,373lb)	1,500kg (3,307lb)
Wing loading	76.5kg/sq m	75kg/sq m
	(15.6lb/sq ft)	(15.3lb/sq ft)
Power loading	3.4kg/hp (7.5lb/hp)	3.26kg/hp (7.1lb/hp)
Maximum speed	162kt (187mph)	162kt (187mph)
Climb to	3,000m (9,843ft)	—
in	4min	—
Service ceiling	9,000m (29,527ft)	—
Endurance	2hr	—

Two prototypes built May–June 1928; five pre-production 1929-31. 320 Type 91-1 built 1931–March 1934; one experimental aeroplane built in April 1933; and twenty-two Type 91-2 built July–September 1934. Total built by Nakajima 350. In addition Ishikawajima built 100* Type 91-1 from September 1932 to March 1934.

*US Strategic Bombing Survey states 115 aircraft.

Nakajima-Fokker Ambulance Aircraft

In 1931, after the outbreak of the Manchurian Incident, the Army made arrangements with Kawasaki to convert one of its Kawasaki-Dornier Merkur Transports to an ambulance. This became the publicly funded and well-known *Aikoku No.2*. With this success, the Army considered conversions of the Nakajima-Fokker Super Universals for the same duties.

Under the supervision of Army Senior Surgeon Yoshinobu Teraji, one Super Universal was converted in the autumn of 1932. Dr Teraji had been a strong advocate of air ambulances since about 1922. Modifications made to the normal passenger model were the replacement of the six passenger seats and cargo compartment with two litters and three folding seats. The cabin was provided with soundproofing, temperature control and ventilation. Provisions for two ambulatory and two litter patients included intravenous feeding and oxygen. The crew of three comprised two pilots and a flight surgeon or medical attendant.

This first Nakajima-Fokker ambulance was donated to the Army as *Aikoku No.40 Bocho-go* in October 1932. In May 1938, another Super Universal ambulance was donated as *Aikoku No.268 Nihon Kangofu No.1 (Japanese Nurses No.1)*. This was converted from a later production aeroplane that was powered by the Kotobuki engine. Ambulance aircraft served a vital role from their first use during the Manchurian Incident, and a number, including small aircraft, were active in carrying sick and wounded from front-line battle areas to behind-the-lines.

Nakajima-Fokker Ambulance Aircraft.

Single-engine high-wing cantilever monoplane. Welded steel tube fuselage with fabric covering, wooden wing with fabric and plywood covering. Crew of two pilots and one medical attendant with two ambulatory and two litter patients.

420hp Nakajima Jupiter VI nine-cylinder air-cooled radial engine (1st aircraft), 460hp Nakajima Kotobuki 2-kai-1 nine-cylinder air-cooled radial engine (2nd aircraft), driving fixed-pitch two-bladed metal propellers.

	Jupiter-powered	Kotobuki-powered
Span	15.43m (50ft 7¾in)	15.43m (50ft 7¾in)
Length	11.09m (36ft 4½in)	11.09m (36ft 4½in)
Height	2.819m (9ft 3in)	2.819m (9ft 3in)
Wing area	34.37sq m (369.967sq ft)	34.37sq m (369.967sq ft)
Empty weight	1,640kg (3,615lb)	1,720kg (3,791lb)
Loaded weight	2,700kg (5,952lb)	2,700kg (5,952lb)
Wing loading	78.6kg/sq m (16.1lb/sq ft)	78.6kg/sq m (16.1lb/sq ft)
Power loading	5.2kg/hp (11.4lb/hp)	6.43kg/hp (14.1lb/hp)
Maximum speed	125kt (144mph)	134kt (154mph)
Cruising speed	92kt (106mph)	117kt (135mph)
Climb to	1,000m (3,280ft)	1,000m (3,280ft)
in	4min 16sec	7min 18sec
Service ceiling	—	6,000m (19,685ft)
Range	564nm (649sm)	486nm (559sm)
Endurance	5½hr	5hr

Aikoku No.40 built in October 1932 and *Aikoku No.268* built in May 1938.

Army Type 94 Reconnaissance Aircraft (Ki-4)

To replace the standard Mitsubishi Army Type 92 Reconnaissance parasol-monoplane, in 1933 the Army contracted with Nakajima for a light-weight scout aircraft that would have manoeuvrability equal to that of a fighter in order to effectively fulfil the air-to-ground support role. To ensure that the design met its needs, the Army, for the first time, participated in the development with a civil aircraft company. Taking part in the planning and supervision of the project was Nario Ando, an Army engineer, with Nakajima's engineer Shigejiro Ohwada as the chief designer. The original plans for this aeroplane envisaged it as a sesquiplane with elliptical planform wings for optimum manoeuvrability and with a Nakajima Kotobuki engine. The fuselage was to be an all-metal monocoque structure based on the successful use of this form in the Type 91 Fighter.

The development of the design was a long process involving many changes. The first three prototypes were completed in March, April and May 1934. The Army remained closely involved with the project and flight evaluations were made by Capt Saburo Amakasu and Capt Yozo Fujita, along with Nakajima test pilot Kiyoshi Shinomiya. After flight tests it was determined that the fuselage should be lengthened, and so modified the aeroplane had good manoeuvrability and stability. It was accepted by the Army in July 1934 as the Army Type 94 Reconnaissance Aircraft, with the short designation of Ki-4, and put into production.

Throughout its production and service life, a number of changes were made to the Type 94 Reconnaissance Aircraft. As the Type 94-Ko, or early production model, it

Nakajima Army Type 94 Reconnaissance Aircraft (Ki-4). (H Ando).

could be fitted with wheel spats, depending on the anticipated landing field conditions to be encountered, and under-wing bomb racks were a later addition.

The Type 94-Otsu had an engine exhaust collector ring instead of individual stacks, and bomb racks beneath the wing became standard equipment. During production, low-pressure tyres were adopted, but without spats. This model of the Ki-4 was manufactured primarily by Tachikawa Hikoki and Manshu Hikoki.

To meet a possible requirement for operations from rivers and lakes in mainland China, the 6th prototype was fitted with one main and two wingtip floats. It was tested at the Kasumigaura Naval Kokutai by the Army Air Technical Research Institute. One of the Type 94-Otsu models was fitted with twin floats but these two models were not accepted for service because of doubts about such a requirement.

Recognizing the need for flotation gear in the event of emergencies over water, a Type 94-Otsu Reconnaissance Aircraft was fitted with a pair of compressed-air inflatable flotation bags attached to the sides of the fuselage. This was the same equipment that was installed on the Nakajima Navy Type 90-2-2 Reconnaissance Seaplane and Type 90-2-3 Carrier Reconnaissance Aircraft, and the first of this type of flotation equipment to be tried on Army aircraft, but it did not become standard Army equipment.

There was also the Type 94-T Multi-purpose Aircraft, which was a civil conversion with two seats in the rear position. This aircraft was to be used for general observation and geographical survey.

The Army Type 94-Ko and-Otsu aircraft were assigned to operational units from 1935 to 1937 respectively and were replacements for the Mitsubishi-built Type 92 Reconnaissance Aircraft. They were used in the close air support role at various locations on mainland China from the beginning to the middle stage of the Sino-Japanese Conflict. In addition to general aerial observation, they undertook various missions ranging from light bombing in support of ground operations to message dropping and pick-up using message containers for contact with troops in the field. Because of this hazardous duty, many were lost and, therefore, the service life for this type was relatively short. Because of this wide combat capability, they were one of the more popular aeroplanes to be seen at Army airfields in the early part of the Sino-Japanese Conflict. They had a reputation for being one of the best types for easy maintenance.

The Ki-4 was the last biplane reconnaissance aircraft to be used by the Japanese Army. Following this aircraft, the Army created specific roles for its various types rather than combining them as in a general purpose category. New specific duties became Command Reconnaissance (Strategic Photographic Reconnaissance), Military Reconnaissance (Tactical Reconnaissance) and Direct Co-operation Reconnaissance (Close Air Support).

Single-engine reconnaissance sesquiplane. All-metal monocoque fuselage with fabric-covered wood and metal wing structure. Crew of two in open cockpits.

600-640hp Type 94-1 (Ha-8) nine-cylinder air-cooled radial engine, driving a controllable-pitch two-bladed metal propeller.

Two forward-firing fixed 7.7mm machine-guns and one or two dorsal flexible 7.7mm machine-guns. Bomb load: Not specified.

Span 12m (39ft 4½in); length 7.73m (25ft 4¼in); height 3.50m (11ft 5¾in); wing area 29.7sq m (319.698sq ft).

Empty weight 1,664kg (3,668lb); loaded weight 2,474kg (5,454lb); wing loading 82.5kg/sq m (16.9lb/sq ft); power loading 4.12kg/hp (9lb/hp).

Maximum speed 153kt (176mph) at 2,400m (7,874ft); climb to 3,000m (9,843ft) in 9min; service ceiling 8,000m (26,246ft).

516 built March 1934–February 1939, 333 by Nakajima, 57 by Tachikawa and 126 by Manshu.

*Military Reconnaissance: Close support to ground forces of division size or more; high-speed and long-range. Direct Co-operation Reconnaissance: Close support to ground forces of smaller than regiment size.

Experimental Ki-8 Two-seat Fighter
(Company designation DF)

During the period from 1930 to 1933, a number of two-seat single-engine fighters were tested in several western countries. Typical examples were the United States Curtiss F8C-1, Berliner Joyce P-16 (PB-1) and Grumman FF-1; British Hawker Demon; and the earlier Swedish Junkers K 47. The Japanese Navy was involved with this concept through the Nakajima 6-Shi and 8-Shi, and the Mitsubishi 8-Shi Two-seat Fighters. A similar project was undertaken in 1934 by Nakajima in the hope of interesting the Army in this type of fighter.

Chief designer assigned to the project was Shigejiro Ohwada, assisted by Toshio Matsuda. Their design was an advanced low-wing cantilever monoplane with inverted-gull tapered wing. This wing was a metal structure with metal skin on the forward half and fabric-covered rear portion. The fuselage followed the now-established practice of being an all-metal monocoque structure. The undercarriage was non-retractable but the wheels were enclosed by large spats. The Kotobuki 3 engine was enclosed by a

Nakajima Experimental Ki-8 Two-seat Fighter.

close-fitting ring cowling with blisters above the cylinder heads, a relatively new form that was later applied to the Nakajima AT transport. The pilot's cockpit was semi-enclosed by a rearward sliding canopy, said to be the first of its type for a fighter.

Five of these aircraft were built between March 1934 and May 1935 and an Army team led by Capt Yatsuo Yokoyama evaluated the aeroplanes. During test flights, they were plagued with accidents, none serious, but bad enough to cause damage to the control surfaces which required constant changing. This was mostly aileron damage caused by a wing dropping on landing due to early stalling and it seems that this problem was never completely overcome. A large dorsal fin was added but what effect this had on correcting this control problem is not known.

Although testing and evaluation continued for some time, the Army did not have a policy covering the use of two-seat fighters, and as a consequence the aeroplane was never accepted as standard equipment. It was reported, however, that the general performance of the Ki-8 was almost equivalent to that of the light-weight single-seat 91 Type Fighter.

Single-engine inverted gull-wing cantilever monoplane. Fuselage was all-metal monocoque construction. Metal wing structure with mixed metal and fabric covering. Crew of two in open cockpits with sliding canopy for pilot.

540-710hp Nakajima Kotobuki 3 nine-cylinder air-cooled radial engine, driving a fixed-pitch two-bladed metal propeller.

Two forward-firing fixed 7.7mm machine-guns and one dorsal flexible 7.7mm machine-gun.

Span 12.88m (42ft 3in); length 8.17m (26ft 9¼in); height 3.57m (11ft 8¼in); wing area 28.5sq m (306.781sq ft).

Empty weight 1,525kg (3,362lb); loaded weight 2,111kg (4,654lb); wing loading 74.1kg/sq m (15.1lb/sq ft); power loading 2.82kg/hp (6.2lb/hp).

Maximum speed 177kt (204mph) at 4,000m (13,123ft); climb to 3,000m (9,843ft) in 5min 39sec; service ceiling 8,760m (28,740ft).

Five built from March 1934 to May 1935.

Experimental
Ki-11
Fighter
(Company designation PA)

Because the Army decided not to accept the inverted gull-wing Kawasaki Experimental Ki-5 Fighter as standard equipment in 1934, it asked for a new competition between Kawasaki and Nakajima. Kawasaki reverted to the biplane layout in what became the Ki-10, and Nakajima submitted a low-wing monoplane fighter. This aeroplane bore a strong resemblance to the Boeing P-26, which had entered US Army service the year before and was gaining world-wide attention in the transition from biplane to monoplane fighters.

The design for the Nakajima project was supervised by Yasushi Koyama, with chief designer Shinroku Inoue. It was a stubby looking aircraft, having a wire-braced low wing with rounded tips which gave

The third prototype Nakajima Experimental Ki-11 Fighter.

it an elliptical wing appearance. While previous Nakajima low-wing aircraft had cantilever wings, a thinner aerofoil for greater speed could be attained by using external wire-bracing and Nakajima adopted this method for its new fighter. The non-retractable undercarriage had broad-chord trouser fairings.

Four prototypes were completed between April and December 1935, with some differences between each aircraft. The third prototype was equipped with a three-bladed propeller, while the fourth had two blades and a cockpit canopy. Each had variations in undercarriage fairings and differences in the vertical tail surfaces as well as detail changes due to test results.

The flying competition between the Ki-10 and Ki-11 was made by the flight-test team of the Army Air Technical Research Institute at Tachikawa in mid-1935. Flight evaluation was largely based on the Japanese favoured method of aerial combat, mainly manoeuvrability in dog fighting. This gave the Kawasaki Ki-10 biplane an advantage over the faster strike-and-run Nakajima Ki-11 monoplane, the latter being a better tactic only discovered later. Based mainly upon these differences, the Ki-10 won the competition and became the Army Type 95 Fighter, while the Ki-11 was rejected by the Army in September 1935. The reports favoured the more reliable Kotobuki radial engine used on the Ki-11 over that of the water-cooled BMW series Ha-9 II engine in the Ki-10. Regardless of these results, the Ki-11 established the foundation for the development of the next generation of fighters, the Nakajima Ki-27, known to the Allies during the Pacific War by the code-name Nate.

Attempts were made by Nakajima to manufacture the Ki-11 as an export fighter for southeast Asian countries, but none of the possible customers showed any interest. Thus, production ended with the four prototypes. The first and third were used by Nakajima for research into future fighter designs, while the fourth was sold to *Asahi Shimbun* as a high-speed aircraft with the designation AN-1 Com-

The fourth prototype Nakajima Experimental Ki-11.

munication Aircraft, it was registered J-BBHA.

This sole AN-1 achieved remarkable success while in service with the *Asahi Shimbun.* Piloted by Mosaburo Niino on 31 December, 1935, it set a speed record from Tokyo to Osaka in 1hr 25min. This record was exceeded by only five minutes by the same aircraft when flown on this route by Masaaki Iinuma. At the time of the solar eclipse which was best observed in Hokkaido in June 1936, the AN-1 flown by Iinuma delivered undeveloped film to the Tokyo office of the *Asahi Shimbun* and scooped all other newspapers. This flight was made at an average speed of 215kt. The AN-1 remained the fastest civil aircraft in Japan until the introduction of the Mitsubishi Karigane used by *Asahi Shimbun* as the *Kamikaze* in March 1937. To prepare for the goodwill European flight in the *Kamikaze,* Iinuma used the AN-1 for proficiency flying before that history-making flight. The well known French pilot Marcel Doret, flew the AN-1 at Haneda Airport in September 1937, demonstrating his aerobatic skills with this advanced aeroplane.

Single-engine low-wing wire-braced monoplane fighter. All-metal monocoque fuselage, wood and metal wing with fabric covering. One pilot in open cockpit.

550-700hp Nakajima Kotobuki 3 nine-cylinder air-cooled radial engine, driving a controllable-pitch two or three-bladed metal propeller.

Two forward-firing fixed 7.7mm machine-guns.

Span 10.802m (35ft 5¼in); length 7.452m (24ft 5¼in); height 3.370m (11ft 0¾in); wing area 18sq m (193.756 sq ft).

Empty weight 1,205kg (2,656lb); loaded weight 1,487kg (3,278lb); wing loading 82.6kg/sq m (16.9lb/sq ft); power loading 2.70kg/hp (5.9lb/hp).

Maximum speed 227kt (261mph) at 4,300m (14,107ft); cruising speed 190kt (218mph); climb to 3,000m (9,843ft) in 6min 9sec; endurance 2½hr.

Four prototypes built between April and December 1935.

Army Type 95-2 Trainer (Ki-6)

In December 1935, the Army made a public announcement of its official acceptance of three types of new trainers. These were the Tachikawa Type 95-1 Intermediate Trainer (Allied code-name Spruce), the Nakajima Type 95-2 Crew Trainer and the Tachikawa Type 95-3 Primary Trainer (Cedar). The trainer being supplied by Nakajima

Nakajima Army Type 95-2 Trainer (Ki-6) based on the Fokker Super Universal design.

was simply the Super Universal converted to Army standards for crew training, a design already considered to be obsolete but one that was still functional.

Production models of this aeroplane, known as the Ki-6, were only slightly different externally to the transport version, having a three-bladed propeller and oversize low-pressure tyres. They provided four crew positions for training in navigation, radio communication, aerial photography, and flexible-gunnery in an open cockpit aft of the wing which could be fitted with a 7.7mm machine-gun.

This aeroplane was the counterpart of the Mitsubishi-designed Navy Type 90 Crew Trainer, K3M2 (Pine), and also tested by the Army as the Ki-7. Because the Nakajima trainer was an adaptation of an already proved design, it gave good and reliable service, and therefore was sometimes used for transport and liaison duties. This aeroplane was later replaced by the Tachikawa Ki-54 (Hickory) which was designed specifically for this type of training.

Single-engine high-wing cantilever monoplane. Welded steel tube fuselage with fabric covering, wooden wing covered with fabric and plywood. Crew of two with four students/instructors.

One dorsal flexible 7.7mm machine-gun, optional.

450-580hp Nakajima Jupiter VII nine-cylinder air-cooled radial engine, driving a fixed-pitch three-bladed metal propeller.

Span 15.437m (50ft 7¾in); length 11.09m (36ft 4½in); height 2.819m (9ft 3in); wing area 34.37sq m (369.967 sq ft).

Empty weight 1,640kg (3,615lb); loaded weight 2,700kg (5,952lb); wing loading 78.6kg/sq m (16.1lb/sq ft); power loading 4.65kg/hp (10.2lb/hp).

Maximum speed 133kt (153mph) at 2,800m (9,186ft); cruising speed 94kt (108mph); climb to 3,000m (9,843ft) in 4min 16sec; service ceiling 6,000m (19,685ft), range 566nm (651sm), endurance 5½hr.

Twenty built, one in March 1934 and nineteen December 1935–November 1936.

Nakajima Experimental Ki-12 Fighter.

Experimental Ki-12 Fighter

No sooner had production begun in France of the advanced Dewoitine D.510 fighter in 1935, than Mitsubishi imported two* for study by September of that year. The outstanding appeal of this aeroplane was its new engine-mounted 20mm cannon which fired through the propeller shaft. Taking into consideration this and other features of the Dewoitine, Nakajima designed a comparable fighter but went a major step further by adding a retractable undercarriage, the first to be built in Japan.

Heading this project were two French engineers, Roger Robert and Jean Beziaud who were hired by Nakajima, with Shigenobu Mori as the chief Japanese designer. Although the D.510 served as a reference aircraft in creating the new Nakajima fighter, a number of details were further refined. Using the same 690hp Hispano-Suiza 12Xcrs engine with its 20mm engine-mounted cannon which was imported separately for this project, an oval-shaped radiator was mounted in front of the nose instead of beneath as on the D.510. This reduced the frontal area of this aeroplane as with the similar D.513. The hydraulically-operated undercarriage retracted inwards into the elliptically shaped wing which also had split flaps. The tailwheel was fully retractable. The headrest behind the open cockpit was extended aft to become part of the fin. The result was perhaps one of the most refined fighter airframes in the world at that time.

The aeroplane was completed in October 1936 and moved immediately into the flight-test phase. It

*One for the Army, one for the Navy.

was tested against the Mitsubishi Ki-18 which had been completed fourteen months previously, as well as the Mitsubishi Ki-33, Kawasaki Ki-28 and the Nakajima Ki-27, the last of these being finished about this time. The Nakajima Ki-12 was found to be inferior to all in manoeuvrability, a quality which the Japanese Army placed above all others. Failing this most important test, the design was doomed because it was not thought that a licence manufacturing agreement for the Hispano-Suiza 12Xcrs would be granted, and Japan did not want to rely upon imported engines for its combat aircraft. Consequently, the Ki-12 programme ended with but one prototype, and Nakajima's Ki-27 won the Army's approval to become its next standard fighter. On a trial basis, two Hispano-Suiza 12Xcrs were tested in the normally radial-engined Mitsubishi A5M3a, greatly enhancing its fighter-like lines and adding a little more speed.

Single-engine low-wing cantilever monoplane fighter with retractable undercarriage. All-metal monocoque fuselage, with all-metal multi-spar stressed skin wing. Pilot in open cockpit.

610-690hp Hispano-Suiza 12Xcrs twelve-cylinder vee liquid-cooled engine, driving a fixed-pitch three-bladed metal propeller.

One 20mm engine-mounted cannon firing through propeller shaft, two 7.7mm machine-guns mounted in the wing.

Span 11m (36ft 1in); length 8.30m (27ft 2¾in); height 3.30m (10ft 10in); wing area 17sq m (182.992sq ft).

Empty weight 1,400kg (3,086lb); loaded weight 1,900kg (4,188lb); wing loading 111.9kg/sq m (22.9lb/sq ft); power loading 2.75kg/hp (6lb/hp).

Maximum speed 260kt (229.2mph); cruising speed 200kt (230mph); landing speed 65kt (74.8mph); climb to 5,000m (16,404ft) in 6min 30sec; service ceiling 10,500m (34,448ft); range 433nm (498sm).

One built in October 1936.

Experimental Ki-19 Heavy Bomber

Acknowledging the experience that both Nakajima and Mitsubishi had accumulated with their few earlier designs of twin-engined aircraft, the Army contracted with both companies in 1935 to develop a modern heavy bomber to replace Mitsubishi's Army Type 93 Heavy Bomber, the Ki-1 of 1933 vintage.

Fourth prototype Nakajima Experimental Ki-19 Heavy Bomber after conversion to the N-19.

With this order came a change whereby the military services issued pre-contractual specifications that were to be met in creating new designs.

Among the requirements issued in February 1936 were: maximum speed 216kt at 3,000m; climb to that altitude in less than 8 minutes; take off in less than 300m; normal operating altitude from 2,000m to 4,000m; and endurance of more than five hours at 162kt at 3,000m. Structural strength was specified as well, including a load factor of 6 while at a high angle of attack, and 4 while in a glide. Minimum bomb load for short-range missions was to be 1,000kg with a variety of load configurations. Loaded, the bomber was to have a weight of less than 6,400kg. Other specified requirements were a crew of from four to six; engines to be either the Nakajima Ha-5 or Mitsubishi Ha-6; and three gun positions (nose, dorsal and ventral, each with one flexible 7.7mm machine-gun). The Hi-2 (Type 94) or Hi-5 radio, and other details were also specified.

Rightfully selected for the design team were Ken-ichi Matsumura as chief designer, assisted by Setsuro Nishimura and Toshio Matsuda, all of whom had previous twin-engined design experience on the Nakajima DC-2 commercial airliner project, and the short-lived LB-2 long-range attack bomber project for the Navy. Embodying the latest innovations in bomber design, this aircraft had a bomb bay within a very streamlined fuselage as opposed to carrying the bombs externally. Its cantilever wing was mounted at mid-level on the fuselage, and a Douglas-type hydraulically-operated retractable undercarriage and split-flaps were used.

Two prototypes designated Ki-19 were built by Nakajima. Performance testing by the Army Air Technical Research Institute with the competing Mitsubishi Ki-21 entries lasted from March to May 1937 at Tachikawa. From there, the evaluation moved to the Army's main bomber base at Hamamatsu for bombing and other operational testing which began in June that year. The evaluators closely studied the engines so well as the airframe and

performance. Not completely satisfied with the combinations of airframe and engines, although the Mitsubishi Ki-21 airframe and Nakajima engines had been selected, the Army ordered two additional Ki-19 prototypes from Nakajima to be powered by the Mitsubishi Ha-6, and two prototypes of the Mitsubishi Ki-21 to be powered by Nakajima Ha-5 engines.

Prototypes from the two companies were almost identical in performance, but the Army selected the Mitsubishi Ki-21 officially as the Army Type 97 Heavy Bomber considering that the Nakajima Ha-5 was the more reliable engine in spite of its poor reputation for reliability. Nakajima having lost the Army contract, converted the fourth prototype, one of those powered by the Mitsubishi Ha-6, into a civil aircraft and in April 1939 gave it the new designation N-19. It was commonly referred to as the N-19 Long-range Communication Aircraft and sold to the Domei Tsushin-sha (Domei Press Co), registered J-BACN and named *Domei No.2*.

Twin-engined mid-wing cantilever monoplane heavy bomber. All-metal construction with fabric covered control surfaces. Crew of five consisting of pilot, co-pilot, navigator/bombardier, radio-operator/gunner and gunner.

Two 890hp Nakajima Ha-5 fourteen-cylinder air-cooled double-row radial engine, driving controllable-pitch Hamilton Standard metal propellers.

Span 22m (72ft 2in); length 15m (49ft 2½in); height 3.65m (11ft 11¾in); wing area 62.694sq m (674.854sq ft).

Empty weight 4,750kg (10,472lb); loaded weight 7,150kg (15,763lb); wing loading 113.5kg/sq m (23.2lb/sq ft); power loading 4.1kg/hp (9.1lb/hp).

Maximum speed 190kt (218.65mph); cruising speed 162kt (186.42mph); range 2,160nm (2,485sm).

Four built in 1937-38.

Weights and performance for N-19 with Ha-6 engines.

Navy Aircraft Built by Nakajima

Navy Yokosho Ro-go Ko-gata Reconnaissance Seaplane

This design emanated from the Yokosuka Naval Arsenal and made the Farman pusher seaplanes obsolete. This was a twin-float biplane of wooden construction with fabric covering. Normally it had a crew of two, but some were converted to single-seat aircraft with additional fuel to increase range.

The first prototype was completed at the Naval Arsenal in the autumn of 1917 followed by production augmented by Aichi and Nakajima beginning in 1920. Of the three producers Nakajima built the largest quantity, making 106 by 1924. This was a practical aeroplane, some remaining in service until 1928. (*see* Yokosho for more details of this aeroplane).

Navy Avro 504 Trainer

An aircraft introduced into Japan in 1921 by the British Aviation Mission was the Avro 504K trainer. The Navy was so impressed with this aircraft, that it obtained its manufacturing rights which included drawings and sample aircraft. Navy production was assigned to Nakajima which produced 250 504L landplanes and 504S seaplanes beginning in 1922. Aichi was also given a contract for thirty twin-float equipped models. Many were eventually released to civilian users and some remained in service well into the 1930s. (*see* Yokosho Navy Avro 504 Trainer).

Navy Type Hansa Reconnaissance Seaplane

As German war reparations following the First World War, Japan

Nakajima Navy Avro 504 Trainer.

received a Hansa-Brandenburg W 33 Reconnaissance Seaplane. This was closely studied by the Japanese Navy and later adopted as standard Navy equipment. The aeroplane was a twin-float low-wing monoplane which was unusual in having the fin and rudder below the fuselage. Beginning in 1922, Navy production was placed with Nakajima and 160 machines were produced by 1925. Aichi was also a manufacturer, producing 150 Type Hansa aircraft. (*see* Yokosho Navy Type Hansa Reconnaissance Seaplane).

Navy Type 13 Trainer (K1Y1 and 2)

One of the very basic, and therefore successful trainer aircraft of the mid-1920s was this Navy designed Type 13 Trainer. It was a type easily converted from wheels to twin floats. This was a reintroduction of the tail-float configuration, and it was also the last with this feature. Recognizing the practicality of this aeroplane as a replacement for the I-go Ko-gata and the Avro 504 seaplane trainers, sub-contracts were placed with Nakajima, Kawanishi and Watanabe, who collectively built 104 machines. Beginning in 1925, Nakajima produced approximately forty. (*see* Yokosho Navy Type 13 Trainer.)

Navy Type 14 Reconnaissance Seaplane (E1Y1 to 3)

sance Seaplane failed to meet Navy approval, modifications to its Type 10 Reconnaissance Seaplane produced the desired results. These changes resulted in the Type 14 Reconnaissance Seaplane appearing in three distinct configurations, differing mainly in the type of engine installation. These were twin-float biplanes carrying a crew of three in open cockpits. This need for increased production was shared with Nakajima and Aichi after the initial Yokosho models were built, reaching a combined total of 320 aircraft. Beginning in 1925, Nakajima produced forty-seven of these aircraft over the following two years. (*see* Yokosho Type 14 Reconnaissance Seaplane).

Nakajima-Breguet Reconnaissance Seaplane

In April 1925, Nakajima imported two Breguet 19s from France and assembled them for Japan's first good-will flight to Europe. This was being sponsored by the *Asahi Shimbun.* The aeroplanes were given the names *Hatsukaze* and *Kochi,* (*First Wind* and *East Wind,* respectively). The Breguet 19 had a

reputation for being a sound multi-purpose long-range aeroplane, both for military and long-range civil use.

At this time, but not associated with these two imports, Nakajima had acquired manufacturing rights for the aeroplane to be known as the Nakajima-Breguet 19-A2 Reconnaissance Aircraft. Because of the soundness of this design and the enthusiastic use of the aeroplane in Europe, Nakajima had high hopes of mass-production to meet Japanese military needs. Nakajima built one example and equipped it with a wheel undercarriage as a demonstrator. However, the Army did not see a need for such a high-powered reconnaissance aeroplane, and the Navy, having just adopted the Yokosho Type 14 Reconnaissance Seaplane, showed little interest.

To meet other reconnaissance needs in 1925, the Navy established a requirement for a long-range reconnaissance seaplane, selecting as competitors, Mitsubishi, Nakajima and Kawasaki. Mitsubishi submitted its Ohtori Type, a twin-float adaptation of its Type 13 Carrier Attack Aircraft. Nakajima, still hopeful of its Nakajima-Breguet 19-A2, designed and built all-metal twin floats and fitted them to this aircraft for the competition. This became the 19-A2B. The Kawasaki entry was the Dornier Do D high-wing monoplane reconnaissance seaplane.

When the three types were evaluated by the Navy at Kasumigaura, none of them was equipped with sufficient fuel capacity to adequately meet the long-range requirement specified by the Navy.

Nakajima-Breguet 19-A2B Reconnaissance Seaplane for entry in Navy competition.

As a consequence, the Navy declared all to be unacceptable, although it did purchase the three aircraft to be used for other test purposes. Later, the Nakajima entry was released for civil use and was converted to a wheel-equipped-mailplane by Nakajima, receiving the registration J-BBFO.

The French-built *Hatsukaze* and *Kochi* were powered by 400hp Lorraine 1 water-cooled twelve-cylinder vee type engines, but the Nakajima-built aircraft was powered by the 450hp Lorraine 2 water-cooled W-type. Nakajima intended to licence-manufacture this engine for its planned production of these aeroplanes.

Experience gained by Nakajima with this aeroplane was used to good advantage with its N-35 Experimental Reconnaissance Aircraft for the Army and the civil N-36 Transport.

Single-engine twin-float sesquiplane. Metal structure throughout, with wings, tail and rear-half of fuselage fabric covered, front-half was metal-covered. Crew of two in open cockpits.

450-485hp Lorraine 2 twelve-cylinder W-type water-cooled engine, driving a two-bladed wooden propeller.

One forward-firing fixed 7.7mm machine gun and one or two dorsal flexible 7.7mm machine-guns.

Span, upper 14.83m (48ft 8in); lower 11.24m (36ft 10½in); length 11.52m (37ft 9½in); height 4m (13ft 1½in); wing area 50sq m (538.213sq ft).

Empty weight 1,380kg (3,042lb); loaded weight 3,240kg (7,143lb); wing loading 64.8kg/sq m (13.2lb/sq ft); power loading 7.2kg/hp (15.8lb/hp).

Maximum speed 108kt (124.28mph); climb to 3,000m (9,843ft) in 18min 25 sec; service ceiling 5,000m (16,404ft); endurance 10hr.

One built in 1925.

Navy Type 15 Reconnaissance Seaplane (E2N1 and E2N2)

In parallel with the Navy's 1925 requirement for a long-range reconnaissance seaplane for which Nakajima used its Breguet 19-A2B in

Nakajima Navy Type 15-1 Reconnaissance Seaplane (E2N1).

competition with Mitsubishi and Kawasaki, the Navy had a second seaplane requirement. This was to replace the Type Hansa Reconnaissance Seaplanes and be capable of catapult-launching from battleships and cruisers for short-range missions. Selected for the competition were Aichi, Nakajima and Yokosho.

Within a year of the competition announcement all three producers submitted their aircraft for evaluation. Aichi and Yokosho used the proven Type Hansa low-wing monoplane design but with modifications that would eliminate known deficiencies. The Aichi entry was the Experimental Type 15-Ko Reconnaissance Seaplane, *Mi-go*, and the Yokosho aircraft was the Experimental *Tatsu-go* Reconnaissance Seaplane. Chief designer for Nakajima, Takao Yoshida, departed from this design and created a sesquiplane with better downward view than its two competitors. All three were powered by the 300hp Mitsubishi Type Hi engine. After flight trials by the Navy's chief test pilot, Lieut-Cdr Hisakichi Akaishi, the Nakajima entry was selected as better than the other two and became Japan's first originally-designed shipboard reconnaissance seaplane.

After the decision was made to accept the Nakajima design, modifications and tests continued. It was not until May 1927 that the Navy officially adopted the aircraft as the Type 15-1 Reconnaissance Seaplane (E2N1) and Type 15-2 Re-

connaissance Seaplane (E2N2), the latter being an intermediate seaplane trainer with dual controls and provision for a hood for instrument training. They were widely used for training at Kasumigaura until replaced by the Type 93 Intermediate Seaplane Trainer. The reconnaissance model, E2N1, was intended for short-range operational missions from battleships and cruisers, while for more distant missions, the Navy relied upon the Type 14 Reconnaissance Seaplane built by both Yokosho and Nakajima. The E2N1 was armed with one flexible machine-gun in the rear cockpit.

Nakajima produced the E2N1 from 1927 to 1928, and the E2N2 from 1928 to 1929, with later production being transferred to Kawanishi. These aeroplanes became the Navy's first-line shipboard reconnaissance seaplanes, the first to use the newly developed catapult systems, replacing such aeroplanes as the Aichi Type 2 that took off under their own power from the top of gun turrets. The E2Ns were the last of the all-wooden Navy aircraft, and were eventually replaced by various models of Nakajima Type 90s.

Several were used by civil operators for air mail services and fish spotting, the latter being described as the Nakajima Fishery Seaplane.

Single-engine twin-float reconnaissance sesquiplane. All wooden construction with fabric covering. Rearward folding wings for stowage. Crew of two in open cockpits.

300-340hp Mitsubishi Type Hi eight-cylinder vee water-cooled engine, driv-

This view of the Type 15-1 Reconnaissance Seaplane clearly shows the frontal radiator and strut arrangement.

ing a two-bladed wooden propeller.

One dorsal flexible 7.7mm machine-gun (E2N1).

Span 13.52m (44ft 4¼in); length 9.565m (31ft 4½in); height 3.688m (12ft 1in); wing area 44sq m (473.627 sq ft).

Empty weight 1,409kg (3,106lb); loaded weight 1,950kg (4,299lb); wing loading 44.3kg/sq m (9lb/sq ft); power loading 6.5kg/hp (14.3lb/hp).

Maximum speed 93kt (107mph); climb to 3,000m (9,843ft) in 31min 37sec; endurance 5hr.

Forty-seven built by Nakajima from 1927 to 1929 and two or three civil aircraft in 1930. Thirty built by Kawanishi 1929–30.

Navy Type 3 Carrier Fighter (A1N1 and 2)

The ageing Mitsubishi Type 10 Carrier Fighters accepted by the Navy in 1921 were in need of replacement and in April 1926, the Navy asked competing manufacturers, Mitsubishi, Nakajima and Aichi, to submit proposals for a replacement.

Nakajima placed an order with the Gloucestershire Aircraft Company (later Gloster Aircraft) in England to construct a modified version of its year-old Gamecock Gambet, that would have increased structural strength and be suitable for carrier operations. For this purpose, the wing of the original Gamecock was increased in span from 9.18m to 9.70m which increased the wing area from 24.4sq m to

Nakajima Navy Type 3-2 Carrier Fighter (A1N2) of the Tateyama Naval Kokutai.

26.3sq m for better performance in manoeuvrability and carrier-deck take offs and landings. To assist with the necessary modifications, Nakajima assigned Takao Yoshida as chief designer to work with Gloster.

Competing aircraft, the Mitsubishi Taka-type and the Aichi H-type, were powered by water-cooled engines, and incorporated such features as a jettisonable undercarriage and flotation system for emergency alightings on water, all of which led to overweight and reduced manoeuvrability. The Nakajima G (for Gloster), although not equipped with flotation devices, used the air-cooled Jupiter VI engine. This was lighter in weight, had increased manoeuvrability and provided a very stable gun platform. These features made the aeroplane attractive to the Navy, and it was officially accepted in April 1929 as the Type 3 Carrier Fighter, with short designation A1N1.

In 1930, an improvement was made by using the 460hp Kotobuki engine with a metal propeller. This became the Type 3-2 Carrier Fighter (A1N2), making the earlier Jupiter-powered version the Type 3-1 Carrier Fighter (A1N1). This was the first Nakajima naval fighter, although not purely Japanese because of its Gloster origin. It was considered the best fighter in Japan at that time.

When Japan became involved in the Shanghai Incident, so did the Japanese Navy's A1N2 fighters, the first Japanese fighters to engage in combat. On 22 February, 1932, the aircraft carrier *Kaga's* three A1N2s led by Lieut Nogiji Ikuta, from the land base in Shanghai, shot down a Boeing P-12 flown by the American pilot Robert Short, after two minutes of combat. On 26 April during an attack on Hangchow airfield, N1N2s scored several victories and probables on Chinese flown aircraft, making it the classic fighter during the Shanghai Incident.

Single-engine single-seat fighter biplane. All-wooden structure with fabric covering. Pilot in open cockpit.

420hp Nakajima Jupiter VI nine-cylinder air-cooled radial engine, driving a two-bladed wooden propeller (A1N1), 450hp Nakajima Kotobuki 2 nine-cylinder air-cooled radial engine, driving a fixed-pitch two-bladed metal propeller (A1N2).

Two forward-firing side-mounted 7.7mm machine-guns. Bomb load: Two 30kg (66lb) bombs.

	Type 3-1 Cr Ftr (A1N1)	*Type 3-2 Cr Ftr (A1N2)*
Span	9.678m (31ft 9in)	9.70m (31ft 10in)
Length	6.491m (21ft 3½in)	6.50m (21ft 3¾in)
Height	3.25m (10ft 8in)	3.30m (10ft 10in)
Wing area	26.3sq m (283.1sq ft)	26.3sq m (283.1sq ft)
Empty weight	950kg (2,094lb)	882kg (1,944lb)
Loaded weight	1,450kg (3,196lb)	1,375kg (3,031lb)
Wing loading	55.1kg/sq m (11.3lb/sq ft)	52.3kg/sq m (10.7lb/sq ft)
Power loading	3.45kg/hp (7.6lb/hp)	3.05kg/hp (6.7lb/hp)
Maximum speed	129kt (148mph)	130kt (149.6mph)
Cruising speed	80kt (92mph)	—
Landing speed	43kt (49.5mph)	—
Climb to	3,000m (9,843ft)	3,000m (9,843ft)
in	7min 18sec	6min 10sec
Service ceiling	7,440m (24,409ft)	7,000m (22,965ft)
Range	200nm (230sm)	—
Endurance	2½hr	2½ to 3hr

Approximately 150 built excluding prototype. About fifty A1N1s 1929–30 and about 100 A1N2s 1930–1932.

Navy Type 90 Carrier Fighter (A2N1)
(Company designation NY)

In 1928 the Japanese Navy imported and tested a Boeing 69B fighter powered by a 420hp Pratt & Whitney R-1340-B Wasp engine. This was the export version of the US Navy F2B-1 carrier fighter. As Nakajima had completed its contract for building the Type 3 Carrier Fighter, it was now free to investigate a new design as a replacement, and used the Boeing 69B as an example.

Takao Yoshida, designer of the A1N1, was assigned design responsibility for the new fighter and used many of the features of the Boeing fighter in his design. Within the company, it was called the 'Type 3 Carrier Fighter Performance improvement model,' soon optimistically changed to 'Type 90 Carrier Fighter' with the assumption of Navy acceptance. Structurally, the fuselage was very similar to that of the Type 3 Carrier Fighter, and the wing was tapered like the Boeing 69Bs. The undercarriage and empennage resembled those of the later Boeing F4B-1, one of which had just been imported as the Boeing Model 100 Export Fighter.

Two prototypes were construc-

Nakajima Navy Type 90-2 Carrier Fighter (A2N1-2).

ted, the first of which was completed in December 1929. They were powered by the Nakajima Jupiter VI. The next year, the fighters were submitted to the Navy for evaluation, but it was considered that there was little improvement over the earlier Type 3 Carrier Fighter and the new type was rejected.

In 1929 Nakajima imported a Bristol Bulldog, a design that was planned for development into an Army fighter. Hoping to salvage something of its investment in its rejected Navy fighter, features of the Bulldog were incorporated into the design. This model was referred to as the 'Yoshida Bulldog'.

In May 1931, under the design leadership of Jingo Kurihara, a new prototype was designed and completed. Its wing with rounded tips closely resembled that of the F4B, it was lighter, and was powered by the later Kotobuki 2 engine. A second prototype was completed with even greater improvements, and in early 1932 it was submitted to the Navy for evaluation. It was soon recognized as a remarkable improvement over that of the Type 3 Carrier Fighter and was officially accepted in April 1932 as the Type 90 Carrier Fighter, with short designation A2N1. It was put into production immediately.

Several models evolved during its production. The first form of the Type 90-1 Carrier Fighter (A2N1-1) had the fuel tank inside the fuselage as had the F4B. Armament consisted of two 7.7mm machine-guns, and the upper wing had no dihedral. The first change was the Type 90-2 Carrier Fighter (A2N1-2) which became the main production version. It had saddle fuel tanks located on both sides of the fuselage like the Vought Corsair, and two 7.7mm machine-guns on top of the fuselage. The Type 90-3 Carrier Fighter (A2N1-3) was identical to the previous model except that 5 degrees dihedral was added to the upper wing. There was also a two-seat trainer version which was officially adopted in June 1934 as the Type 90 Carrier Fighter Trainer, A3N1.

About 100 Type 90 Carrier Fighters were produced by Naka-jima and the Sasebo Naval Arsenal until the Type 95 Carrier Fighter went into fleet service in 1936. The A2Ns were the first Japanese-designed carrier fighters which could meet on equal terms the rest of the world's best fighters. This type was used by the Naval aerobatic team of Genda, Okamura and Nomura.

Single-engine single-seat fighter biplane. All-metal fuselage structure with wood and metal wing, fabric covered. Pilot in open cockpit.

460-580hp Nakajima Kotobuki 2 nine-cylinder air-cooled radial engine, driving a Hamilton Standard fixed-pitch two-bladed metal propeller.

Two forward-firing fixed 7.7mm machine-guns.

Span 9.37m (30ft 9in); length 6.183 m (20ft 3¼in); height 3,025m (9ft 11in); wing area 19.74sq m (212.486sq ft).

Empty weight 1,045kg (2,303lb); loaded weight 1,550kg (3,417lb); wing loading 78.5kg/sq m (16.1lb/sq ft); power loading 3.37kg/hp (7.4lb/hp).

Maximum speed 158.2kt (182mph) at 3,000m (9,843ft); cruising speed 90kt (103.6mph); climb to 3,000m (9,843ft) in 5min 45sec; service ceiling 9,000m (29,527ft); range 270nm (311 sm); endurance 3hr.

About one hundred A2N1-3s built 1932-1936 and sixty-six A3N1s 1936-1939.

Nakajima Navy Type 90-2-1 Reconnaissance Seaplane converted to civil use for Tokyo Koku Yuso KK, and named Giyu-11.

Navy Type 90-2-1 Reconnaissance Seaplane (E4N1) (Company designation NZ)

It was recognized by 1930 that a successor was needed for the Type 15 Reconnaissance Seaplane that had gone into service in 1927.

The Type 15 had been powered by the water-cooled Hispano-Suiza engine, but by 1930 the far superior Nakajima-built Bristol Jupiter VI air-cooled radial was available and the Navy specified the Jupiter for the new Nakajima design for a reconnaissance seaplane to be catapult-launched from battleships and cruisers.

Chief designer for this project was Shinobu Mitsutake. It was a very conventional biplane for the period and its design was much influenced by the Vought O2U Corsair of which one was taken to Japan for study. The Nakajima fuselage had a welded chromium molybdenum steel tube structure covered with aluminium sheet over the forward portion and fabric to the rear. The wings were of wood with fabric covering. The twin-floats were all-metal and were close copies of the Vought single-float design. They were attached separately under each wing so that bombs could be suspended from the underside of the fuselage without interference from cross-bracing. Structurally the new type was a marked improvement over the preceding Type 15 Reconnaissance Seaplane.

Two prototypes were built and submitted to the Navy for evaluation in December 1930. These were known as the Navy Type 90-2-1 Reconnaissance Seaplane, with short designation E4N1. (An Aichi Reconnaissance Seaplane was accepted the same year and identified as the Type 90-1). Tests showed that the E4N1 had relatively poor manoeuvrability which was attributed to its massive twin-float configuration. Consequently, further development was abandoned early, because the company had already embarked upon a similar but single-float seaplane which was a licence-manufactured Vought O2U Corsair with minor refinements.

Lacking Navy acceptance, one of the two E4N1s was converted to a two-passenger transport with an enclosed canopy. This was purchased by Kaibo Gikai, given the name *Giyu-11*, and lent to Tokyo Koku Yuso Kaisha for use on its route between Tokyo's Haneda Airport and Shimizu and Shimoda. Some sources indicate that several aircraft of this type were built and used operationally, but the truth is that only these two were built.

Single-engine twin-float reconnaissance biplane. Fuselage of welded chromium molybdenum steel tube with forward portion covered with sheet aluminium and aft section with fabric. Wooden wings with fabric covering. Rearward folding wings for stowage. Crew of two in open cockpits for reconnaissance; pilot and two passengers in enclosed cabin as a transport.

420-520hp Nakajima Jupiter VI nine-cylinder air-cooled radial engine, driving a two-bladed wooden propeller.

One forward-firing fixed 7.7mm machine-gun and one dorsal flexible 7.7mm machine-gun. Bomb load: two 30kg (66lb) bombs.

Span 12m (39ft 4½in); length 9.05m (29ft 8½in); height 3.75m (12ft 3½in); wing area 35.78sq m (385.145sq ft).

Empty weight 1,256kg (2,769lb); loaded weight 1,950kg (4,229lb); wing loading 54.5kg/sq m (11.1lb/sq ft); power loading 4.65kg/hp (10.25lb/hp).

Maximum speed 113.4kt (130.5 mph); cruising speed 80kt (92mph); climb to 3,000m (9,843ft) in 12min 50sec; service ceiling 5,160m (16,929 ft); range 397m (457sm); endurance 5hr.

Two built beginning in December 1930.

Navy Type 90-2-2 and-3 Reconnaissance Seaplane (E4N2 and 3) (Company designation NJ)

After the acquisition of manufacturing rights for the Vought O2U Corsair, of which a sample had been imported from the United States by the Japanese Navy for research purposes, Nakajima produced this type with minor changes. These changes were made by Nakajima engineer Kiyoshi Akegawa, and included extending the wing by 500mm to increase the area, and repositioning the inter-

Nakajima Navy Type 90-2-2 Reconnaissance Seaplane (E4N2).

plane struts further outboard. The rudder area was increased, giving it a more rounded appearance, and the engine was changed from the 420hp Pratt & Whitney Wasp to the licence-built Nakajima Jupiter VI.

The prototype was completed towards the end of 1930 but was found to lack sufficient structural strength. After repeated modifications and evaluation for about a year, the aeroplane was officially accepted by the Navy in December 1931 as the Type 90-2-2 Reconnaissance Seaplane, short designation E4N2. It was put into production, first with the Kotobuki 1 engine followed by the Kotobuki 2, having 450hp and 580hp respectively. A Townend cowling was added and licence-manufactured Hamilton Standard metal propellers were used.

When compared with its predecessor, the twin-float E4N1 Reconnaissance Seaplane, this later single-float short-range reconnaissance seaplane was more manoeuvrable. It established a good reputation aboard battleships and cruisers, because it demonstrated manoeuvrability equal to that of a fighter, and had the structural strength of a dive-bomber, a mission it was capable of performing.

The Vought Corsair could easily be changed from seaplane to landplane and this feature was also built into the E4N2. On wheels it was the Type 90-2-3 Reconnaissance Seaplane, E4N3, the designation disregarding the existence of the wheels! Several were built and fitted with carrier arresting-gear and designated Type 90-2-3 Carrier Reconnaissance Aircraft, E4N2-C. These did not become operational and their service ended soon after ship-borne trials.

Production continued until 1936 during which time they remained active as the main ship-borne reconnaissance seaplanes until replaced by the Nakajima Type 95 Reconnaissance Seaplane, Allied code-name Dave, which saw service in the Pacific War. A small number of E4N2s were very active in the Shanghai Incident, some being acquired through donations as *Hokoku-go* aircraft. Some became

Nakajima Navy Type 90-2-3 Reconnaissance Seaplane (E4N3) when equipped for land-based operations.

civil aircraft after Navy service, including the P-1 Mailplane which was a development of this design.

Single-engine single-float reconnaissance biplane. Fuselage of wood and metal construction and wings of wood. Fabric covered except for forward part of the fuselage which was metal covered. Rearward folding wings for stowage. Crew of two in open cockpits.

460-580hp Nakajima Kotobuki 2-kai-1 nine-cylinder air-cooled radial engine, driving a Hamilton Standard fixed-pitch two-bladed metal propeller.

One forward-firing fixed 7.7mm machine-gun and one dorsal flexible 7.7mm machine-gun. Bomb load: Two 30kg (66lb) bombs.

Span 10.976m (36ft); length 8.87m (29ft 1¼in); height 3.967m (13ft); wing area 29.66sq m (319.268sq ft).

Empty weight 1,252kg (2,760lb); loaded weight 1,800kg (3,968lb); wing loading 60.7kg/sq m (12.4lb/sq ft); power loading 3.75kg/hp (8.2lb/hp).

Maximum speed 125.2kt (144mph); cruising speed 80kt (92mph); alighting speed 52kt (60mph); climb to 3,000m (9,843ft) in 10min 34sec; service ceiling 5,740m (18,832ft); range 550 nm (633sm).

Approximately eighty-five built by Nakajima, about eighty floatplanes from 1931 to 1936 and about five carrier aircraft from 1933 to 1936. Kawanishi built sixty-seven floatplanes from 1932 to 1934.

Experimental 6-Shi Carrier Two-seat Fighter
(Company designation NAF-1)

As early as 1931, the Navy began investigating the advantages of two-seat fighter concept as was being practised in other major countries. For this purpose, the Navy ordered one prototype which was to be the 6-Shi Two-seat Carrier Fighter. Specifications for this aircraft demanded that in addition to being a two-seat fighter it would have dive-bombing capability with structural strength to withstand a 270-knot dive for dropping small bombs. Armament would be two fixed forward-firing machine-guns and one dorsal flexible gun, and it was to carry a drop

Nakajima Experimental 6-Shi Carrier Two-seat Fighter.

tank for long-range scouting missions. It would also be equipped for carrier service by having an arresting hook and wheel-brakes.

Kiyoshi Akegawa was Nakajima's designer for this project which was given the internal designation of NAF, meaning Nakajima Akegawa Fighter. By the summer of 1932, the prototype was completed, but it was soon found that a number of modifications were required. This delayed evaluation by the Navy until 1933, and then on its official acceptance flight on 8 April the aeroplane was lost during an emergency landing.

Further development of the two-seat fighter concept began with a new design in the form of the 8-Shi Two-seat Fighter, and much that was learned with the 6-Shi was included in this design, as well as in the Type 95 Reconnaissance Seaplane and the Type 95 Carrier Fighter.

The 6-Shi Fighter was one of the lesser-known Japanese aircraft, yet it had a number of interesting innovations. Recognizably, this was a two-seat version of the single-seat Type 90 Carrier Fighter, using the same type of engine. Even though this was a two-seater it had a maximum speed equivalent to that of the Type 90, and slightly longer range. It was inferior in climb, which was inevitable due to the heavier weight with the same power. Its lower wing was an inverted gull-type. These wings were hinged with ball joints to facilitate rearward folding for stowage. A removable N strut was inserted for support at the wing root for folding. The aerofoil was the M-6 with 14 percent thickness. This was one of Japan's earliest aeroplanes capable of inverted flight. For dive-bombing, it would dive at an 80-degree angle, and could safely attain 250 knots. A 280-litre external tank could be fitted to its under-side for extended range.

Single-engine two-seat fighter biplane. All-metal structure with fabric covering. Rearward folding wings for stowage. Crew of two in open cockpits.

460-530hp Nakajima Kotobuki 2 nine-cylinder air-cooled radial engine,

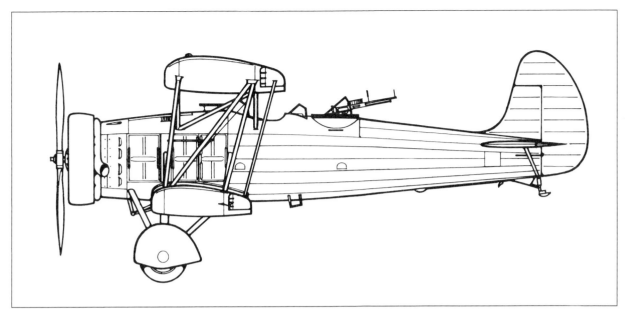

driving a Hamilton Standard-type 3-AN fixed-pitch two-bladed metal propeller.

Two forward-firing fixed Vickers 7.7mm machine-guns, 600 rounds each, one dorsal flexible Lewis 7.7mm machine-gun with 582 rounds in 6 cartridges. Bomb load: four 30kg (66lb) bombs.

Span 10.725m (35ft 2¼in); length 7.19m (23ft 7in); height 2.82m (9ft 3in); wing area 29.39 sq m (316.361sq ft).

Empty weight 1,270kg (2,800lb); loaded weight 1,844kg (4,065lb); wing loading 62.7kg/sq m (12.8lb/sq ft); power loading 3.6kg/hp (7.9lb/hp).

Maximum speed 150kt (172.6mph); cruising speed 95kt (109.39mph); minimum speed 50kt (57mph); climb to 3,000m (9,843ft) in 7min 30sec; service ceiling 5,500m (18,044ft); range 874nm (1,005sm); endurance 8hr with external fuel.

One built in 1932.

Experimental Kusho 6-Shi Special Bomber

In 1931, the Japanese Navy placed an order with Nakajima to build a carrier-based dive-bomber, the first such type in Japan.* The primary design for this aircraft was made by Jun-ichiro Nagahata, an engineer with the Aircraft Department of the Navy Technical Research Institute,

*For security purposes, the term 'dive-bomber' was not used, but instead it was described as a 'Special Bomber.'

who had just returned the year before from visiting Curtiss and Chance Vought in the United States, taking special interest in their Navy dive-bombers. Although this was decidedly a Kusho project, detail design was the responsibility of Nakajima, led by their designer, Royozo Yamamoto.

This dive-bomber was to be a single-seat biplane with negative stagger, and the lower wing was to be carried below the fuselage and connected to it by struts. A symmetrical aerofoil was also planned, the first of its kind to be used in Japanese engineering designs. The reason for this unusual wing arrangement was to adjust the centre of gravity in relation to lift, and use an aerofoil that would not produce lift during the dive.

Two prototypes were built as two-seaters. The inverted gull lower wing was joined to the fuselage but had supporting struts. The first prototype was completed in November 1932 followed a few months later by the second. With the designation 6-Shi Tokushu Bakugekiki (6-Shi [1931] Special Bomber), the Navy began its evaluation of the new aircraft, but found many problems in longitudinal stability and control. On 26 November, 1932, Nakajima test-pilot Tsuneo Fujimaki was unable to recover from a test drive. The aircraft crashed in a rural area, killing the pilot. It is said the impact caused the aircraft to penetrate two metres into

the ground. Observers reported that the pilot made several attempted recoveries but each time the nose pitched down to the vertical.

Because of this accident, further evaluation on the 6-Shi was suspended, but design would begin again in the form of an Experimental 7-Shi Special Bomber. (*see* Yokosho Navy Experimental Kusho 6-Shi Special Bomber).

Nakajima Experimental Kusho 6-Shi Special Bomber. (Shorzoe Abe).

Single-engine carrier dive-bomber biplane with negative stagger. Metal fuselage structure with wood and metal wing having fabric covering. Crew of two in open cockpits.

460-580hp Nakajima Kotobuki 2 nine-cylinder air-cooled radial engine, driving a fixed-pitch two-bladed metal propeller.

One forward-firing fixed 7.7mm machine-gun and one dorsal flexible 7.7mm machine-gun.

Span 11m (36ft 1in); length 8.20m (26ft 11in); height 3.20m (10ft 6in); wing area 32sq m (344.456sq ft).

Empty weight 1,500kg (3,307lb); loaded weight 2,300kg (5,070lb); wing loading 71.9kg/sq m (14.7lb/sq ft); power loading 5kg/hp (11lb/hp).

Maximum speed 125kt (143.8mph) at 3,000m (9,843ft); minimum speed 52kt (59.8mph); climb to 3,000m (9,843ft) in 3min; service ceiling 6,500m (21,325ft); range 450nm (518sm).

Two built in 1932-33.

Nakajima Experimental 7-Shi Carrier Fighter.

Experimental 7-Shi Carrier Fighter
(Company designation NK1F)

At the beginning of the 1930s, the Japanese Navy began a Continuous Development Programme for design development of its operational aircraft. As a result, the Navy placed orders with Mitsubishi and Nakajima in April 1932 to compete for a replacement for the Type 90 Carrier Fighter which had only been in service for a year. It was to be designed and built exclusively in Japan.

For Nakajima, Yasushi Koyama was appointed chief designer for the project. As the 7-Shi Carrier Fighter, this was to be a parasol-monoplane because of the success that Nakajima had just achieved in producing the Army Type 91

Fighter of this configuration. There was very little difference between the two aeroplanes. The main difference was that the Navy aeroplane had the Kotobuki 5 engine with a Nakajima-built Hamilton Standard three-bladed propeller and contained standard naval equipment along with an arrestor hook.

The prototype was completed in the autumn of 1932. When evaluated by the Navy, it reported that this aeroplane, as well as Mitsubishi's entry, failed to meet the general performance requirements, which included a maximum speed of 180 to 200kt. For this 7-Shi aeroplane, the Navy had expected something revolutionary, considering the long development time for this project, and was not interested

in a modification of an existing operational aeroplane as this was.

Single-engine single-seat parasol monoplane fighter. All-metal monocoque fuselage with aluminium wing structure covered with fabric. Pilot in open cockpit.

460-560hp Nakajima Kotobuki 5 nine-cylinder air-cooled radial engine, driving a Hamilton Standard fixed-pitch three-bladed metal propeller.

Two forward-firing fixed 7.7mm machine-guns.

Span 11m (31ft 1in); length 7.20m (23ft 7½in); height 3.20m (10ft 6in); wing area 20sq m (215.285sq ft).

Empty weight 1,100kg (2,425lb); loaded weight 1,600kg (3,527lb); wing loading 80kg/sq m (16.3lb/sq ft); power loading 3.48kg/hp (7.6lb/hp).

Maximum speed 160kt (184mph) at 3,500m (11,483ft).

One built in 1932.

Experimental 7-Shi Carrier Attack Aircraft (B3N1)
(Company designation Y3B)

As part of the Navy's Continuous Development Programme, it placed an order with Mitsubishi and

Nakajima Experimental 7-Shi Carrier Attack Aircraft (B3N1)

Nakajima in April 1932 for a new carrier attack bomber to replace the ill-reputed Mitsubishi Type 89 Carrier Attack Aircraft. The Nakajima design, which was the responsibility of Takao Yoshida, was far from conventional in that this non-staggered biplane had its wings attached to the fuselage in both gull and inverted-gull wing fashion, forming an X at the fuselage. Its non-retractable undercarriage was attached to the lower wing at the bottom of the gull attachment-point. Saddle-type fuel tanks were fitted on the sides of the fuselage as on the Chance Vought influenced Type 90-2 Reconnaissance Seaplane and the Type 90-2 Carrier Fighter.

Two prototypes were built in 1933 with the short designation B3N1, and delivered to the Navy for evaluation but they failed to win Navy approval. Mitsubishi submitted its 7-Shi Carrier Attack Aircraft but it crashed on take off due to engine failure. Because of these failings, the Navy began with a new design competition for a 9-Shi Carrier Attack Aircraft.

This was a time when the major aircraft companies, Mitsubishi, Nakajima, Aichi and Kusho, were attempting to develop a three-seat carrier-based aircraft, but because of the increase in size and weight of these aircraft, a suitable powerplant remained a problem. For the Nakajima entry the company used the new 700hp Nakajima Hikari, but at this early stage it had yet to achieve reliability.

Single-engine biplane carrier attack bomber. Fuselage of welded steel tube construction, metal frame wings, with fabric covering. Rearward folding wings for stowage. Crew of three; pilot, bombardier/navigator and radio operator/gunner.

700hp Nakajima Hikari 2 nine-cylinder air-cooled radial engine, driving a fixed-pitch three-bladed metal propeller.

One dorsal flexible 7.7mm machine-gun. Bomb load: One 800kg torpedo, or one 800kg bomb, or one 500kg bomb, or two 250kg bombs or equivalent.

Span 14m (45ft 11¼in); length 10m (32ft 9½in); height 3.80m (12ft 5½in); wing area 50sq m (538.213sq ft).

Empty weight 2,000kg (4,409lb); loaded weight 3,800kg (8,377lb); wing loading 76kg/sq m (15.5lb/sq ft); power loading 5.4kg/hp (11.9lb/hp).

Maximum speed 120kt (138mph); minimum speed 50kt (57.5mph); climb to 3,000m (9,843ft) in 12min; service ceiling 5,500m (18,044ft); endurance 6hr.

Two built in 1933.

Experimental 7-Shi Special Bomber

Taking into consideration the fatal crash of the Experimental 6-Shi Special Bomber, the 7-Shi was a cautious redesign of its stagger-wing predecessor. Presumably, a more conventional biplane configuration was adopted in the new aircraft. Designers were again Navy engineer Jun-ichiro Nagahata and Nakajima's Ryozo Yamamoto.

One prototype was built in 1933 and delivered to the Navy. Evaluation revealed that further improvements were necessary, causing the design to be deferred to the 8-Shi Special Bomber competition.

Single-engine carrier dive-bomber biplane. Metal framework construction with fabric covering. Rearward folding wings for stowage. Crew of two in open cockpits.

460-580hp Nakajima Kotobuki 2-kai-1 nine-cylinder air-cooled radial, driving a fixed-pitch two-bladed metal propeller.

One forward firing fixed 7.7mm machine-gun and one dorsal flexible 7.7mm machine-gun. Bomb load: 250kg (550lb).

Span 11m (36ft 1in); length 8.50m (27ft 10½in); height 3.50m (11ft 5¾in); wing area 30sq m (322.927sq ft).

Empty weight 1,500kg (3,307lb); loaded weight 2,300kg (5,070lb); wing loading 76.7kg/sq m (15.7lb/sq ft); power loading 5kg/hp (11lb/hp).

Maximum speed 130kt (149.6mph) at 3,000m (9,843ft); minimum speed 50kt (57.5mph); climb to 3,000m (9,843ft) in 10min; service ceiling 6,500m (21,325ft); range 450nm (518sm).

One built in 1933.

Navy Fokker Reconnaissance Aircraft (C2N1 and 2)

Because the Nakajima-built Fokker Super Universal was considered a very practical passenger transport, having been used by Nihon Koku Yuso KK since 1931, it was regarded as having many applications for the Army and Navy. In May 1933 the Navy officially adopted this aircraft as both a landplane and seaplane with some structural changes as part of the Navy specifications.

These aeroplanes became the Fokker Land-based Reconnaissance Aircraft, as the C2N1, and the Fokker Reconnaissance Seaplane, C2N2. About 20 aircraft were built for the Navy in these configurations during 1933 and 1934. Basically, the structure was the same as the civil version, but the cabin area was extended approximately one metre rearward, with an additional window. Nakajima Kotobuki 1 and 2 engines powered these aircraft and were the latest power-plants for the Super Universals.

The aircraft were equipped for geographical observation and aerial photography and used primarily for aerial survey, but they served as transports and liaison aircraft for which they were originally designed. Their Army counterparts were the Army Type 95-2 Trainer (Ki-6), and the Ambulance Aircraft, but with different engines and equipment.

Because of their relatively low speed and short range, they were unsuited for the combat role, so their use was mostly limited to within Japan. They served this purpose well and retained a good reputation as multi-purpose aircraft.

Single-engine high-wing cantilever monoplane. Welded steel tube fuselage with fabric covering, wooden wing structure covered with fabric and plywood. Crew of two with variable interior configurations.

460hp Nakajima Kotobuki 1 or 2 nine-cylinder air-cooled radial engine, driving a fixed-pitch two-bladed metal propeller.

Span 15.43m (50ft 7½in); length 11.09m (36ft 4½in); height 2.819m (9ft

Nakajima Navy Fokker Reconnaissance Aircraft (C2N1).

3in); wing area 34.37sq m (369.967 sq ft).

Empty weight 1,720kg (3,792lb); loaded weight 2,700kg (5,952lb); wing loading 78.6kg/sq m (16.1lb/sq ft); power loading 6.43kg/hp (14.1lb/hp).

Maximum speed 125kt (143.85mph); cruising speed 100kt (115mph); climb to 2,000m (6,562ft) in 17min 53sec; service ceiling 6,000m (19,685ft).

Twenty built in 1933–1934.

Navy Type 95 Carrier Fighter (A4N1)
(Company designation YM)

As the new and more powerful Nakajima Hikari 1 became both reliable and available, a new generation of aircraft was designed around it. Using this engine to improve fighter performance over that of the Type 90 Carrier Fighter, Nakajima and engineer Shigenobu Mori completely redesigned the earlier aeroplane in 1933.

The design was completed in the spring of 1934 and the first prototype was finished by the autumn. In appearance, it closely resembled the Type 90-3 Carrier Fighter, but a noticeable difference was the larger diameter engine which was also cowled. Slipper-type fuel tanks could be attached inboard beneath each lower wing when required to extend range and to provide flotation in the event of an emergency alighting.

The development of this new aircraft took longer than expected,

Nakajima Navy Type 95 Carrier Fighter (A4N1).

and when it was officially accepted by the Navy in January 1936, the next generation fighter, the Mitsubishi 9-Shi Single-seat Fighter, was already being developed. However, the Type 95 was put into production and served as the immediate replacement for the Type 90 Carrier Fighter. Performance improvement was noticeable over that of its predecessor, increasing maximum speed from 158kt to 190kt.

At the time of the Sino-Japanese Conflict, these new fighters were used for air defence over Japanese occupied bases. They also served as short-range scout aircraft, and, with two 60kg bombs, they undertook the close air support role as well. During that conflict in 1936-37 many of these fighters were donated as *Hokoku-go*. One in particular that was identified on the Chinese front was *Hokoku Dai-86-go, Jogakusei-go*, meaning Hokoku No.86 donated by high school girl students.

The Type 95 Carrier Fighter was the last of the biplane fighters for the Navy. A mere ten months after the official acceptance of this aircraft, the low-wing monoplane fighter, the Mitsubishi 9-Shi, became the replacement as the Type 96 Carrier fighter. These were the A5Ms, with Allied code-name Claude, that saw service in the early stages of the Pacific War. Being replaced in front-line service, the Type 95 Carrier Fighters were then assigned to training units as fighter-trainers.

Single-engine carrier-based fighter biplane. Metal structure with fabric covering. Pilot in open cockpit.

670-730hp Nakajima Hikari 1 nine-cylinder air-cooled radial engine, driving a Hamilton Standard fixed-pitch two-bladed metal propeller.

Two forward-firing fixed 7.7mm machine-guns. Bomb load: Two 30 or 60kg (66-132lb) bombs.

Span 10m (32ft 9½in); length 6.64m (21ft 9¼in); height 3.07m (10ft 1in); wing area 22.89sq m (246.393sq ft).

Empty weight 1,276kg (2,813lb); loaded weight 1,760kg (3,880lb); wing loading 76.9kg/sq m (15.74lb/sq ft); power loading 2.62kg/hp (5.7lb/hp).

Maximum speed 190kt (218.6mph) at 3,200m (10,500ft); cruising speed 126kt (145mph); climb to 3,000m (9,843ft) in 3min 30sec; service ceiling 7,740m (25,393ft); range 457nm (526sm); endurance 3½hr.

221 built from 1935 to 1940.

Experimental 8-Shi Carrier Two-seat Fighter
(Company designation NAF-2)

The successor to the 6-Shi Experimental Carrier Two-seat Fighter, the NAF-1, was the 8-Shi which was known within the company as the NAF-2. This was designed for a new competition for two-seat fighters in 1933 but limited to only

Nakajima Experimental 8-Shi Carrier Two-seat Fighter.

Mitsubishi and Nakajima. Because the earlier aircraft had sustained damage during tests, its good and bad qualities were never fully evaluated. Picking up where that project ended, Nakajima engineer and designer Kiyoshi Akegawa continued with the two-seat fighter concept but created an entirely new design.

Two prototypes were built, the first being completed in March 1934 and the other a few months later. The outline of the new aeroplane was considerably refined. The aerofoil was changed from the M-6 to the USA-27 and the upper wing was swept back. One prototype had conventional N interplane struts, while the other had I struts. The smoothly faired undercarriage was of the single-leg configuration. The structure was strengthened, and emphasis was placed upon manoeuvrability and controllability. Both Nakajima prototypes had the Kotobuki 2 engine.

During the evaluation between aircraft of the two companies, the Mitsubishi entry disintegrated in flight. The pilot safely parachuted, but the rear seat observer died in the crash, thus influencing the Navy in bringing further development competition to an end. The Navy remained undecided about the two-seat concept and refrained from creating a category for this type. As a result, the two prototypes of the Nakajima 8-Shi Two-seat Fighters were later released to the *Asahi Shimbun*. They were known as the AF Communications Aircraft, and the one with I interplane struts was registered J-BAAC.

Single-engine two-seat carrier fighter biplane. Metal frame construction with fabric covering. Crew of two in open cockpits.

460-580hp Nakajima Kotobuki 2 nine-cylinder air-cooled radial engine, driving a Nakajima-Hamilton Standard fixed-pitch two-bladed metal propeller.

Two forward-firing fixed 7.7mm machine-guns and one dorsal flexible 7.7mm machine-gun.

Span 10.3m (33ft 9½in); length 7.26m (23ft 9¾in); height 2.85m (9ft 4¼in); wing area 26.35sq m (283.638sq ft).

Empty weight 1,233 kg (2,718lb); loaded weight 1,710kg (3,770lb); wing loading 65kg/sq m (13.3lb/sq ft); power loading 3.7kg/hp (8.1lb/hp).

Maximum speed 162kt (186.4mph) at 3,000m (9,843ft); cruising speed 100kt (115mph) at 3,000m (9,843ft); climb to 3,000m (9,843ft) in 9min 40sec; service ceiling 6,250m (20,505 ft); range 459nm (528sm); endurance 4½hr.

Two built beginning in March 1934.

Note: Weights and performance for civil conversion.

Experimental 8-Shi Special Bomber (D2N1)
(Company designation RZ)

The 8-Shi Special Bomber project in 1933 was a competition between Aichi and a joint effort by Nakajima and Navy Kusho. Designer of the earlier Kusho Nakajima 6-Shi and 7-Shi Special Bombers, Junichiro Nagahata, now an engineer at the Naval Air Arsenal, was retained as chief designer for this 8-Shi project as well, working again with Ryozo Yamamoto of Nakajima who was in charge of production.

Two prototypes were built in 1934. When compared with the earlier 7-Shi design, this later aircraft had an increase in wing area and an improved strut-bracing system for both the wings and the undercarriage. Flight evaluations were disappointing, showing it to be poor in stability and generally inferior to Aichi's D1A1, a development of the Heinkel He 66. The Aichi D1A1 was the aircraft accepted by the Navy as the Type 94 Carrier Bomber (denoting 1934 acceptance), and the Nakajima project was therefore cancelled, making this the last attempt by Nakajima to produce an experimental biplane carrier dive-bomber. From this time, Aichi became the exclusive builder of carrier dive-bombers for the Japanese Navy.

For the competition for the 8-Shi Experimental Special Bomber, Naval Air Headquarters listed the following designs and modifications. Kusho D2Y1, Aichi D1A1, and the Nakajima D2N1, 2, and 3; the last being modifications of the two prototypes.

Single-engine biplane dive-bomber. Metal structure with fabric covering. Wings folded rearward for stowage. Crew of two in open cockpits.

460-580hp Nakajima Kotobuki 2-kai-1 nine-cylinder air-cooled radial engine, driving a fixed-pitch two-bladed metal propeller.

Two forward-firing fixed 7.7mm machine-guns and one dorsal flexible 7.7mm machine-gun.

Span 11.50m (37ft 8¾in); length 9m (29ft 6¼in); height 3.50m (11ft 5¾in); wing area 35sq m (376.749sq ft).

Empty weight 1,500kg (3,307lb); loaded weight 2,500kg (5,511lb); wing loading 71.4kg/sq m (14.6lb/sq ft); power loading 5.4kg/hp (11.9lb/hp).

Maximum speed 140kt (161mph) at 3,000m (9,843ft); climb to 3,000m (9,843ft) in 11min; service ceiling 6,500m (21,325ft).

Two built from March 1934.

Experimental 9-Shi Single-seat Fighter
(Company designation PA-kai)

Following the failure of the 7-Shi carrier-based fighter competition between Nakajima and Mitsubishi, the Navy placed orders again with both companies in February 1934 for their designs of a 9-Shi single-seat fighter. Specifications developed by Lieut-Cdr Hideo Sawai of the Engineering Department of Naval Air Headquarters were simple in that they specified only the desired speed, rate of climb, fuel capacity, armament, radio, maximum dimensions, and only described a 'single-seat' fighter instead of 'carrier-based' fighter. It was the Naval Air Headquarters intention to maximize this fighter's capability in speed and climb, and not have it restricted by other requirements for carrier operations.

Following the procedure Nakajima had followed with the earlier 7-Shi carrier-based fighter competition by submitting a modified version of the Army Type 91 Fighter, Nakajima built a companion to what it was developing for the Army as the Ki-11 as its Navy entry in the 9-Shi Single-seat Fighter competition. This was known to Nakajima as its PA-kai

and, like the Ki-11, looked very much like the Boeing P-26. As with the Ki-11, this design was produced by Yasushi Koyama and Shinroku Inoue. The construction of the four prototypes of the Ki-11 and the one 9-Shi Navy fighter was completed in 1935. The difference between the two types was primarily in the use of the 560hp Kotobuki 5 that was specified for the Navy aeroplane, along with cockpit configuration to Navy standards.

This design for the 9-Shi fighter produced a sturdy aeroplane with a wire-braced low wing and faired non-retractable undercarriage. It achieved a maximum speed of 220kt (253mph) and had excellent manoeuvrability. But the competing Mitsubishi 9-Shi fighter showed better performance and was further developed into the Type 96 Carrier Fighter through pre-production models with various engines. This became the well-known and the world's first operational carrier-based monoplane fighter, with Allied code-name Claude. Followed by Mitsubishi's Zero fighter, this Nakajima 9-Shi prototype was the company's last attempt at creating a Navy fighter.

For technical data, see Nakajima Army Ki-11.

Nakajima Experimental 9-Shi Single-seat Fighter. (Shorzoe Abe).

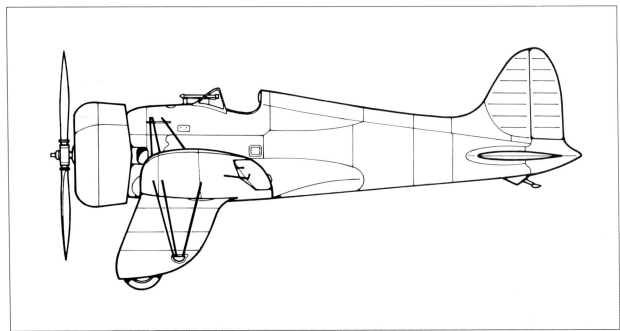

Nakajima Experimental LB-2 Long-range Attack Aircraft.

Experimental LB-2 Long-range Attack Aircraft (Nakajima-type Long-range Land-based Medium Attack Aircraft)
(Company designation LB-2)

At the time this aeroplane was being developed by Nakajima, it was considered out of character for that company. During this development period, Nakajima was absorbed in manufacturing the Type 90 Carrier Fighter, Type 90 Reconnaissance Seaplane, Type 91 Fighter, Type 94 Reconnaissance Aircraft, Fokker Super Universal, and P-1 mailplane, all of which were single-engine aircraft. Mitsubishi was the exclusive builder of large Army aircraft, with technical assistance from Junkers for the Type 92 and Type 93 Heavy Bombers, and the Type 93 Twin-engine Light bomber. The Navy had also developed long-range attack bombers such as the Type 93, Type 95, and the Type 96 which was a development of the 8-Shi Special Reconnaissance Aircraft, all being designed and manufactured by Mitsubishi except for the Type 95 which was built by the Hiro Naval Arsenal.

Nakajima's attempt at this large aircraft market began with licence-manufacturing rights for the Douglas DC-2. From this short but practical experience came the concept and design of the LB-2, a designation that stood for Long-range Bomber number 2, the number 1 being a project that was never completed. There were reports that the LB-2 was classified as the 9-Shi Land-based Attack Aircraft in competition with a similar Mitsubishi entry of that type, but this is unconfirmed.

Chief designer for the aeroplane was Ken-ichi Matsumura and this was the first all-metal twin-engined monoplane designed by Nakajima. It was similar in appearance to the Douglas B-18 and B-23, but had a more tapered wing. The influence of Douglas and Northrop designs was apparent in the wing to centre section attachment technique using an external flange covered with a fairing. The centre and outer wing panels of ALC17ST aluminium with a B-2209/2218 aerofoil employed the structural design of the Douglas wing, particularly in having three centre-section spars that continued through the fuselage. This provided space for the fuel tanks within these wing compartments. The undercarriage was a close match to that of the DC-2, but 20 percent stronger to meet planned increase in loaded weight. Like the early Douglas transports, this undercarriage was retracted hydraulically by a manually-operated pump.

The fuselage was of all-metal monocoque construction with a bomb bay located under the wing centre-section. Above the wing was the cabin passageway and auxiliary fuel tank. The LB-2 had a larger fuselage than the DC-2 but the weights of the two fuselages were nearly the same. This is an indication of the quickly learned practical weight-saving technique that was applied by the Nakajima engineers in this design. Flexible gun turrets were located at the top and centre of the fuselage, and one retractable gun station was in the underside behind the entry door.

The LB-2 was completed in March 1936 at the Ohta plant and was evaluated by the Navy. By this time, the Mitsubishi G3M held the Navy's interest, having helped to develop the project from the beginning. As a consequence, Nakajima's LB-2 was not accepted by the

Navy, and a year later, after considerable modification, it was sold to Manshu Koku KK (Manchurian Airways Company Ltd) as a long-range transport.

For this conversion, the bombardier's section in the nose was converted for baggage stowage. The bomb bay was closed and contained the auxiliary fuel tank formerly on top of the centre section. In its place were seats providing accommodation for six passengers. The crew consisted of two pilots, flight engineer and radio operator.

Before entering commercial service, tests were made with the aircraft by the Aviation Bureau in the spring of 1937. When delivered to Manshu Koku KK, it was called the Nakajima Twin-engine Transport, given the name *Akatsuki-go* (*Dawn*). At that time, the vice-president of Manshu Koku, Tsuneo Kodama, was planning to develop the shortest route between Asia and Europe by flying over the Tien Shan mountain range in China for which two imported Heinkel He 116 four-engined transports were originally intended. But the chance was lost for both the He 116s and the converted LB-2 because of the outbreak of the Sino-Japanese Conflict and Nomonghan Incident. Since this plan had to be abandoned, the *Akatsuki-go* was parked at North Airfield at Mukden (also Shen-yang, China), until about 1941, at which time it was scrapped.

Twin-engined all-metal monoplane bomber and later transport, with retractable undercarriage. Crew of six or seven. As transport, crew of four and six passengers.

Two 700-840hp Nakajima Hikari 2 nine-cylinder air-cooled radial engines, driving Hamilton Standard two-position three-bladed metal propellers.

Span 26.685m (87ft 6½in); length 19.33m (63ft 5in); height 5.45m (17ft 10½in); wing area 97.96sq m (1,054.674 sq ft).

Empty weight 5,750kg (12,676lb); loaded weight 9,630kg (21,230lb); wing loading 98.3kg/sq m (20.1lb/sq ft); power loading 6.88kg/hp (15.1lb/hp).

Maximum speed 177kt (203.69mph)

at 1,850m (6,069ft); cruising speed 130kt (149.6mph), 2,600m (8,530ft); climb to 3,000m (9,843ft) in 8min 45sec; range 6,000km (3,728sm).

One built in March 1936.

Note: Dimensions, weights and performance for transport version.

Experimental 9-Shi Carrier Attack Aircraft (B4N1)
(Company designation Q)

At the beginning of the design competition for the 9-Shi Carrier Attack Aircraft in 1934, the Navy reflected upon the good results that had been achieved in 1923 with the Mitsubishi Type 13 aircraft. The competition, in 1932, did not prove a success, for the 7-Shi Carrier Attack Aircraft was plagued by failures by both the Nakajima and Mitsubishi designs. As a result of their inadequacies, the Navy began its own development programme in February 1934 for a replacement aircraft.

However, the Navy changed its policy and reinstated the competition practice, selecting Nakajima and Mitsubishi for a 9-Shi Carrier Attack Aircraft development. For Nakajima the design of the new aircraft was shared by Takao Yoshida and Yasuo Fukuda. Two prototypes were completed in 1936, one powered by a Kotobuki 3 engine, and the other by the Hikari 1.

At the time of the 9-Shi design, in 1934, other major countries were developing all-metal low-wing monoplanes, a concept already recognized in Japan for carrier fighters and land-based attack bombers. But for this carrier-based attack bomber, the Navy decided to stay with the obsolete but proven biplane concept to achieve the required strength for this type of aircraft. This configuration easily facilitated folding the wings, a desirable feature for carrier stowage.

Nakajima and Mitsubishi delivered their prototypes to the Navy for testing within the time schedule. As in the case of the previous 7-Shi competition, the Kusho aeroplane was late in being completed, giving the designers the opportunity to incorporate design features noted in the two competing prototypes. As a result, the Kusho B4Y1 aircraft had the best combination of design features and was declared the winner in November 1936. Both the Kusho B4Y1 and the Nakajima B4N1 had quite similar exterior lines. The winning Kusho design, however, became the Type 96 Carrier Attack Aircraft. Production of this new Navy bomber was allocated to Nakajima, Mitsubishi and Hiro Naval Arsenal. The Allies expected to meet these aircraft in combat at the outset of the Pacific War, and gave them the code-name Jean. By that time however, only a few remained in use for training.

Single-engine biplane carrier-borne torpedo bomber. Fuselage of welded steel tube construction with wooden frame wings and fabric covering. Rearward folding wings for stowage. Crew of three in open cockpits.

660-820hp Nakajima Hikari 1 nine-cylinder air-cooled radial engine, driving a fixed-pitch three bladed metal propeller.

One forward-firing fixed 7.7mm machine-gun and one dorsal flexible 7.7mm machine-gun. Bomb load: One 800kg (1,763lb) torpedo, or one 500kg (1,102lb) bomb, or two 250kg (551lb) bombs, or six 30kg (66lb) bombs.

Two built in 1936.

Navy Type 97 Carrier Reconnaissance Aircraft (C3N1)
(Company designation S)

In the summer of 1935, Nakajima entered into two simultaneous design proposals for Navy carrier-borne aircraft. The first in this 10-Shi series of aircraft was the carrier-borne reconnaissance aeroplane for which Nakajima was the sole contender. The companion aeroplane was the carrier-borne attack-bomber for which Mitsubishi was a competitor. These two designs by Nakajima were quite similar except that the reconnaissance aircraft had less wing area than the bomber and had a faired non-retractable undercarriage. The bomber became the Type 97 Carrier Attack Aircraft, B5N1, that fought in the Pacific War under the Allied code-name Kate.

Chief designer for the reconnaissance aircraft was Yasuo Fukuda. For this low-wing cantilever monoplane design, the Hikari engine was selected, although the Navy would have allowed the Mitsubishi-built Kinsei engine to have been used. Other requirements were for a wing span of less than 14m, a length of not more than 10m, and a crew of three. Maximum speed was to exceed 200kt, minimum speed to be less than 60kt and range more than 1,200nm. The necessities of excellent visibility for deck and night operations were also required. The wings were to fold for carrier stowage, and consideration of buoyancy was a design factor for emergency ditchings.

The design and manufacture of the prototype was undertaken at the Experimental Factory of Nakajima at Ohta along with the 10-Shi Carrier Attack Aircraft. Many new design concepts were interchanged between these two aircraft as they were being developed. By October 1936, the first prototype of the C3N1 reconnaissance aeroplane was completed. The second in this series soon followed and both were delivered to the Navy for evaluation. Testing, with occasional modifications, continued for about a year until it was officially adopted as the Type 97 Carrier Reconnaissance Aircraft in September 1937.

Soon after the prototype of the 10-Shi Carrier Attack Aircraft was delivered and both types completed their carrier qualifications, they were sent to central China for tactical evaluation. After two months of operations, the B5N1 was officially adopted and became the Type 97 Carrier Attack Aircraft. It also served in its secondary mission of scouting so that it could double for the Type 97 Carrier Reconnaissance Aircraft, and as a consequence the C3N1 was not put in production.

For a considerable time from 1937 both of the C3N1 prototypes were used as land-based reconnaissance aircraft in the Shanghai and Hankow areas.

Nakajima Navy Type 97 Carrier Reconnaissance Aircraft (C3N1).

Single-engine low-wing reconnaissance monoplane. All-metal construction. Upward folding wings for stowage. Crew of three in covered cockpit; pilot, observer and radio/gunner.

750-840hp Nakajima Hikari 2 nine-cylinder air-cooled radial engine, driving a constant-speed three-bladed metal propeller.

One forward-firing fixed 7.7mm machine-gun and one dorsal flexible 7.7mm machine-gun.

Span 13.95m (45ft 9in); length 10m (32ft 9½in), wing area 30sq m (322.927 sq ft).

Empty weight 1,805kg (3,979lb); loaded weight 3,000kg (6,613lb); wing loading 100kg/sq m (20.4lb/sq ft); power loading 3.57kg/hp (7.9lb/hp).

Maximum speed 209kt (240.5mph); service ceiling 6,670m (21,885ft), range 1,230nm (1,415sm).

Two built in 1936.

Experimental 11-Shi Carrier Bomber (D3N1)
(Company designation DB)

In 1936 the Navy initiated a competition for a new 11-Shi low-wing monoplane carrier bomber to replace the biplane Type 96 Carrier Bomber built by Aichi. Formerly, these had been classed as Tokushu Bakugekiki or Special Bomber by the Navy, but its new designation was Kanjo Bakugekiki which meant Carrier Bomber.* The manufacturers involved were Aichi, Mitsubishi and Nakajima.

Mitsubishi abandoned its project in the summer of 1937 after the mock-up was completed, leaving only Aichi and Nakajima in the competition. Chief designer Ryozo Yamamoto led the Nakajima team

*See Kusho 6-Shi Special Bomber for further explanation.

for the new aeroplane. They drew a very similar airframe to its forerunners, 10-Shi Carrier Attack Aircraft (B5N1) and 10-Shi Carrier Reconnaissance Aircraft (C3N1), but with a unique undercarriage design. The undercarriage rotated 90-degrees to rest flat against the bottom of the wing when retracted rearward. For the dive, it was to be extended with the wheel rotated 90 degrees to the line of flight to serve as a dive-brake. During the development of the prototype the Navy changed its required terminal dive speed from 240kt to 200kt. At this lower speed the drag of the undercarriage was insufficient and a pair of perforated spoilers were added beneath the wing to serve as dive-brakes.

The first prototype was completed in March 1937 having the Navy designation D3N1. The test period was protracted because completion of the second prototype was not possible until early 1939 and the third prototype only followed that autumn. Each went through a series of changes based upon discoveries made from the earlier models. However, by December 1939, Nakajima lost the competition, for none of these prototypes was able to surpass the performance of Aichi's second prototype which was developed into the D3A1, to become better known by the Allied

Nakajima Experimental 11-Shi Carrier Bomber (D3N1). (Shorzoe Abe).

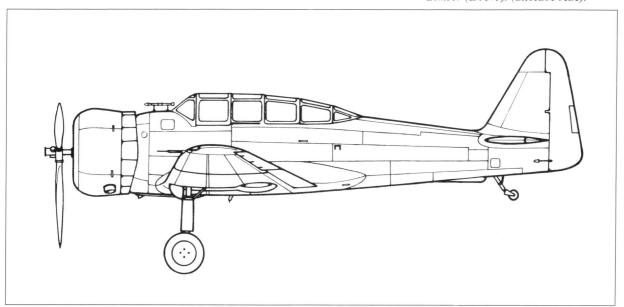

code-name Val.

Although this Nakajima design failed to gain Navy acceptance as a dive-bomber, these aeroplanes were paid for by the Navy. At the request of Nakajima, the second prototype stayed with the company and served as a test vehicle for the Sakae and Homare engines and their related accessories. The testing of thrust-type exhaust stacks was undertaken with this aeroplane, beginning in the spring of 1941. The aeroplane survived until the end of the Pacific War, yet no photographs are known to exist.

Single-engine low-wing monoplane carrier-borne dive-bomber with retractable undercarriage. All-metal construction. Upward folding wings for stowage. Crew of two in covered cockpit.

660-820hp Nakajima Hikari 1-kai nine-cylinder air-cooled radial engine, driving a controllable-pitch two-bladed metal propeller, later changed to a constant-speed three-bladed metal unit.

Two forward-firing fixed 7.7mm machine-guns and one dorsal flexible 7.7mm machine-gun. Bomb load: One 250kg (551lb) bomb and two 30kg (66lb) bombs.

Span 14.50m (47ft 7in); length 8.80m (28ft 10½in); height 2.80m (9ft 2¼in) tail down; wing area 34sq m (365.984sq ft).

Empty weight 1,800kg (3,968lb); loaded weight 3,400kg (7,495lb); wing loading 100kg/sq m (20.4lb/sq ft); power loading 5.15kg/hp (11.4lb/hp). Maximum speed 190kt (218.65 mph) at 3,000m (9,843ft); cruising speed 140kt (161mph); landing speed 60kt (69mph); climb to 3,000m (9,843ft) in 8min; service ceiling 7,000m (22,965ft); range 820nm (944sm); endurance 6hr.

Three built from 1937 to 1939.

Experimental 12-Shi Two-seat Reconnaissance Seaplane (E12N1)

In June 1937, the Navy asked Nakajima and Aichi to design and build sample aircrafts as the 12-Shi catapult-launched two-seat reconnaissance seaplanes. In addition to the reconnaissance mission, the 12-Shi aeroplanes were to be capable of anti-shipping dive-bombing with a 250kg bomb, with a diving angle of 60 degrees.

Nakajima's design work on the new aeroplane began in the summer of 1937 with Shinroku Inoue as chief designer. To make possible the added dive-bombing ability, Aichi and Nakajima adopted the twin-float configuration to facilitate carrying the bomb. A feature that Nakajima developed was a bomb displacement arm that swung the bomb clear of the propeller arc before release. A recess in the underside of the fuselage housed half the bomb to reduce drag.

Two prototypes of all-metal construction were completed in the summer of 1938. These were low-wing monoplanes having tapered wings and the two floats supported by conventional N-struts and diagonal struts. The large slotted-flaps were a new feature at the time in that they added lift for alighting as well as catapult-launchings.

Because of this practical design, the aeroplane had considerable advantages in performance over the earlier biplane reconnaissance seaplanes, namely Nakajima's own Type 95 Reconnaissance Seaplane (Dave). However, this new design

lacked the controllability and stability that the Navy expected. As a consequence, these aeroplanes, known as the E12N1, were unacceptable to the Navy as was the competing Aichi E12A1. Aichi had placed considerable confidence in its E12A1, and continued with its development as a three-seat aircraft. This became the Type O Three-seat Reconnaissance Seaplane, E13A1, to become known by its Allied code-name Jake. For Nakajima, however, the E12N1 was its last reconnaissance seaplane.

Single-engine twin-float low-wing reconnaissance monoplane. All metal construction. Upward folding wings for stowage. Crew of two in covered cockpits.

850-870hp Mitsubishi Zuisei fourteen-cylinder air-cooled double-row radial engine, driving a constant-speed two-bladed metal propeller.

Two forward-firing fixed 7.7mm machine-guns and one dorsal flexible 7.7mm machine-gun. Bomb load: One 250kg (551lb) bomb, or two 60kg (132lb) bombs.

Span 13m (42ft 8in); length 10.50m (34ft 5¼in); height 3.5m (11ft 5¾in); wing area 27.5sq m (296sq ft).

Empty weight 2,100kg (4,629lb); loaded weight 2,850kg (6,283lb); wing loading 103.6kg/sq m (21.2lb/sq ft); power loading 3.35kg/hp (7.3lb/hp).

Maximum speed 195kg (224.4mph) at 1,900m (6,233ft); cruising speed 150kt (172.6mph) at 2,000m (6,561ft); climb to 3,000m (9,843ft) in 5min; service ceiling 8,150m (26,738ft); range 575nm (661sm) endurance 3.8hr.

Two built in 1938.

Nakajima Experimental 12-Shi Two-seat Reconnaissance Seaplane (E12N1). (Shorzoe Ab ·

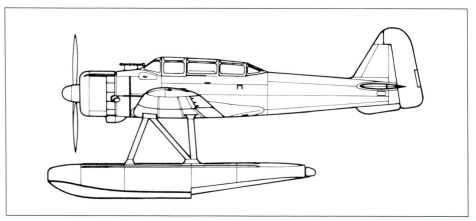

The mid-1930s was a time of great advancement in aircraft of Japanese manufacturers. It was a time that all-metal construction of cantilever low-wing monoplanes flourished with designs ranging from the 9-Shi to 11-Shi projects. Nakajima examples were the 10-Shi Carrier Reconnaissance (C3N1) by designer Fukuda, the 10-Shi Carrier Attack Aircraft (B5N1) by Nakamura, the 11-Shi Carrier Bomber (D3N1) by Yamamoto, and the PE Fighter (Ki-27) by Koyama. Although some of these did not develop beyond the prototype stage, others became the Type 97 Carrier Attack Aircraft (Kate) and the Type 97 Fighter (Nate) as the most advanced aircraft of their type throughout the world for their time period.

Nippi (Nihon Aeroplane Co Ltd) (Nihon Hikoki KK)

The Japanese Navy saw a need for an independent aircraft factory to serve it when called upon. To generally fill this requirement, the Nihon Hikoki KK, better known as Nippi,* was established in October 1934 under the directorship of Rear Admiral (Reserve) Nagamasa Tada. To be near its primary customer, it was located at Tomioka-cho, Isogo-ku, Yokohama, adjacent to the Yokohama Naval Kokutai and Tokyo Bay from which it planned to operate the seaplanes it intended to produce. In October 1935, however, it began by accepting the sub-contracting repair work of three Navy aircraft wrecked at Kasumigaura, the location of the First Naval Air Arsenal. This was soon followed by contracts for the manufacture of wings and other components of aircraft ordered by the Navy.

As a sideline, the company purchased the manufacturing licence from France for the Pou du Ciel, an unorthodox single-seat light aeroplane for the amateur pilot market. This project ended soon after because of the frequent accidents, not only involving Nippi-built aircraft but those of other countries. Another project was the conversion by Nippi of a Supermarine Southampton twin-engined flying-boat that had been imported in 1936 and made into a 16-passenger transport. This large flying-boat was operated by Nippon Koku Yuso Kenkyusho as J-BAID *Kirin-go.*

Starting in 1937, the company transferred its main interest from repair and conversion to that of aircraft manufacture. With this change, the company was registered on the Navy's procurement list as an airframe manufacturer and began sharing the Navy production schedule with Kawanishi. In June 1937 Nippi received an order to build the Kawanishi Navy Type 94 Reconnaissance Seaplane (E7K1 and 2), later to be known by the Allies as Alf. By September 1938 the company was placed under the control of the Navy, and the following December it was recognized by the Minister of Communication which allowed it to obtain additional contracts, sharing Navy production with still more aircraft companies.

Nippi NH-1 Hibari Light Aeroplane

In October 1935 Nippi acquired the manufacturing licence for the Pou du Ciel (Flying Flea) designed by Henri Mignet. This licence was negotiated through the director of the Japan-France Culture Association, Motokazu Sakurazawa.

Two imported samples were assembled and flown for the first time at Haneda on 10 February, 1936. A licence-manufactured aircraft made its first flight on 6 March of that year and no difference in performance was noticed from that of the French models. Although the prototype Pou du Ciel was powered by a 30hp AVA engine, the two imported aircraft as well as those manufactured in Japan used the 27hp Poinsard B engines imported from France.

The configuration of this single-seat aircraft was unique in that it had two wings of different span, in tandem and that the rear wing also served as the tailplane. It had neither elevators nor ailerons, control in pitch being maintained by changing the incidence of the forward wing, and directional control by the rudder alone. Although this control was rather unusual, it was advertised as a safety feature that allowed anyone to fly the aircraft.

In Japan it was called the NH-1 Hibari (Skylark) Model 1. Nippi expected a large volume of sales in the civil market and priced the aeroplanes at approximately 1,200 yen each. The first fifteen Hibaris were given registration letters assigned by the Aviation Bureau of the Department of Communications. Of these, two were sold to the

Nippi NH-1 Hibari Light Aeroplane.

Asahi Shimbun, and several to private buyers. Before long, the Pou du Ciel received adverse publicity because of numerous fatal accidents, and the type soon lost favour or was banned. As a result, Nippi suspended manufacture after producing twenty-five.

Single-engine tandem-wing sports aeroplane. Wooden structure with ply-covered fuselage and fabric-covered wings and rudder. Pilot in open cockpit.

25-27hp Poinsard B four-cylinder air-cooled horizontal-opposed engine, driving a two-bladed wooden propeller.

Span 6m (19ft 8¼in) front, 4m (13ft 1½in) rear; length 4m (13ft 1½in); height 1.74m (5ft 8½in); wing area 11.9sq m (128.093sq ft), 7.50 and 4.4sq m (80.731 and 47.362sq ft) respectively.

Empty weight 133kg (293lb); loaded weight 224kg (493lb); wing loading 18.82kg/sq m (3.84lb/sq ft); power loading 8.3kg/hp (18.3lb/hp).

Maximum speed 56kt (64.48mph); cruising speed 46.9kt (54mph); landing speed 21.5kt (24.74mph); climb to 1,000m (3,280ft) in 12min; service ceiling 1,800m (5,905ft); range 69nm (79sm); endurance 3hr.

Twenty-five built, beginning in March 1936.

Experimental 12-Shi Primary Seaplane Trainer (K8Ni1)

In 1937 the Navy placed orders for a 12-Shi Experimental Primary Seaplane Trainer with Kawanishi, Watanabe and Nippi, as a replacement for the Yokosho Type 90

Nippi Experimental 12-Shi Primary Trainer Seaplane (K8Ni1).

Primary Seaplane Trainer. One stipulation was that the new aircraft was to be powered by the 130hp Jimpu 2 engine.

This was the first time that Nippi designed and manufactured a new aeroplane of its own. Assigned to the task as chief designer was Yoshimoto Tajima, who used as the basic concept the Yokosho Type 90 Primary Seaplane Trainer, but dispensed with the bracing wires and used a new system of struts for attaching the twin-floats to the lower wing. During the mock-up stage and at the insistence of the Navy, however, the wing's cross-bracing wires were retained

The first prototype was completed in November 1938. Because of the company's lack of experience, too long was taken for the design and construction of the prototype, causing the firm to miss the specified completion date and be disqualified. When the already started second prototype was completed in January 1939, Nippi asked the Department of Flight Experiment at the Naval Air

Arsenal at Yokosuka to test the engineering and performance of its aircraft, to which the Navy agreed. During the test period from 29 February to 28 December, 1940, the Navy determined that the general requirements were met after several modifications, but there were still some difficulties with alighting and spin recovery.

Single-engine twin-float biplane trainer. Welded steel tube fuselage, with wooden structure wing, fabric covered. Student and instructor in open cockpits.

130-165hp Gasuden Jimpu 2 seven-cylinder air-cooled radial engine, driving a Kawanishi Model 2 two-bladed wooden propeller.

Span 10.806m (35ft 5½in); length 8.619m (28ft 3¼in); height 3.625m (11ft 11in); wing area 26sq m (279.87sq ft).

Empty weight 810kg (1,785lb); loaded weight 1,075kg (2,370lb); wing loading 41.35kg/sq m (8.4lb/sq ft); power loading 6.52kg/hp (14.3lb/hp).

Maximum speed 75.5kt (86.88mph) at 3,000m (9,843ft); take off and alighting speed 41.5kt (47.75mph); climb to 3,000m (9,843ft) in 27min 42sec; service ceiling 3,270m (10,728ft).

Two built in 1938-39.

Experimental 13-Shi Small Transport (L7P1)

In 1938, the Navy placed an order with Nippi for a small general purpose amphibian as its 13-Shi Small Transport to be used for personnel carriage and liaison duties. This was to be Nippi's second attempt at creating an aircraft of its own design. This type was proposed by Nagamasa Tada, executive direc-

Nippi Experimental 13-Shi Small Transport (L7P1).

tor of Nippi, and retired Navy Rear Admiral. He had been the manager of the Department of Science at the Naval Air Arsenal (Kusho), and therefore was able to put his proposal to the Naval Air Headquarters for the development of an amphibious transport.

Asaji Tsunashima was invited to be chief engineer for the project because he had considerable experience as a Naval assistant engineer with flying-boats at the Hiro Arsenal. In creating this design, Nippi relied to a large extent on the Fairchild XA-942B amphibian (LXF1), an example of which had been imported from the United States in 1936. It was intended that this would be an all-metal aircraft, but the plan was changed to use a wooden wing and this involved much time in re-engineering. Recognizing an overall increase in the weight of the aeroplane, Nippi proposed changing the wing aerofoil from the Sikorsky 23012 series to that of a Boeing series, but the Navy insisted that the design continue without any change because of the time factor. As a result, and as soon as the earlier K8Nil seaplane trainer project was completed, manufacture of the new amphibian began. This was given the short designation L7P1, using P for Nippi instead of Ni to avoid confusion with Nakajima.

Although begun in 1938, it was not until February 1942 that the first of two prototypes was completed. The aeroplane had a striking resemblance to the Sikorsky S-43, although smaller in size. Instead of being pylon mounted, the parasol wing was supported above the hull

by four struts. Two Nakajima Kotobuki 41 engines were installed in the wing leading edge. As with the S-43, the undercarriage retracted flush with the sides of the hull. The cabin provided seating for eight passengers, each with its own round window.

Test flights were made by Navy Commander Sukemitsu Itoh who pointed out the difficulties with water take offs. This was partially due to the increased weight caused by the wooden wing which in turn increased the stalling speed of the aircraft. In general, all other performance figures were close to those calculated. The aircraft was accepted by the Navy in 1943 as the L7P1, but it was never recognized as an official Navy type. This was the only Japanese-built amphibian.

Twin-engined parasol monoplane amphibian. All-metal stressed skin hull. Wooden wing with plywood skin. Retractable undercarriage with non-retractable tailwheel. Crew of three and eight passengers.

Two 680-710hp Nakajima Kotobuki 41 nine-cylinder air-cooled radial engines, driving constant-speed three-bladed metal propellers.

Span 19.60m (64ft 3½in); length 14m (45ft 11¼in); height 4.70m (15ft 5in); wing area 50.10sq m (539.29sq ft).

Empty weight 3,705kg (8,168lb); loaded weight 5,899kg (13,005lb); wing loading 117.7kg/sq m (24.1lb/sq ft); power loading 4.88kg/hp (10.7lb/hp).

Maximum speed 179.4kt (206.45 mph) at sea level; landing speed 59.7kt (68.7mph); climb to 3,000m (9,843ft) in 6min 51sec; service ceiling 7,100m

(23,293ft); endurance 6hr at 150kt.

Two built beginning in February 1942.

As production demands by the Navy for existing types continued to increase, Nippi again directed much of its efforts to building trainers designed by the Naval Air Arsenal. It remained a producer for the Navy throughout the Pacific War. Today, this company's name in English is Japan Aircraft Manufacturing Co Ltd.

Nozawa Aviation Research Institute (Nozawa Koku Kenkyusho)

This little-known company, established in 1939, was formerly the Aviation Department of Nozawa-gumi, a general construction company but also undertaking architectural work. Its aviation activities were located at Tachikawa, using the flying facilities of Susaki Airfield in Tokyo.

Nozawa Z-1 Light Aeroplane

In April 1939 the company created

Nozawa Z-1 Light Aeroplane, patterned closely on the Taylor J-2 Cub.

a light aeroplane which was a copy of the Taylorcraft J-2 Cub imported from the United States. It is not clear as to the rights of manufacture in Japan. With the exception of the Z-1's 40hp Continental A-40-4 engine, 3hp more than its American production counterpart with an A-40-3 engine, it was manufactured exclusively from Japanese materials.

The first flight was made by Suetomi Kumano on 2 August, 1940, at Susaki Airfield, the aeroplane carrying the registration J-BBGR. It was advertised that the manufacturing cost of the airplane was 30,000 yen, but lowered to 5,000 yen when mass-produced. However, for unrecorded reasons, production ended with this first and only prototype.

Single-engine strut-braced high-wing cabin monoplane. Steel tube fuselage and wooden wing and empennage with fabric covering.

Two seats in tandem

40hp Continental A-40-4 four-cylinder horizontally-opposed air-cooled engine, driving a two-bladed wooden propeller.

Span 10.731m (35ft 2½in); length 6.775m (22ft 2½in); height 2.088m (6fto 10¼in); wing area 16.6sq m (178.686sq ft).

Empty weight 255kg (562lb); loaded weight 441kg (972lb); wing loading 26.6kg/sq m (5.4lb/sq ft); power loading 11kg/hp (24.2lb/hp).

Maximum speed 76kt (87.5mph); cruising speed 58kt (66.7mph); landing speed 26kt (30mph); service ceiling 3,660m (12,007ft); range 184nm (212 sm).

One built in 1939.

Nozawa X-1
Light Aeroplane

Nozawa Koku Kenkyusho began another design for a light aeroplane in October 1940, this one being a two-seat low-wing cantilever monoplane. Chief designer was Saburo Tsuchihashi. Built at Tachikawa, the aircraft was completed in November 1941. It was termed a sports-trainer and embodied the latest light aeroplane technology. It had an inverted gull wing, allowing a shorter and simple single-strut non-retractable undercarriage. Landing flaps were incorporated into this design. Some of its features were unusual for light aircraft at that time, but it was planned to compete with the best in world markets.

The engine was the British 75hp Pobjoy R. Although this was an air-cooled radial engine, it had a single-stage reduction gear and propeller shaft located above the main crankshaft. The aerofoil used for the wing was the NACA 4418.

The first flight was made in December 1941 by company pilot Suetomi Kumano at the Furukawa Pilot Training Centre of the Aviation Bureau in Ibaragi Prefecture. Further developments were considerations for different types of engines but, with the start of the Pacific War, production was suspended after the single prototype. Registered J-BBGD, the aeroplane was used for training and as a glider tug at the Furukawa Centre.

Single-engine low-wing cantilever monoplane. Semi-monocoque wooden fuselage, wooden wing covered with fabric and plywood. Two seats in

Nozawa X-1 Light Aeroplane.

tandem in closed cockpits.

75hp Pobjoy R seven-cylinder air-cooled radial engine, driving a two-bladed wooden propeller.

Span 10.60m (34ft 9¼in); length 7.14m (23ft 5in); height 2.16m (7ft 1in) tail down; wing area 15sq m (161.463sq ft).

Empty weight 412kg (908lb); loaded weight 632kg (1,393lb); wing loading 42kg/sq m (8.6lb/sq ft); power loading 8.42kg/hp (18.5lb/hp).

Maximum speed 100kt (115mph); cruising speed 90kt (103.6mph); landing speed 35kt (40.3mph); range 378nm (435mph).

One built in 1941.

Shirato Aeroplane Research Studio (Shirato Hikoki Kenkyusho)

Einosuke Shirato, the founder of this aeroplane manufacturing company, was born in the northernmost part of Honshu in 1886. He enlisted in the Army Balloon Corps in 1906 and worked under Capt Yoshitoshi Tokugawa, noted for being the first person to fly an aeroplane in Japan. After leaving the Army in 1910, Shirato became an assistant to Sanji Narahara through an introduction by Capt Tokugawa. While with Narahara, a builder of aeroplanes and a flying instructor, he learned to fly, and became the second civilian aviator, preceded only by Narahara.

After Narahara retired from aviation in April 1912, Shirato began a series of paid flying exhibition engagements as the exclusive pilot of the Narahara No.4 Aeroplane. Later he worked as a flying instructor at the Nihon Kyodo Hiko Renshusho (Japan Co-operative Flight Training Centre) at Inage in Chiba Prefecture, which had been established by Narahara. He trained several students including Otojiro Itoh (a future manufacturer of aeroplanes) and Saken Kawabe. This school was the first to train civilian aviators in Japan.

In January 1915 Shirato obtained a 50hp Green engine from Takehiko Sonoda who had taken it to Japan from England. Aero-engines were a rare commodity, for in these early days the few on hand were all imported and very expensive. At the request of Shirato, Otojiro Itoh built the first Shirato aeroplane which was completed in April 1915 and named the *Asahi-go*. With this aeroplane he made exhibition flights in Hokkaido, the first on that island.

In December 1916 he transferred his Shirato Flying Training Ground, which was associated with the Japan Co-operative Flight Training Centre in Inage, to Shinjuku Beach, Samukawa in Chiba Prefecture, where he completed his first practical aeroplane without major outside assistance, the Shirato *Takeru-go*, in 1918. The war caused Shirato to be recalled into the Army and he served in Siberia where he became ill and was discharged in December 1918. During his absence, his flying students maintained his airfield and training school. It was at this time in 1918 that he established a new name for his company, Shirato Hikoki Kenkyusho. This was prompted by Shirato becoming more involved in the commercial building of aeroplanes for exhibition flying and flying training. All these activities centred on the flying field at Inage, such as Shirato's flying school and aircraft building, were collectively referred to by the popular name Shirato Airfield.

Shirato Asahi-go Aeroplane.

Shirato Anzani (Ground Taxi-ing) Trainer.

Shirato *Asahi-go* Aeroplane

When Takehiko Sonoda returned from England after having his aeroplane built there in 1912, he brought with him only the 50hp Green engine that powered it. This engine was then sold to Einosuke Shirato in January 1915 to power the first Shirato aeroplane of what was to be a long line of aircraft. Shirato asked Otojiro Itoh to design and build this aeroplane for him. At that time, Itoh was 23 years old and had worked with Shirato when both were assistants of Sanji Narahara.

Itoh started this first of what would be many designs on 11 March, 1915, and the aeroplane was completed on 17 April with the assistance of Toyokichi Daiguchi and Toyotaro Yamagata. The first flight was made on 24 April by Itoh himself. The aeroplane passed into Shirato's ownership after he flew it for the first time on 6 May. Shirato named the aeroplane *Asahi-go* after his birthplace at Asahi-yama, Kanagi Village in Aomori Prefecture in northern Honshu.

A number of commercial exhibition flights were made over a two-month period from June 1915, at many locations in Niigata, Fukushima and Aomori Prefectures, before crowds of people who had never before seen an aeroplane.

Single-engine tractor biplane. All-wooden construction with fabric covering. Pilot in open cockpit.

50hp Green four-cylinder water-cooled inline engine, driving a two-bladed wooden propeller.

Span 11m (38ft 1in); length 7.20m (23ft 7½in); height 2.60m (8ft 6½in).

Empty weight 320kg (705lb).

One built in 1915.

Shirato Anzani (Ground Taxi-ing) Trainer

After extensive touring with his first aeroplane, Einosuke Shirato borrowed from Tetsusaburo Tsuzuku a 50hp Anzani engine which had powered his Tsuzuku No.1 Aeroplane. With this engine, Shirato built a trainer in 1915, designed by Kiyoshi Shiga, and assisted by Toyokichi Daiguchi. Helping with the construction of the new aeroplane were students from the Nihon Kyodo Hiko Renshusho (Japan Co-operative Flight Training Centre).

Shirato Iwao-go *Aeroplane.*

When completed, the aeroplane could just manage to fly with one person on board, or make short hops when occupied by an instructor and a student. As a result, the aeroplane was relegated to use as a taxi-ing trainer. Performance was later improved when fitted with a semi-circular engine cowling, Kichinosuke Tsukamoto's idea. In addition to this taxi-ing trainer, Shirato also built a 25hp Anzani powered trainer.

Single-engine biplane taxi-ing trainer. All-wooden construction with fabric covering. Student and instructor in open cockpit.

50hp Anzani five-cylinder air-cooled rotary engine, driving a two-bladed wooden propeller.

One built in 1915.

Shirato *Iwao-go* Aeroplane

Having a close working relationship with Otojiro Itoh and recognizing his success with the design of the *Asahi-go,* Shirato asked Itoh to design another aeroplane for him. This was a seaplane, the first Japanese-built civil seaplane.

The design was begun in late December 1915 and completed late the next month. It was a twin-float tractor biplane powered by a 60hp Indian rotary engine which was lent to Shirato by his friend Yuzo Umeda who often assisted with his work. Construction of the new aeroplane began on 28 January, 1916, with Shirato making the first flight on 3 March. Two weeks later, Shirato took this aeroplane, the *Iwao-go,* on the first of many exhibition flights, making the first from Lake Suwa in Nagano Prefecture.

After other flights and exhibitions, Shirato encountered a series of problems after one of the floats struck a floating log on Lake Biwa near Ohtsu in Shiga Prefecture, and the exhibition had to be cancelled. The promoter of the event, *Kyotsu Nippo* (a newspaper company) placed a lien against Shirato for failing to honour his contract. Umeda, the owner of the engine, filed a counter suit with the Takamatsu District Court, and the case was settled out of court for 400 yen. Somehow this passed the ownership of the aeroplane to 19-year-old Yukichi Goto, one of Shirato's assistants, who had obtained money from his father. Goto took the aeroplane to his home in Nobeoka-cho, Miyazaki Prefecture, where he planned to fly it. Because special skills were required to fly a seaplane, apart from having general flying ability, Goto soon tired of the aeroplane and returned it to Umeda in February 1917 and went to Tokyo where he joined the Imperial Flying Association as a flying student to improve his skill as a pilot.

Single-engine twin-float tractor biplane. All-wooden construction with fabric covering. Pilot in open cockpit.

60hp Indian nine-cylinder air-cooled rotary-engine, driving a two-bladed wooden propeller.

Span 11m (36ft 1in); length 7.50m (24ft 7¼in); wing area 29sq m (312.163 sq ft).

Empty weight 400kg (881lb).

One built in 1916.

Shirato Takeru-go *Aeroplane, also known as the Tamura Tractor and Ichimori Tractor.*

Shirato *Takeru-go* Aeroplane
(Also known as Tamura Tractor and Ichimori Tractor)

This was the first Shirato aeroplane that proved to have satisfactory performance from the beginning. It was built at the request of Toshikazu Tamura and completed in July 1918. Known as the Shirato *Takeru-go*, it was an improved landplane version of the earlier *Iwao-go* seaplane. It was a rather large aeroplane yet of sufficiently light weight for its 50hp Gnome rotary engine. Emphasis was on safety rather than performance. The pilot and passenger/student sat in tandem in a large single open cockpit. This was the first aeroplane to carry Shirato's target-like design on its wings and fuselage.

As with so many early Japanese aircraft, having an engine around which to build it was the key element. Tamura obtained his engine for this aeroplane by having it rebuilt from spares formerly owned by the American aviator Frank Champion who died in a crash while performing aerobatics over the city of Kouchi in October 1917.

After gaining flying experience, Tamura demonstrated his skills by proudly flying over his home town of Sumoto on Awaji Island, an often used sign of achievement for early pilots.

After several modifications made in the autumn of 1918, the aeroplane became known as the Tamura Tractor to distinguish it from pusher types. Following exhibition tours with his aeroplane that took him to points in northern Honshu and most of Hokkaido, Tamura had to retire from aviation because of illness and died in February 1919. Yoshinori Ichimori then became the owner and he rebuilt the aeroplane under the guidance of his older and experienced friend, aviator Ginzo Nojima. It was renamed the Ichimori Tractor.

Arrangements were made whereby Noburu Fujiwara was to fly this aeroplane for a demonstration at

Shirato Kaoru-go *(Shirato 16) Aeroplane after modification.*

Kobe in January 1920, but immediately after taking off from the Osaka Joto Military Parade Grounds, the aeroplane failed to gain sufficient height because of loss of power, and the port wing struck a lightning rod at the Army Ordnance Arsenal, causing the aeroplane to crash and be destroyed. Fujiwara survived the crash but sustained injuries. (*see* other Fujiwara mishaps under Itoh Emi 6 Aeroplane).

Single-engine tractor biplane. All-wooden construction with fabric covering except for aft portion of the fuselage. Pilot in open cockpit.
50hp Gnome seven-cylinder air-cooled rotary engine, driving a two-bladed wooden propeller.
Span 8.90m (29ft 2¼in); length 7.10m (23ft 3½in).
Empty weight 305kg (672lb).
One built in 1918.

Shirato *Kaoru-go* (Shirato 16) Aeroplane

With the assistance of Otojiro Itoh, this Shirato *Kaoru-go (Fragrance)* Aeroplane owed much to the experience gained with the *Takeru-go*. It was a simple two-bay tractor biplane with slight backward stagger,

and originally it had a skid attached to the undercarriage to prevent nosing over, but this was later removed. It also had later changes made to the engine cowling as well as shortening of the wing span.

When first built, the aeroplane carried its name, *Kaoru-go*, in Japanese on the sides of the fuselage. When modifications were completed and its designation justifiably changed, it then carried the well-known Shirato circular insignia in place of the name, and 16 for Shirato 16 was added to the rudder.

In 1919 Nobuo Takahashi from Hokkaido used the aeroplane to make exhibition flights at various locations in Hokkaido and Karafuto (now Sakhalin in the USSR). In August 1920 the aeroplane was entered in the First Prize-winning Flight Competition at Susaki Airfield in Tokyo where it recorded an altitude of 650m (2,132ft) and a speed of 35.5kt when flown by Takeo Shimada. Although it was the lowest powered aircraft entered, it took 5th place in both of these events.

Single-engine two-bay tractor biplane. All-wooden construction with fabric covering. Pilot in open cockpit.
50hp Gnome seven-cylinder air-cooled rotary engine, driving a two-bladed wooden propeller.

	Shirato Kaoru-go	*Shirato 16*
Span	11m (36ft 1in)	10m (32ft 9½in)
Length	7.90m (25ft 11in)	7.90m (25ft 11in)
Height	2.50m (8ft 2½in)	2.20m (7ft 2½in)
Empty weight	290kg (639lb)	380kg (837lb)

One built in 1918.

Shirato 20 Aeroplane

In early 1920, the trading company Sale & Frazar Ltd, in Yokohama, imported a number of aircraft engines from France. Shirato bought a 120hp Le Rhône and a 180hp Hispano-Suiza with which to power the Shirato 20 and 25 racing aircraft.

The Shirato 20 was a two-seat aircraft developed from the *Kaoru-go*. It was completed in July 1920, and flight tested by Nobuo Takahashi who reportedly found the aeroplane quite satisfactory. It was to participate in the First Prize-winning Flight Competition the following month. However, during preparation for flight on the morning of the competition, the aircraft overturned and was damaged because of an undiscovered defect in the design. Too late for the competition, the aeroplane was eventually repaired with major modifications so that it could be used as a trainer at the Shirato Airfield.

Single-engine biplane. All-wooden construction with fabric covering. Two seats in open cockpit.

120hp Le Rhône nine-cylinder air-cooled rotary engine, driving a two-bladed wooden propeller.

Span 10.30m (33ft 9½in); length 8m (26ft 3in); height 2.70m (8ft 10¼in).

Empty weight 410kg (903lb).

One built in 1920.

Shirato 25 Kuma-go *Racing Aeroplane.*

Shirato 25 *Kuma-go* Racing Aeroplane

Hoping to capture the Japanese speed record, Shirato asked Tomotari Inagaki, the talented designer of Itoh Aeroplanes, to design aircraft for this purpose. The aeroplane was to be powered by the 180hp Hispano-Suiza engine.

In early 1920 Inagaki designed a fighter-like aeroplane which resembled the SPAD XIII. The engine was bought through donations from sponsors in Kumamoto Prefecture where Takeo Shimada originated, thus the special name for the craft, *Kuma-go*, after the largest river in that prefecture, the Kuma River.

At the Osaka-Kurume Second Prize-winning Airmail Flying Contest in November 1920, the *Kuma-go* flew the full course in the impressive time of 3hr 58min, piloted by Nobuo Takahashi, Shirato Airfield's leading pilot. However, on landing an undercarriage strut failed and the aeroplane was disqualified from the contest.

In May 1921 at the Second Prize-winning Flight Competition, held at Susaki Airfield in Tokyo, Takahashi entered the *Kuma-go* in the speed category. Great attention was given to the final engine adjustments made by Aijiro Hara and the installation of a small auxiliary radiator to compensate for higher engine running speed over a longer duration. Hara was a graduate and faculty member of Electrical Engineering, Tokyo Imperial University, but was known for his enthusiasm for aeronautical matters. The aeroplane won first prize with a speed of 221.97km/h (119.86kt), equivalent to that of fighters at that time. It also won first prize in the aerobatic category. In the competition for distance the *Kuma-go* flew 385km and came in third. These records were impressive and demonstrated the quality of the aeroplane.

Following these events, Takeo Shimada entered his aeroplane in the Tokyo–Morioka Airmail Flying Contest in August 1921. He covered the distance in 5hr 8min, but was disqualified because of deviations from the prescribed course. In November the next year, his aeroplane won for him the first prize in the Tokyo–Osaka Airmail Round-robin Flight Competition with a record of 7hr 46min. The normal endurance of the *Kuma-go* was 6hr with just the pilot, but with the removal of one fuel tank to make room for a second crew member or to carry mail, endurance was reduced to 2hr.

In January 1923, the Tozai Teiki Kokukai (East-West Regular Air Transport Association) was begun under the sponsorship of the *Asahi Shimbun*. The *Kuma-go* was put into service, again flown by Shimada, but while en route from Hamamatsu to Tokyo on 22 February, a snow storm was encountered over Hakone east of Mt Fuji, forcing Shimada to alter course and the *Kuma-go* crashed into Myojinga-take, a 3,800ft mountain. This was the first fatal accident on a regular Japanese air service.

Single-engine two-bay biplane. All-wooden construction with fabric covering. Pilot in open cockpit. Capable of carrying a second person.

180hp Hispano-Suiza eight-cylinder vee water-cooled engine, driving a two-bladed wooden propeller.

Span 9.80m (32ft 2in).

Loaded weight 932kg (2,054lb).

Maximum speed 120kt (138.5mph); climb to 1,000m (3,280ft) in 3min.

One built in 1920.

Shirato 26 Trainer

In the years following the First

World War it became quite easy to obtain Army surplus 70hp Renault engines that had been installed in the Maurice Farman 1914 (Type Mo-4) aeroplanes. Efforts were made by Itoh, Akabane and Nakajima to develop and manufacture tractor-type trainers using these pusher-type engines turned round. One example of these Renault-engined types was the Shirato 26 which was designed by Aijiro Hara and built at the Shirato Airfield. In the engine area the Shirato 26 resembled Akabane's Kishi No.5 *Tsurugi-go* Aeroplane.

Single-engine tractor biplane. All-wooden construction with fabric covering. Two seats in tandem in open cockpit.

70hp Renault eight-cylinder vee air-cooled engine, driving a two-bladed wooden propeller.

Span 9.80m (32ft 2in); length 6.90m (22ft 7¾in); height 2.40m (7ft 10½in).

Empty weight 410kg (903lb).

Maximum speed 38kt (43.75mph).

One built in 1921.

Shirato 28 Trainer

When the assets of the American Barr's Flying Circus were seized in 1921 because the lack of gate receipts made them unable to pay their expenses while in Japan, Shirato acquired one Standard R-1. After minor changes, it was used as a trainer. That same year, Aijiro Hara, who was working for Shirato,

Shirato 28 Trainer.

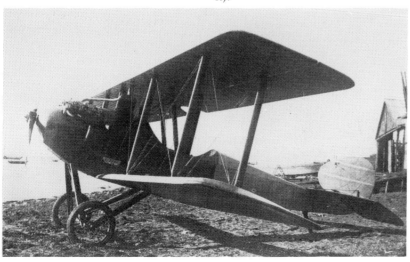

designed the Shirato 28 trainer which used the Curtiss engine from this Standard R-1.

Because of the 'bath tub' type cockpit in the Shirato 28, communication between the student and instructor was good because of the close proximity of the two tandem seats. Ailerons were on the upper wing only and a balance tab was installed on its oval-shaped rudder. There was no fin. A pair of radiators were attached on either side of the nose.

Single-engine two-bay biplane. All-wooden construction with fabric covering. Student and instructor in tandem in large open cockpit.

90hp Curtiss OX eight-cylinder vee water-cooled engine, driving a two-bladed wooden propeller.

Span 9.10m (29ft 10¼in); length 7.50m (24ft 7¼in); height 2.40m (7ft 10½in); wing area 26sq m (279.87sq ft).

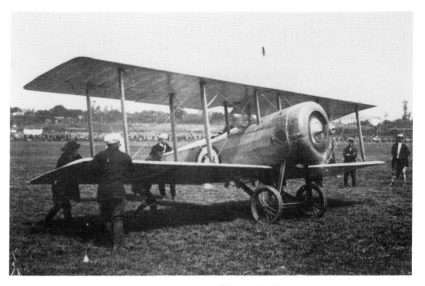

Shirato 31 Trainer.

Empty weight 410kg (903lb).

Maximum speed 49kt (56.4mph).

One built in 1921.

Shirato 31 Trainer

The Shirato 31 was designed in 1921 and expected to become the standard two-seat trainer for civil use. It was designed for simplicity in manufacture and repair.

The two-bay wings were of equal span and without taper. Major components were standardized for ease of replacement. This interchangeability of parts was also a feature of the earlier Shirato 32. The 120hp Le Rhône engine was selected for this design because war surplus stocks were expected to be available for some time.

This aeroplane was used for training, aerial advertising, sightseeing flights and other purposes until 1923, the time of the major earthquake in Tokyo, when many contracts were cancelled. The Shirato 31 Trainer was considered the most practical of Shirato's aircraft.

Single-engine two-bay biplane. All-wooden construction with fabric covering. Crew of two in open cockpits.

120hp Le Rhône nine-cylinder air-cooled rotary engine, driving a two-bladed wooden propeller.

Span 10.30m (33ft 9½in); length 7.90m (25ft 11in); height 2.80m (9ft 2¼in).

Empty weight 550kg (1,212lb);

Shirato 32 Racing Aeroplane.

loaded weight 750kg (1,653lb).
  Endurance 2hr.
  One built in 1921.

Shirato 32
Racing Aeroplane

Like the Shirato 31, the Shirato 32 was also designed using the experience gained with the Shirato 25. For unknown reasons it was completed in 1920, a year or so earlier than the preceding model. Also a two-seat aircraft, it was intended primarily for various categories of flying competition.

In November 1920, the aeroplane was entered in the Osaka–Kurume Second Prize-winning Airmail Flying Contest, and flown by Takeo Shimada. Soon after take off, it suffered engine problems and returned to the take off point with a hard landing causing serious damage. After repairs were made, Shimada entered the aeroplane in the Second Prize-winning Flight Competition in May 1921, at Susaki Airfield in Tokyo where it recorded a speed of 75kt, taking sixth place, and in the distance category it flew 279.5km and was placed fifth.

Single-engine biplane exhibition aircraft. All-wooden construction with fabric covering. Crew of two in open cockpits.

120hp Le Rhône nine-cylinder air-cooled rotary engine, driving a two-bladed wooden propeller.

Span 10.30m (33ft 9½in); length 7.9m (25ft 11in); height 2.80m (9ft 2¼in).

Empty weight 550kg (1,212lb); loaded weight 750kg (1,653lb).

Maximum speed 75kt (86.3mph); climb to 1,000m (3,280ft) in 3min; endurance 2hr.

One built in 1920.

Shirato 37
Racing Aeroplane

The Shirato 37 was regarded as the masterpiece of the Shirato produced aircraft. It was designed by Aijiro Hara and Shuzo Kurahashi, and was considered one of the most refined aeroplanes in Japan in 1921.

The aerofoil selected by Hara was RAF 15, giving it a maximum lift coefficient of 1.21 and a maximum lift drag ratio of 26. The larger upper wing carried the ailerons, and the wing and tail tips were rounded in a further effort to reduce drag. A circular radiator was very cleanly fitted to the front of the 220hp Hispano-Suiza engine giving it an appearance very like the SPAD XIII.

At the Tokyo–Aomori Airmail Flying Contest on 21 August, 1921, Nobuo Takahashi flew the Shirato 37 to Aomori, in northern Honshu, in 3hr 35min, ranking second in elapsed time and recognized as the best entry. Immediately after take off from the Morioka Military Parade Grounds for the return flight to Tokyo, a wingtip struck an object reported as a monument, and was damaged but landed safely. As part of the necessary repairs, co-designer Kurahashi modified the wing from a single- to a two-bay structure with increased span. It was then designated Shirato Kaizo (Modified) 37.

Nobuo Takahashi flew this aeroplane in the Fourth Kanazawa–Hiroshima Airmail Flying Contest in November 1921. He came first with a record of 4hr 6min.

Before the modifications, the Shirato 37 recorded a maximum speed of 230km/h, and in fact, was the fastest Japanese civil aeroplane. It was slightly faster than the Army Type Hei 1 Fighter (220km/h) and the Navy Type 10 Carrier Fighter (213km/h).

By 1922 the Shirato Modified 37 was relegated to training and used by Shirato students.

Single-engine racing biplane. All-wooden construction with fabric covering. Crew of two in open cockpits.

220hp Hispano-Suiza eight-cylinder vee water-cooled engine, driving a two-bladed wooden propeller.

Shirato 37 Racing Aeroplane.

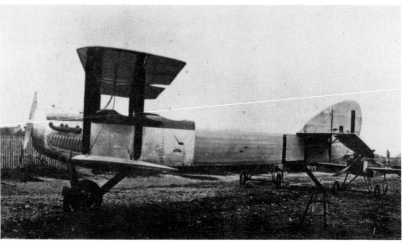

	Shirato 37	Shirato Modified 37
Span	8.60m (28ft 2½in)	9.15m (30ft)
Length	6.86m (22ft 6in)	6.86m (22ft 6in)
Height	2.74m (9ft)	2.74m (9ft)
Wing area	21.5sq m (231.431sq ft)	23.2sq m (249.73sq ft)
Loaded weight	890kg (1,962lb)	950kg (2,094lb)
Maximum speed	125kt (143.85mph)	87kt (100mph)
Endurance	4hr	4hr

One built in 1921.

Shirato 38 Trainer.

Shirato 38 Trainer

The Shirato 38 was a trainer developed from the Shirato 31 and 32, designed by Shuzo Kurahashi and built at the Shirato Airfield in 1922. It differed from most earlier Shirato biplanes in that its wings were staggered and unlike some had a fixed fin. It had a semi-circular engine cowling round its 120hp Le Rhône which resembled some Sopwith and Nieuport cowlings.

The aeroplane was entered in the Third Flight Rally for holders of pilot 3/c civil licences that was held at Shimoshizu Airfield in Chiba Prefecture in June 1922. Flown by Hanji Noriike, the aeroplane won first prize when it climbed to a record altitude for this meeting of 5,900m (19,357ft). This trainer remained in operation until the closing of the Shirato Airfield.

Single-engine two-bay biplane trainer. All-wooden construction with fabric covering. Crew of two in open cockpits.
120hp Le Rhône nine-cylinder aircooled rotary engine, driving a two-bladed wooden propeller.
Span 10.90m (35ft 9in); length 6.82m (22ft 4½in); height 2.42m (7ft 11¼in); wing area 30.3sq m (326.149sq ft).
Empty weight 650kg (1,433lb); loaded weight 800kg (1,763lb).

Maximum speed 74kt (85.2mph); landing speed 32.5kt (37.5mph); climb to 1,000m (3,280ft) in 3min; service ceiling 5,000m (16,404ft).
One built in 1922.

Shirato 40 Trainer

The last aeroplane manufactured at the Shirato Airfield was the Shirato 40 Trainer. Although it was powered by the same 120hp Le Rhône engine as earlier aircraft, its airframe was smaller than the Shirato 38. It was designed as a two-seat trainer but was actually used as a single-seat long-range mailplane, with space for the fuel tank and mail load in the front cockpit area.

Shirato 40 Trainer

When entered in the week-long Tokyo–Osaka Airmail Round-robin Flight Competition in November 1922, it was flown by Kikumasa Koide as one of the relay team members. When taking off from the Yoyogi Military Parade Grounds in Tokyo, and having flown more than half the distance to Osaka, the aeroplane developed engine trouble and Koide made an emergency landing on the Nikawacho dry river bed near Toyohashi City. The aeroplane was damaged, and therefore disqualified from the competition.

Single-engine two-bay biplane trainer. All-wooden construction with fabric covering. Pilot in open cockpit.
120hp Le Rhône nine-cylinder aircooled rotary engine, driving a two-bladed wooden propeller.
One built in 1922.

Following this line of Shirato Aeroplanes, there came a time when a flood of surplus Japanese military aeroplanes became available to the civil market at lower prices than new ones. As a result, this ended Shirato aircraft production. In addition the earthquake of 1 September, 1923, in the Kanto area heavily damaged Shirato's property, dealing the final blow after ten years in aviation. Shirato Airfield and the aircraft construction facilities were closed, and Shirato changed his business to the manufacture of wooden furniture. He died on 24 March, 1938, at the age of 52.

Tachikawa Aeroplane Co Ltd (Tachikawa Hikoki KK)

The Tachikawa Aeroplane Company had its beginning in 1924 as the Aeroplane Factory of Ishikawa-jima Shipbuilding Company in Tokyo. It was renamed Tachikawa Aeroplane Co Ltd in July 1936, having as its president, C Kadono, and managing director, M/Gen (Ret) T Yokoyama. Details of those early years of the company and the aircraft built are described in this work under Ishikawajima.

Tachikawa Army Small and Light Ambulance Aircraft (KKY)

The Japanese Army had a requirement for a small and light-weight ambulance aircraft, and placed an order for such an aeroplane with

Ishikawajima in August 1932. Based on the company's experience with the R-5 trainer, and design concepts found in the imported de Havilland D.H. 83 Fox Moth light transport, chief designer Ryokichi Endo, with the supervision of Moriyuki Nakagawa, undertook the project.

The company designated this aeroplane KKY, which stood for Kogata Kei Kanja Yusoki or Small Type Light Patient Transport. This 'small type' ambulance was to supplement the 'standard type' which at that time was the Naka-jima-Fokker Super Universal converted for ambulance use. The KKY carried a pilot, stretchers for two patients, a seat for one medical attendant, and medical supplies and equipment stipulated by the Army's Senior Surgeon, Yoshinobu Teraji. The KKY type was designed to operate from small airstrips for emergency evacuations. Low-pressure tyres, having a wider footprint, were fitted when these aeroplanes were to be operated from unprepared airstrips.

Although the first prototype was completed in December 1933, it took a long time to complete flying and serviceability evaluations and make the necessary modifications,

and it was not until February 1935 that this first KKY was considered acceptable. After still further, but minor modifications, to the first aircraft, a small number of additional aircraft were manufactured from 1936 to 1940.

The aircraft was designed for, and first built with, the Cirrus Hermes Mk.IV inverted inline engine with a metal propeller. Problems continued with the Cirrus engine, and later models from October 1938 were powered by the 150hp Gasuden Jimpu seven-cylinder air-cooled radial and equipped with a fixed-pitch two-bladed wooden propeller. The wings, with Clark Y aerofoil, had the area increased to improve short-field performance. This later version was the KKY-2, Kogata Kei Kanja Yusoki Kaizogata, the last word meaning modified version. By this time the company name had changed to Tachikawa and these aeroplanes were known by that name.

The KKYs were put into service as *Aikoku-go* aeroplanes (purchased through private donations) and

Tachikawa Army Small and Light Ambulance Aircraft (KKY) with Aikoku-go *lettering to show purchaser's name.*

Tachikawa Army Small and Light Ambulance Aircraft (KKY-2) powered by a 150hp Gasuden Jimpu radial air-cooled engine.

were widely used in air-evacuation duties during the Sino-Japanese conflict up to the early stage of the Pacific War.

Single-engine cabin biplane. Welded steel tube fuselage, wooden wing structure, and aluminium empennage, fabric covered. Pilot, two patients and one medical attendant. (The following data pertain to the first prototype).

120-135hp Cirrus Hermes Mk.IV four-cylinder inline inverted air-cooled engine, driving a fixed-pitch two-bladed metal propeller.

Span 10m (32ft 9½in); length 7.90m (25ft 11in); height 2.38m (7ft 9¾in); wing area 22sq m (236.813sq ft).

Empty weight 560kg (1,234lb); loaded weight 977kg (2,154lb); wing loading 44.4kg/sq m (9.1lb/sq ft); power loading 7.24kg/hp (15.9lb/hp).

Maximum speed 98kt (112.8mph); cruising speed 84kt (96.7mph); landing speed 43kt (49.5mph); take off/landing distance approx 250m (820ft); climb to 2,000m (6,562ft) in 14min; service ceiling 4,500m (14,763ft); range 620km (385sm).

Twenty-three built 1933-1940. (Seventeen of these were built in Fiscal year 1939.)

Tachikawa KS Small Survey Aircraft

The Department of Railways had a requirement for a replacement of its earlier survey aircraft, and ordered

two from Tachikawa. These would be used primarily for the survey to be made of the Shin Tokaido Line which was begun in 1939. To meet this requirement, modifications were made to the KKY-2, including an enlarged rear window and the addition of one in the cabin floor. With these changes, the interior of the cabin was further modified for mapping and aerial photography with a large automatic aerial camera. Three seats were provided for surveyors. In appearance there was a striking resemblance to the Waco C series aircraft but this was purely a coincidence.

These two aeroplanes were allotted the Tachikawa designation KS-1, meaning Kogata Sokuryoki, or Small Survey Aircraft. The first received the identity *Tetsudosho No.5* or Ministry of Railways No.5, and was registered J-AARD.

Single-engine cabin biplane. Welded steel tube fuselage, wooden wing structure, and aluminium empennage

Tachikawa KS Small Survey Aircraft.

fabric covered. Pilot and three survey crew.

150-160hp Hitachi Jimpu 3 seven-cylinder air-cooled radial engine, driving a two-bladed wooden propeller.

Span 9.996m (32ft 9½in).

Empty weight 722kg (1,591lb); loaded weight 1,140kg (2,513lb); power loading 7.15kg/hp (15.7lb/hp).

Maximum speed 100kt (115mph) at 1,000m (3,280ft); cruising speed 73kt (84mph) at 1,000m; landing speed 43kt (49.5mph); climb to 3,000m (9,843ft) in 33min 35sec.

Two built in 1939.

Tachikawa-Beechcraft C-17E Light Transport

In 1936 and 1937, Nihon Koku Yuso KK (Japan Air Transport Company Ltd) showed an interest in the Beechcraft C-17E for use as small transports for the network of air routes it was establishing for passengers and mail. One aeroplane of this type had been imported from the United States and made its first flight in Japan on 29 September, 1936, with impressive performance. These four-passenger backward-staggered biplanes appeared to be quite practical for this type of work because they were achieving great popularity in the United States as corporate aircraft and on charter service. Tachikawa expected to find the same demand within Japan and therefore purchased the manufacturing rights from Beechcraft.

The first aeroplane received by Tachikawa was in dismantled form for study and experience in assembly. When completed it made its

Tachikawa-Beechcraft C-17E Light Transport.

first flight on 21 June, 1938. Production was set in motion, and twenty licence-built aeroplanes were delivered to Dai Nihon Koku KK (Greater Japan Airways Co Ltd)*, Manshu and Chuka Koku, and other government agencies up to April 1939.

The aeroplanes proved to have excellent performance for airline work in comparison with other single-engine transports in service. For example, the cruising speed of the Nakajima-Fokker Super Universal was 92kt, while the Beechcraft cruised at 135kt. Fuel consumption for the Fokker was 110lit/hr, but only 66lit/hr for the Beechcraft.

Problems developed however. The aeroplane was not designed for operating out of unprepared airfields as necessary in Japan. This caused a number of problems with the undercarriage retracting mechanism. The wing construction was rather complex, making repairs quite difficult. More importantly, the engines and the Curtiss metal propellers for the Beechcraft were

*Dai Nihon Koku KK was established on 1 December, 1938, as a joint partnership of Nihon Koku Yuso KK and Kokusai Koku KK (International Airways Co Ltd), both of which were government controlled companies. Kokusai Koku KK had been established on 20 May, 1937, to open a new air route between Japan and Germany, but this did not happen.

imported from the USA, making replacements and spare parts difficult to obtain.

One of these Beechcraft C17Es was used by the provincial police headquarters in Pyong-an Pok-do, Korea, for the Korea-Manchuria border patrol. Named *Hayate (Gale)* and registered J-ACHE, this aeroplane was actually equipped with a light machine-gun and could carry small bombs. It remained operational in this form from April 1938 until the end of the Pacific War. Others served liaison duties in central-China after the ending of domestic local services in Japan.

Single-engine staggered wing cabin biplane with retractable undercarriage. Welded steel tube fuselage structure with wings of wood and metal construction, fabric covered. Pilot and three or four passengers.

285hp Wright Whirlwind R-760E-1 seven-cylinder air-cooled radial engine, driving a Curtiss DWG fixed-pitch two-bladed metal propeller.

Span 9.75m (32ft); length 7.528m (24ft 8½in); height 2.465m (8ft 1in); wing area 24.8sq m (266.953sq ft).

Empty weight approx 1,000kg (2,200 lb); loaded weight 1,630kg (3,593lb); wing loading 66kg/sq m (13.5lb/sq ft); power loading 5.8kg/hp (12.7lb/hp).

Maximum speed 152kt (174.9mph); cruising speed 136kt (156.5mph); landing speed 43kt (49.5mph); climb to 1,000m (3,280ft) in 5min 30sec; service

ceiling 6,000m (19,685ft); range, 1,500km (932sm); endurance 6hr.

Twenty built, fourteen in 1938, five in 1939 and one in 1940.

Tachikawa TS-1 Experimental Ultra-light Aircraft

With the expectation that Japan would experience the same light sports-plane enthusiasm that existed in Europe, Tachikawa planned to compete in Japan for this market, beginning in 1937. Already, Nihon Hikoki KK (Nippi) had imported a sample of the Pou du Ciel from France with the intention of producing it in Japan.

Tachikawa's aeroplane would be one of its own design and was designated TS-1, meaning Tachikawa Sport. It was a single-seat aircraft with low purchase price, economic to operate, and easy to fly. Chief designer for the project was Ryokichi Endo.

By August 1937, what was hoped to be only the first of the TS-1 series was completed. It was a cantilever low-wing monoplane with manually-operated rearward-retracting undercarriage. It was well streamlined with a narrow nose made possible by its two-cylinder inline engine. Its lightweight 16hp engine gave it the impressive cruising speed of 90kt (103mph) at

Tachikawa TS-1 Experimental Ultra-Light Aircraft.

Tachikawa R-38 Experimental Trainer

By 1938, Tachikawa was already heavily involved in production of its very successful Army Type 95-1 and Type 95-3 biplane trainers. As a separate project it developed a parasol-monoplane trainer for use by civil flying schools. This was to be the first monoplane pilot trainer in Japan, and the experience gained by Tachikawa's R-series trainers was incorporated into this new design. It owed much to the Fairchild 22 which had been imported by Okura Shoji (Okura & Co Ltd, a trading company) from the United States and assembled by Tachikawa before the name was changed from Ishikawajima. This new aeroplane was the R-38, a major jump in R-series numbering, the 38 referring to 1938, the year of its design development. Supervising the project was Moriyuki Nakagawa, and chief designer was Ryokichi Endo.

The aeroplane made its first flight on 22 February, 1939, carrying the registration J-BBFE.* The 150hp Jimpu 6 engine was identical

*Although the aeroplane was registered J-BBFE, a photograph shows that some time it had J-BBFF on the fuselage.

1,000m (3,280ft).

But it was this two-stroke air-cooled engine that caused continuous problems. In addition, the aeroplane was difficult to take off and land on grass surfaces because of its very small wheels, the small size being essential for retraction. There was little if any public interest shown in this aeroplane, and therefore the project was abandoned with this one example. It should be noted as well that few of the single-seat aeroplanes that were designed in many parts of the world gained much popularity.

Single-engine single-seat low-wing cantilever monoplane with manually operated retractable undercarriage. Wooden structure with fabric and thin-ply-wood covering.

16-28hp Scott Flying Squirrel two-cylinder air-cooled inverted inline two-stroke engine, driving a two-bladed wooden propeller.

Span 7.75m (25ft 5in); length 5.955m (19ft 6¼in); height 1.60m (5ft 3in); wing area 10sq m (107.642sq ft).

Empty weight 218kg (480lb); loaded weight 309kg (681lb); wing loading 30.9kg/sq m (6.3lb/sq ft); power loading 11kg/hp (24.2lb/hp).

Maximum speed 92kt (106mph) at sea level; cruising speed 66kt (76mph); climb to 3,000m (9,843ft) in 43min 7sec; service ceiling 3,300m (10,826ft); range 488km (303sm); endurance 4hr.

One built in August 1937.

Tachikawa R-38 Experimental Trainer.

to that being used in the Army Type 95-3, but the R-38 was lighter in weight and therefore superior to the Type 95-3 in speed, climb and manoeuvrability. When evaluated by the Army Air Technical Research Institute and the Aviation Bureau Central Pilot Training School, they agreed that the R-38 was superior. But by that time the Army had quantities of the Type 95-1 and -3 trainers and concluded that there was no requirement for the R-38.

Earlier, in September 1937, Tachikawa had merged with Kosokudo Kikan KK (High Speed Engine Co Ltd) and had planned to develop and manufacture the KO-4 four-cylinder air-cooled inverted inline 120hp engine to be manufactured by Kosokudo Kikan KK. There were years of delay in developing and producing the first of these engines but eventually one was available and a KO-4 was installed in the second prototype of the R-

38, greatly enhancing the aeroplane's lines. Known as the R-38 Kai Trainer, and registered J-ALTB, it made its first flight in July 1941.

With the Army's rejection of this aeroplane, a market failed to develop, so this one example was experimentally used by the Aviation Bureau's Matsudo Central Pilot Training School.

As a result of the tighter control that the military was gaining over aircraft and engine manufacturing, the Army directed that the R-38 Kai would not be produced, and manufacture of the KO engine was to be suspended because there was no military application for it.

It is interesting to note that in postwar Japan, Shin Tachikawa Kokuki (New Tachikawa Aircraft) built R-52 and R-53 parasol-monoplane trainers in 1952 and 1953 respectively, using much of the experience gained with the R-38.

Single-engine strut-braced parasol monoplane trainer. Welded steel tube fuselage structure, wood and metal wing, aluminium empennage frame with fabric covering. Student and instructor in open cockpits.

150-160hp Gasuden Jimpu 6 seven-cylinder air-cooled radial engine, driving a two-bladed wooden propeller (R-38). 120-130hp Kosoku KO-4 four-cylinder air-cooled inverted inline engine, driving a two-bladed wooden propeller (R-38 Kai).

	R-38	R-38-kai
Span	10.8m (35ft 5¼in)	10.8m (35ft 5¼in)
Length	7.62m (25ft)	7.889m (25ft 10½in)
Height	2.78m (9ft 1½in)	2.57m (8ft 5¼in)
Wing area	19sq m (204.52sq ft)	19sq m (204.52sq ft)
Empty weight	599kg (1,320lb)	580kg (1,278lb)
Loaded weight	837kg (1,845lb)	818kg (1,803lb)
Wing loading	44kg/sqm (9lb/sq ft)	43kg/sq m (8.8lb/sq ft)
Power loading	5.23kg/hp (11.5lb/hp)	6.29kg/hp (13.8lb/hp)
Maximum speed	111kt (127.7mph)	100kt (115mph)
Cruising speed	82kt (94.4mph)	79kt (91.9mph)
Service ceiling	6.35m (20,833ft)	—
Range	280km (174sm)	230km (143sm)
Endurance	2hr 12min	1hr 30min

Two built, one in February 1938 and one in July 1941.

Aircraft designed by other companies were put into wartime production by Tachikawa, reaching one thousand aircraft a year by 1940, after that year's great expansion programme had been introduced. Once involved in production of first-line combat aircraft, Tachikawa added factories at Kofu, 70 miles west of Tokyo, and Okayama, in southern Honshu. By the end of the war, Tachikawa was producing several types of large and high-performance aircraft of its own design to meet Army needs. These are listed in Appendix A.

Tokyo Aviation Company Ltd (Tokyo Koku KK)

Generally referred to by its shortened name, Tokyo Koku, this company was established in December 1935 by Tamotsu Aiba as Tokyo Koku Yuso Sha (Tokyo Air Transport Company). The company operated passenger and mail seaplane services between Tokyo, Itoh, Shimoda, and Shimizu, as well as sight-seeing flights from the Tokyo Haneda Airport seaplane base, using Japanese-built aeroplanes.

In 1936, the company established an aeroplane factory inside the area of the company-owned Nippon Hiko Gakko (Nippon Flying School) and Nippon Jidosha Gakko (Japan Automobile School) at Kamata, a southern section of Tokyo. Its purpose was to manufacture light passenger aircraft and trainers. Renamed in 1936 as Tokyo Koku KK (Tokyo Aviation Co Ltd), its plan was, first, to replace its ageing airline equipment with its own products to avoid dependence upon converted military aircraft, and second, to manufacture civil aeroplanes at low cost in the hope that they would be used extensively in Japan and elsewhere.

Tokyo Koku Aiba-Tsubame 6 and 7 Light Passenger Transport

As part of its plan to build low-cost passenger aircraft, Tokyo Koku began with the Aiba-Tsubame 6 (Swallow). This aircraft was sponsored by the Imperial Flying Association, which placed an order for one. This aeroplane was powered by a 150hp Gasuden Jimpu Kai-1 engine. Although the wooden fuselage was a totally new design to carry a pilot and three passengers, the wings, horizontal

Tokyo Koku Aiba-Tsubame 6 Light Passenger Transport.

tail surfaces and undercarriage were those taken from the Navy Type 3 Primary Trainer. The vertical tail surfaces were similar to those of the Navy Type 10 Carrier Reconnaissance Aircraft. Final assembly was completed in September 1936 and the aeroplane was registered J-BABC.

Modifications were made to the next model which was then known as the Aiba-Tsubame 7. For this aircraft, the passenger cabin was extended further aft, resulting in some changes to internal fittings. One additional window was provided on each side at the rear of the cabin. This second aeroplane was completed in December 1936 and registered J-BABE.

The Aiba-Tsubame 6 was named *Teikoku Hiko Kyokai No.13 Peru Doho-Go* meaning Imperial Flying Association No.13 Japanese in Peru. The two aeroplanes were used for air taxi services or, more frequently, sight-seeing flights from Haneda Airport. For these joy-rides, the price was 10 yen for three passengers for five minutes. Although both aeroplanes were slow, they were considered to have excellent stability, control and reliability. In their time they became the most widely seen aircraft at Haneda, the 6 being recognized by its orange fuselage, and the 7 by its entirely orange finish.

Single-engine two-bay cabin biplane. Wooden fuselage structure covered with fabric and plywood. Wings of wooden construction with fabric cover-

ing. Pilot in open cockpit, three passengers in cabin.

150-160hp Gasuden Jimpu Kai-1 seven-cylinder air-cooled radial engine, driving a Kawanishi 5 two-bladed wooden propeller.

Span 11.165m (36ft 7¾in); length 8.43m (27ft 8in); height 3.14m (10ft 3½in); wing area 30.4sq m (327.233sq ft).

Empty weight '6' 686kg (1,512lb), '7' 713kg (1,571lb); loaded weight '6' 1,071kg (2,361lb), '7' 1,100kg (2,425 lb); wing loading for '6' 36.2kg/sq m (7.2lb/sq ft); power loading 6.69kg/hp (14.7lb/hp).

Maximum speed 82.5kt (94.94mph); cruising speed 54kt (62mh); climb to 3,000m (9,843ft) in 22min 5sec; service ceiling 4,100m (13,451ft); range 232nm (267sm); endurance 3.9hr.

Two built in 1936.

Tokyo Koku Aiba-Tsubame 8 Trainer

For sub-contracted training for the Aviation Bureau, Tokyo Koku designed a new trainer that could be used for primary and intermediate flying training as a replacement for the obsolete Avro 504K, Hanriot 28, Navy Type 3 Primary Trainers.

Tokyo Koku Aiba-Tsubame 7 Light Passenger Transport, identified by the additional cabin window.

Tokyo Koku Aiba-Tsubame 8 Trainer.

This replacement trainer was an original design with a wooden structure, good visibility from the two open cockpits, and stressed for aerobatics. It was powered by the 150hp Gasuden Jimpu 3 radial engine.

Completed in April 1938 at the Kamata Factory at a cost of 23,800 yen, it was registered J-BABJ. Although it was intended to be used for rapid, mass training of civil pilots, the aeroplane was no match for the Tachikawa Army Type 95-1 and 95-3 trainers already being mass-produced at much lower cost. The prototype Tsubame 8 was retained and used at the Nippon Flying School, and later modified as the Tsubame 9, but no further details are known.

Single-engine biplane trainer. Wooden structure throughout with fabric and some plywood covering. Student and instructor in open cockpits.

150-160hp Gasuden Jimpu 3 seven-cylinder air-cooled radial engine, driving a Mitsubishi Reed fixed-pitch two-bladed metal propeller, or Nihon Gakki (Japan Music Instrument) two-bladed wooden propeller.

Span 8.90m (29ft 2¼in); length 7m (22ft 11½in); height 2.65m (8ft 8¼in); wing area 22sq m (236.808sq ft).

Empty weight 650kg (1,433lb); loaded weight 900kg (1,984lb); wing loading 40.9kg/sq m (8.3lb/sq ft); power loading 5.63kg/hp (11.6lb/hp).

Maximum speed 87kt (100mph); cruising speed 79kt (90mph); landing speed 30kt (34.5mph); climb to 3,000m (9,843ft) in 19min; service ceiling 4,400m (14,435ft); range 314nm (362 sm).

One built in 1938.

Tokyo Koku Aiba 10 Trainer

Based upon the experience gained with the Tsubame 8 Trainer, in May 1939 the Kamata Factory of Tokyo Koku developed another primary/intermediate trainer, the Aiba 10. In comparison with the Tsubame 8, the wing area of this new aircraft was slightly smaller, and although the Tsubame 8 had 5-degree sweep-back on the upper wing only, the Aiba 10 had 5-degree sweep on both wings. Ailerons were on the lower wing only. There was little difference in empty weight between the two

types, but the maximum speed of the newer trainer was increased from 87 to 97.5kt.

Little else is recorded about this aeroplane other than that it was used as a trainer at the Nippon Flying School along with the Tsubame 8.

Single-engine biplane trainer. Wooden structure covered with fabric and some plywood. Student and instructor in open cockpits.

150-180hp Gasuden Jimpu 3 seven-cylinder air-cooled radial engine, driving a Nihon Gakki two-bladed wooden propeller.

Span 9m (29ft 6¼in); length 7.47m (24ft 6in); height 2.83m (9ft 3¼in); wing area 21.39sq m (230.247sq ft).

Empty weight 648kg (1,428lb); loaded weight 902kg (1,988lb); wing loading 42.1kg/sq m (8.6lb/sq ft); power loading 5.01kg/hp (11lb/hp).

Maximum speed 97.5kt (112mph) at 500m (1,640ft); cruising speed 81kt (93.2mph) at 500m; climb to 2,000m (6,562ft) in 11min 30sec; service ceiling 4,400m (14,435ft); range 373nm (429sm); endurance 4½hr.

One built in 1939.

Tokyo Koku Aiba 10 Trainer.

Tokyo Koku Aiba 11 Light Passenger Transport.

Tokyo Koku Aiba 11 Light Passenger Transport

Developed from the Aiba 10 Trainer, the Aiba 11 was a light passenger aeroplane that could carry three passengers. It was completed in June 1941. The general structure of the aeroplane was identical to that of the Aiba 10, and was quite similar to the Gasuden KR-2, with its three seat cabin located in front of the pilot's open cockpit.

As an air taxi operated by Tokyo Koku, the aeroplane was used mostly for sight-seeing flights from Haneda Airport. It had excellent stability and control, and could be flown hands-off, a feature that some earlier aircraft could not claim. It was also noted for its short take off and landing run as well as being an efficient aircraft to operate.

Single-engine cabin biplane. Wooden semi-monocoque fuselage with ply covering forward and fabric rear half. Wooden wing with fabric covering. Pilot in open cockpit and three passengers in cabin.

150-180hp Gasuden Jimpu 3 seven-cylinder air-cooled radial engine, driving a Nihon Gakki two-bladed wooden propeller.

Span 9.199m (30ft 2¼in); length 7.683m (25ft 2½in); height 3.22m (10ft 6¾in); wing area 21.2sq m (228.202sq ft).

Empty weight 653kg (1,439lb); loaded weight 1,035kg (2,281lb); wing loading 48.82kg/sq m (9.99lb/sq ft); power loading 5.75kg/hp (12.6lb/hp).

Maximum speed 97.5kt (112mph); cruising speed 81kt (93.27mph); landing speed 43.5kt (50mph).

One built in June 1941.

Because of the changed military situation, in 1941 Tokyo Koku changed over to the building of Army trainers. Its first type in this category was the Toko-12 low-wing primary trainer designed by Shinroku Inoue. This became the wartime Ki-107.

Tokyo Imperial University (Tokyo Teikoku Daigaku)

A student group at Tokyo Imperial University interested in aviation formed the Student Aviation Research Club. One of their objectives in the late 1930s was to design and build a light-plane, not only as a school project, but for their own use as well. This became the one and only project by the club that resulted in a completed aeroplane.

LB-2 Light Aeroplane

The LB-2 was produced under the supervision of Prof Hidemasa Kimura* of the Aeronautical Research Institute of Tokyo Imperial University, who guided club members on this two-year design project which began in 1936. Student leader for the project was Shin-ichiro Aso. Early on, the project was designated LB-2, the LB standing for light blue, the school colour. The 2 identified this as their second aeroplane project, the first being a side-by-side two-seater that was abandoned early in the design stage, giving way to a tandem-seat arrangement for the second design.

The LB-2 differed from most of the contemporary designs in that

*Noted designer and aviation historian for many years. He died in 1986.

the outer half of the wing was noticeably elliptical in planform. Its smooth cowled 60hp six-cylinder inline engine was decidedly different from similar designs, being of horizontally-opposed layout.

Some of the construction may have taken place at the University, but for the most part the Hiratsuka Factory of Nihon Koku Kogyo KK is credited with the work, completing it in December 1939. The maiden flight took place at Tokyo's Haneda Airport on 18 December, with Shigejiro Takahashi as the pilot.

While the design was considered to be a success, the aeroplane was flown very little because of recurring problems with the French-built Train engine, imported for the project by Nihon Hikoki KK of Yokohama. Only the one aeroplane, J-BBFI, was built.

Single-engine high-wing strut-braced monoplane. Wooden structure with fabric covering. Two seats in tandem in enclosed cabin.

60hp Train 6C-01 six-cylinder air-cooled inverted inline engine, driving a two-bladed wooden propeller.

Span 13m (42ft 8in); length 7.59m (24ft 11in); height 3.09m (10ft 1¾in); wing area 16sq m (172.228sq ft).

Empty weight 264kg (582lb); loaded weight 460kg (1,014lb); wing loading 28.8kg/sq (5.9lb/sq ft); power loading 7.6kg/hp (16.7lb/hp).

Maximum speed 95kt (109.3mph); cruising speed 78kt (90mph); rate of climb 2.9m/sec (570ft/min) at sea level; climb to 1,000m (3,280ft) in 6min 15sec; service ceiling 4,800m (15,748ft); range 564km (350sm).

One built in December 1939.

Tokyo Imperial University LB-2 Light Aeroplane.

Watanabe Iron Works Ltd. (KK Watanabe Tekkosho)

The Watanabe Iron Works, situated on the island of Kyushu near Fukuoka, was founded in 1886 by Tokichi Watanabe, as his private business for manufacturing coal-mining equipment and machines. When Watanabe transferred the management of the company to his adopted son Fukuo (Fukuo Fuji-shiro before adoption in 1903, the company then began the manufacture of precision weapons parts as a sub-contractor. Fukuo Watanabe was well suited to this type of engineering for he had a graduate degree in Mechanical Engineering from Tokyo Polytechnic.

By 1916 Watanabe was registered as an unlimited company, and by 1919 it became a limited company named KK Watanabe Tekko-sho. In 1921 the company was awarded contracts by the Navy for the manufacture of torpedoes because of the standard of its high precision work. The next year it received a contract from the Army for the manufacture of wheel hubs and undercarriage parts. By 1925, it became a supplier of these parts to the Navy through which they went to Mitsubishi, Nakajima, Kawanishi, Aichi and Hitachi aircraft.

As aviation continued to develop in Japan, Watanabe realized that there was no aircraft-manufacturing activity on the island of Kyushu other than the small-scale production then taking place at the close-by Sasebo Naval Arsenal. This led to the start of an aircraft manufacturing section of the iron works.

Because of his close association with the Navy, Watanabe sought orders from Naval Headquarters in 1926 for the manufacture of complete aircraft. Despite repeated attempts, orders were not forthcoming until 1929 when Vice Admiral Masataka Ando, then the chief of Naval Air Headquarters, offered the Navy's full co-operation in establishing a new plant in 1930 in which Watanabe was to manufacture aircraft for the Navy. The site chosen for the new plant was at Zasshonokuma on the southeastern outskirts of Fukuoka. It was here that Watanabe began manufacture of aircraft in 1931 beginning with the Navy-designed Type 3 Land-based Primary Trainer.

Difficulties encountered in the construction and operation of the new plant were overcome with the help of the Navy which supplied engineers and technical specialists. Furthermore, only a limited number of Watanabe personnel were trained in aircraft production techniques which they learned at the Sasebo Naval Arsenal.

In 1934, the expanding company built another new factory called the Tachiarai Branch Factory, used exclusively for the repair of Army aircraft. By 1937, this factory became independent as the KK Tachiarai Seisakusho (Tachiarai Manufacturing Works Limited). By this time, Watanabe came into its own with the successful design of a submarine-based reconnaissance aeroplane which the Navy accepted and ordered from Watanabe. This was the Type 96 Small Reconnaissance Seaplane, (E9W1).

Other types followed. With rapid military expansion in Japan, the company came under the direct control of the Navy in 1938, at which time it began manufacture of the Mitsubishi A5M carrier-based fighter, a very effective fighter which the Allies called Claude.

By 1940, the factory grounds had been fully built on, and in order to accommodate additional expansion, the acquisition of more land and the construction of further plants were envisioned. In 1941, the Kashii plant of the company was constructed on reclaimed land to the northeast of Fukuoka, and in the following year undercarriage-wheel manufacture was transferred from Zasshonokuma to a newly constructed plant at what, in post-war years, became known as Itazuke Air Base, one mile north of Zasshonokuma.

Navy Type 3-2 Land-based Primary Trainer

This Navy trainer was the first aero-plane produced by Watanabe, but was not its own design. It had been designed by the Yokosuka Arsenal to replace the highly successful Avro 504 trainer of 1921. The new design fulfilled the needs of the Navy for an improved primary trainer, and was therefore put into production by several manufacturers. Among these was Watanabe which produced 114 between 1931 and 1937. (see Yokosho Navy Type 3 Land-based Primary Trainer).

Navy Type 90 Seaplane Trainer (K4Y1)

To upgrade its flying training programme with a replacement for the Yokosho Type 13 Seaplane Trainer, the Navy created its own replacement design in 1930. After building two prototypes at the Yokosuka Arsenal and proving its practicality, a production order was placed with Watanabe which produced 156 from 1932 to 1939. (see Yokosho Navy Type 90 Seaplane Trainer).

Navy Type 96 Small Reconnaissance Seaplane (E9W1)

The Japanese Navy took very seriously the design of submarines which could carry a reconnaissance seaplane on board in watertight compartment. To meet the aircraft requirement, the Navy developed the Yokosho 1-go and 2-go Reconnaissance Seaplanes in 1927 and 1929 respectively, the latter becoming operational as the Type 91 Reconnaissance Seaplane. However, these were basically experimental single-seat aircraft and had relatively poor performance as operational aircraft.

In January 1934 the Navy planned the construction of large submarines having high speed and long range, and known as the Jun

Watanabe Navy Type 96 Small Reconnaissance Seaplane (E9W1).

Sen Type 3,* to act as flagships for the submarine flotilla. Being larger than the others, they were able to carry a two-seat reconnaissance seaplane. To provide for such an aeroplane at the time the submarine was conceived, Watanabe was given the chance to design and build such an aeroplane, known then as the 9-Shi Submarine Reconnaissance Seaplane. Watanabe assigned Ryohachiro Higuchi as the chief designer for the project. Design was begun in March 1934 and completed the following August. One airframe was constructed purely for structural testing which was finished in November, followed by the first prototype to be completed in February 1935. Features of the aeroplane were that it could be assembled and dismantled quickly aboard moving submarines and be stowed in the hangar on the submarine's deck. The entire operation for assembling the aeroplane took *2 minutes 30 seconds,* and it could be dismantled in *1 minute 30 seconds.*

After the completion of the structural-test airframe and three prototypes, the manufacture of pre-production aircraft was begun in October 1935. By July 1936, the aeroplane was officially accepted by the Navy as the Type 96 Small Reconnaissance Seaplane, (the word reconnaissance soon being deleted) with the short title E9W1. Deliveries were made to the Jun Sen Type 3 submarines beginning with the I-7 and I-8. Other newly built

*Jun Sen means Cruiser Submarine.

E9W1s were sent to the Jun Sen Type Ko and Jun Sen Type Otsu submarines in 1937. Although Watanabe had been manufacturing aircraft designed by Yokosho and other companies for some time, this was the first aeroplane designed solely within the Watanabe company. It performed well and was deemed quite adequate for submarine use. They continued in production at the same rate as the three types of Jun Sen Class submarines were built, thirty-three aircraft in all, being assigned to each submarine as it was completed over the next six years.

The Type 96 Small Seaplane, E9W1, became the last biplane to be used aboard Japanese submarines, and was replaced by the new low-wing monoplane, the Type 0 Small Reconnaissance Seaplane (Allied code-name Glen) in 1940, also built by Watanabe.

Single-engine twin-float sesquiplane. Metal and wooden structure with fabric covering. Crew of two in open cockpits.
300-340hp Gasuden Tempu 11 or 12 nine-cylinder air-cooled radial engine, driving a two-bladed wooden propeller.
One dorsal flexible 7.7mm machine-gun.
Span 9.98m (32ft 9in); length 7.64m (25ft 0¾in); height 3.29m (10ft 9½in); wing area 22.08sq m (237.674sq ft).
Empty weight 847kg (1,867lb); loaded weight 1,210kg (2,667lb); wing loading 54.8kg/sq m (11.2lb/sq ft); power loading 3.56kg/hp (7.8lb/hp).
Maximum speed 126kt (145mph) at sea level; cruising speed 80kt (92mph); alighting speed 50kt (57.5mph); climb to 3,000m (9,843ft) in 9min 41sec;

service ceiling 6,740m (22,112ft); range 320-395nm (368-454sm); endurance 4.9hr.
Thirty-three built between 1934 and 1940.

Navy Type 92 Carrier Attack Aircraft (B3Y1)

The Navy recognized the shortcomings of the Navy Type 89 Carrier Attack Aircraft produced by Mitsubishi, and undertook a replacement design at Yokosuka Arsenal in 1932. After evaluating one prototype of its new design and finding it acceptable, production was awarded to Aichi and Watanabe, followed by the Hiro Arsenal. Watanabe built twenty-three of these bombers between 1933 and 1936. (*see* Yokosho Navy Type 92 Carrier Attack Aircraft).

Experimental 11-Shi Intermediate Seaplane Trainer (K6W1)

In February 1936 the Navy requested Kawanishi and Watanabe to develop the 11-Shi Intermediate Seaplane Trainer, to be powered by a Kotobuki engine. This aeroplane was to replace the Type 93 Intermediate Seaplane Trainer which had been manufactured under contract to the Navy by Kawanishi and Watanabe. Design work began in April 1936 and was completed the following October. The earlier design of the 9-Shi Submarine-borne Reconnaissance Seaplane had considerable influence in the design of this new trainer. The first prototype K6W1 was completed in May 1937 and two additional prototypes followed.

After a prolonged evaluation by the Navy, it was determined that both the Kawanishi and the Watanabe aeroplanes were unacceptable because of poor take off and alighting characteristics. Although these aeroplanes were to replace the Type 93 Intermediate Seaplane Trainer, handling characteristics never matched the earlier aircraft despite numer-

Watanabe Experimental 11-Shi Intermediate Seaplane Trainer (K6W1).

ous modifications. As a possible solution to meet its requirement, the Navy recommended modernization of the earlier trainer and designated it Type 93 Intermediate Seaplane Trainer Kai (Type 93-12 Intermediate Seaplane Trainer or K5Y3), but this failed to show much improvement, and only one test aircraft was built by Kusho.

Single-engine, twin-float biplane trainer. Metal structure with fabric covering. Crew of two in open cockpits.

460-580hp Nakajima Kotobuki 2-kai 1 or -kai 2 nine-cylinder air-cooled radial engine, driving a fixed-pitch two-bladed metal propeller.

One forward-firing 7.7mm machine-gun and one dorsal flexible 7.7mm machine-gun. Bomb load: two 30kg (66lb) or four 10kg (22lb).

Three built in 1937.

Watanabe Siam Navy Reconnaissance Seaplane.

Siam Navy Reconnaissance Seaplane

In 1935, the Royal Siamese Navy (now the Royal Thai Navy) placed an order with Japan for two gun-boats, two corvettes and two sub-marines. Watanabe Iron Works was awarded the contract for the reconnaissance seaplanes to be carried aboard the corvettes. Ryohachiro Higuchi, Watanabe's chief aircraft designer, began the planning in December 1935, using the 9-Shi Submarine-borne Reconnaissance Seaplane as the basic design. The actual re-design work lasted from June 1936 through April 1937. This produced the first prototype in February 1938 which was kept as a test aircraft by Watanabe, and six more were built during that year for delivery to the Royal Siamese Navy.

After delivery, they were taken aboard the two Siamese corvettes, *Tacheng* and *Mekong*, each displacing 1,400 tons, with the remaining aircraft kept in reserve. Sufficient

strength was designed into these aircraft so they could be catapult-launched. They had similar performance to the Type 96 Small Seaplane, and therefore were regarded as successful. Experience obtained from designing these aeroplanes was useful in making modifications to the earlier Experimental 11-Shi Intermediate Seaplane Trainer.

Single-engine twin-float biplane. Metal structure with fabric covering. Crew of two in open cockpits.

300-340hp Gasuden Tempu 12 nine-cylinder air-cooled radial engine, driving a fixed-pitch two-bladed metal propeller.

One forward-firing fixed 7.7mm machine-gun and one dorsal flexible 7.7mm machine-gun. Bomb load: two 30kg (66lb) bombs.

Span 9.59m (31ft 5½in); length 8.10m (26ft 7in); height 3.45m (11ft 3¾in); wing area 20.97sq m (225.726sq ft).

Empty weight 1,148kg (2,530lb); loaded weight 1,420kg (3,130lb); wing loading 67kg/sq m (13.7lb/sq ft); power loading 4.7kg/hp (10.3lb/hp).

Maximum speed 125kt (143.85mph) at 2,000m (6,562ft); cruising speed 81.7kt (94mph) at 1,000m (3,280ft); alighting speed 52.9kt (60.87mph); climb to 3,000m (9,843ft) in 10min 32sec; service ceiling 4,900m (16,076 ft); range 252nm (290sm), 400nm (460sm) with maximum fuel load without ordnance.

Seven built in 1938.

Experimental 12-Shi Primary Seaplane Trainer (K8W1)

Competition to win a contract for the 12-Shi Primary Seaplane Trainer began in April 1937 when the Navy asked for such an aircraft from Nippi, Watanabe and Kawanishi. The new design was to replace the Type 90 Primary Seaplane Trainer and be powered by a 130hp Jimpu engine.

Designers at Watanabe began their work in May 1937 and completed the design the following November. The first prototype was completed in August 1938. All three aeroplanes from the competing companies were almost identical because

Watanabe Experimental 12-Shi Primary Seaplane Trainer (K8W1).

there was little latitude in designing such a straightforward twin-float trainer. They were basically a redesigned Type 90 Primary Seaplane Trainer which was already in service. Kawanishi won the competition and its entry was adopted as the Type 0 Primary Seaplane Trainer, K8K1.

By this time the Navy had also started using the Type 93 Intermediate Seaplane Trainer for primary training. As a result, and with sufficient numbers of the Type 90 Primary Seaplane Trainer on hand, production of the Kawanishi K8K1, Type 0 Primary Seaplane Trainer ended after only fifteen were built.

Single-engine twin-float biplane trainer. Metal fuselage and wooden wing structure with fabric covering. Crew of two in open cockpits.

130-160hp Gasuden Jimpu 2 seven-cylinder air-cooled radial engine, driving a two-bladed wooden propeller.

Span 10m (32ft 9½in); length 8.7m (28ft 6½in); wing area 25sq m (269sq ft).

Empty weight 750kg (1,653lb); loaded weight 1,015kg (2,237lb).

Maximum speed 91.8kt (105.6 mph); cruising speed 64.8kt (74.56 mph); alighting speed 40.5kt (46.6 mph); climb to 3,000m (9,843ft) in 20min; service ceiling 3,500m (11,482 ft); endurance 4hr.

Three built in 1938.

Experimental Research Aircraft (MXY1 and 2)

In 1935 the Naval Air Headquarters Engineering Department established guidance for new aircraft projects and placed the responsibility for various test functions upon the Aeroplane Department of Kusho. As a result a flight-test vehicle was designed and built exclusively for aerodynamic research and testing. This unusual angular parasol monoplane was designed and built at the Watanabe Iron Works, under the designer direction of Shigeki Naito, supervised for the Navy by Naval engineer Jun-ichiro Nagahata. Design work began in November 1937 and lasted until the following July. The first of two aeroplanes was completed in September 1939.

This strut-braced parasol-monoplane was based upon the British Parnall Parasol features for the wing angle of incidence and tailplane settings for different test measurements found on the Parnall were incorporated into the Watanabe aeroplane. Many types of aerodynamic test equipment were installed in the fuselage of this flying laboratory that was, for some odd reason, unoffocially called the 'Glasgow Test-plane' by the people in charge of the project. There was provision for a pilot and a test crew of four.

This aeroplane was plagued by severe vibration during ground run-ups, thought to be too severe to go uncorrected before test flying. Modifications were made but to no avail, and further development was suspended. A second, and different, aeroplane followed, known as the Experimental Research Aircraft No.2 and officially designated XXY2 (later MXY2) but work was terminated after the structural strength tests had been completed.

These were the first Japanese aeroplanes designed exclusively for research, yet little has been recorded about them. Too much time was consumed on design and construction and, as a consequence, they were not developed sufficiently to serve the purpose intended for them and were considered obsolete by the time the first was completed. They were dismantled and their components used for research purposes.

Single-engine strut-braced parasol-monoplane with non-retractable undercarriage. Wood and metal construction with fabric covering. Pilot and four technicians in enclosed cockpits.

670-730hp Nakajima Hikari 1 nine-cylinder air-cooled radial engine, driving a ground-adjustable two-bladed metal propeller.

One completed in 1939.

Design work at Watanabe continued with Navy guidance for a 12-Shi Small Reconnaissance Seaplane for submarine use. The Navy's Yokosho design, the E14Y1 was accepted in 1939 and Watanabe was awarded the contract to build the aeroplane that became known to the Allies as Glen, previously mentioned under the Type 96 Small Reconnaissance Seaplane. There were no further Watanabe designs and from October 1943 the company became known as the Kyushu Hikoki KK (Kyushu Aeroplane Company Ltd).

Watanabe Experimental Research Aircraft (MXY1)

Yokosho, Kusho and Kugisho (Naval Air Arsenal at Yokosuka)

This Naval Air Arsenal was referred to by more names than any other Japanese aircraft manufacturer, each depending upon a given period of its existence and related circumstances. Most terms used were acronyms derived from its military name or designation, one that was often changed, but throughout, the name Yokosuka prevailed, even though it is a geographical location only and not part of the arsenal name except in its very early days.

The aircraft construction facility at Yokosuka has a very complicated background that goes back to the establishment of a Naval arsenal for the Imperial Japanese Navy in late 1869. This arsenal at Yokosuka, 13 miles south of Yokohama on Tokyo Bay, was established as the focal point for Naval shipbuilding, ship repairs, storage of munitions and the procurement of assorted naval supplies. When the first aeroplanes such as the Maurice Farmans and Curtiss types were imported by the Navy they were processed through this facility. They had to be assembled and periodically repaired, which logically led to modifications to existing designs, the building of new aeroplanes patterned on the old, and eventually creating and building new designs. To facilitate this work, the Aeroplane Factory, Ordnance Department, was formed at the torpedo plant of the Yokosuka Naval Arsenal in May 1913. There were no civil aircraft firms in Japan at that time to call upon for this type of work. It was during the following year, 1914, that the first acronym used in conjunction with Navy-built aircraft was formed, Yokosho, meaning Yokosuka Kaigun Ko-sho (Yoksuka Naval Arsenal).

To render further assistance in the development of Naval aircraft,

the Navy established, in December 1919, the Kaigun Koku Shikensho (Naval Establishment for Aeronautical Research). This was located at Tsukiji, in the central part of Tokyo, in close proximity to other agencies doing aeronautical research.

(Up until this time, there was a similar organization located at a branch of the Tokyo Imperial University at Etchujima, Tokyo, known as the Aeronautical Research Institute. This Institute had been established in 1908 and, while being very small, it was regarded as an extension of the University laboratory. However, by July 1921 with greater interest being shown in aviation, this Institute became independent of the University and developed into an important facility).

By April 1923, with fast growing emphasis on aviation, the Navy organized the Kaigun Gijutsu Kenkyusho (Naval Technical Research Institute) by grouping together several Naval support units. These included the Kaigun Koku Shikensho, Kaigun Kankei Shikensho (Naval Hull Testing Facility) and Tsukiji Kaigun Zoheisho (Tsukiji Naval Ordnance Arsenal), all of which were located at Tsukiji. Five months later, however, on 1 September 1923, their facilities were completely destroyed by the earthquake. Gone were Japan's early wind tunnels, the first of which was an Eiffel type and the second was a Göttingen type.

To restore this Navy establishment, it built a more advanced and larger technical research institute at Meguro, Tokyo, for ships and ordnance research. The aircraft research group was separated and moved to a corner of the Kasumigaura Naval Air Base, northeast of Tokyo, in January 1924, as the Kasumigaura Branch, Naval Technical Research Institute.

The first test equipment installed at Kasumigaura was the German Göttingen type wind tunnel designed and supervised in construction by Dr Wiselsberger of the Aerodynamische Versuchsanstalt Göttingen (Göttingen Aerodynamic Laboratory).* Research work began on 28 November, 1924, with the evaluation of aircraft performance and struc-

tures, as well as materials used in aeroplanes, airships and aero-engines.

On 1 April, 1927, the Naval Air Headquarters was established, at which time the management of all Naval aviation projects came under its control. Under this command on 1 April, 1932, the Kaigun Koku-sho (Naval Air Arsenal) was formed at Yokosuka. Included was the Yokosuka Kokutai at Oppama Naval Air Base which undertook operational evaluation of newly developed aircraft in addition to its activities as the district Naval air base. Amalgamated units from the Ordnance Department of the Yokosuka Naval Arsenal were the Aeroplane Factory, Aero-engine Factory and Flight Experiment Group, along with the Kasumigaura Branch of the Naval Technical Research Institute. Design engineers and a large number of draftsmen from the Hiro Arsenal were transferred to the Naval Air Arsenal, leaving as Hirosho's last design the G2H1 of 1932.

Throughout its existence until the end of the Second World War, this Navy air arsenal was most often referred to by its geographical name Yokosuka, which was not specific as to which of the several functions assigned at this Naval facility was being referred to. For the purpose of specific identification, it progressively had four distinct and significant names and acronyms. In addition to Yokosho these were

Starting date	Name	Acronym
1 April, 1932	Kaigun Koku-sho (Naval Air Arsenal)	Kusho
1 April, 1939	Kaigun Koku-Gijutsu-Sho (Naval Technical Air Arsenal)	Kugisho
15 February, 1945	Dai-Ichi Kaigun Gijutsu-sho (1st Naval Technical Arsenal)	Ichi-Gisho

*Wiselsberger also designed and supervised the wind tunnel at Tsukiji, as well as those at the Army Tachikawa Air Technical Research Institute and Kawanishi.

The acronyms were used officially as the identification of the manufacturer for these air arsenal aircraft, depending upon the acronym in use at that time. As a letter identifier for aircraft designations, the Y for Yokosuka was used in all these cases, i.e. E5Y1, and therefore loosely referred to as Yokosuka being the manufacturer. The acronym Ichi-Gisho was not used in conjunction with an aircraft since none entered production during the short period of its use.

A very large engineering staff was assigned at the Naval Air Arsenal, both civil and military. By the end of the war, this total work force of Ichi-Gisho reached 31,700 for all branches. It was not only here that the Navy designed many of its own aircraft in competition with civil manufacturers, but it provided technical assistance as well as guidance to these manufacturers in the production of Naval aircraft. Many of the Yokosho, Kusho and Kugisho designs were contracted for manufacture by civil companies, yet retained the Y identifier.

Navy Type Mo Small Seaplane

The first two Maurice Farman Seaplanes were imported into Japan by the Navy and assembled at Oppama for initial flying demonstrations in October and November 1912. An additional two were purchased and used for flying training over a considerable period. The relatively simple construction was soon copied by the Yokosuka Naval Arsenal which added a small number to the four already imported. Being of the same type as that of the Army, they received the same short designation Type Mo Small Seaplane. These had fabric-covered wooden structures and were equipped with twin Tellier-type wooden floats. The two seats were in tandem in a fuselage pod, with a 70hp Renault pusher engine in the rear.

When the Tsingtao Campaign erupted in September 1914, three of the imported Type Mo Small Seaplanes, together with one imported Type Mo Large Seaplane, were

Yokosho Navy Type Mo Small Seaplane.

carried by the seaplane tender *Wakamiya* to participate in the campaign. They were soon joined by a fourth aircraft which was a Japanese-made Type Mo Small Seaplane of the same type. These aeroplanes, manned by seven pilots during this two-month operation, succeeded in making 49 sorties during which they dropped 199 bombs. Working with Army aircraft in these air operations, they were unsuccessful in attacks on their most important target, the cruiser *Kaiserin Elisabeth,* but did succeed in sinking one small torpedo-boat with bombing attacks.

Single-engine twin-float pusher biplane reconnaissance/bomber. Wooden structure with fabric covering. Crew of two in open cockpit.

70hp Renault eight-cylinder vee air-cooled engine, driving a two-bladed wooden propeller.

Span 15.50m (58ft 10¼in); length 10.14m (33ft 3in); height 3.80m (12ft 5½in); wing area 56sq m (602.798sq ft).

Empty weight 650kg (1,433lb); loaded weight 855kg (1,884lb).

Maximum speed 46kt (53mph) at sea level; climb to 500m (1,640ft) in 11min; service ceiling 1,500m (4,921ft); endurance 3hr.

Several built beginning in July 1913.

Navy Type Ka Seaplane (Curtiss 1912 Seaplane)

Having been ordered to return early from a flying school in the United States, Lieut Sankichi Kohno was only halfway through his training at the time. Along with a Farman Seaplane, the Curtiss Seaplane which Kohno brought with him was to be demonstrated during a naval review

Yokosho Navy Type Ka Seaplane.

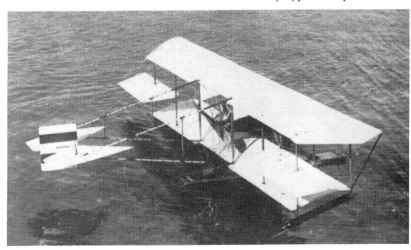

on 12 November, 1912, to give official recognition to aviation as part of the Japanese Navy. Hastily assembled, the Curtiss was first flown by Kohno on 2 November, but a few flights later, while he was gaining experience and carrying a passenger, the aeroplane overturned when struck by a wave and had to be hastily dismantled and repaired.

Recognizing that the water around Oppama was too rough for his limited experience, Kohno decided to leave for the Naval demonstration from the calmer waters around Yokohama. The British trading firm, Sale & Frazar Ltd, co-operated by providing a building for the re-assembly of the aeroplane and a ramp for its launching. As a result the demonstration flight over the Japanese fleet by Lieut Kohno was made without incident, marking the first of the official Navy flights, with the Farman flown by Lieut Kaneko. The flights covered 17 nautical miles and lasted 35 minutes.

In addition to the two Curtiss 1912 Seaplanes imported from the United States, other aircraft of the type were built at the Department of Ordnance, Yokosuka Naval Arsenal, under the designation Type Ka Seaplane, later re-designated I-go Otsu-gata Seaplane. Their service life was short, being phased out of the Navy inventory by mid-1915.

Single-engine pusher biplane seaplane. Wooden structure with fabric covered wings and tail. Pilot and one passenger in open seats.

75hp Curtiss O eight-cylinder vee water-cooled engine, driving a two-bladed wooden propeller.

Span 11.348m (37ft 2¾in); length 8.458m (27ft 9in); height 2.496m (8ft 2in); wing area 33sq m (355.22sq ft).

Empty weight 535kg (1,180lb); loaded weight 745kg (1,642lb).

Maximum speed 43kt (50mph); endurance 3hr.

Several built.

Experimental Japanese-Navy-Type Seaplane

This aeroplane is claimed to be the Japanese Navy's first aeroplane of original design. It closely followed the lines of the classic Curtiss pusher. Differences were that it had unequal span with the ailerons mounted on the top wing. The cockpit nacelle design was influenced by Maurice Farman aeroplanes. It was a tandem-seat aircraft for two crew, with the engine placed behind the cockpit in a pusher configuration. Like the Curtiss, this too had a single broad beam centreline float. From this first Navy aeroplane Lieutenant (Engineering) Chikuhei Nakajima was in charge of the design and construction of this and other aircraft, giving him the experience to later start his own aircraft manufacturing company.

This aeroplane was completed in the autumn of 1913, and test flown by Lieut Tadaharu Yamada, a qualified instructor who had obtained his flying experience from the Curtiss Flying School. Only one aeroplane of this type was built because during test flights it was found to have quite heavy controls. By this time, the Japanese Navy

Yokosho Experimental Japanese-Navy-Type Seaplane.

owned three Curtiss seaplanes and four Maurice Farman seaplanes, therefore this Navy built aeroplane became unofficially known as the Navy No.8 Aeroplane. This is one of the rare incidences that an American design influenced the design of an early Japanese aircraft.

Single-engine single-float pusher sesquiplane. Wooden structure with wings, empennage and crew nacelle covered with fabric. Crew of two in open cockpit.

75hp Curtiss O eight-cylinder vee water-cooled engine, driving a two-bladed wooden pusher propeller.

Span, upper 14.02m (46ft), lower 10.97m (36ft).

One built in 1913.

Navy Type Mo Large Seaplane (Maurice Farman 1914 Seaplane)

This was a large seaplane with a 100hp engine which the Navy imported from France in 1914. Designated Type Mo Large Seaplane, it was superior in general performance to the Type Mo Small Seaplane, particularly in its operational altitude of 3,000m (9,843ft). The aeroplane was larger than the 1912 model and could carry a crew of three.

Soon after its arrival from France the aeroplane was deployed aboard the seaplane tender *Wakamiya* in support of the Tsingtao Campaign in September 1914, along with the three Type Mo Small Seaplanes. They were used in this operation for reconnaissance, spotting of German mines, and bombing missions.

Production of the Type Mo Large Seaplane was undertaken by the Yokosuka Naval Arsenal with few changes. Most noteworthy was the change of engine to the 100hp Benz instead of the 100hp Renault installed in the imported example. Eventually these Type Mo Large Seaplanes were redesignated Ro-go Otsu-gata.

It was only natural to continually test the capabilities of these and other aircraft with long-distance and duration flights. On 4 March,

Yokosho Navy Type Mo Large Seaplane.

1915, Lieut Kishichi Umakoshi piloted one of the Ro-go Otsu-gata (serial No.2) for nearly eight hours over a closed course Oppama, Yokosuka, Yokohama, Bohsou coastline, Miura Peninsula, and back to Oppama. This endurance record was soon broken by a similar aircraft that recorded a duration of 10hr 5min, covering 434nm (500 sm), and, with another, an altitude of 3,500m (11,500ft) was recorded.

The first fatal accident involving Japanese Naval aviators occurred with one of the Yokosho-made aircraft (serial No.15) when it crashed at sea on 6 March, 1915, with Sub-Lieuts Tozaburo Adachi and Takao Takerube along with W/O 3/c Hisanojo Yanase on board, killing all three.

Single-engine twin-float pusher biplane reconnaissance/bomber with enclosed crew nacelle. Wooden structure with fabric covering. Crew of three in open cockpit.

100hp Benz six-cylinder inline water-cooled engine, driving a two-bladed wooden propeller.

Span 19.02m (62ft 5in); length 9.43m (30ft 11¼in); height 4m (13ft 1½in); wing area 50sq m (538.213sq ft).

Empty weight 995kg (2,193lb); loaded weight 1,363kg (3,004lb).

Maximum speed 52kt (59.8mph) at sea level; climb to 1,000m (3,280ft) in 25min; endurance 4½-6½hr.

At least fifteen built.

Experimental Yokosho Nakajima Tractor Seaplane

By 1914 Chikuhei Nakajima was the chief designer of the Navy's Aeroplane Factory, part of the Ordnance Department at the Yokosuka Naval Arsenal. He created the first tractor float biplane in Japan, having closely studied Farman and Deperdussin aircraft designs. Completed in February 1915, this seaplane was known as the Nakajima-type Tractor. On its initial flight, when Lieut Fumio Inoue had only reached about 5m (16ft 6in) it went out of control and crashed, but a second example was built in September 1915 and successfully flight tested.

Tests of performance and reliability were made in comparison with a Yokosho-built and modified Farman seaplane. Having proved successful, a third aeroplane of the Nakajima-type Tractor was completed in June 1916, this one powered by an imported 160hp Salmson engine. The aeroplane proved to be less practical than the Ro-go Otsu-gata three-seat pusher aeroplane, the Japanese-built larger version of a Maurice Farman with modifications.

The Yokosho Nakajima Tractor was the first original design by Chikuhei Nakajima.

Single-engine twin-float tractor biplane. Wooden structure with fabric

Experimental Yokosho Nakajima Tractor Seaplane.

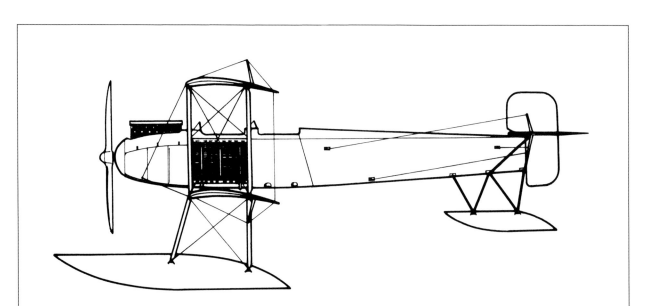

Experimental Yokosho Nakajima Tractor Seaplane. (Shorzoe Abe).

covering. Crew of two in open cockpit.

100-115hp Benz F-D six-cylinder water-cooled inline engine, driving a two-bladed wooden propeller.

Span 15m (49ft 2½in); length 9m (25ft 6in); height 4m (13ft 1½in); wing area 69sq m (742.734sq ft).

Maximum speed 54kt (62mph) at sea level.

Three built in 1915 and 1916.

Experimental Yokosho Twin-engined Seaplane

This aeroplane not only has significance in being the first twin-engined aeroplane built in Japan, but, once completed, no one would fly it. Few pilots in Japan, if any, had ever seen a twin-engined aeroplane. However, it did influence future designs as a result of the experience gained in its design and ground testing.

Intrigued with the idea of launching torpedoes from aircraft, Nakajima pursued this idea, beginning in about 1914. To explore this concept, he designed an aeroplane for

this purpose in April 1916 at the Yokosuka Naval Arsenal. This twin-float biplane could carry a modified version of a 14-inch torpedo which was shortened from a standard torpedo-boat weapon.

When the aeroplane was completed it was claimed to be the most powerful and the fastest aeroplane in Japan. But their claims were never substantiated, since none of the thirty Navy pilots stationed at the Oppama Naval Air Base would volunteer to fly the aeroplane. None had acquired twin-engine flying experience even while studying in other countries. As a result,

Experimental Yokosho Twin-engined Seaplane. (Shorzoe Abe).

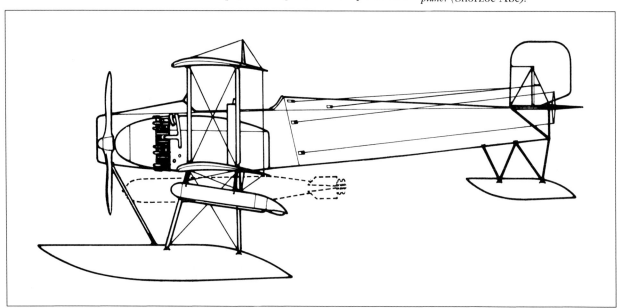

only water taxi-ing tests were made, and the aeroplane was eventually stored in the South Hangar at Oppama.

Twin-engined twin-float biplane with tail float. Wooden structure with fabric covering. Crew of two in open cockpit.

Two 200hp Salmson 2M-7 seven-cylinder water-cooled radial engines, driving two-bladed wooden propellers.

Torpedo weighing 350kg (771lb) having a range of 500 to 600m (1,640 to 1,968ft).

Span 20m (65ft 7½in); length 12m (39ft 4¾in); aspect ratio 12.

Estimated maximum speed 70kt (81mph) at sea level; endurance 4hr.

One built in April 1916.

Experimental Yokosho Ho-go Otsu-gata Seaplane

Based upon the experience gained with the Yokosho Nakajima Tractor Seaplane, two experimental reconnaissance bomber seaplanes were completed in January 1916. These single-engined aeroplanes had larger wings than the earlier type. They were powered by the 200hp Salmson engine, claimed to be the most powerful aircraft engine at that time. Once again Nakajima was the chief designer. His assistant was Sub-Lieut Kishichi Umakoshi, an aircraft designer as well as a test pilot.

The design was a success and two additional aeroplanes were built in 1919 and 1920 respectively. Both were powered by the newer 220hp Peugeot engines. All four aircraft were used for research into long-range reconnaissance and bombing. Compared with the Short Reconnaissance Seaplane imported in 1916, the Japanese aeroplanes had better performance.

They were unfortunately aeroplanes without a purpose, because the Japanese Navy had not yet been organized with air units. Consequently, they were never put into production for operational use although the design was accepted in June 1918 as the Experimental Yokosho Ho-go Otsu-gata Seaplane.

Experimental Yokosho Ho-go Otsu-gata Seaplane.

Single-engine twin-float unequal-span biplane. Wooden structure with fabric covering. Rearward folding wings for stowage. Crew of two in open cockpits.

200hp Salmson 2M-7 seven-cylinder water-cooled radial engine, driving a two-bladed wooden propeller (first two aircraft); 200–230hp Peugeot eight-cylinder vee water-cooled engine, driving a two-bladed wooden propeller (last two aircraft).

One bomb could be carried beneath the fuselage.

Span 21m (68ft 10¾in); length 9.60m (31ft 6in); height 4.122m (13ft 6in).

Maximum speed 52kt (60mph) at sea level; endurance 11.7hr.

Four built in 1916-1920.

Yokosho Navy Short Reconnaissance Seaplane.

Navy Short Reconnaissance Seaplane (Short 225 Seaplane, Type S.184)

Recognizing the capability of the Royal Navy's Short 184 seaplane, the Japanese Navy dispatched Capt Shiro Yamauchi to England to purchase one, as well as a Sopwith fighter seaplane. The Short arrived in Japan in November 1916 and was referred to as the Short Reconnaissance Seaplane, even though the British used it as a torpedo bomber from 1915 to the end of the First World War.

The Japanese Navy used the aeroplane extensively for testing various engines such as the 230hp Salmson A9, 220hp Renault V8, 225hp Sunbeam V12, and the 200hp Peugeot V8. As an experiment, the Aero-

Yokosho Navy Ha-go Small Seaplane.

One nose-mounted fixed 7.7mm machine-gun.

Span 7.223m (23ft 8¼in); length 6.634m (21ft 9in); height 3m (9ft 10in); wing area 22.3sq m (240sq ft).

Empty weight 528kg (1,164lb); loaded weight 697kg (1,536lb).

Maximum speed 78kt (90mph) at sea level; climb to 1,500m (4,921ft) in 13min; endurance 2½hr.

Ten built beginning 1921.

Weights and performance with Gnome engine.

plane Factory, Department of Ordnance, Yokosuka Naval Arsenal, built a few of these aeroplanes with various engine installations but it was not put into quantity production.

Single-engine twin-float reconnaissance three-bay biplane. Wooden structure with fabric covering. Auxiliary floats beneath wingtips and tail. Rearward folding wings for stowage. Crew of two in open cockpits.

One dorsal flexible 7.7mm machine-gun. Bomb load: Maximum 235kg (518lb), or one 14in torpedo.

Various engines driving two-bladed wooden propellers. The data here are for the 230hp Salmson powered aircraft.

Span 19.50m (63ft 11¾in); length 12.735m (41ft 9¼in); height 3.76m (12ft 4in); wing area 63.9sq m (687.836 sq ft).

Empty weight 1,472kg (3,245lb); loaded weight 1,976kg (4,356lb).

Maximum speed 63kt (72.5mph); climb to 1,000m (3,280ft) in 11min 20sec.

Three built.

Navy Ha-go Small Seaplane (Sopwith Schneider Fighter Seaplane)

Capt Shiro Yamauchi acquired a Sopwith Schneider fighter floatplane while on his aviation inspection tour in England in August 1915. As a direct descendant of the famous Schneider Trophy winner it became known as the Schneider and bore a close resemblance to its predecessor, the Tabloid, which

could also be float equipped. Also known as a Sopwith Baby, the aeroplane arrived in Japan by ship in May 1916 and became the Japanese Navy's first fighter seaplane.

Originally this aeroplane was powered by a 100hp Gnome engine, but those manufactured by Aichi under the Naval designation Ha-go Small Seaplane were powered by the 110hp Le Rhône engine. Training for aerial combat with this aeroplane was begun in March 1918 by Sub-Lieut Shirase, and the first loop by a Japanese Naval officer was made by Lieut Torao Kuwahara with one of these aeroplanes.

Single-engine twin-float fighter biplane. Three-float undercarriage. Wooden structure with fabric covering. Pilot in open cockpit.

100hp Gnome nine-cylinder air-cooled rotary engine, or one 110hp Le Rhône eleven-cylinder air-cooled rotary engine, driving a two-bladed wooden propeller.

Experimental Yokosho Ho-go Small Seaplane

In addition to the larger Ho-go aeroplane previously described, a smaller seaplane design was created in 1917 in an attempt to achieve better manoeuvrability. Sub-Lieut Kishichi Umakoshi was the designer, and the aeroplane was completed in 1918. Features of the Short Reconnaissance Seaplane and Sopwith Fighter Seaplane were incorporated into the design.

At that time pilots were being trained in the Farman Small (I-go) and Large (Ro-go) pusher aircraft. However, the Ho-go Small Seaplane had a higher speed, especially noticeable on take off and alighting and pilots found the aeroplane very difficult to handle. As a consequence, only one aeroplane of this type was built, but it provided valuable experience for the design of the Ro-go Ko-gata which followed.

Experimental Yokosho Ho-go Small Seaplane.

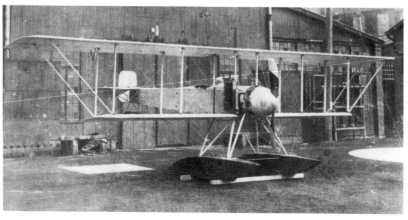

Single-engine twin-float biplane. Wooden structure with fabric covering. Rearward folding wings for stowage. Crew of two in open cockpit.

130hp Salmson M-9 nine-cylinder water-cooled radial engine, driving a two-bladed wooden propeller.

Span 14.60m (47ft 11in); length 9.955m (32ft 8in); height 3.62m (11ft 10½in).

Empty weight 884kg (1,948lb); loaded weight 1,364kg (3,007lb).

Maximum speed 67kt (77mph) at sea level; climb to 3,000m (9,843ft) in 60min; endurance 6½hr.

One built in 1918.

Navy Yokosho Ro-go Ko-gata Reconnaissance Seaplane with Hispano-Suiza E engine.

Navy Yokosho Ro-go Ko-gata Reconnaissance Seaplane

During the First World War a number of Yokosho seaplane designs were created by Lieut Nakajima with the assistance of Lieut Kishichi Umakoshi, and there was much test flying associated with the improvement of these designs. Using foreign techniques, Umakoshi designed a reconnaissance seaplane with the emphasis on stability and control. The first prototype was completed in the autumn of 1917 and flight tests began in early 1918. Better performance was achieved with this aeroplane than with any previous Japanese Navy aircraft.

Production began immediately at the Yokosuka Naval Arsenal and four aeroplanes were built in 1918. Confirming acceptance as a Navy type, they were officially designated Ro-go Ko-gata. Originally powered by a 140hp Salmson engine, the engine was soon changed to the newer 200hp Salmson, followed by the 200hp Mitsubishi type Hi (Hispano) engines which were used in production aircraft. The Ro-go Ko-gata was the first of the Japanese Navy's aircraft to be put into production.

In April 1919 three of these aeroplanes were converted from two-seaters to single-seaters to increase their fuel capacity. In this configuration they made a record-breaking long-distance flight from Oppama, to Kure near Hiroshima, Chinhae (22 miles west of Pusan in Korea), Sasebo in western Kyushu, and return to Oppama. On this flight, Sub-Lieut Kanjo Akashiba set a record by flying from Sasebo to Oppama on 20 April, 1919, an indirect distance of 1,300km (808 sm) in 11hr and 35min at an average speed of 61kt.

The manufacture of these aircraft continued at Yokosuka Naval Arsenal until 1921. In 1920 production was begun by Aichi and Nakajima, making this the first Naval aeroplane built by Nakajima. In November 1923, to conform with a new Navy designation system for aircraft, the official Navy designation for these aeroplanes was changed to Yokosho-Type Reconnaissance Seaplane.

This first mass-produced aeroplane for the Navy was widely used together with the Hansa Reconnaissance Seaplane over the period 1921 to 1926.

In appreciation of his success, which began with the prototype design, Lieut Kishichi Umakoshi was given special recognition by the Minister of the Navy, the first for an aeroplane designer.

The entry into service of the Yokosho Ro-go Ko-gata, with its increased speed and manoeuvrability, made the Farman pusher seaplanes obsolete, and they were taken out of service. In time, a number of this newer type was released for civil use on such duties as mail carriage. Some were in service as late as 1928.

Navy Yokosho Ro-go Ko-gata Reconnaissance Seaplane with Salmson engine used on early models.

Single-engine twin-float biplane. Wooden structure with fabric covering. Rearward folding wings for stowage. Crew of two in open cockpits.

130-140hp Salmson M-9 (Type Sa) nine-cylinder water-cooled radial engine, driving a two-bladed wooden propeller (prototype); 200hp Salmson 2M-7 nine-cylinder water-cooled radial engine, driving a two-bladed wooden propeller (pre-production); 200-220hp Mitsubishi Type Hi (Hispano-Suiza E) eight-cylinder vee water-cooled engine, driving a two-bladed propeller (production).

One dorsal flexible 7.7mm machine-gun.

Continued

	Prototype	Production
Span	15.53m (50ft 11½in)	15.692m (51ft 6in)
Length	10.172m (33ft 4½in)	10.16m (33ft 4in)
Height	3.68m (12ft 1in)	3.666m (12ft)
Wing area	48.22sq m	48.22sq m
	(519.052sq ft)	(519.052sq ft)
Empty weight	1,211kg (2,669lb)	1,070kg (2,358lb)
Loaded weight	1,676kg (3,694lb)	1,628kg (3,589lb)
Wing loading	34.75kg/sq m	33.76kg/sq m
	(7.1lb/sq ft)	(6.9lb/sq ft)
Power loading	12.9kg/hp (28.4lb/hp)	8.1kg/hp (17.8lb/hp)
Maximum speed	75kt (86.36mph)	84kt (96.72mph)
Climb to	500m (1,640ft)	500m (1,640ft)
in	4min 12sec	4min
Range	—	420nm (483sm)
Endurance	—	5hr

218 built: thirty-two Yokosho (1917 to 1921) Type Sa and Type Hi engines, eighty Aichi (1920 to 1924) Type Hi engine and 106 Nakajima (1920 to 1924) Type Hi engine.

Navy Yokosho I-go Ko-gata Seaplane Trainer

As the replacement for the pusher I-go (Farman Small Model), a new design for a tractor seaplane trainer was created by chief designer Lieut Kishichi Umakoshi in 1920. Based on experience of previous Yokosho aeroplanes, he adopted the staggered wing configuration used on the popular Avro 504K.

Various engines were tried including the 70hp and 100hp Renaults, 200hp Hispano-Suiza and the more popular 100hp, 110hp and 130hp Benz engines. The twin-float arrangement with an auxiliary float beneath the rear fuselage was similar to that of the Ro-go Ko-gata which was standard at that time. This was the Japanese Navy's first real seaplane trainer and was influential on the designs of this type that followed.

These seaplanes remained in operational service until around 1924 at which time many were released for civil use. As civil aeroplanes they were known as *Chidori-go* (Plover) and Nippon Koku Yuso Kenkyusho (Japan Air Transport Research Association), established in 1922, used six of them successfully for cargo and mail transport. Others were converted as civil aircraft with 160hp Daimler engines.

Single-engine twin-float two-bay biplane trainer. Wooden structure with fabric covering. Student and instructor in open cockpits.

130hp Gasuden Benz F-D six-cylinder water-cooled inline engine, driving a two-bladed wooden propeller.

Span 13.784m (45ft 2¾in); length 9.755m (32ft); height 3.25m (10ft 8in); wing area 41.1sq m (442.411sq ft).

Empty weight 873kg (1,924lb); loaded weight 1,124kg (2,478lb); wing loading 27.3kg/sq m (5.6lb/sq ft); power loading 8.64kg/hp (19lb/hp).

Navy Yokosho I-go Ko-gata Seaplane Trainer.

Maximum speed 67kt (77mph) at sea level; climb to 1,000m (3,280ft) in 5min; endurance 3hr.

Seventy built: twenty-four in 1920 (ten with 130hp Benz, ten with 70hp Renault, two with 100hp Benz, two with 100hp Renault); forty-two in 1921 (thirty-six with 110hp Benz and six with 200hp Hispano-Suiza); and four in 1922 with 130hp Benz.

Navy F.5 Flying-boat

The British Aviation Mission, which visited Japan in 1921 to instruct the Japanese Navy in the application of airpower, left its mark with its introduction of modern aircraft into the country. Among these was the very advanced Felixstowe F.5 flying-boat for which the Japanese Navy obtained manufacturing rights. The first six of these large, twin-engined biplanes were built from components sent to Japan from England and assembled at the Aeroplane Factory, Ordnance Department of the Yokosuka Naval Arsenal, in April 1921. This led to the manufacture of four more at Yokosuka, a total of ten, until production was moved to the Hiro Arsenal as well as to Aichi where the largest number was produced. (*see* Hirosho Navy F.5 Flying-boat).

Navy Avro 504 Trainer

In 1921 The Master of Sempill's British Aviation Mission took thirty Avro 504 primary trainers to Japan for use by the Japanese Navy. These consisted of twenty Avro 504K landplane trainers (now called 504L), and ten seaplane trainers (504S), both types being outstanding in their class. The Japanese Navy decided to adopt these as its standard primary trainer and put them into production.

To prepare for production, the Navy sent several of its officers to Avro to study the process. Among them were Capt (Ordnance) Ryuzo Tanaka, Capt (Ordnance) Tomasu Koyama, Lieut Kishichi Umakoshi, Lieut Misao Wada, and Engineer Katsusuke Hashimoto. The Navy purchased the manufacturing rights

Navy Avro 504L Land-based Trainer.

from A V Roe, and supplied both Nakajima and Aichi with actual sample aircraft and manufacturing drawings for their production when placing its orders. The Avro trainer for the Navy was in Nakajima production from 1922 to 1924 during which time the company built 250 in various versions.

Aichi built thirty 504s fitted as twin-float seaplane trainers. The land-version was generally referred to simply as the Avro L and the seaplane model was the Avro S; however, the official Navy designation was Avro Land-based Trainer and Avro Seaplane Trainer.

After the introduction of this aircraft by the Sempill Aviation Mission, it had a long life as the Japanese Navy's typical primary trainer. The later model, the 504N, developed into the Navy Type 3 Primary Trainer. Around 1927-28, a number of these Avro-designed trainers were released for civil use and were highly regarded. They had good stability and control, and

Navy Avro 504S Seaplane Trainer.

were good aerobatic aircraft. A few were still flying as late as 1937 and were the last of the rotary-powered aircraft in regular flying operations.

Single-engine land- and seaplane trainer biplane. Wooden structure with fabric covering. Student and instructor in open cockpits.

120hp-130hp Le Rhône nine-cylinder air-cooled rotary engine, driving a two- or four-bladed wooden propeller.

One dorsal flexible 7.7mm machine-gun, (optional).

Span 10.98m (36ft); length 8.57m (28ft 1½in); height 3.03m (9ft 11¼in); wing area 30.7sq m (330.462sq ft).

Empty weight 557kg (1,228lb); loaded weight 830kg (1,830lb); wing loading 27kg/sq m (5.5lb/sq ft); power loading 6.9kg/hp (15.2lb/hp).

Maximum speed 78kt (90mph); cruising speed 64kt (73.6mph); landing speed 30kt (34.5mph); climb to 3,000m (9,843ft) in 23min; service ceiling 4,340m (14,238ft); endurance 3hr; range 185nm (213sm).

250 built by Nakajima 1922 to 1924 (wheel and float versions), thirty by Aichi from 1922 (float version).

Navy Type Hansa Reconnaissance Seaplane

After the First World War, the Japanese Navy received from Germany a Hansa-Brandenburg W 33 reconnaissance seaplane as part of war reparations.* By 1922, the Navy decided to adopt this aeroplane as standard equipment and placed orders for their production with Nakajima and Aichi. The original Hansa seaplane, designed by Dr Ernst Heinkel, was considered to be very advanced structurally and have excellent performance. To make it better suited to Japanese needs, modifications were made in the Nakajima production model.

The Type Hansa was adopted to replace the Navy Type Yokosho Ro-go Ko-gata Reconnaissance Seaplane. This was the Navy's first low-wing ship-based monoplane. They were easily identifiable by their unusual tail configuration, having the vertical surfaces below the tailplane. Pilots who flew these aeroplanes disliked their water-handling because of poor directional control and inadequate downward visibility. They also had other shortcomings.

These were the first reconnaissance seaplanes to be carried on the battleship *Nagato*, beginning in 1926. Many remained in Navy service until around 1927 and 1928 when they were replaced with the Yokosho and Nakajima-built Type 14 and Type 15 Reconnaissance Seaplanes.

When the Hansas became surplus the Ando Aeroplane Research Studio and Japan Air Transport Research Association converted some of them into cabin passenger aircraft with three to five seats.

Single-engine twin-float low-wing monoplane. Wooden structure with fabric covered wing and tail, with plycovered fuselage. Crew of two in open cockpits.

170-210hp Mitsubishi Type Hi twelve-cylinder water-cooled vee en-

*War reparations made to the Allied nations, of which Japan was one, included the dividing and delivering of German aircraft and engines and their manufacturing rights, including Hansa seaplanes and BMW engines.

Navy Type Hansa Reconnaissance Seaplane.

gine, driving a two-bladed wooden propeller.

One dorsal flexible 7.7mm machine-gun.

Span 13.57m (44ft 6¼in); length 9.287m (30ft 5½in); height 2.996m (9ft 10in); wing area 31.3sq m (336.921 sq ft).

Empty weight 1,470kg (3,240lb); loaded weight 2,100kg (4,629lb); wing loading 67.1kg/sq m (13.7lb/sq ft); power loading 10.5kg/hp (23.1lb/hp).

Maximum speed 91kt (104.7mph); climb to 3,000m (9,843ft) in 23min; service ceiling 4,500m (14,763ft).

Approximately 310 built with 160 by Nakajima 1922–25 and 150 by Aichi.

Navy Type 10 Reconnaissance Seaplane

A new design for a high performance reconnaissance seaplane was begun in 1921 as a replacement for the Ro-go Ko-gata type. This aeroplane called the 10th Year Type (meaning 10th year of Taisho) two-seat reconnaissance seaplane, was designed to have the very powerful 400hp Lorraine engine, the first in Japan with this engine. Another first in Japan was the use of long single-step floats which eliminated the need for a tail float. The design was a co-operative effort by Lieut Misao Wada,* Sub Lieut (Ordnance) Jun Okamura and Engineer Masasuke Hashimoto, under the leadership of Mr Fletcher, a member of a visiting Short Brothers' team from England, which in turn was under the leadership of

*Later Vice Admiral Wada, Chief of the Naval Air Headquarters, by the end of the Pacific War.

an engineer named Dodd.

Two prototypes were completed in 1923, but these were disappointingly unusable because of excessive weight. A modified version was completed the following year, known as the Model A, but this showed only slight improvement and therefore remained unacceptable for Navy use. This setback temporarily suspended further work on the project.

By 1925, however, Lieut-Cdr Kiyosaku Shimura and Engineer Masasuke Hashimoto recognized the finer points of the design, and built another example referred to unofficially as the 10th Year Type Reconnaissance Seaplane Model B. By correcting the faults of over-weight as well as the poor stability and control problems of the former, a satisfactory prototype emerged and several pre-production aircraft followed. This type was never officially adopted by the Navy, but the Model B was again redesigned and later developed into the Navy Type 14 Reconnaissance Seaplane, E1Y1.

Single-engine twin-float reconnaissance biplane. Wooden construction with fabric covering. Wooden floats. Crew of two in open cockpits.

400hp Lorraine 1 twelve-cylinder vee water-cooled engine, driving a two-bladed wooden propeller.

One dorsal flexible 7.7mm machine-gun.

	Prototype	Model B
Span	16.822m (55ft 2½in)	16.164m (53ft 0¼in)
Length	12.167m (39ft 11in)	11.77m (38ft 7¼in)
Height	4.244m (13ft 11in)	4.308m (14ft 1½in)
Wing area	74.3sq m (799.784sq ft)	66sq m (710.441sq ft)
Empty weight	1,920kg (4,232lb)	1,912kg (4,215lb)
Loaded weight	3,010kg (6,636lb)	2,878kg (6,344lb)
Wing loading	40.5kg/sq m (8.3lb/sq ft)	43.6kg/sq m (8.9lb/sq ft)
Power loading	7.52kg/hp (16.5lb/hp)	7.19kg/hp (15.8lb/hp)
Maximum speed	79kt (91mph)	85kt (97.8mph)
Climb to	—	2,500m (8,202ft)
in	—	60min
Range	1,125nm (1,295sm)	—
Endurance	12½hr	—

Two prototypes built in 1923, one Model A built in 1924 and several Model B built in 1925.

Yokosho Navy Type 10 Reconnaissance Seaplane.

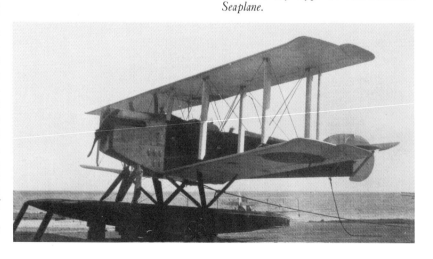

Yokosho Navy Type 13 Seaplane Trainer (K1Y2).

Navy Type 13 Trainer (K1Y1 and 2)

In 1924 as a replacement for the I-go Ko-gata and the Avro 504 seaplane trainers, the Navy asked for a new design, one that would have an interchangeable wheel and twin-float undercarriage. Chief designer for the project was again Masasuke Hashimoto. The first prototype was completed in 1925 and it proved to have good flying qualities and was accepted in October 1925 as standard equipment for the Navy. Production of the new aeroplane was placed with Nakajima, Kawanishi and Watanabe which together produced about one hundred by 1935.

This new Navy trainer was representative of the late Taisho reign to the early Showa period (1926/27). The land version was

Yokosho Navy Type 13 Land-based Trainer (K1Y1).

designated Type 13 Land-based Trainer (K1Y1) and with twin-floats it was the Type 13 Seaplane Trainer (K1Y2). This design reverted to the use of a tail float, but it was the last to do so. In about 1930 many were released for civil use as trainers and general purpose aeroplanes. Some survived until the early part of the Pacific War.

Single-engine twin-float and/or land-based biplane trainer. Wooden structure with fabric covering. Student and instructor in open cockpits.

130hp Gasuden Benz six-cylinder water-cooled inline engine, driving a two-bladed wooden propeller.

	Landplane (K1Y1)	Seaplane (K1Y2)
Span	10.205m (33ft 5¾in)	10.205m (33ft 5¾in)
Length	7.90m (25ft 11in)	8.68m (28ft 5¾in)
Height	3.15m (10ft 4in)	3.47m (11ft 4½in)
Wing area	32.65sq m (351.453sq ft)	32.65sq m (351.453sq ft)
Empty weight	670kg (1,477lb)	872kg (1,922lb)
Loaded weight	928kg (2,046lb)	1,056kg (2,328lb)
Wing loading	28.6kg/sq m (5.85lb/sq ft)	32.3kg/sq m (6.61lb/sq ft)
Power loading	7.13kg/hp (15.7lb/hp)	8.12kg/hp (17.9lb/hp)
Maximum speed	77.5kt (89mph)	70kt (80.6mph)
Climb to	3,000m (9,843ft)	2,000m (6,562ft)
in	52min 4sec	42min
Endurance	—	3hr

About 104 built: six by Yokosho in 1925, approximately forty by Nakajima in 1925, forty-eight by Kawanishi as Type 0 in 1928-33, and ten by Watanabe in 1933–34.

Navy Type 14 Reconnaissance Seaplane (E1Y1 to 3) Type 14 Modified Transport Seaplane

After modifications made to the earlier 10th Year Type Reconnaissance Seaplane Model B, it was officially accepted by the Navy in January 1926 as the Navy Type 14 Reconnaissance Seaplane. Over several years it was developed into three distinct models. The 400hp

Yokosho Navy Type 14-2 Reconnaissance Seaplane (E1Y2), with 450hp Lorraine 2 engine.

Lorraine powered model was the Navy Type 14-1 Reconnaissance Seaplane, E1Y1; the Model B previously described. It was originally a two-seater, later changed to have three seats. The Navy Type 14-2 Reconnaissance Seaplane, E1Y2, was powered by a 450hp Lorraine engine with newly designed all-metal twin-floats. This came into being in January 1926 at the same time as the E1Y1. The last of the series was the Type 14-3 Reconnaissance Seaplane, E1Y3, accepted in January 1931. In addition to its 450hp geared Lorraine with four-bladed propeller, it had many refined details, particularly a newly designed tail unit. It showed a marked increase in general performance and proved to be a very practical aeroplane.

In addition to these three production models there were two experimental versions. These were the Type 14-2 Reconnaissance Seaplane Model Kai-1-C and Model Kai-1-D which became the prototypes for the Navy Type 90-3 Reconnaissance Seaplane.

The E1Y2 and E1Y3 were the most successful of the so-called

Yokosho Type reconnaissance seaplanes. They were the first of the long-range three-seaters for which the Japanese Navy was noted. Replacements were designed but proved unsatisfactory and as a consequence these Type 14s remained in service for many years.

Although by then obsolete, the Type 14s were very active in the Shanghai Incident, being carried aboard the seaplane tender *Notoro*. They remained operational up to the early stage of the Sino-Japanese Conflict together with the Type 90 Reconnaissance Seaplanes. As late as 1932 when the Type 90-3 Reconnaissance Seaplanes were put into operational service, Type 14s remained on battleships and seaplane tenders as the main reconnaissance seaplane equipment of the fleet. They were widely used by shore-based Kokutais and training Kokutais.

Many of these Type 14s were eventually released for civil use and converted to multi-purpose seaplanes or passenger transports from 1932 up to the early stage of the Pacific War. The most popular conversion of many was in making a three/four-seat cabin at the rear while leaving the pilot's open

Yokosho Navy Type 14-3 Reconnaissance Seaplane (E1Y3), with 450hp Lorraine 3 geared engine and four-bladed propeller.

cockpit unchanged. Some, however, were unmodified or only embodied small changes while others were re-engined with the 450hp Napier Lion. The main uses for these converted aeroplanes were sight-seeing, advertising and aerial photography. The main user of the type was the Nippon Koku Yuso Kenkyusho (Japan Air Transport Research Association) in Sakai near Osaka.

Yokosho Experimental Tatsu-go *Reconnaissance Seaplane.*

Single-engine twin-float reconnaissance biplane. Wooden structure with fabric covering. Rearward folding wings for stowage. Crew of three in open cockpits.

400hp Lorraine 1 twelve-cylinder vee water-cooled engine (E1Y1); 450hp Lorraine 2 twelve-cylinder water-cooled W engine (E1Y2), both driving two-bladed wooden propellers; 450hp Lorraine 3 twelve-cylinder water-cooled W geared engine, driving a four-bladed wooden propeller.

One dorsal twin-flexible 7.7mm machine-gun. Bomb load: two 110kg (242lb) or four 30kg (66lb) bombs.

	E1Y1	E1Y2
Span	13.994m (45ft 11in)	14.224m (46ft 8in)
Length	10.91m (35ft 9½in)	10.59m (34ft 9in)
Height	4.15m (13ft 7½in)	4.15m (13ft 7½in)
Wing area	54.31sq m (584.63sq ft)	54.21sq m (583.53sq ft)
Empty weight	1,660kg (3,659lb)	1,889kg (4,164lb)
Loaded weight	2,600kg (5,732lb)	2,750kg (6,062lb)
Wing loading	47.87kg/sq m (9.8lb/sq ft)	50.7kg/sq m (10.4lb/sq ft)
Power loading	6.5kg/hp (14.3lb/hp)	6.1kg/hp (13.4lb/hp)
Maximum speed	96.5kt (111mph)	96kt (110mph)
Cruising speed	75kt (86mph)	70kt (80.5mph)
Climb to	3,000m (9,843ft)	3,000m (9,843ft)
in	35min 25sec	28min 13sec
Service ceiling	3,500m (11,482ft)	4,000m (13,123ft)
Range	530nm (610sm)	624nm (718sm)
Endurance	7hr	9hr

	E1Y3	Transport with Napier engine
Span	14.232m (46ft 8½in)	13.994m (45ft 11in)
Length	10.735m (35ft 2½in)	10.91m (35ft 9½in)
Height	4.15m (13ft 7½in)	4.15m (13ft 7½in)
Wing area	54.312sq m (584.628sq ft)	54.312sq m (584.628sq ft)
Empty weight	1,930kg (4,255lb)	1,680kg (3,703lb)
Loaded weight	2,800kg (6,172lb)	2,600kg (5,732lb)
Wing loading	51.5kg/sq m (10.5lb/sq ft)	47.8kg/sq m (9.8lb/sq ft)
Power loading	6.2kg/hp (13.6lb/hp)	5.7kg/hp (12.5lb/hp)
Maximum speed	102kt (117mph)	97kt (111.6mph)
Cruising speed	75kt (86.3mph)	73kt (84mph)
Climb to	3,000m (9,843ft)	3,000m (9,843ft)
in	20min	35min 25sec

320 built, seventeen E1Y1 by Yokosho 1925–28, six E1Y2 by Yokosho 1929–30, forty-seven E1Y1 and E1Y2 by Nakajima 1925–27, 148 E1Y1 and E1Y2 by Aichi 1926-27 and 102 E1Y3 by Aichi 1931-34.

Experimental *Tatsu-go* Reconnaissance Seaplane

The Navy used the Type Hansa reconnaissance seaplanes which were produced by Aichi and Nakajima until 1925 and in that year Aichi, Nakajima and Yokosho all experimented with improved designs based on the Hansa low-wing floatplane. Yokosho's version designated *Tatsu-go*, closely resembled the Hansa but its chief designer, Narihisa Yokota, decided to built it completely of metal, using Dornier techniques, and it was the first all-metal seaplane built in Japan.

Like the Hansa it was a twin-float cantilever low-wing monoplane with the tailplane mounted on top of the fuselage and the rudder protruding some way below the fuselage. The rectangular-section fuselage had external longitudinal stiffeners and, as on Dornier designs there were auxiliary surfaces above and ahead of the ailerons.

Flight tests proved it to be very unstable, causing the entire project to be abandoned at an early stage. The *Tatsu-go*'s shortcomings were due to lack of experience in this type of construction.

Single-engine low-wing monoplane reconnaissance seaplane. All-metal structure and skin. Crew of two in open cockpits.

300-320hp Mitsubishi Type Hi eight-cylinder vee water-cooled engine, driving a two-bladed wooden propeller.

One dorsal flexible 7.7mm machine-gun.

Span 15m (49ft 2½in); length 9.15m (30ft); height 3.60m (11ft 9½in).

Empty weight 1,445kg (3,185lb); loaded weight 2,100kg (4,629lb).

Maximum speed 93kt (107mph); climb to 3,000m (9,843ft) in 44min 40sec.

One built in 1925.

Navy Yokosho 1-go Reconnaissance Seaplane.

Navy Yokosho 1-go Reconnaissance Seaplane (Experimental Submarine-borne Reconnaissance Seaplane)

The Japanese Navy had a strong interest in the use of submarine-borne reconnaissance seaplanes, and one of several designs for this type was begun at the Yokosuka Arsenal in 1925, based on a Heinkel U 1 submarine-borne seaplane designed by Carl Caspar, former owner of the Hanseatischen Flugzeugwerke in Germany. One of these aircraft, better known as the Caspar U 1, had been imported in 1923 and the Yokosho design was a near duplicate in layout and dimensions.

This Yokosho design was a cantilever biplane having one-piece upper and lower wings without interplane struts. The twin-floats and wings were detachable from the fuselage and these components could be stowed in a tubelike hangar 7.4m long and 1.7m in diameter. The aeroplane could be assembled in 4min by five mechanics and become airborne in a total of 15 to 16min. Dismantling was accomplished in 2min by five mechanics.

Completed in 1927, this was the smallest aeroplane in Japan. Although so small, it was a rugged aircraft of good design with light-weight metals. During 1927-28 it was tested aboard the I-21 submarine which was equipped with a hangar for this purpose, but the aeroplane was not developed further. The experience gained with this project was useful in the later development of the Yokosho 2-go Reconnaissance Seaplane. Similar research at this time was being conducted in the United States and Britain, but none of the projects was developed to an operational level.

Single-engine twin-float reconnaissance biplane. Structure of metal and wood, with light metal fuselage skinning and fabric-covered cantilever wings. Detachable wings and floats for submarine stowage. Pilot in open cockpit.

80hp Gasuden-Le Rhône nine-cylinder air-cooled rotary engine, driving a four-bladed wooden propeller.

Yokosho Navy Type 3 Land-based Primary Trainer (K2Y1) with 130hp Mitsubishi Mongoose five-cylinder engine.

Span 7.20m (23ft 7½in); length 6.205m (20ft 4¼in); height 2.39m (7ft 10in); wing area 15.2sq m (163.616sq ft).

Empty weight 400kg (881lb); loaded weight 520kg (1,146lb); wing loading 34.2kg/sq m (7lb/sq ft); power loading 6.5kg/hp (14.3lb/hp).

Maximum speed 83kt (95.57mph); endurance 2hr.

One built in 1927.

Navy Type 3 Land-based Primary Trainer (K2Y1 and 2)

In 1928 when the Avro 504 became obsolete the Navy began a new trainer design at the Yokosuka Arsenal as a replacement. Listed as an experimental aircraft in April 1929, it was officially accepted as the Type 3 Land-based Trainer in January 1930. It was also tested on twin-floats but was not accepted as operational equipment.

In essence, this was a modernized version of the Avro 504, using a Mitsubishi-built 130hp Armstrong Siddeley Mongoose radial engine in place of the former 110hp Le Rhône rotary. Other noticeable differences were an entirely new undercarriage and tail unit. Manufacture of the new trainer was entrusted to Kawanishi which completed its first aircraft in June 1930. Further production was also undertaken by Watanabe and Mitsubishi.

Development of this design continued at Yokosho and in February 1930 the original engine was replaced by a Jimpu. This proved to be a better combination and became standard as the Type 3

Land-based Trainer Kai-1. When officially adopted with this engine in March 1932 it became the Type 3-2 Land-based Trainer (later changed to Land-based Primary Trainer), and was put into production by the same three manufacturers and later by Nippi and Showa. The Jimpu-powered aircraft had the short designation K2Y2, while the Mongoose-powered earlier version was the K2Y1.

This type gained a good reputation as a Navy primary trainer from 1930 to the early stage of the Pacific War. They were stable and easily controlled trainers and good aerobatic aircraft commensurate with their limited power. Many were eventually released to civil users, the Students' Aviation League being the largest user. A number were supplied to the Air Corps of the Manchurian National Military Force.

Single engine primary trainer biplane. Wooden construction with fabric covering. Student and instructor in open cockpits.

130-150hp Mitsubishi Mongoose five-cylinder air-cooled radial engine, driving a two-bladed wooden propeller (K2Y1), 130-160hp Gasuden Jimpu 2 seven-cylinder air-cooled radial engine driving a two-bladed wooden propeller (K2Y2).

	K2Y1	K2Y2
Span	10.97m (36ft)	10.90m (35ft 9in)
Length	8.67m (28ft 5½in)	8.60m (28ft 2½in)
Height	3.11m (10ft 2½in)	3.13m (10ft 3in)
Wing area	29.43sq m	29.43sq m
	(316.792sq ft)	(316.792sq ft)
Empty weight	590kg (1,300lb)	657kg (1,448lb)
Loaded weight	865kg (1,906lb)	890kg (1,962lb)
Wing loading	29.4kg/sq m	30.7kg/sq m
	(6lb/sq ft)	(6.2lb/sq ft)
Power loading	6.66kg/hp (14.6lb/hp)	6.93kg/hp (15.2lb/hp)
Maximum speed		
at sea level	84.5kt (97.5mph)	87.3kt (100.4mph)
Cruising speed		
at 1,000m	55kt (63mph)	55kt (63mph)
Landing speed	30kt (34.5mph)	35kt (40.3mph)
Climb to	3,000m (9,843ft)	3,000m (9,843ft)
in	18min 35sec	21min 10sec
Service ceiling	4,400m (14,435ft)	4,600m (15,091ft)
Range	—	226nm (260sm)
Endurance	—	4.2hr

360 built: six by Yokosuka Arsenal 1929–30, sixty-six by Kawanishi 1930–32, 114 by Watanabe 1931–37, forty-five by Mitsubishi 1934, 126 by Nippi 1939–40 and three by Showa 1938–39.

Yokosho Navy Type 90 Seaplane Trainer (K4Y1).

Navy Type 90 Seaplane Trainer (K4Y1)

In 1930 the Navy asked for a new design to replace the Yokosho Type 13 Seaplane Trainer. The aeroplane that emerged was designed under the leadership of Lieut-Cdr (Eng) Jiro Saha and Engineer Tamefumi Suzuki. It was unusual in that it had a welded steel tube fuselage, and Saha became known for designing the first aeroplane of this type in Japan, the method having only been tried experimentally before by Ishikawajima. The aeroplane was powered by an inverted four-cylinder inline air-cooled 90hp Hatakaze, a very unusual design for a Japanese-made engine.

Two prototypes were completed in 1930, and flight tests proved the design to be practical. After acceptance of this trainer for Navy use, it was decided that a 130hp Gasuden Jimpu powered version was more practical. This became the standard version beginning in May 1933 as the Type 90 Seaplane Trainer, short designation K4Y1, when production was awarded to Watanabe and Nippi. These replaced the much used Type 13 Seaplane Trainer which remained in service until the early part of the Pacific War along with the Yokosho Navy Type 3-2 Land-based Primary Trainer. Although it could be used as a landplane, all operational K4Y1 trainers were equipped with twin floats. Eventually, a small number were released for civil use.

Single-engine twin-float biplane trainer. Welded-steel tube fuselage with fabric covering, wooden wing with fabric covering. All-metal twin-floats. Student and instructor in open cockpits.

130-160hp Gasuden Jimpu 2 seven-cylinder air-cooled radial engine, driving a two-bladed wooden propeller.

Span 10,90m (35ft 9in); length 9.05m (29ft 8½in) (seaplane), 8.191m (26ft 10½in) (landplane); height 3.51m (11ft 6in) (seaplane), 3.25m (10ft 8in) (landplane); wing area 29.5sq m (317.545sq ft).

Empty weight 740kg (1,631lb); loaded weight 990kg (2,182lb); wing loading 33.5kg/sq m (6.8lb/sq ft); power loading 7.6kg/hp (16.7lb/hp).

Maximum speed 88kt (101mph) at

sea level; cruising speed 50kt (57.5 mph); alighting speed 43kt (49.5mph); climb to 3,000m (9,843ft) in 29min 20sec; service ceiling 3,460m (11,350 ft); range 170nm (196sm); endurance 3½hr.

211 built: two by Yokosuka Arsenal 1930, 156 by Watanabe 1932-39 and fifty-three by Nippi 1939-40.

Navy Type 90-3 Reconnaissance Seaplane (E5Y1)

In an effort to catch-up with the world's aeronautical engineering progress, the Navy planned in 1927 to modernize its reconnaissance seaplane technology with the increased use of metal construction. While the Navy issued orders to Aichi, Nakajima and Kawanishi, for a new three-seat reconnaissance seaplane to replace its outdated Type 14 Reconnaissance Seaplane, the Yokosuka Arsenal undertook a similar plan as an independent programme. For this new project, Jiro Saha designed this aeroplane with technical reference being made to the imported Heinkel HD 28, along with improvements recommended by Aichi still in the process of evaluating and developing this design. (see Aichi Experimental Three-seat Reconnaissance Seaplane).

One of the Yokosho designed aeroplanes was completed in August 1928 and given the designation Type 14-2 Reconnaissance Seaplane Kai-1 experimental-aircraft. It differed greatly from previous designs in this category, had the greatly respected 450hp Jupiter VIII radial engine, and a welded steel tube fuselage structure which was stepped on the lower surface to provide for a ventral downward-firing gun. The wings and empennage were an entirely new design, the wings being rigged with slight stagger.

After this prototype was completed, the Type 14-2 Reconnaissance Seaplane Kai-1-C was put into production with the 450hp Lorraine engine, as was the similar Kai-1-D which was powered by a 450hp Jupiter installed in a lengthened nose. Two pre-production models of the Kai-1-D were built by Kawanishi, with deliveries in October 1931 under the company designation Type G. After these were evaluated by the Navy and a few minor modifications made, the design was adopted officially as the Type 90-3 Reconnaissance Seaplane, short designation E5Y1. (see Yokosho Navy Type 14 Reconnaissance Seaplane).

Initially, a small number of these aircraft were built by Kawanishi as

Yokosho Navy Type 90-3 Reconnaissance Seaplane (E5Y1).

E5K1s. Finding that there was little or no improvement in capability over that of the Type 14-2, a 500hp Type 91 water-cooled engine was installed in some of these aeroplanes but with negligible change in performance. Kawanishi only manufactured seventeen of these reconnaissance aircraft with a mix of both powerplants.

Although noted for being the first three-seat reconnaissance seaplane to have a welded steel tube fuselage structure, it was also noted for being in the test and evaluation phase longer than any of the Type 90 Reconnaissance Seaplanes under consideration. Only about twenty were built; however their entry into service was timely because of the outbreak of the Shanghai Incident. These aeroplanes equipped battleships and seaplane tenders such as the *Notoro* which then left immediately for Shanghai. The activities of these aeroplanes were given impressive newspaper coverage. Two which were publicized in these reports were the first of the donated *Hokoku-go* aircraft, *Hokoku No.1 (Nikke-go)* [Nikke = Nihon Woollen Co Ltd] and *Hokoku No.2 (Hyogo-go)* donated by the citizens of Hyogo Prefecture.

Single-engine twin-float reconnaissance biplane. Fabric-covered welded-steel fuselage, wooden wing structure with fabric covering. All-metal floats. Rearward folding wings for stowage. Crew of three in open cockpits (pilot, dorsal gunner/navigator and radio operator/lower gunner).

450-520hp Nakajima Jupiter VIII nine-cylinder air-cooled radial engine, 450-520hp Jupiter IX both driving two-bladed wooden propellers.

Two forward-firing fixed 7.7mm machine-guns, one dorsal flexible 7.7mm machine-gun and one ventral flexible 7.7mm machine-gun. Bomb load: two 125kg (275lb), or three 60kg (132lb), or three 30kg (66lb) bombs.

	Type 14 Kai-1-D	Type 90-3, E5Y1
Span	14.50m (47ft 7in)	14.46m (47ft 5¼in)
Length	10.552m (34ft 7½in)	10.812m (35ft 5¾in)
Height	4.10m (13ft 5½in)	4.74m (15ft 6¾in)
		with wings folded
Wing area	55sq m (592.034sq ft)	55sq m (592.034sq ft)
Empty weight	1,800kg (3,968lb)	1,850kg (4,078lb)
Loaded weight	3,000kg (6,613lb)	3,000kg (6,613lb)
Wing loading	54.5kg/sq m	54.5kg/sq m
	(11.1lb/sq ft)	(11.1lb/sq ft)
Power loading	6.67kg/hp (14.7lb/hp)	6.67kg/hp (14.7lb/hp)
Maximum speed	96kt (110.5mph)	96kt (110.5mph)
Cruising speed	70kt (80.6mph)	70kt (80.6mph)
Climb to	—	3,000m (9,843ft)
in	—	33min 20sec
Service ceiling	—	4,050m (13,287ft)
Endurance	—	6½hr

About twenty built: some Yokosho Type 14 Kai-1 1928–29, five by Kawanishi in 1931 and twelve in 1932.

Navy Type 91 Reconnaissance Seaplane (E6Y1) (Navy Yokosho 2-go Reconnaissance Seaplane)

In 1929, following experiments with the Yokosho 1-go Reconnaissance Seaplane for submarine use, the Navy sponsored another project of this type with hopes of greater success. Design work for what was at first called the Yokosho 2-go, was again under the leadership of Jiro Saha and Tamefumi Suzuki. This new design had a marked similarity to the British Parnall Peto reconnaissance seaplane which was powered by a 130hp Armstrong Siddeley Mongoose and had been successfully tested aboard the Royal Navy's submarine M2.

The Mongoose engine was also used in the Yokosho design, but minor changes were apparent. Initially there were V interplane struts and the fin and rudder were behind and below the fuselage. When the design was changed in 1931 to take the Jimpu engine, N-struts were fitted and additional fin and rudder area was added by extending them upward in the more conventional fashion. This aeroplane was successfully launched from the catapult of the I-51 submarine in May 1928, and submarine related testing was completed by September 1931. As a proved and practical design, it was officially adopted in January 1932 as the Type 91 Reconnaissance Seaplane. After the second prototype, with minor modifications, production was passed to Kawanishi as its Type N.

With the short designation E6Y1, this was the first submarine-borne reconnaissance seaplane officially accepted by the Japanese Navy. It was around this time that Aichi built its AB-3 small reconnaissance seaplane of a similar size and design, but it was not regarded as intended for submarine use.

Single-engine twin-float submarine-borne reconnaissance sesquiplane. Metal frame fuselage with fabric covering, wooden structure wing with fabric covering. Detachable wings and floats for submarine stowage. Pilot in open cockpit.

130-150hp Mitsubishi-built Mongoose five-cylinder air-cooled radial engine (Yokosho-2); 130-160hp Gasuden Jimpu seven-cylinder air-cooled radial engine (Type 91), both driving two-bladed wooden propellers.

Span 8m (26ft 3in); length 6.69m (21ft 11½in); height 2.87m (9ft 5in).

Empty weight 570kg (1,256lb); loaded weight 750kg (1,653lb); power loading 5.77kg/hp (12.7lb/hp).

Maximum speed 91kt (104.7mph); climb to 3,000m (9,843ft) in 20min 14sec; endurance 4.4hr.

Ten built: one Yokosho 2-go 1929, one Yokosho 2-go-kai 1931, and eight Type 91 by Kawanishi 1932–34.

Yokosho Navy Type 91 Reconnaissance Seaplane (E6Y1), also referred to as the Navy Yokosho 2-go Reconnaissance Seaplane.

Yokosho Navy Type 91 Intermediate Trainer.

Navy Type 91 Intermediate Trainer

As performance of operational aircraft progressed rapidly, the Navy planned in 1930 to develop an intermediate trainer with a 300hp engine for transitioning students from the 100hp class primary trainer to the more advanced 500hp category operational aircraft. This was the first Japanese intermediate trainer designed for this purpose, for in the past, the Type 10 Reconnaissance Aircraft and the Type 15 Reconnaissance Seaplanes were converted and used as intermediate trainers.

Jiro Saha and Tamefumi Suzuki were responsible for the design. This aeroplane, powered by the 300hp Tempu engine, was completed in April 1931 as an experimental project, but soon achieved an official designation as the Navy Type 91 Intermediate Trainer. Further evaluation revealed that it was too close a match in aerobatic performance to operational aircraft at that time and its speed was nearly equivalent to reconnaissance aircraft. However, it lacked stability, and as a result, the project was suspended with only two prototypes. Later, this basic design was developed into the Type 93 Intermediate Trainer (Allied code-name Willow) after modifications to the wings and tail for improved stability.

Single-engine intermediate trainer biplane. Fuselage of welded steel tubing with wooden formers covered with fabric. Wooden wings with fabric covering. Student and instructor in open cockpits.

300-340hp Gasuden Tempu 11 nine-cylinder air-cooled radial engine, driving a two-bladed wooden propeller.

One fixed forward-firing 7.7mm machine-gun. Bomb load: Two 30kg (66lb) bombs.

Span 11.10m (36ft 5in); length 7.89m (25ft 10½in); height 3.316m (10ft 10½in); wing area 27.7sq m (298.17sq ft).

Empty weight 1,000kg (2,204lb); loaded weight 1,500kg (3,306lb); wing loading 54.2kg/sq m (11.1lb/sq ft); power loading 5kg/hp (11lb/hp).

Maximum speed 110kt (127mph); climb to 3,000m (9,843ft) in 15min 10sec.

Two built in 1931.

Experimental Kusho 6-Shi Special Bomber

In 1930, the US Navy was demonstrating a new category of naval aircraft called carrier dive-bombers and using in particular the Curtiss XF8C-2 Helldiver, Vought O2U, and Martin XT5M-1. Of these, the Helldiver held the greatest interest with its 500lb bomb dropping accuracy. These demonstrations were observed by Engineer Junichiro Nagahata, sent to the United States for this purpose by the Japanese Navy, and immediately upon his return he began design work on the Kusho 6-Shi Special Bomber.*

The construction of this new biplane with negative stagger was turned over to Nakajima as a very top secret project. Two were built

in 1932-33 and one crashed when the pilot was unable to recover from a dive. This terminated further testing of the design and corrections attempted in the next two efforts also failed, the Nakajima 7-Shi and 8-Shi Special Bombers. (*see* Nakajima Navy Experimental Kusho 6-Shi Special Bomber).

Experimental Kusho 8-Shi Special Bomber (D2Y1)

In addition to placing an order with Aichi for a new dive-bomber project, the Kusho design staff undertook a parallel project which it termed the Experimental 8-Shi Special Bomber, begun in 1933. The new design was thought to correct the deficiencies of the 6-Shi design, and production was again passed to Nakajima, with two prototypes being built in 1934. Tests showed that this design was flawed as well, and it was outclassed by Aichi's 8-Shi Special Bomber derived from the Heinkel He 66. Thus, the Aichi design was accepted and from this time Aichi held a monopoly on building the Japanese Navy's carrier-based dive-bombers (*see* Nakajima Navy Experimental 8-Shi Special Bomber.)

Navy Type 92 Carrier Attack Aircraft (B3Y1)

Recognizing the need to replace the poorly performing Mitsubishi Navy Type 89 Carrier Attack Aircraft, the Navy decided in 1932 to design and produce its own replacement at the Air Arsenal. This was being done at the same time that competitive designs were contracted with Mitsubishi and Nakajima for a 7-Shi Carrier Attack Aircraft. With hopes of creating a practical carrier attack bomber design like that of the very early Mitsubishi Type 13,

*The Japanese Navy avoided using the designation Dive Bomber from its inception to the end of the Pacific War. Since this new concept was so revolutionary, the Japanese preferred to keep secret their efforts in these designs. Instead, they used the term Tokushu Bakugekiki, meaning Special Bomber, and later the term Kanjo Bakugekiki or Carrier Bomber.

the new aeroplane was initially given the designation Type 13 Carrier Attack Aircraft Modified, even though it was a completely new design.

Under the design guidance of Tamefumi Suzuki, the new aeroplane had an all welded steel tube fuselage, and a 600hp Type 91 engine which had recently been adopted by the Navy. Flight tests were disappointing, not only with stability and control, but unreliability of the new engine. On the other hand, it did not have some of the major problems that were encountered in the 7-Shi Attack Aircraft created by Mitsubishi and Nakajima. As a result of modifications made by Tokuichiro Gomei of Aichi, the aeroplane was officially accepted by the Navy in August 1933. It received the designation Navy Type 92 Carrier Attack Aircraft, with short identification B3Y1. Production was placed with Aichi, followed by Watanabe and the Hiro Arsenal after the prototype built at the Yokosuka Arsenal.

With great expectations for this new bomber, they were deployed with operational units. Engine prob-

Yokosho Navy Type 92 Carrier Attack Aircraft (B3Y1).

lems continually plagued them and they were often grounded while possible corrections were studied. In the early stages of the Sino-Japanese Conflict, these aeroplanes became noted for their success in level bombing against small targets. Gradually they were retired from combat when they were replaced by newer equipment that remained operational until the early phases of the Pacific war, namely the Aichi Navy Type 94 and Type 96 Carrier Bombers (D1A1 and D1A2) and the Kusho Type 96 Carrier Attack Aircraft (B4Y1).

Single-engine biplane carrier-borne attack bomber. Welded steel tube fuselage structure with fabric covering. Wings of wooden structure covered with fabric. Rearward folding wings for stowage. Crew of three in open cockpits (pilot, bombardier/navigator and radio operator/gunner).

600-750hp Type 91 twelve-cylinder W water-cooled engine, driving a two or four-bladed wooden propeller.

One fuselage forward-firing fixed 7.7mm machine-gun and one dorsal flexible 7.7mm machine-gun. Bomb load: One 800kg (1,763lb) torpedo, or one 500kg (1,102lb) bomb, or two 250kg (551lb) bombs, or six 30kg (66lb) bombs.

Span 13.506m (44ft 3¾in); length 9.50m (31ft 2in); height tail down 3.73m (12ft 2¾in); wing area 50sq m (538.213sq ft).

Empty weight 1,850kg (4,078lb); loaded weight 3,200kg (7,054lb); wing loading 64kg/sq m (13.1lb/sq ft); power loading 5kg/hp (11lb/hp).

Maximum speed 118kt (135.8mph); endurance 4½hr.

Approximately 129 built: one Kusho Type 13 Kai 1932, seventy-five by Aichi 1933–36, twenty-three by Watanabe 1933–36 and about thirty by Hiro Arsenal.

Experimental Kusho 12-Shi Special Flying-boat (H7Y1)

In 1937, the Navy recognized the need to develop a long-range flying-boat for reconnaissance missions that was capable of flying nonstop from Japan to Hawaii and return. Because this was a very sensitive top secret project, the Navy decided to create this design within its own facilities at Kusho. Chief designer was Lieut-Cdr (Engineering) Jun Okamura.

Design requirements for the aircraft were generally simple except for the need for maximum

range. This called for 5,000nm (5,750sm), a range which exceeded that of all other aircraft at that time. The only contender was the Dornier Do 26 which was said to have a range of 4,880nm (5,620sm). As a result, the specifications established by the Japanese Navy were similar to those of that German design.

This new flying-boat was to be a high wing monoplane, weigh eighteen tons when loaded, and carry a crew of four. Power was to be provided by two Junkers diesel engines because of their low fuel consumption. These six-cylinder Junkers Jumo 205s, rated at 510hp at 2,100rpm each, would be imported by the Navy. The wing would have a high aspect-ratio with retractable outrigger floats for drag reduction. The hull was to be quite slim for the same reason, and considerable attention was to be paid to weight reduction. Structural requirements were to meet Navy Strength Category 1 (2.0–3.0g).

The first and only prototype was completed in 1939. Test flights were disappointing in that the structure lacked rigidity, and excessive vibration developed within the wing centre section. Oscillations persisted in the tail section and were carried forward to the cabin. Take-off power was inadequate for the fuel load expected to be carried. Directional stability was poor along with other defects in the design.

While these shortcomings were being studied and attempts made to correct them, the Navy had misgivings about the requirements for this type of aircraft, and decided to abandon the project. Because of the sensitive nature of this aircraft requirement, no photographs, drawings or other data were saved.

Experimental Research Aircraft (MXY1)

This aeroplane was purely a test vehicle to study new airborne systems and aerodynamic characteristics for the Aircraft Department of Kokusho. The design was started in 1937 and carried the unusual designation MXY1, meaning Special Purpose (M), Experimental (X), by Yokosho (Y), first model (1). Although the Y designator was used, it was actually designed and built by Watanabe at the request of Yokosho, and by existing standards, should have been designated W for Watanabe. This was a parasol-wing monoplane, configured very much like the British Parnall Parasol that had been developed for the same flight-test purposes. Only one aircraft was built, in 1939. (see Watanabe Experimental Research Aircraft MXY1).

Aircraft designs at the Technical Air Arsenal at Yokosuka continued to be developed, and follow-on designs were used all through the Pacific War. The most noted types not already mentioned were the 13-Shi Carrier-borne Bomber, known as the D4Y1 Judy, configured first with an inline engine, and later with a radial engine that made it an even more effective dive-bomber. A very advanced twin-engined land-based bomber for the 15-Shi requirement was the Ginga with short designation P1Y1 which the Allies called Frances. The Arsenal, better known at that time as Kugisho, remained responsible for all types of development and testing of advanced aircraft as well as reciprocating engines and turbojets. All related equipment was developed at the Arsenal, making Yokosuka the focal point of Japanese Naval aircraft development to the end of the Pacific War.

Appendix A

Japanese Aircraft of the Pacific War Period

Japanese aircraft listed here are those that are recorded as Pacific War aircraft and are therefore not covered in this book but described in detail in René Francillon's *Japanese Aircraft of the Pacific War*. These aircraft are listed to show the scale of diversified development of Japanese types, as well as to record the completion date of the prototypes, many of which are within the time frame of this book but far too numerous to describe in this one volume. Production of many of the aircraft listed here was shared by other companies. The sequence shows the Short Designation, followed by the Type Designation, Allied code-name and completion date for first aircraft.

Short designation	Type designation	Allied code-name	First completed
Aichi			
D1A1	Navy Type 94 Carrier Bomber		12.34
D1A2	Navy Type 96 Carrier Bomber	Susie	Autumn 36
D3A1	Navy Type 99 Carrier Bomber	Val	12.37
E11A1	Navy Type 98 Reconnaissance Seaplane	Laura	6.37
E13A1	Navy Type 0 Reconnaissance Seaplane	Jake	Autumn 38
H9A1	Navy Type 2 Flying-boat Trainer		9.40
E16A1	Navy Reconnaissance Seaplane *Zuiun*	Paul	5.42
B7A1	Experimental 16-Shi Carrier Attack Aircraft *Ryusei*	Grace	5.42
M6A1	Experimental 17-Shi Special Attack Aircraft *Seiran*		11.43
Kawanishi			
E7K1	Navy Type 94 Reconnaissance Seaplane	Alf	2.33
H6K1	Navy Type 97 Flying-boat	Mavis	7.36
H6K3	Navy Type 97 Transport Flying-boat	Mavis	39
H8K1	Navy Type 2 Flying-boat	Emily	12.40
H8K2-L	Navy Type 2 Transport Flying-boat *Seiku*	Emily	43
E15K1	Navy Type 2 High-speed Reconnaissance Seaplane *Shiun*	Norm	9.41
N1K1	Navy Fighter Seaplane *Kyofu*	Rex	5.42
N1K1-J	Navy Interceptor Fighter *Shiden*	George	12.42
N1K2-J	Navy Interceptor Fighter *Shinden-kai*	George	12.43
P1Y2-S	Navy Night Fighter *Kyokko*	Frances	6.44
Kawasaki			
Ki-10	Army Type 95 Fighter	Perry	3.35
Ki-32	Army Type 98 Light Bomber	Mary	3.37
Ki-45-kai	Army Type 2 Two-seat Fighter *Toryu*	Nick	1.39
Ki-48	Army Type 99 Twin-engined Light Bomber	Lily	7.39
Ki-56	Army Type 1 Freight Transport	Thalia	11.40
Ki-60	Experimental Fighter		3.41
Ki-61	Army Type 3 Fighter *Hien*	Tony	12.41
Ki-64	Experimental High-speed Fighter	Rob	12.43
Ki-66	Experimental Dive Bomber		11.42
Ki-78	Experimental High-speed Research Aircraft *Ken-3*		12.42
Ki-96	Experimental Twin-engined Fighter		9.43
Ki-100	Army Type 5 Fighter		1.45
Ki-102a	Experimental High-altitude Fighter	Randy	6.44
Ki-102b	Army Type 5 Assault Aircraft	Randy	3.44
Ki-108	Experimental High-altitude Fighter		7.44
Kayaba			
Ka-1	Army Ka-go Observation Autogyro		5.41
Kokusai			
Ki-86	Army Type 4 Primary Trainer	Cypress	7.43
Ki-59	Army Type 1 Transport	Theresa	4.39
Ki-76	Army Type 3 Command Liaison Aircraft	Stella	5.41
Ki-105	Experimental Transport *Ohtori*		11.45
—	Experimental *Ta-go* Suicide Attacker		45

Kugisho (Formerly Yokosho)

H5Y1	Navy Type 99 Flying-boat	Cherry	7.38
K5Y1	Navy Type 93 Intermediate Trainer	Willow	12.33
B4Y1	Navy Type 96 Carrier Attack Aircraft	Jean	12.35
E14Y1	Navy Type 0 Small Reconnaissance Seaplane	Glen	Autumn 41
D4Y1	Navy Carrier Bomber *Suisei*	Judy	11.40
D4Y1-C	Navy Type 2 Carrier Reconnaissance	Judy	11.40
P1Y1	Navy Land Based Bomber *Ginga*	Frances	8.43
D3Y1-K	Experimental Bomber Trainer *Myojo*		7.44
R2Y1	Experimental 18-Shi Land-based Reconnaissance Aircraft *Keiun*	7.45	
MXY7	Navy Suicide Attacker *Ohka* Model 11	Baka	9.44

Kyushu

K9W1	Navy Type 2 Primary Trainer *Koyo*	Cypress	8.41
A5M4-K	Navy Type 2 Fighter Trainer	Claude	6.42
K11W1	Navy Crew Trainer *Shiragiku*		11.42
Q1W1	Navy Land-based Patrol Aircraft *Tokai*	Lorna	12.43
J7W1	Experimental 18-Shi Interceptor Fighter *Shinden*		7.45

Manshu

Ki-71	Experimental Reconnaissance/Assault Aircraft		41
Ki-79	Army Type 2 Advanced Trainer		12.41
Ki-116	Experimental Fighter	Frank	8.45

Mitsubishi

Ki-15	Army Type 97 Command Reconnaissance Aircraft	Babs	5.36
Ki-21	Army Type 97 Heavy Bomber	Sally	12.36
Ki-30	Army Type 97 Light Bomber	Ann	2.37
Ki-46	Army Type 100 Command Reconnaissance Aircraft	Dinah	11.39
Ki-51	Army Type 99 Assault/Tactical Reconnaissance Aircraft	Sonia	6.39
Ki-57	Army Type 100 Transport	Topsy	7.40
Ki-67	Army Type 4 Heavy Bomber *Hiryu*	Peggy	12.42
Ki-83	Experimental Long-range Fighter		10.44
Ki-109	Experimental Interceptor Fighter		8.44
K3M1	Navy Type 90 Crew Trainer	Pine	5.30
A5M1	Navy Type 96 Carrier Fighter	Claude	1.35
G3M1	Navy Type 96 Land-based Attack Aircraft	Nell	6.35
B5M1	Navy Type 97-2 Carrier Attack Aircraft	Mabel	10.36
C5M1	Navy Type 98 Land-based Reconnaissance Aircraft	Babs	38
F1M1	Navy Type 0 Observation Seaplane	Pete	6.36
K7M1	Experimental 11-Shi Crew Trainer		38
A6M1	Navy Type 0 Carrier Fighter	Zeke	3.39
G4M1	Navy Type 1 Land-based Attack Aircraft	Betty	9.39
G6M1	Navy Type 1 Land-based Large Trainer	Betty	8.40
J2M1	Navy Interceptor Fighter *Raiden*	Jack	2.42
A7M1	Experimental 17-Shi Carrier Fighter *Reppu*	Sam	4.44
J8M1	Experimental 19-Shi Interceptor Fighter *Shusui*		6.45

Nakajima

Ki-27	Army Type 97 Fighter	Nate	10.36
Ki-34	Army Type 97 Transport	Thora	9.36
Ki-43	Army Type 1 Fighter *Hayabusa*	Oscar	12.38
Ki-44	Army Type 2 Fighter *Shoki*	Tojo	8.40
Ki-49	Army Type 100 Heavy Bomber *Donryu*	Helen	8.39
Ki-84	Army Type 4 Fighter *Hayate*	Frank	3.43
Ki-87	Experimental High Altitude Fighter		2.45
Ki-115	Army Suicide Attacker *Tsurugi*		3.45
E8N1	Navy Type 95 Reconnaissance Seaplane	Dave	3.34
B5N1	Navy Type 97 Carrier Attack Aircraft	Kate	12.36
J1N1-C, -R	Navy Type 2 Land-based Reconnaissance Aircraft	Irving	3.41

J1N1-S	Navy Night Fighter *Gekko*	Irving	3.41
G5N1	Experimental 13-Shi Land-based Attack Aircraft *Shinzan*	Liz	12.39
A6M2-N	Navy Type 2 Fighter Seaplane	Rufe	12.41
B6N1	Navy Carrier Attack Aircraft *Tenzan*	Jill	4.41
C6N1	Navy Carrier Reconnaissance Aircraft *Saiun*	Myrt	4.43
P1Y1	Navy Land Based Bomber *Ginga*	Frances	8.43
J5N1	Experimental 18-Shi Interceptor Fighter *Tenrai*		7.44
G8N1	Experimental 18-Shi Land-based Attack Aircraft *Renzan*	Rita	10.44
	Experimental Special Attacker *Kikka*		6.45

Rikugun
| Ki-93 | Experimental Heavy Fighter and Ground Attack Aircraft | | 3.45 |

Showa
| L2D2 | Navy Type 0 Transport | Tabby | 7.41 |

Tachikawa
Ki-9	Army Type 95-1 Intermediate Trainer	Spruce	12.34
Ki-17	Army Type 95-3 Primary Trainer	Cedar	7.35
Ki-36	Army Type 98 Direct Co-operation Aircraft	Ida	4.38
Ki-54	Army Type 1 Twin-engined Advanced Trainer	Hickory	6.40
Ki-55	Army Type 99 Advanced Trainer	Ida	3.39
SS-1	Army Type Lo-B High Altitude Research Aircraft		8.43
Ki-70	Experimental Command Reconnaissance Aircraft	Clara	2.43
Ki-74	Army Long-range Reconnaissance Bomber	Patsy	3.44
Ki-77	A-26 Long-range Research Aircraft		10.42
Ki-94-II	Army High Altitude Fighter		8.45
—	Army Type Lo-14Y Transport		11.40
Ki-92	Experimental Large Transport		9.44
Ki-106	Experimental Fighter	Frank	9.44

Appendix B

Calendar Conversion for Japanese Army and Navy Aircraft Type Numbers

Nengo Calendrical Eras	Navy Type Numbers	Army and Navy Type Numbers (Based upon year of Japan)	Year of Japan	Gregorian Calendar
Taisho 10	Type 10		2581	1921
Taisho 11			2582	1922
Taisho 12			2583	1923
Taisho 13	Type 13		2584	1924
Taisho 14	Type 14		2585	1925
Taisho 15	Type 15		25.12 2586	25.12 1926
Showa 1			26.12 2586	26.12 1926
Showa 2		Type 87	2587	1927
Showa 3	Navy Shisaku	Type 88	2588	1928
Showa 4	Numbers	Type 89	2589	1929
Showa 5		Type 90	2590	1930
Showa 6	6-Shi	Type 91	2591	1931
Showa 7	7-Shi	Type 92	2592	1932
Showa 8	8-Shi	Type 93	2593	1933
Showa 9	9-Shi	Type 94	2594	1934
Showa 10	10-Shi	Type 95	2595	1935
Showa 11	11-Shi	Type 96	2596	1936
Showa 12	12-Shi	Type 97	2597	1937
Showa 13	13-Shi	Type 98	2598	1938
Showa 14	14-Shi	Type 99	2599	1939
Showa 15	15-Shi	Type 0	2600	1940
Showa 16	16-Shi	Type 1	2601	1941
Showa 17	17-Shi	Type 2	2602	1942
Showa 18	18-Shi	Type 3	2603	1943
Showa 19	19-Shi	Type 4	2604	1944
Showa 20	20-Shi	Type 5	2605	1945
Showa 60				1985
Showa 64				7.1 1989
Heisei 1				8.1 1989

Appendix C

Bibliography

The following books were consulted in the preparation of this work.

English language sources:

Pictorial History of Japanese Military Aviation, by Eiichiro Sekigawa, Ian Allan Ltd, London, 1974

The Fifty Years of Japanese Aviation, by Katsu Kohri, Ikuo Komori, and Ichiro Naito, Kantosha Co Ltd (Airreview), Tokyo, 1961

Jane's All the World's Aircraft, various publishers, inclusive years

Japanese language sources:

Encyclopedia of Japanese Aircraft 1900-1945, Shuppan-Kyodo, Tokyo
Volume 1 *Mitsubishi*, by Tadashi Nozawa and Takashi Iwata, 1958
Volume 2 *Aichi, Kugisho*, by Tadashi Nozawa, 1959
Volume 3 *Kawanishi, Hirosho*, by T. Nozawa and Takashi Iwata, 1959
Volume 4 *Kawasaki*, by Tadashi Nozawa, 1960
Volume 5 *Nakajima*, by Tadashi Nozawa and Takashi Iwata, 1963
Volume 7 *Tachikawa, Rikugun and others* by Tadashi Nozawa, 1980
Volume 8 *Kyushu, Hitachi, Showa, Nippi and others*, by Tadashi Nozawa, 1980

Aireview's Japanese Army Aircraft 1910-1945 by Issaku Imagawa, et al, Kantosha Co Ltd, Tokyo 1962

Aviation History of Japan, by Maj-Gen Yahei Ohba, Lieut-Cdr Takao Katoh, Hidemasa Kimura, Tatsuhiko Kohri, et al, Umi To Sora Sha, Tokyo, 1935.

Aviation History of Japan, Vol I (1877-1940), by Kunio Hiraki, Katsuhiro Fujita and Toshio Fujita, Asahi Shimbun Publishing Co, Tokyo, 1983

General View of Japanese Aeronautical Engineering: Vol I, II, by Jun Okamura, et al, Nippon Shuppan Kyodo Co Ltd, Tokyo 1953 (Vol I), 1955 (Vol II)

History of Japanese Naval Wings, by Masataka Nagaishi, Shuppan Kyodo Co Ltd, Tokyo, 1961

History of Nakajima Aero Engines, By Ryoichi Nakagawa and Sotaro Mizutani, Kantosha Co Ltd, Tokyo, 1987

Medium Attack Bombers: Vol I, II, by Fumio Iwaya, Shuppan Kyodo Co, Ltd, Tokyo, 1956 (Vol I), 1958 (Vol II)

Nangoku Icarus Ki, by Kunio Hiraki, Kantosha Co Ltd, Tokyo, 1987

Zero Fighter, by Jiro Horikoshi and Masatake Okumiya, Nippon Shuppan Kyodo Co Ltd, Tokyo, 1953

Zero Fighter, by Kunio Yanagida, KK Bungei Shunju, 1980

Historical articles in monthly magazine, *Aireview* by Kunio Hiraki, Kantosha Co Ltd, Tokyo, 1986-1988.

Appendix D

Glossary

English Terms

AVIATOR: one who flies, but not licensed (*see* pilot).

CADET: Military pilot trainee.

FAI: Fédération Aéronautique International.

PILOT: one with an authoritatively issued pilot's certificate.

PILOT FIRST-CLASS: the highest civil pilot rating for the time of issue. Also written as pilot l/c.

PILOT THIRD-CLASS: the most junior civil pilot rating. Also written as pilot 3/c.

SPECIAL BOMBER: Name given to Navy Carrier-based dive-bomber. (*see* Kusho 6-Shi Special Bomber).

STUDENT PILOT: civilian pilot trainee.

Japanese Words and Translations

GOUSHIKAISHA: or Goushi Kaisha. A smaller company than a stock issuing company as in the case of a Kabushiki Kaisha.

GUNYO: Military

HATSUDOKI: Engine, Ha-(number) for type identification.

HIKO: Flight or flying

HIKOKI: Aeroplane (*see* kokuki)

KABUSHIKI KAISHA: used as KK (Co Ltd)

KAI: (*see* Kaizo)

KAISHIKI: Association Type

KAIZO: Modified (Kai is abbreviation)

KANJO BAKUGEKIKI: Carrier-Borne Bomber.

KANSAI: Osaka, Nara, Kyoto Area.

KANTO: Flat area including Tokyo and surrounding area.

KANTO DAI SHINSAI: Tokyo earthquake of September 1923

KENKYU: Research

KIKAN-HO: cannon, Ho-(number) for type identification.

KIKYU: Balloon

KITAI: Airframe, Kitai number, i.e. Ki-18. (Used to identify in progression, Army aircraft types)

KOKUKI: Aircraft (later word than hikoki)

KOKUTAI: Air Wing (Navy)

KOSHIKI: School Type

RINJI: Provisional, temporary

RYOKAKU-KI: Passenger Transport

SEISHIKI: Standard Type or Official Type

SHIBU: astringent juice

SHIMBUN: Newspaper (also Shinbun)

SUSAKI AIRFIELD: An airfield formerly at 1-chome and 2-chome, Fukagawa, Koto-ku, Tokyo

TEISATSUKI: Reconnaissance Aircraft

Japanese Organizations and Companies

AJIYA KOKUKIKAN GAKKO: Asian Aero-Engine School

ASAHI SHIMBUN: Asahi Newspaper KK

KK ASAHI SHIMBUN SHA: Asahi Shimbun Publishing Company

CHUKA KOKU KK: China Airways Co Ltd

DAI NIHON KOKU KK: Greater Japan Airways Co Ltd (as at 1 December, 1938)

KAIGUN KOKUJUTSU KENKYU KAI: Naval Aeronautical Research Association

KOSOKUDO KIKAN KK: High Speed Engine Co Ltd

MITSUI BUSSAN KK: Mitsui & Co, one of Japan's largest trading companies

NIHON GAKUSEI KOKU REMMEI: Japanese Students' Aviation League

NIHON HIKO KENKYUKAI: Japan Flight Research Association (Torigai)

NIHON HIKOKI KK: Nippi (Nihon Aeroplane Co Ltd)

NIHON HIKOKI SEISAKUSHO: Japan Aeroplane Works Co Ltd (Nakajima and Kawanishi)

NIHON KOKU KYOKAI: Aviation Society of Japan

NIHON KOKU YUSO KK: Japan Air Transport Co Ltd (Government owned)

NIHON KOKUSAI KOKU KOGYO KK: Japan International Aviation Industry Co Ltd

NIHON KYODO HIKO RENSHUSHO: Japan Co-operative Flight Training Centre

NIHON KEI HIKOKI KURABU: Japan Light Aeroplane Club (Itoh)

NIPPI: Nihon Aeroplane Co Ltd

NIPPON HIKO GAKKO: Nippon Flying School, 'NFS' (Tamai and Aiba)

NIPPON HIKOKI SEISAKUSHO: Japan Aeroplane Manufacturing Works (Tachibana)

NIPPON KOGATA HIKOKI KK: Japan Small Aeroplane Co Ltd

NIPPON KOKU KK: Japan Aviation Co Ltd (Kawanishi owned)

NIPPON KOKU YUSO KENKYUKAI: Japan Air Transport Research Society (Bando and Goto)

NIPPON KOKU YUSO KENKYUSHO: Japan Air Transport Research Association (Inoue at Sakai, Osaka)

RIKUGUN KOKUBU, HOKYUBU, TOKOROZAWA SHIBU: Tokorozawa Branch, Department of Supply, Army Department of Aviation

TAIWAN GIYU GAKKO: Taiwan Volunteers School

TAIWAN KOKUBO GIKAI: Taiwan National Defence Volunteer Association

TEIKOKU HIKO KYOKAI: Imperial Flying Association, also Imperial Aviation Association, Imperial Aerial Society, Imperial Aeronautics Association, and others formed 23 April, 1913

TEIKOKU KAIBO GIKAI: Imperial Maritime Defence Volunteer Association

TOKOROZAWA RIKUGUN KOKU GAKKO: Tokorozawa Army Aviation School

TOYO HIKOKI SHOKAI: Oriental Aeroplane Company (Narahara)

TOZAI TEIKI KOKUKAI: East-West Regular Air Transport Association

Index

A number of entries appear within sub-sections in the index, thus, for example, Breguet aircraft is listed within the section AIRCRAFT. The sub-sections are as follows: Aircraft (foreign), Aviation associations, Contests and flying meets, Conflicts, Engines, Flying facilities, Flying schools, Newspapers, Structure systems.